THIRD EDITION

SMALL BUSINESS MANAGEMENT:

An Entrepreneur's Guidebook

William L. Megginson
University of Oklahoma

Mary Jane Byrd
University of Mobile

Leon C. Megginson
Emeritus
University of Mobile

Mc Graw Hill **Irwin McGraw-Hill**

Boston   Burr Ridge, IL   Dubuque, IA   Madison, WI   New York   San Francisco   St. Louis
Bangkok   Bogotá   Caracas   Lisbon   London   Madrid
Mexico City   Milan   New Delhi   Seoul   Singapore   Sydney   Taipei   Toronto

McGraw-Hill Higher Education

*A Division of The **McGraw-Hill** Companies*

SMALL BUSINESS MANAGEMENT: AN ENTREPRENEUR'S GUIDEBOOK

Copyright © 2000, 1997, 1994 by The McGraw-Hill Companies, Inc. All rights reserved. Printed in the United States of America. Except as permitted under the United States Copyright Act of 1976, no part of this publication may be reproduced or distributed in any form or by any means, or stored in a data base or retrieval system, without the prior written permission of the publisher.

This book is printed on acid-free paper.

international   1 2 3 4 5 6 7 8 9 0 QPD/QPD 9 0 9 8 7 6 5 4 3 2 1 0 9
domestic   1 2 3 4 5 6 7 8 9 0 QPD/QPD 9 0 9 8 7 6 5 4 3 2 1 0 9

ISBN   0-07-303564-5 (book)
ISBN   0-07-233484-3 (CD-ROM)
ISBN   0-07-234652-3 (book bound with CD-ROM)

Vice president/Editor-in-chief: *Michael W. Junior*
Publisher: *Craig S. Beytien*
Sponsoring editor: *Karen M. Mellon*
Editorial assistant: *Jade Emrich*
Marketing manager: *Kenyetta Giles Haynes/Chris Witt*
Project manager: *Maggie Rathke*
Production supervisor: *Kari Geltemeyer*
Senior designer: *Michael Warrell*
Senior photo research coordinator: *Keri Johnson*
Supplement coordinator: *Becky Szura*
Compositor: *Carlisle Communications, Ltd.*
Typeface: *10/12 Times Roman*
Printer: *Quebecor Printing Book Group/Dubuque*

Library of Congress Cataloging-in-Publication Data

Megginson, William L.
   Small business management: an entrepreneur's guidebook/William
L. Megginson, Mary Jane Byrd, Leon C. Megginson.—3rd ed.
     p.   cm.
   Rev. ed. of: Small business management/William L. Megginson . . .
[et al.].
   Includes bibliographical references and index.
   ISBN 0-07-303564-5
   1. Small business—Management. 2. Small business—Management—
Case studies. I. Byrd, Mary Jane. II. Megginson, Leon C.
III. Title.
   HD62.7.M44   2000
   658.02´2—dc21   99-12822

INTERNATIONAL EDITION ISBN 0-07-117907-0
Copyright © 2000. Exclusive rights by The McGraw-Hill Companies, Inc. for manufacture and export. This book cannot be re-exported from the country to which it is consigned by McGraw-Hill. The International Edition is not available in North America.

www.mhhe.com

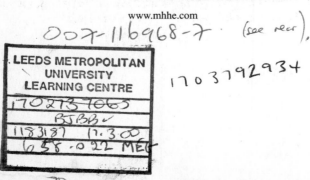

■

DEDICATION

This third edition of *Small Business Management* is dedicated to the memory of Charles Ralph Scott, our former coauthor.

Scotty—as he was known to friends and colleagues—died October 29, 1996, at the DCH Regional Medical Center in Tuscaloosa, Alabama, after a short illness. A memorial service was held on the following Sunday at the Trinity United Methodist Church. The family, including his widow, Addie M. Scott; his daughter, Sandy Scott Smith; his son, Charles Eugene Scott; and his brother, Sidney Scott, received friends at the church after the service. Also surviving him are three grandsons, Chris Scott, Kevin Smith, and Alex Smith. Scotty was buried in the family crypt at Memory Hill Gardens.

After graduating from Cornell University, Scotty worked in industry a few years before returning to teach in Cornell's College of Engineering and its V-12 program during World War II. Later, he moved to the University of Alabama in Tuscaloosa, where he taught in the College of Commerce and Business Administration. He retired from there in 1980.

During leaves of absence from the University of Alabama, Scotty taught in Korea, New Zealand, and Peru. Former students and colleagues from those countries communicated with Scotty until his death.

Scotty made enormous and outstanding contributions to his profession. He was the coauthor of 11 books in the management and computer science fields, and researched and wrote numerous business articles and cases. He was a cofounder of the Southern Case Writers Association, and became an Honorary Fellow in its successor, the North American Case Research Association. He was also president and an Honorary Fellow in the Southern Management Association.

Instead of relaxing when he retired, he counseled many small business owners as a member of the Service Corp of Retired Executives. He also served on the administrative board and as a teacher of youth and adult classes at the Trinity United Methodist Church.

Scotty and Addie, believing so strongly in the value of education, established the Addie M. and Charles R. Scott Endowed Scholarship in the University of Alabama's College of Commerce.

It can honestly be said that Charles R. Scott was a true gentleman and scholar. This, and future editions of this text, will be the poorer for his passing.

APPRECIATION

Our sincerest appreciation goes to our spouses, Peggy, Jerry, and Joclaire, without whose encouragement, help, and forbearance this book would not have been written.

PREFACE

The twenty-first century should be a stimulating and exciting time to be involved in small business—either as an owner or as a student studying to become an owner. Events since the publication of the Second Edition of *Small Business Management* have drastically changed the environment in which entrepreneurs and small business owners now operate—and especially the way they will operate beyond the year 2000!

While operating any business—small *or* large—will probably be more complex and challenging, it should also provide more interesting, creative, and rewarding experiences. Current events indicate that the first few years of the new century will present ever more stimulating, challenging, and rewarding—and no doubt at times frustrating—opportunities to those millions of intrepid men and women who own and/or manage these essential enterprises.

Success will require commitment, desire, knowledge, and hard work on your part—plus a certain amount of luck, as in any endeavor. This text provides essentials of the knowledge required.

To the Student

This Third Edition of *Small Business Management: An Entrepreneur's Guidebook*—like the Second Edition—takes a practical, down-to-earth approach to conceiving, planning, organizing, and managing a small business. Based on current research, theory, and practice, the material in the Third Edition is presented from a "how-to"

perspective, with many practical examples and applications from the business world. All three authors have had meaningful experience in the "real world" as owner, manager, or employee of one or more small businesses.

The text explores the role and growing importance of small business. It discusses the arguments both for and against owning a small firm. It presents up-to-date thinking about preparing, starting, organizing, and operating a small business. And it explains how to achieve optimum benefits from the limited resources available to small firms and also how to plan for growth and succession in a business.

The chapter-opening Profiles are especially useful examples from the real world that highlight actual entrepreneurs' experiences. Sometimes it may be as helpful to present the "how not to" as the "how to" of small business and the Profiles, and numerous other examples, look at all sides of small business issues and experiences. Web site addresses for organizations are given throughout.

Note that the Web sites included in this text are those that were in use at the time of writing and may or may not still be in use; however, they should give guidance as to what types of information can be gathered on the information superhighway.

Organization of the Book

Part I, The Challenge of Owning and Managing a Small Business, dramatizes the important role of small business in the United States and world economies; the chief characteristics of entrepreneurs and small business owners; the reasons why you should or should not own a small business; some current opportunities and challenges in small business; and the legal forms you can choose for your business.

Part II, Planning for and Organizing a Business, explains in detail how to become the owner of a small business—including how to do strategic and operational planning—as well as the growing opportunities in franchising; how to prepare and present a winning business plan, along with a Sample Business Plan; and how to obtain the right financing for your business.

Part III, Marketing Goods and Services, discusses how to develop marketing strategies for producing a product (either a good or service) and selling and distributing it—including developing global markets, marketing research, and other related activities.

Part IV, Organizing and Managing the Business, explains the important role played by human resources in a business, showing how to recruit, select, train, and compensate the required number of capable employees. Students are encouraged to learn how to communicate with, motivate, and maintain good human relations with employees—and their union, when one is involved.

Part V, Operating the Business, deals with such important operating factors as locating and laying out facilities, purchasing and maintaining inventory, and assuring quality control.

Part VI, Financial Planning and Control, explains what profit is, and how to plan for it; how to budget and control operations; and how to deal with taxes and record keeping. Finally, much new information is provided concerning the use of computer technology and management information systems to do these things more effectively. Considerable insight is provided into the operation of the Internet.

Part VII, Providing Present and Future Security for the Business, tells how to use insurance and crime prevention for better risk management and how to deal with laws affecting small businesses; and it discusses social responsibility and acting ethically, the role of family-owned businesses, and how to plan for the future—including tax and estate planning.

Following Part VII, we have included a Workbook for Developing a Successful Business Plan. The Workbook provides a discussion of what a business plan is and how to develop a business plan, and instructions on how to use the Workbook to develop your own plan, using the case provided, or developing your own case.

This Workbook should help you apply what you have learned in the text.

Aids to Learning

The text, which was written with the "computer generation" in mind, provides many insightful visuals, photos, tables, figures, charts, checklists, and cartoons to illustrate the concepts being discussed. Throughout, real-life examples are provided, with their Web sites. Important terms or concepts that are defined in the chapter are boldfaced in the text for easy recognition and then defined in the margins. These terms are listed in a Glossary at the end of the book.

Each chapter begins with relevant, thought-provoking quotations, along with numbered Learning Objectives that set the stage for what should be learned in the chapter. Then follows a Profile describing an actual business and its business owner and how she or he operates that illustrates and gives a vivid, hands-on sense of the material to be covered.

End-of-chapter features include a summary—called "What You Should Have Learned"—which is coordinated with the numbered Learning Objectives at the chapter's beginning to help review the text material; Questions to test mastery of the chapter; and two interesting Cases that analyze, amplify, and apply the material learned.

With the Third Edition, we are also providing a free CD-ROM that contains Microsoft Word and Excel templates to help you outline and create a business plan. The CD also includes Power Point student lecture notes to help you better prepare for class discussions and exams.

We think the Third Edition of *Small Business Management* will stimulate your interest in small business. We hope you will identify with the individuals in the Profiles and the Cases and throughout the discussions and through them and their experiences learn to be a better owner or manager of a small firm yourself.

To the Instructor

As an instructor, you will find this new edition of *Small Business Management: An Entrepreneur's Guidebook* easy and interesting to teach from.

The outstanding strengths of the Third Edition include its simple, clear, and concise conversational writing style, numerous and varied visuals, and numerous and relevant examples throughout the text to reinforce the basic ideas being presented. The prevailing current topics of interest to small business owners, such as diversity, global issues, improving and expanding quality, franchising, computer operations, the Internet and the mind-boggling implications it poses for small businesses, taxes and government regulations, estate planning, ethics and social responsibility, how to prepare and present a meaningful business plan, risk management, and—of course—how to plan for and make a profit, are discussed in sufficient depth to be meaningful to you and your students, while still being concise and short enough to be interesting and quickly comprehended.

Each chapter begins with philosophical, thought-provoking quotations to pique students' interest in the main concepts presented in the chapter. Next, Learning Objectives prepare students for what they should learn from the chapter. These objectives are coordinated by number with the chapter-ending summary, "What You Should Have Learned." The Learning Objectives are followed by a Profile, which is a close-up view of a business and its owner(s) or manager(s). The Profile and "real-world" Cases in each chapter give helpful and colorful portraits of small businesses in operation. The Profiles feature actual business situations and events in small firms, although some are small businesses that have become large. The Profile provides the tone and focus for the chapter, giving a grounding for what is to follow in entrepreneurs' actual experiences.

All chapters contain visuals—photographs, figures, tables, and, where they give an appropriate touch to discussions, cartoons. In the text, examples, illustrations, and real-life vignettes are set apart from the text to bring out for students how the material they are learning has been applied to actual business situations. The most important words and/or phrases defined in the text are boldfaced for easy recognition and the definitions are highlighted in the margins. These terms are listed in a Glossary at the end of the book. Thorough endnotes provide authority for and cite the sources of the material discussed so that readers can get further information if desired. The endnotes are grouped at the end of the book to prevent "clutter" on the text pages.

Several end-of-chapter features aid learning. We have mentioned the summaries, called "What You Should Have Learned," that are coordinated with the numbered Learning Objectives to provide for a better review of the material. Short-answer and review Questions for Discussion can be used for student assignments, class discussion, or quizzes. Finally, two

pertinent and interesting Cases at the end of each chapter help students analyze the text material from the point of view of real-world situations.

To help you as an instructor plan, teach, and evalute your course, we have put together a valuable package of supplements that includes the following:

- **Instructor's Manual/Test Bank/Transparency Masters-**This manual provides materials and ideas for each chapter in the Third Edition. Each chapter discussion contains a Chapter Overview with teaching suggestions, lecture outlines, answers to discussion and case questions, and numbered Learning Objectives which are coordinated with the end-of-chapter Summary. In addition, the Test Bank contains true/false and multiple choice questions, wach with correct answeres and page references in the text where the subject is dicussed in the chapter. About 150 transparency masters of the images in the text and original material are also included.
- **Computerized Test Bank-**Diploma 97 Software from Brownstone give you simple ways to write tests that can be administered on paper, over a campus network, or over the Internet.
- **Video-**This video offers two segments featuring Specialized Bicycle Components. The first segment discusses Specialized's approach to strategic management and long-term planning, while the second segment shows strategic implementation and key philosophies of the company.

Important Current Issues Facing Small Business People

We have featured many topics small business owners and managers will be concerned with in the twenty-first century. These include taxes and their payment; business laws; social responsibility and managerial ethics; marketing and global marketing; developing and presenting a business plan; and the use of computer technology—especially the Internet.

We have discussed from a practical, applications-oriented point of view the issues of location and purchasing, especially in retailing and services; the expanding roles of small businesses; franchising; diverse groups; and sources of financing. Finally, the functional areas of a business are covered from a small business perspective. These features of the text discussion make this an excellent, up-to-date teaching tool, relevant to the twenty-first century's changing environments.

An innovative feature is the Workbook for Developing a Successful Business Plan at the end of the book, which provides a hands-on guide for developing an actual business plan. This is in addition to the Sample Business Plan, which is an Appendix to Chapter 5.

Acknowledgments

We wish to give our sincere thanks to those who contributed suggestions, cases, profiles, and examples to the text. Where appropriate, recognition is shown by the sources at the end of each Case or Profile. Our thanks also go to the many teachers, entrepreneurs, managers, professional people, and members of the North American Case Research Association who made contributions.

Our special thanks go to Dr. Walter H. Hollingsworth, of the University of Mobile, for his expert contribution to the computer technology and management information systems areas. We also appreciate the research and writing contributions of Ragan and Jay Megginson.

Helpful comments and contributions from colleagues around the country and the following reviewers are gratefully acknowledged: David L. Carter, MS, CPA/PFS, CFP—Abilene Christian University; Charles N. Toftoy—George Washington University; Charles N. Armstrong—Kansas City Kansas Community College; Mary Lou Lockerby—College of DuPage; Richard Randall—Nassau Community College; Dr. Fred A. Ware, Jr.—Valdosta State University; and Joseph F. Salamone—University of Buffalo.

We are pleased and grateful to give a resounding vote of thanks and praise to our spouses, Peggy Megginson, Jerry Byrd, and Joclaire Megginson. Their support, suggestions, and patience have lightened our task. In addition, Joclaire Megginson was of tremendous assistance with her computer, phone, printer, and Internet searches. She was the intermediary who took the authors' ideas and converted them into more usable form for Suzanne S. Barnhill's drafting of the final text, which was then sent to Irwin/McGraw-Hill.

There is no adequate way we can express our gratitude and appreciation to Suzanne, except to say that this text would not have been possible without her help in editing, correcting, revising, typing, and proofreading our efforts. Her final drafts were the best we have seen in our years of publishing. In addition, her suggestion—and in some cases drafting—of additional text material was very helpful. Her contributions have been of inestimable value in making the production of this book possible.

Also, thanks go to J. B. Locke, who coordinated the logistics involved in copying and shipping the material to Irwin/McGraw-Hill. We thank Marina Nyman, Mike McCord, Erika Young, Heather Steward, Shannon Wynn, and Lisa Bevill for the assistance they gave us in preparing the text materials, and for providing other meaningful assistance.

Suzanne Hagan, Joseph Payne, and Darrell Waldrup made a great contribution with their preparation of the Sample Business Plan, which appears as an Appendix to Chapter 5.

Not enough can be said about the excellent and professional preparation of the *Instructor's Manual* by Gayle M. Ross. It should be of considerable assistance to teachers in presenting the text material.

We would also like to express our thanks and appreciation to our supportive colleagues and friends at Irwin/McGraw-Hill. Special thanks to our book team for this edition: Karen Mellon, sponsoring editor; Kenyetta Giles Haynes and Chris Witt, marketing managers; Jade Emrich, editorial assistant; Maggie Rathke, project manager; Michael Warrell, senior designer; Kari Geltemeyer, production supervisor; and Becky Szura, supplement coordinator.

Finally, we would like to offer our thanks to the following people from the University of Mobile: Dr. Mark Foley, President; Dr. Audrey Eubanks, Vice President for Academic Affairs; Dr. Anne Lowery, Dean of the School of Business; and Mrs. Kathy Dunning, CPA. We also gratefully acknowledge the J. L. Bedsole Foundation for their generous support. Without it, we could not have completed this important work.

If we can be of assistance to you in developing your course, please contact any one of us.

William L. Megginson
Mary Jane Byrd
Leon C. Megginson

BRIEF CONTENTS

CONTENTS

Chapter 3

LEGAL FORMS OF OWNERSHIP   48

PART

II

PLANNING FOR AND ORGANIZING A BUSINESS   65

Chapter 4

HOW TO BECOME THE OWNER OF A SMALL BUSINESS   66

Chapter 5

■

THE ROLE OF PLANNING IN ORGANIZING AND MANAGING A SMALL BUSINESS   94

Chapter 6

■

OBTAINING THE RIGHT FINANCING FOR YOUR BUSINESS   142

PART

IV

ORGANIZING AND MANAGING THE BUSINESS   217

Chapter 9

MANAGING HUMAN RESOURCES AND DIVERSITY IN SMALL FIRMS   218

Chapter 10

MAINTAINING RELATIONSHIPS WITH YOUR EMPLOYEES AND THEIR REPRESENTATIVES   248

P A R T

V

OPERATING THE BUSINESS   275

Chapter 11

LOCATING AND LAYING OUT OPERATING FACILITIES   276

Chapter 12

PURCHASING, INVENTORY, AND QUALITY CONTROL   296

P A R T

VI

FINANCIAL PLANNING AND CONTROL   319

Chapter 13

■

PLANNING FOR PROFIT   320

Chapter 14

■

BUDGETING AND CONTROLLING OPERATIONS AND TAXES   340

Chapter 15
■

USING COMPUTER TECHNOLOGY IN SMALL BUSINESSES 364

PART
VII

PROVIDING PRESENT AND FUTURE SECURITY FOR THE BUSINESS 389

Chapter 16
■

RISK MANAGEMENT, INSURANCE, AND CRIME PREVENTION 390

THE CHALLENGE OF OWNING AND MANAGING A SMALL BUSINESS

You cannot escape being involved with small business, for it is everywhere! When you think of "business," you may think of large corporations—Fortune 500 companies—but if you look around you, where you work and live, you will realize that the vast majority of businesses are small. And these small businesses are not only numerically significant; they are also important as employers, as providers of needed (and often unique) goods and services, and as sources of satisfaction to their owners. For these and many other reasons, there is hardly anyone who has not at some time or other been tempted to start a small business.

Part I of this text is designed to show what is involved in forming and/or owning a small business. The material covered should help you decide whether pursuing a career in small business is the right course of action for you.

The dynamic and challenging role of small business is covered in Chapter 1. Chapter 2 discusses reasons for starting a small business, describes some characteristics of successful small business owners, and explores some opportunities in small firms, especially for many diverse groups. Finally, the more popular forms of ownership available to small businesses are presented in Chapter 3.

1

THE DYNAMIC ROLE OF SMALL BUSINESS

There is an entrepreneurial revolution sweeping this country, and it's a great time for all of small business.

June Nichols, entrepreneur

The good health and strength of America's small businesses are a vital key to the health and strength of our economy. . . . Indeed, small business is America.

Former President Ronald Reagan

LEARNING OBJECTIVES

After studying the material in this chapter, you will be able to:

1. Explain why now is an interesting time to study small business.

2. Define what is meant by the term *small business*.

3. Name some of the unique contributions of small businesses.

4. Describe some current problems small businesses face.

5. Discuss some current trends challenging entrepreneurs and small business owners.

Trillium House: A Blue Ridge Mountain Country Inn

Trillium House, a country inn located on a mountaintop in the Blue Ridge Mountains of Virginia, is no ordinary rustic lodge on an ordinary mountaintop. The inn is nestled in a setting where birds, squirrels, and deer come to call on the guests. Frequently, as many as nine deer appear outside the dining room window—not 15 feet away from the diners. Located in the middle of the 11,000-acre Wintergreen Resort, Trillium House (www.trilliumhouse.com) has a vast array of recreational choices.

Designed and built by Ed and Betty Dinwiddie, the inn features floor-to-ceiling windows, outside of which the birds and animals entertain guests; a garden room; and a brick terrace. Beyond a picturesque gazebo is the seventeenth fairway of Devil's Knob Golf Course. Closer by are indoor and outdoor swimming pools, tennis courts, and a fitness center. Ski lifts are only minutes away.

Most new innkeepers are inclined to buy an established inn, or at least an existing landmark building, for their operations. Instead, the Dinwiddies built a new inn of their own design. But it was not a haphazard adventure! Rather, they brought to the venture an intimate knowledge of the area, where the Dinwiddie family had lived for generations, as well as the experience gathered in their prior lifestyles and occupations.

After meeting in college and marrying, Ed and Betty settled in the area, where they raised their children. Ed had been active in the textile industry and served for 13 years as Executive Vice President of Development for the Colgate Darden Graduate Business School Sponsors of the University of Virginia. Then he and Betty decided to go into business for themselves. As they wanted to stay in the area, work for themselves, and "be with people," it seemed that running a country inn offered the most appealing prospect. In fact, an occupational test Ed had taken as a high school student had showed that he "would do well in the hotel business."

Betty had also been preparing for this career development. "For example," she said, "we were always entertaining. We were either giving dinner parties for students or faculty, or I was in charge of food at various church functions."

Realizing that Wintergreen was the ideal place for their unique inn, the Dinwiddies negotiated a 40-year lease—with an option to buy after five years—on space in the resort. They then engaged a well-known architectural firm in Charlottesville to design the inn "from the ground up," in order to blend the sylvan setting with the latest modern amenities. They succeeded in acquiring not just a business but a lifestyle! For an investment of $800,000, they built an attractive wood-frame building, with modern facilities, set on a mountain with a beautiful view of the surrounding countryside.

Ed and Betty started their business in 1982, with a complete and detailed business plan. Construction cost $500,000, with groundbreaking on April 13, 1983. The Dinwiddies, with their three children, moved into the uncompleted inn during the Thanksgiving holidays. Carpeting was still being installed as their first guests arrived on December 23. Betty and Ed's dream was fulfilled. Five years later, they exercised the option to buy the land for $166,000.

Although the inn was a family affair in its early days, a staff of six full-time and six part-time employees now permits the Dinwiddies to resume "normal lives complete with vacations." They have moved out of the inn and into a home nearby.

As you enter Trillium House you find yourself in a 23-foot-high "great room" with a chimney that towers above a stone fireplace. A library of over 8,000 volumes includes the complete works of Agatha Christie. The inn has 10 rooms and two suites—all furnished with family antiques and one-of-a-kind items. Betty achieved a "homey feeling" by mixing family furnishings with treasured memorabilia and family heirlooms. All guest rooms are equipped with phone and cable TV and have private baths and individually controlled heating and cooling.

"But our important asset," says Ed, "is our highly qualified staff. We operate on the honor system, with no tolerance of theft or other forms of misconduct. We've never had a lost-time injury or had to pay out workers' compensation."

A full breakfast—included in the price of the room—is offered each morning. Gourmet dinners are served—by reservation—on Friday and Saturday nights and selected other evenings.

Since 1992, Betty and Ed—with extremely mixed feelings—have considered selling Trillium House. While it has been a successful venture—breaking even at about $25,000 a month, bringing in around $50,000 in "good months," and losing money during several weak months—the future is uncertain. The bed-and-breakfast business is still growing rapidly, they point out. "There are 22 quality B&Bs within an hour's drive of us, all of which have opened since 1982." As a result, running the inn is "now very expensive and not as attractive." Furthermore, their children are not interested in going into the B&B business with their parents—at least not at this time.

Trillium House is listed or featured in *The Innkeepers' Register,* as a member of the elite Independent Innkeeper Association (IIA); *Country Inns & Back Roads;* Andrew Harper's *Hideaway Report;* Condé Nast articles; *Rural Living: The Discerning Traveler;* and *Washingtonian* magazine. Mobil Travel Club gave Trillium a "three stars" rating, while AAA gave it three diamonds.

What do Ed and Betty like least about their business? "Restrictions on our time." What do they like most? "Meeting and working with interesting people." "In summary," said Ed, "it's a great life!"

You have probably never heard of the Dinwiddies and their country inn. Neither had we until we started revising the second edition of our popular book about entrepreneurs and small business owners. But you *have* heard of companies such as Wal-Mart, Sears, McDonald's, Dell Computer, Intel, and Microsoft. All of them were started as small businesses by then-unknown entrepreneurs such as Sam Walton, Richard Sears, Ray Kroc, Michael Dell, Andrew Grove, and Bill Gates. By capitalizing on their imagination, initiative, courage, dedication, hard work, and—often—luck, these entrepreneurs turned an idea into a small struggling business that became a large, successful one. In fact, Bill Gates, known as "the richest person in America," was worth over $81 billion in 1999.[1] The other richest people in the technology field are Paul Allen, of Microsoft, worth $21 billion; Steve Ballmer, also of Microsoft, over $8 billion; Larry Ellison, of Oracle, over $8 billion; and Gordon Moore, of Intel, nearly $8 billion.

Now it is your turn to see if you can start (or restart) your career as an entrepreneur—by converting an idea into a small business. According to Joseph Nebesky, who has served as an adviser to the U.S. Agency for International Development, the Small Business Administration (SBA) (www.sba.gov), and the National Council on the Aging, these small firms "are the backbone of the American economy." Apparently he is right, for firms with fewer than 500 employees employ 53 percent of the total private nonfarm work force, contribute 47 percent of all sales in the country, are responsible for 51 percent of the gross domestic product, and produce around two out of every three new jobs each year.[2] They also account for over half of U.S. gross domestic product.[3]

■ IT'S AN INTERESTING TIME TO BE STUDYING SMALL BUSINESS

As you can see, this is an interesting, challenging, and rewarding time to be studying small business, for owning and operating such a firm is one of the best ways to fulfill the "great American dream," and many Americans believe this is one of the best paths to riches in the United States. Apparently this is true, for a study by the U.S. Trust found that nearly 40 percent of the top 1 percent of the wealthiest Americans* got there by building a small business. Every year, around three-quarters of a million Americans turn this dream of owning a business into a reality. And most of these dreams become true success stories.

As an indication of this popularity, SBA-sponsored research found that about 16 million Americans are in some type of part- or full-time entrepreneurial activity. This figure represents about 13 percent of all nonagricultural U.S. workers.[4]

The following are some reasons for the increased interest in small business:

- The number of small businesses is growing rapidly.
- Small firms generate most new private employment.
- The public favors small business.
- There is increasing interest in small business entrepreneurship at high schools and colleges.
- There is a growing trend toward self-employment.
- Entrepreneurship is attractive to people of all ages.

The Number of Small Businesses Is Growing Rapidly

The development of small business in the United States is truly an amazing story. The value of goods and services they produce and the new jobs they generate make the small business sector one of the greatest economic powers in the world, accounting for trillions of dollars' worth of commerce annually. As an economic power, U.S. small businesses rank third in the world, behind only the U.S. economy as a whole and the Japanese economy.[5] If small business is this important, how many small firms are there in the United States? According to IRS Statistics of Income, there were approximately 23.3 million nonfarm businesses in 1996. The SBA estimated that 99 percent of those were small businesses, according to its size standards.[6] Thus, *it can be assumed that there are now around 23 million small businesses in the United States.*

More important than the number of small businesses, though, is the fact that the number of such firms is growing by about three quarters of a million each year. For example, SBA-sponsored research found 842,357 new employer firms in 1996—2.8 percent more than the record set in 1995.[7] Growth was particularly strong in the South Atlantic states as well as California and Massachusetts. Also significant is the fact that about nine new firms were organized for every one that failed.[8]

During recent years, a myth has arisen that small firms have a high failure rate.[9] This perception is not true. To the contrary, a recent Dun & Bradstreet census of 250,000 businesses found that "almost 70 percent of all firms that started in 1985 were still around" in 1995.[10]

---

*Those individuals earning $200,000 or more a year, or with $3 million or more in assets.

A 1998 national poll of 300 small business owners tends to confirm this conclusion. The survey, conducted by the New England Business Service (www.nebs.com), found that 49 percent of small businesses reported profitability during their first year of operations; and 30 percent of the others reached profitability after three or more years.[11]

In an earlier study of 814,000 businesses started in 1977 and 1978, Bruce A. Kirchoff of the New Jersey Institute of Technology found that over half survived more than eight years. While 18 percent had actually failed—*that is, they did not have assets to cover their liabilities*—28 percent had closed voluntarily. Of the others, 28 percent were operated by their original owners, and 26 percent had new owners. Kirchoff concluded that "entrepreneurs aren't stupid. They look around and realize their chances of success are far better than those proclaimed by the 'experts.' "[12] Recent SBA-sponsored research tended to verify these findings. It found that "of every seven businesses that shut their doors, only one actually fails—that is, leaves unpaid obligations."[13]

Small Firms Generate Most New Private Employment

From various government and private sources it can be concluded that small businesses contribute greatly to employment, especially in the creation of *new jobs*. According to the U.S. Departments of Commerce and Labor, "Small-business-dominated industries (those with fewer than 500 employees) produced an estimated 64 percent of the 2.5 million new jobs created in 1996."[14]

Findings similar to these were recently reported by David Birch, of Cognetics, Inc., a reputable research firm. He found that most new jobs come from a relative handful of fast-growing companies. While some of these companies "are behemoths and are all the more noticeable because so many other giant companies are slashing payrolls, . . . the vast majority of job-creating businesses are fast-growing smaller companies."[15] For example, while profits of the Forbes 500 rose 14 percent in 1996,[16] and revenues rose 8.3 percent,[17] their employment rose only 3 percent, to 20.9 million.[18]

The information in Figure 1–1 tends to verify these findings. It shows that business establishments with less than 500 employees employed 80 percent of all employees in 1994, while the larger establishments employed only 20 percent.

Robert L. Bartley, editor of *The Wall Street Journal,* called the decade of the 1980s the heyday of "an expanding, entrepreneurial economy."[19] Some new names that exploded onto the business landscape during that time were Microsoft, Lotus, Apple, Sun Microsystems, Liz Claiborne, and McCaw Cellular. The employment figures in Figure 1–1 tend to confirm his conclusion. Notice that the smaller firms (those with fewer than 500 employees) had around 73 percent of all employees in 1974, but this figure had increased to 78 percent in 1984 and 80 percent by 1994. This trend is expected to continue into the twenty-first century.

Finally, small businesses are a particularly good source of jobs for women and teenagers and especially for older workers. According to a classic study for the SBA, businesses with fewer than 25 employees *account for more than two-thirds of new hiring of workers age 65 and over.*[20] Also, small employers provide around two-thirds of all initial job opportunities. Thus, they are responsible for most on-the-job training in basic skills.[21]

The Public Favors Small Business

Generally, small business owners and managers believe in the free enterprise system, with its emphasis on individual freedom, risk taking, initiative, thrift, frugality, and hard work. In fact, a Gallup survey of 600 adults for the Center for Entrepreneurial Leadership in Kansas City, Missouri (www.celcee.edu), found that half of the respondents expressed an interest in owning a small business.[22]

Figure 1–1
Percent Distribution of Employees by Size of Employer

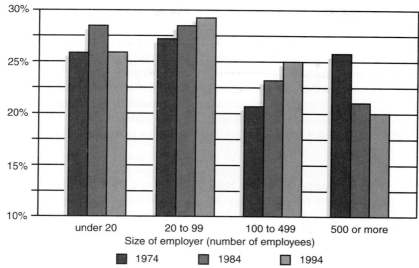

Source: U.S. Bureau of the Census, *Statistical Abstract of the United States, 1985,* 105th ed. (Washington, DC: U.S. Government Printing Office, 1985), Table 874, p. 518; 108th ed. (1988), Table 831, p. 499; and 117th ed. (1997), Table 846, p. 544.

Another indication of interest in small business and entrepreneurship is the large number of magazines aimed at that market. These include older ones, such as *Black Enterprise* (www.blackenterprise.com), *Entrepreneur, Inc.,* and *Hispanic Business* (www. hispanicbusiness.com), and many new ones. Some of these journals are targeted for specific markets. *Family Business* targets family-owned businesses; *Entrepreneurial Woman* aims at female business owners; and *Your Company,* sent free by American Express (www.americanexpress.com) to the million or more holders of its small-business corporate card, targets small firms. Other journals include *Journal of Small Business Management, Small Business Journal* (www.tsbj.com), *New Business Opportunities,* and *Business Week Newsletter for Family-Owned Businesses* (www.businessweek.com).*

Interest Increasing at High Schools, Colleges, and Universities

Another indication of the growing popularity of small business is its acceptance as part of the mission of many high schools, colleges, and universities, where entrepreneurship and small business management are now academically respected disciplines. Virtually unheard of 20 years ago, courses in entrepreneurship are now offered at hundreds of U.S. colleges and universities, thanks to the efforts of the federal School-to-Work Opportunities Act of 1994 and New York City's National Foundation for Teaching Entrepreneurship.[23]

This trend is evident not only at small schools but also at the larger ones.

> For example, most of the 1974 graduates of Harvard Business School (www.hbs.harvard.edu) headed for medium-sized to large employers. But 18 years later, more than a third of a 115-person sample had been fired or laid off, and 62 percent were working for small firms.[24]

*Please note that the *Business Week* site requires registration and a fee in order to view the entire file.

The considerable interest at colleges and universities is also shown by the formation of many student organizations to encourage entrepreneurship. For example, the Association of Collegiate Entrepreneurs (ACE), founded in 1983 at Wichita State University, now has hundreds of chapters throughout the world. Other organizations include the University Entrepreneurial Association (UEA) and Students in Free Enterprise (SIFE) (www.sife.org).

Community colleges, especially, are now offering courses for small business owners. One study found that 90 percent of community colleges offer such courses, while 75 percent of public community colleges also provide training courses. This activity is one of the fastest-growing areas in the community college field. Many colleges and universities are now offering specialized business courses, such as programs in family business, franchising, and international operations, as well as job fairs and career days.

> This growing interest in entrepreneurship has had a profound effect on graduate students. Now some campus career centers and student-run organizations try to place MBAs with small companies where they can get the appropriate experience to start and run their own businesses. In fact, MBA Central, a new Palo Alto, California start-up, specializes in placing MBAs at no cost to the candidate. The interested small firm receives a stack of résumés from prospective employees for a flat fee.[25]

Finally many students are now starting businesses while still in school to finance their own educations or to provide a product or service not otherwise available.[26] Student-run businesses are not, however, a new phenomenon:

> The venerable Harvard Cooperative Society, better known as the Coop, was established in 1882 by Harvard junior Charles H. Kip and fellow students "to protect themselves from the rapacity of Harvard Square coal dealers and booksellers." Today, the Coop operates six stores, including a 90,000-square-foot department store in Harvard Square and branches at MIT and Harvard's professional schools. In September 1995, the Society signed a 15-year management agreement with Barnes and Noble Bookstores, Inc., but students still hold half the seats on the board of directors (the rest are Harvard faculty, officials, and alumni). The Coop retains its name and continues to operate as a cooperative, paying an annual rebate to all its members.[27]
>
> Similarly, Harvard Student Agencies, Inc., was born in 1957 out of Gregory Stone's idea to start a company incorporating the businesses that enterprising students operated out of their dorm rooms. The objectives of the business were to provide employment opportunities to needy Harvard undergraduates, valuable products and services to the Harvard community, and business experience to students. Entirely run by students, HSA provides catering and dry cleaning services, assistance in computer services and graphic design, and furniture and equipment rental and publishes the popular *Unofficial Guide to Harvard.* Its subsidiary, Let's Go, Inc., publishes the *Let's Go* travel guide series and operates the Let's Go travel agency. Employing one in every five Harvard undergraduates, HSA is one of the world's largest student-run organizations, generating over $4.3 million in revenue and paying over $1.5 million in wages annually.[28]

According to a long-running survey by the Higher Education Research Institute at the University of California at Los Angeles (www.gseis.ucla.edu/heri/heri.html), America's students are still attracted to the entrepreneurial life. As shown in Figure 1–2, 41.1 percent of college freshmen in 1997 said succeeding in their own business was essential or very important to them. While this figure was less than the 52 percent in 1985, it was still at about the same level as in the early 1970s. An interesting finding of the 1997 study was that 63.2 percent of all African-American college students wanted to go into business for themselves.

Not only college and university students but also students in lower-level schools are interested in small business and entrepreneurship. Nearly 70 percent of high school students

Figure 1–2

Tomorrow's Entrepreneurs (Share of College Freshmen Who Say Succeeding in Their Own Business Is Essential or Very Important)

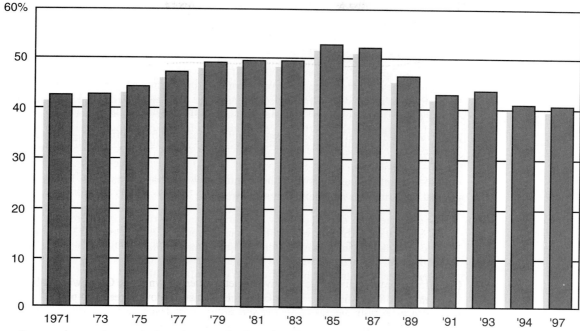

Source: Correspondence and communication with personnel at the Higher Education Research Institute at UCLA.

are interested in launching their own businesses, according to the previously mentioned Gallup survey.[29] One of the reasons given by the students was distrust of government and big business.

> For instance, one student was quoted as saying, "If you work for yourself, you reap more benefits than you would if you worked underneath someone." This student planned to open a computer graphics business of her own and not rely on a big company for her pay.[30]

Trend toward Self-Employment

The growth rate for self-employment is greater than the growth rate of the general work force. Small business grew rapidly from the mid-1980s to the mid-1990s as investors became more willing to assume the risk of starting or revitalizing small businesses. Many of these were middle-aged executives from large corporations who were eager to put their management skills to work in reviving smaller companies in aging industries.

This trend is still alive. For example, a recent national poll found that 55 percent of us want to be our own boss. Advances in technology have helped make this dream come true.[31]

Entrepreneurship Is Attractive to All Ages

Entrepreneurship knows no age limits! From the very young to the very old, people are starting new businesses at a rapid rate. Particularly heartening is the large number of young people who are entrepreneurs. In 1994, the U.S. Bureau of Labor Statistics (www.stats.bls.gov) found that 272,000 young people, ages 20 to 24, were self-employed—up 10 percent in only one year. Another study at Babson College indicated that nearly 10 percent of Americans between the ages of 25 and 34 were trying to start their own businesses. Also, 3.3 percent of 18–24-year-olds, 3.0 percent of 35–44-year-olds, 2.1 percent of 45–54-year-olds, and 0.3 percent of those 55 and over were trying to start a business.[32]

> Age is not a requirement for success in starting small businesses. Megan Crump is a good example of a young entrepreneur. At age seven she found an exciting way to make money. After a successful evening of trick-or-treating, Megan took all her candy to school and sold it to her schoolmates for a handsome profit of $3 the first day and $1 the second day. She later held a yard sale where, among other things, she sold her sister's used bicycle for $9. The resourcefulness of youngsters such as Megan should continue to stimulate our economy well into the twenty-first century.[33]

Older people are also involved in forming new companies, as small businesses offer the most opportunities and flexibility to retirees.

> For example, after devoting nearly 30 years to the law—rising to partner in charge of the London office of Rogers & Wills—Joni Nelson quit in 1991 at age 53 to turn her love of gardening into a new career. Chelsea American Flower Shows, the company she formed, organizes flower shows around the country. She says of her second career, "I'm a capitalist at heart. I want to work till I'm 80."[34]

Many groups, such as the American Association of Retired Persons (AARP) (www.aarp.org), colleges, and private consultants now offer classes—and, more important, support groups—specifically for retirement-aged potential and actual entrepreneurs.[35] Also, 40 percent of those who form new businesses each year already have some management experience, and one-fourth of them have managed or owned a business before.

A word of caution is needed at this point. If you start a business, you can't just "turn it on and off" like a light switch; that is, you can't take time off whenever you want to. If your business is to succeed, you can't shut down for holidays or vacations or when things aren't going well. As one discouraged small business owner said at a recent conference, "A small business is wonderful: you only have to work half a day—and you get to choose which 12 hours it is that you will work!"

■ DEFINING SMALL BUSINESS—NO EASY TASK

Now that we've seen how much interest there is in small business, what *is* a small business? There is no simple definition, but let's look at some definitions that are frequently used.

What Is Small?

What is a small business? At first, this question appears easy to answer. Many places of business that you patronize—such as independent neighborhood grocery stores, fast-food restaurants, hair stylists, dry cleaners, video or record shops, and the veterinarian—are examples of small businesses. However, even with 8,500 employees, American Motors was once considered a small business: the SBA deemed it eligible for a small business loan. Why? Because American Motors *was* small compared to its giant competitors—General Motors, Ford, and Chrysler. Chrysler bought the company in 1987.

Qualitative factors are also important in describing small businesses. To be classified as "small," *a small business must have at least two of the following features:*

Table 1–1
Classification of Business by Size, According to SBA

Under 20 employees	Very small
20–99	Small
100–499	Medium
500 or more	Large

Source: Small Business Administration.

- Management is independent, since the manager usually owns the business.
- Capital is supplied and ownership is held by an individual or a few individuals.
- The area of operations is primarily local, although the market isn't necessarily local.
- The business is small in comparison with the larger competitors in its industry.

Perhaps the best definition of small business is the one used by Congress in the Small Business Act of 1953, which states that *a small business is one that is independently owned and operated and is not dominant in its field of operation.*[36] We'll use that definition in this text, unless otherwise indicated.

As will be shown in Chapter 6, the SBA, for loan purposes, uses different size criteria by industry. In general, however, it uses the size classification shown in Table 1–1.

Distinguishing between Entrepreneurial Ventures and Small Businesses

We also need to distinguish between small businesses and entrepreneurial ventures. The rapidity of the rate of growth of a business is one useful way to distinguish between small business owners and entrepreneurs.

An **entrepreneurial venture** is one in which the principal objectives of the entrepreneur are profitability and growth. Thus, the business is characterized by innovative strategic practices and/or products. The entrepreneurs and their financial backers are usually seeking rapid growth, immediate—and high—profits, and a quick sellout with—possibly—large capital gains.

> In an **entrepreneurial venture,** the principal objectives of the owner are profitability and growth.

Trillium House (see the opening Profile) is a classic example of an entrepreneurial venture. Notice that the owners started the business for achievement, profit, and growth; they introduced many innovative practices and products; and they are now seeking to sell the business.

A **small business** (or mom-and-pop operation), on the other hand, is any business that is independently owned and operated, is not dominant in its field, and does not engage in many new or innovative practices. It may never grow large, and the owners may not want it to, as they usually prefer a more relaxed and less aggressive approach to running the business. They manage their business in a normal way, expecting normal sales, profits, and growth. In other words, they seek a certain degree of freedom and—ideally—a certain degree of financial independence.

> A **small business** is independently owned and operated, is not dominant in its field, and doesn't engage in new or innovative practices.

As opposed to Trillium House, the Caudle House, a small B&B in Wadesboro, North Carolina, with four bedrooms, is an example of a small business. The owners, who use only word-of-mouth advertising, do all the work themselves. They enjoy visiting with their guests—especially over a full-course breakfast. The business closes over the main holidays unless there is a special event that they are catering. The owners say they are "running the business for fun."[37]

A **small business owner** establishes a business primarily to further personal goals, including making a profit.

The goals of an **entrepreneur** include growth, achieved through innovation and strategic management.

It is not always easy to distinguish between a small business owner and an entrepreneur, for the distinction hinges on their intentions. In general, a **small business owner** establishes a business for the principal purpose of furthering personal goals, which *may* include making a profit. Thus, the owner may perceive the business as being an extension of his or her personality, which is interwoven with family needs and desires.

On the other hand, the **entrepreneur** starts and manages a business for many reasons, including achievement, profit, and growth. Such a person is characterized principally by innovative behavior and will employ strategic management practices in the business, as the following example illustrates.

> Court L. Hague (or "Corky," as he is known), has a driving compulsion: he loves to start new businesses. While most entrepreneurs start one, two, or three enterprises in their lifetime, by age 47 Hague had founded—or acquired with the intent to expand—28 companies.
>
> In the early 1970s, after one year teaching algebra and earning a degree in accounting from the University of Texas, he started his "acquisition binge." By the mid-1980s, he was simultaneously running 12 companies.
>
> He selected most of his companies by leafing through the Yellow Pages to find "solid businesses that could benefit from splashier ads." He has owned a sign business, an air conditioner factory, a dry-wall supplier, travel agencies, bike stores, pawnshops, and software companies—just to mention a few.
>
> Hague bases his success on three guiding principles: (1) get good people, (2) stick to what you know best, and (3) watch the business like a hawk.[38]

Of course, the owner's intentions sometimes change, and what started out as a small business may become an entrepreneurial venture.

Size, Sales, and Employment

The Internal Revenue Service classifies 96 percent of American businesses as small.* Yet those small businesses generate only 12 percent of the total receipts each year, while the 4 percent of firms that are classified as large generate 88 percent of all revenues.[39]

Still, as has been shown, one of the greatest advantages of small businesses is their ability to create new jobs. Figure 1–1 showed that small businesses account for 80 percent of all private employees in the United States. Note that those firms account for over 99 percent of all private businesses, as shown in Figure 1–3.

As you can see from Figure 1–4, small firms are more prevalent in contract construction and wholesale and retail trade, where they provide over 90 percent of all employment. Yet they generate the largest number of actual jobs in services (24,701,000 employees), retail trade (19,683,000), and manufacturing (11,911,000). These figures show how important small firms are in generating employment opportunities.

■ SOME UNIQUE CONTRIBUTIONS OF SMALL BUSINESS

As indicated throughout this chapter, small firms differ from their larger competitors. Let's look at some major contributions made by small businesses that set them apart from larger firms.

Smaller firms tend to:

- Encourage innovation and flexibility.
- Maintain close relationships with customers and the community.
- Keep larger firms competitive.

---

*The definition of small is based on the amount of annual revenue—$1 million or less.

Figure 1–3
Percent Distribution of Business Establishments by Size of Employer

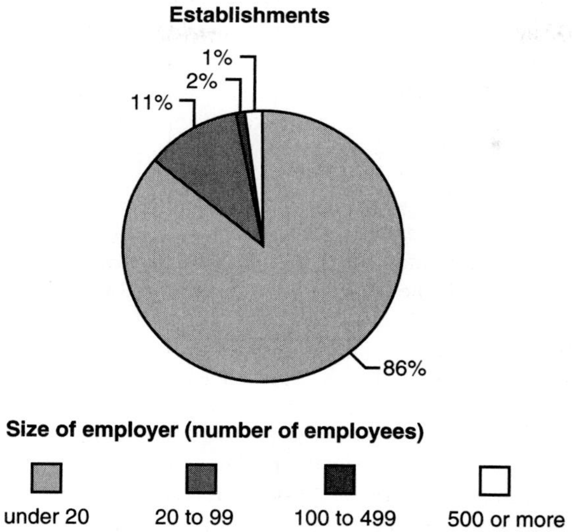
Establishments
1%
2%
11%
86%
Size of employer (number of employees)
under 20
20 to 99
100 to 499
500 or more

Source: U.S. Bureau of the Census, *Statistical Abstract of the United States, 1997,* 117th ed. (Washington, DC: U.S. Government Printing Office, 1997), Table 846, p. 544.

- Provide employees with comprehensive learning experience.
- Develop risk takers.
- Generate new employment.
- Provide greater employee job satisfaction.

Encourage Innovation and Flexibility

Smaller businesses are often sources of new ideas, materials, processes, and services that larger firms may be unable or reluctant to provide. In small businesses, experiments can be conducted, innovations initiated, and new operations started or expanded. In fact, small firms produce 55 percent of all innovations and twice as many innovations per employee as large firms.[40] This trend is especially true in the computer field, where most initial developments have been carried on in small companies.

> For example, it is no coincidence that IBM didn't produce the first electronic computer, as it already owned 97 percent of the then-popular punched-card equipment, which the computer would tend to make obsolete. Instead, the Univac was conceived and produced by a small firm formed by John Mauchly and J. Presper Eckert. However, while they were design experts, they lacked production and marketing skills, so they sold out to Remington Rand, which controlled the remaining 3 percent of the punched-card business. So the first giant computers at organizations such as the U.S. Census Bureau and General Electric's Appliance Park in Kentucky in January 1954 were Univacs. Nonetheless, IBM's marketing expertise overcame Remington's production expertise, and IBM soon dominated the computer industry.
>
> Also, it is no coincidence that two design geniuses, Steven Jobs, 21, and Steve Wozniak, 19, essentially started the PC industry by founding Apple Computer in 1976 with capital obtained by selling Jobs's Volkswagen microbus and Wozniak's Hewlett-Packard scientific calculator. And Michael Dell, 19, started Dell Computer Corporation by selling computer parts from his dorm room at the University of Texas. He started out to "make it big."[41]

Figure 1–4

Percent Distribution of Employees in Large and Small Firms in Selected Industries

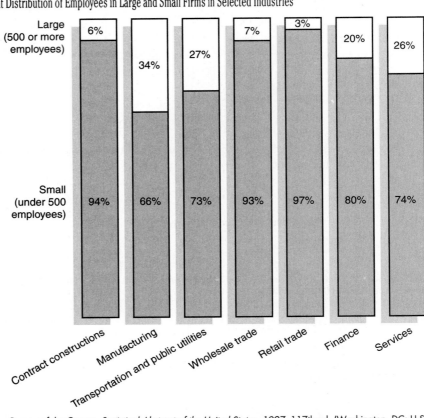

Source: Bureau of the Census, *Statistical Abstract of the United States, 1997,* 117th ed. (Washington, DC: U.S. Government Printing Office, 1997), Table 846, p. 544.

Maintain Close Relationships with Customers and Community

Small businesses tend to be in close touch with their communities and customers. They can do a more individualized job than big firms can, thereby attracting customers on the basis of specialty products, quality, and personal services rather than solely on the basis of price. While competitive prices and a reputation for honesty are important, an atmosphere of friendliness makes people feel good about patronizing the business and encourages them to continue shopping there.

Keep Larger Firms Competitive

Smaller companies have become a controlling factor in the American economy by keeping the bigger concerns on their toes. With the introduction of new products and services, small businesses encourage competition—if not in price, at least in design and efficiency, as happened in the area of California now called Silicon Valley, where the personal computer was developed.

Provide Employees with Comprehensive Learning Experience

A small business provides employees with a variety of learning experiences not open to individuals holding more specialized jobs in larger companies. Along with performing a greater variety of functions, small business employees also have more freedom to make decisions, which can lend zest and interest to their work experience. So small businesses train people to become better leaders and managers and to develop their talents and energies more effectively. This reality has led more college graduates to seek full-time jobs with small businesses, according to a survey by the National Association of Colleges and Employers. The reason for this trend is that small companies "tend to offer broader experiences because of their smaller staffs." Thus, employees "get more responsibility, more quickly," according to one graduate applicant.[42]

Develop Risk Takers

Small businesses provide one of the basic American freedoms—risk taking, with its consequent rewards and punishments. Small business owners have relative freedom to enter or leave a business at will, to start small and grow big, to expand or contract, and to succeed or fail, which is the basis of our free enterprise system. Yet founding a business in an uncertain environment is risky, so much planning and study must be done before start-up.

Generate New Employment

As repeatedly emphasized throughout this chapter, small businesses generate employment by creating job opportunities. Small firms also serve as a training ground for employees, who, because of their more comprehensive learning experience, their emphasis on risk taking, and their exposure to innovation and flexibility, become valued employees of larger companies.

Provide Greater Job Satisfaction

Also, small companies provide greater employee job satisfaction. For example, the 1997 *Inc.*/Gallup survey of American workers found that employees in smaller workplaces have higher job satisfaction than those in larger firms. But the greatest satisfaction comes to those who own their own workplaces.[43]

■ SOME CURRENT PROBLEMS FACING SMALL BUSINESSES

Just as small companies make unique contributions, there are special problems that affect them more than larger businesses. These problems can result in limited profitability and growth, the decision to voluntarily close the business, or financial failure.

According to Bruce Phillips, chief economist for the SBA, start-up firms don't fail as often as some people think. In a landmark study, he found that 4 out of 10 new businesses survive at least the first six years.[44] He also found that *the vast majority of businesses that close do so for voluntary reasons,* such as the owner's desire to enter a more profitable business, legal changes, owner's disenchantment, or a family's decision to end the business after the owner's death.

Why do new businesses fail? While we don't always know the exact reasons, an early Minota Corporation survey of 703 businesses with fewer than 500 employees found that the main reasons were (1) lack of capital (48 percent), (2) no business knowledge (23 percent), (3) poor management (19 percent), (4) inadequate planning (15 percent), and (5) inexperience (15 percent). As you can see, the last four reasons can be summarized as *inadequate management.*[45] An additional problem cited by many small business owners is the burden of government regulations and paperwork.

Inadequate Financing

Notice in the list above that inadequate financing is the primary cause of new business failure. *It cannot be stressed enough that the shortage of capital is the greatest problem facing small business owners.* Without adequate funds, one is unable to acquire and maintain facilities, hire and reward capable employees, produce and market a product, or do the other things necessary to run a successful business. Therefore, a study for the SBA, done by CERA Economics Consultants, Inc., found that most start-ups fail because of undercapitalization.[46]

Inadequate Management

Inadequate management, in the forms of limited business knowledge, poor management, inadequate planning, and inexperience, is the second problem facing small firms. Many owners tend to rely on one-person management and seem reluctant to vary from this managerial pattern. They tend to guard their position very jealously and may not select qualified employees, or may fail to give them enough authority and responsibility to manage adequately. Most small businesses are started because someone is good at a specific activity or trade, not because she or he has managerial skill.

Managers of small firms must be generalists rather than specialists. Because they must make their own decisions and then live with those choices, managers are faced with a dilemma. Because the business's resources are limited, it can't afford to make costly mistakes; yet because the organization is so small, the owner can't afford to pay for managerial assistance to prevent bad decisions.

Burdensome Government Regulations and Paperwork

If you want to upset small business managers, just mention government regulations and paperwork. That is one of their least favorite subjects—and with good reason. At one time, smaller firms were exempt from many federal regulations and even some state and local ones. Now, small firms are subject to many of the same regulations as their larger competitors. These regulations are often complex and contradictory, which explains why small business managers find it so difficult to comply with governmental requirements. While most businesspeople do not purposely evade the issues or disobey the law, they are often just unaware of the regulations and requirements. As will be shown in Chapter 17, however, small businesses often benefit from many of these regulations.

■ SOME CURRENT TRENDS CHALLENGING SMALL BUSINESS OWNERS

Small firms like large ones are now experiencing fundamental changes and new trends in the ways business is conducted and people are being employed. If small businesses are to overcome the problems just discussed, they must also be prepared to recognize and cope with these current trends that are potentially rewarding but which will challenge them and require their best performance. The most important trends are: (1) a more diverse work force, (2) emphasis on empowerment and team performance, (3) exploding technology, (4) occupational and industry shifts, and (5) global challenges.

Diversity in the work force is achieved by employing more members of minority groups, women, and older workers.

A More Diverse Work Force

Entrepreneurs and owners of small firms must develop more effective human relations skills if they are to successfully deal with the growing **diversity** in the work force. For example,

Figure 1–5

Distribution of the Labor Force by Race, 1994 and Projected 2005*

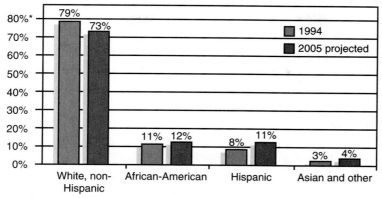

*Does not necessarily add to 100 percent because of rounding.

Source: U.S. Department of Labor, "Tomorrow's Jobs," *Occupational Outlook Handbook,* 1996–97 edition, p. 6.

while nearly half of the work force in 1975 was white males, they will compose only about 12 percent of *all net new hires* by the year 2005. White males' share of the work force is expected to fall to about 29 percent by that year, while the share of workers categorized as African-American, Hispanic, and Asian and Other (including Native American) is expected to rise significantly. So the future work force will look more nearly like that shown by the right-hand bars in Figure 1–5 than like its 1994 composition, shown by the left-hand bars.

While women are entering the work force at about the same rate as men, the men, who have been in the work force longer, are retiring at a faster rate. Thus, like racial and ethnic minorities, women will assume an even greater role in entrepreneurship and small business, as will be shown in Chapter 2.

The work force is aging, along with the rest of the population. For example, about 40 percent of the workers in 1990 were 35–54 year olds. By the year 2005, this age group will increase to about 50 percent. At the other end of the spectrum, since women are having fewer children, there will be fewer young workers than at present, causing a further shift in the work force.

Thus, tomorrow's entrepreneurs must be particularly sensitive to the need for, and ways to provide, more effective employment for a diverse group of employees. Unfortunately, both small and large companies are finding it increasingly difficult to hire well-qualified employees. All the more reason to seek the potential rewards in the challenge of diversity.

Empowerment and Team Performance

As small businesses seek **empowerment** for their employees by equipping them to function more effectively on their own, owners and managers will increasingly be using work teams. Small firms, as well as large, are increasingly organizing teams or cells that study problems and recommend changes intended to make better things happen or to make things run more smoothly. These teams are not an end in themselves but a means to an end, which is better performance than team members would achieve working on their own. Thus, the owner-manager becomes a leader who facilitates activities by presenting ideas in a group setting, by running different kinds of meetings, and by sharing skills knowingly, willingly, and freely, while letting employees make many decisions that the owner formerly made. Managers let subordinates learn by making decisions, stepping in to take control only when it becomes necessary.

Empowerment is giving employees experiences and responsibilities that equip them to function more effectively on their own.

A word of caution to owners of small businesses is appropriate here. While some workers do enjoy the idea of "being their own boss," many do not. Recent research shows that many workers "hate the headaches" that come with empowerment. They don't like "fixing broken machines and having to learn a variety of jobs."[47]

Exploding Technology

Few jobs in small firms are unaffected by improvements in communications and computer technology. Small business management is being drastically changed as automated robotics are introduced in production departments, accounting departments become heavily dependent on computer support, and marketing people use computer-aided promotional and sales programs.

A recent study by Access Media International found that companies with fewer than 100 employees spent $138 billion in 1997 just on information technology and telecommunications. This figure was 17 percent more than was spent in 1996. See Figure 1–6 for more details.

The primary challenge of exploding technology for small companies will be to improve the selection and training of workers and overcome their resistance to change. Therefore, owners and managers must keep up to date themselves on the latest technologies so they can effectively train their people to use these technologies, including telecommuting.

For example, Cynthia McKay, owner of Le Gourmet Gift Basket, allows distributors of her custom gift baskets to work from their homes. Distributors have 24-hour toll-free support and can be found at www.legift.com.[48]

Occupational and Industry Shifts

Technological advances in automation, computers, robotics, and electronic communication, along with changing markets resulting from cultural, demographic, and economic changes, have caused drastic shifts in occupations and industries. There is a declining

---

Figure 1–6
Small Business Spending on Technology

Small businesses* spent $138 billion on information technology and telecommunications in 1997, up 17% from 1996. Types of spending, in billions:

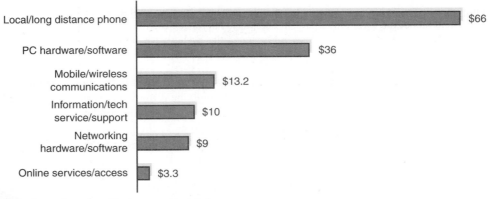

Local/long distance phone	$66
PC hardware/software	$36
Mobile/wireless communications	$13.2
Information/tech service/support	$10
Networking hardware/software	$9
Online services/access	$3.3

*Fewer than 100 employees, home-based businesses not included.

Source: Access Media International (USA), as reported in *USA Today*, March 30, 1998, p. 1B.

emphasis on traditional "smokestack" industries, with a concurrent shift toward more people-related activities, to which small business enterprise is exceptionally well suited, such as health care, banking and financial services, retail trade, transportation, and computer services.

Among these shifts, **reinvention,** particularly including a reduction in the size and markets for businesses, has led to fewer job opportunities for those who are less well trained and educated. At the same time, many larger companies have **reengineered** their activities, which has involved wiping the slate clean as far as current operations are concerned and asking, "If we blew this place up and started over, what would we do differently? What should we eliminate? What can we do that would make things easier for our customers?" The result is **downsizing** (sometimes called **rightsizing**), whereby an organization reduces the number of people it employs as it strives to become leaner and meaner and consolidates departments and work groups. According to an estimate by Professor Richard Florida at Carnegie Mellon University (www.cmu.edu), 40 percent of U.S. manufacturers have adopted this effort to "white-collarize" factories.[49]

This movement is giving people more responsibility for making more decisions and the chance to escape acting like automatons, but they must work harder and are under more pressure. A survey of a dozen big employers showed that two-thirds of workers were stretched so thin that they could not take advantage of flexible work schedules, personal leave, or other benefits, as "they're just hoping to retain what they've got."[50] *These shifts help smaller firms, as many highly skilled workers and managers leave to join the ranks of small business owners and managers.*

Reinvention is the fundamental redesign of a business, often resulting in reduction in size and markets.

Reengineering is the redesign of operations, starting from scratch.

Downsizing (rightsizing) is reducing the number of employees in order to increase efficiency.

Global Challenges

The trend in business is to become more active globally and those interested in small business management need to understand at least what the challenge is and what the rewards may be. We are entering an age of global competition and a one-world market. Consequently, *we estimate that up to half of all today's college graduates will work in some type of global activities in the future.*

One result of this global challenge is the large number of large and small U.S. businesses that are or become foreign owned. And these foreign-owned companies tend to have different management styles from their original American owners. This means small business owners and managers must learn to adjust and adapt to nontraditional styles. While foreign ownership may lead to new management styles, the American consumer may not realize the change.

> For example, few Americans know or care that consumer products for sale with RCA and GE brand names are owned by a French company, Thompson S.A. Magnavox and Sylvania are owned by Philips Electronics of the Netherlands, and Quasar is made by Japan's Matsushita Electric Industries. Even Zenith, the last TV sets to be "Made in America," are now made in South Korea by L. G. Electronics. But it really doesn't seem to make that much difference to consumers.

WHAT YOU SHOULD HAVE LEARNED

1. This is an interesting, challenging, and rewarding time to be studying small business because the field is so popular and is expected to continue growing in employment and productivity. The public attitude toward small business is favorable, and self-employment is so popular that around three-quarters of a million people—young and old—start their own businesses each year.

2. Defining *small business* is difficult because the definition of smallness varies widely. In general, a small business is independently owned and operated and is not dominant in its field of operation. It is difficult to draw a clear distinction between a *small business* and an *entrepreneurial venture,* as the distinction depends on the intentions of the owners. If they start a small business and want it to stay small, it is a small business. If, on the other hand, they start small but plan to grow big, it is an entrepreneurial venture. Although small businesses generate only 12 percent of the total receipts each year, according to the IRS, around 96 percent of U.S. businesses are small, and firms with fewer than 500 employees account for 80 percent of existing jobs.

3. Small firms differ from larger ones in many ways, but their unique contributions include (*a*) flexi-bility and room for innovation, (*b*) the ability to maintain close relationships with customers and the community, (*c*) the competition they provide, which forces larger companies to remain competitive, (*d*) the opportunity they give employees to gain experience in many areas, (*e*) the challenge and freedom they offer to risk takers, (*f*) the employment opportunities they generate, and (*g*) the job satisfaction they provide.

4. Some current problems that plague small companies more than larger ones—and limit their development—are (*a*) inadequate financing, (*b*) inadequate management (especially as the firm grows), and (*c*) burdensome government regulation and paperwork.

5. Some current trends challenging small businesses are (*a*) a more diverse work force, (*b*) the new emphasis on empowerment and team performance, (*c*) exploding technology, (*d*) occupational and industry shifts, and (*e*) the move to global operations.

QUESTIONS FOR DISCUSSION

1. Do you agree that this is an interesting time to be studying small business? Why are you doing so?

2. All of us have had personal experiences with small business—as an owner, employee, friend, or relative of an owner, or in other relationships. Explain one or more such experience(s) you have recently had.

3. What comes to your mind when you think of a small business? How does your concept differ from the definition given in this chapter?

4. Distinguish between a small business and an entrepreneurial venture. If you were to start your own business, which would you wish it to be? Why?

5. How do you explain the growing interest young people have in small business? Relate this to your personal small business experience.

6. What are the unique contributions of small businesses? Give examples of each from your own experience of owning or working in a small business or from small businesses that you patronize.

7. What are some problems facing small businesses? Again, give example from your experience.

8. Name and explain some current trends challenging small businesses.

CASE 1–1

THE BIG WASH

Henry Gibson, a 68-year-old retired file clerk, enjoyed sitting on his front porch on Belmont Street in Washington, D.C., on summer evenings watching his neighbors go by. But the sight of them lugging their laundry to two coin-operated laundries a half-mile on each side of him—one uphill, one downhill—caused him distress. With no business education or experience, nevertheless he had an idea: Why not start a laundry in the neighborhood?

Gibson knew he could not do this alone, especially raising the $250,000 needed to set up a good-sized coin laundry business. So he sought the help of Reuben McCornack, an adviser with Hope Housing, a nonprofit group located in the same block. Together they formed the Belmont Investment Group (BIG) and started selling 300 shares at $100 per share. Many investors came from the Community of Hope Church, where Gibson is an usher. Two shareholders sing in its choir. Some bought only one share, while others bought up to 50. (One neighbor invested his life's savings in 50 shares.)

Once the two men had sold 600 shares ($60,000), McCornack raised $60,000 in grants from seven foundations. With this backing, the two men were able to get a loan from a local bank and a District of Columbia government agency for a total of $300,000.

The Big Wash (the "Big" comes from the initials of their investment group) opened during the summer of 1995 in a well-designed and refurbished building on the same block where Gibson lives. (Even with its inner-city location, but without bars or a roll-down iron fence, the place had not been robbed or vandalized by early 1998.) The laundry has much going in its favor, especially the official criterion for success, according to the Coin Laundry Association: a densely populated neighborhood, with lots of kids and renters.

With 30 washers, 28 dryers, and 8 staff members—four of whom are paid attendants—operating from 7 A.M. to midnight, Big Wash usually grosses over $20,000 a month. This puts it in the top ranks of all the 35,000 self-service coin-operated laundries in the United States, which gross between $15,000 and $300,000 a year.

Since its opening in 1995, each of the laundry's shareholders has received $175 back on his or her $100 investment. For most of them, this is the first experience receiving dividend checks, which are issued quarterly by the investment group.

Questions

1. Evaluate Henry Gibson's approach to starting a new business.

2. Could there have been another source of funding? Explain.

3. How do you explain the fact that Big Wash has not been robbed?

Source: Prepared by Leon C. Megginson from various sources, including "Odds and Ends: It Took a Laundry to Clean the Area," *Mobile* (Alabama) *Register,* February 13, 1998, p. 2A.

CASE 1–2

SUE THINKS OF GOING INTO BUSINESS

Sue Ley had been a truck driver for a local oil company for about four years. Before that, she had worked as a forklift truck operator in the same company. In a recent interview, she said, "I was getting fed up with this type of work. I like working with people and thought I'd like to get into selling. One day a friend in Personnel, when I indicated interest in getting into marketing, called my attention to the company's education program, which pays tuition for employees taking college courses. So I applied for it and was accepted."

Sue, whom the interviewers found to be a woman of above-average intelligence, personality, and drive, enrolled in the marketing program at the local university. She completed her marketing coursework and graduated in three years with a business administration degree. She had continued driving the truck while working on her degree.

When she approached her employer about the possibility of transferring to the marketing department, she was told it would be four or five years before there would be an opening for her.

A short time later, Sue's uncle suggested she go into business for herself. The uncle, who had taken over Sue's grandfather's steel oil drum cleaning business about 200 miles away, advised her that she could make around $100,000 a year ($300,000 by the third year) if she started and ran a business of that sort. He offered to help her form a business and get it started.

Sue, who had been married and had two grown children, said, "I could not see any future in marketing with the oil company, and I did not want to drive trucks the rest of my life. I had saved $25,000 that I could put into the business. Why not?"

Questions

1. What do you see as Sue's alternatives?

2. What are Sue's qualifications for going into business for herself?

3. What are Sue's deficiencies?

4. What do you think of Sue's uncle's profit predictions?

5. What do you recommend that Sue do?

Source: Prepared by William M. Spain, Service Corps of Retired Executives (SCORE), and Charles R. Scott, University of Alabama.

2

OPPORTUNITIES AND CHALLENGES IN SMALL BUSINESS

The role of small and midsized firms . . . has never been more important to America's future.

Tom Peters, coauthor of *In Search of Excellence*

Guts, brains, and determination—key ingredients of the American entrepreneurial spirit—[have] sustained this nation through good times and bad, and launched it on an economic journey unlike any ever witnessed in history.

John Sloan, Jr., President and CEO, National Federation of Independent Business

LEARNING OBJECTIVES

After studying the material in this chapter, you will be able to:

1. Explain why people start small businesses.

2. Describe the characteristics of successful entrepreneurs.

3. Define the requirements for success in owning and managing a small business.

4. Analyze your qualifications for becoming a small business owner.

5. Describe where the opportunities are for small businesses.

6. Define some of the growing opportunities in small business for women and minorities.

7. Identify some of the areas of concern for small business owners.

Bob and Mai Gu: Making It in America!

Mai and Bob Gu are a perfect example of the adage "Hard work pays off." Married for 11 years, the couple has gone from working in other people's restaurants to owning and operating Shanghai Restaurant, the successful small business they opened in 1988. Their first establishment was a modest operation, serving only takeout Chinese and South Vietnamese cuisine. Mai was the sole cook for the business, coming in at 9 A.M. and working until at least 10 at night, except on Sundays.

Business was very good, so the couple decided to expand their operation. They moved to a larger building where they were able to include dining space and table service. Since their opening day there, Bob says, business has been good.

The couple used personal experience in the restaurant industry and a sharp business sense to successfully launch their own enterprise. They had both held various jobs in restaurants long before they met in early 1988. Mai had always loved to cook, so in 1972, when she divorced her South Vietnamese husband in order to "find my fortune in America," she looked for work in the restaurant field. Not satisfied with the jobs she found in Los Angeles, she moved to Mobile, Alabama, in 1975. For several years she worked in the kitchen of a suc-cessful Hunan restaurant. Although working behind the scenes, she was learning all she could about the operation. Then Bob Gu, who had come to Mobile from China, entered the picture. It wasn't long before the two were married and had started their own business.

Bob was the planner, Mai the implementer. Bob took care of the "paper" end of the business, managing the books and ordering supplies and equipment, while Mai ran things in the kitchen and on the restaurant floor. Greeting customers with genuine graciousness when they enter the front door, cooking Oriental dishes with an expertise that comes only from years of hands-on culinary experience, and taking time out to chat with the regulars, Mai and Bob are the perfect hosts. It is quite obvious that they enjoy what they are doing.

Employees of the restaurant, from the cooks in the kitchen to the waitresses, are family members lending a hand to make the operation a success. Mai seems especially proud of the fact that all of her children work for her in one capacity or another. This family involvement adds another dimension to the dining experience for the patron; when you see the same friendly faces each time you visit a restaurant, it eventually feels as if you were eating a meal at home.

Hoping to attract new customers, Mai and Bob obtained a liquor license for the restaurant. They also advertised in the local newspaper and the local *Chinese Business Directory* in an effort to increase revenues.

Their enterprise, hard work, and dedication have paid off. A few years ago, Mai was able to visit her family in Vietnam to show them that she had indeed "made it in America." She was glad she had made the trip, as her mother died shortly thereafter.

In the early years Bob and Mai had opened a small Oriental market adjacent to the restaurant. It offered everything from special Oriental teas and spices to hand-carved clocks. According to Mai, the market occasionally drew a curious restaurant customer but didn't attract very much business on its own. The couple recently expanded this sideline into an international market and relocated it several blocks from the restaurant, on another busy thoroughfare. It features Spanish and Chinese food and related items imported from China and Latin America by their other business, the Shanghai Trading Corporation. In addition, they cater to the local market by stocking Mardi Gras goods such as beads, toys, masks, balloons, and other novelties. Their customers include wholesalers, retailers, and the general public.

Continuing their successful division of work, Mai manages the restaurant while Bob manages the market, except during the lunch and dinner hours, when he helps out in the restaurant.

Source: Prepared by Ragan Workman Megginson, owner and president of Compliments of the Chef, LLC.

Now that you've seen the dynamic role played by small business, it's time to see what is needed to succeed in owning such a business. It's also time to see if there are really opportunities in small business and, if so, what and where they are. Next, you should be interested in any special areas of concern for small firms. Finally, it's time for you to determine whether you have the qualities needed to succeed in a small business.

■ WHY PEOPLE START SMALL BUSINESSES

One contribution to the explosion of new entrepreneurs discussed in Chapter 1 is the current trend of corporate downsizing. Many of today's corporate professionals are leaving their companies to start their own businesses. The changing environment in large firms is leaving employees frustrated and uncertain about their future. So they leave to find a better job or—as many are now doing—to start their own company, using the expertise they learned at the larger firm.[1]

As these employees who go out on their own are aware, owning a small business provides an excellent opportunity to satisfy personal objectives while achieving the firm's business objectives. Probably in no other occupation or profession is this as true. But there are almost as many different reasons for starting small businesses as there are small business owners. Those reasons can be summarized as (1) to satisfy personal objectives and (2) to achieve business objectives.

To Satisfy Personal Objectives

Small business owners have the potential to fulfill many personal goals. In fact, owning a small business tends to satisfy most of our work goals. According to a survey by Padgett Business Services USA, Inc. (www.dbtech.net/padgett), the best things about owning a small business are independence (cited by 72 percent of those surveyed), control (10 percent), satisfaction (10 percent), and other factors (8 percent). The worst parts of such ownership are the long hours (mentioned by 23 percent of respondents), taxes (22 percent), risk (17 percent), responsibility (17 percent), and other factors (12 percent).[2]

Similar results were found in a study by the National Bureau of Economic Research in Great Britain, where 46 percent of the self-employed were "very satisfied," versus 29 percent of those working for others. In the United States, the numbers were 63 percent versus 27 percent.[3]

The personal objectives of owners of small businesses differ from those of managers of larger firms. Managers of large companies tend to seek security, place, power, prestige, high income, and benefits. By contrast, the primary objectives of small business owners are to:

- Achieve independence.
- Obtain additional income.
- Help their families.
- Provide products not available elsewhere.

In summary, the personal objectives of small business owners tend to be achievement oriented, as opposed to those of managers of large firms, who tend to be power and prestige oriented. How these personal objectives are achieved depends on the knowledge, skills, and personal traits these owners bring to the business.

> For example, Bob and Susan Shallow operate a hot air balloon ride business within a 250-mile radius of their home base. Susan gave up a career in real estate so she could devote full time to running the enterprise, called Gulf View Balloon Company. Gulf View's revenue comes from balloon rides, sales, and service. Susan explained their success by saying, "We really love balloons and ballooning. It's something Bob and I can do together, and ballooning is something people can do with their families."[4]

To Achieve Independence   While all the above objectives may lead someone to own a small business, the owner's primary motive is usually independence, that is, freedom from interference or control by superiors.[5] Small business owners tend to want autonomy to exercise their initiative and ambition; this freedom often results in innovations and leads to greater flexibility, which is one of the virtues of small businesses. People who operate small firms know they are running a risk when they strike out on their own, but they hope to realize their goal of independence. In essence, owning your own business provides a feeling of satisfaction that may be missing if you work for someone else. As you can see from Figure 2–1, this is the choice the prospective entrepreneur must make.

To Obtain Additional Income   Many people start a business to obtain needed income. This need obviously varies with different people in different life stages or situations. For example, a

Figure 2–1
Which Road to Take?

retired person may want to earn just enough to supplement Social Security payments and possibly provide a few luxuries. Such a person may be content with a business that provides a small supplement to retirement income, as the following example illustrates.

> Margaret Williamson began sewing when she was 10. She learned much from her mother and from home economics classes in high school. In the mid-1930s, she was employed by a government works program, the WPA, and later she sewed for her own family, making all her daughter's school clothes.
>
> In the 1960s, Mrs. Williamson began making and selling handicrafts to boost her Social Security income. The Alabama Cooperative Extension Service (www.reeusda.gov) advised her on marketing her crafts, with instructions on how to participate in craft shows and how to make effective displays. This training gave her the opportunity to participate in many local craft shows and school bazaars, and she has displayed items in local beauty shops and schools.
>
> Now 83, Mrs. William has completed her afghans for 1999 Christmas sales. She's looking forward to producing them into the twenty-first century.

On the other hand, owning a business can provide the opportunity to make a great deal of money and to take advantage of certain tax benefits.* In fact, you are 10 times more likely to become a millionaire by owning your own business than by working for someone else.[6] Yet not all small business owners and managers make a lot of money; nor do they all intend to.

As we said at the outset, people start small businesses after being unable to find employment elsewhere or being discharged from a larger firm. Professional athletes, whose bodies are a wasting asset and who must retire early, often find a second career in small businesses they have formed. For example, Earvin "Magic" Johnson, the former Los Angeles Lakers star player, is investing in inner cities that have been ignored or abandoned by other entrepreneurs. His Magic Johnson Theaters have created at least 100 new jobs at each of their locations in Atlanta, Houston, and Los Angeles. His mission is "to revitalize the underserved communities." The result has been one of the highest-grossing theater complexes in the nation.[7]

To Help Their Families   Small business owners are probably motivated as much by personal and family considerations as by the desire for profit. Students may return home to operate the family business so their parents can retire or take life easier. They may take over the firm on the death of a parent or form a business to help their family financially.

> For example, some years ago, Rebiya Kader secretly made and sold children's clothes to supplement her husband's income, which was insufficient to feed their six children. At the time, private enterprise was illegal in China, where she lived. In addition, the Muslim culture to which she belonged looked down on women working outside the home. But she persisted, and soon she was managing a $10.4 million organization and was the richest woman in Xinjiang.[8]

To Provide Products Not Available Elsewhere   The saying "Necessity is the mother of invention" applies to the beginning of many small firms. In fact, as shown in Chapter 1, most American economic development has resulted from innovations born in small firms. Relative to the number of people employed, small firms produce two-and-a-half times as many new ideas and products as large firms. The first air conditioner, airplane, automobile, instant camera, jet engine, helicopter, office copier, heart pacemaker, foam fire extin-

---

*You should consult your lawyers and tax accountants, though, to make sure you stay on the right side of tax laws, which have been modified to remove many of these benefits.

guisher, quick-frozen foods, sliced and wrapped bread, vacuum tube, zipper, and safety razor—not to mention the first giant computer, as well as many other breakthroughs—either resulted from the creativity found in small companies or led to the creation of a new business, as the following example illustrates.

> Lloyd Mandel recognized a need for more economical funerals. As most funeral homes began to offer more services such as expensive seals and elaborate ceremonies, he identified a growing need for basic rituals. Mandel opened such a "funeral store" in a Skokie, Illinois, mall nine years ago.
>
> He was so successful that he was bought out by the huge Service Corporation International (SCI). He is now a regional vice president who does research and similar ventures for Service Corp.[9]

To Achieve Business Objectives

One of the most important functions the business owner must perform is setting **objectives,** which are the ends toward which all the activities of the company should be aimed. Essentially, objectives determine the character of the firm, for they give the business its direction and provide standards by which to measure individual performance.

Among the objectives that are important to a business are service, profit, social, and growth objectives. These objectives tend to be interrelated. For example, the service objective must be achieved to attain the profit objective. Yet profits must be made if the business is to continue to reach its social and service objectives. Growth depends on attaining both profit *and* social objectives, which are not necessarily incompatible.

Service Objective   In general, the objective of a business is to serve customers by producing and selling goods or services (or the satisfactions associated with them) at a cost that will ensure a fair price to the consumer and adequate profits for the owners. Thus, a person who aspires to operate a small business *must set service as the primary objective—but seek profit as a natural consequence.* The pragmatic test for a small firm is this: If the firm ceases to give service, it will go out of business; if there are no profits, the owners will cease operations.

Profit Objective   Profit is the revenue received by a business in excess of the expenses paid. We expect a private business to receive a profit from its operations because profit is acceptable in a free-enterprise economy and is considered to be in the public interest. Simply stated, the **profit motive** is entering a business to make a profit, which is the reward for taking risks. Profits are needed to create new jobs, acquire new facilities, and develop new products. Profits are not self-generating, however; goods or services must be produced at a cost low enough to permit the firm to make a profit while charging customers a price they are willing and able to pay.

Profits, then, are the reward for accepting business risks and performing an economic service. They are needed to assure the continuity of a business.

Social Objective   As will be discussed further in Chapter 17, successful small businesses must have **social objectives,** which means helping various groups in the community, including customers, employees, suppliers, the government, and the community itself. Even small firms have a responsibility to protect the interests of all parties as well as to make a profit. Profit and social objectives are not necessarily incompatible.

Growth Objective   Owners of small firms should be concerned with growth and should select a growth objective, which will depend on answers to questions such as "Will I be satisfied for my business to remain small?" and "Do I want it to grow and challenge larger

Objectives are the goals toward which the activities of the business are directed.

Profit is the revenue received by a business in excess of the expenses paid.

The **profit motive** is expecting to make a profit as the reward for taking the risk of starting and running the business.

Social objectives are goals regarding assisting groups in the community and protecting the environment.

firms?" and "Do I seek a profit that is only 'satisfactory,' considering my effort and investment, or do I seek to maximize profits?"

Need to Mesh Objectives

Personal and business objectives can be integrated in a small business. In fact, there is often
a close connection between profitability, customer satisfaction, manager satisfaction, and
nonfinancial rewards. Also there is an increased chance of success when the objectives of
the business—service at a profit—are meshed with the owner's personal objectives.

■ CHARACTERISTICS OF SUCCESSFUL ENTREPRENEURS

The abilities and personal characteristics of the owner(s) exert a powerful influence on the
success of a small company. Also, the methods and procedures adopted in a small firm
should be designed not only to offset any personal deficiencies the owner may have but also
to build on his or her strengths.

What characterizes owners of successful small companies? A set of characteristics for
small business entrepreneurs was suggested in a definitive study by the U.S. Trust Company
(www.ustrust.com) of mostly longtime small business owners. Nearly half of those studied
were from poor or lower-middle-class families. On the average, they had started their careers
with a part-time job, such as a paper route or babysitting, at age 10. They were working full
time by 18, and by 29 they owned their own businesses. While 6 percent had dropped out
of high school, 23 percent had earned a high school diploma, another 27 percent had some
college, 29 percent had finished college, and 17 percent had completed professional or graduate school. *Three out of four had financed their own college education by working.*[10]

By and large, small business owners are reasonably well educated. A Padgett Business
Services survey of business owners with fewer than 20 employees found that 97 percent of
them had at least a high school education. Half had at least a college education. (See Figure
2–2 for more details.) The U.S. Trust study found that, in general, women business owners
were better educated than their male counterparts; 58 percent were college graduates as
compared to only 45 percent of male business owners.[11]

Figure 2–2
Education Level of Small Business Owners*

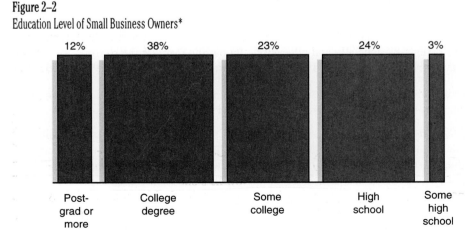

*Those that employ fewer than 20 people.

Source: Padgett Business Services USA, Inc., survey, as reported in *USA Today,* September 25, 1995. Copyright
1995, *USA TODAY.* Reprinted with permission.

From these and many other sources, we conclude that the characteristics of successful owners of small businesses are that they:

- Desire independence.
- Have a strong sense of initiative.
- Are motivated by personal and family considerations.
- Expect quick and concrete results.
- Are able to react quickly.
- Are dedicated to their businesses.
- Enter business as much by chance as by design.

Desire Independence

As shown earlier in the chapter, those people who start small businesses seek independence and want to be free of outside control. They enjoy the freedom that comes from "doing their own thing" and making their own decisions—for better or for worse.

Have a Strong Sense of Initiative

Owners of small businesses have a strong sense of initiative that gives them a desire to use their ideas, abilities, and aspirations to the greatest degree possible.[12] They are able to conceive, plan, and carry to a successful conclusion ideas for a new product. This is not always true in a larger organization.

Another aspect of initiative usually seen in small business owners is their willingness to work long, hard hours to reach their goals. They tend to be capable, ambitious, persevering individuals.

Are Motivated by Personal and Family Considerations

As shown earlier, small business owners are often motivated as much by personal and family considerations as by the profit motive. They start and operate their businesses to help their parents, children, and other family members. It's interesting to note that 34 percent of the families of small business owners "always" have dinner at home together, and another 34 percent do so "frequently."[13] The flexibility afforded small business owners is a great advantage in planning family activities such as this.

As will be discussed in Chapter 18, there now seems to be a trend toward children helping their parents—financially and otherwise—by putting them on the payroll[14] or helping them start small firms. This trend builds on the past practice of parents helping their children, as the following classic example shows.

John H. Johnson, one of the nation's leading black entrepreneurs, founded Johnson Publishing Company (www.ebonymag.com), which owns *Ebony* and *Jet* magazines, radio stations, and a cosmetics firm. When asked what was the key to his success, Johnson answered, "My mother . . . made so many sacrifices. . . . She even let me mortgage her furniture [for $600] . . . to start my business. . . . I couldn't let her down."[15] Now he's one of the nation's richest individuals, and his daughter, Linda Johnson Rice, heads the company. She says, "I was exposed to the company at an early age. While other kids played after school, I'd come work in my dad's office."[16]

Another interesting trend is the shift toward more couples doing business together, as several of our previous examples have shown. According to the SBA's Office of Advocacy, this was expected to be the fastest-growing category of new businesses by the turn of the twenty-first century.[17]

Expect Quick and Concrete Results

Small business owners expect quick and concrete results from their investment of time and capital. Instead of engaging in the long-range planning that is common in large businesses, they seek a quick return on their capital. And they become impatient and discouraged when these results are slow in coming.

Are Able to React Quickly

Small businesses have an advantage over larger firms in that they can react more quickly to changes occurring both inside and outside the company. For example, one characteristic of a small business is its vulnerability to technological and environmental changes. Because the business is small, such changes have a great effect on its operations and profitability. A small business owner must therefore have the ability to react quickly, as the following example illustrates.

> In 1995, while selling color printers for Hewlett-Packard, Judy MacDonald dreamed of producing a new product that would let children use computer software to make crafts such as jewelry, iron-on decals, calendars, and holiday ornaments. When her best friend, Irit Hillel, a French business consultant, visited her in January 1995, she was captivated by the idea and said, "Let's do it!"
>
> Soon after that, Hillel called her after seeing a huge line of computer-generated iron-on T-shirt decals at a trade show. She told MacDonald, "We have to jump on this!" After a week of faxes and phone calls, MacDonald invited another friend, Rosie Welch, a freelance designer, to join the team.
>
> MacDonald invested $50,000—her life savings—and quit her job. Hillel invested $25,000, and Welch kicked in $15,000 and closed her design business. Their company, PrintPaks Inc., was in business by May 1995. MacDonald was CEO, Hillel was vice president for international sales, and Welch was creative director.
>
> Needing additional funds, the friends obtained $1.7 million from venture capitalists and were operating successfully. Wanting a big company to invest in PrintPaks, in 1996 MacDonald started negotiating with Mattel, which soon paid $20 million for the new company. After paying off investors and generously rewarding their 32 employees, the three entrepreneurs made a profit of $6 million.[18]

Are Dedicated to Their Businesses

Small business owners tend to be fiercely dedicated to their company. With so much of their time, energy, money, and emotions invested in it, they want to ensure that nothing harms their "baby." Consequently, they have a zeal, devotion, and ardor often missing in managers of big companies.

Enter Business as Much by Chance as by Design

An interesting characteristic of many small business owners is that they get into business as much by chance as by design. These are the owners who quite frequently ask for assistance in the form of management training and development. This type of individual differs sharply from those who attend college with the ambition to become professional managers and who gear their programs toward that end.

For example, 17-year-old Levi Strauss emigrated from Bavaria to America in 1847. After peddling clothing and household items from door to door in New York for three years, he sailed by clipper ship to California with a load of denim to make tents for gold miners. There was little demand for tents but great demand for durable working clothes, so the ever-adaptable Strauss had a tailor make the unsold cloth into waist-high overalls, called them "Levi's," and was in business (www.levistrauss.com).[19]

■ WHAT LEADS TO SUCCESS IN MANAGING A SMALL BUSINESS?

Although it is difficult to determine precisely what leads to success in managing a small business, the following are some important factors:

- Serving an adequate and well-defined market for the product.
- Acquiring sufficient capital.
- Recruiting and using human resources effectively.
- Obtaining and using timely information.
- Coping effectively with government regulations.
- Having expertise in the field on the part of both the owner and the employees.
- Managing time effectively.

Serving an Adequate and Well-Defined Market

As will be shown in Part II of this book, there must be an adequate demand for your product. One of the greatest assets you can have is the ability to detect a market for something before others do and then devise a way of satisfying the market. A company providing venture capital to small business entrepreneurs found that 90 percent of the 2 million U.S. millionaires owned their own firms. The primary reason for this was that larger firms rejected the new—and often superior—ideas of employees, who then went out and started their own companies.[20] It also helps if you can find a market that is not being satisfied and design a unique product for it.

In 1961, for example, Ross Perot (www.perot.org) suggested to IBM, his employer, that they emphasize software rather than hardware. After being turned down by top management the second time, Perot left his lucrative job and founded EDS, a data processing firm. He later sold it to GM for several million dollars.

Acquiring Sufficient Capital

As shown in Chapter 1, a major problem for small business owners is obtaining sufficient capital, at a reasonable price, to acquire the resources needed to start and operate a business. Owners who become successful have been able to obtain needed funds, either from their own resources or from others. They are willing to delay satisfying the desire for profit or dividends now, in the long-run interest of the business.

Although lack of investment capital is a problem for small firms, even worse is a shortage of working capital. In fact, probably *the biggest crisis for a small business is a lack of cash,* as will be discussed in Chapter 14.

Recruiting and Using Human Resources Effectively

The effective recruitment and use of human resources are especially important to owners of small businesses, who have a closer and more personal association with their employees than do managers of larger businesses. Workers in a small firm can be a good source of information and ideas, and their productivity should increase if you allow them to share ideas with you, especially if you recognize and reward their contributions.

Obtaining and Using Timely Information

You need to stay informed of financial and marketing conditions affecting your business. You must analyze and evaluate information and develop plans to maintain or improve your position. The "information explosion" of the 1980s has not been accompanied by an increased ability to interpret and use all the data available. Instead, information's increased complexity sometimes overwhelms small business owners. There are limits to the amount and types of information owners can absorb and use in their operations.

Coping with Government Regulations

As discussed in Chapter 1, the days when small businesses were exempt from most governmental regulation have passed. Now the cost in time and money to comply with the regulations is of major concern to small business owners, whose responses are varied and often negative (see Figure 2–3). Not only must small business owners be able to handle red tape effectively, but it is especially important that they become involved in governmental activities, as will be discussed in Chapter 17.

Having Expertise in the Field

If you are to succeed in a business of your own, ambition, desire, drive, capital, judgment, and a competitive spirit are not enough. In addition, you'll need technical and managerial know-how and expertise to perform the activities necessary to run the business. Some types of business, such as general retail establishments, may need only general skills. But the more technical and complex the business is, the greater the need for specialized skills, which can be acquired only through education, training, and experience. In other words, "Become an expert before becoming a business owner."[21]

Managing Time Effectively

The effective use of time is especially important to small business owners because of the many and varied duties that only they can perform. While managers of large firms can delegate activities to others, freeing time for other uses, small business owners are limited in their ability, or willingness, to do so. They often prefer to do things themselves rather than delegate authority to others. Another problem is the long hours worked by new business owners.

While there is no magic formula for effective time management, the following are some specific methods for saving your time:

- Organizing the work, including delegating to subordinates as many duties as feasible.
- Selecting a competent person to sort out unimportant mail, screen incoming calls, and keep a schedule of appointments and activities.
- Using electronic equipment for letters and memos.
- Adhering to appointment and business conference times.
- Preparing an agenda for meetings, confining discussion to the items on the agenda, and making follow-up assignments to specific subordinates.

Figure 2–3
Coping with Government Regulation

■ DOING AN INTROSPECTIVE PERSONAL ANALYSIS

Now that you have seen some characteristics of successful small business owners, do you think you have enough of those characteristics to be successful? The following personal evaluation will help you decide this important question. No one of these items is more important than any other; rather, you need to determine whether the combination of qualities you have will help you succeed as a small business owner.

Analyzing Your Values

To manage your firm effectively, you need a set of basic principles to serve as guidelines for managerial decision making. The more important questions you need to ask are the following: What are your true motives? What real objectives do you seek? What relative weights do you give to service, profit, and social responsibilities? What type of interpersonal relations do you want to establish with employees and customers?

Everyone has a philosophy—that is, a conviction of what is right or wrong, desirable or undesirable. That personal philosophy will more than likely become your management philosophy. Your business objectives and resulting policies and procedures will be based on it. In the business world, the greatest esteem seems to be granted to those people viewed as builders—that is, the ones who create a product and a company to produce it.

Analyzing Your Mental Abilities

Next, you should analyze your mental abilities to determine the type of business that will satisfy your objectives. Ask questions such as these: Can I see my choice of a business in its entirety—physically and economically? Can I see things logically, objectively, and in perspective? Can I generate ideas about new methods and products? Can I interpret and translate ideas into realistic activities? Can I accurately interpret the feelings, wants, and needs of others?

Remember, *you don't have to have all these abilities to be a successful small business owner. But an analysis of them can help you understand what you can do if you try. It helps determine how you can move toward succeeding in business.*

Analyzing Your Attitudes

Another way to determine whether you should become a small business owner is to analyze your attitudes. Ask questions such as these: Am I willing to accept responsibility? Am I mentally and emotionally stable? Am I committed to the idea of operating a small business? Am I willing to take risks? Can I tolerate irregular hours? Am I self-disciplined? Self-confident? Let us again emphasize that you will not—and need not—have all the necessary attitudes, but you should be able to develop as many of them as feasible.

If your answer to the questions in this section was yes, or if you feel that you can make it yes in the near future, you may have the qualities that would make an entrepreneurial venture a satisfying and rewarding activity for you. The self-test in Figure 2–4 should help you decide whether you have these qualities. To utilize an interactive entrepreneurial self-test on the World Wide Web, go to *www.innonet.ch/_pages/sp_e/service_ utest_frames.html.* This international Web site includes sidebars with detailed checklist to test your entrepreneurial spirit and analyze the qualities necessary in any successful small business owner.

Figure 2–4

Test Your Potential as an Entrepreneur

Do you have what it takes to be a success in your own business? Below is a list of 20 personality traits. Consider each carefully—and then score yourself by placing a check under the appropriate number with 0 being the lowest and 7 being the highest. Tally your score and find out what kind of entrepreneur you would make, using the key below.

	0	1	2	3	4	5	6	7
I have the ability to communicate.	—	—	—	—	—	—	—	—
I have the ability to motivate others.	—	—	—	—	—	—	—	—
I have the ability to organize.	—	—	—	—	—	—	—	—
I can accept responsibility.	—	—	—	—	—	—	—	—
I can easily adapt to change.	—	—	—	—	—	—	—	—
I have decision-making capability.	—	—	—	—	—	—	—	—
I have drive and energy.	—	—	—	—	—	—	—	—
I am in good health.	—	—	—	—	—	—	—	—
I have good human relations skills.	—	—	—	—	—	—	—	—
I have initiative.	—	—	—	—	—	—	—	—
I am interested in people.	—	—	—	—	—	—	—	—
I have good judgment.	—	—	—	—	—	—	—	—
I am open-minded and receptive to new ideas.	—	—	—	—	—	—	—	—
I have planning ability.	—	—	—	—	—	—	—	—
I am persistent.	—	—	—	—	—	—	—	—
I am resourceful.	—	—	—	—	—	—	—	—
I am self-confident.	—	—	—	—	—	—	—	—
I am a self-starter.	—	—	—	—	—	—	—	—
I am a good listener.	—	—	—	—	—	—	—	—
I am willing to be a risk taker.	—	—	—	—	—	—	—	—

Key:

110–140	Very strong
85–109	Strong
55–84	Fair
54 or below	Weak

Source: Prepared by Sherron Boone and Lisa Aplin of the University of Mobile.

■ WHERE ARE THE OPPORTUNITIES FOR SMALL BUSINESSES?

Up to this point, we have shown you the challenges of becoming an entrepreneur and explained the requirements for succeeding as the owner of a small business. Now it is time to explain what your opportunities are.

What Are the Fastest-Growing Industries?

According to the Bureau of Labor Statistics (www.stats.bls.gov), no industry is growing faster than services, and this trend is expected to continue at least into the twenty-first century. This trend is evident in both the number of new businesses being created and, as Figure 2–5 shows, the number of new jobs being created. Most of the growing industries are dominated by small private companies. According to the SBA's Office of Advocacy (www.sba.gov), only construction and personnel/supply services tend to be dominated by larger businesses.

Figure 2–5
Where the New Jobs Will Be

These industries are expected to produce the most new jobs by the year 2000.

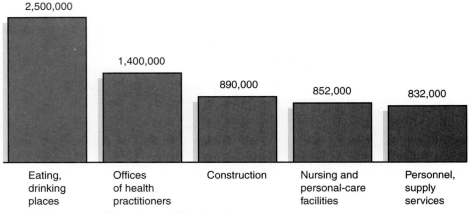

Source: U.S. Department of Labor, Bureau of Labor Statistics.

No discussion of job growth would be complete without mentioning the role of technology, especially in the computer industry. Not only is the number of new companies exploding, but they are also quite profitable. In fact, according to *Forbes,* 45 of the 500 American corporations most prized by Wall Street are in the computer industry.[22] Also, globalization, downsizing, consolidations, interorganizational cooperation, and the use of new technologies such as the World Wide Web are causing a phenomenal growth in the telecommunications industries.[23] A related trend is occurring in the computer industry. In December 1997, 190,000—or one in 10—information technology jobs were vacant. The industry was "opening its arms to cops, waitresses, and retirees in a mad scramble to combat a dire shortage of high-tech employees."[24]

Factors Affecting the Future of an Industry or a Business

Many changes are now occurring that will affect the future of an industry or business, and small business owners should study them intently in order to adjust to them. These changes can cause slow-growing industries to speed up or fast-growing ones to slow down. For instance, one recent study found that the more professional technicians or other "knowledge workers" an industry has, the greater the chance that it will create new jobs. The study defined such **high-knowledge industries** as those in which 40 percent or more of workers are high-knowledge workers.[25]

Another important reality to consider is that a change that provides an opportunity for one industry or business may pose a threat to others. For example, aging of the population may increase the need for retirement facilities but hurt industries supplying baby needs.

Figure 2–6 shows some selected examples of factors that affect various industries and businesses. These factors will be discussed more fully in Chapters 4 and 5.

Some Practical Ideas for Small Businesses

Recent Bureau of Labor Statistics figures indicate that around 71 percent of future employment in the fastest-growing industries (such as medical care, business services,

High-knowledge industries are those in which 40 percent or more of human resources are professionals, technicians, or other "knowledge workers."

Figure 2–6
Examples of Factors Affecting Industry and Business Trends

1. *Economics*—gross national product (GNP), interest rates, inflation rates, stages of the business cycle, employment levels, size and characteristics of business firms and not-for-profit organizations, and opportunities in foreign markets.
2. *Technology*—artificial intelligence, thinking machines, laser beams, new energy sources, amount of spending for research and development, and issuance of patents and their protection.
3. *Lifestyle*—career expectations, consumer activism, health concerns, desire to upgrade education and climb the socioeconomic ladder, and need for psychological services.
4. *Political-legal*—antitrust regulations, environmental protection laws, foreign trade regulations, tax changes, immigration laws, child-care legislation, and the attitude of governments and society toward the particular type of industry and business.
5. *Demographics*—population growth rate, age and regional shifts, ethnic moves and life expectancy, number and distribution of firms within the industry, and size and character of markets.

and the environment) will likely come from small businesses—and these are areas where small firms are quite competitive. One reason for this is that, as shown in Chapter 1, entrepreneurs tend to be innovative and to develop new ideas. Some innovative ideas currently being developed, such as the following, should lead to the big businesses of tomorrow.

- Career counseling.
- Catering.
- Computer and office machine repair.
- Day care.
- Educational services and products.
- Financial planning.
- Home health care.
- Marketing, promotion, and public relations.
- Senior fitness and recreation.
- Specialized delivery services.

> For example, Cuisine Express (www.westchestermenus.com/cexpress/index.html) provides fast, effective home or office delivery of meals from 40 restaurants in Westchester County, New York. Customers choose the restaurant and meal they desire and place an order with Cuisine Express's operator or via the Internet. The meal is ordered from the restaurant, and a driver picks it up, delivers it, and collects payment by cash, Visa, MasterCard, American Express, Discover, or Diner's Club.

■ GROWING OPPORTUNITIES FOR WOMEN AND DIVERSE ETHNIC GROUPS IN SMALL BUSINESSES

Starting a small business provides an excellent chance for women and members of diverse ethnic groups to gain economic freedom. The opportunities for women, African-Americans, Hispanics, Asians, and Native Americans are escalating in number and frequency, as will be shown by several examples in this chapter.

Increasing Opportunities for Women

The 1980s were called the "decade of women entrepreneurs."[26] In fact, the last two decades of the twentieth century can be called that, for during that time female entrepreneurs have been the fastest growing segment of the small business sector, creating firms at a rate twice that of their male counterparts.[27] For example, the number of women-owned businesses increased 78 percent nationwide from 1987 to 1996, outpacing overall business growth by nearly two to one.[28] Women now own about 35 percent of all the nation's businesses.[29] In fact, it has been projected that by now women probably own half of all U.S. small firms.[30]

A study by the National Foundation for Women Business Owners (NFWBO) and Dun & Bradstreet found that in 1996 nearly 8 million women-owned firms provided jobs for 18.5 million persons—more than were employed in the Fortune 500 industrial firms—and generated $2.28 *trillion* in sales.[31]

(*Source:* Reprinted from *The Wall Street Journal* by permission of Cartoon Features Syndicate.)

Most women entrepreneurs are still concentrated in the more traditional areas, such as public relations, retailing, marketing, data processing, business services, and human resources. In fact, 52 percent of all women-owned businesses are in service industries, compared to 44 percent for all U.S. firms.[32] However, according to the NFWBO, the change in women-owned businesses is occurring faster in the nontraditional industries such as manufacturing, transportation, communications, finance/real estate, and construction.[33] The federal government is encouraging this trend by specifying that 5 percent of all U.S. procurement spending should go to women-owned firms.[34]

An earlier poll of National Association of Women Business Owners members found that these owners were not the mythical women who inherited the family, or their spouse's, business. Instead, 90 percent of them either started the business for themselves, bought a business, or bought a franchise—primarily to prove that they could succeed, to earn more money, or to control their work schedule. The surveyed women entrepreneurs were highly educated: only 5 percent of those responding had only a high school education or less.[35] A later study found that roughly three out of four home-based women business owners are college educated.[36]

Globally, women are rapidly advancing by becoming entrepreneurs. As the economic status of women is expanding worldwide, we are learning that many women are discovering talents for running businesses. The United Nations Development Program encourages women in developing nations to launch small businesses.

> For instance, Kamala Lamechhane opened a restaurant in a mountainous tourist area one hour from Katmandu, Nepal. With a beautiful panoramic view and a steady flow of customers, she was earning $40 to $60 a week, which she used to supplement her family's farm income.[37]

Yet there are many problems still facing women entrepreneurs, including getting a loan, dealing with male employees and clients, getting moral support in the industry, and dealing with female employees and clients. To overcome some of these problems, the Women's Business Ownership Act, passed in late 1988, extended antidiscrimination laws to include commercial and personal credit for women.[38]

Increasing Opportunities for Diverse Ethnic Groups

Small business ownership also provides growing opportunities for many ethnic groups. Small business has traditionally owed a great deal to immigrants, who have been responsible for much of the surge in new firms. A flood of immigrants poured into the United States around the turn of the century, and many of our great companies were started by newcomers.

Now, the situation is quite similar, as millions of people moved to the United States in the last quarter-century. About 80 percent of these immigrants came from Latin America, the Caribbean, and Asia.[39] These promising entrepreneurs, with their bilingual skills, family ties, and knowledge of how things are done in other countries, have much to contribute— especially to the growing Asian and Latin American markets. But the influence of immigrants is also felt at home. For example, the computer industry today is highly dependent on microprocessor chips made by Intel, whose former chairman, Andrew Grove, came to the United States in 1957 at age 20. A refugee from Hungary, he was unable to speak English and had only the clothes on his back and $20.[40]

Now, according to a survey, about 14 percent of U.S. businesses are owned by members of minorities.[41] The U.S. economy is increasingly feeling the impact of ethnic entrepreneurs as big corporations step up efforts to market their wares to minority-owned businesses. As businesspeople have learned the importance of communications, they have found that minority business communities, with their linguistic and cultural complexities, aren't easy to navigate. New and more sophisticated ways of selling to target markets result from these findings.

> For example, Pacific Telesis Group opened a unit in San Francisco for Vietnamese customers. They can order phone services in Vietnamese, and Pacific Telesis can send out Vietnamese-speaking sales representatives or mail bilingual information to Vietnamese-American business owners.[42]

One particularly interesting trend is the rapid growth of businesses owned by minority women. One of the fastest-growing small business categories, the number of these companies recently surged to 1.1 million.[43] This 153 percent increase in nine years was more than three times the percentage growth (47 percent) of U.S. business in general. The report by the NFWBO indicated that the sales total for this group was $184.2 billion. The number of businesses owned by Hispanic women increased 206 percent; those owned by Asian, Native American, and Alaska natives rose by 138 percent, and those by African-American women, by 135 percent.[44]

Opportunities for African-Americans   There are many good opportunities for African-Americans in small business since small firms hire about 10.5 times as many blacks as do large firms. According to the Commerce Department's Minority Business Development Agency (www.mbda.gov), the number of black-owned businesses grew rapidly during a recent period, showing a 46 percent increase as compared to a 26 percent increase for all businesses.[45]

Yet there is still much room for improvement. According to Barbara Lindsey, founder of the Los Angeles Black Enterprise Expo, while African-Americans make up about 11–12 percent of the U.S. population, they account for only 3 percent of its business owners.[46] And most black-owned businesses are small. While they account for 3 percent of all U.S. companies, they employ only 1.1 percent of U.S. workers.

The role of black entrepreneurs is rapidly changing. Once engaged primarily in mom-and-pop businesses such as barbershops, cleaners, and grocery stores, they are now moving into such fields as electronics, advertising, real estate development, insurance, health care, computers, publishing, and automobile dealerships.

An example of this trend is Carolyn Colby, founder of Colby Care Nurses, Inc., who provides health care services to clients in predominantly black and Hispanic areas. "Because we're a black-owned company, we can cover areas that other companies cannot and will not cover," she says. Many black entrepreneurs like Ms. Colby are fulfilling social needs as well as making a profit.[47]

Black entrepreneurs—including many ambitious, well-educated, and influential young African-Americans—are now organizing for empowerment in order to help others reach success.[48] For instance, there is "The Network," an informal, but powerful, system of contacts and relationships that is helping drive economic growth in the black business community. It draws in successful people, from entrepreneurs to business executives to entertainers. Some of its members are the previously mentioned Earvin "Magic" Johnson, former basketball star and co-owner of Pepsi-Cola of Washington, D.C.; Oprah Winfrey, TV personality and owner of Harpo Productions; J. Bruce Llewelyn, owner of Queen City Broadcasting, Philadelphia Coca-Cola Bottling, and Garden State Cable; and Earl Graves, owner of *Black Enterprise* magazine and co-owner of Pepsi-Cola of Washington.[49]

Another organization that encourages entrepreneurship among disadvantaged young people—especially inner-city blacks—is the National Foundation for Teaching Entrepreneurship, Inc. The mission of this organization, founded in 1987, is to bring basic business and entrepreneurial skills to these young people, using the principles taught by one of U.S. history's most remarkable figures, Booker T. Washington. The foundation has 800 entrepreneurship teachers who preach Washington's simple principles, including: "Become entrepreneurial. Make yourself indispensable."[50] The National Urban League, as well, building on earlier foundations, is expanding its emphasis on encouraging business ownership and wealth creation by African-Americans.[51]

Big companies are also helping blacks start small businesses. They do it through creating joint ventures, lending their personnel to help start—or advise—the business, providing low-cost facilities, and providing an assured market, as the following example illustrates.

As part of its minority supplier program, McDonald's asked George Johnson and David Moore to start a business making croutons for the new line of salads it planned to introduce. Johnson and Moore, managers at a brewing company, had never run a business, knew nothing about baking, and had only one client—McDonald's. They invested $100,000 each and, with such an assured market, persuaded a Chicago bank to lend them $1.6 million. Also, a McDonald's bun and English muffin supplier bought a Chicago pork-processing plant and leased it back to their company, Quality Croutons, Inc. Sales for the first year exceeded $4 million, including sales to McDonald's, United Airlines, Kraft Foods, and Pizza Hut.[52]

Opportunities for Hispanics   Hispanics are also forming small businesses at a record rate. These businesses are now booming particularly in the food area. This field was previously dominated by mom-and-pop grocers, but supermarkets are now invading the field because of the Hispanic view of shopping as a social event. Also, the national appetite for Hispanic foods is rapidly growing.

The Hispanic market represents one of the fastest-growing groups of customers in the country. The Hispanic population now accounts for 10 percent of the U.S. population and is expected to reach 25 percent by the year 2050.[53] Hispanic entrepreneurs are trying to capitalize on this growth, especially in the high-tech field, as the following example illustrates.

In the mid-1990s, *Hispanic Business* magazine (www.hispanicbusiness.com) recognized Mevatec Corporation (www.mevatec.com) as the fastest-growing Hispanic-owned high-technology company in the country. Mevatec also made the *Inc.* 500 list as the 43rd-fastest-growing U.S. small business. This growth occurred under the leadership of Nancy Archuleta, Mevatec's president for the previous 10 years.[54]

Another rapidly growing area of Hispanic small business is radio. The number of Hispanic-owned stations is increasing at a rate of about 10 percent per year.[55]

Opportunities for Asians   During the past decade, the U.S. Census Bureau found that the total Asian and Pacific Islander population in the United States increased around 11 percent per year.[56] The greatest increase was among the Chinese (104 percent), Filipinos (82 percent), Japanese (21 percent), Asian Indians (126 percent), Koreans (126 percent), and Vietnamese (135 percent).

This flood of immigrants has resulted in a wave of small mom-and-pop businesses; according to the Census Bureau, there are 57 Asian-owned firms per 1,000 Asians, compared to 21 Hispanic-owned firms per 1,000 Hispanics and 15 black-owned ones per 1,000 African-Americans.[57] Koreans have the highest rate of self-employment of any ethnic or racial group.[58]

These immigrants are also helping to ensure the future growth of knowledge industries in the United States. For instance, one-third of our engineers and computer chip designers are foreign born. And Asians constitute over 20 percent of students at our elite universities.[59]

A key factor in Asians' success is their tradition of self-employment. Also, they are motivated to open their own businesses because language and cultural barriers often prevent them from obtaining ordinary wage or salary jobs. Hence Asians go into business for themselves, even if it means setting up a street stand or opening a store in a poor, run-down neighborhood. Also, as shown in Figure 2–7, Asian immigrants receive considerable support from cultural networks when they try to set up a small business.

Cultural factors alone do not explain the outstanding success of Asian entrepreneurs. Instead, a study of small businesses in California—the state with the highest concentration of Asian businesses—found several important differences between businesses owned by Asians and those owned by non-Asians. While only 69 percent of non-Asians had a business plan when they started their company, 84 percent of Asians did. Also, Asians were more prone to use personal computers and to use outside attorneys and accountants to assist them. According to a spokesman for Pacific Bell Directory (www.smallbizpartners.com/

Figure 2–7
Asians Benefit from Networking

Recently arrived Asian immigrants establishing U.S. business enterprises gain support from cultural networks.

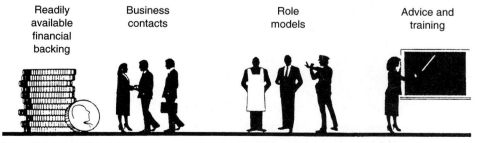

| Readily available financial backing | Business contacts | Role models | Advice and training |

Source: U.S. Department of Commerce, as reported in Robert Lewis, "Asian Immigrants Find Large Profits in Small Stores," *Mobile* (Alabama) *Press Register,* March 5, 1989, p. G-1. Adapted with permission of Newhouse Graphics.

partners), which sponsored the study, Asian businesspeople are prospering not because they are Asians but because they understand the key ingredients of running a successful business. Also, Asian-Americans have learned to work the affirmative action system. During the past decade, Asian-American–owned businesses have more than doubled their share of SBA's so-called 8a program, from 10.5 percent of all loans in 1986 to 23.7 percent in 1996.[60]

Opportunities for Native Americans   Because of the historically harsh treatment and banishment to reservations of Native Americans, opportunities for them have not been favorable. According to the U.S. Bureau of Indian Affairs (www.doi.gov/bia), the unemployment rate for the nation's 2 million Indians has run about 35 percent in recent years.[61] Average annual household incomes were less than $7,000. Now, however, several development groups are trying to change this pattern.

> One of the most prominent of these is the Lakota Fund, which was established during the 1980s on the Pine Ridge Indian Reservation in Kyle, South Dakota. It serves members of the reservation's Oglala Sioux tribe. During its first six years of operation, it lent over $428,000 to 200 individuals.[62]

■ SOME AREAS OF CONCERN FOR SMALL BUSINESS OWNERS

So far, we have indicated that opportunities abound for anyone with a good idea, the courage to take a chance and try something new, and some money to invest. That's what small business is all about. But, as shown in Chapter 1, the success of smaller firms tends to be limited by factors such as inadequate management, shortages of capital, government regulation and paperwork, and lack of proper record keeping. Two other concerns are (1) poorly planned growth and (2) the threat of failure.

Poorly Planned Growth

Poorly planned growth appears to be a built-in obstacle facing many small businesses. Clearly, if the owners are incapable, inefficient, or lacking in initiative, their businesses may flounder and eventually fail, or if the owners are mediocre, their businesses remain small. However, if the owners are efficient and capable and their organizations succeed and grow, but in a poorly planned way, they risk losing the very things they seek from their companies.

For instance, as small businesses succeed, their owners may begin to feel trapped. Instead of feeling on top of the world, they feel like prisoners of long hours and hard work. Todd Logan, who owned and operated a publishing and trade show company, cites five core symptoms that entrepreneurs must understand and change if they are to deal with this syndrome.

- Despair over the loss of closeness in important personal relationships.
- Unshakable anxiety despite accomplishments.
- Anger toward family, employees, and customers.
- Frustration that the lack of significant current progress is preventing forward movement.
- The paradox itself: You own your own business, yet you don't enjoy it.[63]

Loss of Independence or Control   With growth, owners must please more people, including employees, customers, and the public. There are new problems, such as hiring and rewarding managers and supervising other people—exercising the very authority small business owners may resent in others.

Many otherwise creative entrepreneurs are poor managers. They can generate ideas and found the business but are unable to manage it on a day-to-day basis. If the firm becomes large enough to require outside capital for future success and growth, the owner may lose control over the company, as the following example shows.

> As mentioned in Chapter 1, Steven Jobs and Steve Wozniak founded Apple Computer in 1976. They managed its growth until 1980, when they sold stock in it to the public. Although Jobs and Wozniak were worth $165 million and $88 million, respectively, they could not manage the day-to-day operations, so they hired John Sculley away from PepsiCo to manage the floundering firm.
>
> But both men were unhappy when Apple grew so big that they lost control. In 1985, after a dispute with Sculley, Wozniak sold his Apple stock and founded another company, Cloud 9. And when Jobs was ousted as chairman by the directors representing the outside stockholders, he sold all but one share of his stock and also formed a new company, NeXT, Inc.

Typical Growth Pattern   Historically, the ownership and management of small businesses have tended to follow a growth pattern similar to that shown in Figure 2–8. During stage 1, owners manage the business and do all the work. In stage 2, the owners still manage their companies but hire employees to help with routine and/or management activities. In stage 3, the owners hire managers to run the firms. The length of service of professional managers (as opposed to owner-managers) in small businesses tends to be relatively short; they move from one company to another as they progress upward in rank and earnings. Often, owners must give managers a financial interest in the business to hold them. Thus, the business takes on the form, the characteristics, and many of the problems of a big business. If entrepreneurs plan poorly, and fail to foresee these growth patterns, they may run into trouble.

Threat of Failure

As shown in Chapter 1, the threat of failure and discontinuance is a reality for many small businesses. A **discontinuance** is a voluntary decision to quit. A discontinuance may result from any of several factors, including health, changes in family situation, and the apparent advantages of working for someone else.

A **failure** results from inability to make a go of the business; things just don't work out as planned. There are two types of failure: (1) **formal failures,** which end up in court with some kind of loss to the creditors, and (2) **personal (informal) failures,** where the owner cannot make it financially and so voluntarily calls it quits. Personal failures are far more

A **discontinuance** is a voluntary decision to terminate a business.

A **failure** results from inability to succeed in running a business.

Formal failures are failures ending in court with loss to creditors.

In **personal (informal) failures,** the owner who cannot succeed voluntarily terminates the business.

Figure 2–8
Stages in the Development of a Small Business

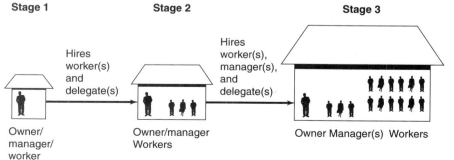

Stage 1	Stage 2	Stage 3

Hires worker(s) and delegate(s)

Hires worker(s), manager(s), and delegate(s)

Owner/manager/worker

Owner/manager Workers

Owner Manager(s) Workers

numerous than formal ones. People put their money, time, and effort into a business only to see losses wipe out the investment. Creditors usually do not suffer, as the owners tend to absorb the losses. The owners are the ones who pack up, close the door, and say, "That's it!"

Studies of the behavior of people who choose careers in small business show that, all too often, discontinuance or failure results from one or more of the following weaknesses: (1) too much was left to chance, (2) too many decisions were based on a hunch or intuition, (3) crucial obstacles went unnoticed for too long, (4) the amount of time and/or physical effort demanded of the small business manager were not recognized and/or planned for, and (5) the amount of capital needed was either not estimated or grossly underestimated.

While looking for data on failure rates and trends in failure rates, the latest available information seems to indicate a decrease. The data available are sketchy at best due to the lack of consistent collection vehicles. For example, many hobbiests, mom-and-pop ventures, and other small undertakings open and close every day without any documentation for tracking their success or failure rate. Many fail to consult with the Small Business Administration, obtain licensing, or report results to the Internal Revenue Service, which makes tracking the non-surviving entities next to impossible.

The SBA Office of Advocacy's latest report of Small Business Economic Indicators revealed that reported business terminations decreased by 1.6 percent while small-firm-dominated industries added 1.5 million net new jobs. Long-term trends since 1986 support marked declines in both bankruptcies and failure rates and indicate more stability for business births than for business terminations.[64]

WHAT YOU SHOULD HAVE LEARNED

1. People start businesses for many personal and business reasons. While income is an important consideration, the primary reason is to achieve independence. The need to exercise initiative and creativity also leads entrepreneurs to take the risk involved in striking out on their own. Many small business owners are also motivated by family considerations, such as taking over a family business to permit parents to retire or starting a family business to have more time with their families. Also, some people start businesses chiefly to provide a product or service not readily available elsewhere. Finally, some entrepreneurs start businesses to achieve business objectives such as providing services to their customers; making a profit; providing social benefits to society; and growing into large, profitable organizations.

2. The characteristics most typical of the more successful business owners are that they (*a*) desire independence, (*b*) have a strong sense of enterprise, (*c*) tend to be motivated by personal and family considerations, (*d*) expect quick and concrete results, (*e*) are able to react quickly to change, (*f*) are dedicated to their businesses, and (*g*) often enter business as much by chance as by design.

3. The most prevalent factors leading to success in owning and managing a small business are (*a*) serving an adequate and well-defined market, (*b*) acquiring sufficient capital, (*c*) recruiting and using human resources effectively, (*d*) obtaining and using accurate information, (*e*) coping effectively with government regulations, (*f*) having expertise in one's chosen field, and (*g*) managing time effectively. In essence, it is sticking to the basics that leads to success rather than using gimmicks or catering to fads.

4. If you are interested in becoming an entrepreneur, you should carefully examine your values, mental abilities, and attitudes to see if you have the characteristics required for success. Your ability to think logically, generate new ideas, translate these ideas into a useful product, do effective planning, and relate to the feelings and needs of customers and employees is also important. Your success in any business depends on your level of aspiration, willingness to accept responsibility, ability to

handle setbacks and disappointments, commitment to the business, willingness to take risks, ability to live with an irregular schedule, self-discipline, and self-confidence.

5. There are many opportunities for prospective small business owners, especially in eating and drinking establishments, offices of health practitioners, and nursing and personal care facilities. The best opportunities are found in small firms, limited in scope, that involve long, hard hours working to satisfy basic human needs.

6. Opportunities in small business abound for women and diverse ethnic groups. Women are starting new businesses at a rapid rate. They are expected to own half of all small firms by the year 2000. Women owning small firms tend to be well educated, capable, and committed owners.

   While African-American entrepreneurs are progressing in small business, their firms tend to be smaller and less profitable than other firms. The role of black entrepreneurs is changing, as they are moving into fields such as publishing, electronics, insurance, health care, and real estate development.

The Hispanic market is growing rapidly and is expected to provide many opportunities in the future, especially in supermarkets, high-tech industries, and radio and TV.

Cultural networks, along with shrewd business practices—such as having a business plan, hiring professional consultants, and using computers—are aiding Asian entrepreneurs.

Native Americans do not so far enjoy many of the benefits of entrepreneurship, but many groups are now trying to assist them.

7. Poorly planned growth and the threat of failure should concern small business owners. Failure to grow can mean the death of a business, but poorly planned growth and the failure to foresee the stages of growth a typical company may go through can also pose a real problem.

   Some businesses discontinue for health, family, or other personal reasons, while others fail. Although relatively few failures are formal failures, personal failures resulting from unprofitability or general discouragement can be just as devastating for small business owners.

QUESTIONS FOR DISCUSSION

1. Discuss the four personal objectives that people seek when starting a new business.

2. Explain the four business objectives small business owners try to achieve.

3. Explain the interrelationship between the *service* and *profit* objectives.

4. What are some characteristics found in successful small business owners? Evaluate the importance of each of these.

5. How did you make out with the self-test in Figure 2–4? Do you think the results accurately reflect your potential? Explain.

6. Name the fastest-growing small businesses listed in Figure 2–5, as indicated by the number of jobs. Explain their growth.

7. Evaluate the opportunities in small business for women, African-Americans, Hispanics, Asians, and Native Americans.

8. How does success cause concern for small businesses? Can you give examples from your experience or suggest ways to avoid the problems of growth?

CASE 2-1

JUDY JONES'S TRY J. ADVERTISING AGENCY

Judith Anne Jones's advertising agency, Try J. Advertising, of Carlsbad, California, sells service. It specializes in automobile dealerships such as Toyota Carlsbad and Lexus Carlsbad. When asked what started her in business, Jones gave the following answer:

I was attracted to creative writing by my father, Scott W. Erwin, who was an announcer, copywriter, advertising manager, and manager of a radio station in Baton Rouge, Louisiana. My mother's career, library work, also influenced my career, as her dedication to her field set an example to me and gave me the opportunity to go to college. I studied advertising in the School of Journalism at Louisiana State University, including taking extra courses during summers to achieve a certificate of specialization in public relations.

After graduating in 1976, I became a field reporter for the *Louisiana Contractor* magazine, which led to my first pair of work boots and hard hat. After three years, I transferred to the *San Diego Contractor* magazine. My stay there was brief, as I had to sell ads in Los Angeles two weeks out of every month. Its smog and crowded freeways energized me to start my own business in Carlsbad.

After being marketing director for Wendy's Old-Fashioned Hamburgers' San Diego County Region, I joined the Ad Group, an advertising agency, as the account executive for one of its main accounts, the San Diego Toyota Dealers'

Advertising Association. One of the dealers appreciated my work so much he offered me a position at his store, Toyota Carlsbad, from which I started my own ad agency in 1981.

Try J. Advertising, Inc., was incorporated with Judy Jones as president and equal shareholder with Louis V. Jones, president of Toyota Carlsbad. The two later married, and Judy bought out his interest. In addition to Ms. Jones, the agency's staff consists of two full-time account executives; a computer technician, who develops graphic cuts; and a bookkeeper who works as an independent contractor.

Jones and her people continue to (1) provide for clients' printing needs by acting as their agent; (2) prepare items such as business cards, letterheads, and stationery; (3) prepare and distribute newsletters to clients' employees and customers; (4) write and print direct-mail pieces; (5) produce training videos; (6) write and produce radio, newspaper, and television ads; and (7) plan special events, such as grand openings and new model introductions.

Questions

1. Was Judy Jones's preparation adequate and appropriate for a small business owner? Explain.

2. Could you suggest ways for her to profitably expand her business? Explain.

Source: Author's correspondence and communication with Judith Anne Jones.

CASE 2-2

VICTOR K. KIAM II—HOW TO SUCCEED AS AN ENTREPRENEUR

In a famous TV commercial, Victor Kiam says, "I was a dedicated blade shaver until my wife bought me this Remington Microscreen shaver. . . . I was so impressed with it, I bought the company." Whether or not that was the reason for his purchase of Remington Products, Inc., Kiam did pick up the firm from Sperry Corporation in 1979 for a "mere" $25 million, most of which was provided by Sperry and various banks. Since then, sales

have increased manyfold. Market share has more than doubled, and profits have skyrocketed. Since 1988, Kiam has been the majority owner of the New England Patriots.

Kiam's success has been based on the guiding principles he has followed since 1935, when he became an entrepreneur at the age of eight. That summer, when people stepped off the streetcar named *Desire* near his home in New Orleans, they looked as if they would drop if they didn't have something cold to drink. Victor's grandfather staked him $5 to buy 100 bottles of Coca-Cola to sell to the suffering passengers. The young entrepreneur set his price at 10 cents, a 100 percent markup, expecting to make a substantial profit. Sales zoomed, and his supply of drinks was soon sold out. He and his grandfather were both shocked when Victor learned he had only $4 to show for his efforts. Since this new venture was launched during the Depression, most customers couldn't pay the 10 cents; being softhearted, Victor couldn't turn them away. While this business was a financial disaster, it did build much goodwill for him and taught him some valuable business lessons.

After acquiring an MBA degree from Harvard in 1951 and after 18 years of selling foundation garments for Playtex and toothpaste for Lever Brothers, Kiam bought an interest in the Benrus Corporation, where he sold watches and jewelry for another 11 years. These 29 years of experience, not to mention his years as CEO at Remington, demonstrate that he fits the profile of a successful entrepreneur—a profile Kiam developed in his best-selling book *Going for It! How to Succeed as an Entrepreneur.*

In the book, Kiam says a person has "the right stuff" if he or she can answer the following questions affirmatively:

- Am I willing to sacrifice?
- Am I decisive?
- Do I have self-confidence?
- Can I recognize an opportunity when it presents itself and capitalize on it?
- Do I have confidence in my proposed venture?
- Am I willing to lead by example?

In his book *Live to Win,* Kiam explains how you can figure your "Personal Balance Sheet" and your "Intangible Balance Sheet."

Remington continued to transform itself from a brand synonymous with electric razors by entering the small innovative electronic appliance field. With an extensive campaign of TV advertising and infomercials, it introduced the Soundmate Personal Safety Siren.

Questions

1. What business and personal needs might Victor Kiam have been attempting to satisfy when he decided to risk millions on Remington Products, Inc.?

2. How, and to what degree, has Kiam's background and personal business experience helped him build Remington Products into the profitable company that it is?

3. Consider some of the risks and obstacles Kiam had taken and overcome in 1979 just before he bought Remington Products. Would you have been willing to take a multimillion-dollar chance? Why or why not?

4. What personal and entrepreneurial qualities might Kiam possess that have helped him achieve his success? Which of these would you classify as the most important?

Source: Based on Victor Kiam, *Going for It! How to Succeed as an Entrepreneur* (New York: William Morrow, 1986) and *Live to Win* (New York: Harper & Row, 1989); "Remington Considers Acquisition Proposals," *The Wall Street Journal,* March 8, 1995, p. C17; and author's correspondence with Remington Products.

3

LEGAL FORMS OF OWNERSHIP

Good order is the foundation of all good things.
   Edmund Burke

To me, going public [incorporating] *would be like selling my soul.*
   Carlton Cadwell, manufacturer

LEARNING OBJECTIVES

After studying the material in this chapter, you will be able to:

1. Name the legal forms of ownership a small business can have.

2. Explain the reasons for and against forming a proprietorship.

3. Explain the reasons for and against forming a partnership.

4. Explain the reasons for and against forming a corporation.

5. Discuss some other legal forms a business can take.

Henry E. Kloss—Proprietor, Partner, and Corporate Owner

As an undergraduate at Massachusetts Institute of Technology, Henry E. Kloss first ventured into business by designing, making, and selling cabinets for stereos. He did this to pay his way through school.

After military service, Kloss returned to Cambridge, where his skills as a cabinetmaker, combined with his interest in electronics and sound, led him to Edgar Villchur, who had an idea for an acoustic suspension system. They formed a partnership, Acoustic Research, in 1954 and pioneered the production of acoustic suspension speakers, which made all other types of loudspeakers obsolete. Half the company stock went to Kloss and two other investors, while the other half went to Villchur. Disagreement over day-to-day management eventually required a separation, so Kloss and the two top managers left. They sold their interest for about $56,000 and formed KLH Corporation to produce low-cost, full-range speakers. Later, they expanded their product base by adding items such as the Dolby® noise reduction system. Their sales doubled from $2 to $4 million in the year after they were the first to use transistors in a consumer product—a portable stereo.

In 1964, KLH was sold to Singer for $4 million, of which Kloss received $1.2 million in stock. (Unfortunately for him, Singer stock was the second-biggest loser on the New York Stock Exchange the next year.) Over three years, however, he had sold most of his stock on the open market. Kloss ran KLH for Singer until 1967; but when Singer chose not to enter the TV market, Kloss left and sold the rest of his stock to Singer for $400,000. Kloss then spent two years developing a working model of a large-screen TV set—called Videobeam—in the basement of his home. By then he was out of money, so he founded Advent Corporation to produce projection TVs and high-quality, low-priced speakers as well as the Videobeams. Advent had constant financial problems due to its low prices for its high-quality speakers and TV sets. By 1975, its bankers forced Advent to raise new capital, which resulted in Kloss's being demoted from president to chief scientist—and then leaving the company.

Kloss spent the next two years perfecting a low-cost method of manufacturing the tubes for his large-screen TV. In 1979, he founded Kloss Video with $400,000 of his own money and $400,000 from private sources. Kloss became president and treasurer of the company. Its two-piece, large-screen projection set, the Novabeam—which sold for about $3,000—had sharper and brighter images than those of its competitors. Because of insufficient public interest in big-screen TV, Kloss Video reentered the speaker market. Kloss Video's stock declined after reaching its top price in 1983, when Kloss's 60 percent share was worth about $15 million.

By 1987, Kloss Video was interested in emphasizing consumer sales, so the directors asked Kloss to search for a new president from outside the company. Instead, they chose one of their own for the position and appointed Kloss as head of research and development.

Kloss left to start a new company, Cambridge SoundWorks (www.hifi.com), in nearby Newton, Massachusetts. Its total capital was a $250,000 no-equity loan from Dr. Henry Morgan, who had been associated with Kloss for several years. Its Ensemble Speaker System comprised four separate units: two woofers and two tweeters. The speakers were known for "quality and affordability." The company now manufac-

tures 33 different models of home and car stereos and home theater and computer speakers.

Kloss continues to be an innovative entrepreneur. His vision and genius were rewarded on October 7, 1997, when the National Academy of Television Arts and Sciences awarded him an Emmy for "Outstanding Achievement in Technological Advancement—Pioneering Development of 3-CRT Video Projectors." The award recognized his pioneer efforts in developing big-screen projection television.

Source: Author's correspondence with Henry Kloss and Kloss Video; Kloss Video 10-K filings and proxy statements; Hans Fantel, "Henry Kloss's Mail-Order Speakers," *New York Times,* February 19, 1989, p. H32; Alan Deutschman, "How to Invest in a Startup Business," *Fortune,* Fall 1989, pp. 115–22; and a company press release dated October 8, 1997.

■ SELECTING THE RIGHT LEGAL FORM

Going into business for yourself and being your own boss is a dream that can become either a pleasant reality or a nightmare. Though it may be satisfying to give the orders, run the show, and receive the income, other factors must be considered when choosing the legal form to use for the business. Income tax considerations, the amount of free time available, responsibility for others, and family wishes—as well as the amount of available funds—must also be considered in choosing a proprietorship, partnership, corporation, or other legal form for the business.

Factors to Consider

When choosing the proper legal form for your business, you should ask several basic questions. For example, to what extent is your family able to endure the physical, psychological, and emotional strains associated with running the business? Second, how easy is it to start, operate, and transfer to others your interest in the company? Third, to what extent are you and your family willing to accept the financial risks involved, including being responsible for not only your own losses and debts but also those of other people? Finally, how much information about yourself, your family, and your economic status are you willing to make public? For example, if you choose the corporate form, information about the business—including profits and/or losses—may have to be made public knowledge.

The choice of legal form does not have to be final. The usual progression is to start as a proprietorship or partnership and then move into a corporation. For example, in the CleanDrum case on page 21, Sue Ley started her business as a proprietorship, but when she needed extra capital, she brought in a partner.

Relative Importance of Each Form

As you can see from Figure 3–1, the proprietorship is by far the most popular form of business in the United States. Around 73 percent of all businesses are proprietorships, while only 20 percent are corporations, and 7 percent are partnerships. Notice in Table 3–1 that

Figure 3–1

Relative Position of U.S. Proprietorships, Partnerships, and Corporations

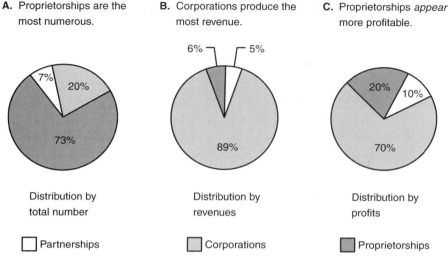

A. Proprietorships are the most numerous.

B. Corporations produce the most revenue.

C. Proprietorships *appear* more profitable.

Distribution by total number

Distribution by revenues

Distribution by profits

☐ Partnerships   ▢ Corporations   ▆ Proprietorships

Source: U.S. Department of Commerce, *Statistical Abstract of the United States, 1997* (Washington, DC: U.S. Government Printing Office, 1997), Table 833, p. 537.

the proprietorship is most popular in all industries. Finance, insurance, and real estate use the partnership more frequently than do the other industries.

While the proprietorship is the most popular form, it accounts for only a small share of total revenues. As Figure 3–1 shows, proprietorships generate only around 6 percent of all revenues, while corporations account for 89 percent, and partnerships provide around 5 percent.

Table 3–1 shows that corporations dominate the business receipts in all areas except services, where proprietorships dominate. Proprietorships also account for significant revenues in construction.

Figure 3–1 shows that proprietorships appear to be the most profitable form; they received 20 percent of profits on only 6 percent of revenues. Partnerships accounted for 5 percent of revenues and 10 percent of profits. Corporations received only 70 percent of the profits on 89 percent of the sales. These numbers should be interpreted with caution, however, since proprietorship "profits" include net financial return to owners. In a corporation, much of that return would be included in wage and salary expense and deducted from profit.

■ WHY FORM A PROPRIETORSHIP?

A **proprietorship** is a business that is owned by one person. It is the oldest and most prevalent form of ownership, as well as the least expensive to start. Most small business owners prefer the proprietorship because it is simple to enter, operate, and terminate and provides for relative freedom of action and control—as shown in Figure 3–2. Finally, the proprietorship has a favorable tax status. As will be shown in Chapter 14, it is taxed at the owner's personal income tax rate. In these respects, you may find it an attractive form to use, as millions of proprietors now do.

A **proprietorship** is a business that is owned by one person.

> Notice in the opening Profile how easy it was for Henry Kloss to begin operating as a proprietor while a student at the Massachusetts Institute of Technology. All he had to do was find a place to produce and sell his cabinets. He probably did not even have to pay taxes. Also, he was independent, with no co-owners to cause him problems.

Table 3–1
Comparison of Proprietorships, Partnerships, and Corporations in Selected Industries

Industry	Percentage of firms in the industry			Percentage of industry's business receipts		
	Proprietorships	Partnerships	Corporations	Proprietorships	Partnerships	Corporations
Services	73	7	20	67	5	28
Trade	70	4	26	6	3	91
Construction	80	3	17	16	4	80
Finance, insurance, real estate	47	29	24	3	7	90
Manufacturing	54	14	32	*	3	97

*Less than 1 percent.

Source: U.S. Department of Commerce, *Statistical Abstract of the United States, 1997* (Washington, DC: U.S. Government Printing Office, 1997), computed from Tables 833 and 834, p. 537.

Figure 3–2 also shows some negative factors that should be considered. First, from a legal point of view, the business and its owner are one and the same and cannot be separated. Consequently, the business legally ends with the proprietor's death, and some legal action must be taken to restart it. Second, if the business does not have enough funds to pay its obligations, the owner must use personal assets to pay them. The figure summarizes the major advantages and disadvantages of owning a proprietorship.

■ WHY FORM A PARTNERSHIP?

A **partnership** is a business owned by two or more persons who have unlimited liability for its debts and obligations.

A **partnership** is a voluntary association of two or more persons to carry on as co-owners a business for profit. As shown in Figure 3–3, the partnership is similar to the proprietorship but is more difficult to form, operate, and terminate. As with the proprietorship, profits are taxed only once—on each partner's share of the income—not twice, as in the corporation. Partnerships, however, are generally more effective than proprietorships in raising funds and in obtaining better ideas, management, and credit. Mel Farr is an example of this type of arrangement.

Mel Farr was All-American when he played football for the UCLA Bruins from 1963 to 1967. The number one draft choice of the Detroit Lions in 1967, he was named the NFL's "Rookie of the Year." After being on the All Pro Team in 1967 and 1972, he retired from the NFL in 1974 because of extensive injuries.

Farr started preparing for his post-football career early. He worked in Ford's Dealer Development Division, played football, and in 1971 earned his college degree from the University of Detroit. After retiring from the NFL, he remained with Ford to help set up its training program for minority dealers.

In 1975, Farr and a partner bought a bankrupt Ford dealership in Oak Park, Michigan. By 1978 Farr was able to buy out his partner. He then came up with a brilliant and successful marketing coup for his dealership. For years he starred in a series of TV ads, dressed in a crimson cape and asking viewers to "See Mel Farr, Superstar, for a Farr better deal!" They did! He became the youngest honoree in the "Top 100 Black Businesses in America" when it was first published by *Black Enterprise* magazine in 1978. In 1978 he was cited by President Carter for outstanding achievements in business, and he has received numerous other awards and recognitions since then.

Figure 3–2
Weighing the Advantages and Disadvantages of a Proprietorship

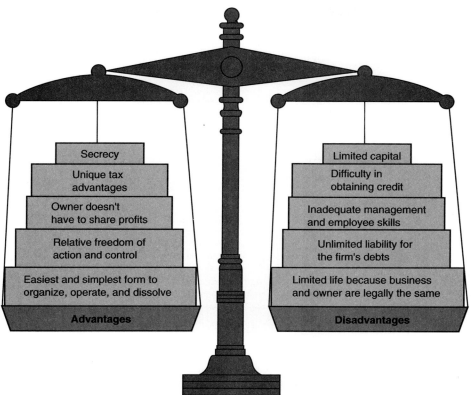

Advantages
- Secrecy
- Unique tax advantages
- Owner doesn't have to share profits
- Relative freedom of action and control
- Easiest and simplest form to organize, operate, and dissolve

Disadvantages
- Limited capital
- Difficulty in obtaining credit
- Inadequate management and employee skills
- Unlimited liability for the firm's debts
- Limited life because business and owner are legally the same

Farr was inducted into the prestigious UCLA Sports Hall of Fame in 1988 and in 1992 headed the Ford-Lincoln-Mercury Dealers Association (www.lincolnmercury. com). Through the selective acquisition of 10 unprofitable dealerships, Mel Farr Automotive Group had become the top Ford dealership in the Detroit metropolitan area by 1997.[1]

Figure 3–3 also shows that the partnership has many drawbacks. For example, the death of any one of the partners legally terminates the business, and legal action is needed to revive it. This disadvantage may be overcome, however, by an agreement among the partners stating that the remaining partner(s) will purchase the interest of the deceased partner. Further, the partnership itself usually carries insurance to cover this contingency.

How a Partnership Operates

The Uniform Partnership Act (UPA) governs the operations of partnerships *in the absence of other expressed agreements.* The Act has done much to reduce controversies in integrating the laws relating to partnerships.[2]

Each partner is responsible for the acts of all the other partners. Thus, all partners—except in a limited partnership (see next section)—are liable for all the debts of the firm; even the personal property of each partner can be used to satisfy the debts of the partnership. Nor

Figure 3–3
Weighing the Advantages and Disadvantages of a Partnership

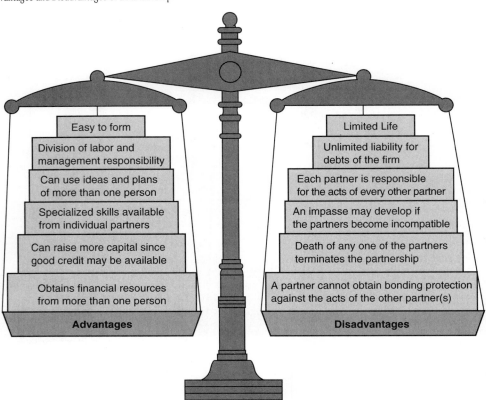

can a partner obtain bonding protection against the acts of the other partner(s). Therefore, each partner is bound by the actions of the other partners, as the following example illustrates.

> Edward Nickles, a 37-year-old Bostonian, was delighted when his small accounting firm, Pannell Kerr Forster, made him a partner. But his joy was short-lived; after the firm paid $1 million of a $5 million legal settlement, his annual income plummeted from $145,000 to $65,000. Later, the firm dropped its partnership structure and reorganized itself into six separate professional corporations in five states.[3]

An impasse can easily develop if the partners can't agree on basic issues. Consequently, the business may become inoperative (or even dissolve).

> This is what happened at Acoustic Research, as described in the Profile. When there was a disagreement over day-to-day operations, Kloss and the others pulled out and sold their interest, but one partner stayed in.

Types of Partnerships

Partnerships may be general or limited. In a **general partnership,** each partner is known to the public and held liable for the acts of the other partners. In a **limited partnership,** there are one or more general partners and one or more limited partners, whose identity is not generally known. The firm is managed by the general partners, who have unlimited per-

In a **general partnership,** each partner actively participates as an equal in managing the business and being liable for the acts of other partners.

In a **limited partnership,** one or more general partners conduct the business, while one or more limited partners contribute capital but do not participate in management and are not held liable for debts of the general partners.

sonal liability for the partnership's debt. The personal liability of the limited partners is limited to the amount of capital they have contributed. Limited partners may be employees of the company but may not participate in its management.

Limited partnerships were quite popular during the rapid business expansion of the 1980s. But their popularity has diminished during the 1990s, as many of the highly speculative deals have soured.

> For example, in 1995 a federal judge in New York granted preliminary approval of a $110 million settlement against Prudential Securities (www.prudential.com), a subsidiary of Prudential Insurance Company, for selling "highly speculative partnerships to investors in the 1980s."[4] Including other investor claims against the company for "soured partnerships," Prudential will likely pay out over $1.5 billion in legal claims and costs resulting from various partnerships it sold to investors during the 1980s.

Rights of Partners

Articles of copartnership are drawn up during the preoperating period to show rights, duties, and responsibilities of each partner.

If there is no agreement to the contrary, each general partner has an equal voice in running the business, which can lead to difficulties between the partners, as shown in the Figure 3–4. While each of the partners may make decisions pertaining to the operations of the business, the consent of all partners is required to make fundamental changes in the structure itself. The partners' share of the profits is presumed to be their only compensation; in the absence of any agreement otherwise, profits and losses are distributed equally.

Ordinarily, the rights, duties, and responsibilities of the partners are detailed in the **articles of copartnership.** These should be agreed on during the preoperating period and should spell out the authority, duties, and responsibilities of each partner.

A partnership is required to file Form 1065 with the IRS (www.irs.gov) for information purposes. The IRS can, and sometimes does, challenge the status of a partnership and may attempt to tax it as a separate legal entity.

"Doctor, our business partnership is so shaky, we don't even talk shop during the TV commercials."

(*Source:* Courtesy J. Nebesky.)

■ WHY FORM A CORPORATION?

In one of the earliest decisions of the U.S. Supreme Court, a corporation was defined as "an artificial being, invisible, intangible, and existing only in contemplation of the law." In other words, a **corporation** is a legal entity whose life exists at the pleasure of the courts. The traditional form of the corporation is called a **C corporation.**

The formation of a corporation is more formal and complex than that of the other legal forms of business. The minimum number of persons required as stockholders varies with individual state laws, but it usually ranges from three to five. The procedure for formation is usually legally defined and requires the services of an attorney. Incorporation fees are normally based on the corporation's amount of capital.

The corporate form offers several advantages, as shown in Figure 3–4. Since the corporation is separate and distinct from the owners as individuals, the death of one stockholder does not affect its life. Also, each owner's liability for the firm's debts is limited to

A **corporation** is a business formed and owned by a group of people, called stockholders, given special rights, privileges, and limited liabilities by law.

The **C corporation** is a regular corporation that provides the protection of limited liability for shareholders, but its earnings are taxed at both the corporate and shareholder levels.

Figure 3–4
Weighing the Advantages and Disadvantages of a Corporation

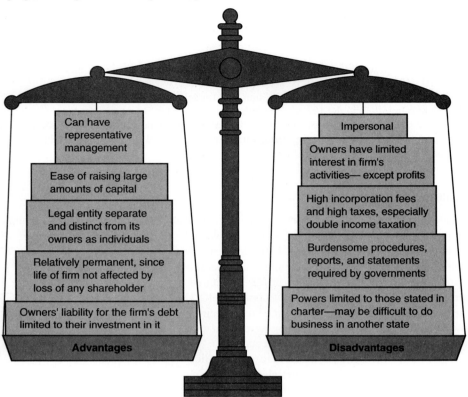

the amount invested, so personal property can't be taken to pay the debts of the business (with certain limited restrictions, such as loan guarantees, nonpayment of taxes, and malfeasance). Finally, since the owners are not required to help run the firm's operations, large amounts of capital can be raised relatively easily.

> Notice in the Profile that Henry Kloss decided to incorporate when he needed more capital but wanted to restrict his liability and reduce the chances of disruption from partners. This made it easier for him to sell his interest to Singer and to raise money from friends when he organized Kloss Video.

The many disadvantages of the corporation, also shown in Figure 3–4, might keep you from choosing it for your business. The main problem is double taxation, as the corporation pays taxes on its profit, and then individual owners pay taxes on their dividends. (As will be shown later, this is one reason for using an S corporation.) Also, the area of operations is limited by the corporation's charter, and the process of incorporation is complex and costly.

How to Form a Corporation

Articles of incorporation are the instrument by which a corporation is formed under the corporation laws of a given state.

A **corporate charter** states what the business can do and provides other organizational and financial information.

To form a corporation, **articles of incorporation** must be prepared and filed with the state in exchange for a **corporate charter,** which states what the business can do and provides other information. Also, the procedures, reports, and statements required for operating a corporation are cumbersome, and because the owners' powers are limited to those stated in the charter, it may be difficult for the corporation to do business in another state.

Because the legal requirements for incorporating vary from state to state, it might be advantageous to incorporate in a state favorable to business, such as Delaware. Delaware's incorporation requirements are so lenient that, despite its small size, it charters more corporations than any other state. Corporations can also reduce legal risks by relying on the extensive case law built up in Delaware's Chancery Court, one of the only state courts in the nation solely dedicated to hearing business cases.[5] It is also the best state in which to file for federal bankruptcy.[6] Texas, however, has fewer filing requirements and simpler forms than any other state.

One danger in any business is that one of the owners will leave and start a competing business. Even if trade secrets are not stolen, the new competitor will have acquired business knowledge at the corporation's expense. It may not be possible to prevent such defections, but incorporators can make provisions during the incorporation process for recovering damages for any loss the firm suffers.

One way is to include a **buy-sell agreement** in the articles of incorporation. This arrangement details the terms by which stockholders can buy out each other's interest. Also, if the success of the venture is dependent on key people, insurance should be carried on them. This type of insurance protects the resources of the firm in the event of the loss of these people (see Chapter 16).

A **buy-sell agreement** explains how stockholders can buy out each other's interest.

Adequate bond and insurance coverage should be maintained against losses that result from the acts of employees and others.

How a Corporation Is Governed

The initial incorporators usually operate the corporation after it is formed. But they are assisted by other stockholders, directors, officers, and executives.

Stockholders   The stockholders are the corporation's owners. In a small company, one or a few people may own most of the stock and therefore be able to control it. In a large corporation, however, holders of as little as 10 percent may be able to control the company. Often, the founders have the controlling interest and can pick the people to be on the board of directors.

Board of Directors   The board of directors represents the stockholders in managing the company. Board members can help set goals and plan marketing, production, and financing strategies. However, some owners prefer to run the company alone, without someone "looking over their shoulder."

There are many sources of effective outside directors, such as experienced businesspeople, investors, bankers, and professionals such as attorneys, CPAs, or business consultants. It is becoming difficult, however, to obtain competent outsiders to serve on boards—especially of small companies—because liability suits may be filed against them by disgruntled stockholders, employees, customers, or other interested parties.[7]

Corporate Officers   While their titles and duties vary, corporate officers usually include the chairman, president, secretary, and treasurer. Within limits set by stockholders and the board, these officers direct the day-to-day operations of the business. As the business grows, others are often added to constitute an executive committee, which performs this function.

The S Corporation

A form of business ownership receiving growing attention in recent years is the **S corporation,** a special type of corporation that is exempt from multiple taxation and excessive

An **S corporation** is a special type of corporation that is exempt from multiple taxation and excessive paperwork.

paperwork. Any business with fewer than 75 stockholders, none of whom are corporate shareholders, can form such a corporation.[8] The S corporation eliminates multiple taxation of income and the attendant paperwork, as well as certain other taxes. For example, regular corporations must deduct Social Security taxes on income paid to owners employed by the firm, as well as pay the employer's share of the taxes. But if an owner receives an outside salary above the maximum from which such taxes are deducted, the S corporation neither deducts nor pays Social Security taxes on the owner's income.

If the income from corporate operations is distributed to the stockholders of an S corporation, they pay taxes on it at their individual rates. While the payment process is similar to that of a partnership, the corporation must file a special federal income tax return.

There are, however, significant costs to electing S corporation status. These corporations can issue only one class of stock—common. This may limit equity financing in some cases, because other forms of stock, which can't be issued by the S corporation, are preferred by many venture capitalists. Another disadvantage is that all shareholders must be individuals, estates, or some type of personal trust. Therefore, no other corporation or partnership may invest in the company. Also, only shareholders who are individuals or estates and are U.S. citizens or permanent residents can belong. Finally, tax rules for S corporations are very tough and confusing, as the following example shows.

> In 1990, Dallas-based Hartfield & Co., a wholesale distributor of industrial valves, reorganized as an S corporation. While savings in taxes more than justified the switch, George Boles, Hartfield's chief financial officer, had to cope with "one of the murkiest and most volatile aspects of the tax code." According to him, "The Subchapter S rules have got to be some of the toughest in the land."[9]

As an indication of the growing popularity of this form, the IRS received about 2.5 million S corporation tax returns in 1997, compared to 367,200 in 1975, 736,900 in 1985, and 2,161,000 in 1995. S corporation returns accounted for 48 percent of all corporate returns filed in 1997, up from 17 percent in 1975, 21 percent in 1985, and 45 percent in 1995.[10]

S corporations lost much of their appeal in the early 1990s for two reasons. First, federal tax laws increased the top rate for their owners. Second, individual states began passing laws creating limited-liability companies, which have similar appeal.[11]

■ OTHER FORMS OF BUSINESS

Other legal forms can be used by a small business owner. The most popular of these are the limited-liability company (LLC), the cooperative, and the joint venture.

The Limited-Liability Company (LLC)

The **limited-liability company (LLC)** combines the advantages of a corporation, such as liability protection, with the benefits of a partnership, such as tax advantages.

Since 1977, a rapidly growing number of states have authorized the formation of **limited-liability companies (LLCs)** to help entrepreneurs gain the benefit of limited liability provided by the corporation along with the tax advantages of a partnership. LLCs provide benefits similar to the S corporation, without the special eligibility requirements. By 1996, all but a few states had enacted LLC statutes. Some state statutes now also provide for limited-liability partnerships (LLPs), which are similar to LLCs.[12] This type of organization is becoming increasingly popular for professional groups.[13]

Billed as the "business entity of the future," the LLC is attractive to many small business owners, for without some shield from personal liability, an owner can be held personally liable for the company's debts, which is a major deterrent to prospective proprietors and partners. Like a partnership, an LLC distributes profits and losses directly to owners and investors, who must report them on their personal income tax return. But, like a corporation, it provides limited liability for members even if they participate in management.

> Because of worries about environmental problems and the liabilities associated with them, clients of F. B. Kubic, a Wichita, Kansas, accounting firm, used an LLC for an oil and gas venture. They needed the limited-liability protection because of potential lawsuits arising from environmental problems.[14]
>
> In July 1994, KPMG Peat Marwick (www.kpmg.com) announced its intention to reorganize its U.K. operations from partnership status to a limited-liability corporation. The reasons for the change include the fact that professional liability insurance coverage had become almost unavailable.[15]

Because of its newness and the fact that some states still do not recognize LLCs, you may run into difficulty if you operate in one of these states. Also, the Securities and Exchange Commission (SEC) (www.sec.gov) has joined the states to ensure that LLCs are not used to avoid U.S. securities laws.[16]

The Cooperative

A **cooperative** is a business composed of independent producers, wholesalers, retailers, or consumers that acts collectively to buy or sell for its clients. Usually the cooperative's net profit is returned to the patrons at the end of each year, resulting in no profits and no taxes to it. To receive the advantages of a cooperative, a business must meet certain requirements of federal and state governments. The cooperative form of business is usually associated with farm products—purchasing, selling, and financing farm equipment and materials, and/or processing and marketing farm products.

A **cooperative** is a business owned by and operated for the benefit of patrons using its services.

> Delta Pride Catfish Inc. (www.deltapride.com) of Indianola, Mississippi, the farm-raised catfish capital of the United States, is such a cooperative. Catfish farming, the nation's largest aquaculture industry, is done primarily by small farmers who don't have the expertise or resources to do their own marketing. So they join cooperatives that provide aggressive marketing and financing. Delta Pride, the largest U.S. processor of fresh fish, is a farmer-owned cooperative with nearly 200 members, each of whom receives one share of stock for each acre of land in production. Delta Pride's members own 64,000 acres of catfish ponds.[17]

The Joint Venture

Working relationships between noncompeting companies are quite popular these days and may become even more so in the future. The usual arrangement is a **joint venture,** which is a form of temporary partnership whereby two or more firms join in a single endeavor to make a profit. For example, two or more investors may combine their finances, buy a piece of land, develop it, and sell it. At that time, the joint venture is dissolved.

A **joint venture** is a form of temporary partnership whereby two or more firms join in a single endeavor to make a profit.

Many small businesses are using their research and development capabilities to form joint ventures with larger companies that provide them with marketing and financial clout, as well as other expertise.

According to Toby Walters, research manager for the Joint Venture Database, corporate partnering arrangements are increasing. He says, "It's more common in high-tech industries, companies involved with the information superhighway, and the communications companies."[18] Those who are interested in finding a corporate partner to form a joint venture are advised to contact the executive director of the trade association representing the industry they are targeting.

Figure 3–5
Checklist for Evaluating Legal Forms of Organization

- Under what legal form of organization is the firm now operating?
- What are the major risks to which the firm is subjected?
- Does the legal form of organization give the proper protection against these risks?
- Does the firm supplement its legal form of protection with public liability insurance?
- Is unlimited liability a serious potential problem?
- Has the present form limited financial needs in any way?
- What is the relative incidence of the firm's major risks?
- Are there tax advantages available by changing the legal form of organization?
- Have you considered the management advantages of alternative legal forms?
- Are you aware of the features of a Subchapter S corporation? Would they be beneficial?
- Is the company using all the advantages of the present legal form of organization?

Source: Verona Beguin, ed., *Small Business Institute Student Consultant's Manual* (Washington, DC: U.S. Small Business Administration, 1992), Appendix F5.

Joint ventures are becoming quite popular in both domestic and global operations. As evidence of this, consultant Coopers & Lybrand (www.coopers.com) reports that from 1993 to 1996 over half of America's fastest-growing companies teamed with others to improve products or create new ones.[19] This trend is especially noticeable in China and Vietnam, as well as Russia, since those areas are trying to attract U.S. capital.[20] As you can see from the following example, they appear to have succeeded.

Six Russian joint ventures involving Western partners received tax breaks on oil exports in late 1994. While five of the partners were relatively well-known companies, the sixth was Aminex PLC, a small firm registered in Dublin, Ireland, but operating from the United Kingdom. It exported 380,000 barrels of Russian crude to the West from the Komi Republic during December 1995.[21]

In summary, in an endeavor where neither party can achieve its purpose alone, a joint venture becomes a viable option. Usually, income derived from a joint venture is taxed as if the organization were a partnership.

HOW TO EVALUATE THE LEGAL FORM OF ORGANIZATION

A small business may change its legal form many times during its life. There are many and varied factors that influence these decisions. Figure 3–5 provides a checklist that owners of small firms should consider using when making this type of decision.

WHAT YOU SHOULD HAVE LEARNED

1. Although your choice of legal form is important, it is not final, for many businesses progress from one form to another, as the opening Profile illustrates. While most small businesses are proprietorships, they generate only a small proportion of business revenues; yet they seem to be quite prof-

itable. Most other U.S. businesses are corporations and partnerships. Corporations account for most of the revenues and profits.

2. A proprietorship is a business owned by one person. It is simple to organize, operate, and dissolve and gives the proprietor much freedom. The owner gets all the profits (if any), is not required to share information with anyone, and has some unique tax advantages. Since the business is legally inseparable from its owner, it ends when he or she dies. As the owner is personally liable for all the debts of the business, he or she may find it hard to raise money or get credit.

3. A partnership is jointly owned by two or more people and is automatically dissolved by the death of any partner. The partners share its profits, its management, and its liabilities. The partnership can combine the resources of several people but can also be difficult to manage if the partners disagree. Moreover, except for limited partners, all partners bear responsibility for the actions of the other partners, and bonding protection against such actions is not available.

4. A corporation is a legal entity separate from its owners. Because owners aren't personally responsible for its liabilities, the corporate form makes it possible to raise large amounts of capital, provides representative management, and assures the continuity of the business regardless of what happens to individual owners. Its main disadvantages are double taxation, the expense and paperwork of incorporation, and the limitations of its charter, which may make it difficult to operate in another state.

Stockholders have the right to make decisions submitted to them for a vote but may be dominated by a majority of the owners. The board of directors, which is elected by the stockholders, is responsible for running the company, but day-to-day operations are directed by company management.

For simple businesses, with 75 or fewer shareholders and no corporate shareholders, the S corporation offers relief from multiple taxation and some of the burdensome paperwork required of the traditional C corporation.

5. Other forms of business include limited-liability companies (LLCs), cooperatives, and joint ventures.

QUESTIONS FOR DISCUSSION

1. What are some basic questions to ask when deciding on the legal form to choose for a small business?

2. Define proprietorship, partnership, corporation, limited-liability company, cooperative, and joint venture.

3. What are some advantages and disadvantages of a proprietorship?

4. What are some advantages and disadvantages of a partnership?

5. What are some advantages and disadvantages of a corporation?

6. Distinguish between a general partnership and a limited partnership.

7. Distinguish between a C corporation, an S corporation, and a limited-liability company (LLC).

C A S E   3 – 1

THE MARTIN FAMILY GROWS A BUSINESS

In 1989, Dot and Jiggs Martin, along with their married daughters, Michele Statkewicz and Renee Thompson, started a small business—named Bloomin' Lollipops, Inc.—to supplement their retirement income and provide future income for their children—and grandchildren, one of whom worked in the business. They specialized in making chocolate flowers, hard candy lollipops, candy animals, a caramel-chocolate-pecan dipped gourmet apple "drizzled" with white chocolate, and eight varieties of gourmet popcorn. These were arranged in gift baskets, mugs, vases, and other containers. Their unique arrangements were sold in the store, delivered by van within a 15-mile radius, and shipped beyond that range by UPS. The owners advertised on local radio and TV and in local upscale magazines.

The aspiring entrepreneurs did extensive research for about six months before opening their store. The family members worked closely together on all aspects of organizing, promoting, opening, and operating the store. They searched for and tried many recipes for candy, then developed their own by combining the best aspects of the ones they liked. Although each person specialized in one particular job—such as making candy, arranging items creatively in containers, serving customers and answering the phone, or delivering the wrapped items—each one helped in all the activities as demand dictated.

The organizers also studied what form of ownership would be best. They wanted to form an S corporation but for technical reasons decided on a C corporation with the Martins holding 50 percent of the stock (25 percent each), Michelle 30 percent, and Renee 20 percent. There was a buyout clause in the charter, which permitted the other stockholders to buy the stock of anyone leaving the business. This occurred a few years later when Renee left to return to her "first love," being a dental technician.

The business grew so rapidly that the stockholders opened a satellite location, which was immediately successful, and expanded into wholesaling on a limited basis. Even with the normal growing pains, the family

not only did an outstanding job of running the business but also enjoyed social interaction with each other and the employees, many of whom were friends or relatives.

A few years ago, however, the volume of business and the resulting record keeping were so great that something had to be done. The family realized they would either have to sell out or hire more people, build a separate "kitchen" to make the products, and expand the wholesaling activities. Because she had a growing family, Michele had little time to give to the business, and Jiggs and Dot didn't look forward to at least five more years of "working around the clock" before Michele could return to full-time employment. For these and other reasons, they sold the business.

While Dot is enjoying the role of grandmother to her many grandchildren, Jiggs and Michele have started another small business. They provide a select group of high-volume service stations with car-washing machinery, sophisticated automobile vacuum cleaners, and coin-operated pneumatic tire pumps. Michele and Jiggs buy the equipment and provide it to their clients under a lease, profit-sharing, or financing arrangement.

As a result of the Martin family's vision, enterprise, and hard work, Bloomin' Lollipops has continued to expand and prosper. By 1999, its new owners had a kiosk in one of the city's shopping malls and have built a new production facility and expanded their wholesaling operation to include major retailers in New York and other large cities.

Questions

1. Do you think the Martins did the right thing in selling out? Why or why not?

2. Do you think the decision to incorporate as a C corporation rather than an S corporation was correct? Explain.

3. What—if anything—would you have done differently from the Martins?

Source: Author's conversations with members of the Martin family.

CASE 3-2

DB BIKES

David recently opened a small bike shop after completing a course in small business management at a local community college. At first he needed no assistance as business was slow and he had all the skills needed to run the business. As the business began to flourish, however, he could no longer do everything himself. Also, he was frequently in a financial bind.

In order to solve both problems—but especially to gain more capital—David asked Becky to join him in the venture. They formed DB Bikes as a general partnership. They each had an equal share in the business and drew the same amount of salary. They used the profits from operations to expand the business. They also shared liabilities equally as they arose.

As the business continued to expand, however, they realized they could not manage it alone, as they didn't have enough funds to meet the growing customer demand. So they decided to incorporate and sell shares to the public. Since there were only 15 stockholders, David and Becky decided to become an S corporation. The business became DB Bikes, Inc.

Questions

1. What form of business was DB Bikes when David owned it alone?

2. What kind of business did it become when Becky joined the business?

3. What kind of partnership did David and Becky have? Explain the difference between this and other kinds of partnerships.

4. What kind of business did it become when they sold shares and became an S corporation? Do you think they made the proper decision? Why or why not?

II

PLANNING FOR AND ORGANIZING A BUSINESS

Part I showed some opportunities in small business, as well as the characteristics of small businesses and their owners. It included some thoughts on studying the economic environment in order to increase the chances of success, but those suggestions presented general ideas rather than precise details. In Part II, more specific ideas for planning and organizing a small business are covered. The information presented is considerably more detailed, taking a practical "how to" approach to the activities involved in starting such a business.

Owners and managers of small firms must get things done through others, allocate scarce resources, and make decisions so that their objectives are reached. In doing these things, they perform the same five functions as managers in an organization of any size: planning, organizing, staffing, leading, and controlling. Some business textbooks organize individual chapters around these functions, but we will discuss them all in their proper context throughout the text.

We will, however, devote specific chapters to detailed discussion of the more important activities involved in starting a business. Chapter 4 explains how to become a small business owner; Chapter 5 shows how to do strategic and operational planning; and Chapter 6 discusses ways of obtaining the proper financing for the business.

4

HOW TO BECOME THE OWNER OF A SMALL BUSINESS

There is no such thing as growth industries. There are only companies organized and operated to create and capitalize on growth opportunities.

Theodore Levitt

Franchising is changing not only our marketing system, but also our way of life.

Peng S. Chan and Robert T. Justis

Buying a franchise is probably the quickest, easiest, and most successful way of becoming an entrepreneur.

Harlan Sanders, founder of Kentucky Fried Chicken

LEARNING OBJECTIVES

After studying the material in this chapter, you will be able to:

1. Explain how to go into business for yourself.

2. Describe the steps involved in the procedure recommended for going into business.

3. Describe how to search for and identify a product needed by the public—that is, how to find your niche.

4. Decide whether to start a new business, buy an existing one, or buy a franchise.

5. Describe the growing opportunities in franchising.

6. Explain how to tell if a franchise is right for you.

7. Explain the future of franchising.

Ray Kroc—Father of Franchising

Ray Kroc probably made more people millionaires than anyone else in history. And he did it after he was 52 years old and in poor health. Now his "brainchild"—McDonald's (www.mcdonalds.com)—has about 237,000 employees working in more than 23,000 restaurants in 109 countries, with over $33 billion in systemwide sales. The company has about 42 percent of the $36 billion U.S. fast-food market.

Kroc, a high school dropout, sold everything from paper cups in Chicago to real estate in Florida before he wound up selling electric milkshake mixers in the early 1950s. At that time, a hamburger and a shake took about 15 to 30 minutes to prepare at any of the thousands of small, independent drive-ins scattered across the country.

In 1954, Kroc received an order from a drive-in in San Bernardino, California, for eight machines that could make five milkshakes at a time. His curiosity led him to visit Richard and Maurice McDonald to see why they needed to make 40 shakes at a time. He found people lining up at a window, ordering, and leaving in about 30 seconds with bags of hamburgers, fries, and shakes—all for under a dollar. He thought the assembly-line operation, based on clean, instant service with a family atmosphere, was the most amazing merchandising operation he'd ever seen. Kroc persuaded the brothers to let him set up a complete franchising operation, including finding operators and locations, building drive-ins, and ensuring that they maintained the McDonalds' high standards. He left with a contract to franchise McDonald's worldwide and pay the brothers 0.5 percent of restaurant sales.

Kroc opened his first drive-in under this arrangement in Des Plaines, Illinois, in 1955. By 1961, there were 323 of the golden-arches stores, and the McDonalds wanted to retire. Kroc bought their rights for $2.7 million. At the time, sales were $54 million and earnings were around $175,000. Also, the company had some company-owned restaurants. When he died in 1984, at age 81, Kroc was a billionaire. And his franchisees were doing quite well, too. Average store sales were over $1 million and there were before-tax profit margins of 15 to 20 percent. By 1998, there were 23,500 restaurants, serving an average of 38 million people per day in 109 countries.

Kroc did for the fast-food industry what Henry Ford had done for the automobile industry. He was truly the "Father of Franchising."

Source: Reprinted with permission from McDonald's Corporation.

Figure 4–1
How a Business Is Formed and Operates

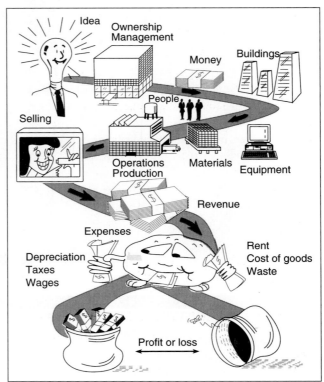

As you can see from the Profile, many opportunities exist for enterprising people to go into business for themselves. As shown in Figure 4–1, the process begins when you have an idea for a new product,* such as an innovative computer game. Then you decide on the owner-ship and management of the business and obtain resources—in the form of people, build-ings and equipment, materials and supplies, and the money to finance them. You then begin producing and selling the product to obtain revenues to pay expenses and provide you with a profit, so you can repeat the cycle.

While the concept is simple, the actual process is not as easy as it may appear from the figure. In fact, the actual process of choosing a business to enter is quite complex, as will be shown in this and the following chapters.

■ HOW TO GO INTO BUSINESS FOR YOURSELF

Chapter 2 cites many reasons for starting a small business and describes some available opportunities. Those who decide to take the important step of starting their own business must do extensive planning in order to increase their chances of success. Now we would like to explain how to actually go into business—if that is what you would like to do.[1]

---

*Technically, a product can be either a physical good or a service. To prevent repetition, we will use the term *product* to mean both.

Once the decision is made to go into business, proper planning becomes essential. While there is no one tried-and-true procedure that will work for everyone, you should at least follow some logical, well-thought-out procedure.[2]

If you *really want to start a new business, how do you do it?* We've tried to compress all the details into the following eight steps:

1.   Search for and identify a needed product.
2.   Study the market for the product, using as many sources of information as feasible.
3.   Decide whether to start a new business, buy an existing one, or buy a franchise.
4.   Make strategic plans, including setting your mission, strategic objectives, and strategies.
5.   Make operational plans, including setting policies, budgets, standards, procedures, and methods, and planning the many aspects of producing and marketing the product.
6.   Make financial plans, including estimating income and expenses, estimating initial investment, and locating sources of funds.
7.   Develop these plans into a detailed business plan.
8.   Implement the plan.

The first three of these steps are covered in this chapter. Steps 4 through 8 are covered in Chapter 5. Implementing the business plan is also covered throughout the text.

■ FINDING YOUR NICHE BY IDENTIFYING A NEEDED PRODUCT

Many business owners fail because they see the glamour of some businesses—and the apparent ease with which they are run—and think, "I know I can make a lot of money if I start my own business." While a few do succeed without adequate preparation, the majority fail. Although proper planning does not ensure success, it does improve the chances of succeeding.

Planning starts with searching for a good or service to sell. According to William A. Sahlman, who teaches entrepreneurial finance at Harvard, "Being bright-eyed and bushy-tailed isn't necessarily a barometer of success. If people succeed, it's because they really understand an industry and perceive some need or service that no one else has seen."[3] So first find your product!

The list of possible products is almost unlimited, considering the variety of goods and services offered by the over 23 million U.S. businesses. What types of businesses are available? Not all the fields are open, but there is very likely a potential new business; you just have to find it. The best place to start searching is to find your appropriate market niche. This process is called **niche marketing,** which is the process of finding a small—but profitable—demand for something, then producing a custom-made product for that market, as the following example illustrates.

> **Niche marketing** is the process of finding a small—but profitable—demand for something and producing a custom-made product for that market.

> Gwendolyn Johnson and her son, Eric, of Cleveland, Ohio, specialize in caring for "bedridden people in bad neighborhoods." And their company, Geric Home Health Care, Inc. (www.geric.com), mostly hires single welfare mothers to do the work.
>
> Although motivated partly by charity, the Johnsons, who are deeply religious people, are also "hard-driven entrepreneurs." By recruiting inner-city workers to serve an inner-city market, they use two problems to solve each other. "We hire from the 'hood to serve the 'hood," they say. The Johnsons' motto is: "Give us the cases nobody else will take." So their clients tend to be quadriplegics, people on ventilators, cases where drugs and alcohol are mixed with paralysis or terminal illness, and so forth.

> Their system seems to be working. They have "a clean report card from Medicare," annual sales of $12 million, and expanding operations in Cleveland, Detroit, and Gary, Indiana. Geric Home Health Care was named Northeast Ohio's 1996 "Socially Responsible Entrepreneur of the Year."[4]

Some of the most successful small firms find a "niche within a niche" and never deviate from it. This is what Ray Kroc did with McDonald's.

How to Decide on a Product

How can the right product be found? Most new businesses were at one time uncommon or innovative, such as selling front pouches for parents to carry children in, selling or renting videotapes, and selling computer software. Talking to large companies may help you identify opportunities that can be handled better by a small business. Newspapers are filled with advertisements for "business opportunities"—businesses for sale, new products for sale by their inventors, and other opportunities to become one's own boss. Bear in mind, though, that *these ideas are not always feasible, so proceed with caution.*

Don't forget to look to the past for a "new" product. Consumer tastes run in cycles, so it may be time to reintroduce an old product.

> For example, the magazine *Victoria* is devoted to Victorian-style decorating; and old-fashioned clothes for children—at thoroughly modern yuppie prices—are sold in trendy stores and catalogs. "High Tea"—old-fashioned English tea, scones, French pastries, and fruit trifle—is served on summer afternoons in the lobby of Chateau Lake Louise in Banff, Alberta, Canada. Accompanied by harp music, it gives one "a sense of independence and grandeur."[5]

Hobbies, recreation, and working at home require study, training, and practice that can lead to products of new design or characteristics. In addition, the subject of needed products and services often comes up in social conversation. Bankers, consultants, salespeople, and anyone else can be good sources of ideas. But it takes observation, study, vision, and luck to recognize the appropriate product for your business. Or sometimes it takes only a phone call, as the following example illustrates.

> Maggie and Gary Myers made a lot of long-distance calls in 1994 while Gary was working for a geological consulting company in east Texas and Maggie was working at South Baldwin (County, Alabama) Hospital. In one conversation, Gary learned that Maggie had to travel an hour either east or west to find a satisfactory selection of uniforms. This suggested a market niche for a business that would reunite them.
>
> Now, after much research, and with the aid of a member of **SCORE (Service Corps of Retired Executives)** (www.score.org), sponsored by the SBA and Small Business Development Centers, they are the proud owners of Specialty Uniforms, opened in January 1995. They specialize in hospital and restaurant uniforms and special-order hard-to-find items.[6]

SCORE (Service Corps of Retired Executives) is a group of retired—but active—managers from all walks of life who help people develop their business ideas.

The search for and identification of a product require innovative and original thinking, including putting the ideas together in an organized form. For example, if the chosen product is now being provided by competitors, what change is necessary for you to compete successfully or avoid competition?

Looking into the future requires extensive reading and making contacts with a wide variety of people. Constant questioning of changes that are occurring and critical analysis of products and services being received provide ideas. Innovation is alive and well and will continue its surge ahead. Each new idea spawns other ideas for new businesses.

Figure 4–2
Questions to Ask to Help Eliminate Possible Businesses That Are Wrong for You

- How much capital is required to enter and compete successfully in this business?
- How long will it take to recoup my investment?
- How long will it take to reach an acceptable level of income?
- How will I live until that time?
- What degree of risk is involved? Am I willing to take that risk?
- Can I make it on my own, or will I need the help of my family or others?
- How much work is involved in getting the business going? In running it? Am I willing to put out that much effort?
- Do I want to acquire a franchise from an established company, or do I want to start from scratch and go it on my own?
- What is the potential of this type of business? What are my chances of achieving that potential?
- Is sufficient information available to permit reaching a meaningful decision? If so, what are the sources of information?
- Is it something I would enjoy?

Choosing the Business to Enter

In choosing the business to enter, first eliminate the least attractive ideas from consideration and then concentrate on selecting the most desirable one. It is important to eliminate ideas that will not provide the challenges, opportunities, and rewards—financial and personal—that you are seeking. Be ruthless in asking, "What's in it for me?" as well as, "What can I do to be of service to others?" Questions like those in Figure 4–2 will be helpful. Also, concentrate on the thing(s) you would like to do—and can do—not on what someone else wants for you.

> For example, Dairl M. Johnson found his niche when he started a business as a result of hurting his back. After 20 years of back pain, his physician sent him to a Relax The Back retail store. Johnson was so pleased with the success of the products the store offered—office chairs, beds, car seats, and portable seats providing postural support—that he quit his job with IBM and started a chain of Relax The Back franchise stores (www.relaxtheback.com). He expected sales of $10 million by 1997. His success, says Johnson, was "a natural chain of events."[7]

After eliminating the unattractive ideas, get down to the serious business of selecting the business to which you plan to devote your energy and resources. One way of doing this is to talk to friends, various small business owners, relatives, financial advisers, or lawyers to find out what kinds of products are needed but not available. Try to get them to identify not only existing types of businesses but also new kinds. Then consider the market for the kinds of products and businesses they have suggested.

Several self-help groups of entrepreneurs in various parts of the country can be called on at this stage, as well as later stages. These groups help potential entrepreneurs find their niche and then assist them in surviving start-up, operating, and even personal problems. SCORE members can also be important sources of information. In addition to its Washington, D.C., headquarters office, SCORE now has about 388 chapters located in the United States and its territories.

It is a good idea for all prospective business owners to get help and advice from as many people as possible. The following are good sources of information:

Figure 4–3
Business Selection Survey Checklist

Capital required	Degree of risk involved	Amount of work involved	Independent ownership or franchise	Potential of the business	Source of data

- Small Business Administration.
- State Economic Development Agencies.
- *Directory of Trade Associations in the United States.*
- U.S. Department of Commerce (Office of International Trade).
- Local colleges.
- Public libraries.
- Chambers of commerce.

The last of these—chambers of commerce—are particularly effective sources of information. Being private associations of local (or regional) business and professional people, they are usually quite familiar with the area's needs. Also, the members have a vested interest in expanding business opportunities.

When obtaining advice from outsiders, though, remember it is your resources that are at stake when the commitment is made, so the ultimate decision must be yours. *Don't let someone talk you into something you are uncomfortable with.*

After discussing the need for the product with other people, select the business that seems best for you. To be more methodical and objective in your evaluation, you might prepare a checklist similar to the one in Figure 4–3. It is used by a consultant with the MIT Enterprise Forum (www.mitforum-cambridge.org) to help people decide what business to enter. You could use these criteria to help you decide whether suggestions you've received are appropriate for you. If not, make other lists until you find an idea that matches your ability, training, experience, personality, and interests.

Initially you may want to make more than one choice and leave yourself some options. Remember to consider your personal attributes and objectives in order to best utilize your capabilities. Let your mind—not your emotions—govern your decisions.

■ STUDYING THE MARKET FOR THE PRODUCT

After selecting the product and business, look at the market potential for each one. If a market does not exist—or cannot be developed—don't pursue the project any further. On the other hand, there may be a market in a particular location or a segment of the population that needs your product.

For example, a number of entrepreneurs have discovered a market that has not been adequately served—"plus-sized" individuals. Having discovered that there was a

9 percent increase in the number of overweight people, who were being forced to accept clothing and other products designed for average-sized customers, many companies are now developing products and services especially for this market.

In one case, Jan Herrick, a large-sized person herself, began publishing *Royal Resources,* a sort of Yellow Pages for plus-sized products and services. It includes over 1,200 items ranging from "dating services and toilet seats to wigs and motorized gear."

In another instance, Ann Kelly enjoyed working out at the gym, but was tired of trying to find plus-sized activewear. To compensate, she developed a catalog carrying all types of athletic items.[8]

Small businesses usually select one segment of the population for their customers, or choose one product niche, since they do not have sufficient resources to cover the whole market. Also, small businesses cannot include as large a variety of products in their efforts as large businesses can. Hence, a small business must concentrate its efforts on the customers it can serve effectively.

Methods of Obtaining Information about the Market

There are many ways to identify a market, and all can be generally classified as marketing research. As will be discussed in Chapter 7, **market research** consists of gathering, recording, classifying, analyzing, and interpreting data related to the marketing of goods and services. Formal research programs can be very valuable in giving direction, but they can also be expensive. Computers are helping to increase the amount of information gathered while reducing the cost.

Market research is the systematic gathering, recording, and analyzing of data related to the marketing of goods and service.

Another means of collecting data is a search of existing literature. The first places to look in a library are the "technical section" and the "government documents section." You should examine Census Bureau data on subjects such as population, business, and housing.

The U.S. Department of Commerce is another good source of information, as its district offices have well-stocked libraries of census data. The department publishes many useful books on planning and organizing small businesses.

Methods Used to Study the Market

There are three things you need to do when estimating your sales and market share. First, determine the size of the industry and market segment you want to enter. Second, estimate your competition and determine how you stack up against it. Finally, estimate your own share of the market.

Estimating the Size of the Market   Before launching a business, you should find out, by asking questions similar to the following, whether the market for it is large enough to accommodate a newcomer:

- How large is the industry?
- Where is the market for the company, and how large is it?
- Are sales to be made to a selected age group, and, if so, how large is that group?
- What are the size and distribution of income within the population?
- Is the sales volume for this kind of business growing, remaining stable, or declining?
- What are the number and size of competitors?
- What is the success rate for competing businesses?
- What are the technical aspects (state of the art) of the industry?

Estimating the Competition   In studying the market area, the number of similar businesses that have gone out of business or merged with a competitor should be determined. A high number of these activities usually signals market weakness. Analysis of competitors' activities may also indicate how effectively a new company can compete. Is the market large enough for another firm? What features—such as lower price, better product, or more promotion—will attract business? Can these features be developed for the new firm?

While the biggest worry for small businesses is their large national or global competitors, the natural advantage goes to the "excellent" companies—large *or* small—that strive for low overhead, use no-frills assets, and look for a better real estate deal. Small, growing companies should stay out of the path of focused market leaders and deliver unprecedented value to the chosen customers in their market niche.

Estimating Your Share of the Market   By now, you should be able to arrive at a ballpark figure for your sales volume and share of the market. First, determine the geographic boundaries of the market area and estimate how much of your product might be purchased. Finally, make an educated guess as to what part of this market you might attract as your share.

■ DECIDING WHETHER TO START A NEW BUSINESS, BUY AN EXISTING ONE, OR BUY A FRANCHISE

By now, you have probably decided what type of industry you want to enter and have done an economic feasibility study of that industry and the potential business. The next step is to decide whether to start a new business from scratch, buy an established business, or buy a franchise. As shown in Figure 4–4, many prospective business owners find themselves in a quandary over which direction to take. The material in this section may be helpful in making the choice more effectively.

To Start a New Business?

Many successful small business owners start a new business because they want others to recognize that the success is all theirs. Often, the idea selected is new, and the businesses

Figure 4–4
Which Road to Take?

for sale at the time do not fit the desired mold. Also, the size of the company, fresh inventory, new personnel, and a new location can be chosen to fit the new venture.

All this is exciting and—when successful—satisfying. But the venture is also challenging because everything about it is new, it demands new ideas, and it must overcome difficulties. Moreover, because everything is newer, a larger investment may be required.

Reasons FOR Starting a New Business   Some reasons for starting a new business lie in the owner's freedom to:

- Define the nature of the business.
- Create the preferred type of physical facilities.
- Obtain fresh inventory.
- Have a free hand in selecting and developing personnel.
- Take advantage of the latest technology, equipment, materials, and tools to cover a void in acceptable products available.
- Select a competitive environment.

> For example, Cindy and Bob Maynard started Vermont Country Cyclers in 1977. By 1988, the business had grown too big—bringing in $2 million a year by taking 6,000 people on bike trips throughout the world. The Maynards felt that cycling was falling behind the times. Also, the population was aging, and people wanted to get back to basics. So the couple sold the business.
>
> In 1990, they founded Country Walkers (www.countrywalkers.com/countrywalkers/welcom.htm), which offered walking vacations in the United States and a dozen other countries around the world. While they now serve more than 1,600 clients a year, the couple intend to keep their business "small and personal."[9]

Reasons for NOT Starting a New Business   Some reasons for not starting a new business are:

- Problems in finding the right business.
- Problems associated with assembling the resources, including the location, building, equipment, materials, and work force.
- Lack of an established product line.
- Production problems associated with starting a new business.
- Lack of an established market and channels of distribution.
- Problems in establishing basic management systems and controls.
- The risk of failure is higher in small business start-ups than in acquiring a franchise or even buying an existing business.

To Buy an Existing Business?

Buying a business can mean different things to different people. It may mean acquiring the total ownership of an entire business, or it may mean acquiring only a firm's assets, its name, or certain parts of it. Keep this point in mind as you study the following material. Also remember that many entrepreneurs find that taking over an existing business isn't always a "piece of cake."

Reasons FOR Buying an Existing Business   Some reasons for buying an established business are:

- Personnel are already working.
- The facilities are already available.
- A product is already being produced for an existing market.

- The location may be desirable.
- Relationships have been established with banks and trade creditors.
- Revenues and profits are being generated, and goodwill exists.

> For example, when the owner of the Speedy Bicycle Shop suddenly decided to sell the business, Don Albright, the manager, arranged to buy it. He alerted all the customers who had Christmas layaways to come and collect their purchases before the owner closed the shop. This gained Don a lot of goodwill when he reopened the shop as his own. Although he had to come up with a lot of capital to purchase new inventory, he already had the experience of managing the shop.

Reasons for NOT Buying an Existing Business   Some reasons for not buying an ongoing business are:

- The physical facilities may be old or obsolete.
- The employees may have a poor production record or attitude.
- The accounts receivable may be past due or uncollectible.
- The location may be bad.
- The financial condition and relations with financial institutions may be poor.
- The inventory may be obsolete or of poor quality.

Some Questions to Ask before Buying   *A word of caution is needed here.* Even if there are several businesses to choose from, the evaluation finally comes down to one business that must be thoroughly evaluated before the final decision is made. Past success or failure is not sufficient foundation for a decision about whether or not to buy a given business. Instead, you must make a thorough analysis of its present condition and an appraisal of what the business might do in the future. Table 4–1 suggests some important questions to be asked when making the decision to buy an ongoing business.

To Buy a Franchise?

As you will see later in this chapter, franchising is expanding rapidly and appears to be very successful.[10] Yet franchisers have failed, and some franchisees have suffered severe losses. So the decision to buy a franchise is a serious one.

Reasons FOR Buying a Franchise   Franchise agreements normally spell out what both the franchiser and franchisee are responsible for and must do. Each party usually desires the success of the other. The franchiser brings proven and successful methods of operation and business images to aid the franchisee. If you decide to become a business owner, you can obtain guidance from experienced people by obtaining a franchise. Franchises are available in a wide range of endeavors, so you may be able to find one that combines your talents and desires, as the following example shows.

> David and Tamara Kennedy, of Sausalito, California, once made their living as skipper and chef aboard yachts around the world. Then they were drawn by an ad for a nautical bookstore franchise—Armchair Sailor Bookstore (www.seabooks.com)— seeking to expand nationally. "Must have a love of the sea and know how to sail," it said. "While we won't become millionaires," they confessed after buying a franchise, "we love what we're doing and are doing something we know about. It's been a learning experience for both of us."[11]

Another reason for buying a franchise is that it probably has many of the requirements for success. The market niche has been identified, and sales activities are in place. Also, the

Table 4–1

Questions to Ask before Buying an Existing Business

- **Why is the business available for purchase?** This question should help establish the validity of the owner's stated reason for selling the business. Some reasons suggest a challenging opportunity.
- **What are the intentions of the present owners?** After selling a business, former owners are free to do what they wish unless restricted by contract. What has been said before the sale and what happens afterward may not be the same. Some questions needing answers are: Will the present owner remain in competition? Does he or she want to retire or leave the area?
- **Are environmental factors changing?** The demand for a firm's product may rise or fall, or the niche may change, because of such factors as changes in population characteristics, neighborhood, consumer habits, zoning, traffic patterns, environment, tax law, or technology.
- **Are physical facilities suitable for present and future operations?** To be suitable, facilities must be properly planned and laid out, effectively maintained, and up-to-date.
- **Is the business operating efficiently?** Will the business need to be "whipped into shape" after purchase? Are the personnel effective? Is waste excessive or under control? Is the quality of the product satisfactory, and is the inventory at the proper level and up-to-date?
- **What is the financial condition of the firm?** Will the business be a good financial risk? This can be determined by checking variables such as the validity of financial statements, the cash position, the cash flow, various financial ratios, the amount and terms of debt, and the adequacy of cost data.
- **How much investment is needed?** Remember, the investment includes not only the purchase price of the existing firm but also capital needed for renovations, improvements, and start-up activities.
- **What is the estimated return on investment?** This estimate should be realistic and not based on wishful thinking. It should include potential losses as well as potential gains.
- **Is the price right?** One important factor that should always be considered is the price asked for the firm. Sometimes, a successful ongoing business can be bought at a fraction of its value. But while you may be lucky enough to get such a bargain, be wary of pitfalls. For example, a retailer may offer to sell a business for "the current price of assets—less liabilities." But the accounts receivable may be in arrears, while the inventory consists of unsalable goods.
- **Do you have the necessary managerial ability?** Some people have a special talent for acquiring ongoing businesses that are in economic difficulty and turning them around. If you have—or can develop—this special talent, the ability is valuable to society and profitable to you, the new entrepreneur.

business may already be located, managed, and running. The questions to ask about franchises are: How much help do I need? Can a franchise help me enough to more than cover the costs of the franchise?

Most potential small business owners do not have the competencies or resources to get started successfully. But the franchiser can provide supplemental help through its experience and concentrated study of the field. These talents come from both successes and failures in the past. A study of the services listed in the contract, in relation to your needs, shows the value to you.

Reasons for NOT Buying a Franchise   Buying a successful franchise is probably beyond the means of the ordinary entrepreneur, as the best ones are quite costly. Expenses include initial investments and fees, as well as royalty payments. A recent Gallup survey found that the average investment in a franchise, including fees and additional expenses, was $143,260.[12] Also, new franchisees face far greater financial risks than well-established ones.[13] And even the best franchise is not a guarantee of success. The costs may outweigh the benefits from its purchase. It may not fit the owner's desires or direction, or it may not

Table 4–2
How Franchising Benefits Both Franchisee and Franchiser

Selected Benefits to the Franchisee	Selected Benefits to the Franchiser
1. Brand recognition	1. Faster expansion and penetration
2. Management training and/or assistance	2. Franchisee motivation
3. Economies of large-scale buying	3. Franchisee attention to detail
4. Financial assistance	4. Lower operating costs
5. Share in local or national promotion	

give the franchisee enough independence. Finally, overpriced, poorly run, uninteresting, and "white elephant" franchises are potentially disastrous, as the following example illustrates.

> An enterprising young woman and her younger brother put up $2,000 as a guaranteed investment for candy machines after the franchiser promised to find good locations for them. These failed to materialize, however, because all the desirable locations were already in use. The franchiser disappeared, and the entrepreneurs lost their $2,000.

Even under the best of conditions, franchisers tend to hold an advantage, as shown in Table 4–2. Usually, this relates to operating standards, supply and material purchase agreements, and agreements relating to the repurchase of the franchise. Also, there are constraints as to the size of the territory and the specific location. Moreover, you sometimes have no choice about the layout and decor. However, careful study of franchisers' past records and contract offerings can lead to selection of a potentially successful franchise operation.

■ GROWING OPPORTUNITIES IN FRANCHISING

The Profile of Ray Kroc illustrates the many exciting opportunities in one of the fastest-growing and most important segments of U.S. business: franchising. As Harlan Sanders indicates in one of the opening quotations, this alternative to starting a new business has helped tens of thousands of entrepreneurs achieve their dream of owning a business of their own. However, while many franchising opportunities exist, they do not automatically spell success. Caution is called for especially in dealing with franchisers who promise a guaranteed return on your investment. Contracts with elusive or vanished companies often prove worthless.

What Is Franchising?

We will define franchising by describing the process and parties involved, and then discuss the two most popular types of franchises. These are (1) product and trademark franchising and (2) business format franchising.

Franchising is a marketing system based on a legal arrangement that permits one party—the franchisee—to conduct business as an individual owner while abiding by the terms and conditions set by the second party—the franchiser.

The **franchise** is the agreement granting the right to do business and specifying the terms and conditions under which the business will be conducted. The **franchiser** is the company that owns the franchise's name and distinctive elements (such as signs, symbols, and patents) and that grants others the right to sell its product. The **franchisee** is usually an

Franchising is a marketing system whereby an individual owner conducts business according to the terms and conditions set by the franchiser.

A **franchise** is an agreement whereby an independent businessperson is given exclusive rights to sell a specified good or service.

The **franchiser** owns the franchise's name and distinctive elements and licenses others to sell its products.

The **franchisee** is an independent businessperson who agrees to sell the product according to the franchiser's requirements.

independent local businessperson who agrees with the franchise owner to operate the business on a local or regional basis. While the franchisee is given the right to market the franchiser's designated goods or services, that marketing must be done according to the terms of the licensing agreement. The contract specifies what the franchisee can and cannot do and prescribes certain penalties for noncompliance.

Extent of Franchising

According to Arthur Karp, chairman of the International Franchise Association (IFA) (www.franchise.org), the only international trade association serving franchisers in more than 50 countries, U.S. franchises create around 300,000 *new jobs* each year, as each new franchise creates about 8 to 10 new jobs, many of which go to younger and older workers who otherwise would be unable to find jobs.[14]

The IFA also estimates that a new franchised business opens in the United States every eight minutes.[15] These franchises are responsible for nearly 41 percent of all U.S. retail sales.[16]

Types of Franchising Systems

Figure 4–5 shows the two main types of franchising systems: product and trademark franchising; and business format franchising. **Product and trademark franchising** is an arrangement under which the franchisee is granted the right to sell a widely recognized product or brand. Most such franchisees concentrate on handling one franchiser's product line and identify their business with that firm. Familiar examples include automobile and truck dealerships, gasoline service stations, and soft-drink bottlers. The franchiser exercises very little control over the franchisee's operations; what control there is has to do with maintaining the integrity of the product, not with the franchisee's business operations.

Business format franchising is a relationship in which the franchisee is granted the right to use an entire marketing system, along with ongoing assistance and guidance from the franchiser. The industry groups with the largest volume of sales in this type of franchising are restaurants, retailing (nonfood), hotels and motels, business aids and services, automotive products and services, and convenience stores.

> When Ray Kroc set up McDonald's as a franchiser (see the opening Profile), he controlled the trade name (McDonald's), symbol (golden arches), and operating systems. In turn, he permitted franchisees to use them under controlled conditions— for a fee. Kroc also controlled all aspects of quality that characterized the successful operations of the original drive-in.

Product and trademark franchising grants the franchisee the right to sell a widely recognized product or brand.

Business format franchising grants a franchisee the right to market the product and trademark and to use a complete operating system.

■ WHY FRANCHISING IS GROWING IN IMPORTANCE

Franchising has been one of the fastest-growing areas of U.S. business during the past decade or so. And if you think of all the franchises you've interfaced with during the past week, you can see why they're growing in importance.

Recent Rapid Growth

The number of franchise establishments increased over 400 percent during the last two decades,[17] and this trend is expected to continue into the twenty-first century. Business format franchising has accounted for most of this growth. Earlier, product and trademark franchising dominated the franchise field, but its role has declined rapidly during the past two decades as business format franchising has skyrocketed.

Figure 4–5
Types of Franchising Systems

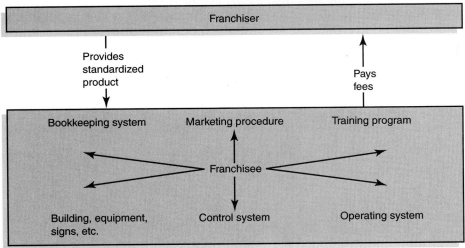

A. Product and trademark franchising

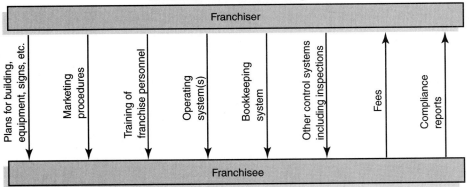

B. Business format franchising

For example, a revolution is occurring in the business of selling cars, and not all dealers will survive. Investment bankers and venture capitalists are rapidly moving into the car business. As big investors consolidate the nation's 22,000 new-car dealerships, many traditional dealers are retiring or selling their dealerships to the big chains. Corporate giants, with their "no-haggle" pricing and customer-friendly sales approach, are the latest trend in auto selling. According to the National Automobile Dealers Association, franchised new car dealers are disappearing at a rate of about 50 per year.[18]

Adding to this trend for the last three years has been the mushrooming growth of auto-selling Web sites. These sites permit purchasers to review, select, finance, insure, and take delivery of a new vehicle without leaving their homes.[19]

Causes of Rapid Growth

There are many reasons franchising, especially business format franchising, has become so popular. First, a franchiser has already identified a consumer need and created a product to meet that need, as well as a convenient and economical method of marketing it. For example, in single-parent or dual-career homes, few people want to spend precious time preparing meals, so they head for a fast-food outlet such as Wendy's. Reluctance to make dental or doctor's appointments far in advance—with a good chance of spending hours in the waiting room—has led to franchising of walk-in health care services, such as LensCrafters (www.lenscrafters.com) and United Surgical Centers. Increasing leisure time has resulted in franchising of recreational and exercise activities, such as Jazzercise (www.jazzercise.com). In other words, franchises have emerged to cater to many consumer and business needs that were not being recognized or satisfied elsewhere.

Second, as Harlan (Colonel) Sanders said in the chapter's opening quotation, one of the best ways to succeed in small business is to buy an established franchise. This is because, according to SBA estimates, the failure rate for franchises is much lower than for small independent businesses.[20]

A third reason for franchising's popularity is that franchisees have the support of established management systems for bookkeeping, marketing, operations, and control. These systems give franchisees the benefit of business experience without their having to acquire it for themselves.

A major drawback to franchising, though, is the voluminous paperwork needed to provide disclosure documents to potential franchisees. These statements, required by the Federal Trade Commission (FTC) (www.ftc.gov), provide background and financial position information about the franchiser and the franchise offering.

■ HOW TO TELL WHETHER A FRANCHISE IS RIGHT FOR YOU

While franchising opportunities abound, intensive study and evaluation are needed before you enter into such an arrangement. When you buy a franchise, you're relying not only on your own business expertise and experience but also on the franchiser's business ideas, skills, capital, and ethics. While nothing is guaranteed to protect you in buying a franchise, you can reduce your risks by taking the actions discussed in this section. See Figure 4–6 for specific questions to ask when checking out a potential franchise.

In investigating franchises, learn which ones are growing the fastest so as to get in on growth possibilities. You can do this by studying such sources as *Entrepreneur* magazine's annual listing of the best performers and the U.S. Commerce Department's *Franchise Opportunities Handbook,* published annually. Also, your local SBA office or SCORE chapter, schools with small business development centers, chambers of commerce, and libraries can be of great help.

See What the Franchise Can Do for You

While you may cherish your freedom to operate as you choose, you might prefer to receive the management training and assistance provided by the franchiser. You should consider whether you're willing to give up some of your independence in exchange for such training and assistance. For entrepreneurs with little business experience, the assistance they can get from the franchiser justifies some sacrifice of their independence.

When you buy a franchise, you'll pay up front to buy a building or rent space, renovate a store or office, lease or buy equipment, buy inventory, and receive other facilities. Then you'll pay the franchiser a one-time franchise fee and regular royalty fees. For these fees and costs—ranging from around 3 to 7 percent—you can expect the kind of help shown in Figure 4–7 on page 83. Those considering buying a franchise should ask themselves if they are willing to pay these fees, accept the franchiser's regulations, and give up a certain amount of their independence.

Figure 4–6
How to Check Out a Franchise

The franchise

1. Does your lawyer approve of the franchise contract being considered?
2. Does the franchise call on you to take any steps that your lawyer considers unwise or illegal?
3. Does the franchise agreement provide you an exclusive territory for the length of the franchise, or can the franchiser sell a second or third franchise in the territory?
4. Is the franchiser connected in any way with any other franchise handling similar merchandise or services?
5. If the answer to question 4 is yes, what is your protection against the second franchiser?
6. Under what circumstances and at what cost can you terminate the franchise contract if you decide to cancel it?
7. If you sell your franchise, will you be compensated for goodwill?

The franchiser

8. How many years has the franchiser been operating?
9. Has it a reputation among local franchisees for honesty and fair dealing?
10. Has the franchiser shown you any certified figures indicating net profit of one or more franchisees that you have personally checked?
11. Will the franchiser assist with:
    - *a.* A management training program?
    - *b.* An employee training program?
    - *c.* A public relations program?
    - *d.* Capital?
    - *e.* Credit?
    - *f.* Merchandising ideas?
12. Will the franchiser help find a good location for the new business?
13. Is the franchiser adequately financed to implement its stated plan of financial assistance and expansion?
14. Does the franchiser have an experienced management team trained in depth?
15. Exactly what can the franchiser do for you that you can't do for yourself?
16. Has the franchiser investigated you carefully enough to be sure of your qualifications?
17. Does your state have a law regulating the sales of franchises, and has the franchiser complied with that law?

The franchisee

18. How much equity capital will you need to purchase the franchise and operate it until it reaches the break-even point? Where are you going to obtain it?
19. Are you prepared to give up some independence to secure the advantages offered by the franchise?
20. Do you really believe you have the qualifications to succeed as a franchisee?
21. Are you ready to spend much or all of your remaining business life with this franchise company?

The market

22. Have you determined that an adequate market exists in your territory for the good or service at the prices you will have to charge for it?
23. Is the population in the territory expected to increase, remain the same, or decrease over the next five years?
24. Will the good or service be in greater, about the same, or less demand five years from now than it is today?
25. What is the competition in the territory for the good or service:
    - *a.* From nonfranchised firms?
    - *b.* From franchised firms?

Source: Franchising Opportunities Handbook (Washington, DC: U.S. Department of Commerce, January 1988), pp. xxxii–xxxiv.

Figure 4–7
Services Provided by Competent Franchisers

- Start-up assistance, such as market information, site location, building and equipment design and purchase, and financial advice.
- A proven and successful system for operating the business.
- A standardized accounting and cost control system for business records. These records are audited periodically by the franchiser's staff. In many instances, standard monthly operating statements are required. The franchiser develops a set of standard performance figures based on composite figures of reporting franchisees and returns a comparative analysis to the franchisee as a managerial aid.
- In some instances, financial assistance to cover land, building, equipment, inventory, and working capital needs.
- Assistance in the purchase of the site and the construction of a standardized structure with a design identified with the franchise.
- A training program to help prepare employees to operate and manage the unit. (The more successful franchisers have their own special training schools, such as McDonald's Hamburger University and the Holiday Inn University.)
- A well-planned and well-implemented national or regional advertising program to establish and maintain a uniform image.
- A set of customer service standards created by the franchiser and its professional staff, who make regular inspection visits to assure compliance by the franchisee.
- Sensitivity and responsiveness to changing market opportunities.
- The advantage of discounts for buying in large quantities.

Investigate the Franchise

You should investigate the franchiser and the franchise business as thoroughly as possible. First, be sure to look at more than one franchise and investigate similar franchises in the same line of business. Review the brief descriptions of franchises in the Commerce Department's *Franchise Opportunities Handbook,* and consult other guides and literature available from your library or the other sources mentioned above.

The Federal Trade Commission requires that a franchise give prospective franchisees a formal agreement and a Uniform Franchise Offering Circular (UFOC) at least 10 days before the contract is executed or before any money is paid.[21] This **prospectus** or **disclosure statement** should provide background on the franchiser and its financial position; the financial requirements for a franchisee; and the restrictions, protections, and estimated earnings of the franchise. Since 1997, a franchiser's formal offering circular can be downloaded from the World Wide Web.[22]

A **prospectus** or **disclosure statement** provides background and financial information about the franchiser and the franchise offering.

Contact several of the franchise owners listed in the disclosure statement and ask about their franchising experiences. Preferably, seek those who have been in the business for several years. They should be able to give the best advice about what to expect in the first year of operation—typically the period during which the success or failure of a new franchise is determined.

Obtain Professional Advice

The legal requirements of franchising are such that both franchiser and franchisee should "work with a franchise attorney from day one."[23] The potential franchisee especially should obtain professional assistance in reviewing and evaluating any franchise under consideration.

The financial statements will reveal to a professional accountant, banker, or financial analyst whether the franchiser's financial condition is sound or whether there is a risk that it will be unable to meet its financial and other obligations. It's also important to check to see whether you'll be required to stock items that you don't need or can't sell, or whether the contract can be terminated for insufficient reason. Incidentally, while some terms of a franchise agreement are negotiable, *some are not.* For example, *trademarks, royalty rates, and assignment or termination provisions are usually not negotiable.*[24]

Legal advice is the most important professional assistance you need before investing in a franchise. A lawyer can advise you about your legal rights and obligations in relation to the franchise agreement and may be able to suggest important changes in it that will protect your interest better. A lawyer should also tell you of any laws that may affect the franchise, especially taxation and personal liability aspects.

Know Your Legal and Ethical Rights

The IFA, mentioned earlier, has a code of ethics that covers a franchiser's obligations to its franchisees. Each member company pledges to comply with all applicable laws and to make sure its disclosure statements are complete, accurate, and not misleading. Furthermore, it pledges that all important matters affecting its franchise will be contained in written agreements and that it will accept only those franchisees who appear to possess the qualifications needed to conduct the franchise successfully. The franchiser agrees to base the franchisee's compensation on the sale of the product, not on the recruitment of new franchisees.

In considering the franchisee's rights, what happens if the franchiser attempts to buy back the franchise when it becomes very profitable? Should the franchisee be required to sell, as happened in the following example?

> One of the contract provisions of Subway's tight control of franchisees was so restrictive that the SBA intervened. In an unusual action, the SBA refused to guarantee loans to buyers who signed what had become the standard contract offered by Doctor's Associates Inc., Subway's franchiser (www.subway.com). The offending provision, apparently unprecedented in the contracts of other large franchisers, gave Doctor's the right to repurchase franchises "at any time." It also made it easier to oust "difficult" or "underperforming" franchisees. Critics said it "drastically undermines franchisees' ownership rights." Doctor's agreed to amend the provision, but only for those who seek SBA assistance.[25]

Other problem areas for franchisees include (1) the high price of supplies that must be bought from the franchiser,[26] (2) inadequate servicing,[27] (3) slashing technical support and services,[28] (4) fraud,[29] and (5) encroachment, whereby a franchiser opens another outlet "too close."

> Franchise outlets, especially fast-food restaurants, are multiplying so rapidly that new ones occasionally open just a mile or so away from an established one. While the franchisers and courts have tended to ignore the problem in the past, franchisees were given hope by a recent ruling by the Ninth U.S. Circuit Court of Appeals (www.ce9.uscourts.gov). A three-member panel concluded that Naugles, Inc., a Mexican restaurant chain, "breached its covenant of good faith and fair dealing" with franchisee Vylene Enterprise Inc. by building a new site [only] 1.4 miles from Vylene's restaurant.[30] The court upheld a lower court's award of $2.2 million in damages, plus attorney's fees and other costs of $550,000.

Franchisees got another boost in October 1994, when Congress passed a law requiring the SBA to provide clients with information on the risks and benefits of franchising. However, the agency has been slow complying with the law.[31]

■ THE FUTURE OF FRANCHISING

The future of franchising is indeed bright, and the number and variety of U.S. franchises are expected to continue to grow. As indicated earlier, franchises now account for nearly 41 percent of all retail trade, and the Commerce Department expects this figure to increase to 50 percent by the year 2000.

Expected Areas of Growth

The industries that especially lend themselves to franchising are restaurants; motels; convenience stores; electronics; and automotive parts, accessories, and servicing. Not all franchises in these categories are of a quality worthy of selection, nor are these categories the only ones worthy of consideration; but they do appear to be good growth areas.

Restaurants   The success of restaurants, especially those offering fast foods, is related to many variables, including demographic factors such as the high percentage of young adults and singles in the population and the increasing number of women working outside the home. The changing gender distribution will affect demand at various fast-food outlets. For example, a study by Maritz Marketing Research (www.maritz.com) found that men eat more burgers and pizzas at fast-food restaurants than women; women eat more Mexican, chicken, and other foods, including Chinese, deli, salads, and seafood.[32]

Other factors that seem to have had a positive influence on franchised restaurant success are product appeal to a growing segment of the market, fast service, a sanitary environment, and buildings and signs that are easily recognizable. You may think of restaurant franchises such as McDonald's (www.mcdonalds.com), Burger King (www.burgerking.com), Wendy's (www.wendys.com), and other fast-food outlets, but franchising is also becoming dominant in the traditional restaurant market as well. "Chains such as Chili's (www.chilis.com), the Olive Garden (www.olivegarden.com), and Outback Steakhouse (www.outback.com) are now creating their own revolution in full-service dining." Earlier successful chains such as Howard Johnson's (www.hojo.com) and Big Boy (www.frischs.com) were deposed by McDonald's, but the new restaurant franchises, aiming at a narrow market niche, are posing a serious threat to established independent restaurants.[33]

Motels   The motel industry has experienced explosive growth since the interstate highway system began in 1956 and the growing affluence and mobility of Americans created a market for quality motels. The industry has grown from mom-and-pop units (with an often questionable image) to one dominated by large corporate empires. These corporations not only sell franchises to independent businesspeople but also operate some of the most profitable units themselves. Best Western is considered to have the largest number of establishments.

Convenience Stores   While the term *convenience store* is usually associated with food outlets, it can cover other types of specialty shops. Some examples of these franchises are the Bread Basket, T-Shirts Plus, and Health Mart.

Electronics   With the rapid growth in electronics fields such as music, video, TV, and computers, franchising has naturally followed. Radio Shack (www.radioshack.com) has long been a franchise, and its computers are standard equipment for school and business applications. Some other well-known franchises are Circuit City (www.circuitcity.com), Babbage's (www.babbages-etc.com), American Software (www.amsoftware.com), and Muzak (www.muzak.com).

Automotive Parts, Accessories, and Servicing   Automotive franchises have been around for a long time as retail outlets for parts and accessories. Some of the units have been affiliated with nationally known tire manufacturers such as General Tire (www.generaltire.com). A comparatively recent entry into the automotive franchise field is the specialty service shop. Some examples are shops specializing in muffler and shock absorber repairs and parts, such as Midas International (www.midas.com); shops providing technical assistance and specialized parts for "customizing" vans; and diagnostic centers with sophisticated computerized electronic equipment. Also, the number of automotive service franchises, such as Precision Tune (www.precision-tune.com) and Jiffy Lube (www.jiffylube.com), has been growing as gasoline stations shift from full service to self-service, and many of these franchises use former service station facilities. According to the president of Valvoline Instant Oil Change Franchising, Inc. (www.vioc.com), "It was the decline of the neighborhood service station that gave rise to our business. . . . Many of the original sites used for our centers were such stations."[34]

Other Areas of Expected Development

A growing number of small business owners are finding that they do not have the expertise, the resources, or the time to package and ship their wares. This trend has led to the expansion of franchises to address these needs for local outlets. In addition to packaging and shipping, these franchises offer other services, such as private mailbox rentals, faxing, photocopying, and quick printing.

> One such franchise is Pak Mail of America Inc. (www.pakmail.com). Its activities solve the need of small companies for effective service while keeping costs low.[35]

Changing demographics are also creating a need for new franchises. There have been many franchises for health care and fitness. Now there is a need to merge these activities, as there are more single parents and less physical activity on the streets and playgrounds.

Another trend is toward mergers of franchises in related fields. These mergers can result in stronger and more powerful franchises.

> One example of this trend was when four profitable multi-unit franchisees of Pennzoil Company's Jiffy Lube International merged to form Heartland Automotive Services Inc. Located in Omaha, Nebraska, Heartland had 66 outlets in 1995.[36]

Synergy is the concept that two or more people, working together in a coordinated way, can accomplish more than the sum of their independent efforts.

In **combination franchising (multiformat franchising, dual branding, complementary branding)** big-name franchise operations offer both companies' products under the same roof.

There is a growing emphasis on **synergy** among U.S. small businesses as they try to *reengineer* and *rightsize* themselves. One way they are doing this is by combining noncompeting franchises into one location. This latest rage in franchising goes by many names, such as **combination franchising, multiformat franchising, dual branding,** and **complementary branding.** The concept, however, is the same by any name: Big-name franchise operations team up with each other to offer both companies' products under the same roof. Figure 4–8 lists some of the many franchisers using the dual-brand concept. Notice that the products carried under this arrangement tend not to be directly competitive.

There can, however, be "cultural clashes" that lead to the breakup of these arrangements.

> For example, when, in 1995, Arby's (www.arbysrestaurant.com) and ZuZu Inc. planned to share at least 85 of their restaurants by 1998, they thought they had "a winner." But only "a handful" of the two-menu restaurants ever appeared, and they were short-lived because of "cultural clashes from the start."[37] Arby's sandwiches came in simple paper wrappings, but ZuZu dishes came on crockery plates with metal utensils. Some customers, confused by the difference, threw ZuZu's plates and utensils in the trash along with Arby's paper.

Another aspect of synergy is the trend toward ownership of a large number of franchise outlets. Franchisers find it speeds their growth and simplifies their work to place multiple

---

Figure 4–8
Teaming Up

Franchisers currently using the dual-brand concept include:
- Arby's/Sbarro
- Baskin-Robbins/Dunkin' Donuts
- Blimpie/I Can't Believe It's Yogurt/Java Coast Coffee
- Carl's Jr./Green Burrito
- Carl's Jr./Long John Silver's
- Denny's/Baskin-Robbins
- El Pollo Loco/Foster's Freeze
- KFC/Taco Bell
- Rally's Hamburgers/Green Burrito
- Taco Bell/T. J. Cinnamons

Some of the big-name fast-food franchisers now found in convenience stores:
- Blimpie
- Burger King
- McDonald's
- Subway
- Taco Bell

Source: Lynn Beresford, "Seeing Double," *Entrepreneur*, October 1995, pp. 166–67. Reprinted with permission.

units in the hands of "big boys," as those owning 20 or more stores are called. This trend has led to the practice of some franchisers of shunning "mom-and-pop" franchisees entirely.[38]

Global Franchising

The success achieved by some U.S. franchises has resulted in growing global interest and opportunity. One survey found that an estimated 20 percent of U.S. franchisers operate internationally by means of company units, master licenses, individual franchises, or joint ventures.[39]

Franchises also help the U.S. balance of trade. For example, in 1994, franchising accounted for $458 million in exports but only $10 million in imports, and the favorable gap is widening each year. Germany, Canada, Japan, the United Kingdom, and Mexico are our biggest sources of export revenue.[40]

Global operations also help the franchisers. For example, McDonald's revenues from foreign sales topped 50 percent of the total, and that figure was expected to be 60 percent by the beginning of the twenty-first century. McDonald's is obviously committed to global expansion: it is opening two foreign stores for every new U.S. outlet.[41]

Another global operator is KFC International (formerly Kentucky Fried Chicken) (www.kfc.com), which has close to 5,000 restaurants in 73 countries on six continents outside the United States. Although it owns more than 1,000 of those units, KFC's global units are operated primarily through franchise and joint-venture arrangements. In these arrangements, KFC holds an equity stake in the operations, from which it earns a percentage of profits.[42]

U.S. franchisers have been quite successful in Eastern Europe. Many U.S. law firms specializing in franchising are already setting up branches abroad, such as East Europe Law Ltd., in Budapest, Hungary.

Fast-food franchises have been particularly successful abroad. Because the fast-food industry isn't as well developed in other countries, U.S. franchises have a great opportunity to be leaders in many markets. For example, franchises such as McDonald's, Pizza Hut (www.pizzahut.com), and Pepsi (www.pepsi.com) are flourishing in Eastern European countries and Russia.[43]

Expansion into other countries is not always smooth, however, and problems can develop easily. For instance, when McDonald's offered its non-kosher Quarter Pounder in its first unit in Jerusalem, Orthodox Jewish protesters surrounded the store. Still, the store, which opened in May 1995, did a brisk business.[44] On the other hand, when it opens stores in India, where Hindus regard cows as sacred, McDonald's will substitute veggie burgers for its traditional "all-beef patties."[45]

McDonald's also made news when city officials demanded that it vacate its central Beijing site—on which the franchise held a 20-year lease. After the case drew international condemnation, the central government intervened. McDonald's used a new, smaller design.[46]

Burger King is also facing problems with its European, African, and Middle East franchises. Many franchisees say they need more guidance and support—as well as lower prices for franchiser-approved paper goods and food supplies from Burger King.[47]

But there is also good news. Chick-fil-A, the Atlanta-based franchiser, announced plans to open franchises in Africa during the 1990s. The company planned to open more than 50 restaurants scattered over 10 countries in the southern end of the continent.[48]

According to Joseph R. Lunsford, chairman of Franchise Concepts, Inc., an Atlanta-based management company for four franchise chains, Africa is an attractive market for franchises. He said the relatively untapped continent "is one of the more lucrative markets . . . for master licensees and franchisees."[49]

Growing franchise industries also include maid and personal services; home improvements; business aids and services (such as accounting, collections, and personnel services); automobile products and services; weight-control centers; hair salons and services; and private postal services.

> For example, the California-based Mail Boxes, Etc.® (www.mbe.com) franchise was recently granted an exception to the Mexican constitution's ban on private postal services. Each MBE unit in Mexico pays $1,000 to register as an official post office.[50]

Minority Ownership of Franchises

Minority ownership of franchises has made steady progress over the years, especially in automobile and truck dealerships. According to a study of 366 franchise chains in 60 businesses, about 10 percent of franchises were operated by members of minorities.[51]

While the major barriers continue to be lack of financing and expertise, minority ownership is now growing. According to Shingler-Hollis Investment Group, a small business development/franchise consultant, the minority community is insisting on getting more information from franchisers.[52] The result is that franchise executives and government agencies are increasingly alerting potential franchisees to franchise opportunities, including financing, training, and support activities, as the following examples illustrate.

> Shoney's, Inc. (www.shoneys.com), which franchises Shoney's (www.shoneysrestaurants.com), Captain D's Seafood (www.captainds.com), Fifth Quarter Steakhouse (www.5thquarter.com), and Pargo's (www.pargos.com) restaurants, defers a big chunk of the initial franchise fee and slashes initial royalties for minority owners. KFC reduces liquidity requirements by over one-half and guarantees loans made by local banks to minority operators of its restaurants.

The primary group that implements federal policies benefiting minority entrepreneurship is the Minority Business Development Agency (MBDA) (www.mbda.gov). Among its many other activities, it operates the **Minority Vendor Profile System,** a computerized database listing minority firms. The system is designed to match minority entrepreneurs with available marketing opportunities.

You have probably heard comments about so many new jobs during the past two decades being just "burger flippers."[53] There may be a grain of truth to such statements, but fast-food franchises provide excellent opportunities for upward mobility for new, inexperienced workers. This mobility is particularly impressive for immigrants and minorities.[54] Dennis Perdomo, the Hispanic manager of a Pizza Hut in South Central Los Angeles, explained this mobility by saying, "We teach people team building, time management, basic math [and] even how to assimilate." The following examples illustrate the opportunities franchises can offer.[55]

> In 1965, Ed Rensi, McDonald's current president and CEO, started at $0.85 an hour in Columbus, Ohio. And at Pizza Hut, 40 percent of the managers at its 6,000 company-owned stores started as part-time crew members. Every one of them is now a salaried employee with health insurance. Some 54 percent of Pizza Hut's assistant managers also started as crew members. They also have health insurance.

The reason franchise operations are so desirable as a training ground was explained by Herman Cain, president of Godfather's Pizza (www.godfathers.com). He said, "The people . . . our industry is able to hire are not as educated . . . experienced . . . and skilled as other people. There are very few other people who *would* hire and train them."

The **Minority Vendor Profile System** is a computerized database designed to match minority entrepreneurs with available marketing opportunities.

■ TURNING YOUR DREAM INTO A REALITY

We've presented much information to help you decide whether or not you want to go into franchising. You've also been told how to investigate whether a franchise is right for you or not. Figure 4–9 provides a step-by-step review of what is required for you to become a franchisee. It also estimates the time required for each of the steps. While all these steps may not be required, and the time spans are not universal, the information is a good overview of the activities required by many franchisers and the time it takes to do each of them.

WHAT YOU SHOULD HAVE LEARNED

■

1. The first thing to do in becoming a small business owner is to decide whether it is what you *really want to do*. Then, proper planning becomes essential to chart your new venture. The time of starting your new business is also important.

2. Although there is no set procedure for starting a business, there are steps that can be taken to help ensure success. They are (*a*) search for a needed product; (*b*) study the market for the product; (*c*) decide whether to start a new business, buy an existing one, or buy a franchise; (*d*) make strategic plans, including setting a mission, objectives, and

strategies; (*e*) make operational plans, including setting up policies, budgets, procedures, and plans for operating the business; (*f*) make financial plans, including estimating income, expenses, and initial investment, and locating sources of funds; (*g*) prepare a business plan; and (*h*) implement the plan. The first three steps were discussed in this chapter.

3. The product to sell can be found by (*a*) reading books, papers, and other information; (*b*) having social and business conversations with friends, support groups, businesspeople, and others; and

Figure 4–9
What's Needed to Become a Franchise Owner

Step-by-step review of what needs to be done and how long it will take to turn the dream of owning your own business into the reality of opening day.

Phase	1 Decide to become a franchisee	2 Make decision and invest $____	3 Real estate	4 Construction	5 Equipment and inventory
Action items	Investigate and select your franchise	Decide, buy, sign contract; pay $____	Look for proper store site: *a.* Storefront type *b.* Build to specs, freestanding	Conform to franchise contract: *a.* Leasehold improvements *b.* Construct building per drawings	Order and install all equipment; order opening inventory—goods
Time span	3 months to 2 years	3 months	2 to 12 months	3 to 11 months	1 to 3 months

Phase	6 Hiring	7 Training	8 Pre-opening final check	9 Opening and operations	10 Contract term
Action items	Hire manager or assistant manager; hire crew; fill out state and federal forms	Get your training in franchiser's school; learn procedures and methods	Construction; punch list; permits; bank accounts; marketing plan; inventory	First soft opening; later grand opening Employee daily work schedule Daily sales reports Cash register tapes, money Deposit cash in bank nightly Insurance accuracy Pay royalty and advertising fees	Work and manage your own franchise
Time span	2 to 6 weeks	2 weeks to 2 months	1 day to 2 weeks	Select a Friday, Saturday, or Sunday	

Source: Ralph J. Weiger, "Franchise Investigation Time Span," *Franchising World,* March/April 1989, p. 18. Copyright International Franchise Association, Washington, DC.

(*c*) using checklists, questioning people, and doing marketing research. You should then study the market to estimate (*a*) its size, (*b*) the competition and its share of the market, and (*c*) your own share of the market.

4. Next, you should decide whether to (*a*) start a new business, (*b*) buy an existing one, or (*c*) buy a franchise. There are compelling arguments for and against each of these alternatives. Starting a new business means it is your own, but the process is time-consuming and quite risky.

When you buy an existing business, you acquire established markets, facilities, and employees. But you must be sure when you buy that all aspects of the business are in good shape and that you are not inheriting someone else's problems.

Buying a franchise may help bring success in a hurry, since it provides successful management and operating procedures to guide the business. But you must be able to succeed on your own, for a franchise does not ensure success. Also, the cost may be high, or the franchiser may not perform satisfactorily.

5. Franchising is a marketing system that permits the franchisee to conduct business as an individual owner under the terms and conditions set by the franchiser. The two most common franchising systems are (*a*) product and trademark franchising and (*b*) business format franchising. In the first, franchisees acquire the right to sell the franchiser's product and use its trademark, but they are relatively free to use their own operating methods. In the second, the franchiser determines virtually every aspect of the franchisee's operations, including management policies, accounting methods, reporting forms, designs, and furnishings. The number of product and trademark franchises has declined, particularly in auto dealerships and gasoline service stations. Business format franchising has increased steadily because it provides a ready market and management system, and the failure rate is lower than for inde-

pendent businesses. Franchising sales have more than doubled in the last decade, and the number of establishments is also increasing. Franchising is strongest in retailing, accounting for about 41 percent of retail sales.

6. Franchising is a good way for someone to enter business. But you should carefully research the industry and investigate the particular franchise to determine whether the assistance provided by the franchiser is worth the sacrifice of independence. You should study the franchise offering circular, check with existing franchisees, and obtain professional advice to understand your rights and obligations. Franchisers who belong to the International Franchise Association (IFA) subscribe to a code of ethics that provides protection to their franchisees.

7. The future of franchising looks good, especially for restaurants; motels; convenience stores; electronics; automotive parts, accessories, and servicing; packaging and shipping; health care and fitness; combination franchising; and catering to home-based small businesses. International franchising is one of the fastest-growing areas of franchising. Minority ownership of franchises is also growing, and special efforts are being made to encourage minority franchising.

QUESTIONS FOR DISCUSSION

1. What are some important factors to consider in choosing the type of business to enter?
2. How can you identify a business you would like to own? What characteristics do you have that would help make that business successful?
3. How do you determine the market for a product? Your share of that market?
4. What are some characteristics you should consider in studying the potential market for a proposed business?
5. *a.* What are some reasons for and against starting a new business?
   b. What are some reasons for and against buying an existing business?

c. What are some reasons for and against buying a franchise?
6. What distinguishes a franchise from an independent small business?
7. What are the two most important forms of franchising? Describe each.
8. Describe why franchising is growing in importance.
9. What are some expected areas of growth for franchising in the future?
10. Why is franchising growing internationally?
11. What is happening to opportunities in franchising for minorities?

CASE 4-1

TIM LEWIS FILLS A NICHE

■

Tim Lewis owns T. A. Lewis and Associates in Birmingham, Alabama, a consulting firm that designs telephone, data, and video systems. In this information age, Lewis's success might seem inevitable, but it is based on experience, hard work, and finding a market niche.

The Lewis story begins in his hometown of Tuscaloosa, about 35 miles southwest of Birmingham, where Lewis gained both business and technical skills. While in high school he worked as a salesman at a local shoe store and served as business manager for the James Brown Singers, a local community choir.

After earning an electrical engineering degree from the University of Alabama, Lewis became an account manager and sales trainer for TMC, a new and growing long-distance phone company. When he went to companies such as Rust Engineering in Birmingham to sell long-distance service, executives would ask him many questions and seek his advice. The buyers wanted his opinion on fax machines, voice-mail systems, and copy machines. They wanted some knowledgeable person to give them fair and unbiased answers. Lewis offered suggestions, and most of the time his advice turned out to be right, so they kept asking him.

It occurred to Lewis that a market niche might exist that no one was filling. When he studied the market, he learned that it was very difficult for small to medium-sized firms to get objective information on products. Most "consultants" were representatives of particular manufac-

turers; if clients weren't interested in buying the products they were selling, they weren't interested in giving advice.

After about 18 months of research, Lewis prepared a comprehensive business plan. Then, with the help of the Birmingham Business Assistance Network (an incubator organization for small businesses), he took the plunge and ventured out on his own. The contacts he had made while working with TMC provided a springboard. When he left TMC, he had accounts at seven Birmingham-area hospitals, and the business he got from them spread. That's why a third of his customers are in the health care industry.

He now has 18 full-time employees and is planning to expand by adding a training facility.

Lewis continues to live in Tuscaloosa and drives 90 minutes to and from his facility in Birmingham. Of this commuting time, he says, "I've got a cellular phone and a beeper, so I can work on the way up and work on the way back."

Questions

1. What do you think of Lewis's method of finding an unfilled niche?

2. What growth possibilities are there for him in this expanding technological age?

3. What suggestions would you make to him as to where to live? Explain.

Source: Gilbert Nicholson, "Filling a Niche," *The Tuscaloosa* (Alabama) *News,* October 22, 1995, p. 1E.

CASE 4-2

LA-VAN HAWKINS: URBAN ENTREPRENEUR

When you think of hamburgers, the words that come to mind are more likely to be "pickles, ketchup, and mustard" than "economic empowerment." It may sound odd at first—burgers helping to build neighborhoods—but that's what one man is determined to accomplish.

La-Van Hawkins, president and chief executive officer of Inner City Foods Incorporated, is one of America's most successful, but extraordinary, entrepreneurs. His story demonstrates both the potential and the importance of entrepreneurship to the continued success of American business, especially minority entrepreneurship.

Hawkins grew up in one of Chicago's poorest and most dangerous areas, the Cabrini Green housing project. His first job was sweeping floors at a local McDonald's. He concluded early in his career that many businesses would not locate in mostly African-American urban neighborhoods. Unlike others, however, he saw that harsh reality as an opportunity, not only for his own benefit but also as a way to provide employment and income for people in inner-city communities.

In contrast to most businesses that avoid poor, largely black urban neighborhoods, Hawkins and his Inner City Foods Incorporated seek out such neighborhoods. He now owns over 30 Checkers restaurant franchises in the inner-city areas of Atlanta, Baltimore, and Philadelphia. All provide jobs and income to communities that are usually considered too great a risk by national chains and fast-food outlets.

Hawkins was recently given a seat on the board of directors of the Checkers Corporation. His growing fast-food empire is providing a fast track into the business world for hundreds of African-American men and women.

Questions

1. How do you explain Hawkins's success?
2. Do you think his program of opening franchises in inner-city areas would work for others? Explain.
3. What future do you see for La-Van Hawkins?

Source: Adapted from William G. Nickels, James M. McHugh, and Susan M. McHugh, *Understanding Business,* 4th ed. (New York: Richard D. Irwin, 1996), p. 27.

5

THE ROLE OF PLANNING IN ORGANIZING AND MANAGING A SMALL BUSINESS

Businesses don't plan to fail, they just fail to plan.

Old business adage

After you have made up your mind just what you are going to do, it is a good time to do it.

Josh Billings

A completed business plan is a guide that illustrates where you are going, and how to get there.

Charles J. Bodenstab

LEARNING OBJECTIVES

After studying the material in this chapter, you will be able to:

1. Tell why planning is so important—yet so neglected—in small businesses.

2. Explain the role of strategic and operational planning, and give some examples.

3. Explain the role of financial planning, and give some examples of it.

4. Tell why a business plan is needed and what purpose it should serve.

5. Prepare a sample business plan.

Sam and Teresa Davis Do Their Homework before Launch

When Sam and Teresa Davis decided it was time for a career change, they opted to start their own business rather than work for someone else. After considering the options, Sam, who had 18 years of marketing and managing experience with a large regional department store, and Teresa, who was a veteran teacher, chose to open a school supply store in Northport, near the university. Knowing that many small businesses fail because of poor planning, the Davises chose to start their venture the right way—by doing extensive strategic and operational planning.

One of the first steps the Davises took early in their endeavor was to seek the services of the university's Small Business Development Center (www.business.uab.edu/school/sbdc/index.html). Sam cites the Center's *Small Business Handbook* as an invaluable asset that answered questions concerning such important details as taxes, business licenses, zoning problems, and advertising.

Before getting in over their heads, the Davises knew they had to do extensive research and write a comprehensive business plan. This step would not only assist their fund-raising efforts but also serve as a blueprint for the process of making their dream a reality. The key word, according to Sam, was research. "The biggest problem was gathering the facts to write a detailed business plan."

The Davises did their homework well. First, they made numerous trips to school supply stores in surrounding cities. They also took their idea directly to their potential clients—teachers and school administrators. Finally, after carefully assembling the needed information, they wrote a detailed business plan.

One thing the Davises learned from their research was that there was little or no diversity among school supply stores. To avoid being just another run-of-the-mill school supply store—and risk market saturation—they needed to find a unique twist, something to set their store apart from the others. They found their niche by adding a work area that includes a letter and shape cutter, a laminator, and a copier to produce transparencies.

This unique idea proved to be the solution to one of the most difficult problems new businesses face—getting customers in the door. "Sometimes we have as many as six university students at a time working on some school project here," Teresa says. Others using the center include junior and senior high school students working on science and social studies projects, as well as church workers. Through their research, the Davises also discovered that the growing home schooling trend had been virtually ignored by other supply stores; this opened a new market for their products. The Davises cite this as another key factor in their success.

As a result of their painstaking research and creative ideas, the Davises' store, Learning Experiences, has been tremendously successful. Now, as they advise potential entrepreneurs, the Davises emphasize two points about formulating a good business plan and running an effective business: (1) entreprenuers *must* have firsthand knowledge of the product or service they plan to offer, and (2) they must create a distinctive niche by making the business unique in some fashion.

Source: Gilbert Nicholson, "By the Book . . . Entrepreneurs Do Homework Before Launch," *The Tuscaloosa* (Alabama) *News,* May 7, 1995, p. E1.

The Profile illustrates some of the problems and steps involved in planning, organizing, and developing a new business. The first three of those steps were discussed in Chapter 4, and others will be explained in detail in this chapter.

■ WHY IS PLANNING SO IMPORTANT TO SMALL BUSINESSES?

To become an effective business owner-manager, *you must look ahead.* In selecting the business to enter, as discussed in Chapter 4, you are doing just that—planning for the future. As shown in Figure 5–1, planning should be the first step in performing a series of managerial

Figure 5–1
How Planning Relates to Other Managerial Functions

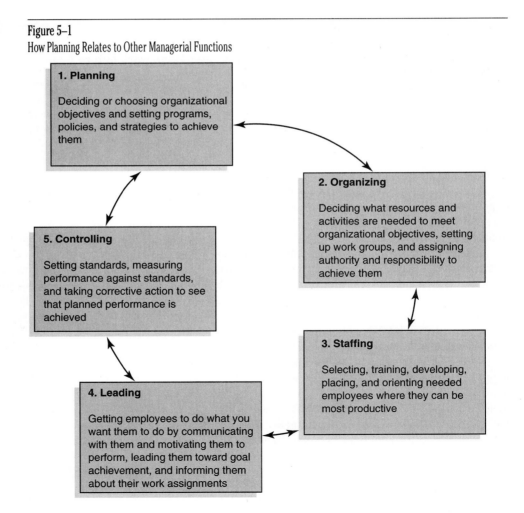

functions because it sets the future course of action for all aspects of the business. **Planning,** which is the process of setting objectives and devising actions to achieve those objectives, answers such questions as these: What business am I in? What finances do I need? What is my sales strategy? Where can I find needed personnel? How much profit can I expect?

Planning is the process of setting objectives and determining actions to reach them.

Why Small Business Owners *Need* to Plan

Planning is one of the most difficult activities you must do. Yet it is essential that you do it because, before taking action, you must know where you are going and how to get there. Outsiders who invest or lend money need to know your chances of success. Plans provide courses of action, information to others, bases for change, and a means of delegating work. In summary, well-developed plans can (1) interest moneyed people in investing in your business, (2) guide the owner and managers in operating the business, (3) give direction to and motivate employees, and (4) provide an environment to attract customers and prospective employees.

Why Small Business Owners *Neglect* Planning

Although planning is so important, it is one of the most difficult managerial activities to perform. Many small business owners neglect planning, because (1) day-to-day activities leave them little or no time for planning, (2) they fear the problems and weaknesses planning may reveal, (3) they lack knowledge of how to plan, and (4) they feel that future changes cannot be planned for.

Planning requires original thinking, takes time, and is difficult to do, but it does help one prepare to take advantage of promising opportunities and cope with unexpected problems. Table 5–1 illustrates and explains strategic planning.

Table 5–1
Some of the Most Important Types of Plans and Planning Functions

Types of Plans and Planning Functions	Examples
Strategic planning:	
Mission: The long-term direction of the business.	To provide financial security at low cost.
Objectives: Shorter-term ends to help achieve the mission.	
For total firm.	Earn a 20% return on investment in 2000.
For functional area.	Increase penetration of market by 25% by 2001.
Strategies: Means to achieve an end, or courses of action needed to achieve objectives.	
For total firm.	Establish control procedures to control costs by 2000.
For functional area.	Use 1 percent of sales to improve and expand service.
Operational planning:	
Policies: Guides to action that provide consistency in decision making, particularly in repetitive situations.	*Personnel policy:* Promote from within, giving preference to promotions for present employees.
Methods and procedures: Prescribed manner of accomplishing desired output.	*Employee selection procedure:* Complete application form, test, interview, investigate, select.
Budgets and standards: Plans for future activities using measures for control.	*Cash budget:* For planning use of money.

■ THE ROLE OF STRATEGIC PLANNING

Strategic planning provides comprehensive long-term direction to help a business accomplish its mission. Table 5–1 shows that strategic planning consists of two parts: the firm's mission and objectives, and its strategies. The following are some examples of strategic planning:

- Selecting the type of business to enter.
- Formulating the mission of the company.
- Deciding whether to start a new business, buy an existing one, or buy a franchise.
- Choosing the product or service to sell.
- Deciding on the market niche to exploit.
- Choosing the type of organization to use.
- Determining financial needs.
- Selecting the location for the business.

> For example, a recent study by three CPAs indicated the significance of location to small businesses. They studied which small firms in their areas were succeeding and which were failing.
>
> Jacqueline L. Babicky's consulting group found that the types of business doing well in the Portland, Oregon, area were those that had taken steps to differentiate themselves and/or their products from others in the mainstream. Larry Field's firm found a growing number of small high-tech businesses were moving into the Phoenix, Arizona, region to provide secondary parts to larger manufacturers.
>
> On the other hand, C. Norman Pricher and his staff found that one type of business in Orlando, Florida, was not doing well. They learned that indoor foliage, the region's biggest industry concentration, was doing poorly.[1]

Mission and Objectives

The **mission** is the long-range vision of what the business is trying to become. It is concerned with broad concepts such as the firm's image, with the basic services the firm plans to perform (e.g., "entertainment" instead of just "movies"), and with long-term financial success. Once set, missions are rarely revised.

A clear definition of your mission enables you to design *results-oriented objectives and strategies.* A good mission statement defines exactly the identity of your business and allows all of your planning to flow from it. Figure 5–2 illustrates the "umbrella" structure of strategic planning. The umbrella shows graphically how important it is to have a mission statement and major objectives that will interrelate and provide guidance for a cohesive and meaningful organizational structure.

Frequently when small business owners are closely tied to their business, the mission becomes very personal.

> For example, Leslie Godwin, owner of Parent Support Services in Calabasas, California, which develops work-family programs, sees mission statements as combining values, priorities, and service in a single sentence. Hers includes: "To live a life of personal integrity, and use my writing abilities to offer businesspeople examples of how they can make a difference."[2]

Objectives are the goals that give shorter-term direction to the business and serve as benchmarks for measuring performance. Examples of objectives might include: "To increase total sales by 8 percent a year" and "To introduce within the next two years a new product aimed at the middle-class consumer." Notice in Figure 5–2 how the objec-

Strategic planning provides comprehensive long-term direction to help a business accomplish its mission.

A business's **mission** is its long-term vision of what it is trying to become.

Objectives are the purposes, goals, and desired results for the business and its parts.

Figure 5–2
Strategic Umbrella

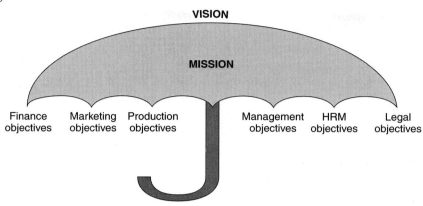

tives flow from the mission statement. Objectives are more specific than missions and are revised more frequently. Table 5–2 illustrates how objectives can be set. Creating the mission and defining objectives for a small business involve two important considerations: the business's external environment and the internal resources that give it a competitive edge.

The External Environment   Many consultants and other advisers are pushing small companies to give more emphasis to their external environment. In a study of 100 companies, the Futures Group of Glastonbury, Connecticut (www.tfg.com), found that "managers who spend more time evaluating external factors such as their competitors, the U.S. market climate, and emerging technology can better manage and forecast business than those who focus on internal factors."[3] This practice was found to improve their strategic plans.

Some other external environmental factors to consider include clients, the economy, legal and political factors, changing demographics, foreign competition, and many other influences. Changes caused by the introduction of videotapes, computer hardware and software, lasers, and population aging, for example, have been a blessing to some companies and a death warrant to others. The expanding communication and transportation systems require that even the smallest companies keep abreast of a constantly widening range of events.

Internal Resources and Competitive Edge   The internal resources found in small businesses include those listed below. Also, to be competitive, the resources must include the characteristics listed.

1. **Human resources** include both management and nonmanagement people and include key operating employees such as production supervisors, sales personnel, financial analysts, and engineers. To keep the company competitive, these people must be motivated, imaginative, qualified, and dedicated.
2. **Physical resources** include buildings, tools and equipment, and service and distribution facilities. For the company to be competitive, these resources must be strategically located, be productive, be low in operating costs, be effective distributors, and make the proper product.

Human resources are the personnel that make up the business's work force.

Physical resources are the buildings, tools and equipment, and service and distribution facilities that are needed to carry on the business.

Table 5–2
Example of How Objectives Can Be Set

Firm's Objectives	2000	2001	2002	2003
Total net profit (income) after taxes	$_____	$_____	$_____	$_____
Return on investment (ROI) (net income after taxes/total assets)	_____	_____	_____	_____
Return on equity (ROE) (net income after taxes/equity)	_____	_____	_____	_____
Total sales volume (units)	_____	_____	_____	_____
Total sales volume ($)	_____	_____	_____	_____
Return on sales (ROS) (net income after taxes/sales)	_____	_____	_____	_____

To attain a _____ percent share of market by the end of 2001.

To have a _____ percent debt-to-equity ratio in the capital structure initially, declining to _____ percent debt-equity at the end of 2002.

To develop a new product by the end of the year 2003.

Financial resources include the cash flow, debt capacity, and equity available to finance operations.

3. **Financial resources** include cash flow, debt capacity, and equity available to run the business. To make the company competitive, company finances must be adequate to maintain current levels of activities and to take advantage of future opportunities. Many accountants suggest that aspiring entrepreneurs get their financial house in order before starting. This includes setting aside funds for taxes and Social Security and as a cushion against financial reversals.[4]

A **competitive edge** is a particular characteristic that makes a firm more attractive to customers than are its competitors.

If a small firm has exceptionally good resources and they are effectively used, it can have a **competitive edge** over its competitors. Therefore, a proper evaluation of available resources may permit you to focus on your customers and provide them with a little something extra, which gives you a competitive edge.

A classic example of this type of competitiveness is provided by a Portland, Oregon, restaurant called Old Wives' Tales (www.busdir.com/oldwives). It has incorporated a 130-square-foot play area for children into the dining room, thus redefining the eating-out experience for parents. This consumer focus did require sacrifices, as the playroom takes up the space of 20 revenue-generating seats. Also, there is less turnover; customers stay longer because their children are happy. But the practice has produced a loyal base of customers who drive there from all over Portland.[5]

As you can see from this example, a small business must align its mission, objectives, and resources with its environment if it is to be effective. The proper evaluation of its competitive edge can make a small firm's planning more realistic and lead to greater profitability.

Strategies

Strategies are the means by which a business achieves its objectives and fulfills its mission.

Strategies are the means by which the mission and objectives sought by a small business can be achieved. A basic question in setting strategies is: How should the business be managed to achieve its objectives and fulfill its mission? To be most effective, strategies should give a business a competitive advantage in the marketplace. They should combine the activities such as marketing, production or operations, research and development, finance, and personnel in order to use the firm's resources most effectively.

Figure 5-3
Mission/Strategy of John Smith, General Agent, Tulsa, Oklahoma

Mission: To provide the maximum amount of personal financial security at the lowest possible cost while maintaining the highest quality of individualized service.

Objective: To serve the financial needs of businesses, individuals, and their families in the Tulsa area through guaranteed income to meet loss from death or disability, through these services and policy coverages.

- Estate tax planning
- Qualified pension and profit sharing
- Group life and health
- Ordinary life
- Business interruption

Figure 5–3 shows how a strategy can be set up to fulfill the mission of a small business. Notice that John Smith will provide certain services and policy coverage to clients so they will have maximum personal financial security at the lowest possible cost.

As we discussed in Chapter 1, an effort is now being made to encourage owners of small businesses to rethink and redesign the way their organization operates. Thus, while top management must still be involved, lower levels of managers and workers seem to be more involved in integrating their company's vision, mission, objectives, and strategies into their strategic planning.[6]

■ THE ROLE OF OPERATIONAL PLANNING

Why do so many small businesses fail? As shown in Chapter 4, the underlying reason in most cases is lack of proper strategic and operational planning. These types of planning are vital because they help potential and new entrepreneurs avoid costly blunders, save time, and result in a more polished final product. Three types of planning will improve a small business owner's chances of success: (1) strategic planning before starting the business; (2) a business plan to attract investors, financiers, and prospective employees; and (3) continuous operational planning and control before and after the business starts operating.

Setting Up Policies, Methods, Procedures, and Budgets

As you can see from Table 5–1, **operational planning** starts with setting policies, methods and procedures, and budgets, which together form the basis for the other part of operational methods and planning.

Policies guide action. They exist so that managers can delegate work and employees will make decisions based on the thinking and wishes of the business owner. **Methods** and **procedures** provide employees with standing instructions for performing their jobs. They comprise detailed explanations of how to do the work properly, and in what order it should be done. **Budgets** set the requirements needed to follow the strategies and accomplish the objectives. For example, a cash budget shows the amount and times of cash income and outgo. It helps the manager determine when and how much to borrow.

Operational planning sets policies, procedures, and standards for achieving objectives.

Policies are general statements that serve as guides to managerial decision making and supervisory activities.

Methods and **procedures** provide standing instructions to employees on how to perform their jobs.

Budgets are detailed plans, expressed in monetary terms, of the results expected from officially recognized programs.

Planning to Operate the Business

The second part of operational planning—planning to operate the business—includes:[7]

- Choosing your location.
- Planning operations and physical facilities.
- Developing sources of supply for goods and materials.
- Planning your human resource requirements.
- Setting up the legal and organizational structure.
- Determining your approach to the market.
- Establishing an efficient records system.
- Setting up a time schedule.

Choosing a Location   The type of business influences most of your location decisions, as they relate to access to customers, suppliers, employees, utilities, and transportation, as well as compliance with zoning regulations and other laws. The mission of the business is also a basic consideration in seeking the right location. As will be shown in Chapter 11, each type of firm has its own factors to consider and gives priority to those that most affect the business.

Planning Operations and Physical Facilities   A firm's ability to sell its product is based on its ability to produce that good or service, as well as on its market potential. Good selection and efficient arrangement of physical facilities, then, are important. Too much capacity increases costs, which can reduce the company's competitive position; too little capacity reduces the availability of goods and causes loss of sales. Therefore, a proper balance between production and sales volume is needed. Planning starts with the estimate of sales and the operations needed to produce the product(s). Using these estimates, the machines and personnel needed for the demand can be determined.

Another important decision is whether to buy facilities or lease them. Any such choice between purchase and lease is based on differences in initial investment cost, operating performance and expense, and tax considerations. A photocopier is an example of an item that should probably be leased rather than purchased. Because of rapid improvements—and the need for prompt and proper maintenance—leased copiers will probably give more dependable service than purchased ones. Chapter 11 provides more details on locating and laying out facilities.

Developing Sources of Supply for Goods and Materials   The largest expense for companies selling products usually is purchasing materials, supplies, and/or goods; this cost is often more than 50 percent of the cost of products sold. Therefore, the ability to purchase these essentials at favorable prices can lead to profitability—or vice versa. Lowest-cost materials do not necessarily mean inferior quality, and small firms should take every opportunity to reduce costs. But small businesses usually find it difficult to compete with large ones on the basis of price alone. Instead, they can more successfully compete on the basis of better quality, service, delivery, and so forth. And as will be shown in Chapter 12, the business must be sure to have sources of supply that meet its standards in all ways, including competitive prices.

Human resource planning is the process of converting the business's plans and programs into an effective work force.

Planning Human Resource Requirements   **Human resource planning** can be one of the most frustrating tasks facing small businesses, when such businesses are not big enough to easily hire the specialized people needed. You, as a small businessperson therefore, need to estimate how much time you will spend in the business, for the less time you can devote to the business, the more important it will be to have capable employees who must be able to work with less supervision than in larger firms. The issue arises of obtaining good employees. Some important questions to ask yourself are: How many workers are needed? Where will they be obtained? How much must I pay them? These and similar questions are discussed in Chapters 9 and 10.

Figure 5–4
An Oversimplified Organizational Structure

"As you see, we are a highly centralized organization."

Setting Up the Legal and Organizational Structure   Your organization structure must be developed taking into consideration the legal and administrative aspects of the business. Both legal and administrative structures offer several options, so you must select the structure that best serves your needs. Many small business owners, especially if they have started as sole proprietors, may have difficulty envisioning a management structure beyond the boss/employee relationship, as shown in Figure 5–4. Retaining too much authority is one of the best ways to kill your small business, so be aware of setting up too rigid an organizational structure.

The legal form of a business, as discussed in Chapter 3, may be a proprietorship, partnership, corporation (C corporation or S Corporation), limited-liability company (LLC), cooperative, or joint venture. The administrative structure of a small business should be based on factors such as (1) the strategic plan, including the business mission and objectives; (2) the owner's personal and business objectives; (3) the plans, programs, policies, and practices that will achieve those objectives; and (4) the authority and responsibility relationships that will accomplish the mission or purpose of the firm. These aspects of organization are discussed in greater detail in Chapter 10.

Determining Approach to Market   The volume of sales and income of a small firm depends on its marketing strategies and activities. If a study of the environment determines that there is a sufficiently large market for the firm's product(s), plans must be made to capture enough of that market to be successful. Even if your company's service is the best, you must tell potential customers about it. Many methods of marketing are in use; the ones used must be chosen for the particular business.

For example, a number of years ago, a man living in New England conceived of a rubber, instead of metal, dustpan. He had a dozen samples of the new product custom-made in a variety of colors and headed to Boston to hawk his wares in Filene's and Jordan Marsh. Neither seemed interested in the dustpan.

> Still, because he was sure that homemakers would buy his product, he decided to test-market the dustpan by calling on them. Pulling into a residential street, he parked his car and set out to ring doorbells. Just 45 minutes later, he returned to his car with only two pans left. Convinced that his idea was good, Earl Tupper developed a company—Tupperware (www.tupperware.com)—to market the product directly to consumers.

Once a target market is chosen, you must provide for sales promotion and distribution to it. The product to be offered should again be studied carefully to determine answers to the following questions: What qualities make it special to the customer? Are there unique or distinct features to emphasize, such as ease of installation or low maintenance? Should the company use newspaper advertising or mailings to publicize the product? These and other marketing questions are discussed in more detail in Chapters 7 and 8.

Establishing an Efficient Records System　Even in a small business, simple records and information systems must be used. But they must be designed to help you control your business by keeping track of activities and obligations and also to collect certain types of information demanded by outside organizations such as government agencies. For example, you must maintain records of such data as (1) the date each employee is hired, the number of hours each one works, and the wages and benefits paid; (2) inventories, accounts receivable, and accounts payable; (3) taxes paid and owed (see Chapter 14); and (4) units of each product sold.

Many records are needed to help make the small business operate successfully. Management information systems, covered in Chapter 15, should be selected and designed to aid management in this respect.[8]

Setting Up a Time Schedule　Once you decide to go ahead with the formation of the business, you should establish a time schedule to provide an orderly and coordinated program. The schedule should probably include the prior planning steps. Many of these steps can be and often are performed simultaneously. A SCORE representative can provide valuable assistance.

■ THE ROLE OF FINANCIAL PLANNING

Financial planning involves determining what funds are needed, where they can be obtained, and how they can be controlled.

Financial planning can be quite simple or very complex, as shown in Chapters 6, 13, and 14, but it should involve at least the following:

1. Estimating income and expenses.
2. Estimating initial investment required.
3. Locating sources of funds.

Estimating Income and Expenses

Net profit is the amount of revenue (sales) over and above the total amount of expenses (costs) of doing business.

The steps described so far set the stage for determining the profit (or loss) from operating your new business. Income from sales (also called *revenue*) can be estimated by studying the market, and expenses (also called *costs*) can be calculated from past experience and other sources, such as knowledgeable people, a library, or a trade association. After all costs have been estimated, they can be totaled and subtracted from the estimated sales income to obtain the expected **net profit** (or loss), as shown in the worksheet for Dover Enterprises* in Figure 5–5. When making your estimates, remember two key points. First, these expense

---

*An actual company, but the name is disguised at the owner's request.

Figure 5–5

DOVER ENTERPRISES
Worksheet for Estimated Annual Income,
Expenses, and Profit (Loss)*

	Units sold		
	10,000	20,000	30,000
Income			
Sales income ($5/unit)	$50,000	$100,000	$150,000
Cost of goods sold:			
Production cost ($1.62/unit)	$16,200	$32,400	$48,600
Shipping boxes and labels ($0.04/unit)	400	800	1,200
Depreciation (mold)	2,500	2,500	2,500
Total production expenses	19,100	35,700	52,300
Gross profit	30,900	64,300	97,700
Other operating expenses			
Salaries	30,000	30,000	30,000
Telephone	3,000	3,500	4,000
Rent	2,100	2,100	2,100
Insurance	400	400	400
Office expense	1,000	1,100	1,200
Sales promotion	7,000	8,000	9,000
Freight	1,000	2,000	3,000
Travel	4,000	4,000	4,000
Taxes and licenses	4,000	4,000	4,000
Miscellaneous	1,000	2,000	3,000
Total operating expenses	53,500	57,100	60,700
Net profit (loss)	($22,600)	$ 7,200	$ 37,000

*Projections for three levels of sales.

and income (or loss) estimates are usually for only the first year of operations. However, if you also make an income analysis for an expected typical year in the future as well as for the first year, the exercise can provide valuable information for planning purposes.

Second, while total expenses do move up and down with sales volume, they do not vary as much. Some expenses, such as materials, which rise in direct proportion to increases in sales volume and drop as sales volume drops, are called **variable expenses.** Other expenses, such as depreciation on buildings, which do not vary in value as sales volume rises or falls, are called **fixed expenses.** Also, there are some expenses, such as supervision, that combine variable and fixed costs.

Changes in sales volume drastically affect the amount of net profit: As sales volume rises (say from 10,000 to 20,000 units), losses are reduced and profits may rise; as sales volume drops (say from 20,000 to 10,000), profits drop and losses may occur.

Don't forget to also prepare a personal budget! As Robert Caldwell, a New York financial planner, emphasizes, "Living below your means is never a mistake, and that is even more true with a start-up business."[9] Therefore, you—and your family—must have enough income to live on during the time you are moving from being an employee to being an employer. If

Variable expenses change in relation to volume of output: when output is low, the expenses are low, and when output is high, expenses rise.

Fixed expenses do not vary with output, but remain the same.

your standard of living drops too drastically, it will probably be devastating to your family. So, in addition to determining the expected income and expenses of the business, also estimate your continuing needs, and where you will get the resources to satisfy them.

Estimating Initial Investment

You will need money and/or credit to start your business. You must pay for items such as buildings, equipment, materials, personnel, inventory, machines, business forms, and sales promotion at the outset before income from sales starts providing the means to pay these expenses from internal sources. Credit may be extended to help sell the products, but this only adds to operating expenses.

The worksheet in Figure 5–6 provides a logical method of calculating the initial cash needs of a new business such as Dover Enterprises. The figures in column 1 are estimates that have already been made for the income statement for the first year. The amount of cash needed is some multiple of each of the values in column 1, as shown in column 3. The total of these multiple values is an estimate of the money needed to start the business and is shown in column 2. This sum can be considerable. For example, Coopers & Lybrand (www.colybrand.com) discovered that founders of 328 fast-growing businesses risked an average of $82,300 to start their companies.[10]

Note that the cash needed to start the business—shown in column 2—represents the delay between paying money out for expenses and receiving it back as revenue. The item called *starting inventory* is an illustration of buying goods in one period and selling them in another. But inventories of goods and supplies—in the form of purchases and recurring inventories—continue to exist for the life of the business. Therefore, funds obtained from investments in the business or from loans must continue for its life unless they are paid off.

Cash flow is the amount of cash available at a given time to pay expenses.

Because cash does not produce revenue, it should not sit idle but should be used to earn income. The amount of cash a business needs, and has, will vary during the year, since most businesses have busy and slack periods. To keep the investment and borrowing low, **cash flow** projections must be made. The worksheet in Chapter 14 (Figure 14–1) is a form that can be used to make such projections, which can then be compared with what actually happens. You might contact your nearest SBA office to get information to help you estimate your start-up costs. Also, various financial firms and certified public accountants have computed some helpful standard figures.

Locating Sources of Funds

Once the amount of funds needed is known, you must find sources for those funds. The many sources from which to obtain funds to start and operate a business boil down to two: the owner and others. These two sources will be discussed in detail in Chapter 6, so only the highlights are discussed here. Before approaching a funding source, decide how much money you and others will put into the business and how much should come from other sources.

For example, William Williams decided in 1989 to open a soul food market and found three food marketing experts to help. Together they came up with $20,000 and started Glory Foods. Later they were able to obtain a $300,000 line of credit, and in 1993 they sold 17 percent of their company to 40 new investors for $1 million. Their strategic planning used for fund raising has paid off, as they expected a profit of $800,000 on revenues of $12 million in 1998.[11]

Using Your Own Funds   Some small business owners prefer to invest only their personal funds and not borrow to start or operate a business. Others believe they should use little of

Figure 5–6

DOVER ENTERPRISES
Estimated Monthly Expenses and Starting Costs
January 1, 20__

Estimated monthly expenses

Item	(1) Estimate of monthly expenses based on sales of $100,000 per year	(2) Estimate of how much cash you need to start your business (see column 3)	(3) What to put in (2) (Multipliers are typical for one kind of business. You must decide how many months to allow for in your business.)
Salary of owner-manager	$2,500	$5,000	2 times column 1
All other salaries and wages	—	—	3 times column 1
Rent	175	525	3 times column 1
Travel		1,000	As required
Advertising	700	2,100	3 times column 1
Delivery expense	100	300	3 times column 1
Supplies	100	300	3 times column 1
Recurring inventory and purchases	—	—	Check with suppliers for estimate
Telephone and telegraph	300	900	3 times column 1
Other utilities	—	—	3 times column 1
Insurance		400	Payment required by insurance company
Taxes, including Social Security	325	1,300	4 times column 1
Interest	—	—	3 times column 1
Maintenance	—	—	3 times column 1
Legal and other professional fees	—	—	3 times column 1
Miscellaneous	200	600	3 times column 1

Starting costs you have to pay only once

Item	(1)	(3)
Fixtures and equipment:		
Telephone, $203; mold, $11,280; computer, $750	$12,233	Enter total from separate list
Decorating and remodeling	—	Talk it over with a contractor
Installation of fixtures and equipment	—	Talk to suppliers from whom you wish to buy these
Starting inventory	5,000	Suppliers will probably help you estimate this
Deposits with public utilities	—	Find out from utilities companies
Legal and other professional fees	—	Lawyer, accountant, and so on
Licenses and permits	(Part of taxes above)	Find out from city offices what you have to have
Advertising and promotion for opening	(Part of advertising above)	Estimate what you'll use
Accounts receivable	1,200	What you need to buy more stock until credit customers pay
Cash	1,000	For unexpected expenses or losses, special purchases, etc.
Other		Make a separate list and enter total
Total estimated cash you need to start with	$31,858	Add up all the numbers in column 2

Source: This basic worksheet is based on *Checklist for Going into Business*, Management Aids No. 2.016 (Washington, DC: Small Business Administration), p. 4.

their own money and instead make as much profit as possible by using their interest in the business as security when obtaining funds from others. Normally, owners control a company; they take the risks of failure but also make the decisions. To maintain control, you must continue to invest more personal funds than all the other investors combined. Moreover, you can maintain control only so long as lenders do not become worried about the safety of their money.

Using Funds from Others   There are several sources of outside funds. These can be generally divided into **equity investors,** who actually become part owners of the business, and **lenders,** who provide money for a limited time at a fixed rate of interest. Both run the risk of losing their money if the business fails, but this gamble is offset for investors by the possibility of large returns if the business is successful. Since the rate of return for lenders is fixed, some security is usually given to offset their risk.

You may be able to find investors interested in a venture opportunity. Such people might be found among relatives, friends, attorneys, bankers, or securities dealers. Building multiple bank relationships early on in your business is important. But you must have a well-prepared business plan and an advocate in the bank on your side; if they tell you "no," make them tell you why.[12]

Equity investors are those who actually become part owners of the business.

Lenders are those outsiders who provide business owners money for a limited time at a fixed rate of interest.

■ THE ROLE OF THE BUSINESS PLAN IN STRATEGIC AND OPERATIONAL PLANNING

As the Davises discovered in the opening Profile, a new business results from the prospective owner's having both a good idea for producing and selling a product and the ability to carry out the idea. Yet other things—such as buildings and machines, human resources, materials and supplies, and finances—are also needed. These needs are developed from the strategic, operational, and financial planning. And all that planning needs to be formalized into a **business plan,** which is a formal plan to serve as a tool for attracting the other components of the business formation package—the people and the money. A well-developed and well-presented business plan can provide small business owners with a much greater chance of success—and reduce their chances of failing.

A **business plan** is a formal plan prepared to serve as a tool for attracting the other components of the business formation package, including people and money.

Purposes of the Plan

The business plan could be the most useful and important document you, as an entrepreneur, ever put together. When you are up to your ears in the details of starting the business, the plan keeps your thinking on target, keeps your creativity on track, and concentrates your power on reaching your goal.

The plan can be a useful money-raising tool to attract venture capital for those entrepreneurs who are willing to dilute control of their company. Although few owners use a plan to attract venture funds, many more use a formal business plan to obtain loans from lending agencies.

But an effective plan does more than just help convince prospective investors that the new business is sound. It provides a detailed blueprint for the activities needed to finance the business, develop the product, market it, and otherwise manage the new business. Business plans are also used for planning the continuing operations of a firm, as the following example illustrates.

Ava DeMarco, a 32-year-old graphics designer, and Robert Brandegee, a 28-year-old who favors torn blue jeans and bandannas as work attire, founded their Pittsburgh-based Little Earth Productions (www.littlearth.com) to help with recycling. Their research convinced them, though, that their business should cater to two powerful market trends—environmental protection and style. Therefore, the accessories they produce and sell—which include notebooks, backpacks, and belts—are not only environmentally friendly but also "hip." Made entirely from recycled materials such as license plates, auto seat belts, soda cans, and bottle caps, these products are commendably "green," but they are also very stylish and attractive.[13]

What the Plan Should Include

Because an effective business plan helps determine the feasibility of an idea, it should include a detailed analysis of factors such as the following:

- The proposed product.
- The expected market for it.
- The strengths and weaknesses of the industry.
- Planned marketing policies, such as price, promotion, and distribution.
- Operations or production methods and facilities.
- Financial aspects, including expected income, expenses, profits (or losses), investment needed, and expected cash flow.

In addition, a properly developed, well-written business plan should answer questions such as the following:

- Is the business formation package complete?
- Would it be attractive to potential investors?
- Does the proposed business have a reasonable chance for success at the start?
- Does it have any long-run competitive advantages to the owner? To investors? To employees?
- Can the product be produced efficiently?
- Can it be marketed effectively?
- Can the production and marketing of the product be economically financed?
- Can the new company's business functions—operations, distribution, finance, and human resources—be properly managed?
- Are the needed employees available?

In summary, a properly developed and written plan provides more than mere facts. It serves as (1) an effective communication tool to convey ideas, research findings, and proposed plans to others, especially financiers; (2) the basis for managing the new venture; and (3) a measuring device by which to gauge progress and evaluate needed changes. Developing and writing a business plan takes much time, effort, and money, but the results can make the difference between the company's success and failure.

■ PREPARING THE PLAN

When developing a business plan, you should consider the firm's background, origins, philosophy, mission, and objectives, as well as the means of fulfilling that mission and attaining those objectives.[14] A sound approach is to: (1) determine where the business is, by recognizing its current status; (2) decide where you would like to be, by clarifying your philosophy about doing business, developing the firm's mission, and setting objectives; and (3) determine how to get to where you want to be, by identifying the best strategies for accomplishing the business's objectives.

Figure 5–7
How to Prepare a Business Plan

- Survey consumer demands for your product(s) and decide how to satisfy those demands.
- Ask questions that cover everything from the firm's target market to its competitive position.
- Establish a long-range strategic plan for the entire business.
- Develop short-term, detailed plans for all those involved with the business, including the owner(s), managers, and employees.
- Plan for every part of the venture, including operations, marketing, general and administrative functions, and distribution.
- Prepare a plan that uses staff time sparingly.

Figure 5–7 shows one approach to preparing a business plan. It is the one we recommend for those who are serious about succeeding in small business ownership.

Who Should Prepare the Plan?

If the prospective owner is the only one involved in the business, he or she should prepare the plan, with the advice and counsel of competent advisers. But if the business is to be organized and run by more than one person, it should be a team effort. You might encourage each manager to prepare a part of the plan. We also recommend having other key employees help in the planning stage, as this will improve communication and motivation.

There are many software packages available to assist one in planning and preparing the business plan. Ideally, such a system should include several key characteristics. To begin with, it should be user-friendly and have plenty of examples to help you. Spreadsheet-like templates for individual data input and automated integration between the modules or sections are also needed. You must remember that a software package is only a helpful tool and that you must formalize your plan.

Developing Action Steps

You can collect needed information from the steps discussed in Chapter 4 and earlier in this chapter, as well as from business associates and from legal, management, and financial consultants. Discussions with people both inside and outside the business are useful in gathering and evaluating this information.

The focus of the plan should be on future developments for the business, with steps set up to deal with specific aspects, such as product development, marketing, production or operations, finance, and management. Realistic, measurable objectives should be set, and the plan's steps should be delegated, monitored, and reported regularly.

Questions such as the following are useful in developing action steps: Who will be responsible for each course of action? What is the time frame for achieving each objective? What are the barriers to achieving the objectives? How can those barriers be overcome? Have the necessary controls been considered?

■ COMPONENTS OF THE PLAN

Because the business plan is such an important document, it should be arranged logically and presented clearly to save the reader time and effort, as well as to ensure understanding. While the information that should be included tends to be standardized, the format to be used is not. (Figure 5–8 presents a typical format.)

Figure 5–8
Typical Business Plan Format

1. Cover sheet
   - Business name, address, and phone number
   - Principals
   - Date
2. Executive summary
   - Abstract—mission statement
   - Objectives
   - Description of products or services
   - Marketing plan
   - Financial budget
3. Table of contents
4. History
   - Background of principals, or company origins
   - History of products or services
   - Organization structure
   - Company history in brief
5. Description of the business
6. Definition of the market
   - Target market/area
   - Market analysis
   - Competitor analysis
   - Industry analysis
7. Description of products or services
   - What is to be developed or produced
   - Status of research and development
   - Status of patents, trademarks, copyrights
8. Management structure
   - Who will enact plan
   - Organizational chart
   - Communication flowchart
   - Employee policies

9. Objectives and goals
   - Profit plan
   - Marketing plans
   - Manufacturing plans
   - Quality control plans
   - Financial plans
10. Financial data
    - Pro forma income statements (three years)
    - Pro forma cash flow analyses (first year, by months)
    - Pro forma balance sheets (three years)
    - Cost-volume-profit analyses where appropriate
11. Appendixes
    - Narrative history of firm in detail
    - Résumés of key employees
    - Major environmental assumptions
    - Brochures describing products
    - Letters of recommendation or endorsement
    - Historical financial data (at least three years)
    - Details of:
      a. Products and services
      b. Research and development
      c. Marketing
      d. Manufacturing
      e. Administration
      f. Finance

Regardless of the specific format chosen, any plan should include at least the following elements: cover sheet, executive summary, table of contents, history of the (proposed) business, description of the business, definition of the market, description of the product(s), management structure, objectives and goals, financial data, and appendixes.

Cover Sheet

The cover sheet presents identifying information, such as the business name, address, and phone number. Also, readers should know at once who the principals are.

Figure 5–9
Sample Outline of an Executive Summary

A. Company
   1. Who and what it is
   2. Status of project/firm
   3. Key goals and objectives
B. Product/service
   1. What it is
   2. How it works
   3. What it is for
   4. Proprietary advantages
C. Market
   1. Prospective customers
   2. How many there are
   3. Market growth rate
   4. Competition (list three to six competitors by name and describe)
   5. Industry trends
   6. How the firm will compete
   7. Estimated market share
      a. In one year
      b. In five years

D. Operations
   1. How product/service will be manufactured/provided
   2. Facilities/equipment
   3. Special processes
   4. Labor skills needed
E. Channels of distribution: how product/service will get to end users
F. Management team
   1. Who will do what
   2. Their qualifications
   3. Availability
G. Sources and application of funds
   1. Present needs
   2. Future needs

One-page profit and loss statement showing annual totals for first three years, including detailed costs of goods sold and overhead (general and administrative) breakdowns.

Source: Entrepreneur Application Profile used by Venture Capital Exchange, Enterprise Development Center, The University of Tulsa, Tulsa, Oklahoma.

Executive Summary

> The **executive summary** is a brief overview of the most important information in a business plan.

The **executive summary** of your plan must be a real "grabber"; it must motivate the reader to go on to the other sections. Moreover, it must convey a sense of plausibility, credibility, and integrity. Your plan may be one of many evaluated by representatives of lending institutions. They tend to evaluate the worth of the plan on the basis of this summary; if it generates sufficient interest, the remainder of the document may be assigned to other persons for review. The executive summary outlines the entire business plan, its major objectives, how these objectives will be accomplished, and the expected results. Therefore, it is sometimes first sent to potential investors to see if they have any interest in the venture; if so, the entire plan will then be sent to them.

Remember, *the executive summary is just that—a summary—so keep it short!* It may be difficult to get so much information on one or two pages, but try to do so. Also, even though the summary is the initial component of the plan, *it should be written only after the rest of the plan has been developed.*

Figure 5–9 presents a sample outline of the executive summary required of individuals and firms seeking equity capital from the Venture Capital Exchange of the University of Tulsa (www.utulsa.edu). We recommend that your summary also contain sections on the ownership and legal form of the business.

Table of Contents

Because the table of contents provides an overview of what's in the plan, it should be written concisely, in outline form, using alphabetical and numerical headings and subheads.

History of the (Proposed) Business

Background information on the person(s) organizing the business, as well as a description of each person's contributions, should be discussed at this point. Explanations of how the idea for the product or firm originated and what has been done to develop the idea should also be included. If the owner or owners have been in business before, that should be discussed, and any failures should be explained.

Description of the Business

It is now time for you to describe your business! More information is needed than just a statement of what the firm does—or plans to do—and a listing of its functions, products, or services. This definition should tell what customer needs the business intends to meet. In writing this component, it might be helpful to distinguish between how you perceive the business and what potential customers might think of it. Think about questions such as these, from the *owner's* perspective:

- What do you think will sell?
- What is your largest line of inventory?
- Where is your greatest profit made?

and from the *customer's* perspective:

- What do you think they need or want to buy?
- What is the best-selling item?
- On what product or service is most personnel time spent?

Ask yourself whether the answers to these questions are closely aligned and compatible or divergent. If they are divergent, the business may be in trouble. If they are compatible—or can be made compatible—there is a good chance of success, as the following example illustrates.

> The sales manager of an FM radio station evaluated the results of efforts to sell advertising and found that advertising customers obtained 45 percent or more of their business volume from the black community. Yet that group made up only a small portion of the station's listening audience, and the station had never attracted the desired volume of advertising. A shift to black disc jockeys and a program format attuned to the black community produced a substantial increase in advertising revenues.

Definition of the Market

While the definition of the market is one of the most important—and most difficult—parts of the plan to develop, it should at least indicate the target of your marketing efforts, as well as the trading area served. It must answer questions such as these: Who buys what and why? What are your customers like? Does the competition have any weaknesses you can exploit?

Description of the Product(s)

This section should describe the firm's existing or planned product(s). The status of all research done and developments under way should be described, along with discussions of any legal aspects, such as patents, copyrights, trademarks, pending lawsuits, and legal claims against the firm. Are any government approvals or clearances needed? Catalog sheets, blueprints, photographs, and other visuals—if available—are helpful and should be included.

Management Structure

This is the place to describe your management structure, especially the expertise of your management team. Explain how its members will help carry out the plan. You could also discuss employee policies and procedures. To repeat: It is important to demonstrate the proven ability and dedication of the owner and staff.

Objectives and Goals

This part outlines what your business plans to accomplish, as well as how and when it will be done and who will do it. Sales forecasts as well as production, service, quality assurance, and financial plans should be discussed. Other items of interest to potential investors include pricing and anticipated profits, advertising and promotion strategies and budgets, a description of how the product(s) will be distributed and sold, and which categories of customers will be targeted for initial heavy sales effort, and which ones for later sales efforts.

Financial Data

One important purpose of the business plan is to indicate the expected financial results from operations. The plan should show prospective investors or lenders why they should provide funds, when they can expect a return, and what the expected rate of return on their money is. At this point in the new business's development, assumptions—or educated guesses—concerning many issues may have to be made. For example, assumptions must be made about expected revenues, competitors' actions, and future market conditions. Assumptions, while necessary, should be designated as such, and financial projections should be realistically based on how increased personnel, expanded facilities, or equipment needs will affect the projections. The budgetary process to be used is an important part of the business plan. And prices should reflect actual cost figures, as the following example illustrates.

> In a college town, a restaurant owner who was in financial difficulty sought aid from the SBA (www.sba.gov). The first question asked by the SCORE (www.score.org) volunteer assigned as a consultant was: "What's the most popular item on your menu?" The owner replied, "Our $6.25 steak dinner." The consultant asked for a scale and a raw steak. He showed the restaurant owner that the raw steak alone cost $5.10. Obviously, the reason for the steak dinner's popularity was the markup of less than 23 percent on the cost of the steak alone. It was also the underlying cause of the business's financial troubles.

Appendixes

Other components needed in the plan are the firm's organizational structure, including organization charts. This part should include résumés of the officers, directors, key personnel, and any outside board members. If any of these have any special expertise that increases the chances of success, this should be mentioned. Historical financial information, with relevant documents, should also be included. Brochures, news items, letters of recommendation or endorsements, photographs, and similar items should be included as well.

■ PRESENTING THE PLAN

We know a SCORE adviser who tells his clients, "Investors decide during the first five minutes of studying the executive summary whether to reject a proposal or consider it further." Therefore, *presenting the business plan is almost as important as preparing it.* All the work is in vain if potential investors aren't interested in it. Presentation involves both writing the plan and presenting it to the targeted audience.

This point was strongly reinforced by Joseph Mancuso, author of a leading book on how to prepare and present business plans. The director of the Center for Entrepreneurial Management in New York asserts that "a good business plan takes a minimum of five months to write, but you've got to convince your readers in five minutes not to throw [it] away."[15]

Writing the Plan

John G. Burch, a writer on entrepreneurship, made the following suggestions for writing an effective plan:[16]

* *Be honest,* not only by avoiding outright lies, but also by revealing what you actually feel about the significant and relevant aspects of the plan.
* *Use the third person,* not the first person ("I" or "we"). This practice forces you to think clearly and logically from the other person's perspective.
* *Use transitional words,* such as *but, still,* and *therefore,* and active, dynamic verbs as a means of leading the reader from one thought to another.
* *Avoid redundancies,* such as "*future* plans," since repetition adds nothing to the presentation.
* *Use short, simple words,* where feasible, so the plan will be easy to understand and follow.
* *Use visuals,* such as tables, charts, photos, and computer graphics to present your ideas effectively.

The plan should be prepared in an 8 ½-by-11-inch format, typed, and photocopied, with copies for outsiders attractively bound. Most business plans can—and should—be presented effectively in 25 to 30 pages—or less. Of course, the plan should be grammatically correct, so have someone proofread it for spelling and grammar before you present it.

The plan should be reviewed by people outside the firm, such as accounting and business consultants, other business people, and attorneys, before it is sent to potential investors or lenders. Other helpful reviewers might include a professional writer, editor, or English teacher.

When pertinent, the cover and title page should indicate that the information is proprietary and confidential. However, there is always the chance that this practice might offend a potential investor.

The Written/Oral Presentation

In an oral presentation, you should present the plan in person to investors or lenders. Presenting your plan involves creative skills on your part to give the impression that you have (or plan to have) a profitable and stable business, and that its chances of continuing that way are good. Your listeners will be looking very carefully at *you,* to see what kind of person *you* are, for *you are the business*—and vice versa. Both written and oral presentations should be very positive and quite upbeat.

The plan should be delivered from the listener's perspective, not yours. Both oral and written presentations should demonstrate that you have a marketable product and that the business has a feasible plan for aggressively marketing it—at a profit. You should provide visual aids for key segments of the plan and be prepared for specific questions concerning the following:

- The adequacy of the research and development behind the product.
- The validity of the market research.
- Your understanding of the business.
- Financial projections and why they will work.
- Relative priority of the objectives.
- Your ability to "make it happen."

The amount of detail in the market data and financial projections will vary according to the plan's purpose. If it is to raise equity or debt financing, more detail is needed; if it is to improve operations and motivate employees, less detail is needed.

You must remember that you are probably the best expert on your product or service and may have only one brief opportunity to present your plan. So be prepared!

Even the best-prepared plan, though, may not be accepted by potential investors. The following example is one of the classic blunders in the history of computers.

> In 1946, J. Presper Eckert, Jr., one of the inventors of the ENIAC, the first digital computer, fired off a business plan to IBM (www.ibm.com), hoping it would yield an investment to produce and distribute the UNIVAC, the first giant electronic computer. IBM President Thomas J. Watson, Sr., after careful review, responded that it was the company's opinion that the world would ultimately need only about 5 or 10 such large computers, and Eckert's machine was therefore of no interest to IBM.

■ IMPLEMENTING THE PLAN

Now you are ready to take the plunge![17] It is time to get a charter, obtain facilities and supplies, hire and train people, and start operating. Using the capital structure plan and the sources of funds you have developed, obtain the funds and put them in a checking account ready for use. Obtain the services of an attorney to help acquire the charter (if the business is to be incorporated), obtain occupational licenses and permits, and take care of other legal requirements.

Once the funds, charter, and permits are in hand, refer to the timetable and start negotiating contracts; purchasing equipment, materials, and supplies; selecting, hiring, and training employees; establishing a marketing program; setting the legal structure in place; and developing an information system to maintain the records needed to run the business.

You are now a small business owner! You are operating your own business, you have all the risks, and you hope to receive the benefits and rewards of being on your own. Be ready for unforeseen problems, however, that may occur during the start-up period.

■ SAMPLE BUSINESS PLAN

A sample business plan is presented as an appendix at the end of this chapter. It is a proposal for a new business center. Notice that it closely follows the form as presented in Figure 5–8.

WHAT YOU SHOULD HAVE LEARNED

1. Planning, one of the key managerial functions, is usually done first, since everything else depends on it. While planning establishes directions and goals for any business, it is especially difficult in small firms, where management is often fully engaged in day-to-day operation and "can't see the forest for the trees." Some barriers to planning in small firms are the fear of learning things you would rather not know, the unpredictability of plans, the uncertainty of plans, and especially the lack of adequate time to plan.

2. Strategic planning—from which other plans are derived—determines the very nature of the business. Next comes operational planning, which sets policies, methods and procedures, budgets and standards, and other operating plans.

3. Financial planning involves estimating income and expenses, estimating investment required, and locating sources of funds. Income and expenses should be estimated to ensure that the proposed business will be feasible. Estimates should be based on the firm's first year of operation, as well as a typical "good" year, since investors may be willing to assume some risk of loss at the beginning to achieve greater gains later. Also, estimates should be made of personal needs during the transition period. These projections permit the prospective new owner to estimate the initial investment needed. Finally, sources of funds must be determined. The two sources are the business owner(s) and others, either private individuals or lending institutions.

4. A business plan is important for obtaining funds and as a blueprint for operating success. The research and analysis required to write an effective plan help you focus on the company's goals, markets, expected performance, and problems that might be encountered. The plan keeps you from jumping into an enterprise without adequate thought and planning, and then serves as a yardstick against which to measure performance.

5. The plan should include at least the following: (a) cover sheet, (b) executive summary, (c) table of contents, (d) history of the (proposed) business, (e) description of the business, (f) definition of the market, (g) description of the product(s), (h) management structure, (i) objectives and goals, (j) financial data, and (k) appendixes. When used to raise funds, detailed financial projections of expected sales, profits, and rates of return should be emphasized.

6. From discussions in this and the previous chapter, you should be able to prepare an effective business plan.

QUESTIONS FOR DISCUSSION

1. Explain why planning is so badly needed by small businesses. Why is it so often neglected?

2. Explain the two overall categories of planning. What are the essential differences between the two?

3. Explain each of the following: policies, methods and procedures, budgets, and standards.

4. In planning to operate the business, what are the factors that must be planned for? Explain each.

5. What is involved in financial planning?

6. What is the purpose of a business plan? Explain.

7. How can a business plan be useful even to a prospective business owner who does not need outside capital?

8. What should the business plan include?

9. Who should prepare the plan? Why? Why should the writer get help from outside professionals and businesspeople?

Appendix
A Sample Business Plan: The Business Center*

■ EXECUTIVE SUMMARY

The Company

The Business Center will provide traveling businesspeople and vacationers with on-site access to office services such as photocopying, Internet access, secretarial services, and other related office needs.

Marketing Strategy

The Business Center will serve hotel clientele and local businesses. The major focus will be on hotel guests traveling in the area with business-related needs. As part of the hotel's informational literature, The Business Center will be featured as a convenient service for the guests. Other advertising will be achieved through placement of The Business Center's brochures inside adjacent hotels and other strategic locations.

Operations

The facility will be housed in the lobby area of the Marriott Courtyard. Using the services of an employment leasing service, one full-time employee will be on site during working hours.

Management Team

The three partners will maintain their current jobs. Management responsibilities will be divided according to their experience in their primary professions. Suzanne Hagan will be responsible for operations; Joseph Payne will be responsible for financial management; and Darrell Waldrup will be responsible for marketing procedures.

The goal of the management team will be to operate near break-even for the first year, expand services to guests at neighboring hotels, and eventually service the needs of local businesses.

Financial Considerations

As shown in Appendix I, the expected profit for the first year is $6,159, with an anticipated 10 percent increase annually.

■ TABLE OF CONTENTS

---

*Prepared by Suzanne Hagan, Joseph Payne, and Darrell Waldrup of the University of Mobile.

III.   Objectives and Goals
    A.   Profit Plans
    B.   Marketing Plans
    C.   Quality Control Plans
    D.   Financial Plans
IV.   Definition of the Market
    A.   Customers
    B.   Competition
       1.   Competitors' Strengths
       2.   Competitors' Weaknesses
    C.   Substitutes
    D.   Barriers to Entry
    E.   Powers of Suppliers
    F.   Growth Strategy
    G.   Marketing Strategy
V.   Description of the Product
    A.   Office Services
    B.   Secretarial Services
    C.   Computer Workstation Rentals
    D.   Pickup and Delivery
VI.   Management Structure
VII.   Environmental Factors
    A.   Demographic
    B.   Economic
    C.   Technological
VIII.   Financial Data
    A.   Pricing Strategy
    B.   Cash Flow Projections
    C.   Income Projections
IX.   Appendixes
    A.   Résumés of Principals
    B.   Hotel Locations
    C.   Location of Competitors
    D.   Demographics of the Area
    E.   Economic Indicators
    F.   Pricing Flyer
    G.   Loan Payment Schedule
    H.   Three-Year Projected Cash Flow
    I.   Three-Year Projected Income Statement
    J.   Three-Year Projected Balance Sheet with Projected Ratios
    K.   Product Layout

■ I. History and Background of the Business

The Business Center will be a limited-liability corporation run by Suzanne Hagan, Joseph Payne, and Darrell Waldrup. The individuals are students at a local university working toward master's degrees in business administration. Their individual professional experiences will be utilized in the operation of the business. (Refer to Appendix A for each principal's professional experience.)

The concept of opening a business center came from the need for office services for businesspeople traveling and staying at hotels and motels in the vicinity. The area of concentration for this facility is proposed as an area along Interstate 65 near Airport Boulevard.

The facility will be housed in the lobby area of the Marriott Courtyard which is part of a complex of Marriott holdings including the Fairfield Inn and the Residence Inn located on three adjacent properties on the Beltline Highway facing the Interstate. In addition, there are 19 other motels located within a two-mile radius of the facility. (Refer to Appendix B for a map of hotel markets in this area.)

The income received from operations will not be the primary source of revenue for the principles. Each partner is currently employed in various business industries that will contribute to the success of this venture.

■ II. Definition of the Business

Every day, people are reinventing the way they do business. The Business Center will support this revolution by providing innovative ways to get the job done in a convenient and timely manner. It will offer a variety of services including photocopies, laser prints, facsimiles, secretarial services, computer workstation rentals, shipping, and office supplies. It will also offer Internet access with an emphasis on offering e-mail access for the businessperson.

■ III. Objectives and Goals

The company will be committed to doing whatever is needed to guarantee customer satisfaction with the organization's products and customer services.

A. Profit Plans

The company's goals will be to maximize profits through efficiency of operations. Through the use of minimum square footage, they will provide minimum overhead and maximum service output; this will provide high return on investment.

B. Marketing Plans

The company will use service advertising and promotional programs to increase exposure to the target market.

C. Quality Control Plans

Through streamlining operations and responding to customers' concerns, the company hopes to narrow any gap seen by the client between their office and the services being provided.

D. Financial Plans

The principals will obtain an unsecured loan in the amount of $10,000, with the first payment not due for 90 days. The first $1,500 of the loan will be used to purchase supplies and equipment. The the rest of the loan will be used as working capital. Each of the principals will supply personal funds of $1,000 toward start-up costs for The Business Center. Future capital will be obtained through a line of credit from the bank for working capital.

■ IV. DEFINITION OF THE MARKET

The area is currently experiencing rapid growth in the hotel and motel market. Lodging facilities are currently operating at 70 percent occupancy. The industry standard for minimum profit is 60 percent capacity. As long as capacity is above 60 percent, there is room for growth. The result is an expanding need of business services for guests staying in these facilities.

A. Customers

The target market is businesspeople visiting the area, either for business purposes such as company business or conventions, or for leisure activities. These are people who cannot afford to be away from the office and the services their office provides to them. The Business Center will become an office away from home, thereby filling this void in services.

The Business Center would also serve the general public, but recognizes that this is not its primary target market.

B. Competition

Direct competitors are three major franchises—Kinko's; Mail Boxes, Etc.; and Printing One—as well as small individually owned operations.

1. Competitors' Strengths

- The major franchises offer name recognition to the customer.
- Franchises also have corporate support in operations, management, accounting, and technological systems.
- The competitors have been in business long enough to target the most profitable services.

2. Competitors' Weaknesses

- The competitors are positioned away from where the customers are located; their location requires driving along major thoroughfares in unfamiliar territories. (Refer to Appendix C for a map showing competitors' locations.)
- Cost of operation of the competitors' facilities is high.
- The competitors, being located away from the hotels, would not be able to offer such personal services.

C. Substitutes

Substitutes for The Business Center include such things as personally owned fax machines and portable computers. Other substitutes could be making copies by hand.

D. Barriers to Entry

Some barriers to entry for The Business Center include the capital required to purchase the necessary business machines and securing a good location for the facility.

E. Power of Suppliers

The power of suppliers to affect The Business Center is relatively low, except in the circumstances of repair of a malfunctioning copier or computer.

F. Growth Strategy

Exhibits 1 and 2 show indicators of potential business for The Business Center. The Mobile Convention Center—located on the Mobile River in downtown Mobile—alone drew 195,000 guests in 1995/1996, with an anticipated annual growth of 10 percent. There are only two major hotels downtown near the convention center. Many guests are required to stay in one of the strip of hotels located along Interstate 65 near Airport Boulevard.

According to these indicators, the county, in 1996, had a growth rate of 2 percent from 1995, indicating a small increase in the number of visitors. An increase in the number of

Exhibit 1
Selected Indicators of Visitors to Mobile County

Year	Enplaned Passengers	I-10 Westbound Welcome Center	I-10 Eastbound Welcome Center	Total
1992	365,777	335,589	492,651	1,194,017
1993	357,289	283,181	426,049	1,066,519
1994	353,626	332,888	423,313	1,109,827
1995	304,859	390,537	390,974	1,086,370
1996	378,706	335,015	392,017	1,105,738

Exhibit 2
Hotels and Motels in Mobile County

Year/ Month	Occupancy rate					
	Downtown	Beltline	I-10 West	City Average	State Average	U.S. Average
1995	N.A.	N.A.	N.A.	62.20	63.70	65.10
1996	N.A.	N.A.	N.A.	60.60	62.03	65.70
1997/1	43.23	57.48	51.70	54.67	51.50	53.70
1997/2	60.93	66.50	68.49	66.04	61.70	62.40
1997/3	52.75	69.87	78.88	67.16	65.00	65.30
1997/4	56.93	71.93	70.44	68.83	67.70	67.00
1997/5	49.40	64.58	74.73	62.54	N.A.	N.A.

visitors indicates an increase in the number of business travelers as well as vacationers. This would indicate an increase in the need of services provided by The Business Center.

G. Marketing Strategy

As mentioned above, the company will use service advertising and promotional programs to increase exposure to the targeted market.

Being part of the hotel complex shown in Appendix B, The Business Center will receive direct advertising from all of the corporate affiliates. As part of the hotel's informational literature, The Business Center will be featured as a convenient service for the guests.

Other advertising will be achieved through placement of The Business Center's brochures inside adjacent hotels and other strategic locations.

The Business Center will conduct periodic mailings to companies located in the two-county area. Corporations will be targeted for business services needed by their visiting associates. These mailings, also, could generate additional revenues from local businesses, helping to offset seasonal variations in volume.

■ V. Description of the Product

The Business Center plans to offer all the convenient services of a conventional office. These services would encompass everything from office supplies to Internet access.

A. Office Services

Customers will have access to basic office supplies, such as pens, paper supplies, folders, report covers, etc. Facsimile services will be available. Photocopying services will include plain-paper copies, color copies, and copying onto transparencies.

B. Secretarial Services

Customers will have access to services of a professional familiar with word processing, dictation, and spreadsheet applications. All work will be printed on laser printers using quality paper or transparencies for presentation. The availability of a service to develop professional presentations using Microsoft *PowerPoint* presentation software will also be available. The presentations could be printed or could be stored on floppy disks for the customers to use in their own computers.

C. Computer Workstation Rentals

Customers will have access to a computer workstation, complete with a laser printer, for their own personal use. The computer will be equipped with a modem to allow customers access to the Internet. A feature that The Business Center intends to offer is e-mail service for the customer. Currently approximately half of all e-mail service providers offer access availability from remote locations, so customers would be able to access their own personal e-mail, receive and send messages, and continue to stay in touch while they are away from home.

D. Pickup and Delivery

Shipping via United Parcel Service and Federal Express will be available for customers. The company plans to establish the location as a drop-off/pickup point for both these services, therefore increasing business traffic.

The company will contract with a local delivery service for off-site pickup and delivery for customers staying at hotels other than the Marriott Courtyard and for local businesses.

■ VI. MANAGEMENT STRUCTURE

The three partners will maintain their current jobs. Using an employment leasing service, one full-time employee will be on site during working hours. During initial start-up, the principals will meet weekly to discuss matters such as operational issues, client concerns, and financial analysis. Management responsibilities will be divided according to their experience in their primary professions.

Suzanne Hagan will be responsible for operations. Her many years of experience in the business sector make her well aware of the needs of the customers. Having managed office staff and worked with office facilities, she will utilize her contacts for purchasing of equipment and supplies, training office personnel, and working with personnel regarding operational problems and procedures.

Joseph Payne will be responsible for financial management. His years of experience in banking will prove to be an asset for the purpose of obtaining initial capital for this venture. Furthermore, his analytical skills in evaluating current trends and future outlooks of the company's financial position will be a valuable tool.

Darrell Waldrup will be responsible for marketing procedures. His understanding of the demands of customers and how to meet those demands will allow him to evaluate the performance of the business and keep operations running smoothly. He will also be responsible for developing new accounts and soliciting new business to continue the growth of the organization.

■ VII. ENVIRONMENTAL FACTORS

A. Demographic

Although The Business Center's primary market is traveling businesspeople, the market that exists for permanent residents of the area cannot be overlooked. The location of The Business Center will allow for quick recognition among some of the city's most business-minded people. The Business Center is within close proximity to the residences of people who tend to be the highest spenders on such services as auto loans, home loans, investments, retirement plans, travel, and health insurance. (Refer to Appendix D.) These people have been targeted as the segment most likely to use these services other than traveling people. The Business Center will focus on maintaining and developing positive and supportive customer relationships with this group of people, especially in the initial introduction and growth stages of the businesses.

B. Economic

Over the past three years, several new corporations and businesses have come into the area. Existing corporations and businesses have been growing tremendously as well. The three largest areas of employment are in the following industries: Services, Retail and Wholesale Trade, and Government. With these new and expanding businesses come needs for business services. The Business Center recognizes the needs of these industries and is willing to serve them. (Refer to Appendix E.)

C. Technological

In today's business world, technology has a strong presence. The ability to use technology efficiently can be a tremendous asset to an organization. Information can be transferred, stored, and presented very quickly and efficiently by electronic means currently available. The Business Center recognizes this fact and uses some of the latest equipment and means to better serve the customer in an accurate, timely, and professional manner.

■ VIII. FINANCIAL DATA

A. Pricing Strategy

Pricing will be competitive as it relates to the convenience of services provided to customers. (Refer to Appendix F for proposed pricing flyer.)

B. Cash Flow Projections

Refer to Appendix G: Loan Payment Schedule.
Refer to Appendix H: Three-Year Projected Cash Flow.

C. Income Projections

Refer to Appendix I: Three-Year Projected Income Statement.
Refer to Appendix J: Three-Year Projected Balance Sheet with Projected Ratios.

■ IX. APPENDIXES

A.   Résumés of Principals.
B.   Hotel Locations.
C.   Location of Competitors.
D.   Demographics of the Area.
E.   Economic Indicators.
F.   Pricing Flyer.
G.   Loan Payment Schedule.
H.   Three-Year Projected Cash Flow.
I.   Three-Year Projected Income Statement.
J.   Three-Year Projected Balance Sheet with Projected Ratios.
K.   Product Layout.

■ APPENDIX A: RÉSUMÉS OF PRINCIPALS

Suzanne C. Hagan

Professional Experience

Vice President of Information Systems ♦ *1991–present*

- Directly responsible for operation of the corporation's mainframe computer system which includes accounting, parts and inventory, and service operations.
- Coordinate all data communications between the mainframe and 35 personal computers throughout the company's four branch locations as well as satellite communications with a major vendor.
- Manage the telephone communication systems at all locations.
- Install software and train staff in usage.
- Monitor hardware and manage a network of PCs.
- Provice technical support to PC and laptop users in sales, repair diagnosis, parts, service, accounting, and general word processing.
- Coordinate the installation of, train staff, and maintain a contact management system used for direct mail and telecommunications.
- Work on the advertising team producing bimonthly direct mail brochures and periodic mail-outs. Publications include in-house and outsourced printing projects. Publish the monthly newsletter.
- Experienced in the procurement of hardware and software.

Vice President of Accounting and Data Processing ♦ *1978–1991*

- Supervised all accounting and computer operations for corporate office and three branches.
- Directed the completion of monthly financial statements and led accountants during annual audits to prepare year-end reports.

Office Manager ♦ *1966–1978*

- Managed office and accounting operations including monthly financial statements.
- Hired and trained office personnel.
- Supervised the installation of the company's first computer as well as three subsequent computer upgrades.

Computer Operator ♦ *1965–1966*

- Operated IBM keypunch machine, card sorter, and IBM computer to prepare life insurance policies as well as reissue policies after changes from field sales personnel.

Suzanne C. Hagan

Page Two

Technical Skills and Professional Development

Computer/software experience:

WordPerfect	Lotus 1-2-3
Alpha 4 Database	Windows 3.1/95
Desktop Publishing	Windows for Workgroups
Telemagic & Sidekick Contact Management Software	

Seminars in:

Performance Appraisals	How to be a Winner at Work
Understanding a Financial Statement	Job Skills for Success
Developing Productive Communications	Reward of Teamwork
Implementation of Inventory	Dealer's User Conference

Education

Master of Business Administration ♦ **1999**

Bachelor of Science (Organizational Management), Summa cum laude ♦ **1995**

Professional Affiliations

National Association of Women Business Owners
Executive Women's Forum
Career Women of Mobile
National Association of Women in Construction
  Chapter Treasurer, Secretary, Vice President, and President

References Available on Request

Joseph Payne

Professional Experience

Financial Sales Manager, Assistant Vice President ♦ *1994–present*

- ♦ Progressively promoted to Branch Manager and Bank Officer following first year accomplishments.
- ♦ Achieved top 1% company sales ranking—first year.
- ♦ Consistently ranked top 10% in sales performance.
- ♦ Lead area in Business Banking relational developments.
- ♦ Regional sales training officer for branch management.
- ♦ Supervise internal operational cash management.
- ♦ Perform daily financial and investment counseling.
- ♦ Responsible for motivational staff management.
- ♦ Personal Banker for a 4,500 customer base.
- ♦ Conduct Prospect and Client sales calls—increased deposit base by 11%.
- ♦ Selected as corporate CRA representative.
- ♦ Headed system update of a computerized financial program.

Buyer/Senior Merchandiser, Major Retail Store ♦ *1989–1994*

- ♦ Managed a $1.33mm department at the district headquarters.
- ♦ Chosen to implement company pilot programs.
- ♦ Designed, developed, and initiated time/cost reduction program saving more than $1mm.
- ♦ Motivational training of 27 associates into a leading sales force.
- ♦ Responsibilities included:

Buying	Inventory Management
Sales and Profit Analysis	Merchandising Layout
Forecasting	Strategic Management
Advertising	Quality Control
Competitive Shopping Analysis	Prospecting
Personnel Training and Development	Marketing Research
Expanding Customer Base	Queuing
Promotional Management	

System Sales/Installation Manager—Radio Shack ♦ *1986–1989*

- ♦ Systemized coordination of damaged inventory.
- ♦ Implemented introductory computer classes.

Technical Skills and Professional Development

Computer/software experience:

PC/Laptop/Mainframe	Database Design
WordPerfect	Lotus 123
Microsoft Word/Works	Microsoft Excel

Joseph Payne

Page Two

Education

Master of Business Administration ♦ **1998**

Bachelor of Science (Operations & Systems Management) ♦ **1989**

Professional Affiliations

University Alumni Board, 1997–Present
Junior Achievement
   Board Member
   Economics Instructor, Project Business
Mentor/year-round Volunteer Teacher, 1993–Present
Sickle Cell Disease Association
   Executive Board Member, 1995–Present
Stone Street Baptist Church
   Sunday School Junior Superintendent/Teacher
   Laymen Organization Treasurer
Alabama Institute of Banking, 1995–Present
   Education Committee Chairman
Midtown Optimist Club
United Way
   Corporate Chairman, 1992–1994
American Diabetes Associations
   Chairman 1994
DECA Regional Competition
   Competition Judge, 1991–1996
   Speaker, 1991

References Available on Request

Darrell E. Waldrup

Professional Experience

Graduate Assistant, School of Business, local university ♦ *1996–present*

- Assist key faculty in research and lecture tasks.

Lead Person, Sport Supply Group ♦ *1994–1996*

- Implemented graphic art and developed managerial abilities.
- Met screen printing production demands.
- Produced quality merchandise within deadlines.
- Trained other employees in the production process.

Partner/Consultant, Southern Merchandise Liquidators ♦ *1994*

- Assisted in developing a successful small business.

Technical Skills and Professional Development

Computer/software experience:

Microsoft Office	Internet; Netscape

Major courses in:

Small Business Management	Managerial Marketing
Human Resource Management	Organizational Behavior

Education

Master of Business Administration ♦ *1998*

Bachelor of Science, Business Management ♦ *1994*

Honors and Activities

Summer Honors Program	Business Management Club
Presidential Leadership Scholarship	Accounting Club
J.L. Bedsole Academic Scholarship	Student Government Association
Mallory-Hand Academic Scholarship	Students in Free Enterprise (SIFE)
Graduate Assistant	Future Business Leaders of America

References Available on Request

■ APPENDIX B: HOTEL LOCATIONS

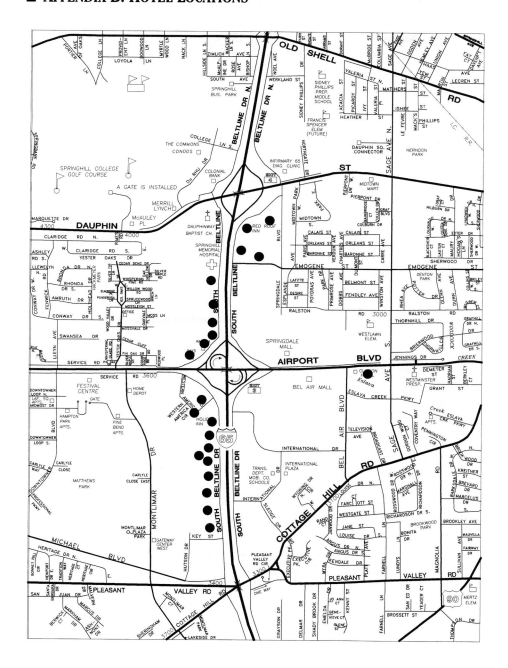

■ APPENDIX C: LOCATION OF COMPETITORS

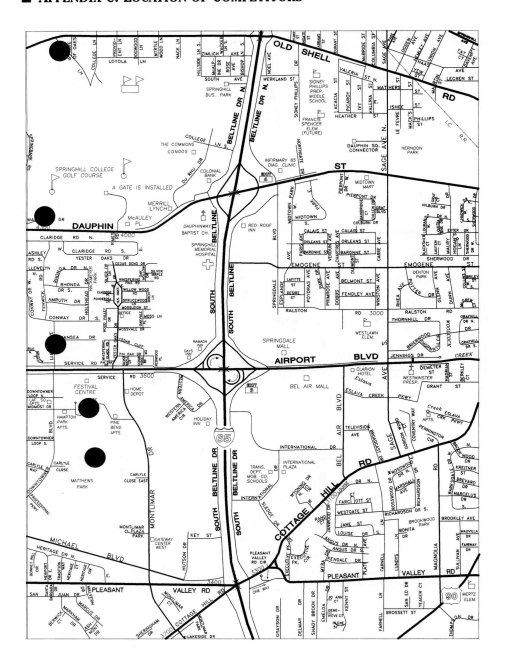

■ APPENDIX D: DEMOGRAPHICS OF THE AREA

Population Change

Zip Code	1980	1990	1996	2001
36606	19,985	18,247	18,507	18,921
36607	9,944	8,610	8,607	8,706
36608	34,622	37,600	39,470	40,952
36609	19,913	23,667	25,518	26,898
36693	14,311	17,704	19,103	20,109
36695	13,898	21,467	25,772	28,485
Total	114,653	129,285	138,973	146,072

1996 Household Income Distribution (%)

Zip Code	Less than $15,000	$15,000 to $24,999	$25,000 to $49,999	$50,000 to $99,999	$100,000 to $149,999	$150,000 or More
36606	25.8	20.4	35.5	16.3	1.5	0.06
36607	37.2	19.2	29.8	11.2	1.2	1.5
36608	18.1	17.0	33.8	21.4	5.5	4.3
36609	16.0	16.9	36.9	22.4	4.4	1.5
36693	12.7	13.0	33.7	31.5	6.3	2.7
36695	9.0	11.8	32.7	35.7	7.4	3.4

1996 Household Income Distribution (%)

Zip Code	Auto Loan	Home Loan	Investments	Retirement Plans
36606	95	89	108	85
36607	92	79	100	76
36608	100	102	110	103
36609	98	99	89	91
36693	104	104	108	106
36695	103	105	81	98

■ APPENDIX E: ECONOMIC INDICATORS

Employment Composition

	1995	1996	Net Change
Construction and Mining	15,100	15,900	+ 800
Manufacturing	27,000	27,100	+ 100
Transportation and Public Utilities	12,900	13,000	+ 100
Retail and Wholesale Trade	56,000	57,000	+ 1,000
Finance, Insurance, and Real Estate	9,000	9,500	+ 500
Services	55,900	57,400	+ 1,500
Government	33,800	33,800	0
Total	209,700	213,700	+ 4,000

Area Economic Indicators

	Sept. 1997	Sept. 1996	Year to Date 1997
Business activity			
Number of new businesses (city)	261	−4.1%	2,377
Number of homes sold (county)	302	−8.0%	2,820
Average price of homes sold	$103,411	+11.2%	
Construction			
Number of building permits	372	+5.1%	3,281
Value of building permits	$10,926,805	−49.0%	$138,141,846
Number of residential permits	18	−33.4%	223
Value of residential permits	$1,540,943	−35.2%	$18,627,691
Employment			
Labor force	264,510	−0.1%	
Employed	252,160	−0.2%	

Unemployment Rate	(1997)	(1996)
City	4.7%	4.6%
State	4.9%	4.7%
U.S.	4.9%	5.2%

	Sept. 1997	Sept. 1996	Year to Date 1997
Trade			
Sales tax revenue (city)	$5,704,449	+9.0%	$66,484,127
Sales tax revenue (county)	$3,446,865	+2.8%	$35,695,810
Lodging tax receipts (city)	$184,209	−0.4%	$1,970,067
Transportation			
Enplaned air passengers	33,508	+12.3%	311,443

■ **Appendix F: Pricing Flyer**

THE BUSINESS CENTER
Marriott Courtyard
Phone: 555-675-5990 / Fax: 555-675-5991

PHOTOCOPIES   Per Copy
Black and White Copies

20 lb., letter and legal	$ .15
Over 100 . . . . .add	$ .10
Special paper . . . . .add	$ .05
Transparencies	$ 2.00

Color Copies

Letter and legal	$ 1.49
Over 100	$ .99
Transparencies	$ 2.49

LASER PRINTS

Letter and legal, per copy	$ .50

FACSIMILE
Transmission—Domestic

Per page	$ 2.00

Transmission—International

Per page	$ 8.00

Reception

Per page	$ 1.00

SECRETARIAL SERVICES

Per hour	$35.00

COMPUTER WORKSTATION
IBM workstations with modems and laser printers

Per hour	$35.00

SHIPPING
We will gladly ship your overnight letters or small parcels via Federal Express or UPS. Please inquire at **The Business Center** for current rates.

OFFICE SUPPLIES
We maintain an inventory of the most often needed office supplies. Please inquire at **The Business Center.**

Pickup and delivery service is available.
Call **The Business Center** *at 555-675-5990 for this service.*

THE BUSINESS CENTER
You're never too far from "the office."

■ APPENDIX G: LOAN PAYMENT SCHEDULE

Amount financed	10,000
Annual interest	9.860
Duration of loan	3.6 years
Monthly payments	277.00
Total number of payments	43
Yearly principal + interest	3,324.00
Principal amount	10,000.00
Finance charges	1,966.40
Total cost	11,966.40

Payment Number	Payment Date	Beginning Balance	Interest	Principal	Balance	Accumulated Interest	Accumulated Principal
1		10,000.00	82.17	194.83	9,805.17	82.17	194.83
2		9,805.17	80.57	196.43	9,608.73	162.74	391.26
3		9,608.74	78.95	198.05	9,410.68	241.69	589.31
4		9,410.69	77.32	199.68	9,211.01	319.01	788.99
5		9,211.01	75.68	201.32	9,009.69	394.69	990.31
6		9,009.69	74.03	202.97	8,806.72	468.72	1,193.28
7		8,806.72	72.36	204.64	8,602.08	541.08	1,397.92
8		8,602.08	70.68	206.32	8.395.76	611.76	1,604.24
9		8,395.76	68.99	208.01	8,187.75	680.75	1,812.25
10		8,187.75	67.28	209.72	7,978.03	748.03	2,021.97
11		7,978.03	65.55	211.45	7,766.58	813.58	2,233.42
12		7,766.58	63.82	213.18	7,553.39	877.39	2,446.60

■ APPENDIX H: THREE-YEAR PROJECTED CASH FLOW

THE BUSINESS CENTER
Projected Cash Flow
First Year of Operation

Summary	Quarter 1	Quarter 2	Quarter 3	Quarter 4	Year End
Opening balance	$3,000	$14,325	$15,214	$17,168	$3,000
Total receipts	$17,000	$7,300	$8,300	$6,600	$39,200
Total disbursements	5,675	6,411	6,346	6,421	24,853
Total cash flow	$11,325	$889	$1,954	$179	$14,347
Ending balance	$14,325	$15,214	$17,168	$17,347	$17,347

Receipts

	Quarter 1	Quarter 2	Quarter 3	Quarter 4	Year End
Cash revenues	$7,000	$7,300	$8,300	$6,600	$29,200
Loans	$10,000				$10,000

Disbursements

	Quarter 1	Quarter 2	Quarter 3	Quarter 4	Year End
Wages	$3,840	$3,840	$3,840	$3,840	$15,360
Leased equipment	$200	$380	$340	$340	$1,260
Advertising	$375	$175	$150	$225	$925
Supplies	$75	$75	$75	$75	$300
Rent	$525	$525	$525	$525	$2,100
Insurance	$150	$150	$150	$150	$600
Telephone	$285	$285	$285	$285	$1,140
Utilities	$225	$150	$150	$150	$675
Loan payments		$831	$831	$831	$2,493

THE BUSINESS CENTER
Projected Cash Flow
Second Year of Operation

Summary	Quarter 1	Quarter 2	Quarter 3	Quarter 4	Year End
Opening balance	$17,347	$17,979	$19,038	$21,269	$17,347
Total receipts	$7,700	$8,030	$9,130	$7,260	$32,120
Total disbursements	7,068	6,971	6,899	6,982	27,920
Total cash flow	$632	$1,059	$2,231	$278	$4,200
Ending balance	$19,979	$19,038	$21,269	$21,547	$21,547

Receipts					
Cash revenues	$7,700	$8,030	$9,130	$7,260	$32,120
Loans					

Disbursements					
Wages	$4,224	$4,224	$4,224	$4,224	$16,896
Leased equipment	$220	$418	$374	$374	$1,386
Advertising	$412	$193	$165	$248	$1,018
Supplies	$81	$83	$83	$83	$330
Rent	$576	$578	$578	$578	$2,310
Insurance	$165	$165	$165	$165	$660
Telephone	$312	$314	$314	$314	$1,254
Utilities	$247	$165	$165	$165	$742
Loan payments	$831	$831	$831	$831	$3,324

THE BUSINESS CENTER
Projected Cash Flow
Third Year of Operation

Summary	Quarter 1	Quarter 2	Quarter 3	Quarter 4	Year End
Opening balance	$21,547	$22,321	$23,570	$26,108	$21,547
Total receipts	$8,470	$8,833	$10,043	$7,986	$35,332
Total disbursements	7,696	7,584	7,505	7,595	30,380
Total cash flow	$774	$1,249	$2,538	$391	$4,952
Ending balance	$22,321	$23,570	$26,108	$26,499	$26,499

Receipts					
Cash revenues	$8,470	$8,833	$10,043	$7,986	$35,332
Loans					

Disbursements					
Wages	$4,646	$4,646	$4,646	$4,646	$18,584
Leased equipment	$241	$460	$411	$411	$1,523
Advertising	$454	$212	$182	$272	$1,120
Supplies	$91	$91	$91	$91	$364
Rent	$635	$635	$635	$635	$2,540
Insurance	$182	$182	$182	$182	$728
Telephone	$345	$345	$345	$345	$1,380
Utilities	$271	$182	$182	$182	$817
Loan payments	$831	$831	$831	$831	$3,324

■ APPENDIX I: THREE-YEAR PROJECTED INCOME STATEMENT

THE BUSINESS CENTER
Projected Income Statement
First Year of Operation

	Quarter 1	Quarter 2	Quarter 3	Quarter 4	Year End
Product Sales					
Office services	$3,000	$3,100	$3,500	$2,800	$12,400
Secretarial services	$2,500	$2,500	$2,700	$2,200	$9,900
Computer rentals	$1,000	$1,200	$1,500	$1,200	$4,900
Pickup and delivery	$500	$500	$600	$400	$2,000
Total sales	**$7,000**	**$7,300**	**$8,300**	**$6,600**	**$29,200**
Operating Expense					
Wages	$3,840	$3,840	$3,840	$3,840	$15,360
Leased equipment	$200	$380	$340	$340	$1,260
Advertising	$375	$175	$150	$225	$925
Supplies	$75	$75	$75	$75	$300
Rent	$525	$525	$525	$525	$2,100
Insurance	$150	$150	$150	$150	$600
Telephone	$285	$285	$285	$285	$1,140
Utilities	$225	$150	$150	$150	$675
Interest		$242	$227	$212	$681
Total operating expense	**$5,675**	**$5,822**	**$5,742**	**$5,802**	**$23,041**
Net Income	**$1,325**	**$1,478**	**$2,558**	**$798**	**$6,159**

THE BUSINESS CENTER
Projected Income Statement
Second Year of Operation

	Quarter 1	Quarter 2	Quarter 3	Quarter 4	Year End
Product Sales					
Office services	$3,300	$3,410	$3,850	$3,080	$13,640
Secretarial services	$2,750	$2,750	$2,970	$2,420	$10,890
Computer rentals	$1,100	$1,320	$1,650	$1,320	$5,390
Pickup and delivery	$550	$550	$660	$440	$2,200
Total sales	**$7,700**	**$8,030**	**$9,130**	**$7,260**	**$32,120**
Operating Expense					
Wages	$4,224	$4,224	$4,224	$4,224	$16,896
Leased equipment	$220	$418	$374	$374	$1,386
Advertising	$412	$193	$165	$248	$1,018
Supplies	$81	$83	$83	$83	$330
Rent	$576	$578	$578	$578	$2,310
Insurance	$165	$165	$165	$165	$660
Telephone	$312	$314	$314	$314	$1,254
Utilities	$247	$165	$165	$165	$742
Interest	$196	$181	$165	$148	$690
Total operating expense	**$6,433**	**$6,321**	**$6,233**	**$6,299**	**$25,286**
Net Income	**$1,267**	**$1,709**	**$2,897**	**$961**	**$6,834**

THE BUSINESS CENTER
Projected Income Statement
Third Year of Operation

	Quarter 1	Quarter 2	Quarter 3	Quarter 4	Year End
Product Sales					
Office services	$3,630	$3,751	$4,235	$3,388	$15,004
Secretarial services	$3,025	$3,025	$3,267	$2,662	$11,979
Computer rentals	$1,210	$1,452	$1,815	$1,452	$5,929
Pickup and delivery	$605	$605	$726	$484	$2,420
Total sales	$8,470	$8,833	$10,043	$7,986	$35,332
Operating Expense					
Wages	$4,646	$4,646	$4,646	$4,646	$18,584
Leased equipment	$241	$460	$411	$411	$1,523
Advertising	$454	$212	$182	$272	$1,120
Supplies	$91	$91	$91	$91	$364
Rent	$635	$635	$635	$635	$2,540
Insurance	$182	$182	$182	$182	$728
Telephone	$345	$345	$345	$345	$1,380
Utilities	$271	$182	$182	$182	$817
Interest	$131	$114	$96	$78	$419
Total operating expense	$6,996	$6,867	$6,770	$6,842	$27,475
Net Income	$1,474	$1,966	$3,273	$1,144	$7,857

■ APPENDIX J: THREE-YEAR PROJECTED BALANCE SHEET WITH PROJECTED RATIOS

THE BUSINESS CENTER
Projected Balance Sheet
Three Years Ending December 31, 20__

	First Year	Second Year	Third Year
Current Assets			
Cash	$17,347	$21,547	$26,499
Total current assets	$17,347	$21,547	$26,499
Current Liabilities			
Notes payable, current	$2,634	$2,905	$2,649
Total current liabilities	$2,634	$2,905	$2,649
Long-Term Liabilities			
Notes payable, long-term	$5,554	$2,649	$00
Total long-term liabilities	$5,554	$2,649	$00
Total liabilities	$8,188	$5,554	$2,649
Net worth	$9,159	$15,993	$23,850
Total Liabilities & Net Worth	$17,347	$21,547	$26,499

THE BUSINESS CENTER
Projected Ratios

	First Year	Second Year	Third Year
Current ratio	6.6:1	7.4:1	10:1
Operating profit margin	21.1%	21.3%	22.2%
Return on equity	67.2%	54.3%	32.7%
Debt to owners' equity	89.4%	34.7%	11.1%
Current liabilities to owners' equity	28.8%	18.2%	11.1%

■ APPENDIX K: PRODUCT LAYOUT

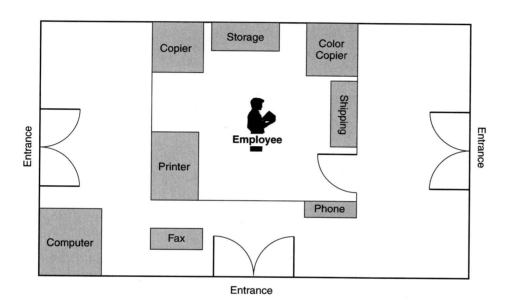

6

OBTAINING THE RIGHT FINANCING FOR YOUR BUSINESS

Money makes money, and the money money makes, makes more money.
Benjamin Franklin

Many of the financial problems plaguing small businesses are avoidable, provided entrepreneurs analyze their own funding needs objectively and with sufficient lead time to act decisively.
Small Business Administration

LEARNING OBJECTIVES

After studying the material in this chapter, you will be able to:

1. Explain the importance of proper financing for a small business.

2. Tell how to estimate financial needs, and explain some principles to follow in obtaining financing.

3. Explain why equity and debt financing are used, and describe the role each plays in the capital structure of a small firm.

4. Distinguish the types of equity and debt securities.

5. Describe some sources of equity financing.

6. Describe some sources of debt financing.

7. Explain what a lender looks for in a borrower.

Roy Morgan—Pioneer in Air Medical Transport Services

Roy Morgan, president of Air Methods Corporation of Englewood, Colorado (www.airmethods.com), was a pioneer in providing rapid air medical transport services. After helping to develop the first hospital helipad in Salt Lake City, at Holy Cross Hospital, he brought in the first patient by helicopter, flying him in on the skids of a Bell 47, which was the method used during the Korean War.

Later, after seeing three seriously burned firefighters waiting for primitive medical attention, he saw the critical need to provide rapid medical response for people working in remote areas. After approaching several Colorado hospitals, Roy interested St. Mary's Hospital in Grand Junction in the project. But first he had to have a helicopter.

Roy and his wife, Dorothy, and friends Austin Clark and Ralph Mulford scraped together enough money to form a corporation and make the down payment on a helicopter. Roy and Dorothy took out a second mortgage on their house; sold a camper, a pickup truck, and stock in Western Airlines; and used their savings account to get the funds. Their friends made similar sacrifices. Air Methods had a Texas company convert the helicopter to provide a medical interior and then started the contract with St. Mary's Hospital AIR LIFE in August 1980.

By 1985, Air Methods had started five new programs in several states. To add another new program with the University of Utah Hospital in Salt Lake City

(www.med.utah.edu/hosp/), Air Methods shareholders expanded to include David and Cheryl Ritchie and Dennis and David Beggrow.

In November 1991, Air Methods merged with Cell Technology (www.celltechnology.com) and became a publicly held corporation. According to Morgan and current chairman and CEO Terry Schreier, "Obtaining access to capital is one big benefit to becoming a public company." By selling shares in 1992, the company raised $7.2 million to help lower debts and increase working capital.

The new arrangement was so successful that by the end of 1992 Air Methods was serving 43 hospitals in 13 states. It had 25 helicopters and five airplanes (all of them medically equipped), 250 employees, and revenues of $18.5 million.

Not surprisingly, success bred competition. By late 1994, there were 217 helicopter ambulance services operating throughout the United States.

Air Methods has managed to remain competitive, however, partly through the judicious use of appropriate financing. In 1995, Air Methods had 19 long-term operating contracts for emergency medical programs in 14 states. Its fleet had expanded to 30 helicopters and 12 airplanes. The average cost of a flight to a hospital was $2,600, which was a small part of the average $160,000 hospital bill of the seriously injured patients the company transported.

By 1997, Air Methods had added a wholly owned subsidiary, Mercy Air Services, Inc. Dedicated flight coordinators, operating out of Mercy Air's Emergency Operations Center in Fontana, California, are available 24 hours a day, seven days a week, to assure prompt response to calls.

Source: Written by Gayle M. Ross from communication and correspondence with Air Methods Corporation. Other sources include Eugene Carlson, "Airborne Medical-Service Firms See Soaring Growth," *The Wall Street Journal,* July 14, 1992, p. B2; Gene G. Marcial, "A Medical Play Gains Altitude," *Business Week,* November 22, 1993, p. 124; Lisa Scott," Air Ambulances, Hospitals Renegotiate," *Modern Healthcare,* May 30, 1994, p. 32; Lee Reeder, "Air Methods Announces New Service," *AirMed,* September/October 1994, p. 32; and the Air Methods home page, accessed March 17, 1998.

The Profile shows the importance of a truth that has been shown repeatedly throughout this text: *Sufficient capital is essential not only for small business start-ups but also for their continued operation.* One main reason for the high failure rate of small businesses is inadequate or improper financing. Too often, insufficient attention has been paid to planning for financial needs, leaving the new business open to sudden but predictable financial crises. Even firms that are sound financially can be destroyed by financial problems, for one difficulty most commonly experienced by rapidly growing firms is that they are unable to finance the investment needed to support sales growth.

■ Estimating Financial Needs

The degree of uncertainty surrounding a small firm's long-term financial needs primarily depends on whether the business is already operating or is just starting, as mentioned in the Profile. If a business has an operating history, its future needs can be estimated with relative accuracy, even with substantial growth.

Even for an existing business, however, an in-depth analysis of its *permanent* financial requirements can be valuable. It may show the current method of financing the business to be unsound or unnecessarily risky. As a general rule, small businesses' long-lived assets, such as buildings and other facilities, should be financed with long-term loans, while short-lived assets, such as inventory or accounts receivable, should be financed with short-term loans.

Principles to Follow

Fixed assets are those that are of a relatively permanent nature and are necessary for the functioning of the business.

Working capital is current assets, less current liabilities, that a firm uses to produce goods and services, and to finance the extension of credit to customers.

A new business, or a major expansion of an existing business, should be evaluated with great care, paying particular attention to its capital requirements. For example, the firm's **fixed assets** should be financed with equity funds, or with debt funds having a maturity approximately equal to the productive life of the asset.

No business, however, can be financed entirely with debt funding, nor would such a capitalization be desirable—even if creditors were willing to lend all the funds required. Such a capital structure would be extremely risky, both for the creditors and for the business. This is especially true of **working capital,** which includes the current assets, less current liabilities, that a firm uses to produce goods and services and to finance the extension of credit to customers. These assets include items such as cash, accounts receivable, and inventories. Management of working capital is always a central concern for managers of small firms because they are often undercapitalized and overdependent on uninterrupted cash receipts to pay for recurring expenses. Therefore, small business managers must accurately estimate their working capital needs in advance and obtain sufficient financial resources to cover these needs, plus a buffer for unexpected emergencies.

Using Cash Budgets

An important tool small business managers can use to project working capital needs is a **cash budget.** Such a budget estimates what the out-of-pocket expenses will be during the next year to produce a product(s) for sale and when revenues from these sales are to be collected. In most businesses, sales are not constant over the year, so revenues vary a great deal from one period to another, while the costs of producing them tend to be relatively constant. For example, most retailers have their greatest sales period from Thanksgiving to Christmas. Yet, if they extend their own credit, payments are not received until the following January or February—or even later. Also, small producers may have produced the goods during the previous summer and had to bear the out-of-pocket costs of production for up to six months before actually receiving cash payments.

In general, therefore, when sales are made on credit, *the firm must carry the costs of production itself for an extended period.* A cash budget can help the manager predict when these financing needs will be the greatest and plan the firm's funding accordingly. An accurate assessment of seasonal financing needs is especially important if commercial bank loans are used, since bankers usually require a borrower to be free of bank debt at least once a year.

> **Cash budgets** project working capital needs by estimating what out-of-pocket expenses will be incurred and when revenues from these sales are to be collected.

■ REASONS FOR USING EQUITY AND DEBT FINANCING

Regardless of the type or size of the business, there are really only two sources of financing: equity financing and debt financing. While **equity** is the owner's share of the firm's assets, the nature of this claim depends on the legal form of ownership. For proprietorships and partnerships, the claim on the assets of the firm is that they are the same as the owner's personal assets. Equity financing in a corporation is evidenced by shares of either common or preferred **stock.**

Common stockholders are the real owners of a corporation, and their financial claim is to the profit left after all other claims against the business have been met. Because they almost always retain the right to vote for company directors and/or on other important issues, common stockholders exercise effective control over the management of the firm.

Preferred stockholders, on the other hand, have a claim to the firm's profits that must be paid before any dividends can be distributed to the common stockholders; but they often pay for this superior claim by giving up their voting rights.

The other kind of capital, or funding, that a firm uses is **debt financing,** which comes from lenders, who will be repaid at a specified interest rate within an agreed-on time span. The lenders' income does not vary with the success of the business—unless the business defaults on its debts—while the stockholders' does.

As discussed in Chapter 3, capital can also be raised by using a limited partnership, which combines the benefits of both debt and equity financing.

> **Equity** is an owner's share of the assets of a company. In a corporation, it is represented by shares of common or preferred stock.
>
> **Stock** represents ownership in a corporation.
>
> **Common stockholders** are the owners of a corporation, with claim to a share of its profits and the right to vote on certain corporate decisions.
>
> **Preferred stockholders** are owners with a superior claim to a share of the firm's profits, but they often have no voting rights.
>
> **Debt financing** comes from lenders, who will be repaid at a specified interest rate within a specified time span.

Role of Equity Financing

The role of equity financing is to serve as a buffer that protects creditors from loss in case of financial difficulty. In the event of default on a contractual obligation (such as an interest payment), creditors have a legally enforceable claim on the assets of the firm. It takes preference over claims of the common and preferred stockholders. From an investor's point of view, common stock investments should have a higher financial return than debt investments because equity securities are riskier.

Role of Debt Financing

With debt financing, principal and interest payments are legally enforceable claims against the business. Therefore, they entail substantial risk for the firm (or for the entrepreneur if the debt is guaranteed by personal wealth). Despite the risks involved, however, small firms use debt financing for several reasons. First, the cost of interest paid on debt capital is usually lower than the cost of outside equity, and interest payments are tax-deductible expenses. Second, an entrepreneur may be able to raise more total capital with debt funding than from equity sources alone. Finally, since debt payments are fixed costs, any remaining profits belong solely to the owners. This last strategy, employing a fixed charge to increase the residual return to common stockholders, is referred to as employing **financial leverage.**

One type of debt financing that is becoming more popular is leasing facilities and equipment from someone outside the business instead of buying them. A **lease** is a contract that permits you to use someone else's property, such as real estate, equipment, or other facilities, for a specified time period. While a lease is not usually classified as debt, it is in many respects financially very similar.

From the small business owner's point of view, the benefits of a lease are that (1) the payments are tax deductible, and (2) it may be possible for the business to lease equipment when it would be unable to secure debt financing to purchase it. A growing number of small firms are signing up for the extra services leasing can provide.

> For example, Ryder Commercial Leasing & Services (www.ryder.com) frees a small company of the paperwork of buying and operating vehicles. It handles the equipment, drivers, routing, and warehousing of trucks—that is, it performs the entire distribution function.[1]

■ TYPES OF DEBT AND EQUITY SECURITIES

Small companies use many types of securities, some of which are described below. This listing is incomplete but sufficient to illustrate the variety of financial sources that is a hallmark of the American financial system. Potential small business owners should remember that if they have a viable project, financing can be obtained from some source!

Equity Securities

To start operating, all firms must have some equity capital. In corporations, **common stock,** which represents the owners' interest, usually consists of many identical shares, each of which gives the holder one vote in all corporate elections. (See Figure 6–1 for an example of a share of stock in a new small business.) Common stockholders have no enforceable claim to dividends, and the liquidity of the investment will depend largely on whether there is a public market for the firm's stock.

A corporation may also issue **preferred stock,** with a fixed par value (the value assigned in the corporation's charter, usually $100 per share). It entitles the holder to a fixed dividend payment, usually expressed as a percentage of par value, such as 8 percent (equal to $8 per year). This dividend is not automatic; it must be declared by the firm's board of directors before it can be paid. Nor is it a legally enforceable claim against the business. However, no dividends can be paid to the common stockholders until preferred stock dividends have been paid. Moreover, preferred dividends that have been missed typically cumulate and must be paid in full before payments can be made to common stockholders. Preferred stock usually conveys no voting rights to its holder.

The 1990s have been called the decade of the stockholder in the United States. In fact, there were more than 85 million Americans who were investors in the stock market

Financial leverage is using fixed-charge financing, usually debt, to fund a business's operations.

A **lease** is a contract that permits use of someone else's property for a specified time period.

Common stock, representing the owners' interest, usually consists of many identical shares, each of which gives the holder one vote in all corporate elections.

Preferred stock has a fixed par value and a fixed dividend payment, expressed as a percentage of par value.

Figure 6–1

A Share of Stock in a Small Business

Source: Courtesy of Dot and Jiggs Martin of Bloomin' Lollipops, Inc.

in January 1999.[2] Part of the reason for this large number is the ease with which one can purchase stock.

> For example, one can use the "Mobile Trader," a cellular phone–sized device, with a wireless modem, that attaches to any laptop, notebook, or desktop computer. Windows-based software enables users to buy or sell stock, bonds, stock options, futures, or mutual funds.[3]

A new and emerging kind of equity financing is the Small Company Offering Registration (SCOR). SCOR (www.scor-net.com) is a uniform registration, permitted in most states, that lets a company raise up to $1 million by selling common stock directly to the public. The price per share must be at least $5. If state laws permit SCOR, companies can trade their common stock on NASDAQ's electronic OTC bulletin board (www.nasdaq.com).[4] SCOR offerings are important to small businesses because they cut through antiquated legal barriers and facilitate buying and selling small business investments.

> For example, when he cofounded Cal-Pearson Corporation in Bristol, Rhode Island, Chris Bent had little more than a few maxed-out credit cards. A year later, however, he had plans to raise $825,000 by selling 165,000 shares of the company for $5 each. He gave much of the credit for his success in his yacht-building business to DataMerge, Inc.'s, *Raising Capital Through SCOR* software package (www.datamerge.com).[5]

Debt Securities

Debt securities are usually in the form of bonds or loans. In general, publicly issued debt (such as bonds or commercial paper) is more commonly used by larger firms, whereas small companies rely more on private loans from financial institutions such as commercial banks, insurance companies, or finance companies.

A distinction is usually made among **short-term securities** (those with maturities of one year or less), **intermediate-term securities** (those with maturities of one to five years), and **long-term securities** (those with maturities of more than five years). As we will discuss more thoroughly in the next section, commercial banks prefer to make short- and intermediate-term loans; other financial institutions, such as insurance companies, prefer to make long-term loans.

If a small business manager negotiates a loan from a bank or other single lender, the amount of the loan is simply the amount borrowed. However, if securities are sold to the public or are privately placed with several lenders, most companies will issue the debt in the form of **bonds.** These have a standard denomination, method of interest payment, and method of principal repayment.

Long-term debt secured by real estate property is a **mortgage loan,** whereas a **chattel mortgage loan** is debt backed by some physical asset other than land, such as machinery, transportation equipment, or inventory. Furthermore, many of the "unsecured" loans that banks extend to small businesses require personal guarantees by the manager or directors of the firm. Such loans are implicitly secured by the personal assets of these individuals.

■ SOURCES OF EQUITY FINANCING

Obtaining sufficient equity funding is a constant challenge for most small businesses, particularly for proprietorships and partnerships. The only way to increase the equity of these two types of firms is either to retain earnings or to accept outsiders as co-owners.

> This is what David Getson did in 1997 when he wanted to start *Icon,* a bimonthly magazine focusing on "ideas" for young men. He brought in a fellow Princeton graduate who invested $25,000 as a partner. After seven issues the magazine had a circulation of 150,000.[6]

For corporations, the choices may be more varied. Some of the more frequently used sources of equity funding are discussed here.

Self

Overall, owners of small firms rely more on their own capital and less on external debt capital than owners of larger firms. Also, small firms are more dependent on short-term debt than on long-term debt. In fact, most small companies use external financing only occasionally. However, those few firms that experience rapid growth, or those that must maintain a high level of accounts receivable, use external financing frequently.[7]

People who start a small business must therefore invest a substantial amount of their own funds in it before seeking outside funding. Outside investors want to see some of the owner's own money committed to the business as some assurance that she or he will not simply give up operating the business and walk away from it. Many owners also prefer using their own funds because they feel uncomfortable risking other people's money or because they do not want to share control of the firm. In summary, for the smallest firms, owner capital is the most important source of financing.

> Dr. Richard Meyer, an Albuquerque, New Mexico, consultant, found that entrepreneurs can commonly finance as much as $100,000 of start-up costs with the help of family and friends. However, he found in the latest National Census of Early-Stage Capital Financing that the gap in financing still unfilled is the gap between $100,000 and $1 million.[8]

Short-term securities mature in one year or less.

Intermediate-term securities mature in one to five years.

Long-term securities mature after five years or longer.

Bonds are a form of debt security with a standard denomination, method of interest payment, and method of principal repayment.

A **mortgage loan** is long-term debt that is secured by real property.

A **chattel mortgage loan** is debt backed by some physical asset other than land, such as machinery, equipment, or inventory.

Small Business Investment Companies (SBICs)

Small business investment companies (SBICs) are private firms licensed and regulated by the SBA to make "venture" or "risk" investments to small firms. SBICs supply equity capital and extend unsecured loans to small enterprises that meet their investment criteria. Because they are privately capitalized themselves (although backed by the SBA), SBICs are intended to be profit-making institutions, so they tend not to make very small investments.

SBICs finance small firms by making straight loans and by making equity-type investments that give the SBIC actual or potential ownership of the small firm's equity securities. SBICs also provide management assistance to the businesses they help finance.

SBICs prefer to make loans to small firms rather than equity investments, so we will discuss them further under the heading "Sources of Debt Financing" later in this chapter.

Small business investment companies (SBICs) are private firms licensed and regulated by the SBA to make "venture" investments in small firms.

"I run a small investment firm. Unfortunately, it used to be a large investment firm!"

(*Source:* Copyright 1989 by Doug Blackwell.)

Venture Capitalists

Entrepreneurs often complain that it is "lonely at the top." If so, a venture capitalist can serve as a form of security blanket when needed. Traditionally, venture capital firms have been partnerships composed of wealthy individuals who make equity investments in small firms with opportunities for fast growth, such as Federal Express (www.fedex.com), Apple Computer (www.apple.com), and Microsoft (www.microsoft.com) once were. In general, they have preferred to back fast-growth industries (usually high-tech ones), since the ultimate payoff from backing a successful new business with a new high-tech product can be astronomical.

> Juniper Networks Inc. (www.juniper.net) is an example of this type of relationship. Juniper is a start-up company that has boldly entered the highly competitive networking and telecommunications industry. The company claims to have the solution to high-speed networking technology that will greatly outpace the current market leader, Cisco (www.cisco.com). Juniper's product is expected to "run a hundred times faster than current models."[9] Backers think the new technology will help deal with the overcrowding of Internet traffic.
>
> Juniper received sufficient venture capital from major telecommunications equipment makers to get started.

Venture capitalists are *not a good source of funding for new businesses—especially the mom-and-pop variety*. At least that seems to be suggested by the fact that more than two-thirds of all venture capital goes to expand existing businesses rather than to start new ones.[10] Also, these investors tend to prefer high-tech areas. For example, in 1997, three out of four dollars of venture capital went to just six such areas.[11] In fact, *29 percent of all such investment* went to firms in Silicon Valley.

However, a new generation of small venture capitalists is jumping in to fill the gap left by the departure of the traditional financiers. These new firms are returning to the more traditional relationship with small businesses: They are acting as business incubators and hands-on advisers.[12] These and other venture capitalists are now "looking South" for investment opportunities. Total investment in the Southeast rose 17 percent in 1996, and the region attracted 10 percent of all such investments during 1997.[13] The reason for the shift is that during the last five years the Southeast has gathered together the critical pieces needed to lure venture capitalists, namely, strong universities—with a focus on engineering research and other aspects of technology—along with accountants, bankers, and lawyers who are adept at start-ups of small businesses.

Foreign stock exchanges are also sources of venture capital. They tend to have easier regulations for listing, require less paperwork, and have lower legal and administrative costs, as the following example shows.

> The Vancouver (Canada) Stock Exchange (VSE) is a popular source of venture capital for many small U.S. firms. The VSE (www.vse.com) specializes in natural resource exploration companies and small new technology firms. The VSE has a proven record of performance, as shown by its fourth-place standing (after the NASDAQ, New York, and Toronto exchanges) in trading volume among North American stock exchanges. It has a two-tier system that recognizes the stages of development of companies as they grow and mature. Its rules and regulations are designed to (1) provide a niche for venture companies and (2) maintain the integrity of the marketplace. Also, by using the VSE—rather than making deals with private U.S. venture capitalists—entrepreneurs can keep greater control of their businesses.[14]

Many venture capitalists rely more heavily on the executive summary of a business plan (see Chapter 5) than on the plan itself in making investment decisions. So many long and complex plans are presented to them that they need a quick way to evaluate proposals in order to quickly discard those they do not want to consider further. The percentage of business plans accepted by venture capitalists for investment purposes is very low.

Yet during 1997, venture capitalists invested a record $13 billion in over two thousand deals.[15] In addition to money, the capitalists provide management skills and business contacts. For example, the Center for Entrepreneurial Leadership, launched in Kansas City in 1992, is also trying to help: it launched a Fellows Program to help venture capitalists and entrepreneurs understand each other's needs.[16]

You should be aware when approaching either a venture capitalist or an SBIC for possible funding that neither will view your business the same way you do. While you may be content to remain relatively small in order to retain personal control, this is the last thing a professional investor will want. An SBIC or a venture capitalist will invest in a firm with the expectation of ultimately selling the company either to the investing public (through an initial public stock offering) or to a larger company. This potential conflict of goals can be very damaging to the new business owner unless the differences are explicitly addressed before external financing is accepted. We alluded to this danger earlier in the book in our discussion of the problems arising from "poorly planned growth."

Angel Capitalists

Angel capitalists or **business angels** are wealthy local businesspeople and other investors who may be external sources of equity funding.

Entrepreneurs have always tapped financial patrons, such as friends, relatives, and wealthy individuals, for beginning capital. These **angel capitalists** or **business angels** are a diverse group of high-net-worth individuals who will invest part of their assets in high-risk, high-return entrepreneurial ventures. The University of New Hampshire's Center for Venture Research estimated that as many as 90 percent of small businesses are started with the financial help of friends and relatives.[17] It has also been estimated that angel capitalists provide up to four times as much total investment capital for small businesses as do the professional venture capital firms. While angels have always been around, fortunes made in the high-tech industries have spawned more angels than ever before.

> For example, when Dina Bitton needed financing for her new software company, DBStar, she shunned venture capitalists in favor of a "Band of Angels." This group of private investors provided $1 million of the fledgling company's $1.5 million in capital. The group—which had 65 members—meets once a month for dinner and to hear the "pitch" from a potential entrepreneur.[18]

Other Sources

In some cases, small business entrepreneurs may be able to acquire financial assistance from business incubators, employee stock ownership plans, their own customers, bartering, and others.

Business Incubators   According to the National Business Incubation Association (NBIA) (www.nbia.org), a private, not-for-profit organization in Athens, Ohio, business incubation is "a dynamic process of business enterprise development."[19] **Business incubators** nurture young firms and help them to survive and grow during the start-up period when they are most vulnerable. Hands-on management assistance, access to financing, and orchestrated exposure to critical business or technical support services are provided. Incubators offer entrepreneurial firms shared office services, access to equipment, flexible leases, and expandable space—all under one roof.

Business incubators are old buildings that have been renovated, subdivided, and rented to new companies by groups desiring to assist young enterprises until they are healthy enough to go out on their own.

The main goal of an incubation program is to produce successful graduates, that is, businesses that are financially viable and freestanding when they leave the incubator. While the usual incubation period is two to three years, 30 percent of incubator clients typically graduate each year.

Like venture capitalists, incubators usually apply some type of selection criteria to prospective clients. Some accept a mix of industries, but others concentrate on specialized industry niches. According to NBIA research, incubator clients may be classified as follows:

- Service—40%.
- Light manufacturing—23%.
- Technology—22%.
- Research—7%.
- Others—8%.

The largest study ever conducted of business incubators was finished in November 1997. It was conducted by the University of Michigan (www.umich.edu), the NBIA, Ohio University (www.ohio.edu), and the Southern Technology Council (www.southern.org/stcindex.htm), and funded by the U.S. Department of Commerce's Economic Development Administration (www.doc.gov/eda). The findings indicated that incubators gave a five-to-one return on investment.[20] Other findings were:

1. The average firm's sales increased more than 400 percent from the time it entered to the time it left the incubator.
2. The average annual growth in sales for firms of all types was $240,000 per year.
3. On average, 84 percent of the firms that "graduate" from incubators remain in the community.
4. While different types of incubators have different effects, firms from technological incubators create more jobs than those from other types.

Business incubators are a relatively new concept in economic development. They were started in 1980 with 12 programs, but by 1997 there were more than 800 of them operating in the United States.[21] Incubators have become so successful that some are themselves attracting venture capital, as the following example illustrates.

> Foundation Capital, a Menlo Park, California, venture capitalist (www.foundationcapital.com), has invested $1 million in Idealab, an incubator formed in 1996 in Pasadena, California, to nurture Internet-related companies.[22] Foundation's infusion of capital partly reflects how eager venture capitalists have become to invest in Internet-related companies.

Employee Stock Ownership Plans (ESOPs)   For existing small businesses, another source of financing is **employee stock ownership plans (ESOPs)**. The company reaps tax advantages and cash flow advantages from selling shares to workers. The plan also makes employees think like owners, tending to make them more productive.

Your Customers   Your customers are another source of financing. It happens often, and in many ways. For example, mail-order vendors, especially those who use TV commercials, require the customer to pay when ordering; they then have that money for operations, while the customer waits several weeks for delivery of the goods. Also, it is customary for artisans and contractors to require a substantial down payment before beginning to produce the product.

> For example, Diane Allen, a portrait artist, requires a down payment of one-third of the total price before she will begin a portrait. This money not only assures that the contract will be honored but also can be used to buy supplies and cover other expenses.

Bartering   **Barter** is an increasingly popular method of financing small businesses. In its simplest form, bartering consists of two companies swapping items of roughly equal value. But as this age-old business practice has become more popular—partly because of the competitive global business environment—bartering has become more creative. Now business owners trade everything from employee perquisites to corporate airfare with barter credits.

Bartering lends itself to many uses, such as (1) business travel, (2) debt collection, (3) closing a sale, (4) employee perks and bonuses, and (5) a line of credit. As bartering has become more popular—and complex—corporate barter networks, or regional trade exchanges, have developed to provide the needed exchange mechanism.

Bartering exchanges were largely considered disreputable in the 1970s and early 1980s because some would brag about "skirting income-tax reporting laws."[23] But a 1982 law required barter exchange, for the first time, to report the value of their transactions to the IRS, where they are subject to the same tax treatment as a cash transaction.

The International Reciprocal Trade Association (IRTA), an industry group located in Chicago (www.irta.net), reported that in 1997 there were as many as 686 barter groups, serving more than 400,000 business clients by brokering products and services valued at an estimated $9.1 billion (see Figure 6–2 for more details).

■ SOURCES OF DEBT FINANCING

Although, as stated earlier, most small business owners rely more on owner funding than on debt financing, research by the SBA and Federal Reserve Board found that a majority of them had used such funding in the past.[24] This is true at least in part because there are so many sources for such financing, several of which are described here.

Trade Credit

Trade credit refers to purchases of inventory, equipment, and/or supplies on an open account in accordance with customary terms for retail and wholesale trade. In general, trade

Figure 6–2
Growth in Bartering

Total dollar amount bartered by North American trade exchanges, in billions.

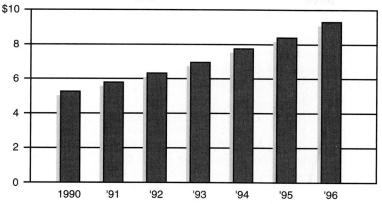

Source: International Reciprocal Trade Association, as reported in Eleena De Lisser and Rodney Ho, "Barter Exchanges Say Future Looks Promising," *The Wall Street Journal,* November 12, 1997, p. B2.

credit is one of the most important sources of debt financing for small business because it arises spontaneously in the normal course of operating the business. Firms seeking new and expanded wholesale and retail markets for goods have the option of using **consignment selling.** Small auto, major appliance, and farm equipment dealers consider consignments a form of trade credit because payments to suppliers are made only when the products are sold rather than when they are received in stock.

With **consignment selling,** payments to suppliers are made only when the products are sold, rather than when they are received in stock.

Commercial and Other Financial Institutions

Traditional financial institutions may provide the small business owner with borrowed funds. The proportion of funds such institutions make available ranges from 25 to 60 percent of the value of the total assets. Usually, the cost of such financing is higher than that of other alternatives, but such funds may be the most accessible.

Commercial Banks   Commercial banks are the dominant supplier of external financing to small firms. In fact, a few years ago, an exhaustive study found that 90 percent of small and midsized businesses identified their local bank as their primary financial institution for banking and other financial services. While commercial banks are still a good source for small borrowers who have funds of their own and proven successful financial experience, rarely will they make conventional loans to a start-up business. Although banks realize that these small firms are a strong market, with strong demand, they also know they don't provide the return sought by banks. In other words, "small business loans are . . . regarded as expensive to service and marginally profitable."[25]

Banking institutions charge a higher rate of interest—usually two or three percentage points above the prime rate*—to small companies to offset the greater risk; the result is a greater return. Additionally, some financial institutions specializing in small business loans become more knowledgeable and therefore more efficient.

---

*The prime rate (the rate banks charge their best commercial customers) is published periodically in *The Wall Street Journal.* In October 1998, the prime rate was 8.25 percent.

The tendency for banks to service only existing accounts for small firms was emphasized by Charles Freeman, CEO of a New York financial services company that specializes in commercial loans backed by the U.S. Small Business Administration. "Banks are looking to expand credit, but they are mostly expanding existing credit lines, not opening new ones."[26] The lack of the collateral required to secure the debt causes many problems for small firms.

During the late 1990s, however, the number of new banks escalated as entrepreneurs sought the new lending opportunities created by consolidations in the banking industry. A new study concluded that these start-ups are more friendly toward small firms.[27] Part of the reason for this change is a "drastic reduction in paperwork made possible—in part—by better computer technology for credit analysis." A related trend has been the interest shown in women business owners.[28]

A **line of credit** permits a business to borrow up to a set amount without red tape.

If your business is successful, you may want to open a **line of credit** with your bank. This is an arrangement whereby the bank permits an ongoing business to borrow up to a set amount—say $50,000—at any time during the year without further red tape. The business writes checks against its account, and the bank honors them up to the maximum amount. Usually, except for firms with an exceptionally high credit rating, the business is required to pay up all unsecured debts for a short period—say 10 to 15 days—each year to prove its creditworthiness. This is usually done when the firm's cash level is at its highest in order not to inconvenience the borrower too much.

A well-prepared business plan, as described in Chapter 5, should help lower a firm's interest rate and possibly even extend the term of the loan. Even then, however, you may find it more advantageous to finance the business with a personal loan.

Credit Cards   Another form of credit line is the use of credit cards to finance your business. In fact, for companies with fewer than 500 employees, the use of credit cards to finance operations increased from about 18 percent in 1993 to around 33 percent in 1997, while bank loans declined from 50 percent to around 38 percent.[29]

Insurance Companies   Insurance companies may be a good source of funds for a small firm, especially real estate ventures. The business owner can go directly to the company or contact its agent or a mortgage banker. While insurance companies have traditionally engaged in debt financing, they have more recently demanded that they be permitted to buy an equity share in the business as part of the total package.

Small Business Administration (SBA)

One primary purpose of the SBA is to help small firms find financing, including those having trouble securing conventional financing, especially at reasonable rates. Many small firms need term loans of up to 25 years, but most lenders limit their lending to short-term loans.

The SBA helps these small firms in several ways, including offering guarantees on loans made by private lenders and offering direct specialized financing.[30] As indicated earlier, it also provides some venture capital through SBICs. The SBA-licensed SBICs also include some **specialized SBICs** (called **SSBICs**) to assist socially or economically disadvantaged enterprises, which, in turn, provide future capital through equity-purchased long-term loans or loan guarantees. Much attention is currently being given to SBICs by Congress and the President.

Specialized small business investment companies (SSBICs) assist socially and economically disadvantaged businesses with venture capital.

Guaranteed Loans   The SBA guarantees 30 to 40 percent of all long-term loans to small businesses under its 7(a) program. The loans can be used to (1) purchase land, buildings, or equipment; (2) provide working capital; (3) refinance existing debt (under certain conditions); or (4) provide seasonal lines of credit. To qualify, a business must be unable to obtain private financing on reasonable terms but must have a good chance of success. Also, the borrower must meet the size standards shown in Table 6–1.

Table 6–1

Eligibility for SBA-Guaranteed Business Loans by Industry Type

Type of Industry	Restrictions
Manufacturing	Maximum number of employees may range from 500 to 1,500, depending on the industry in which the applicant is primarily engaged.
Wholesaling	Maximum number of employees not to exceed 100.
Services	Annual receipts not exceeding $3.5 million to $13.5 million, depending on the industry in which the applicant is primarily engaged.
Retailing	Annual sales or receipts not exceeding $3.5 million to $13.5 million, depending on the industry.
Agriculture	Annual receipts not exceeding $0.5 million to $3.5 million, depending on the industry.

Source: Small Business Administration Web site (www.sba.gov/financing/7aloan.html), accessed July 18, 1998.

With the SBA's guarantee program, a bank actually extends a loan to a small firm, with the SBA guaranteeing repayment for a certain percentage of the loan. The amount guaranteed is usually 75 to 80 percent. The maximum rate the bank can charge is the prime rate plus 2.25 percent on loans for less than seven years or prime plus 2.75 percent on loans for seven years or more.

The procedure to be followed is for the business owner to contact a bank (preferably one with experience in SBA lending) to request an SBA loan. The following documents should already be prepared to expedite the process:[31]

- A narrative business plan with profit/loss projections for three years.
- Résumés for key managers and owners.
- An outline showing how the loan will be used, including an itemized list of assets to be purchased.
- At least three years of historical financial statements on the company and personal financial statements for all owners.
- A proposed collateral structure.

The bank then submits the application directly to the SBA for approval. The SBA also has a few other basic financial requirements. For existing businesses, the SBA generally looks for a debt-to-net worth ratio (that is, total liabilities divided by total assets) of not more than 3:1 (three to one) after the loan is granted. A start-up business must have at least 30 percent equity invested by the owners. The SBA looks for (1) management ability and experience in the field of operations, (2) at least a simple, but feasible business plan, and (3) the ability to repay the loan. Also, all owners of 20 percent or more of a business must personally guarantee SBA loans.

Specialized Programs   The SBA also has several specialized programs. First, there are special government contracts to be awarded to small, disadvantaged business subcontractors, along with counseling and bonding assistance. The small business must be at least 51 percent owned by a "socially or economically disadvantaged individual." Included in this group are African-Americans, Native Americans, Hispanic Americans, Asian Pacific Americans, and Subcontinent Asian Americans.

A second special program is the SBA Low Documentation (LowDoc) Loan Program (www.sba.gov/financing/lowdoc). It can be used for loans of less than $100,000. While the borrower must still work with a bank, the documentation is much less stringent. The LowDoc puts more emphasis on the borrower's credit history, projected cash flow, and character, and less on collateral and equity.

The SBA also has a CAPLine Revolving Line of Credit initiative (called CAPLine for short). Its purpose is to help small companies obtain short-term working capital through an established line of credit (www.sba.gov/financing/frcaplines.html).

Finally, the "Women's Prequalification Loan Program" (www.sba.gov/financing/prequal) allows women business owners to receive prequalification from the SBA for a loan guarantee of up to $250,000 *before* going to a bank. Going directly to the SBA is a great advantage in saved time and effort. As with the LowDoc program, the primary focus is on character, credit history, and experience. The SBA guarantees the bank up to 80 percent in loans up to $100,000 and up to 75 percent on loans from $100,000 to $250,000. To be eligible, the business must be at least 51 percent owned, operated, and managed by women, have sales of less than $5 million, and employ fewer than 100 people.

Small Business Investment Companies (SBICs)

In addition to indirect equity financing, as previously discussed, SBICs also make qualified SBA loans. The SBA matches each dollar an SBIC puts into a loan. Loans are usually made for a period of 5 to 10 years. An SBIC may stipulate that it be given a certain portion of stock purchase warrants or stock options, or it may make a combination of a loan and a stock purchase. The latter combination has been preferred.

Recent changes in SBICs have created a surge in their popularity. They are no longer limited to the sale of debentures but are now permitted to sell securities similar to preferred stock. One must remember, however, that SBA funds are federal government monies and may dry up as attitudes in Washington change.[32]

U.S. Department of Agriculture (USDA)

The U.S. Department of Agriculture (USDA) (www.usda.gov) has also started investing in small business. With its novel programs to develop nonfood, nonfeed uses of farm products, the department has spent millions of dollars on large and small businesses to induce them to come up with innovative products.

A **green product** is an environmentally friendly product offered for sale commercially.

> One example was an enterprising 11-year-old in Mankato, Minnesota, who developed a product—which felt like wood and looked like granite—from shredded newspapers, blended with glue in her mother's blender (which didn't survive the experiment). A local group of investors, which was looking for a "**green product**" to commercialize, adopted the girl's idea. But financing was a problem, so the USDA offered a $1 million loan if the company could raise the same amount, which it easily did.
>
> According to Scott Taylor, vice president of Phenix Biocomposites, Inc. (www.phenixmfg.com), "The stamp of approval from a prestigious body like the USDA helped us raise $4.5 million." The company began full-scale production on May 16, 1994.[33]

■ WHAT LENDERS LOOK FOR

What do lenders look for when considering a loan to a small business? In essence the basics apply today as they did in the past. First, if the loan is for a new business, the lender wants

---

Figure 6–3
How to Improve the Entrepreneur-Investor Relationship

There are at least five steps you should take in order to assure a good working relationship with the investor:

1. Establish the range of funds you will need.
2. Identify the investor's skills and abilities that could help advance your venture.
3. Find an investor with interests and personality traits similar to yours.
4. Find a long-term investor, not one who wants to "make a quick buck" and get out.
5. Find an investor with more to offer you than just money, so that you may avoid having to hire outside consultants.

There are certain things the investor should find out about you:

1. Can you and the investor work together as a team?
2. Do you appear to be flexible and willing to accept new management if the project is highly successful?
3. Are you truly committed to this endeavor, and are you willing to expend the energy and resources to make it a success?
4. Can you accept constructive criticism, feedback, and assistance?
5. Do you have definite, fixed, realistic goals, and where do you plan to be in, say, one year? Five years? Ten years?

Source: International Reciprocal Trade Association, as reported in *The Wall Street Journal,* November 26, 1990. Reprinted with permission of *The Wall Street Journal,* © 1990 Dow Jones & Company, Inc. All Rights Reserved Worldwide.

to see if you can live within the income of the business. Given your expected revenues and expenses, will you be able to repay the loan? How much collateral can you put up to insure the lender against your inability to repay?

Second, if the money is for an existing business, the lender will look at its track record. If there are problems, you will be expected to explain what's going to happen to make a difference in the future. Do you have a new business plan? Are you going to buy new equipment or technology? Is there a new marketing plan?

To a large extent, your ability to attract money will depend on the lender's perception of your character as well as your ability to return the money. First, *income* is important. Second, the lender will also look at your *stability,* to see how long you've lived in a given residence or neighborhood, as well as how long you've worked at a particular job or run a business.

In summary, your request for financing will almost certainly be checked by some major credit company, using computerized reference services. Therefore, knowing that your credit record will be checked immediately by the computer, you should ask for a credit printout (which can be obtained free or for a few dollars) before you apply for funds. This will give you an opportunity to correct any errors or misunderstandings in your credit record.

Figure 6–3 provides some steps to use in developing a better relationship with investors, along with some questions the investor should ask you. Remember, while lenders should have an interest in how financially sound your business is, *they should not have a voice in managing it.* If you permit them to, they in reality become partners and must share responsibility for any failures.

What You Should Have Learned

1. Providing for financial needs is crucial to the success of a small business, which may be under-capitalized and living hand to mouth. Sufficient short- and long-term financing is needed to provide for fluctuations in sales or an unexpected business slump.

2. For a start-up venture, the assets of a business should be financed with equity or with debt funds having a maturity about equal to the productive life of the asset. A useful tool for estimating financial needs is the cash budget, which projects the amounts and timing of expenses and revenue for the year.

3. The two major sources of funds are equity and debt financing. Equity financing never has to be repaid and provides an interest in the business, including a share of the profits and a voice in decision making. Debt financing, which must be repaid whether the company is profitable or not, is less expensive than equity financing, since interest payments are tax deductible, and it does not require as high a rate of return.

4. The most frequently used types of equity securities are common and preferred stock. Common stock conveys voting rights but has no enforceable claim to dividends. Preferred stock entitles the share-holder to a fixed rate of dividend whenever profits are sufficient, but preferred stockholders usually have no voting rights. Debt securities include short-, intermediate-, and long-term loans and bonds. Loans made by a lender in standard denominations are called bonds. Long-term debt secured by real property is a mortgage loan, whereas a chattel mortgage loan is backed by some other physical asset. A lease can also be a form of debt financing.

5. Sources of equity financing include funds from the owner, family and friends, small business invest-ment companies (SBICs), venture capitalists, angel capitalists, business incubators, employees, customers, and bartering.

6. Sources of debt financing include trade credit, commercial and other financial institutions—including commercial banks and insurance companies—the SBA, SBICs, the U.S. Depart-ment of Agriculture, and the Economic Develop-ment Administration (EDA). The SBA finances business ventures through guaranteed loans.

7. When deciding whether or not to finance a small business, lenders look for factors such as ability to repay the debt, the owner's and the business's financial and business track record, and the owner's income, stability, and debt management.

Questions for Discussion

1. Discuss the basic rules to follow in financing a business venture.

2. Why should small business managers assess working capital needs in advance?

3. What are some reasons small business entrepre-neurs use equity financing? Debt financing?

4. What are the factors that determine the classifica-tion of debt securities?

5. List and discuss the primary sources of equity financing.

6. List and discuss the primary sources of debt financing.

7. Compare equity financing to debt financing.

8. Evaluate the role of the SBA in providing operating and venture capital.

CASE 6-1

ELLA WILLIAMS: MAKING IT ON HER OWN

After working for 13 years in various departments at Hughes Aircraft Corporation, Ella Williams, believing in herself, decided to form a small business of her own. With the help of the SBA's Section 8(a), she took out a $65,000 second mortgage on her house and founded Aegir Systems in Oxnard, California, to provide engineering, environmental, multimedia, and computer services to the aircraft industry.

She struggled for three years—often scrounging aluminum cans from dumpsters to earn money to support herself and her two children. Her daughter was mortified, she said. "But she sure was interested in the money when I cashed them in."

It was an uphill battle to convince white-male–dominated firms that a black-woman–owned company could deliver the technical services she offered. Although she eventually proved to them that she could, it took three years to get her first client. The turning point came when she went back to her kitchen and baked cheesecake, breads, and muffins for her prospects. Shortly thereafter she got her first contract.

By 1998 she had 70 employees working in the Oxnard headquarters and regional offices in Los Angeles. Her talent and achievements have been recognized in numerous ways. In 1993, Northrop named Aegir its "Small Business Supplier of the Year." Williams was named one of "The Nation's Ten Most Admired Women Managers of 1993" by *Working Woman* magazine, and AT&T designated her "The 1993 Entrepreneur of the Year." In 1996, she was presented with the "Woman of the Year" award by the Women's Transportation Seminar, and in 1997 she was voted "Business Person of the Year" by *Business Digest* readers.

Questions

1. What kind of financing did Williams use to start her business?

2. How could SCORE have helped?

3. Do you think that this cycle of "uphill battle" is typical for minority-owned businesses?

Source: Andrew Tobias, "You Can Still Make a Million Dollars," *Parade* magazine, October 29, 1995, pp. 14–15; and Kathy A. Price, " 'Business Person of the Year'—Ella Williams," *Business Digest* 38 (Winter 1997) at www.bdigest.com/win38.html; and correspondence with Ella Williams.

CASE 6-2

J&J COMPUTERS: GOING PUBLIC

J&J Computers was started several years ago. When it started growing a few years back, its owners needed more money to expand their business and meet the growing demands of their customers. In an effort to raise more capital, the owners approached the area bank and took out a loan.

They soon realized, however, that they needed more money because their business was growing at a much faster pace than originally predicted. The owners decided to go public and sold an issue of common stock. They were thereby able to raise enough capital to continue operating and were able to meet the demands of their customers—and creditors.

Questions

1. When J&J Computers took out a loan from the bank, what kind of financing was it?

2. Why do you think they preferred to take a loan first?

3. What kind of financing is it when you sell stock?

4. Who are the stockholders, and what are their rights?

III

MARKETING GOODS AND SERVICES

To succeed, a small business must effectively perform a number of essential business functions: marketing, organizing and managing, operations, and financing. The last three functions will be covered in Parts IV, V, and VI; this Part concentrates on the marketing function.

Marketing involves determining customers' needs, developing goods and services to satisfy those needs, and distributing those products to customers through various channels of distribution. It is an essential function because, unless the firm has—or can develop—a market for its product, performing the other business functions is futile.

Chapter 7, "Developing Marketing Strategies," covers the marketing concept; marketing research; strategy development, including marketing objectives, targets, and mix; types of products and their life cycles; marketing strategies for services; packaging; and pricing strategies.

In Chapter 8, "Product Promotion and Distribution," we discuss channels of distribution, global opportunities, using intermediaries or one's own sales force, supporting and controlling sales personnel, promoting the product, credit management, and physical distribution.

7

DEVELOPING MARKETING STRATEGIES

There are really only two important functions in business: marketing and innovations.

Peter Drucker

We don't focus enough attention on adequate product differentiation, much less on distribution channels, service organizations, or the reputation of vendors. We tend to forget that those things tremendously influence what someone buys.

William H. Davidow, venture capitalist and author of *Marketing High Technology*

LEARNING OBJECTIVES

After studying the material in this chapter, you will be able to:

1. Describe the marketing concept, and explain how it can be used by a small business.

2. Show how marketing research can be used to implement the marketing concept.

3. Explain how to develop and implement a marketing strategy.

4. Explain how the product life cycle affects marketing strategies.

5. Explain how packaging affects marketing.

6. Describe how prices are set and administered.

7. Show how marketing services differs from marketing goods.

BSI: Marketing a Service

BSI is a small land surveying corporation established in 1974 that employs between 20 and 25 people. Its primary business is subdivision development and boundary surveys, but the firm also does mortgage loan surveys, percolation tests, and construction layout work.

BSI's president and CEO, Gerald Byrd, is licensed in Alabama, Florida, and Mississippi. As in any professional service organization, ethics is a main concern, and many forms of advertising are not considered ethical for this industry. Opportunities for marketing the services are few because professional associations are used to get the word out about the business and its services.

BSI belongs to the local chamber of commerce and to the Mortgage Bankers Association (www.mbaa.org), and its CEO is a director of the local MBA chapter. He is also "Associate Council Director Emeritus" of the Homebuilders Association and is active in the Realtors Association.

BSI is active in the Alabama Society of Professional Land Surveyors, of which its president is the local chapter treasurer, district nine state director 1995–1999, and a member of the Professional Standards Committee. In addition, he serves as a technical adviser for the state Board of Registration for Professional Engineers and Land Surveyors. As a result of his work with various planning and zoning groups, such as the Mobile City Planning Commis-sion (www.ci.mobile.al.us/html/urban/plan_comm.html), Byrd has been appointed county surveyor.

Such professional associations can mean many extra hours of service and hard work. Because these memberships are a marketing tool, however, BSI employees are active and working members, serving on the various boards and attending meetings and organizational functions. These associations hold many charitable activities, from fishing rodeos to actual construction of buildings and homes. Active members provide services, supplies, and labor for many causes.

To maintain an image of friendly professionalism, Byrd also personally delivers many of his finished jobs. This is a follow-up prospecting function. During this visit to the client, questions can be answered and new projects brainstormed. Pricing, timing, and criteria may also be discussed one-to-one at this time of personal contact. It is also very important that all phone calls and drop-ins be treated with courtesy and respect. "Let's not forget the quality of the finished product," Byrd says. His business creed is: "A satisfied client is a continuing client."

Despite all the hours necessary to own and manage a small business, Byrd still finds time to pursue his favorite hobby—flying!

Source: Prepared by W. Jay Megginson from conversations with Gerald Byrd, his associates, and fellow professionals.

The Profile illustrates an important aspect of the marketing function—marketing a service. It also gives an overview of marketing, including the importance of the marketing concept, product development, and customer service. This chapter is about those and other marketing strategies, including developing a favorable marketing mix of the Four Ps: product, place, promotion, and price.

Companies with a reputation for superior marketing tend to share some basic strategies for successful marketing. These include:[1]

- Moving quickly to satisfy customer needs.
- Using pricing to differentiate the product/service.
- Paying attention to packaging.
- Building customer loyalty.
- Offering samples and demonstrations.
- Educating customers.

■ THE MARKETING CONCEPT

The **marketing concept** involves giving special consideration to the needs, desires, and wishes of present and prospective customers.

The **marketing concept** helps a business focus its efforts on satisfying customer needs in such a way as to make a satisfactory profit. The concept comprises three basic elements: a customer orientation, a goal orientation, and using the systems approach. This concept is based on the truth that the survival of a small business depends on providing service. With such a customer orientation, small firms will try to identify the group of people or firms most likely to buy their product (the target market) and to produce goods or services that will meet the needs of that market. Being consumer oriented often involves exploring consumer needs and then trying to satisfy them, as the following example shows.

> Janet Forti and June Negrycz recognized that both GapKids (www.gapkids.com) and BabyGap ignore a significant market—parents who want to dress their children in something other than T-shirts and denim. To fill that neglected niche, the pair opened Olivia and Sam, a children's specialty store, in the gentrified Cobble Hill neighborhood of Brooklyn, New York. The shop has prospered from the first day because the founders recognized an opportunity and joined forces to design, manufacture, and sell children's clothing. In addition, while the parents shop, children enjoy a Victorian playroom.[2]

In focusing on customer orientation, however, the small firm must not lose sight of its own goals. Goals in profit-seeking firms typically center on financial criteria such as profit, return on investment, or market share, as well as service.

In a **system** all parts of the business work in unison.

The third component of the marketing concept is the systems approach. In a **system** all parts of the business work together. Thus, consumer needs are identified, and internal procedures are set up to ensure that the right goods and services are produced, distributed, and sold to meet those needs.

Meeting Customers' Needs

Your understanding of customers' needs starts with the realization that when people buy something, they purchase satisfaction as well as goods or services. Consumers do not simply choose a toothpaste, for example. Instead, some want a decay preventive, some seek pleasant taste, others desire tooth brighteners, and still others will accept any formula at a bargain price. Thus, understanding customers' needs means being aware of the timing of the purchase, what customers like and dislike, or what "turns them on."

> For example, the owner of a ladies' dress shop in a small town has a good business. Many of her customers live as far as 50 miles away. She knows her customers by name, understands their needs, and buys with them as individuals in mind. When she goes to market, she thinks, "This style is perfect for Mrs. Adams," or "Jane would love this." Then she calls Mrs. Adams or Jane when that style comes in.

The marketing concept should guide the attitudes of the firm's salespeople, who should be encouraged to build personal relationships with customers. A recent American Productivity and Quality Center study found that companies are increasingly converting employee knowledge and participation into bottom-line gains.[3] A good example is the retail salesperson, who, in order to build a following, writes to 20 customers every day, describing new stock that should appeal to the specific customer.

Small firms should add something extra in the way of customer service. Customers want a business to be helpful, and outstanding service will often generate good word-of-mouth advertising.

> For example, Avon Products Inc. (www.avon.com) insists it can sell clothes successfully by offering customers not only convenience but also low catalog shopping prices. In addition, the company offers the services of a personal shopper. Avon has about 440,000 salespeople in the United States, who have developed an extensive network of intimate relationships with customers.[4]
>
> Avon upset those salespeople in late 1997 when it announced the most radical makeover in its history. It announced that it would soon test the notion of selling its products to retail outlets—a move that risks upsetting the doorbell ringers who account for more than 98 percent of U.S. sales. Although the idea sounds foreign to U.S. consumers, it's the way Avon has been doing business in many foreign markets, notably in Asia, where the company reaps 16 percent of its sales. In Malaysia, for instance, Avon already has 145 franchised boutiques, which provide half of its Malaysian sales.[5]

Keeping customers satisfied is more difficult than it seems, because it involves all aspects of the business. Customer satisfaction involves not just employees and customers but other factors as well, such as store design and upkeep, method of employee payment, and methods for providing feedback to and from customers. Unfortunately, as Yankelovich Partners (www.yankelovich.com) found in a recent survey, the vast majority of consumers feel they are not being served properly. Figure 7–1 shows how consumers react to this problem.

Implementing the Marketing Concept

In implementing the marketing concept, you should use the systems approach. As mentioned above, all parts of the business must be coordinated and marketing policies must be understood by all personnel in order to avoid problems such as that in the following example.

> A store sent its customers a flyer urging them to use its credit plan. Yet one customer received the flyer in the same mail with a harsh letter threatening repossession of earlier purchases if the customer's account wasn't paid within 24 hours.

You should try to apply the marketing concept by using one or more of the following ideas:

- Be conscious of image.
- Practice consumerism.
- Look for danger signals.

Be Conscious of Image   You should evaluate the business frequently to see what kind of image it projects—from the customers' point of view. You should ask: Can my customers find what they want, when they want it, and where they want it, at a competitive price?

Figure 7–1
Consumers Talking Back

Eighty-five percent of consumers say they must look out for themselves in the marketplace. Many are seeking product information and giving feedback after buying. Those who have:

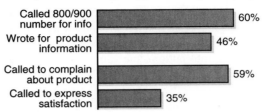

Source: Yankelovich Partners for *USA Weekend* magazine, as reported in *USA Today*, October 19, 1995, p. 1B.

Consumerism
involves prodding businesses to improve the quality of their products and to expand consumer knowledge.

Practice Consumerism   The major concerns of the consumer movement during the last three decades have been the rights of consumers to buy safe products, to be informed, to be able to choose, and to be heard. **Consumerism** recognizes that consumers are at a disadvantage and works to force businesses to be responsive in giving them a square deal. You can practice consumerism by doing such things as performing product tests, making clear the terms of sales and warranties, and being truthful in advertising.

Look for Danger Signals   There are many danger signals that can indicate when the marketing concept is not being followed. Your business is in trouble if, over time, it exhibits one or more of the signs listed in Table 7–1. An uninterested employee—or manager—turns customers off, as the following example shows.

> Thomas Shoemaker was hunting for some Con-Tact paper in a Peoples Drug store in Washington, D.C. He finally gave up the search and was walking out when he saw a man with a Peoples ID badge adjusting some stock on a shelf. When Shoemaker asked him if the store carried Con-Tact paper, the man replied, "I don't know. I don't work here. I'm the manager."[6]

Seeking a Competitive Edge

There is a close relationship between key success factors and the competitive edge that a small business should seek. Some of these key factors, based on industry analysis, were discussed in Chapter 5. Your **competitive edge** (sometimes called *competitive advantage*) is something that customers want and only you can supply, which gives you an advantage over your competitors.

A **competitive edge** (competitive advantage) is a particular characteristic that makes one firm more attractive to customers than are its competitors.

> For example, H&H Embroidery and Promotions (hhembro@iamerica.net) has captured the opportunity to supply other companies with specific casual clothing for "dress-down day." H&H provides in-house catalogs for its customers, from which employees can buy approved items to wear. According to one 1995 survey, 90 percent of all companies allow employees to dress casually at least one day a week. It is predicted that two of every three office workers will be allowed to dress down every day by the year 2000.[7]

Some factors that might provide such an advantage are quality, reliability, integrity, and service, as well as lower prices. In some industries, such as electronics or toys, novelty and innovation provide the most important competitive edge.

Table 7–1

Danger Signals Indicating Marketing Problems

Indicator	Indication
Sales	Down from previous period
Customers	Walking out without buying
	No longer visiting store
	Returning more merchandise
	Expressing more complaints
Employees and salespeople	Being slow to greet customers
	Being indifferent to or delaying customer
	Not urging added or upgraded sales
	Having poor personal appearance
	Lacking knowledge of store
	Making more errors
	Good ones leaving the company
Store image	Of greed through unreasonable prices
	Inappropriate for market area
	Unclear, sending mixed signals

For example, Thomas First and Thomas Scott concocted a libation for parties that included peaches, sugar, and water. They named their product Nantucket Nectars (www.juiceguys.com). Now, a few years later, this innovative duo has sales in excess of $30 million and is contemplating "growing up."[8]

In many small businesses, however, the competitive edge can be something as simple as courtesy, friendliness, and helpfulness. It may also involve developing and managing cost-effective databases that provide timely information indicating *who* should be contacted, *when* they should be contacted, and *how* to contact them.[9]

In looking for a competitive edge or advantage, keep in mind that it is based on providing one or more of three forms of value to customers. Customers prefer goods and services that are better, cheaper, and faster. These forms of value can be summed up as follows:[10]

Better	Quality differentiation
Cheaper	Cost leadership
Faster	Quick response to consumer needs

These forms of competitive advantage create value for the customer, which can, in turn, increase the value of the firm. Be aware, though, that it is seldom possible for a small company to compete in all three areas, but you must find one area in which to compete. If your product costs more or your service takes longer than your competitors', then it must be of recognizably better quality. Or a product or service of moderate quality and average cost may be acceptable if it is available immediately.

■ USING MARKETING RESEARCH TO IMPLEMENT THE MARKETING CONCEPT

Marketing research is the systematic gathering, recording, and analyzing of data relating to the marketing of goods and services. It is an orderly, objective way of learning about customers or potential customers and their needs and desires. By studying customers'

Marketing research
is the systematic gathering, recording, and analyzing of data relating to the marketing of goods and services.

actions and reactions and drawing conclusions from them, you can use marketing research to improve your marketing activities. But bear in mind that marketing research does not solve all problems, as the following examples illustrate.

> When the Ford Edsel was introduced in 1959, it was the most highly researched car in history, and it had innovations galore. It also had problems—from defective power steering to sticking hoods. The estimated loss was $250 million, or almost $1,117 per car.
>   And when Coca-Cola (www.coca-cola.com) introduced "New Coke" to compete with Pepsi's sweeter formula, it provoked a national uproar from diehard loyalists.[11]

Marketing research is helpful at several points in the life of your business. Before starting the business, you can use marketing research to find out whether the location and surrounding population are right for your proposed product. After you open the business, marketing research can help you decide (1) whether to develop new or different products, (2) whether to expand at the original location or open additional locations, and (3) when and where to change emphasis on activities such as channels of distribution and advertising and promotion strategy.

How Does Marketing Research Aid Marketing?

Marketing research is part of a company's overall marketing system. By analyzing marketplace data such as attitudinal, demographic, and lifestyle changes, marketing research can help you plan your strategic efforts. The following are some areas in which marketing research is effective:

- Identifying customers for the firm's products.
- Determining their needs.
- Evaluating sales potential for both the firm and its industry.
- Selecting the most appropriate channel of distribution.
- Evaluating advertising and promotional effectiveness.

> For example, marketing research techniques are available to correlate data from actual customer purchases, using universal product code scanners in supermarkets and drugstores, with advertising information. The business owner can see how the amount and type of advertising and sales promotion lead to actual purchases.[12]

How to Do Marketing Research

Marketing research does not have to be fancy or expensive to meet your needs. It deals with people and their constantly changing likes and dislikes, which can be affected by many influences. Marketing research tries to find out how things really are (not how you think they are or should be) and what people are really buying or want to buy (not what you want to sell them).

> For example, Jennifer Nevitt, a marketing specialist, told apartment managers, developers, and owners at the National Association of Homebuilders International Builders' Show in Dallas in mid-January 1998 that apartments in the future will be "bigger, smarter." Also, the apartments will have more amenities associated with the apartment itself, rather than for community use, and will better accommodate electronic technologies with features such as multiple and high-speed phone lines.[13]

In its simplest form, marketing research involves (1) defining the problem and then (2) gathering and evaluating information. Many small business managers unknowingly do some form of marketing research nearly every day. For example, they check returned items to see if there is some pattern. They ask old customers on the street why they have not been in recently. They look at competitors' ads to find out what the competition is selling and at what prices.

> At a university small business seminar, the owner of a wholesaling firm that sold farm equipment and supplies stated that market research was not relevant in a small business. Later, he told the participants he visited dealers to learn their needs for shovels and other items before ordering these items for his stock. Without realizing it, he was doing marketing research.

Defining the Problem Proper identification of the problem is the most important step in the process, since the right answer to the wrong question is useless. Thus, you should look beyond the symptoms of a problem to get at the real cause. For example, a sales decline is not a *cause* but rather a *symptom* of a marketing problem. In defining the problem, you should look at influences that may have caused it, such as changes in customers' home areas or in their tastes.

Gathering and Evaluating Information Marketing research can use existing (secondary) data or generate new information (primary data) through research. So you must make a subjective judgment and weigh the cost of gathering more information against its usefulness. The cost of making a wrong decision should be balanced against the cost of gathering more data to make a better-informed decision.

Using Existing Information You should "think cheap" and stay as close to home as possible when doing marketing research. Looking at your records and files, such as sales records, complaints, and receipts, can show you where customers live or work or how and what they buy, as the following example illustrates.

> The owner of a fabric shop used addresses on checks and cash receipts to pinpoint where her customers lived. She then cross-referenced the addresses with products purchased, which permitted her to check the effectiveness of advertising and sales promotion activities.

Credit records can also yield valuable information about your market, since customers' jobs, income levels, and marital status can be gleaned from them. Employees are a good source of information about customer likes and dislikes because they hear customers' gripes about the firm's products as well as about its competitors. They are also aware of the items customers request that are not stocked. Outside sources of information include publications such as *Survey of Current Business* and *Statistical Abstract of the United States,* trade association reports, chamber of commerce studies, university research publications, trade journals, newspapers, and marketing journals.

Doing Primary Research Primary research can range from simply asking customers or suppliers how they feel about your business to more complex studies such as direct-mail questionnaires, telephone or "on the street" surveys, and test marketing. **Test marketing** simulates the conditions under which a product will eventually be sold. However, even a small market test is costly.

Test marketing simulates the conditions under which a product is to be marketed.

> For example, Kaufman and Broad Home Corporation (www.kaufmanandbroad.com), in Denver, Colorado, assumed for years that people enjoyed snuggling up in front of a fire on snowy winter evenings. Therefore, fireplaces were standard in all the homes that K&B built. In 1997, however, it asked potential homebuyers which features they actually wanted in a home. It surprised them to find that half the people in Denver would willingly forgo a fireplace, especially if it meant a lower price for the home. K&B no longer offers a fireplace as a standard feature.[14]

Primary research, which includes studies such as surveys, interviews, and question-naires, should usually be left to experts. You might use this type of research, but take care to ask the right questions and obtain unbiased answers.

David Futrell, a consultant with QualPro Inc. (www.qualproinc.com), offers these tips for developing effective surveys:[15]

- Ask your customers what to ask.

- Be sure the answer will tell you what to do.

- Use a combination of different types of questions.

- Develop a user-friendly design.

- Avoid asking customers to rank lengthy lists of items.

- Address only one issue in each question.

Using Specialized Research Techniques   Other techniques include license plate analysis, tele-phone number analysis, coded coupons, and "tell them Joe sent you" broadcast ads, not to mention just plain people-watching.

In many states, license plates give information about where a car's owner lives—what city or county, for instance. By recording the origin of cars parked at the firm's location, the trade area can be estimated. Similarly, telephone numbers and ZIP codes can tell where people live. This type of data can be found on sales slips, prospect cards, and contest blanks, as well as on personalized checks used for payment.

Coded coupons and "tell them Joe sent you" broadcast ads can be effective, too. The relative effectiveness of your advertising media can be checked by coding coupons and by including in broadcast ads some phrase customers must use to get a discount on a given sale item. If neighborhood newspapers are involved, you can also get some idea of the area from which customers are drawn. Where they read or heard about the discount offered in the ads may also give information about their tastes.

Using Computerized Databases

A wide variety of information is available at public libraries or online; many such sources also offer, for a fee, access to computerized databases, such as Standard & Poor's Daily News and Cumulative News (Corporation Records) (www.stockinfo.standardpoor.com). By gathering data on selected kinds of companies (such as electronics firms producing home videocassettes) or specific geographic areas (such as firms moving into a particular state or city), you can learn about companies that are expanding operations. Such informa-tion may be valuable to small retailers, service businesses, wholesalers, and manufacturers in selecting their target markets and marketing strategy.

A variation of computerized databases is now being used by big and small businesses alike—from Federal Express to fast-food franchises to independent cabbies and pharma-cists. Computer programs hooked to a phone with Caller ID can create a database that can increase efficiency, enhance security, control inventory, improve marketing, and simplify contacts with customers.

> For instance, if you call your favorite Domino's pizzeria (www.dominos.com), the person who answers the phone may say something like "Do you want another large deep-dish pepperoni with pineapples and anchovies?" How does the clerk know this much about your tastes? By looking into a convenient high-tech file: a computer that used Caller ID to tell who you are and then called up its records of where you live and what you like.[16]

■ DEVELOPING A MARKETING STRATEGY

As a small business owner, you should develop a marketing strategy early in your business operations. Such a strategy consists of (1) setting objectives, (2) choosing target market(s), and (3) developing an effective marketing mix.

Setting Objectives

Marketing objectives should be tied in with your competitive edge and flow from your mission statement. For example, an image of higher quality than competitors' products at comparable prices may be an objective. To achieve this objective and still make planned profits requires aligning all operations, including the added costs of improved quality, adequate capital, and so forth. Objectives must consider customers' needs as well as the survival of the business. To attain objectives, a target market must be identified and served.

Choosing Target Markets

The **target market** of a business should be the customers most likely to buy or use its product(s). Only when a clear, precise target market has been identified can an effective marketing mix be developed, as the following examples illustrate.

> A **target market** is the part of the total market toward which promotional efforts are concentrated.

The year 2000 is ushering in some classic marketing strategies. One of these is targeted at individuals graduating at the turn of the century. For example, Rich Soergel, of the San Diego–based licensing and marketing company Class of 2000, Inc., is offering this class a way to show off its unique status with a special line of merchandise. Some of the products that he is expecting will go over big with this group are apparel, jewelry, linens, footwear, and the like—all emblazoned with their "Class of 2000" trademark.[17]

M&M Mars has TV commercials that tout M&Ms as the official candy of the new millennium. Why? Because MM = 2000.

Use Market Segmentation   To define a target market requires **market segmentation,** which is identifying and evaluating various layers of a market. Effective market segmentation requires the following steps:

> **Market segmentation** is identifying and evaluating various layers of a market.

1. Identify the characteristics of two or more segments of the total market. Then, distinguish among the customers in each segment on the basis of such factors as their age, sex, buying patterns, or income level. For example, adults desire a table-service restaurant more than do teenagers and young children, who generally prefer a fast-food format.
2. Determine whether any of those market segments is large enough and has sufficient buying power to generate profit for your business.
3. Align your marketing effort to reach the selected segment of the market profitably. This is not always easy to do, as the following example illustrates.

The retail chain Talbots, Inc., has traditionally concentrated on the more conservative line of business attire that professional women prefer. In an attempt to take advantage of the changing "upbeat" fashion market, Talbots changed its marketing stream from conservative navy, black, and brown to a high-fashion spectrum of "hot pinks, lime, and orange." The result: Talbots's conservative clients "ran away," and the company was slow to attract the high-fashion market it wanted. Realizing the error in marketing strategy, Talbots switched back to its conservative clothing lines. That was the easy part. Luring back its former dedicated customers will not be easy.[18]

Figure 7–2
Selling to Older Consumers

The growing ranks of older consumers and a decline in the size of the youth market are leading companies to redesign products and sales appeals to capture the increasingly influential senior citizen and aging baby-boomer markets.

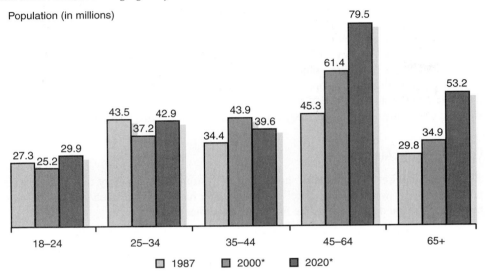

Population (in millions)

	18–24	25–34	35–44	45–64	65+
1987	27.3	43.5	34.4	45.3	29.8
2000*	25.2	37.2	43.9	61.4	34.9
2020*	29.9	42.9	39.6	79.5	53.2

☐ 1987   ◼ 2000*   ◼ 2020*

*Estimated.

Source: U.S. Census Bureau data, as reported in U.S. Department of Commerce, *Statistical Abstract of the United States, 1997,* 117th ed. (Washington, DC: U.S. Government Printing Office, 1997), p. 17, Table 17 (based on the "Middle Series" of projections).

Shifting Target Markets   Choosing and maintaining a target market is becoming more difficult because of changing consumer characteristics. Therefore, small business owners should study the external environment for shifts in such factors as population patterns, age groups, and income levels, as well as regional patterns of consumption.

Population and Age Shifts   The underlying market factor determining consumer demand is the number and type of people with the purchasing power to buy a given product. In general, the U.S. population is shifting from the East and North to the West and South. Other important population factors are household size and formations, education, and the number of married couples, singles, single-parent families, unmarried couples, and children. According to the U.S. Census Bureau, the average size of U.S. households declined from 3.5 persons in 1940 to 3.14 in 1970, 2.63 in 1990, and it is expected to be only 2.5 by the year 2000.[19]

   Age groups also change. The average age of Americans has been rising and is expected to continue to rise in the foreseeable future. From 1990 to 1997 the average age increased from 32.8 to 34.9 years according to the U.S. Census Bureau (www.census.gov).[20]

   Also, the age distribution is shifting. As you can see from Figure 7–2, the number of young people and young adults is declining, while the 35-and-over group—especially the 45-to-64-year-old group—is currently increasing rapidly. Since people in each age group differ in their consumption patterns, different marketing strategies are needed.

> For example, the demographic group that is eligible for senior citizen discounts is exploding. The travel industry has recognized this shift and offers special discounts on airline, car rental, and hotel costs to those 50 years and older. There are now more than 75 million Americans who qualify.[21]

Figure 7–3

Senior Spenders—Percentage of U.S. Population Age 55 and Over

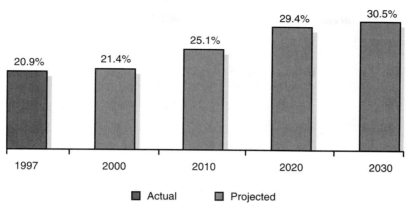

Source: U.S. Census Bureau data as reported in U.S. Department of Commerce, *Statistical Abstract of the United States, 1997,* 117th ed. (Washington, DC: U.S. Government Printing Office, 1997), p. 17, Table 17 (based on the "Middle Series" of projections).

The 55-plus market is expected to grow almost 50 percent in the next 30 years, according to the U.S. Census Bureau. Figure 7–3 illustrates how the explosion is expected to occur. A different set of data and projections from the U.S. Census Bureau forecast that the segment of the U.S. population aged 65 and over is expected to increase 63 percent from 1993 to the year 2020.[22]

The most dramatic population shifts now occurring are the aging of the baby boomers and the need to use and conserve the skills and work ethic of older workers. According to one authority, the aging of the "boomers" coincided with a change in their work ethic. On entering their 40s, they took stock of their lives and decided they wanted "a lifestyle at least as good as their predecessors."[23] Members of this group are looking for more personal fulfillment, including more time with family and friends—and more time alone. This trend may cause a change in their spending habits.

The second trend—the need to use and conserve the skills of older workers—is forcing employers to find productive ways to use those who want to keep on working. During the coming decade, employers will have to choose from an aging work force, as shown in Figure 7–2, since there will be a crunch for younger workers with both basic and technical skills. In fact, *the number of 18-to-35-year-olds will actually decline* until the year 2000, at which time it will begin to increase, but not as rapidly as the 45-and-over group. These shifts in age group-ings will probably require redesigning jobs; rehiring retirees as consultants, advisers, or temporaries; using phased-in retirement programs; and aggressively recruiting older workers.

Regional Differences in Purchases   Purchasing habits and patterns also vary by region. These variations are significant, for where people live is one of the best clues as to what they buy.

> Cracker Barrel Old Country Store Inc. (www.crackerbarrelocs.com) is well known in the South for home-style cooking at modest prices. In a calculated gamble, it is now opening 70 percent of its new restaurants outside its core Southern market.
> Since many of the new restaurants are in the North and West, the menu is being changed from Southern staples such as grits and fried okra to local specialties. For example, when Cracker Barrel opened its first store in Wisconsin, sales were only about 60 percent of those in the Southeast. After closing three restaurants, the company

began to change its menu and now offers dishes such as thick-sliced bratwurst and fried cheese curds in areas such as Germantown, Wisconsin. It has also added a Friday-night fish fry. These changes turned the Wisconsin stores around.[24]

In the mid-1990s, demographic forces dramatically changed the nation's geographic economic balance. In addition to the flood of immigrants into New York, Florida, California, and the Southwest, there was an internal mass migration. People were drawn from California and the Northern states to the Southern and Southwestern states. These latter states are now experiencing an economic boom.[25]

Developing an Effective Marketing Mix

A **marketing mix** is the proper blending of the basic elements of product, price, promotion, and place into an integrated marketing program.

A **marketing mix** consists of controllable variables that the firm combines to satisfy the target market. Those variables are the Four Ps: product, place, promotion, and price. The right *product* for the target market must be developed. *Place* refers to the channels of distribution. *Promotion* refers to any method that communicates to the target market. The right *price* should be set to attract customers and make a profit.

■ THE PRODUCT LIFE CYCLE

You may find that your most effective strategy is to concentrate on a narrow product line, develop a highly specialized product or service, or provide a product-service "package" containing an unusual amount of service. In setting strategy, competitors' products, prices, and services should be carefully analyzed. This is not easy to do because of the large number of new products introduced each year.

Stages of the Product Life Cycle

Products are much like living organisms: They are brought into the world, they live, and they die. When a new product is successfully introduced into the firm's market mix, it grows; when it loses appeal, it is discontinued. A new product may have a striking effect on the life cycle of other products as well.

Phonograph records are a good illustration of the product life cycle. Although 78 RPM records coexisted with the 45s, they gave way to the long-playing vinyl 33s. Then the compact disc (CD) began to dominate the market, threatening all records, even the 45s, which had maintained their hold on jukeboxes. Jukeboxes that play CDs offer vastly superior quality, along with lower maintenance costs. By the early 1990s, although a few audiophiles still maintained that CDs were "cold" and "lifeless" and could not match vinyl LPs in richness of tone, CDs had almost entirely supplanted vinyl records, though they continued to coexist with the cheaper cassette tapes. In 1998, although CDs themselves seemed secure, CD *players* were threatened by new technologies. Most CD-ROM players also play audio discs, and DVD (digital versatile disc) players that can also play CDs looked likely to be the next wave. In fact, DVD-ROM drives are now standard equipment on most new computers.

The **product life cycle** consists of four stages: introduction, growth, maturity, and decline.

As shown in Figure 7–4, the **product life cycle** has four major stages: introduction, growth, maturity, and decline. As a product moves through its cycle, the strategies relating to competition, promotion, distribution, pricing, and market information should be evaluated and possibly changed. You can use the life-cycle concept to time the introduction and improvement of profitable products and the dropping or recycling of unprofitable ones.

Figure 7–4
Sales and Profits during the Product Life Cycle*

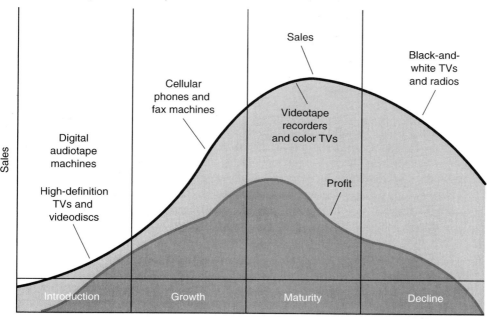

*Note that profit levels start to fall *before* sales reach their peak. When profits and sales start to decline, it's time to come out with a new product or remodel the old one to maintain interest and profits.

Source: William G. Nickels, James M. McHugh, and Susan M. McHugh, *Understanding Business,* 4th ed. (Burr Ridge, IL: Irwin, 1996), p. 449. Reprinted with permission.

Introduction Stage The introduction stage begins when a product first appears on the market. Prices are usually high, sales are low, and profits are negative because of high development, promotion, and distribution costs. In this stage, it is vital to communicate the product's features, uses, and advantages to potential buyers. Only a few new products—such as telephones, microwave ovens, and home computers—represent major innovations. More often, a "new" product is an old one in a new form. Many products never get beyond the introduction stage because of insufficient or poor marketing research, design or production problems, or errors in timing the product's introduction.

Growth Stage During the growth stage, sales rise rapidly and profits peak. As competitors enter the market, they attempt to develop the best product design. During this stage, marketing strategy typically encourages strong brand loyalty. The product's benefits are identified and emphasized to develop a competitive niche.

Maturity Stage Competition becomes more aggressive during the maturity stage, with declining prices and profits. Promotion costs climb; competitors cut prices to attract business; new firms enter, further increasing competition; and weaker competitors are squeezed out. Those that remain make fresh promotional and distribution efforts.

Decline Stage Sales fall rapidly during the decline stage, especially if a new technology or a social trend is involved. Management considers pruning items from the product line to eliminate unprofitable ones. Promotion efforts may be cut and plans may be made to phase out the product, though sometimes it can be saved by repackaging or other changes.

> For example, the Swanson TV Dinner, developed in 1955, had food to be cooked in an oven on an aluminum tray and eaten while watching TV. It flourished at the height of television's Golden Age but has now been relegated to the Smithsonian Institution (www.si.edu) for possible display at the National Museum of American History. As VCRs have facilitated "time shifting" of dinner-hour TV programs, the TV dinner has been replaced as a convenience food by microwavable meals that can be "nuked" in just a few minutes.[26]

Need for a Wide Product Mix

The life-cycle concept indicates that many, if not most, products will eventually become unprofitable. Hence, small firms should investigate and evaluate market opportunities to launch new products or extend the life of existing ones. You should have a composite of life-cycle patterns, with various products in the mix at different life-cycle stages; as one product declines, other products are in the introduction, growth, or maturity stages. Some fads may last only a few weeks or months (such as a new video game or doll), while other products (refrigerators, for example) may be essentially unchanged for years.

Still other products will decline in popularity for a period and then reemerge. This trend provides great opportunities for small business entrepreneurs.

> For example, Trendmasters Inc., of St. Louis, earned $137 million in 1997 from sales of a new line of "Lost in Space" toys. These and other toys, such as Godzilla, are proving to be a bonanza for Russell Hornsby, co-CEO of Trendmaster Toys.[27]

■ PACKAGING

Packaging, because it both protects and promotes the product, is important to you as well as to your customers. Packaging can make a product more convenient to use or store and can reduce spoiling or damage. Good packaging makes products easier to identify, promotes the brand at the store, and influences customers in making buying decisions.

> Many top-selling global brands have a common thread—*and it's not money.*
> Products such as Coca-Cola, Campbell's soup, and Colgate toothpaste all have one very important thing in common—*they're all packaged in red!* Others with red logos or names are Kellogg's, Nabisco, Dole, Del Monte, Lipton, Dentyne, and many other best sellers. Packaging experts and color psychologists say that a product's color and consumer buying preferences are closely linked. Red is considered to be warm and bright.[28]

A better box, wrapper, can, or bottle can help create a "new" product or market. For example, a small manufacturer introduced a liquid hand soap in a pump container, and it was an instant success. Sometimes, a new package improves a product by making it easier to use, such as reclosable plastic containers for motor oil, stand-up tubes and flip-open caps for toothpaste, or zipper-closure bags for cheese or sliced meat. Packaging can also improve product safety, as when drugs and food are sold in child-proof bottles and tamper-resistant packages. Sometimes variations in packaging are a last resort when everything else has been tried. How many times have you seen a "New, Improved" product and suspected that all that has changed is the label?

There now seems to be a reversal in recent packaging trends. Formerly, customers seemed to prefer recyclable packaging material—and lots of it. But *Packaging Digest,* a trade magazine, found that nearly 90 percent of surveyed consumers said no more packaging should be used than is necessary to protect the product. Ease of opening and reclosing the package ranked high with consumers.[29]

■ PRICING YOUR PRODUCT

Pricing can make the difference between success and failure for any business, but it is especially crucial for small businesses. Dr. Anne B. Lowery, a marketing scholar, has concluded that owners of small businesses may not be able to consider all the many and complex economic variables involved in price setting. She has summarized demand, supply, and other variables into four categories, which she calls "the four Cs of pricing."[30] They are:

- Customer.
- Company.
- Competition.
- Constraints.

The customer and company categories are internal and therefore largely within the control of the owner or manager. Competition and constraints, on the other hand, are generally considered external to the business and therefore largely beyond the control of the small business.

In considering these four categories, there are three practical aspects of pricing that you must consider. First, regardless of the desirability of the product, the price must be such that customers are willing—and able—to pay it.

Second, you must set your price to maintain or expand your market share and/or profit. If the new product is successful, competitors will introduce either a better product or a cheaper one.

Third, if you want to make a profit on the new product, the price must be sufficiently greater than cost to cover development, introduction, and operating costs.

Establishing Pricing Policies

As shown in Table 7–2, there's a large variety of pricing policies you can adopt, but the first three deserve particular attention: product-life-cycle, meet-the-competition, and cost-oriented pricing.

Effect of Product Life Cycle   Notice the role played by the product life cycle, as discussed earlier. When you introduce a new product, you have two alternatives: (1) to set a **skimming price,** which will be high enough to obtain the "cream" of the target market before competitors enter, or (2) to set a **penetration price,** which will be low enough to obtain an adequate and sustainable market. Small producers sometimes use a combination approach, setting a realistic price but making an initial purchase more attractive by issuing discount coupons.

> A **skimming price** is one set relatively high initially in order to rapidly skim off the "cream" of profits.

> A **penetration price** is one set relatively low to secure market acceptance.

Meeting the Competition   You can also set prices by meeting the competition, that is, following the pricing practices of competitors. But this practice can lead to severe losses if cost and volume of sales aren't taken into account. Small firms with an attractive, possibly unique product should not be afraid to charge what the product is worth, considering not only what it costs to provide the product but also what the market will bear.

Cost-Oriented Pricing   Cost is basic to all pricing policies. Total costs provide a floor below which prices should not be permitted to go, especially for long periods. Cost-oriented pricing involves adding a markup to the cost of the item.

Markup   **Markup** is the amount added to the cost of the product to determine the selling price. Usually, the amount of the markup is determined by the type of product sold, the amount of service performed by the retailer, how rapidly the product sells, and the amount of planned profit. Markup may be expressed in terms of dollars and/or cents, or as a percentage.

> **Markup** is the amount added to the product's cost to determine the selling price.

Table 7–2
Potential Pricing Policies for a Small Business

Policy Area	Description
Product life cycle:	
Skimming price	Aimed at obtaining the "cream" of the target market at a high price before dealing with other market segments.
Penetration price	Intended to try to sell to the entire market at a low price.
Meet the competition	Below the market price. At the competitors' price level. Above the market price.
Cost-oriented pricing	Costs are accumulated for each unit of product, and a markup is added to obtain a base price.
Price flexibility:	
One price	Offering the same price to all customers who purchase goods under the same conditions and in the same quantities.
Flexible price	Offering the same products and quantities to different customers at different prices.
Suggested retail price	Manufacturers often print a suggested price on the product or invoice or in their catalog.
List prices	Published prices that remain the same for a long time.
Prestige pricing	Setting of high prices used, say, by fur retailers.
Leader pricing	Certain products are chosen for their promotional value and are priced low to entice customers into retail stores.
Bait pricing	An item is priced extremely low by a dealer, but the salesperson points out the disadvantages of the item and switches customers to items of higher quality and price. (This practice is illegal.)
Odd pricing	Prices end in certain numbers, usually odd, such as $0.95—e.g., $7.95, $8.95.
Psychological pricing	Certain prices for some products are psychologically appealing; there can be a range of prices that customers perceive as being equal to each other.
Price lining	Policy of setting a few price levels for given lines of merchandise—e.g., ties at three levels: $8, $16, and $25.
Demand-oriented pricing	Potential customer demand is recognized, and prospective revenues are considered in pricing.

The way to figure markup percentage on cost is:

$$\text{Markup as percentage of cost} = \frac{\text{Dollar amount of markup}}{\text{Cost of the item}}$$

For example, assume a retailer is pricing a new product that costs $6. The selling price is set at $9. Therefore, the total amount of markup is $3: selling price ($9) less cost ($6) equals markup ($3). The markup percentage, then, is:

$$\text{Markup percentage (cost)} = \frac{\$3}{\$6} = 50 \text{ percent}$$

Discounts and Allowances   Sellers often use discounts and allowances to increase sales. **Discounts,** which are reductions from a product's normal list price, are given to customers

A **discount** is a reduction from the list price given to customers as an inducement to buy more of a product.

Table 7–3
Discounts and Allowances Provided by Small Businesses

Reduction	Description
Cash discounts	Given as a reduction in price to buyers who pay their bill within a specified time period (e.g., 2/10, net 30 days).
Functional or trade discounts	List price reductions given to channel members for performance of their functions.
Quantity discounts Noncumulative Cumulative	Reduction in the unit price granted for buying in certain quantities. Apply to individual shipments or orders only. Apply to purchases over a given period (e.g., a year).
Seasonal discounts	Induce buyers to stock earlier than immediate demand would dictate.
Promotional allowances	Provided by manufacturers and wholesalers to retailers for promotion (e.g., point-of-purchase display materials, per case discounts, and cooperative advertisements).
Trade-ins	Allowance provided to customer by retailer in the purchase of, say, a major electric appliance.
Push money or prize money	Allowances provided retailers by manufacturers or wholesalers to be given to salespersons for aggressively selling particular products.

as an inducement to buy the item. **Allowances** are given to customers for accepting less of something or as an adjustment for variations in quality. Some of the more popular discounts and allowances are shown in Table 7–3.

Allowances are given to customers for accepting quality or quantity reductions.

How Prices Are Set by Small Businesses

Prices are set differently by small service firms, retailers, wholesalers, producers, and building contractors. Some of the more popular methods are described here.

By Service Firms   Service firms either charge the "going rate" (that is, the usual rate for a given job) or they may set prices according to those prevalent in their industry. They try to set a price based on the cost of labor and materials used to provide the service, as well as direct charges, such as transportation costs, and a profit margin. Many firms charge customers an hourly rate, based on the time required to perform the services, plus any travel expenses. Others incorporate the labor, materials, and transportation costs into an hourly rate, or a rate based on some other variable.

By Retailers   Different types of products are priced differently. Staple convenience goods, such as candy, gum, newspapers, and magazines, usually have customary prices or use the manufacturer's suggested retail price. **Customary prices** are the prices customers expect to pay as a result of custom, tradition, or social habits.

A **customary price** is what customers expect to pay because of custom, tradition, or social habits.

> For example, Hershey Chocolate Company (www.hersheys.com) sold candy bars for 5 cents in 1940. As cocoa and sugar became scarce and more expensive because of World War II, the price didn't rise for a while. Instead, the size of the bars was cut in half by the end of 1942.

Some discount and food stores discount prepriced items such as candy, gum, magazines, and greeting cards by a set percentage—say 10 or even 20 percent. Food World discounts all prepriced items 10 percent, and Wal-Mart discounts greeting cards 20 percent and sewing patterns nearly 50 percent.

Fashion goods, by contrast, have high markups but are drastically marked down if they do not sell well. High markups are also used on novelty, specialty, and seasonal goods. When the novelty wears off, or the selling season ends, the price goes down.

> Early-bird shoppers after holidays expect to find markdowns up to 50 or even 75 percent on Christmas wraps and toys or on Easter candy and stuffed rabbits. Customers also expect discounts on novelty items marketed as "stocking stuffers," holiday party clothes, and extravagantly priced items intended as gifts.

Unit pricing is listing the product's price in terms of some unit, such as a pound, pint, or yard.

Most grocery stores use **unit pricing** for products such as meats, produce, and deli items, charging so much per ounce or pound for each item. Information about unit prices of other items facilitates comparison shopping by customers.

Although influenced by competitors', vendors', and customary prices, retailers still must determine their own prices for the products they sell. The retailer's selling price should cover the cost of goods, selling and other operating costs, and a profit margin. In some cases, however, a store might use **loss leaders,** or items sold below cost, to attract customers who may also buy more profitable items.

A **loss leader** is an item priced at or below cost to attract customers into the store to buy more profitable items.

By Wholesalers   Wholesalers' prices are usually based on a markup set for each product line. Since wholesalers purchase in large quantities and cannot always immediately pass along price increases, price drops can cause heavy losses. Therefore, they may sometimes quote different prices to different buyers for the same products.

By Producers   While meeting competitors' prices is common among small producers, many set their prices relative to the cost of production, using a break-even analysis. As shown in Chapter 13, their costs include purchasing, inventory, production, distribution, selling, and administrative costs, as well as a profit margin. Those figures are totaled to arrive at a final price.

Cost-plus pricing is basing the price on the basis of all costs, plus a markup for profit.

By Building Contractors   Most building contractors use **cost-plus pricing.** They start with the cost of the land; add expected construction costs for items such as labor, materials, and supplies; add overhead costs; add financing and closing costs and legal fees; and add the real estate broker's fee. They then total the costs and add on a markup for profit.

Other Aspects of Pricing

Product, delivery, service, and fulfillment of psychological needs make up the total package that the customer buys. A price should be consistent with the image the business wants to project. Since customers often equate the quality of unknown products with their prices, raising prices may actually increase sales.

However, the reverse might also be true: Selling at a low price might lead customers to think the product is of low quality. Sometimes, "cheap" can be too cheap, especially when compared to nationally advertised products.

In summary, small business owners commonly make two errors in setting prices for their products. First, they charge less than larger businesses and consider themselves price leaders. Because of their relatively small sales, costs per unit tend to be higher for a smaller business than for a larger one. Therefore, *small firms generally should not attempt to be price leaders.*

Second, many firms offering services performed personally by the owner undercharge during the early period of operation. The owner mistakenly believes prices can be raised later as more customers are secured. However, it is easier to lower prices than to raise them, and raising them usually creates customer dissatisfaction.

■ STRATEGY FOR MARKETING SERVICES

Because the service sector of our economy is so important and has certain unique features, we will cover strategies for marketing services separately from marketing goods.

Nature of Service Businesses

There are two categories of services: personal and business. **Personal services** include activities such as financial services, transportation, health and beauty, lodging, advising and counseling, amusement, plumbing, maid services, real estate, and insurance. **Business services** may include some of these, plus others that are strictly business oriented, such as advertising agencies, market research firms, economic counselors, and certified public accountants (CPAs). Some services include aspects of both, as the following example illustrates.

> Accident and Crime Scene Clean-Up, Inc., doesn't do windows, but it does specialize in housework most homeowners would prefer not to contemplate. Many times, after a messy or violent crime, property owners or their maids or maintenance workers lack either the expertise or the willingness to clean up what the police or ambulance crew refuses to remove. Todd Menzies, owner and sole employee of the company, dons space-suit-like protective clothing and respiratory protection and goes to work, leaving the scene scrubbed, disinfected, and germ and odor free. Menzies says that in many cases insurance picks up at least part of the tab.[31]

Personal services can be performed by individuals or by automated equipment. Two examples of the latter are automatic car washes and computer time-sharing bureaus.

There are many opportunities in service industries because the demand for services is expected to grow faster than for most other types of businesses. Some reasons for increased spending on services include rising discretionary income, services as status symbols, more women working outside the home (and earning more), and a shorter workweek and more leisure time.

On the other hand, service businesses have severe competition, not only from other firms but also from potential customers who perform the services themselves and from manufacturers of do-it-yourself products.

How Services Differ

Since service firms must be chosen on the basis of their perceived reputation, a good image is of utmost importance. There are few objective standards for measuring the quality of services, so they are often judged subjectively. Not only is a service usually complete before a buyer can evaluate its quality, but also defective services cannot be returned.

Services cannot be stored in inventory, especially by firms providing amusements, transportation services, and room accommodations. Special features or extra thoughtfulness that create a memorable experience will encourage repeat business for service firms.

> For example, many modern hotels in Canada and the United States are creating a memorable experience that customers enjoy by offering them "afternoon tea." These hotels offer the tea and refreshments with a sales pitch that "in these hurry-up times, afternoon tea is a relaxing experience."

The level of customer contact required to provide and receive the service also varies. That is, the longer a customer remains in the service system, the greater the interaction between the server and customer. Generally, economies of scale are more difficult to achieve in high-contact services than in low-contact ones. For example, a beauty salon is a high-contact system, with the receptionist, shampoo person, and stylist all interacting with the customer. On the other hand, an automated car wash may have little contact with a customer.

Personal services are performed by a business for consumers.

Business services are provided to another business or professional.

Developing Service Marketing Strategies

Strategies for marketing services differ according to the level of customer contact. For example, in low-contact services the business doesn't have to be located near the customer. But a high-contact service, such as a plumbing firm, must be close enough to quickly meet the customer's needs. Quality control in high-contact services consists basically of doing a good job and maintaining an image and good public relations. Thus, if employees have a poor attitude, the firm may lose customers. Sometimes a company can gain a competitive edge by turning a low-contact service into a high-contact one, departing from the service approach taken by competitors.

> For example, in the early 1990s, Mobil Corporation (www.mobil.com) conducted extensive research to find out why it was suffering major losses in its gasoline retailing business. Results showed that out of five types of gasoline buyers, only one, representing just 20 percent of the total, based their buying decision on price. Moreover, some of the other types (higher-income men who drive 25,000 to 50,000 miles a year and people with moderate-to-high incomes who are loyal to a brand and sometimes to a particular station) were more likely to buy the higher-priced premium gasoline and tended to spend more on convenience store items than those who based their decision on price alone.
>
> Consequently, the focus at Mobil is no longer on price competition but on "blowing the customer away with product quality and service." This new strategy has raised revenue as much as 25 percent at some of the stations experimenting with the new concept.
>
> Adding services, such as helpful attendants providing assistance to customers, has allowed Mobil to raise pump prices, on the philosophy that increased prices will not deter the shoppers they are trying to attract. "Most people don't worry about several cents," said one oil industry analyst. "They'd rather not have the pump nozzle greasy."[32]

Primacy of the Marketing Concept   The marketing concept is more important for service businesses than for other types of businesses, since customers often can perform the service themselves. The business must demonstrate why it is to the customer's advantage to let the service firm do the job.

Pricing Services   The price for a service should reflect the quality, degree of expertise and specialization, and value of its performance to the buyer. As shown earlier, a high price tends to connote quality in the mind of the customer, so lower prices and price reductions may even have a negative effect on sales, particularly in people-based businesses.

The pricing of services in small firms often depends on value provided rather than on cost. Customers will pay whatever they think the service is worth, so pricing depends on what the market will bear. Pricing decisions often consider labor, materials, and transportation costs, as the following example illustrates.

> Lynn Brown's Mini-Maid franchise team takes from 30 to 90 minutes to clean a house: make beds, scour sinks, clean glass doors, sweep and mop or wax floors, vacuum carpets, clean bathrooms, polish furniture, load the dishwasher, wipe cabinets, shine counters, change bed linens, remove garbage, freshen the air, and do general pickup.
>
> Supplies and labor are furnished by Brown, and cleaning prices depend on the size of the house and the amount of work involved. When estimating the price, Brown considers the frequency with which customers use her services. The more often they use Mini-Maid, the better their rate.
>
> Although Brown has an office in her home (with a 24-hour-a-day answering service), she spends most of the workweek in her minivan. She says her success results from doing specific activities, in a specific way, for a specific price—which, as she says, is the Mini-Maid way.[33]

Promoting Services   Word-of-mouth advertising, personal selling, and publicity are usually used by small firms to promote their business. Often, the message will have a consistent theme, which is related to the uniqueness of the service, key personnel, or the benefits gained by satisfied customers. Small service firms typically also use the Yellow Pages, direct mail, and local newspapers, and may use specialty advertising, such as calendars with the firm's name, to promote themselves. Referrals, that is, asking satisfied customers to recommend the service to friends, can be quite effective. Belonging to professional and civic organizations and sponsoring public events are also important in building a firm's revenues and profitability, as the Profile for this chapter illustrates.

■ IMPLEMENTING YOUR MARKETING STRATEGY

Now that you have developed your marketing strategy, how do you implement it? Implementation involves two stages: the introductory stage and the growth stage.

The Introductory Stage

When introducing a new product, you should (1) analyze present and future market situations, (2) fit the product to the market, and (3) evaluate your company's resources.

Analyze Market Situations   This step determines the opportunities that lie in present and future market situations, as well as problems and adverse environmental trends that will affect your company. Because market size and growth are vital, potential growth rate should be forecast as accurately as possible.

Fit Product to Market   You should design your products to fit the market and then find other markets that fit those products. A market niche too small to interest large companies may be available.

> For example, a small firm manufacturing truck springs found that its product was a standard item produced by larger competitors that benefited from economies of scale. Because price competition was so severe, management decided to specialize in springs for swimming pool diving boards. This change in product strategy proved to be highly profitable.

Evaluate Company Resources   Your company's strengths, as well as its limitations, should be determined at each stage of the marketing process. Financial, cost, competitive, and timing pressures must be viewed realistically, and successes and failures need to be understood and regarded as important learning experiences.

The Growth Stage

Once you begin to grow, you can adopt one of three strategies: (1) expand products to reach new classes of customers, (2) increase penetration in the existing target market, or (3) make no marketing innovations but try instead to hold your present market share by product design and manufacturing innovations.

Expand Products to Reach New Markets   To reach new markets, you may add related products within the present product line, add products unrelated to the present line, find new applications in new markets for the firm's product, or add customized products, perhaps upgrading from low-quality to medium- or high-quality goods. This is **diversification**, or product line expansion, which tends to increase profits; contribute to long-range growth; stabilize production, employment, and payrolls; fill out a product line; and lower administrative overhead cost per unit.

Diversification involves adding products that are unrelated to the present product line.

The major pitfall of diversification is that the firm may not have the resources to compete effectively outside its established market niche. But the advantages seem to outweigh the pitfalls in most cases.

Increase Penetration of Present Market   You may want to increase the sales of existing products to existing customers. If so, you might reduce the number and variety of products and models to produce substantial operating economies.

Make No Marketing Innovations   The strategy of retaining current marketing practices without trying to innovate may suit your company if its strength lies in its technical competence. It is often advisable for retail store owners to follow this strategy.

Over the long term, a firm may follow one strategy for several years with the intent to change after certain marketing goals have been reached. But the change should occur if progress is desired.

What You Should Have Learned

■

1. You use the marketing concept when you focus your efforts on satisfying customers' needs—at a profit. Consumer needs and market opportunities should be identified, and the target market(s) most likely to buy your products should be determined. You should seek a competitive edge that sets your firm apart from, and gives it an advantage over, competitors.

2. Market research involves the systematic gathering, recording, and analyzing of data relating to the marketing of goods and services. It is part of the company's overall marketing system. By analyzing marketplace data, such as attitudinal, demographic, and lifestyle changes, marketing research can help small business owners plan their strategic efforts.

3. A marketing strategy involves setting marketing objectives and selecting target market(s) based on market segmentation. It means knowing consumers' needs, attitudes, and buying behavior, as well as studying population patterns, age groups, income levels, and regional patterns. Finally, the marketing mix, which consists of the controllable variables product, place, promotion, and price, should weigh heavily in decision making.

   The marketing strategies you can adopt are to expand products to reach new classes of customers, increase penetration in the existing target market, or make no marketing innovation but copy new marketing techniques instead.

4. A product life cycle has four major stages: introduction, growth, maturity, and decline. Strategies related to competition, promotion, distribution, and prices differ depending on the product's stage of the cycle.

5. Packaging both protects and promotes the product. It not only makes products more convenient and reduces spoiling or damage, but also makes products easier to identify, promotes the brand, and makes the purchase decision easier.

6. Pricing objectives should be set in order to achieve your firm's overall objectives. The "best" selling price should be cost- and market-oriented. Some pricing concerns for small businesses are product life cycle, meeting the competition, and cost orientation. Most small businesses employ cost-oriented pricing methods, using markups, discounts, and allowances. Different types of small firms use varying pricing practices.

7. The marketing of services differs from the marketing of goods. There are few objective standards for measuring service quality, but quality should be emphasized since customers measure services subjectively. Price competition in standardized services is quite severe; however, output of service firms is often difficult to standardize, and services cannot be stored, making thoughtfulness and special features important sources of a competitive edge for service businesses.

QUESTIONS FOR DISCUSSION

■

1. What is the marketing concept, and why is it so important to small firms?

2. How are the key success factors for a firm related to its competitive edge?

3. Why is marketing research so important to a small business—especially a new one?

4. What is market segmentation, and how can it be made more effective?

5. Discuss some characteristics that should be considered in selecting a target market.

6. What controllable variables are combined into a marketing mix to satisfy the target market?

7. What are the major stages of the product life cycle, and how do marketing strategies differ at each stage?

8. In what ways is packaging important to small firms and their customers?

9. What are the three basic considerations in pricing products? Explain cost-oriented pricing. What is markup?

10. Explain how service firms, retailers, wholesalers, manufacturers, and building contractors actually set prices.

11. How does the marketing of services differ from the marketing of goods?

CASE 7–1

PARKVIEW DRUG STORE: ADDING THE "PERSONAL TOUCH"

■

For 36 years, Bert and Barbara English have owned and operated Parkview Drug Store in Tuscaloosa, Alabama. Although not as high profile as Tuscaloosa's two main institutions—University of Alabama football and Dreamland Ribs—Parkview Drug Store is an institution.

The Englishes believe it is the "personal touch" that keeps customers coming back. "Big business has its place, but this is still the place for the personal touch," says Bert.

"We really thrive on the people and the relationships with families we've made throughout the years. Most people who come here know us on a first-name basis," adds Barbara.

Their "personal touch" philosophy definitely does not ring hollow like the marketing ploys and ad campaigns of many big businesses. Bert and Barbara truly foster a family atmosphere, and the effects of this approach are readily evident in their long-term relationship with customers. For example, the great-grandchildren of some of their original customers still patronize the store. Remarkably, five generations of one family have been—and still are—customers of the Englishes.

The bond between the owners and their customers is so strong, in fact, that over the years many customers have joined the Parkview family as employees. "Several

of our customers' children have come back to work for us," says Barbara. "One time we had a grandmother and her three grandchildren working here at the same time."

One aspect of the Englishes' business and personal philosophy of establishing relationships with customers is their policy of never turning away a college student who needs medicine. "There's nothing worse than being in an unfamiliar place, sick, and alone," says Bert. "We decided a long time ago that we would not turn away any student who needed medicine. If a student can't pay for a prescription or over-the-counter medicine, we set up an account and bill the parents. We've been doing that for 35 years, and we've never been burned."

The Englishes were recently awarded a Community Service Award by the family pharmacy division of Amerisource Health Corporation.

Fittingly, Bert and Barbara met at Brown's Drug Store in Selma, Alabama, in 1959, when Bert was the young pharmacist, and Barbara was a college student who worked on weekends and during the summers. Bert says it was a whirlwind courtship. "We met that winter, I gave her a ring on Mother's Day, and married her in July. She didn't get a chance to think about it."

In September of that year, J. W. Brown, the store owner, made Bert an offer he couldn't refuse: Brown would buy Parkview Drug Store in Tuscaloosa if Bert would operate it. "I didn't have any money," Bert explains, "but I had the sweat. He had a lot of faith in me; I was so young and inexperienced." So the young couple was off, and the rest is history.

No success story, though, is complete without a recounting of "the hard times." Those came for the Englishes only two years after they moved to Tuscaloosa. For an entire year, the street facing Parkview Drug was closed to widen it to four lanes. "It was very difficult for anyone to get to us," Bert recalls. "We'd sit here a couple of hours and no one would come in the store." Things got so bad that friends began encouraging the young couple to declare bankruptcy and cut their losses. But Bert says they enjoyed what they were doing. "I figured we were young, our life was before us, and we had a great future mapped out for ourselves. We didn't want to give it up. We just tightened our belts and did a lot of praying and refinancing." Soon "the hard times" were over—they had made it through.

At 59, Bert says he is more than up to the challenges that face a small pharmacy in today's market, namely, insurance policies that require participants to purchase medicine by mail and large chain stores with in-house pharmacies. Because Bert and Barbara are not ready to retire just yet, their son recently suggested that they hire another pharmacist to help out. True to his "personal touch" business approach, Bert responded, "I don't want another pharmacist. I want to deal with my customers myself."

Bert sums up their success: "You treat people the way you want to be treated, and they'll remember you."

Questions

1. Do you think the "personal touch" is still feasible in today's mass-merchandising climate? Explain.

2. What are your thoughts on hiring customers? What are the strengths and weaknesses of this practice?

3. Is the policy of letting students without funds have medicine a practical one?

4. How do you explain the owners' success in using the Golden Rule as an operating philosophy?

Source: Prepared by William Jay Megginson, with heavy reliance on Gilbert Nicholson, "Down-Home Atmosphere," *Tuscaloosa* (Alabama) *News,* January 7, 1996, pp. 1E–2E.

C A S E   7 – 2

AKIM'S LAWN CARE SERVICE

Akim, a high school teacher, wanted to earn some extra money to help provide better care for himself, his wife, and their expected baby. After studying the lawn care business in the local area, he decided there was a place for him to operate a part-time business. His niche would be cutting and caring for private lawns and doing contract work on common ground in prosperous neighborhoods.

Using his credit cards, Akim bought the equipment he needed. Then he used his home computer and printer to make up business cards and circulars to be distributed in the neighborhoods he had selected as his niche.

Akim priced his service by stating a low figure based on the time he thought it would take to finish the job. Then, based on that experience, he'd set a price to do the yard in the future.

Things went well until summer vacation. Then business improved so much that he couldn't handle it all by himself, but he had difficulty finding capable and dependable help. Also, many of his customers wouldn't pay when billed. Finally, unable to find a quick and reasonable source of repairs for his equipment—which he could ill afford, anyway—he called it quits after two years. He was unable to sell his equipment!

Questions

1. What did Akim do right in starting his business?

2. Was there anything he should have done that he didn't do?

3. What marketing concepts apply to a small business of this nature?

8

PRODUCT PROMOTION AND DISTRIBUTION

Don't sell the steak; sell the "sizzle."

Dale Carnegie sales slogan

Sales-management skills are very different from selling skills, and talent in one area does not necessarily indicate talent in the other.

Jack Falvey, management consultant, speaker, and writer

Much of what is included in the phrase "globalization" begins with changing our thinking. The first order of business for decision-makers is to think beyond our native borders and to adopt a mind-set that believes all world markets constitute one economy.

Fred Smith, Federal Express CEO

LEARNING OBJECTIVES

After studying the material in this chapter, you will be able to:

1. Describe different channels of distribution used for marketing products and discuss factors to consider in choosing an appropriate channel.

2. Describe the functions of intermediaries used in selling a product.

3. Describe the creative selling process used in personal selling.

4. Describe the use of advertising to promote the sale of a product.

5. Discuss some opportunities and problems involved in selling to ethnic groups.

6. Describe the opportunities for small firms in global marketing.

7. Explain how physical distribution affects marketing strategy.

8. Discuss some factors and problems involved in granting credit.

Springdale Travel, Inc.

In the late 1970s, Murray E. Cape recognized the profitable opportunities represented by the travel industry. Aware of the imperfections in that marketing niche, he responded on May 22, 1978, by opening Springdale Travel, Inc. Springdale Travel represents all major airlines, tour companies, hotels, and cruise lines—both domestically and globally. Recently Murray decided to semi-retire and is now travel manager/consultant for the company. Steve Cape and Bob Bender are leading the operations as partners into the twenty-first century.

Since 1978, Springdale Travel has evolved into three different operational units: Cruise Quarters, with eight full-time Cruise Counselors; Vacation World, with six full-time Vacation Counselors; and—the heart of the business—Springdale Travel, with 26 full-time corporate agents and 12 supporting services employees. In addition, the agency provides on-site services to five large corporations, with facilities in each of the clients' corporate headquarters.

Agents in the travel industry provide many products and services. Currently, Springdale Travel segments its target markets into the cruise market, vacation tours and packages, personal travel, and corporate travel. The product mix is approximately 65 percent corporate and 35 percent leisure travel.

Travel agents have a responsibility to represent the interests of the companies they serve. However, agents must also ensure that their clients receive the value and service they need. So Springdale Travel is a "go-between" representing the interests of both.

Most of the services provided by the agency are customer requests via the telephone, as all the agents (including the Capes and Bender) have a small workstation with a computer terminal and telephone. There are 30 incoming Essex system phone lines into the main office, with switching capabilities to Cruise Quarters and Vacation World. The beauty of the Essex system is that the lines can be tagged for specific uses, such as a specific number of lines to ring in, a specific number for calling out, and a specific number that are mixed for both incoming and outgoing calls. This system provides an effective control system for nonessential outgoing phone calls.

Another advantage is automatic call distribution (ACD), which assigns specific blocks of lines to particular agents or groups of agents. For example, certain agents are assigned to handle specific corporate accounts, and the system will ring on their lines first. If a given agent is busy, the call will cycle to any other reservation agent; if all other agents are busy, the system offers the client the option of holding or using voice mail. All agents, including the on-site agents, log into the main phone system to receive calls.

Mail, facsimile, a Web page (www.Springdale-Travel.com), and e-mail can also be used by customers to communicate with Springdale Travel. The agents can make and confirm most arrangements at first contact by using sophisticated computerized systems, or customers may choose to book their own arrangements via the Web page, which the agents will verify and "clean up" during working hours. When it is time to issue the ticket(s), the agency will mail the customer's purchases, deliver them (locally), or hold them for pickup either at the agency or at the point of departure. Bob Bender pointed out that in 1999, although many air carriers are moving to ticket-less reservations, at this point that is not usually suitable for the consumer. Nearly 80 percent of all airline reservations are still handled through travel agents.

Many changes are anticipated in Springdale Travel's future. For example, keeping up with communications technology alone will be an awesome task. Changing fee structures will play havoc with the bottom line, as travel providers have moved from paying a percentage commission for agents to a structured fee system. Springdale then must move more into a "consulting, counseling, meeting planning, value-added service industry," according to Murray Cape.

Springdale Travel, Cruise Quarters, and Vacation World are located next to one another in a busy shopping mall. Springdale Travel's main location opens onto the exterior of the shopping complex, while the other two maintain attractive storefronts that open directly into the mall near a main entrance. The storefront locations allow ever-changing window displays to attract the leisure traveler into the offices. Displays are frequently modified or changed to highlight the new attractions or "hot" vacation spots. This practice also allows for seasonal and market segmentation. For example, in 1999, Vacation World had a window display of The Sandals all-inclusive resorts in the Caribbean, which created a great deal of interest among both honeymooners and longer-married couples.

All three locations feature entire walls filled with racks of attractive travel brochures and magazines. This arrangement allows the shopper a chance to browse for points of interest—both domestically and globally.

Source: Prepared by M. Jane Byrd from conversations and correspondence with Murray Cape, Steve Cape, Bob Bender, and Kari Givens.

The Profile illustrates much of the material covered in this chapter. The people at Springdale Travel are creative in their advertising, sales promotion, and personal selling. This chapter deals with those subjects and also covers the channels of distribution to be used, the use of intermediaries for selling your product, other forms of promotion, the importance of considering ethnic groups in marketing products, opportunities in global marketing, physical distribution, and credit management.

■ CHOOSING A DISTRIBUTION CHANNEL

A **distribution channel** consists of the marketing organizations responsible for the flow of goods or services from the producer to the consumer.

One of the first things a small business producer of goods or services must do to promote sales of its product is to choose a distribution channel. A **distribution channel** consists of the various marketing organizations involved in moving the flow of goods and services from producer to user. The distribution channel acts as the pipeline through which a product flows. While the choice of distribution channels is quite important, it is not a simple one because of the many variables involved. Also, the channels for distributing consumer and industrial goods differ.

Factors to Consider in Choosing a Distribution Channel

Small business producers should design their own distribution channels, if feasible, to attain the optimum income. In doing so, they need to seek a *balance between maintaining control over the flow of the product and minimizing the cost involved.* The primary factors to consider include the following:

- Geographical markets and consumer types arranged in order of importance.
- Whether the product will be distributed through many outlets, selected outlets, or exclusive distributors.
- Kind and amount of marketing effort the producer intends to exert.
- Need for receiving feedback about the product.
- Adequate incentives to motivate resellers.

New products commonly require distribution channels different from those used for well-established and widely accepted products. Thus, you may introduce a new product using one channel and then switch to another if the product does not sell well. Also, a new channel may be required if you seek new markets for your products.

Finally, multiple distribution channels can create conflicts, and distribution can be hampered unless these conflicts are resolved. Producers should anticipate and provide for this problem. Choosing the right channel also permits a difference in pricing.

> For example, Hill's Science Diet dog and cat foods are so expensive that they could never compete with other pet foods in grocery stores, so they are sold in pet stores and by veterinarians to people who are evidently willing, on the vet's recommendation, to pay the premium price.

Distribution Channels for Consumer Goods

Figure 8–1 shows the traditional channels for distributing consumer goods. As you can see, a small business has essentially two choices: (1) to sell directly to the consumer or (2) to sell through one or more intermediaries. This decision is usually made (at least initially) when choosing what type of business to enter. The first channel (direct from producer to consumer) is the most frequently used by small firms, probably because it is the simplest.

Figure 8–1
Distribution Channels for Consumer Goods

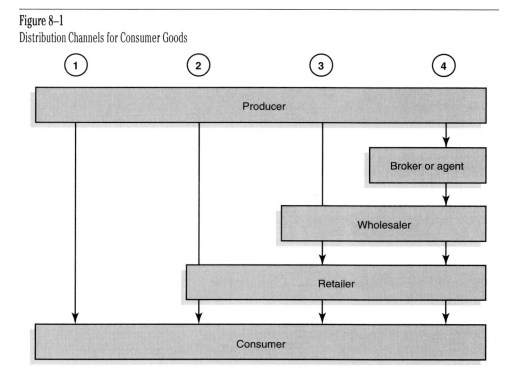

Figure 8–2
Distribution Channels for Industrial Goods

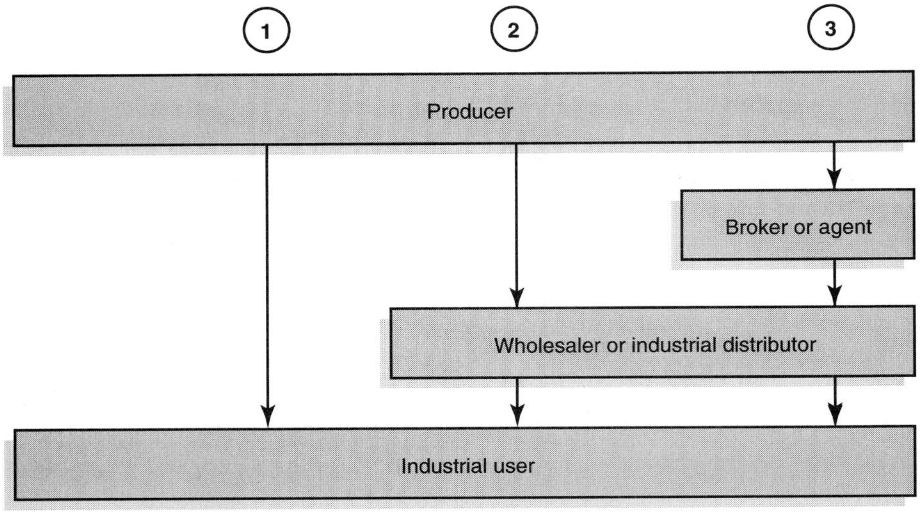

As discussed in Chapter 7, small firms performing services and selling goods at retail usually deal directly with consumers. Most of our discussion in this chapter will concentrate on the remaining channels, which use intermediaries.

> Louisiana strawberries are an interesting example of using channel 4 depicted in Figure 8–1. Because strawberries are so perishable, they must be sold quickly. So they are picked, placed in refrigerated railroad cars, and shipped before they are sold. As they travel north, agents or brokers contact wholesalers in cities along the line to Chicago. As the berries are sold, the cars carrying them are diverted to the appropriate city, where the wholesaler picks them up and sells them through the remainder of the channel.*

Distribution Channels for Industrial Goods

Distribution channels for industrial goods are shown in Figure 8–2. Channel 1 (direct from producer to industrial user) is the most frequently used. In general, items produced in large quantities, but sold in relatively small amounts, move through channel 2. Large, bulky items that have relatively few buyers, or whose demand varies, flow through channel 3.

■ SELLING THROUGH INTERMEDIARIES

Intermediaries are those units or institutions in the channel of distribution that either take title to or negotiate the sale of the product. The usual intermediaries are: (1) brokers, (2) agents, (3) wholesalers, and (4) retailers.

Brokers

A **broker,** for a fee, brings the buyer and seller together to negotiate purchases or sales but does not take title to, or possession of, the goods. The broker has only limited authority to

Intermediaries are those units or institutions in the channel of distribution that either take title to or negotiate the sale of the product.

Brokers bring buyers and sellers of goods together to negotiate purchases or sales.

---

*Sometimes they are not sold by the time they reach Chicago, the train's destination, and must be sold at distressed prices or allowed to rot. Then the farmers not only lose the value of their crop but must pay transportation costs as well.

set prices and terms of sale. Firms using brokers usually buy and/or sell highly specialized goods and seasonal products not requiring constant distribution, such as strawberries or crude oil. Canned goods, frozen-food items, petroleum products, and household specialty products are also often distributed through brokers.

Agents

Because brokers operate on a one-time basis to bring buyers and sellers together, a small business that wants a more permanent distribution channel may use an agent to perform the marketing function. These **agents,** who market a product to others for a fee, are variously called *manufacturers' agents, selling agents,* or *sales representatives (reps),* depending on the industry.

Agents are marketing intermediaries who market a product to others for a fee.

Wholesalers

Wholesalers take actual physical possession of goods and then market them to retailers, other channel members, or industrial users. They maintain a sales force and provide services such as storage, delivery, credit to the buyer, product servicing, and sales promotion.

Wholesalers are intermediaries who take title to the goods handled and then sell them to retailers or other intermediaries.

Retailers

Retailers sell goods and services directly to ultimate consumers. They may sell through store outlets, by mail order, or by means of home sales. Included in this category are services rendered in the home, such as installing draperies and repairing appliances.

Retailers sell goods or services directly to the ultimate consumers.

Services Performed by Retailers   Retailers must essentially determine and satisfy consumer needs. They deal with many customers, each making relatively small purchases. Some major decisions of retailers are what goods and services to offer to customers, what quality of goods and services to provide, whom to buy from and sell to, what type of promotion to use and how much, what price to charge, and what credit policy to follow.

Current Trends in Retailing   The more traditional retail outlets are department stores, mass-merchandising shopping chains, specialty stores, discount stores, factory outlets, supermarkets, and mail-order selling.

A newer version of the discount house is **off-price retailers,** such as T. J. Maxx and Hit or Miss. They buy designer labels and well-known brands of clothing at less than wholesale prices and pass the savings along to the customers, using mass-merchandising techniques and providing reduced services.

Off-price retailers are those who buy designer labels and well-known brands of clothing at low prices and sell them at less than typical retail prices.

Another recent development is self-service fast-food restaurants. Many of these are now following the gasoline companies' move to cheap, self-help "refueling stops."

Even supermarkets now use this approach. First came self-service, with the customers selecting their own items, taking them to the checkout counter, and paying the checker-cashier. Now customers in some stores can select, ring up, and pay for their groceries using handheld scanners.

An experiment with these devices and this arrangement in the Netherlands was quite successful. In fact, the store managers found that the loss of products from store shelves through theft or inventory error actually declined with self-scanning.[1]

Another innovation is similar to automated teller machines (ATMs), namely, computerized video kiosks in shopping malls that replace salespersons. Many retailers are now installing these devices, which utilize existing technologies, such as computer science, video display, laser disks, voice recognition, and sophisticated graphics.

Shopping from television is another escalating trend. The following example illustrates how this relatively new channel of distribution operates.

> The Home Shopping Network (HSN) gets more than 200,000 calls a day from consumers. In answering this demand, HSN created the HSN Institute, a research and development center to help inventors, businesspeople, and manufacturers get their products on the air. Businesses do not have to pay to appear on the network but must be able to provide enough goods to meet the network demand and take back unsold inventory. In the HSN search for products, scouts visit local product fairs searching for products and crafts to offer.[2]

Another emerging marketing channel is the Internet (discussed later in the chapter). People are now using it to swap items and information. And some people are using it to sell information, products, and services.

■ SELLING WITH YOUR OWN SALES FORCE

Selling expertise is needed in all business activities. While advertising may entice customers to desire a product, it alone is not usually sufficient to complete a sale. Customers appreciate good selling and dislike poor service. They believe salespeople should show an interest in them and assist them in their buying. Often, when competing businesses carry the same merchandise, the caliber of the salespeople is the principal reason one outsells the other. The following letter, which came from a homemaker in the Washington, D.C., area, illustrates this point.

> I went to the cosmetic counter at Lord & Taylor [www.lordandtaylor.com], intending to get one or—at the most—two items. Instead, the Estée Lauder area sales rep who was there gave me such an overwhelming sales pitch that I ended up buying a horrifying amount of stuff. In addition, they signed me up for the free workshop next week, where they will make me over to show what I should be wearing. After trying *three* Lauder counters in *three* different stores *with no satisfaction,* it was nice to have someone take *a personal interest in me.*[3]

Need for Personal Selling

In self-service operations, the burden of selling merchandise is placed on the producer's packaging and the retailer's display of the merchandise. Some retailers have found that 80 percent of the shoppers who made unplanned purchases bought products because they saw them effectively displayed. Self-service reduces retail costs by having smaller sales salaries and more effective use of store space. However, risks from pilferage and breakage increase.

Some items are packaged differently for self-service. For example, where film is kept behind the counter, the boxes are stacked in bins; but for self-service, the box has a large extra flap with a hole, permitting it to hang on an arm, which increases its visibility and also cuts down on shoplifting. Similarly, the same pens that stand en masse in a bin display in a small office supplies store are packaged in hanging blister packs in drug, grocery, and variety stores.

A quiet revolution is sweeping department store retailing in an effort to counter such factors as apathy, lack of training, and lack of initiative, which have kept salespeople's productivity (and pay) low. Now many retailers are using straight commission, rather than salary or salary plus commission, to pay their salespeople. They hope that the promise of potentially higher pay will motivate existing staff and attract better salespeople (and encourage them to train and develop themselves to be better producers). It seems to be working, as the following example shows.

John L. Palmerio, a veteran salesman in the men's shoe department at the Manhattan Bloomingdale's store (www.bloomingdales.com), increased his earnings by 25 percent after switching from a straight hourly scale to a 10 percent commission on sales. Similar experiences are being reported at other stores, including the Burdines chain in Florida.[4]

The largest promotional expenditure for small businesses is almost always for personal selling. Effective sales personnel are especially important to small businesses, which have difficulty competing with large ones in such areas as variety, price, and promotion. Personal selling is one activity where small firms, particularly retailers, can compete with larger competitors—and win! But effective selling doesn't just happen. Rather, small business managers must work hard to attain a high level of sales effectiveness.

Steps in the Creative Selling Process

The creative selling process, as shown in Figure 8–3, may be divided into eight steps. You should inform your people that these steps are needed for effective selling—therefore, they should know the steps and use them.

Preparation   Before any customer contact is made, the salesperson should know the company's policies, procedures, and rules; how to operate equipment, such as the cash register; and a great deal about the product, including how and when to use it, its features in comparison with those of other models or brands, and available options (such as color, size, and price).

Prospecting   Prospecting consists of taking the initiative in dealing with new and regular customers by going to them with a new product or service idea.[5] An example of new customer prospecting is when a salesperson contacts a bride-to-be or new mother and tells her about goods or services that might be appropriate. Regular customer prospecting is effective because a firm's best prospects are its current customers. A salesperson should periodically call regular customers to tell them about products and services, but not so often that they lose the sense of being special, or feel they are being badgered. Prospecting for new customers may require a more creative approach.

Prospecting is taking the initiative in seeking out customers with a new product.

For example, when Donna Chaiet needs new students to enroll in the self-defense classes at her New York City–based business, Prepare, Inc., she makes "cold calls" to people she picks out of the phone directory. Her goal is to encourage the listener to drop by and tour her school or sign up for a 20-hour Impact Personal Safety training seminar.[6]

Figure 8–3
Steps in the Sales Process

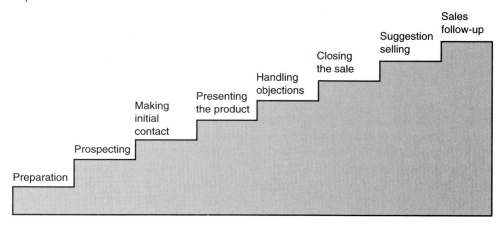

Preparation / Prospecting / Making initial contact / Presenting the product / Handling objections / Closing the sale / Suggestion selling / Sales follow-up

Prospecting has become much easier with the introduction of address and phone information databases on CD-ROM. Many small businesses are beginning to use them to find potential customers. They can gain telemarketing and direct-mail opportunities without using—and paying for—directory assistance calls.

A highly rated CD-ROM phone directory is *Select Phone,* made by Pro CD Inc. (www.procd.com), of Danvers, Massachusetts. Sales at Pro CD doubled in the year after its introduction. Unit sales are growing much faster, since prices of the software are plummeting.[7]

Making Initial Contact   In the initial contact with a customer, the salesperson should begin on a positive note. The salesclerk might ask, "May I help you?" The customer replies, "No, thank you. I'm just looking." This common, automatic greeting shows no creativity on the part of the clerk. Instead, salespeople should treat each customer as an individual, reacting differently to each one. Initial contact also includes acknowledging customers when they enter the sales area, even if they can't be waited on immediately. For example, you could say, "I'll be with you in a moment." When free, you should be sure to say, "Thank you for waiting." These actions will result in fewer customers leaving without being served and produce a higher sales volume.

Whenever possible, serving customers should be given top priority. Nothing is more annoying to a customer than waiting while a clerk straightens stock, counts money, finishes a discussion with another clerk, or continues a phone conversation.

Presenting the Product   In presenting the product to a customer, you should stress its benefits to the buyer. Get the customer involved in the presentation by demonstrating several features and then have the customer handle it. At this stage, you should limit the choices the customer has. For example, you could use the "rule of two"—don't show more than two choices at one time. If more than two items are placed before the customer, the chance of a sale lessens, and the possibility of shoplifting increases. For this reason, many stores limit the number of clothing items that may be taken to a dressing room.

"Canned" sales presentations are generally ineffective. You should therefore try to find out how much the customer already knows about the product in order to adapt the presentation to his or her level of expertise. A sale can be lost both by boring the customer with known facts and by using bewildering technical jargon.

Handling Objections   Objections are a natural part of the selling process. Thus, if the customer presents objections, you should recognize that as a sign of progress, since a customer who doesn't plan to buy will seldom seek more information in this way. In many cases, an objection opens the way for you to do more selling. For example, if the customer says a dress looks out of date, you could answer, "Yes, it does look old-fashioned, but that style is back in fashion." This is more diplomatic than a flat contradiction, such as, "That dress was first shown at the market this season. It's the latest thing."

Closing the Sale   Some closing techniques you can use to help the customer make the buying decision are offering a service ("May we deliver it to you this afternoon?"), giving a choice ("Do you want the five-piece or the eight-piece cooking set?"), or offering an incentive ("If you buy now, you get 10 percent off the already low price.").

Suggestion Selling   You should make a definite suggestion for a possible additional sale. Statements such as "Will that be all?" or "Can I get you anything else?" are not positive suggestions. When a customer buys fabric, you should offer matching thread, buttons, and the appropriate interfacing. A supply of bags is a natural suggestion to a vacuum cleaner buyer. And customers' attention should always be drawn to other items in the product line. Many customers like to receive valid suggestions that keep them from having to come back later for needed accessories.

Figure 8–4
How to Lose a Sale

---

1. *Speak more than your potential client.* If you do all the talking, you won't be able to ascertain the needs of the buyer. The most successful sales reps spend 70 to 80 percent of the time listening.

2. *Wing it.* Don't call without first finding out as much as you can about your potential customer. Research the company's size, history, products, and challenges using *Hoover's Handbook, Dun & Bradstreet, Value Line,* or other such resources, which can be found at the library.

3. *Forget to ask questions.* Most people drift off after five or six minutes of a presentation, so be sure to interject questions to keep clients alert and involved. Focus on your buyer's criteria by asking, "What does the next vendor need to do to earn your business?" "What is your business's biggest challenge?" "What differentiates your company from your competition?"

4. *Rely on your memory.* You can't afford to miss important points, and nobody's memory is perfect. Ask the customer if it's okay to take notes, and use key points the customer made in a follow-up letter after the sales call. Start it with, "Just to make sure we're on the right track, the following is a list of your key needs . . ."

5. *Go off on tangents.* Instead of expounding on every passing thought, stay focused to make a strong case. Before you start your presentation, give your customers an overview of what you'll be telling them, and highlight key points at the end. Don't forget to follow up.

Source: Reprinted from Barry J. Farber, as reported in *AT&T Powersource* 1 (Spring 1995), p. 20.

Sales Follow-Up   Follow-up should be a part of every sale. The close, "Thank you for shopping with us," is a form of sales follow-up if said with enthusiasm and sincerity. Follow-up may also consist of checking on anything that was promised the customer after the sale. If delivery is scheduled for a given day or time, you could check to make sure the promise is met and, if not, notify the customer of the problem.

Attributes of a Creative Salesperson

Many efforts have been made to identify and isolate those personal characteristics that can predict a knack for selling. So far, however, evidence indicates there is no perfect way to determine who will be successful, for salespeople just do not fit a neat pattern.[8] Still, there are some mental and physical attributes that seem to make some people more effective than others at selling. Barry J. Farber, author of the book *State of the Art Selling*[9] and an audio training program of the same name,[10] emphasizes the attributes of a good salesperson by telling salespeople what *not* to do. Figure 8–4 provides his advice.

Mental Attributes   Judgment—often called common sense, maturity, or intelligence—is essential for effective selling. For example, good salespeople don't argue with customers, nor do they criticize the business in front of customers. Tact is also needed. Good salespeople have a positive attitude toward customers, products, services, and the firm.

Physical Attributes   Personal appearance is important for success. For example, a slim salesperson would be more appropriate than a larger person for a health spa. Poor personal hygiene may lead to lost business. An observant manager should watch out for hygiene problems among the staff and, when necessary, counsel offending employees in private.

■ ADVERTISING

Advertising informs customers of the availability, desirability, and uses of products. It also tries to convince customers that the products are superior to those of competitors. Advertising is paid for by the marketer, who also controls the content, appearance, and/or sound

Advertising informs customers of the availability, desirability, and uses of products.

of the message. The advertiser also has considerable authority over when, where, and how often advertising messages reach the target market.

Types of Advertising

Product advertising
calls attention to or
explains a specific
product.

**Institutional
advertising** is selling
an idea about the
company.

Advertising can be either product or institutional. **Product advertising** is self-explanatory; **institutional advertising** is selling an idea about the company. Most advertising by small firms is a combination of the two. Institutional advertising tries to keep the public conscious of the company and its good reputation while also trying to sell specific products, as the following example illustrates.

> R. David Thomas, the founder of Wendy's Old Fashioned Hamburgers restaurants (www.wendys.com), started in the restaurant business as a busboy at age 15 and gained experience as a food service provider as a short-order cook in the U.S. Army. He opened his first restaurant in 1969 and named it after his daughter, Melinda Lou, nicknamed "Wendy" by her brothers and sisters.
>
> In 1989, Thomas began appearing in a series of TV ads built around Wendy. In one ad, he emphasizes quality by saying, "The hamburgers have to be good, or I wouldn't have named the place after my daughter." In another ad, when a voice chides Thomas about his efforts to align a menu board of Wendy's new products, he turns in exasperation and asks, "Wendy, don't you have anything else to do?"
>
> Thomas visits the restaurants and introduces himself with "Hi, I'm Wendy's dad." Market surveys have shown that the consumer identification of Wendy's has jumped tremendously. Thomas is also a noted philanthropist, working with children's hospitals, medical research, and private charities.[11]

Developing the Advertising Program

To be most effective, an advertising program should be used over an extended time period. The advertising should include preparing customers to accept a new product, suggesting new uses for established products, and calling attention to special sales. Such a program requires four basic decisions: (1) how much money to budget and spend for advertising, (2) what media to use, (3) what to say and how to say it, (4) what advertising agency to use, and (5) what results are expected.

Setting the Budget

Advertising costs should be controlled by an *advertising budget.* The most popular bases for establishing such a budget are: (1) a percentage of sales or profits, (2) units of sales, (3) objective (task), and (4) executive decision.

With the *percentage of sales or profits method,* advertising costs have a consistent relationship to the firm's sales volume and/or profit level. Thus, as sales/profits go up/down, advertising expenditures go up/down by the same percentage. One disadvantage of using this method is that advertising may be needed most when sales and profits fall.

Using the *units of sales method,* the firm sets aside a fixed sum for each unit of product to be sold. It is difficult to use this method when advertising many different kinds of products, for sporadic or irregular markets, and for style merchandise. But the method is useful for specialty goods and in situations where outside factors limit the amount of product available.

While the *objective (task) method* is most accurate, it is also the most difficult and least used method for estimating an advertising budget. Specific objectives are set, such as "to sell 25 percent more of Product X by attracting the business of teenagers." Then the medium that best reaches this target market is chosen, and estimates are made concerning costs.

With the most popular method of all, the *executive decision method,* the marketing manager decides how much to spend. This method's effectiveness depends on the manager's experience and/or intuition.

Selecting Advertising Media

The most popular advertising media used by small businesses are display ads in newspapers, store signs, direct mail, circulars and handbills, Yellow Pages ads, outdoor signs, radio, television, and the Internet. Probably the best medium for a small business, though, is word-of-mouth advertising from satisfied customers.

Some Popular Media Used by Small Firms   *Display ads* in the local newspaper are effective for most retail and service businesses. *Store signs* are useful in announcing sales or special events and for recruiting personnel. High postage rates are making the use of *direct mail* more expensive. Offset and instant printing have simplified the preparation of small quantities of *circulars* and *handbills;* however, printing and distribution costs are increasing, and local ordinances limit use of this medium. *Yellow Pages ads* are effective for special products, services, and repair shops. *Outdoor signs* are useful in announcing the opening or relocation of a business.

Radio advertising is helpful for small businesses in thinly populated areas. *Television* has generally been too costly and wasteful for many small firms to use. Now, however, local cable systems and low-power TV stations, broadcasting only 15 to 25 miles, have rates low enough to permit small firms to use them.[12]

By no means a new advertising medium, the **infomercial** is an effective strategy for a small business in a fast-changing, or young, industry to emphasize its competitive advantages. These "omnipresent half-hour TV ads hosted by hyperthyroid 'sellevangelists,' "[13] can be effective in helping small firms keep growing and enter markets once dominated by giant competitors. However, if they are to be effective in sales, infomercials must be produced professionally, by experts.

Infomercials are long, usually half-hour TV ads hosted by a hyper "sellevangelist," selling a relatively new product or service.

> Guthy-Renker (www.guthy-renker.com), based in Palm Desert, California, is such a professional organization, founded by Bill Guthy and Greg Renker. Their first infomercial, an instant hit that grossed nearly $10 million by 1988, featured ex-football great Fran Tarkenton endorsing a success program based on Napoleon Hill's book *Think and Grow Rich.* The partners bought time on six small-market TV stations and gradually expanded.
>
> The partners had decided earlier to make only high-quality productions and to keep their claims honest. The company ran up an impressive string of successes through the 1990s selling cosmetics, personal motivation courses, and weight-loss programs.[14]

The Internet *is* a new advertising medium that is exploding in use as companies are lured by the speed, the cost savings, and the possibility of more personalized pitches.[15] For example, an American International College (www.aic.edu) survey of Forbes 500 CEOs found they expected to generate almost 40 percent of annual sales via this medium within 10 years.[16] But the Internet is also used by small-scale entrepreneurs. Ernst & Young (www.eyi.com), a consulting firm, surveyed 398 entrepreneurs attending the Entrepreneur of the Year Conference in Palm Springs, California, on their present and planned use of the Internet to sell their goods and services. As shown in Figure 8–5, slightly over 80 percent of them were already using the Internet. The primary uses, however, were for e-mail and to give information; only 8 percent were actually using it for commerce. Still, the respondents expected commerce to account for 27 percent of their Internet use within a year and a half.

Figure 8–5
Use of the Internet by a Select Group of Entrepreneurs

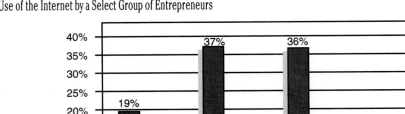

Source: Based on information in Del Jones, "More Entrepreneurs Turning to Internet," *USA Today,* November 25, 1997, p. 2B.

> Some booksellers have completely abandoned traditional bookselling and turned instead to the Internet. For example, Karen Weyant, of Newport, Rhode Island, closed her store—Scribe's Perch—for good in 1996 after finding that her Internet sales were three times greater than her storefront sales. Now, using the Advanced Book Exchange site (www.abebooks.com/home/scribebks/), she sells only via the Net—about $200 worth per day—to customers as far away as Croatia and the Netherlands.[17]

How to Select the Appropriate Medium   The medium (or media) you choose will depend on several factors, including the target market, cost, and availability. The media of choice are those that your *target market* pays most attention to.

> The owners of a Chicago party supplies rental company came up with a unique way to advertise their company. Instead of competing with a lot of "clutter" to advertise locally in newspapers or the Yellow Pages, they decided to use their delivery trucks as on-the-road advertisements. Working with a graphics company, the owners developed two images—costing $3,500 per truck—one a formal dinner setting and one showing a summertime scene, both using products that can be bought or rented from the company.
>
> The ads were quite successful, as more than 80 percent of the subsequent callers had seen the ads. There are two additional costs: (1) repair costs are higher in case of accident, and (2) the trucks "must be kept clean."[18]

When considering media costs, you must look at both absolute cost and relative cost. *Absolute cost* is the actual expenditure for running an ad. *Relative cost* is the relationship between the actual cost and the number of consumers the message reaches (typically, the cost per 1,000 consumers reached). Finding the lower relative cost should be your objective. You should consider not only monetary costs but also public relations costs. For example, many e-mail users have complained loudly and bitterly about the large amount of *spam,* that is, unwanted direct marketing, they receive.[19]

Developing the Message

The ideas or information you want to convey should be translated into words and symbols relevant to the target market. You must decide what is to be said, then how it is to be said, what form it will take, and what its style and design will be. Skilled employees of the chosen medium can help you develop the ads once you have decided on the central idea. Businesses can also get help from an advertising agency or a graphic arts firm.

When and How to Use an Advertising Agency

Most small business managers plan their own ad programs, particularly when they consider the rather high costs of retaining the services of an advertising agency. This practice may be false economy, however, because advertising agencies with experienced specialists can help you by (1) performing preliminary studies and analyses; (2) developing, implementing, and evaluating an advertising plan; and (3) following up on the advertising. Most small agencies tend to specialize in one area.

Measuring the Results of Advertising

Measuring the results of advertising is important. Assume you want to determine whether your advertising is doing the job it was intended to do. You could do so by using some form of immediate-response advertising. **Immediate-response advertising** attempts to entice potential customers to buy a particular product from the business within a short time, such as a day, weekend, or week. The advertising should then be checked for results shortly after its appearance. Some ways of measuring results of these ads are coupons (especially for food and drug items) brought to the store, letters or phone requests referring to the ads, the amount of sales of a particular item, and checks on store traffic. Comparing sales during an offer period to normal sales, tallying mail and phone orders, and switching offers among different media can help determine which medium was more effective.

Immediate-response advertising tries to get customers to buy a product within a short period of time so that response can be easily measured.

■ MERCHANDISING, SALES PROMOTION, AND PUBLICITY

Many businesses use other means and go beyond advertising or support their advertising through merchandising, sales promotion, and publicity.

Merchandising

Merchandising is the promotional effort made for a product in retailing firms, especially at the point of purchase. It is the way the product is presented to customers, including window displays, store banners, product label and packaging, and product demonstrations. Window and counter displays are especially effective if they are attractively done and changed frequently. Some manufacturers and wholesalers provide retailers with advice on how to design better store displays and layouts.

Merchandising is promoting the sale of a product at the point of purchase.

Some retailers, however, use their own initiative in developing an effective merchandising strategy. The following example shows what one entrepreneur did to merchandise his stores.

Richard Ost owns three of the smallest drugstores you probably ever saw, located in one of Philadelphia's "most bombed-out and burned-up" neighborhoods. Yet he was doing $5 million of business a year in the mid-1990s, more than twice the rate of average drugstores.

How did he do it? He's succeeded by weaving himself into the fabric of the community. In retail health care, nothing succeeds like sensitivity. Ost instructs his employees to "be culturally competent." He enforces this idea by labeling prescriptions in Spanish for his Hispanic customers. He's loaded into his computer some 1,000 common regimens in Spanish. With a single keystroke, any one of these can be printed in Spanish rather than English. The program was so popular that he was the first Anglo in the community named "Hispanic Citizen of the Year." Business took off!

After he bought his second location, he found he had an Asian clientele, so he started labeling prescriptions in Vietnamese as well. Soon he was filling over 400 prescriptions a day at just the second location—half in English, 30 percent in Spanish, and 20 percent in Vietnamese.[20]

Sales Promotion

Sales promotion includes marketing activities (other than advertising and personal selling) that stimulate consumer purchasing and dealer effectiveness.

Sales promotion, or activities that try to make other sales efforts (such as advertising) more effective, includes consumer promotions, trade promotions, and sales force promotions. *Consumer promotions* use coupons, discounts, contests, trading stamps, samples, rebates, and so forth. Rebates appeal to many manufacturers because few consumers actually redeem them, but they can also provide a competitive edge for retailers.

For example, Office Max, an office superstore chain based in Cleveland, recently began handling rebate submissions for customers as an added service. This attracts customers to both the product and the retailer.[21]

Trade promotions include advertising specialties, free goods, buying allowances, merchandise allowances, cooperative advertising, and free items given as premiums. *Sales force promotions* consist of benefits, such as contests, bonuses, extra commissions, and sales rallies, that encourage salespeople to increase their selling effectiveness.

There are many examples of such promotions. Retailers usually promote the opening of their business. A premium (or bonus item) may be given with the purchase of a product. During out-of-season periods, coupons offering a discount may be given to stimulate sales by attracting new customers. Holidays, store remodeling or expansion, store anniversaries, special purchases, fashion shows, or the presence in the store of a celebrity are other events suitable for promotions.

In the 1800s, William Wrigley, Jr., left Philadelphia for Chicago to sell soap. He offered baking soda to customers as an incentive to buy soap. Then he tried giving away chewing gum to get people to buy baking soda. Since gum sold best, he concentrated on selling it. When Wrigley first offered Spearmint in 1893, his marketing message was: "Tell 'em quick and tell 'em often." As a promotional gimmick, he sent a stick of gum to every person listed in the U.S. phone book in 1915.[22] Publicly owned since 1919, the Wm. Wrigley Jr. Company (www.wrigley.com) is still innovating. Wrigley brands are now produced in 13 factories around the world and sold in over 140 countries.

Publicity

Publicity is information about a business that is published or broadcast without charge.

Publicity can be considered free advertising. When your product, your business, or you as the owner become newsworthy, publicity may enhance sales. Many local newspapers are interested in publicizing the opening of a new store or business in their area. Take the initiative by sending a well-written publicity release to a news editor for possible use. Also, information about a new product or employees who perform various community services may be interesting to the editor.

■ CONSIDERING ETHNIC DIFFERENCES

There are growing opportunities for small businesses to increase the sales of their products to various ethnic groups, for they are growing much faster than traditional markets.

However, ethnic groups may require special attention in promoting your product. Language differences are an obvious example; more than 10 percent of U.S. families speak a language other than English in their homes. Some areas of the country have an even higher percentage. For example, about one out of three households in Miami and San Antonio speaks Spanish. On the other hand, you should be careful not to regard all members of an ethnic group as a single target market. Some members of minority groups strive for what they perceive as white middle-income features or standards in material goods, while other sectors in ethnic markets disregard these objectives in favor of their traditional values.

The demographics for ethnic groups may vary, too. The median age of most such groups is much lower than that of whites. Since more minorities are in the earlier stages of the family life cycle, they constitute a better market for certain goods, especially durable goods. Separate marketing strategies may be needed for these ethnically or racially defined markets, as the following example illustrates.

> Longo Toyota in El Monte, California—near Los Angeles—is the number one Toyota dealership in the United States. It probably achieved that distinction by having salespeople who speak over 24 languages. In addition to Spanish, there are native speakers of Arabic, Nigerian Ibo, Mandarin Chinese, and many other Asian, African, and European languages.[23]

More and more businesses are advertising on Hispanic TV stations. The two Spanish-language networks, Telemundo Group Inc. and Univision Inc., attract about 5 percent of the total audience during prime-time television viewing. Univision, founded in 1962, reaches about 85 percent of the nation's 6 million Hispanic households. Telemundo, founded in 1986, reaches about 75 percent.[24] Companies such as Domino's Pizza have specialized Hispanic media campaigns for selected areas.

■ OPPORTUNITIES FOR SMALL FIRMS IN GLOBAL MARKETING

The author Heywood Broun stated: "Time and space cannot be discarded. Nor can we ignore the fact that we are citizens of the world." This is so for us as individuals or as small business owners. Think of the products you use every day. Notice how many of them originated outside the United States. Where does your coffee, tea, or cola drink come from? What type of music system do you use? Where was your television set or VCR produced? Look at the remote control to your electronic system and see if it was "Assembled in Mexico" or "Made in Malaysia." If you own a personal computer, chances are good that some of its components were designed, manufactured, or assembled in Japan, South Korea, or Taiwan.

Do you get the point? As students, teachers, consumers, and small business people, we're surrounded by the overwhelming evidence of **global marketing,** which involves buying and selling goods or services that are produced, bought, or sold throughout the world. Because of the growing importance of

"Mama, you take the minutes of the meeting. . . . Let's see, New York wants a good recipe for lasagna. What the heck is lasagna?"

(*Source:* Cartoon by Fred Maes. Copyright by Fred Maes, 1996.)

Global marketing involves products that are produced, bought, sold, or used almost anywhere in the world.

these activities, we estimate that *over half of you will work in some aspect of international activities during your working life.*

Globalization is a challenge not only to large firms but to small ones as well. Andrew S. Grove, an immigrant who became CEO of Intel Corporation (www.intel.com), recently said, "Today's managers [must] adapt to a globalized business world [because] business knows no boundaries." He went on to say, "Every employee, therefore, must compete with every person in the world who is capable of doing the same job."[25]

Global marketing has two faces. One is **importing,** which is purchasing and marketing the products of other nations. The other, **exporting,** consists of marketing our products to other nations. We now explore both of these facets.

Importing involves purchasing and marketing other nations' products.

Exporting involves marketing our products to other nations.

Importing by Small Firms

There are essentially two types of small business importers. First, there are those who engage in actual import activities by importing products and selling them to intermediaries or directly to customers. Second—and much more prevalent—are the millions of small retailers and service businesses that sell international products. Both types are interested in imports for a number of reasons.

Before reading further, take the test in Figure 8–6. The results will show you how knowledgeable you are about one of our trading partners, China. (See Endnote 26 for this chapter at the end of the book for the researchers' findings.)[26]

Reasons for Importing There are various significant reasons for importing. First, imported goods may be the product the company sells to customers or the raw material for the goods it produces. The small company must decide whether to purchase U.S. products, if available, or to import foreign products. If the items are imported, does the company purchase them from a U.S. wholesaler or from firms outside the country?

Second, companies from other countries are just as interested in selling to U.S. markets as our producers are in selling to international markets. Thus, imported goods may form the

---

Figure 8–6
Test Your Trade IQ

Can you go through the day without using something made in China?

Source: Ellen Neuborne's visit to a Minneapolis, Minnesota, mall to see what Chinese-made products U.S. consumers use, as reported in *USA Today,* February 24, 1995, p. 1A.

main source of revenue—or competition—for a small business in all stages of buying, producing, and/or selling a product.

Third, small business owners capitalize on the fact that some Americans have a preference for foreign goods or services. Goods such as English china, Japanese sports cars, Italian leather goods, Oriental carpets, Russian caviar, and French crystal are eagerly sought by American consumers. Also, small U.S. producers should understand that the increasing flow of new and improved products into the country can improve their output or increase their competitive level.

Some Problems with Importing   The benefits of importing must be weighed against the disadvantages. At present, for example, we see foreign goods flooding U.S. markets at the same time that some of our producers are suffering a lack of customers, or even going out of business. This means that foreign-made automobiles, cameras, stereos, TV sets, VCRs, clothing, shoes, calculators, and home computers are being imported in growing numbers. Nevertheless, although manufactured abroad, these imports provide many opportunities for American small firms to sell, distribute, and service them.

While it is probably true that imports generate more jobs than they eliminate, this is small comfort to those small business owners and employees who are adversely affected, as the following example shows.

> Kalart Victor Corporation, the last U.S. maker of 16-millimeter movie projectors, called it quits in 1989, a victim of Japanese competition and the popularity of VCRs. Its projectors had been used in school systems and by government bodies around the world. As these groups switched to VCRs for instructional films, the demand for projectors declined. In 1980, there were five U.S. makers of projectors, with Kalart alone employing 250 people. By 1989, Kalart, the only producer—with fewer than 50 employees—left the market to three Japanese makers.[27]

Another "problem" with imports—if it can be called a problem—is knowing what is "Made in USA" and what is not. Running shoes provide a symbol of how tough it is to figure out what *is* and *is not* made in the United States.

> For example, the New Balance running shoe (www.newbalance.com), often worn by President Clinton and Vice President Gore during their early days in office, was labeled "Made in USA." But according to the Made in the USA Foundation, 29 percent of it was made in China.[28]

Exporting by Small Firms

Along with the fascination we have with foreign business, there are many misconceptions concerning it, including the following:

1. *Only large firms can export successfully.* Small size is no barrier to international marketing. Today's most likely exporters are not the manufacturing giants, but small companies. According to a survey by Cognetics Inc. (www.cogonline.com), 87 percent of the 51,000 exporters it studied employ fewer than 500 workers.[29]

2. *Payment for goods sold to foreign buyers is uncertain.* Not true, as there are fewer credit losses in international sales than there are domestically.

3. *Overseas markets represent only limited sales opportunities.* On the contrary, around 95 percent of the world's population, and two-thirds of its purchasing power, are outside the United States.

4. *Foreign consumers will not buy American products.* Although some goods may not travel or translate well, most American products have a reputation overseas

Figure 8–7
Some Opportunities and Risks in International Operations

Opportunities and challenges for small firms:

Expansion of markets and product diversification

More effective use of labor force and facilities

Lower labor costs in most countries

Availability, and lower cost, of certain desired natural resources

Potential for higher rates of return on investment

Tax advantages

Strong demand for U.S. goods in many countries

Benefits provided to receiving country, such as needed capital, technology, and/or resources

Problems and risks:

Possibility of loss of assets and of earnings due to nationalization, war, terrorism, and other disturbances

Rapid change in political systems, often by violent overthrow

Fluctuating foreign exchange rates

High potential for loss, or difficulty or impossibility of retrieving earnings from investment

Unfair competition, particularly from state-subsidized firms

Lower skill levels of many workers in underdeveloped countries

Difficulties in communication and coordination with the home office

Attitudinal, cultural, and language barriers, which may lead to cultural differences and/or misunderstandings

Source: Adapted from Donald C. Mosley, Paul H. Pietri, Jr., and Leon C. Megginson, *Management: Leadership in Action,* 5th ed. (New York: HarperCollins, 1996), Table 4.1, p. 116.

for high quality, style, durability, and many state-of-the-art features. In fact, some products—such as hamburgers, blue jeans, movies, and music albums—are in demand simply because they are American!

5. *Export start-up costs are high.* Not necessarily, since you can begin exporting your products through exporting intermediaries at little real cost to you.

Some Opportunities and Risks   Many opportunities are available for small firms interested in international or global operations. However, there are also many risks involved, as you can see from Figure 8–7. In general, the *opportunities* are to expand markets, use excess resources, and increase profits from higher rates of return and possible tax advantages.

Exports also help the economic development of our own country. For example, exports account for one-third of the U.S. economy's growth over the past 10 years, and in 1995, we were the world's foremost exporter. For some products, "Made in America" means near-cult status overseas—especially among the young. It has been found that in the emerging world, "many youths splurge, mainly on U.S. goods. Flush with cash and plastic, they load up on Levi's [www.levistrauss.com] and tune in to MTV [www.mtv.com]."[30] These exports translate into job growth here, as the following two examples show.

Paul Jernigan, marketing chief of Gibson Guitar (www.gibson.com), says that "about 50 percent of Gibson's guitars are now exported," and that figure is growing. These exports are expected to increase Gibson's work force by 200 jobs. And Stetson Hats (www.millerhats.com/stetson) ships about 5 percent of its Western headgear to South America, Europe, and Japan. Exports are expected to "boost Stetson's 1,500 plus work force to 2,000."[31]

The *risks* overseas derive from the difficulty of getting earnings out of many countries and the changing political, economic, and cultural conditions there. Among other problems encountered in global operations is the temptation of entrepreneurs to enter international markets because they see "dollar-dominated opportunities." However, when dealing with currency exchanges, fast and radical fluctuations are a constant possibility.

Also, cultural risks and pitfalls do abound. International business etiquette in the context of potential intercultural misunderstandings must be considered. Many books and journal articles warn Americans of the dire consequences of ambiguous or improper gestures, language, dress, gift giving, and business operations.[32]

> For example, Islamic leaders were very upset about the disposable bags used for McDonald's "Happy Meals" in London. The bags featured the national flags of the 24 competitors in the World Cup competition. Saudi Arabia's flag, however, featured sacred words that, according to these leaders, should not be crumpled up and thrown away.[33]
>
> Similarly, the number one chewing gum in Singapore (Wrigley's) hit a snag in sales when chewing gum was banned in Singapore in order to protect its subways.[34]

Another risk, which is beyond the control of the entrepreneur, is economic fluctuation. Exports largely depend on the ability of importers to sell products to local customers, using local currency. But when the importing company's economy "crashes," U.S. exporters must reduce their exports or find other markets.

> For example, that is what happened in 1998 when a recession hit Japan and other Asian countries. Many small U.S. exporters saw their customer bases "dry up" in countries such as Korea, Malaysia, Thailand, and others across the "Pacific Rim." Many of these companies developed strategies for avoiding Asian markets.[35]

Finally, there is a growing problem with copyright and patent violations. This trend is particularly rampant in the electronics and music fields. The Chinese are particularly guilty. Evidently, the Chinese "see nothing wrong with copying or producing any product they have the technology to manufacture."[36]

Deciding Whether or Not to Export   If you expect to export, you must be willing to commit the resources necessary to make the effort profitable. Thus, you should make sure you (1) have a product suitable for export, (2) can reliably fill the needs of foreign countries while still satisfying domestic demand, (3) can offer foreign buyers competitive prices and satisfactory credit terms, and (4) are willing to devote the time and skills needed to make export activities a significant part of your business.

The U.S. Department of Commerce (www.doc.gov) has identified 10 countries that have been predicted to be the best partners for potential trading with the United States. They are Argentina, Brazil, Greater China (People's Republic of China, and Hong Kong), India, Indonesia, Mexico, Poland, South Africa, South Korea, and Turkey.[37] These countries are trying to attract trading partners by rebuilding infrastructure and privatizing selected industries. These efforts enhance the countries' attractiveness for small businesses seeking international targets.

Levels of Involvement   There are at least five levels of involvement in exporting, as shown in Figure 8–8. At level 1, you may not even know you're involved in exporting, since the product is sold to an intermediary, who then sells it to foreign buyers.

At level 2, you actually make a commitment to seek export business. This commitment may be formal or informal, as the following example illustrates:

> Bending Branches Inc. has been shipping hockey sticks across the Canadian border since 1986. The company followed the example of many small U.S. businesses that enter international operations almost intuitively—without getting advice on exporting or importing from any government or private source of information.

Figure 8–8

Five Levels of International Operations

Degree of product control	Level		Risk to your company
Great	5	Producing, as well as marketing, your product overseas	Great
↑	4	Beginning to actually market your product overseas by maintaining an office or subsidiary in a foreign country	↑
	3	Foreign licensing, involving a formal agreement with a foreign country to produce and/or distribute a product or service	
Little	2	Becoming actively involved by making a continuing effort to export	Little
	1	Doing some exporting on a casual or accidental basis, usually through an intermediary	

Source: Adapted from Donald C. Mosley, Paul H. Pietri, Jr., and Leon C. Megginson, *Management: Leadership in Action,* 5th ed. (New York: HarperCollins, 1996), Figure 4.4, p. 120.

There are many unserved market niches in Canada that welcome U.S. businesses, particularly those that deliver products as ordered, and on time, and cut through the border red tape.[38]

Level 3 is reached when you make a formal agreement with a foreign country to produce and/or distribute your product there.

> For example, Ohio-based Vita-Mix (www.vita-mix.com) began operating at level 3 in 1991 when it hired an international sales manager. Now, it sells its high-powered blenders to 20 countries, and faxes are coming in from everywhere, from Norway to Venezuela.[39]

At level 4, you begin to maintain a separate sales office or marketing subsidiary in one or more foreign countries.

Finally, you begin to engage in foreign production and marketing at level 5. You can do this by (1) setting up your own production and marketing operations in the foreign country, (2) buying an existing firm to do your business, or (3) forming a joint venture, as discussed in Chapter 3. These strategic partnerships have had a considerable impact on small business growth and stability.[40]

Help with Exporting Is Available   Despite the barriers facing small firms, help with exporting is available from many sources. This help takes two forms: (1) providing information and guidance and (2) providing financial assistance. The latter is particularly important to small firms because, while they account for 94 percent of all U.S. exporters, they do only 30 percent of the dollar volume of the nation's exports.[41]

Both government and private groups provide practically unlimited information and guidance, including technical expertise. Ten different government agencies and some 200 small business development centers, funded by the SBA (www.sbaonline.sba.gov), offer export counseling. An SBA pamphlet, *Market Overseas with U.S. Government Help,* provides excellent information on overseas marketing. Other SBA help comes from members of SCORE (www.score.com) and ACE, who have many years of practical experience in international trade. Small business institutes also provide export counseling and assistance.

Finally, the U.S. Department of Commerce offers assistance through its Trade Information Center and its Global Export Market Information Service. The department's computerized market data system has information on nearly 200 nations, and the department has contacts in around 75 countries.[42]

Small companies needing export-related electronic data processing services can get help from the Commerce Department's Census Bureau. You can obtain financial assistance for your export program from the Foreign Credit Insurance Association (FCIA) and the Export-Import Bank of the United States (Eximbank).[43]

■ DISTRIBUTION

Because of its many cost-saving potentials, distribution should be important to small companies. **Distribution** includes the whole range of activities concerned with the effective movement of a product from the production line into the hands of the final customer. To perform the complex operation of distribution effectively, you must make decisions in such important areas as protective packaging, materials handling, inventory control, storing, transportation (internally and externally), order processing, and various aspects of customer service. Because of space limitations, we'll discuss only storing, order processing, and transportation.

Distribution involves the effective physical movement of a product from the production line to the final consumer.

Storing

Until sold or used, goods must be stored by manufacturers, wholesalers, and retailers. While some small manufacturers and wholesalers have their own private warehouses, more of them use public warehouses, which are independently owned facilities that often specialize in handling certain products, such as furniture or refrigerated products. Public warehouses are particularly useful to small firms wanting to place goods close to customers for quick delivery, since the firms then avoid investing in new facilities.

Order Processing

Effective order processing improves customer satisfaction by reducing slow shipment and incorrectly or incompletely filled orders. Order processing begins the moment a customer places an order with a salesperson. The order goes to the office, often on a standardized order form. After the order is filled, the goods are sent to the customer.

Transportation

Transportation involves the physical movement of a product from the seller to the purchaser. Since transportation costs are the largest item in distribution, there are many opportunities for savings and improved efficiency. The two most important aspects in terms of cost savings are choosing the transportation mode to be used and understanding delivery terms. **Transportation modes** are the methods used to take products from one place to another. A small producer has many choices of ways to move goods to and from its plant and/or warehouse, and each mode has advantages and disadvantages. Which mode you choose to use will depend on questions of speed, frequency, and dependability required, points served, capability (capacity, flexibility, and adaptability) to handle the particular product, and cost. Whether containers are used affects the choice of transportation system. The various modes can be evaluated as to their effectiveness on each of these variables.[44]

Transportation modes are the methods used to transfer products from place to place.

Railroads, trucks, pipelines, and waterways are popular means of transporting bulky and heavy materials. Although the modes of transportation for heavy materials are changing, these still tend to be the primary systems used by producers.

Railroads continue to be important movers of goods, carrying around 37.6 percent of all tonnage moved each year. Their primary advantage is the capacity to carry large volumes of goods, fairly quickly, at a low cost. The main disadvantage is that they operate only on fixed routes, often on fixed schedules.

Trucks play an important role in shipping because of their flexibility and because of improved highway systems. Trucks carry about 25.6 percent of all tonnage. However, changing traffic configurations and government rules and regulations may affect the efficiency of truck use, as the following example suggests.

> A Nebraska feed-and-seed store owner spent much time, money, and effort to get his city to rescind a recent ordinance prohibiting tractor-trailers from unloading in front of his store. The extra cost of unloading on the edge of town and transporting sacks of feed and seed to the store would have forced him out of business.

Oil pipelines carry about 20.4 percent of all tonnage moved; waterways carry 16.1 percent. The use of air transport is increasing, particularly for products that must be delivered in a hurry, as well as for products with a high unit value and low weight and bulk. In such cases, a site for the firm near an airport should be considered if the costs are not too high.

Intermodal shipping is the use of a combination of truck, rail, or ship to ship goods.

The shipment of freight by a combination of truck, rail, or ship—called **intermodal shipping**—is now used extensively by small firms. Many companies use a combination of trucks and air to expedite service. For example, Gateway (www.gateway.com) and many other mail-order computer vendors work with Federal Express (www.fedex.com). UPS (www.ups.com) is used by many small businesses. These carriers use a system of airplanes and trucks.

Some "products" can be delivered in ways that might not immediately spring to mind in a discussion of modes of transportation. The Internet has revolutionized the sale and distribution of digital products. Most downloadable software is free—Microsoft's Internet Explorer and updates and "patches" to other applications are good examples—but many software vendors have their products for sale in downloadable form. Data transmission (whether of products or of sensitive business documents) has offered a new niche market.

> In 1998, UPS expanded its core delivery business to include "secure electronic delivery" over the Internet. Now, UPS Document Exchange offers customers with a computer, a modem, and access to the World Wide Web "state-of-the-art technology to provide maximum encryption levels, user authentication, proof of delivery, and archiving."[45]

■ CREDIT MANAGEMENT

Credit management involves setting and administering credit policies and practices.

Credit management involves (1) deciding how customers will pay for purchases, (2) setting credit policies and practices, and (3) administering credit operations. The objectives of each of these activities are to increase profits, increase customer stability, and protect the firm's investment in accounts receivable, which is often the largest single asset on the firm's balance sheet.

Methods of Payment

Customers can pay for purchases in a number of ways, and you must decide early in the life of your business which method(s) to accept. Payment methods include cash, checks, and various kinds of credit. Figure 8–9 shows which method is preferred by adult shoppers.

Cash   Given a choice, every business owner would probably prefer to make all sales for cash. Record keeping would be easier, and there would be no bad debts. But it is unrealistic to expect buyers to carry cash for every purchase, especially large purchases. Soon it may

Figure 8–9

Paper or Plastic?

Percentage of adult shoppers who prefer to pay for purchases with cash, checks, or credit cards:

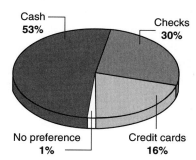

Cash
53%

Checks
30%

No preference
1%

Credit cards
16%

Source: Lutheran Brotherhood, as reported in *USA Today,* July 12, 1995, p. 1B.

not be necessary to carry cash at all, however. Going credit cards and debit cards one step better, companies such as Citibank (www.citibank.com) and Chase Manhattan (www. chase.com), after many trials and delays, have created bank cards that let consumers buy small items such as coffee and newspapers without using coins and bills. These cards have a microprocessor in the plastic called a "smart card" chip that will be able to download funds as the ATM machines do. Smart plastic originated in Europe as the need arose to leapfrog antiquated telephone systems.[46]

Checks   Because accepting checks for payment increases sales, most small business owners think the risks involved are worth it. With proper verification procedures, bad-debt losses can be minimized. Checks can be treated the same as cash in record keeping, and they're actually safer to have on hand than cash and easier to deal with in making bank deposits.

Credit   To stimulate sales, various forms of credit may be used, including installment payment plans and credit cards or a business's own credit plan. Granting your own credit allows you to choose your own customers and avoid fees to credit card issuers. Customer accounts can be paid off every month or can be *revolving charge accounts* such as those used by large department stores. For major purchases, you may give the buyer more time to pay before interest is charged or the account is turned over to a finance company. To extend credit even longer, you may offer an *installment payment plan* that gives the buyer up to a year or more to pay for the purchase. Buyers make a down payment, make regular weekly or monthly payments, and pay interest charges on the unpaid balance.

Whenever you extend credit, though, record keeping becomes more complex. Small firms can use manual or computer methods to maintain their charge accounts internally, or they can turn the accounts over to a service firm for handling. Either way, there are costs for billing and collections, as well as bad-debt losses.

Some of these responsibilities and costs can be avoided by accepting bank or corporate *credit cards,* so-called *plastic money.* Today's consumers have come to expect most firms of any size to accept the major cards, *which are in effect a line of credit granted to the customer by the card issuer.* Acceptance of credit cards is especially necessary in resort areas or other venues where customers are less likely to have large amounts of cash, local checking accounts, or a store charge account.

Although merchants pay a fee to join and a fee on sales, many find it worth the expense; provided they follow required authorization procedures, sellers are guaranteed payment, largely eliminating bad-debt losses. Authorization, once cumbersome, is now almost universally automated through the use of readers that scan the card's magnetic strip, dial the number of a database, get authorization for the charge, and record the sale, all in just a few seconds.

Once a business is set up to accept credit cards, it is generally simple to include debit cards as well. *Debit cards* are issued by banks, look like credit cards, and can be scanned in the same way. Instead of a line of credit, however, debit cards represent a plastic check, as the amount of purchase is immediately deducted from the user's checking account. Many banks now offer ATM cards that can be used in this way.

Setting Credit Policies

While your credit department can contribute to increased sales and profit, several factors should be considered in formulating a credit policy; some factors are beyond your control. Any credit policy should be flexible enough to accommodate these internal and external factors.

Some credit policies you can use are (1) liberal extension of credit with a liberal collection policy, (2) liberal extension of credit with a strictly enforced collection policy, and (3) strict extension of credit with a collection policy adjusted to individual circumstances. Generally, being liberal in extending credit or in collecting bad debts tends to stimulate sales but increase collection costs and bad-debt losses. Strict policies have the reverse effect. Whatever policy is chosen, you should extend a businesslike attitude toward credit customers.

Carrying Out Credit Policies

The person managing credit for you should have ready access to the accounts receivable records and be free from interruptions and confusion. Several tools this person can use in performing the function include the accounts receivable ledger or computer printout, invoices and other billing documents, credit files, account lists, credit manuals, reference material, and various automated aids.

Classifying Credit Risks

You should begin by classifying present and potential customers according to credit risk: good, fair, or weak. These risks can be determined from information in the customer's file, trade reports, financial reports, and previous credit experience.

Good credit risks may be placed on a preferred list for automatic approval within certain dollar limits. Periodic review of these accounts usually suffices. Fair credit risks will require close checking, particularly on large amounts or in case of slow payment. While weak credit risks may be acceptable, they should be closely watched. You ask for problems when you unwisely extend credit.

Investigating Customers' Creditworthiness

A major cause of bad-debt losses is making credit decisions without adequate investigation. Yet prompt delivery of orders is also important. Thus, your credit-checking method should be geared to need and efficiency to improve the sales and delivery of your product. For new accounts, a complete credit application may be desired. Direct credit inquiry can be effective in obtaining the name of the customer's bank and trade references. Outside sources of valuable credit information include local credit bureaus, which are linked nationally through Associated Credit Bureaus, Inc. (www.acb-credit.com), and others who provide guidelines and mechanisms for obtaining credit information for almost any area in the United States.

Establishing Collection Procedures

The collection of unpaid accounts is an important part of credit management. The collection effort should include systematic and regular follow-up, which is vital to establish credibility with the customer concerning credit terms. The follow-up should be timely, which is now feasible since most businesses have computer capacity to show the age of a bill.

When an account is past due, prompt contact with the customer, made tactfully and courteously, generally produces results. If this doesn't work, holding customers' orders can be effective. But you should respond rapidly when the customer clears the account so that unnecessary delays in shipping are avoided.

WHAT YOU SHOULD HAVE LEARNED

∎

1. Marketing a product begins with deciding how to get it into the users' hands through a distribution channel. A small business essentially has the choice of selling directly to the customer or selling through intermediaries. In making the choice, you should be guided by the nature of the product, traditional practices in the industry, and the size of the business and of its market.

2. The usual intermediaries are brokers, independent agents, wholesalers, and retailers. A broker receives a commission for sales of merchandise without physically handling the goods. Independent agents, such as selling agents and manufacturers' agents (manufacturers' representatives), also represent clients for a commission, but they may do more actual selling than brokers.

   Wholesalers take physical possession of the goods they sell and provide storage, delivery, credit to the buyer, product servicing, and sales promotion. Retailers buy goods from manufacturers or wholesalers and sell them to the ultimate consumer. Retailers determine customer needs and satisfy them with choice of location, goods, promotion, prices, and credit policy. The current trends in retailing are toward more self-service, more automation or computerization, and using TV and the Internet.

3. Personal selling is required at all levels of the marketing process. All sales personnel should know the steps in the creative selling process, namely, preparation, prospecting, making initial contact, presenting the product, handling objections, closing the sale, suggestion selling, and following up on the sale. A creative salesperson should possess judgment, tact, and a good attitude toward customers, products, services, and the firm.

4. Advertising should be continuous and governed by an advertising budget based on (a) a percentage of sales or profits, (b) a given amount per unit of desired sales, (c) the actual amount required to accomplish the sales objective, or (d) an executive decision. Advertising media include newspapers, store signs, direct mail, circulars and handbills, Yellow Pages ads, outdoor signs, radio, television, and the Internet. Infomercials are now extensively used to advertise specialty products.

   Some factors affecting a company's choice of media are target market, cost, and availability. Using an advertising agency to develop and place advertisements may be desirable. The results of advertising should be measured to determine its effectiveness by some form of immediate-response advertising.

5. Ethnic groups in the United States may require special attention in the promotion of goods and services, but you should not lump all members of an ethnic group together into one target market, since many members of new groups adopt the

values and tastes of middle America while others cherish the traditional preferences of their culture.

6. The opportunities in global marketing are growing rapidly. All of us—students, teachers, consumers, and members and owners of large and small businesses—are already involved. Millions of small businesses are importing and selling foreign products. While these imports provide many opportunities for some small firms, they may force some others out of business.

Some opportunities provided by exporting are: (*a*) expansion of markets, (*b*) more effective use of resources, particularly personnel, (*c*) potentially higher rates of return on investment, and (*d*) tax advantages. Some problems are (*a*) the difficulty of getting earnings out of the host country, (*b*) political or economic conditions in the form of unfair competition from state-subsidized firms and favorable treatment given to local firms and products, (*c*) unstable political climates, and (*d*) fluctuations in currency exchange rates and in economic conditions in general.

Small firms can become involved in international marketing at one of five levels, namely: (*a*) casual, or accidental, exporting; (*b*) active exporting; (*c*) foreign licensing; (*d*) overseas marketing; and (*e*) foreign production and marketing.

7. Distribution, which is moving the product from the seller to the buyer, includes the vital functions of storing, order processing, and transporting the product.

8. Credit management includes deciding on customer payment methods, establishing credit policies, and administering credit operations. A credit policy should be flexible and help increase revenues and profits. Customers should be classified according to their creditworthiness—good, fair, or weak. Credit investigations should be conducted, and the collection of outstanding receivables should be systematic and include regular follow-up. The overall results of the credit functions and collection efficiency should be evaluated to see that they are achieving their objectives.

QUESTIONS FOR DISCUSSION

1. What factors should be considered in choosing a channel of distribution?
2. Describe the traditional channels of distribution for consumer goods.
3. Describe the traditional channels of distribution for industrial goods.
4. Name two types of independent agents. What are the advantages and disadvantages of using them?
5. Describe the eight steps in the creative selling process.
6. What basic decisions should be made about an advertising program?
7. Describe some opportunities and problems in catering to ethnic differences.
8. Do you believe international marketing is as important as stated? Explain.
9. What are some reasons for importing? What are some problems?
10. List the opportunities available in exporting.
11. Describe some risks and problems involved in exporting.
12. Explain the five levels of involvement in exporting.
13. What is credit management, and why is it so important to small business? Why is the acceptance of credit cards by small businesses increasing?

CASE 8–1

TAKING YOUR STORE TO YOUR CUSTOMERS

There are several channels that producers can use to get their products to the market. Sometimes these distribution channels may be long and complicated, using several intermediaries between the producer and consumer. However, as Sarah Hammet, owner of Feeling Special Fashions, has shown, it does not have to be that complicated.

Hammet sells clothing specially designed for senior citizens. It is called "adaptive" clothing—dresses and separates for seniors whose mobility and dexterity are restricted. Hammet bypasses the usual intermediaries, such as retail stores, and takes her product directly to the customers. She sells clothing at 50 nursing homes and retirement communities in two states and the District of Columbia.

Four days out of the week, every spring and fall, Hammet and an assistant load half a dozen racks of clothes into the back of a van and hit the road. She conducts fashion shows and offers individual consultations at every facility they visit. This type of personal selling has been effective for Hammet, who thought up the idea in the early 1980s while visiting her elderly father in a Kentucky nursing home. She was appalled by the careless and drab manner in which patients were dressed. Hammet perceived a need and stepped in to fill it.

The clothing she sells is manufactured by Comfort Clothing, Inc., which is located in Canada. The items are stylishly designed and come in various colors and prints. The clothing is different in that armholes are bigger, buttons often hide Velcro® fastenings, and waists are uncinched and come with optional belts. The garments can be stepped into rather than pulled on over the head. They are washable and cost between $40 and $60. Through a combination of creative merchandising and personal selling, Hammet has established a growing business.

Questions

1. What type of distribution channels does Feeling Special Fashions use?

2. Should Sarah Hammet consider selling through intermediaries, such as retailers? Discuss the advantages and disadvantages.

3. How would you rate Hammet's selling strategy? Recommend ways she could increase sales.

4. Should Feeling Special Fashions advertise? Discuss the advantages and disadvantages.

5. How do you rate Hammet's chances for success? Why?

CASE 8–2

CLARK COPY INTERNATIONAL CORPORATION'S CHINA EXPERIENCE

In the early 1980s, China's powerful State Economic Commission launched a major effort to attract small Western enterprises. It was dissatisfied with large firms that sell expensive consumer items such as VCRs that do little to aid China's economy.

This policy helped Clark Copy International Corporation, a small company making plain-paper copiers in a cramped plant in Melrose Park, Illinois, beat out the industry's world leaders to sign a lucrative contract with China. At that time, it had only 14 employees and had earned only $58,000 on $1.5 million of sales for 1982. Clark agreed to sell 1,000 CMC 2000 copiers assembled and ready to use, as well as to provide parts and instructions for the Chinese to assemble into another 5,000

machines. Also, Clark would train 1,600 Chinese technicians to manufacture the copiers and other Clark products for domestic and export sales in a new plant in Kweilin in the south of China.

How did Clark do it? According to Clark's founder and president, Otto A. Clark, a Slovak who emigrated to the United States in 1950, "You can't do business in China on a simple buy-and-sell basis, like most multinationals do. Instead, you have to establish a close human relationship and a commitment to stay." That relationship was established with the help of David Yao, Clark's Far East representative, who was born in Shanghai and speaks fluent Chinese.

Yao and Clark went to China eight times to negotiate before closing with China's National Bureau of Instrumentation Industries in April 1982. In the mid- to late 1980s, the Chinese attitude toward private enterprise and foreign investments changed, and Clark wasn't permitted to complete the agreement. By 1991, it was out of business.

Questions

1. Evaluate the procedure followed by Otto Clark in his effort to enter global operations.

2. What went wrong? Explain.

3. What—if anything—would you have done differently?

Source: Correspondence with Clark Copy International; the Melrose Park, Illinois, Chamber of Commerce; and others.

IV

ORGANIZING AND MANAGING THE BUSINESS

Many management texts begin with a statement such as "Management is getting things done through people." And the annual reports of most companies include statements such as "Our people are our most important asset." Both of these statements are correct: Whether the business is large or small, its success or failure depends on having a capable, well-trained, and motivated work force.

In essence, all owners of small businesses are human resource managers. They must decide what work is to be done, determine the type and number of employees needed to do it, recruit and employ those employees, train and develop them, reward them with adequate pay and benefits, and lead and motivate them to perform effectively. How well—or poorly—owners handle these important activities determines the success or failure of their businesses.

Chapter 9 looks at the overall problem of managing human resources in small firms and covers such topics as planning personnel needs, recruiting employees, selecting the right people for the jobs, training and developing them, and compensating them, as well as providing a safe and healthy working environment and complying with equal employment opportunity laws.

Chapter 10 deals with maintaining relationships with employees and their representatives. It includes topics such as setting up organizational relationships, maintaining good human relations with employees, leading and motivating employees to produce more effectively, communicating with employees, appraising their performance, counseling disturbed employees, handling employee complaints and grievances, exercising discipline, dealing with unions, and the difficulty of terminating ineffective employees.

9

MANAGING HUMAN RESOURCES AND DIVERSITY IN SMALL FIRMS

Small businesses must make wooing and keeping employees as high a priority as attracting and retaining customers.

John L. Ward, Loyola University of Chicago

Good ideas and good products are "a dime a dozen" but good execution and good management—in a word, good people—are rare.

Arthur Rock, venture capitalist

The key to . . . success is superior customer service, continuing internal entrepreneurship, and a deep belief in the dignity, worth, and potential of every person in the organization.

Tom Peters, coauthor of *In Search of Excellence*

LEARNING OBJECTIVES

After studying the material in this chapter, you will be able to:

1. Explain how small business managers plan personnel needs and develop sources from which to recruit personnel.

2. Name some methods used for recruiting personnel, and describe the steps in the employee selection process.

3. Explain the importance of personnel development, and discuss some development methods.

4. Tell how selection of managers differs from selection of nonmanagerial personnel, and describe some methods of manager development.

5. Discuss the laws that affect personnel recruiting, selection, and development.

6. Describe how to compensate employees with money and employee benefits.

7. List some factors influencing employee health and safety, and tell how to safeguard employees in small firms.

Mary H. Partridge and Michael Levy: Even Small Companies Merge!

Michael Levy and Mary H. Partridge, a married couple in Austin, Texas, operated separate businesses for over 12 years. He was owner and president of Michael Levy & Associates, consultants in training and organization development; she was owner and president of Impact Consulting, consultants in human resource administration and development.

When they moved to Austin from Houston in 1994, they set a goal to develop a clientele in Austin, a fast-growing, high-tech environment. Having relied on repeat business and word-of-mouth referrals for years, they realized they would have to have a more aggressive marketing plan in the new environment. To maximize the return on advertising and promotional dollars, they decided to focus their efforts on marketing one company—Impact Consulting. So, after 18 years of marriage and more than a decade of operating two separate companies, they decided to "merge."

As they planned the "merger," they asked themselves what they would advise a client to do in a similar situation. Following their own advice, they arranged for their college intern to facilitate a "planning meeting" to define the goals and strategies of the new, consolidated company. In addition, they identified the concerns that each of them had about "merging" and their core competencies. Using that approach, they divided functional responsibilities such as marketing and technology planning.

One benefit of the two companies had been autonomy of operation and their ability to make decisions without delay or consultation with a second decision maker. But many of the services they offered were of equal interest to both Partridge and Levy. The solution they found was to divide clients between themselves in such a way that each client had a designated "Account Executive" who had primary responsibility for all decisions, planning, coordination, and account management.

Much of their time is spent on executive coaching and 360-degree feedback. The latter involves individual consultations with managers to help them improve their management approach, communication abilities, and leadership style.

Practicing what they preach, the two consultants avoid hiring staff and incurring burdensome overhead. Instead, they use a network of familiar independent contractors, as needed, to supplement the owners' efforts. Levy and Partridge have developed workable relationships with their own personnel—each other and hired freelancers—and are able to translate their knowledge and experience to benefit the companies they serve.

By 1999, they had established a strong client base in Austin and a comfortable, successful partnership in business, which reflected and enriched their partnership in life.

Source: Author's correspondence and discussions with Mary H. Partridge and Michael Levy.

The Profile emphasizes the importance of managing human resources in a small firm. You must have a sufficient supply of adequately trained and motivated employees if you are to succeed as the owner or manager of a small business. In the late 1800s, a young entrepreneur, Andrew Carnegie, expressed this thought when he said, "Take away all our factories, our trade, our avenues of transportation, and our money, but leave our organization, and in four years, I will have reestablished myself." In other words, while physical and financial resources are *important* to any business, large or small, *human resources are vital.*[1] While larger firms have professional human resource managers to perform these activities, owners of small businesses must do it themselves—in addition to their many other duties.

Being able to identify and hire good employees can mean the difference between having a successful and an unsuccessful business. This basic management function of **staffing** involves (1) planning for, (2) recruiting, (3) selecting, and (4) training and developing employees, as well as compensating them and providing for their health and safety. That's what is discussed in this chapter.

Staffing involves planning for, recruiting, selecting, and training and developing employees, as well as compensating them and providing for their health and safety.

■ PLANNING FOR HUMAN RESOURCE NEEDS

You can't wait until you need a new employee to think about your human resource needs. Like larger competitors, small businesses must (1) determine which human resources are needed and (2) develop sources from which to recruit future employees, especially women and people from diverse ethnic groups. As shown in Chapters 1 and 2, women and minority workers—and owners—of small businesses are growing in numbers much more rapidly than white male workers and business owners. Figure 1–5 dramatically illustrated the shift being brought about by government and employers' efforts.

Small businesses find it difficult to plan for human resource needs, since many are facing absolute labor shortages because of the declining work force. For example, a recent survey by the National Federation of Independent Business of 1,600 of its members found that fully 30 percent of them had "hard to fill" openings.[2] To a large extent, this shortage has been brought on by the aging of the U.S. population. According to the U.S. Bureau of the Census (www.census.gov), the average age of Americans had increased from 26 in 1966 to around 35 in 1998.[3] It is expected to rise to over 37 by the year 2010.[4]

The number of Americans aged 16 to 24 was expected to decrease by more than 7 percent by the year 2000. Because small businesses employ two-thirds of these entry-level workers, they are the first to feel the shortage. In fact, "finding qualified workers" was one of the top five concerns of small business owners in the 1990s, according to a Dun & Bradstreet survey of 296 such owners.[5]

Compounding the problem is the fact that blue-collar jobs were down from 40 percent of the labor force at the end of World War II (1945) to only 27 percent in 1997.[6] And because we are in a "postindustrial society," where 80 percent of all jobs require higher-level skills and knowledge, many workers, especially entry-level applicants, lack the education and flexibility needed to transfer from one job to another. Another problem for small business owners is that most people now expect to change jobs and careers seven times in their working lives.[7]

This shortage of skilled workers has created a paradox for many small employers. Thousands of prospective employees are being rejected because of inadequate skills. This trend leaves many unhappy employers (because jobs remain unfilled), not to mention frustrated job seekers.

To meet this declining supply of potential employees, many small businesses are changing the way they operate. They are spending more on technology,[8] using new methods to attract more applicants, making their workplaces more attractive, and using employee

---

Figure 9–1

Components of a Simplified Job Description and Job Specification

---

- *Identification of job:* Job title, department, code, salary range, supervisor, etc.
- *Job description:*
  a. Physical demands of the job and the minimum physical requirements needed to fill it.
  b. Working conditions, including psychological conditions such as relationships with others and responsibilities for other people, money, and equipment.
  c. Summary of the duties and responsibilities of the job.
  d. Days and hours of work.
  e. Machines, tools, formulas, and equipment used.
- *Job specifications:*
  a. Educational background and knowledge, skills and techniques, and training and experience required to perform the job, as well as special training and development needed.
  b. Personal characteristics such as sociability, articulateness, or aggressiveness.

---

benefits and other incentives to retain valued employees. Finally, small companies are also stepping up automation and even subcontracting out part of their work to reduce the number of employees needed.

Determining Types of Employees Needed

When business owners want to construct a building, they obtain a set of blueprints and specifications. When they buy merchandise, materials, and supplies, they develop specifications for those items. In the same way, even the smallest businesses should have some type of **job specifications,** which are statements of the mental, physical, and other qualifications required of a person to do the job. Drawing up job specifications begins with a **job description,** which is a list of the job's duties, responsibilities, and working conditions, as well as relationships between it and other jobs in the organization. When the personal qualities, education, training, and experience needed to perform the job are added, the result is a set of job specifications that forms the basis for recruiting and selecting new employees, as shown in Figure 9–1.

Just a word of caution: *Job descriptions should be flexible in very small firms to give the owner more freedom in assigning work to available employees, whether the work fits their job description or not.*

Don't ask for more than is needed to do the job properly! Ask yourself, "Is a college education really needed, or can a high school graduate do the job?" Or again, "Are three years' experience required, or can an inexperienced person be trained to do the work?" "If an inexperienced person can be trained, is there someone to do the training?" Increasing education and experience levels raises the starting pay expected, and you may actually be better off training someone to do things your own way.

Job specifications are detailed written statements of work assignments and the qualifications needed to do the job acceptably.

A **job description** lists the duties and responsibilities of a given job.

"Welcome aboard. You're just what we're looking for—not too bright, no ambition, and content to stay on the bottom of the ladder and not louse things up!"

(*Source:* Cartoon courtesy of J. Nebesky, from *Savant,* February/March 1988.)

Figure 9–2
Where to Find Needed Employees

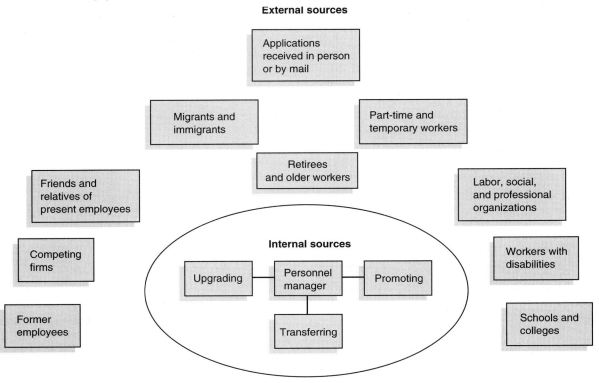

Developing Sources from Which to Recruit Potential Employees

As with purchasing supplies for building and running the business, you need sources from which to seek new workers. Some of these sources are shown in Figure 9–2. Not all of them will be appropriate for all small businesses.

Internal Sources   Filling job openings with present employees rather than going outside the business makes good sense. This method raises morale and improves employees' motivation, since they know they can move up in your firm. It also saves time, effort, and money, since outside recruiting is time-consuming and costly. For example, a study by the Bureau of National Affairs found that the cost of replacing a good employee "ranges from half to several times [an employee's annual pay]."[9] Another study of 206 companies by William M. Mercer, Inc., found the cost to be between "$10,000 or less" and "over $40,000."[10]

Filling jobs from within is also effective because the worker's performance has been observed and evaluated. Further, this method leads to stability. Employees can be upgraded, transferred, or promoted to fill job openings.

Upgrading involves retraining workers so they can do increasingly complex work.

Upgrading occurs when an employee who is presently not capable of doing a job that has become more difficult receives training to enable him or her to do the work successfully, as the following example illustrates.

A small service organization replaced its typewriter with a word processor. The present typist, age 52, had been with the firm for 20 years but didn't know how to use a word processor. Instead of hiring a new operator, management sent the typist to a training program. She mastered word processing in a short time and was soon back at the company using her new skills.

Transferring is moving an employee from one location or department to another, without necessarily changing job title or pay. **Promoting** is moving a person to a higher position, frequently with increased responsibilities, greater status or prestige, a new title, and a higher salary. If the company is family owned, the owners' children can be "promoted" as they become capable of assuming more responsibility.

External Sources   You may need to use external sources as the business grows, especially to fill lower-level jobs. External sources may also be used to provide new ideas and perspectives and to obtain needed skills when necessary, especially for scientific, technical, and professional positions.

Many small firms keep a list of *former employees* as a potential source of trained workers. If a worker left voluntarily and for good reason, is in good standing, and seeks reemployment, rehiring may be a good idea.

Diane Allen worked for an art supply store. When her husband started teaching at a college 40 miles away, she resigned. Later, when the store moved to a new location and its business increased, Diane was asked to come back, and she agreed.

As will be shown later, *friends and relatives* of present employees may also be a good source of dependable people. But remember, if a friend or relative is hired but doesn't work out and must be terminated, you've lost a friend as well as an employee.

You should make it a habit to keep *applications that come in either through the mail or in person.* Also, in some areas (especially in shopping centers), workers change jobs frequently, so attracting workers from *other businesses*—even competitors—is another good source.

Managers and technical and professional personnel may be found in various *social and professional organizations.* Also, *schools and colleges* can be a good source for skilled personnel and part-time employees.

With the unprecedented increase in corporate consolidations, downsizing, and outsourcing, there is a large pool of *retirees and older workers* now available. The mandatory retirement age has been outlawed, and a shift toward more favorable retirement programs now rewards workers who stay in the work force longer. So the number of workers ages 55 to 64 who are reentering the work force has been rising since 1994. These trends are providing small firms with the opportunity to hire experienced, seasoned employees who are ready to return to gainful employment.[11]

Other sources of employees are *migrants and immigrants* and *workers with disabilities.* Few of us realize the role played by migrant workers in the United States, especially in agriculture. In the late 1990s, the U.S. Congress tried to "prevent immigration reform from devastating an important segment of U.S. agriculture—the fruit, vegetable, and nursery growers who depend on seasonal labor . . . to harvest their crops."[12]

Part-time and temporary workers (temps), who provide scheduling flexibility, as well as a way of reducing hiring (and benefit) costs, will become even more important in the future. No longer is part-time employment only for students seeking summer jobs or homemakers supplementing the family income. Instead, recent college grads, retirees, corporate dropouts (or those pushed out), and others are taking temporary jobs. In fact, research by the National Association of Temporary and Staffing Services (NATSS) (www.natss.org) shows that older people are increasingly represented in the temporary ranks.[13] One group of such workers are those who wish to work less than 40 hours a week "in order to suit their lifestyles and workstyles."[14] Thus, they may be hired to work a few hours each day (e.g., as a clerk in a store) or a few days each week (e.g., as an industrial engineer or accountant).

Transferring is moving an employee from one job to another, without necessarily changing title or pay.

Promoting is moving an employee to a higher position, usually with increased responsibilities, title, and pay.

The number of temporary workers in the United States has nearly doubled over the last five years. In fact, more than 2.6 million temporary workers were employed in the United States on an average day during the third quarter of 1997.[15] At about 2 percent of the average daily employment, temporary employees are rapidly becoming an increasingly important segment of our work force.[16] Another study by NATSS indicated that the nature of temporary employment is changing. It showed that industrial and professional jobs were increasing, as opposed to office/clerical, technical, and health care, which decreased.[17]

Leased manpower is another source of part-time employees. These workers may work full time for the leasing firm and only part time for the small employer. This is an especially useful source of employees for clerical, maintenance, janitorial, and food service tasks. Leasing saves labor costs for a business, because the employees' health insurance and other benefits are paid by the agency that supplies the needed labor. Also, it permits greater flexibility to cut back on staff when business is slack. This group is also fast becoming a permanent part of the American work force.

Economic conditions have reshaped our work force in recent years, establishing a smaller "core" of permanent employees surrounded by a flexible border of temporary and part-time workers. This trend is now a global phenomenon, especially in Europe, where the temporary work force grew 18 percent in 1997, especially in the technology areas.[18]

■ RECRUITING AND SELECTING EMPLOYEES

Once the number, types, and sources of employees needed are known, the small business manager starts looking for the people. Don't limit applications to people who drop in and ask for a job; instead, *go out and recruit them!*

Methods of Recruiting Employees

Recruitment, as shown in Figure 9–3, is reaching out to attract a supply of potential employees. It's generally done by advertising but may also be accomplished using employee referrals, temporary help services, **networking,** state and private employment agencies, and scouting. A study by Olsten Forum for Information Management found that while "networking" was the fastest-growing method used, Help Wanted ads were the most frequently used—by 89 percent of respondents. Employee referrals were second, with 77 percent, followed by temporary help services (63 percent), networking (57 percent), and employment firms (51 percent).[19]

Studies over the last 10 years indicate that, on average, employees attracted by a highly creative, motivational recruitment ad remain on the job two to three times longer than those attracted by executive recruiters and employment agencies.[20]

Another rapidly growing recruitment vehicle is the Internet. An employer's job announcement on the Net can gain "an instant audience that can run into the thousands."[21] Some company Web sites even match job openings with the qualifications of candidates who have previously visited the company's site and notify them by e-mail of the opportunities. Using a Web site can considerably speed up the recruitment process.

> An example of this process is the Paradise Pizza Café in West Des Moines, Iowa. It now accepts job applications at its Web site.[22]

Methods of Selecting the Right Person for the Job

Selection is the process of determining whether an applicant has personal qualities that match the job specifications for a given position. Some of the qualities that working men and women say helped them get ahead are hard work, ability, and high standards.

Leased manpower refers to employees obtained from an outside firm that specializes in performing a particular service.

Recruitment is reaching out to attract applicants from which to choose one to fill a job vacancy.

Networking is the process of establishing and maintaining contacts with key persons in one's own or another organization as informal development or promotion systems.

Selection involves choosing the applicant who has the qualifications to perform the job.

Figure 9–3
Methods Used to Recruit Employees

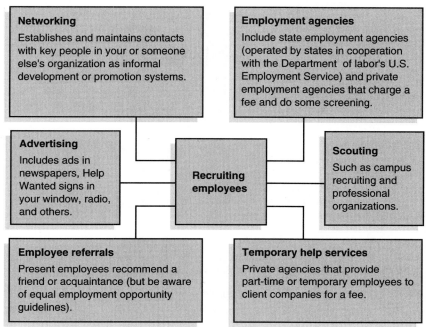

No potential employee is perfect! So don't expect to find someone with all the qualities you ideally want. Instead, find people who have the qualities you need, and be willing to accept qualities you don't need or want, so long as those qualities don't harm the business. The selection procedure involves (1) gathering information about the applicant, (2) making a job offer, and (3) orienting the new employee.

Gathering Information about the Applicant   Many people applying for a job will not be qualified, so try to find out all you can about what they can—and can't—do. *In general, what a person has done in the past best indicates future performance.* You should therefore use the most appropriate techniques to help discover a person's past performance and future possibilities.

The amount of information you need to know about an applicant depends on the type of employee being recruited. Figure 9–4 shows some selection techniques that are frequently used to gather the information, but not all are needed for every job. Also, these techniques are based on having several applicants for each job, which is not always true of most small businesses.

Using Employee Input   When selecting human resources, it helps to bring present employees into the process—in an advisory capacity. The consequences of hiring an incompatible worker in a small company can be very disruptive.

> Jody Wright learned this lesson the hard way a few years ago. As president of Motherwear, a $5 million catalog company in Northampton, Massachusetts (www. motherwear.com), Wright hired a worker who was incompatible with her existing staff. After the dust had settled, she instituted a system whereby present employees helped hire new co-workers. Having helped in the selection, they had a greater commitment to working with the new hires.[23]

Figure 9–4
Techniques for Gathering Information about Potential Employees

Techniques used to gather data	Characteristics to look for	Applicants who are available as potential employees
Preliminary screening or interview	Obvious misfit from outward appearance and conduct	
Biographical inventory from application blank, résumé, etc.	Lacks adequate educational and performance record	
Testing Intelligence test(s)	Fails to meet minimum standards of mental alertness	
Aptitude test(s)	Lacks specific capacities for acquiring particular knowledge or skills	
Proficiency or achievement test(s)	Unable to demonstrate ability to do job	
Interest test(s)	Lacks significant vocational interest in job	
Personality test(s)	Lacks the personal characteristics required for job	
In-depth interview	Lacks necessary innate ability, ambition, or other qualities	
Verifying biographical data from references	Unfavorable or negative reports on past performance	
Physical examination	Physically unfit for job	
Personal judgment	Overall competence and ability to fit into the firm	

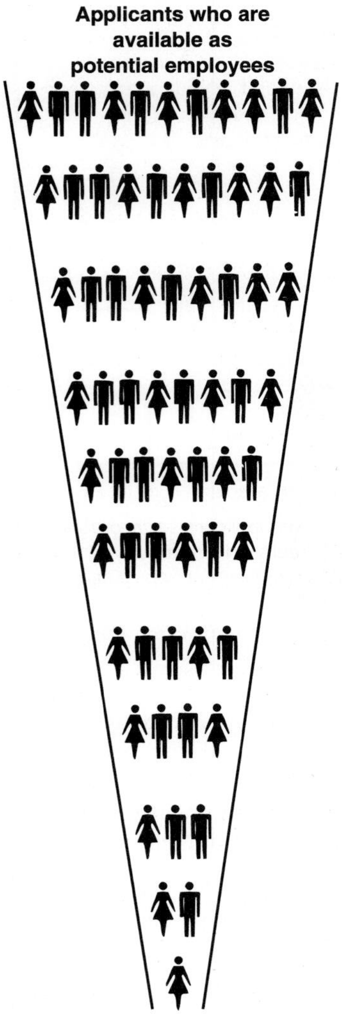

Source: Leon C. Megginson, Geralyn M. Franklin, and M. Jane Byrd, *Human Resource Management* (Houston, TX: Dame Publications, 1995), Figure 6–5, p. 154.

Preliminary Screening You should do some form of preliminary screening of applicants early in the selection procedure. This can be done in a formal interview or informally through reviewing a candidate's application form, letter, résumé, or other submitted material. Most firms use some form of interviewing at this point. You should look for such obvious factors as voice, physical appearance, personal grooming, educational qualifications, training, and experience. Many applicants are eliminated at this stage for reasons such as inappropriate dress, attitude, education, or experience.

It is at this stage of selection that many small business owners or managers inadvertently—or intentionally—run afoul of equal employment opportunity (EEO) laws (to be discussed in detail later). Table 9–1 presents some questions to avoid asking applicants at this stage—or at any other time before a job offer is made.

Table 9–1
Topics to Avoid When Interviewing Applicants

Here is an up-to-date summary of 10 of the most dangerous questions or topics you might raise during an interview.

1. *Children.* Do not ask applicants whether they have children, plan to have children, or have child care.
2. *Age.* Do not ask an applicant's age.
3. *Disabilities.* Do not ask whether the candidate has a physical or mental disability that would interfere with doing the job.
4. *Physical characteristics.* Do not ask for such identifying characteristics as height or weight on an application.
5. *Citizenship.* Do not ask applicants about their citizenship. However, the Immigration Reform and Control Act does require business operators to determine that their employees have a legal right to work in the United States.
6. *Name.* Do not ask a female candidate for her maiden name.
7. *Lawsuits.* Do not ask a job candidate whether he or she has ever filed a suit or a claim against a former employer.
8. *Arrest record.* Do not ask applicants about their arrest records.
9. *Smoking.* Do not ask whether a candidate smokes. While smokers are not protected under the Americans with Disabilities Act (ADA), asking applicants whether they smoke might lead to legal difficulties if an applicant is turned down because of fear that smoking would drive up the employer's health care costs.
10. *AIDS and HIV.* Never ask job candidates whether they have AIDS or are HIV-positive, as these questions violate the ADA and could violate state and federal civil rights laws.

Source: Adapted with permission from Janine S. Paulist, "Topics to Avoid with Applicants," *Nation's Business,* July 1992. Copyright 1992, U.S. Chamber of Commerce.

Gathering Biographical Information   Biographical information comes from application forms, résumés, school records, military records, credit references, and so forth. You should look for solid evidence of past performance, concrete information on which to base the decision instead of depending on opinions or assumptions. Having applicants fill out an application form in your presence—in longhand—serves as a simple performance test of their neatness and communications ability, or even simple literacy. No matter how good an applicant's record appears, don't base a decision on her or his unconfirmed statements. Unfortunately, there's a trend toward inflating résumés, so you should make it a point to verify education and employment history and check references.

For example, a study of 1,200 job applicants by Certified Reference Checking, of St. Louis, found that 34 percent of them had lied on their résumés.[24]

Several "red flags" may indicate a phony résumé: gaps in dates or sequences that do not add up, such as the time between getting a degree and a job; degrees from unknown schools; vagueness; and accomplishments that don't make sense, such as years of education and experience that are greater than possible for the applicant's age.

Giving Preemployment Tests   Since 1971, when the U.S. Supreme Court ruled that preemployment tests must be job related, most small firms have minimized their use because of the cost involved and the possible legal hassles. Also, some experts in the field warn that testing may be based on the false assumption that a test can determine whether an applicant fits a given "profile." Human relations is too complex and vital to be determined with "a simple 20-minute screening test."[25]

The **polygraph** is an instrument for simultaneously recording variations in several different physiological variables.

A word of caution is needed about the use of a special test, the **polygraph,** or "lie detector." Before 1989, many companies used the polygraph. Because of conflicting results, Congress has since passed a law barring most private employers from using polygraph tests. Now, written and computerized tests for assessing employee honesty are increasingly being produced and sold.

Interviewing Applicants in Depth   Applicants who have survived the procedure this far are often subjected to an **in-depth interview** at this time. Sometimes called a **preemployment** or **diagnostic interview,** its purpose is to probe the applicant's character, motivation, and other aspects of personality. Some suggestions for improving the interview process are:

In-depth, preemployment, or **diagnostic interviews** are detailed, probing, and penetrating interviews seeking to determine the applicant's character and other aspects of personality.

- Don't ask the obvious questions.
- Don't ask legally indefensible questions.
- Do ask the right questions, but be sure to know how to evaluate the answers.
- Do try not to focus too much attention on the candidate's self-evaluation.
- Don't be afraid of probing the applicant.
- Don't be overly influenced by first impressions.
- Don't miss important clues.
- Don't rely too much on past credentials.

Checking References   References play an important role in gathering information about an applicant. The three most frequently used types of references are: personal, academic, and past employment. For applicants with any work history, the most valued references are from former employers. Using a personal visit, a telephone call, or a personal letter, you can verify work history, educational attainments, and other information the applicant has presented. By law, former employers may, if they choose, limit their responses to information about dates and title of the most recent job and total period of employment. Be sure to get the applicant's permission before contacting the present employer, who may not know the employee is job hunting.

Just as some applicants are not honest with their prospective employer, neither are the persons giving them a reference always entirely candid.

For instance, a Robert Half International (www.rhii.com) poll of 150 executives found that many of them admitted to erring on the favorable side when discussing an applicant. Their primary reasons for shading the truth were (1) fear of lawsuits (80 percent) and (2) bias due to friendship with the applicant.[26]

Giving Physical Examinations   In the past, the final step in selecting employees was some type of physical exam. Now, however (as you can see in Table 9–2 in the section "Laws Providing for Equal Opportunity"), the Americans with Disabilities Act (ADA) limits the use of such exams in hiring by employers with 15 or more employees. To prevent possible discrimination against the disabled, the law prohibits asking questions about an applicant's medical history or requiring an exam *before* a preliminary job offer is made.

Making a Job Offer   When you have decided to hire an applicant, you should make him or her a firm job offer. It should include details of working conditions, such as pay, work hours, holidays, vacations, and other employee benefits, as well as the new employee's duties and responsibilities. Given the increasing tendency for workers to sue their employers, you should put job offers in writing and get the applicant to sign, indicating his or her understanding and agreement.

Orienting the New Employee   Selection also should include orienting new employees to the job. Starting a new job is usually a difficult and frustrating experience, even for the best-qualified people. Thus, orientation should include, at a minimum, an introduction to co-workers; an explanation of the business's history, policies, procedures, and benefits; and working closely with the new employee during at least the first pay period. More employees leave a firm during that period than at any other time during their employment, as the following example shows.

> After more than 20 years as a full-time wife and mother, Elaine Reeves* accepted her first job outside the home. When she reported for work on Monday morning, Elaine was greeted by the business's owner and shown the word processor, other office machines, and the supply cabinet. Then she was left on her own while the owner went to call on several contractors. In these unfamiliar surroundings and with the other employees wrapped up in their own work, which made them seem unfriendly and unhelpful, she felt shaken and discouraged and was thinking of turning around and going home. The owner walked in just in time to stop her.

■ TRAINING AND DEVELOPING EMPLOYEES

The effectiveness of a small business results not only from the ability of the owner but also from (1) the inherent abilities of its employees; (2) their development through training, education, and experience; and (3) their motivation. The first of these depends on effective recruiting and selection. The second results from personnel development. The third, motivation, which will be covered in Chapter 10, results from the manager's leadership abilities.

Not only must new employees be trained, but the present ones also must be retrained and upgraded if they are to adjust to rapidly changing job requirements. Some of the results of training and developing workers include (1) increased productivity, (2) reduced turnover, (3) increased earnings for employees, (4) decreased costs of materials and equipment due to errors, (5) less supervision required, and (6) improved employee satisfaction. A recent report by *Business and Legal Reports* (www.blr.com) found that U.S. employers spend an average of over $55 per employee annually on employee training.[27]

Ways of Training Nonmanagerial Employees

You can use many methods to train nonmanagerial employees including (1) on-the-job training (OJT), (2) apprenticeship training, and (3) internship training.

On-the-Job Training   The most universal form of employee development, **on-the-job training (OJT),** which is in reality **on-the-job learning (OJL),** occurs when workers perform their regular job under the supervision and guidance of the owner, a manager, or a trained worker or instructor. Thus, while learning to do the job, the worker acts as a regular employee, producing the good or service the business sells. Whether consciously planned or not, this form of training always occurs. While the methods used vary with the trainer, OJT usually involves:

On-the-job training (OJT) or **on-the-job learning (OJL)** has the worker actually performing the work, under the supervision of a competent trainer.

- Telling workers what needs to be done.
- Telling them how to do the job.
- Showing them how it must be done.
- Letting them do the job under the trainer's guidance.

---

*Name disguised at her request.

- Telling—and showing—them what they did right, what they did wrong, and how to correct the wrong activity.
- Repeating the process until the learners have mastered the job.

The main *advantages* of OJT are that it results in low out-of-pocket costs and production continues during the training. Also, there is no transition from classroom learning to actual production. Research and experience have repeatedly shown that OJT is a cost-effective and proven alternative to formal training programs, as it both educates *and* motivates employees.[28] Do you remember from Chapter 4 that 40 percent of Pizza Hut managers learned their jobs as part-time crew members? And that 70 percent of McDonald's restaurant managers, and over 50 percent of its middle and senior managers, began their careers performing hourly restaurant jobs?[29]

On the other hand, the *disadvantages* of OJT are excessive waste caused by mistakes and the poor learning environment provided by the production area. While most OJT is done by owners and managers, they are not necessarily the best ones to do it, since their primary focus is on running the business. For this reason, another capable employee or even an outside trainer should be assigned this responsibility, if possible.

Apprenticeship training blends OJT with learning of theory in the classroom.

Apprenticeship Training   For workers performing skilled, craft-type jobs, **apprenticeship training** blends the learning of theory with practice in the techniques of the job. If the job can best be learned by combining classroom instruction and actual learning experience on the job, this training method should be used. It usually lasts from two to seven years of both classroom learning and on-the-job training. For young people who can't—or won't—finish a high school program, an effective apprentice program can put a good job within their reach.

Internship training combines OJT with learning at a cooperating school or college.

Internship Training   **Internship training** combines education at a school or college with on-the-job training at a cooperating business. It is usually used for students who are prospective employees for marketing, clerical, technical, and managerial positions. Co-op programs prepare students for technical positions, provide income to meet the cost of their education, and give them a chance to see if they would like to go to work for the company. This method also gives the small business owner a chance to evaluate the student as a prospective full-time employee.

> For example, auto shop students at 12 high schools in the Kansas City, Missouri, area can participate in an internship program called "Jump on Life." Sponsored by local Jiffy Lube (www.jiflube.com) franchises, it gives the students technical and management training. After graduation, all 15 of its first graduates were hired by local Jiffy Lube franchises.[30]

Cross-training involves workers learning many job skills so they are more versatile.

Cross-Training   With the shortage of skilled job applicants, some small businesses are turning to **cross-training** to make their employees more versatile—and keep them more satisfied. While specialized training tends to improve performance, it may also result in boredom and fatigue. Cross-training, which has employees learn many kinds of jobs, may reduce turnover by keeping workers more interested in their jobs.

> At Motor Technology (www.motortech.com), for instance, training—especially cross-training—is seen as "the prerequisite to delivering excellent customer service . . . , [helping] reduce turnover . . . , [and fostering] pride of workmanship." Thomas Ryan, president of Motor Technology, believes this type of training has helped "the family business grow as competitors had to shut down."[31]

Outside Help with Training

Many outside programs are available to help you train your employees. For example, the National Apprenticeship Act of 1937, administered by the U.S. Labor Department's Bureau of Apprenticeship and Training (www.doleta.gov), sets policies and standards for apprenticeship programs. Write to this bureau for help in conducting such a program. Vocational-technical schools, business schools, junior colleges, and small private firms help small companies by conducting regular or special classes. Through such programs, potential employees can become qualified for skilled jobs such as machinist, lathe operator, computer operator, and legal assistant.

■ SELECTING AND DEVELOPING MANAGERS

Determining the job requirements for someone to be a manager is more difficult than filling other positions because managerial jobs differ so greatly. But one generalization usually applies: *The employee who is a good performer at the nonmanagerial level does not necessarily make a good manager, because the skills needed at the two levels differ drastically.* Adding to this difficulty is the constant change in managerial methods and terms. Many small businesses can't always be abreast of these changes. Therefore, such concepts as total quality management (TQM), reengineering, benchmarking, and rightsizing might be desirable goals, but are often unattainable.

Selecting Managers

In small firms, managers are usually promoted from within, but many businesses hire college graduates for management trainee programs. We have found in directing and teaching in management development programs that the characteristics to be developed to produce good managers are creativity, productivity, innovativeness, communication skills (including oral, written, nonverbal, and telephone), self-motivation, and the drive and energy to motivate and energize others to achieve consistently large amounts of high-quality work. You can see that these tend to be the same qualities that lead to success as an entrepreneur, as shown in Chapter 2.

Developing Managers

In addition to the usual methods used to develop all employees, some special techniques are used to develop managerial personnel. These include (1) coaching, (2) planned progression, (3) job rotation, and (4) executive development programs, as shown in Figure 9–5. Also, many franchisers, such as McDonald's and Holiday Inn (www.holidayinn.com), have their own schools at which their franchise owners and managers learn the desired system and how to make it work.[32]

The small company owner's need for ways to train a person to become a supervisor or manager is often overlooked. Yet the move up from being an employee to being "an overseer is one of the most difficult in people's careers."[33]

■ COMPLYING WITH EQUAL EMPLOYMENT OPPORTUNITY (EEO) LAWS

Federal and state laws and regulations affect almost all aspects of personnel relations. Since state laws vary so widely, only the most significant federal laws affecting recruiting and selecting employees are discussed here.

Laws Providing for Equal Employment Opportunity

Since 1963, Congress has passed various acts to create equal employment opportunity and affirmative action. Table 9–2 summarizes the most significant legislation in this area.

Figure 9–5
Methods Used to Develop Managers

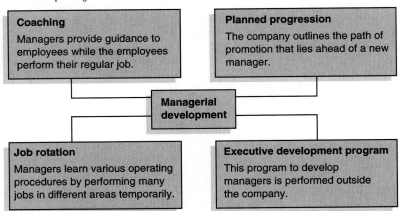

Special mention should be made of the **Americans with Disabilities Act (ADA)** of 1990, for it changed the way employers must deal with the 33.8 million U.S. citizens who have physical or mental disabilities. This law has probably had greater impact on small business management than any other law, for it requires positive actions on the part of employers. Employers' fears of the effect of this law have been borne out, for claims against the EEOC increased from 15,099 in 1993 to more than 18,000 in 1997.[34]

The act mandates the removal of social and physical barriers against the disabled, two-thirds of whom are unemployed. It covers disabilities such as cancer, blindness, arthritis, chemical dependency, speech and hearing impairment, learning disabilities, and mental illness, and also protects employees infected with the HIV virus. The act specifically excludes sexual behavior disorders, gambling, kleptomania, and others. This act, which targets employers with 15 or more workers, is particularly hard on small business owners because it assumes that they can comprehend and act on the needs of the mentally ill. Yet employers have enough difficulty just understanding the intent of the law. Questions still requiring answers are: Are obese workers disabled? What about alcoholic employees?[35]

Enforcing EEO Laws

You must remember that *all employees—temporary as well as permanent—are entitled to equality in all conditions of employment.* Hiring, training, promotions and transfers, wages and benefits, and all other employment factors are covered. Posting available job openings on a bulletin board to give present employees a chance to bid on them has been found to be a good method of complying with EEO laws. There must be no discrimination in rates of pay, including pensions or other deferred payments. Recreational activities—company sports teams, holiday parties, and the like—should be open to all employees on a nondiscriminatory basis.

As shown in Table 9–2, the **Equal Employment Opportunity Commission (EEOC)** (www.eeoc.gov) is the primary enforcing agency for most EEO laws. Figure 9–6 shows some regulations it has issued to prevent discrimination such as age discrimination.

Table 9–2

Legal Influences on Equal Employment Opportunity (EEO) and Affirmative Action

Laws	Coverage	Basic Requirements	Agencies Involved
Title VII of Civil Rights Act of 1964, as amended	Employers with 15 or more employees and engaged in interstate commerce; federal service workers; and state and local government workers.	Prohibits employment decisions based on race, color, religion, sex, or national origin.	Equal Employment Opportunity Commission (EEOC)
Executive Order 11246, as amended	Employers with federal contracts and subcontracts.	Requires contractors who underutilize women and minorities to develop affirmative action plans (AAPs), including setting goals and timetables; and to recruit, select, train, utilize, and promote more minorities and women when contracts exceed $50,000 a year.	Office of Federal Contract Compliance Programs (OFCCP) in the Labor Department
Age Discrimination in Employment Act of 1967	Employers with 20 or more employees.	Prohibits employment discrimination against employees aged 40 and over, including mandatory retirement before 70, with certain exceptions.	EEOC
Vocational Rehabilitation Act of 1973	Employers with federal contracts or subcontracts.	Prohibits discrimination and requires contractor to develop affirmative action programs to recruit and employ handicapped persons. Requires development of an AAP.	OFCCP
Vietnam-Era Veterans Readjustment Act of 1974	Employers with federal contracts or subcontracts.	Requires contractors to develop AAPs to recruit and employ Vietnam-era veterans and to list job openings with state employment services, for priority in referrals.	OFCCP
Americans with Disabilities Act of 1990 (ADA)	Employers with 15 or more employees.	Prohibits discrimination based on physical or mental handicap, including HIV infection (affirmative action required).	EEOC
Civil Rights Act of 1991	Same as Title VII	Amends Title VII and ADA to allow punitive and compensatory damages in cases of intentional discrimination and permits more extensive use of jury trials.	EEOC

Source: Various government and private publications.

Another difficult issue for small—and large—businesses is how to cope with sexual harassment. According to the EEOC, this is the fastest-growing employee complaint—increasing 150 percent from 1990 to 1996.[36] The term is difficult to define because the nature of the act lies as much in the reaction of the victim as in the intentions or actions of the offender; that is, what makes a gesture, remark, or pinup photo "harassment" is that it is "unwelcome."[37] Small employers should therefore install an effective prevention program, for the U.S. Supreme Court ruled in June 1998 that if the harassment results in a

Figure 9–6
Principal EEOC Regulations

- Sex discrimination guidelines
- Questions and answers on pregnancy disability and reproductive hazards
- Religious discrimination guidelines
- National origin discrimination guidelines
- Interpretations of the Age Discrimination in Employment Act
- Employee selection guidelines
- Record keeping and reports
- Affirmative action guidelines
- EEO in the federal government
- Equal Pay Act interpretations
- Policy statement on maternal benefits
- Policy statement on relationship of Title VII to 1986
- Immigration Reform and Control Act
- Policy statement on reproductive and fetal hazards
- Policy statement on religious accommodation under Title VII
- Policy guidance on sexual harassment
- Disabilities discrimination guidelines

Source: James Ledvinka and Vida Gulbinas Scarpello, *Federal Regulation of Personnel and Human Resource Management,* 2d ed. (Belmont, CA: Wadsworth Publishing/ITP, 1992).

job loss, such as firing or demotion, the employer is legally responsible, even if unaware of the behavior. If the employee's job was not threatened, the employer can still be held liable unless the company can show it had effective anti-harassment policies in place and complaint procedures that the employee did not invoke.[38]

Religious discrimination is another employee issue that must be scrupulously dealt with by small business owners. In essence, employers (or potential employers) must cope with two essential questions. First, can a business force an employee, while in the workplace, to remove clothing with religious significance, or can it refuse to hire an employee who will not make such concessions? Second, if a business honors the request of a client or consultant to exclude employees of certain religious persuasions from certain positions, can the employer be held liable? In answering these and related questions, the employer should consider how it treats employees of religious persuasions different from that of the employee alleging discrimination.[39]

Language is another job-related activity that is causing problems for small businesses. The EEOC has decreed that English-only rules may violate EEO laws "unless an employer can show they are necessary for conducting business."[40]

The enforcement of these laws—as desirable as they may be—is causing problems for the EEOC. In turn, those filing charges, and those charged, are suffering long waits—often of more than a year—for decisions.[41]

Affirmative action programs (AAPs)
provide guidelines to help firms eliminate discrimination against women and minorities.

The Labor Department's Office of Federal Contract Compliance Programs (OFCCP) (www.oalj.dol.gov) requires employers with government contracts or subcontracts to have **affirmative action programs (AAPs)** to put the principle of equal employment opportunity into practice. The OFCCP can cancel a guilty firm's contract or prohibit it from getting future contracts if a violation is blatant.

■ COMPENSATING EMPLOYEES

Another aspect of managing human resources and diversity is providing what employees consider fair pay for their activities. Their earnings should be high enough to motivate them to be good producers, yet low enough for you to maintain satisfactory profits.

Legal Influences

There are many federal and state laws that affect how much small business owners pay their employees (see Table 9–3 for the primary federal laws involved). According to the Wage and Hour Law, 14 is the minimum working age for most nonfarm jobs. Thus, you can hire workers aged 14 and 15 for nonhazardous jobs for up to three hours on a school day and eight hours on any other day, but no more than 18 hours per week from 7:00 AM to 7:00 PM during the school term. Those aged 16 and 17 can work an unlimited time on nonhazardous jobs.

Certain retail and service companies don't have to comply if their annual sales are less than $500,000. Laundry, fabric care, dry cleaning, and some construction firms also qualify for exemptions, while employers of "tipped employees" must pay a cash wage of at least $2.13 per hour if they claim a tip credit against their minimum wage obligations. "If an employee's tips, combined with the employer's cash wage of at least $2.13 per hour, do not equal the minimum hourly wage, the employer must make up the difference."[42]

Since state laws vary so much from each other and from the federal law, we won't try to discuss them. You should check the laws for the state in which you operate.

Setting Rates of Pay

In addition to legal factors, many variables influence what employees consider a *fair wage*. First, they think they should be paid in proportion to their physical and mental efforts on the job. The standard of living and cost of living in the area also matter. And unions help set wages in a geographic area through collective bargaining, whether the company itself is unionized or not. The economic factors of supply and demand for workers help set wages, but the employer's ability to pay must ultimately be the deciding factor.

In actual practice, most small businesses pay either the minimum wage (which was set at $5.15 per hour on September 1, 1997)[43] or the same wages that similar businesses in the area pay. If you pay less than the prevailing wage, you will have difficulty finding employees. Conversely, you cannot afford to pay much more unless your employees are more productive. In the final analysis, you pay whatever you must to attract the people you really need—and can afford.

Using Money to Motivate

Many small businesses use some form of financial incentive to motivate their employees to use their initiative and to perform better. Some of the more popular financial incentives are (1) merit increases, (2) incentive payments, and (3) profit sharing. A few years ago, a Conference Board survey of 382 companies found that around three-quarters of them provided some type of incentive pay, including bonuses for cost-saving suggestions or for learning new skills.[44]

Merit Increases   **Merit increases,** which base a person's wage or salary on ability and merit rather than on seniority or some other factor, tend to be effective motivators. Merit programs identify, appraise, and reward employees for outstanding contributions toward your company's profits. Thus, an employee's wage or salary relates directly to that

Merit increases are based on the employee's ability and performance.

Table 9–3

Legal Influences on Compensation and Hours of Work

Law	Coverage	Basic Requirements	Agencies Involved
Public Construction Act of 1931 (Davis-Bacon Act)	Employers with federal construction contracts or subcontracts of $2,000 or more.	Employers must pay at least the prevailing wages in the area, as determined by the Secretary of Labor; overtime is to be paid at 1½ times the basic wage for all work over 8 hours per day or 40 hours per week.	Wage and Hour Division of the Labor Department
Public Contracts Act of 1936 (Walsh-Healy Act)	Employers with federal contracts of $1,000 or more.	Same as above.	Same as above
Fair Labor Standards Act of 1938 (wage and hour law)	Private employers engaged in interstate commerce; retailers having annual sales of $325,000. (Many groups are exempted from overtime requirements.)	Employers must pay a minimum of $4.25 per hour and 1½ times the basic rate for work over 40 hours per week and are limited (by jobs and school status) in employing persons under 18.	Same as above
Equal Pay Act of 1963	All employers.	Men and women must receive equal pay for jobs requiring substantially the same skill, working conditions, effort, and responsibility.	Equal Employment Opportunity Commission
Service Contracts Act of 1965	Employers with contracts to provide services worth $2,500 or more per year to the federal government.	Same as Davis-Bacon.	Same as Davis-Bacon
Family and Medical Leave Act of 1993	Employers with 50 or more employees within a 75-mile radius; certain employees are exempted.	Employers must provide workers up to 12 weeks of unpaid leave during a 12-month period for (1) birth of a child; (2) placement of a child for adoption or foster care; (3) caring for a spouse, child, or parent with a serious health condition; and (4) a serious condition of the employee. Health coverage must be continued during the leave period and same or comparable job be available upon return.	Department of Labor

Source: Various government and private publications.

person's efforts to achieve your objectives. Many companies—large as well as small—are basing employee pay on observed competence. These employers recognize that with global competition they can no longer pay employees whose performance does not support business strategies and organizational goals.[45]

An **incentive wage** is the extra compensation paid for all production over a specified standard amount.

Incentive Payments   Incentive payments can be paid in the form of incentive wages, bonuses, commissions, and push money.

An **incentive wage,** which is the extra compensation paid for all production over a specified amount, is effective in situations in which a worker can control the volume of sales or production. Piece rates, commissions, and bonuses are forms of incentive payments. Under a *piece-rate system,* an employee's earnings are based on a rate per unit times the number of units produced. But you should give some form of guaranteed base rate to ensure that the employee earns at least a minimum amount. Piece-rate systems, which are usually used in production- or operations-type activities, can be quite effective, as the following example illustrates.

> A pilot study of the use of piece rates in the corrugated shipping container industry found that 16 of 18 operations showed significantly increased productivity after use of such incentives. On the average, productivity per employee increased about 75 percent.[46]

Commissions, which consist of a given amount per sale or a percentage of sales, are used extensively to reward salespeople, especially in retailing. They are particularly useful in rewarding door-to-door selling of items such as encyclopedias and magazine subscriptions, but they are also used by most department stores and similar retail outlets and are the only form of compensation for real estate agents.

> A **commission** is incentive compensation directly related to the sales or profits achieved by a salesperson.

Bonuses are amounts given to employees either for exceeding their production quotas or as a reward on special occasions. Many production or sales personnel have work quotas and receive bonuses if they exceed that amount.

> A **bonus** is a reward—not specified in advance—given to employees for special efforts and accomplishments.

> For instance, during a recent 10-year period, the sales of W. K. Buckley, Ltd., a family-run cough medicine maker, which still markets its original formula, increased over fourfold—with the same number of employees. To keep employees motivated and focused on helping the firm grow, the owners pay competitive wages, provide excellent working conditions, and have a unique bonus system that "rewards everyone from the shop floor people to the highest level of management."[47]

Another form of incentive payment is called **push money (PM),** or **spiff,** which is a reward given to employees for selling an item the business is making a special effort to sell—in other words, pushing.

> **Push money (PM),** or **spiff,** is a commission paid to a salesperson to push a specific item or line of goods.

Profit Sharing   In **profit sharing,** employees receive a prearranged share of the company's profits. Profit sharing can be effective in motivating employees by tying rewards to company performance. Not only does it reward good performance,[48] but a good plan can also reduce turnover, increase productivity, improve communication, and reduce the amount of supervision needed. The oldest, best-known, and most successful profit-sharing plan is that of the Lincoln Electric Company of Cleveland, Ohio (www.lincolnelectric.com).[49]

> **Profit sharing** is an arrangement—announced in advance—whereby employees receive a prescribed share of the company's profits.

If you can afford to do so, you might want to use an **employee stock ownership plan (ESOP),** which is a modification of profit sharing. In general, an ESOP borrows money, purchases a block of the company's stock, and allocates it to the employees on the basis of salaries and/or longevity. These plans are particularly attractive to small companies because they provide a source of needed capital, boost the company's cash flow, raise employee morale and productivity, and provide a very beneficial new employee benefit.

> An **employee stock ownership plan (ESOP),** a form of profit sharing, borrows money, purchases some of the company's stock, and allocates it to the employees on the basis of salaries and/or longevity.

Compensating Managerial and Professional Personnel

In general, managers of small businesses are paid on a merit basis, with their income based on the firm's earnings. Many small companies also use profit sharing, bonuses, or some other method of stimulating the interest of managerial and professional personnel.

■ PROVIDING EMPLOYEE BENEFITS

Employee benefits (sometimes called **fringe benefits**) are the rewards and services provided to employees in addition to their regular earnings. Some of them are required by

> **Employee benefits,** or **fringe benefits,** are the rewards and services provided to workers in addition to their regular earnings.

Figure 9–7
Some of the Most Popular Employee Benefits

Legally required
Social Security/Medicare
Unemployment insurance
Workers' compensation
Family and medical leave

Voluntary, private
a. Health and accident insurance
    Eye care and eyeglasses
    Chiropractic care
    Dental and orthodontic care
    Health maintenance—diagnostic
        visits/physical exams
    Major medical/hospitalization
    Psychiatric and mental care
    Accident and sickness insurance
b. Life and disability insurance
    Accidental death and dismemberment
    Group term life insurance
    Long-term disability
c. Sick leave, including maternity leave
d. Income maintenance
    Severance pay
    Supplemental unemployment benefits
        (SUBs)
    Pensions
e. Pay for time off
    Holidays
    Personal time
    Sabbatical leaves
    Union activities
    Vacations

f. Employee services and others
    Alcohol and drug rehabilitation
    Auto insurance
    Child care and day care centers for other
        family members
    Christmas bonuses
    Clothing and uniforms
    Company car
    Credit unions
    Discount privileges on organization's
        products or services
    Loans and financial assistance
    Food services and cafeteria
    Group tours and charter flights
    Gymnasium and physical training center
    Legal assistance
    Liability coverage
    Matching gifts to charitable organizations
        or schools
    Matching payroll deductions and savings
        plans
    Moving and transfer allowances
    Personal counseling and financial advice
    Recreation center
    Service awards
    Stock purchase and profit-sharing plans
    Transportation and parking
    Tuition for employee and/or family
        members

Source: Various government and private publications.

law, while others are offered voluntarily by the employer. Figure 9–7 lists some of the most popular of these benefits.

In general, these benefits increase in importance as employees' lifestyles expand and it takes more than just wages to satisfy them. But benefits are costly. For example, while wages were increasing at the rate of 4 percent in 1998, rising benefits were adding an additional 3.3 percent to the employer's compensation cost.[50] And once given, they are difficult—if not impossible—to take back. In addition to the actual cost of the benefits, the cost of administering them is tremendous. Still, employees want and expect them, almost as much as they do their salary!

Legally Required Benefits

Small employers are legally required by the Social Security Act to provide retirement, disability, survivors, and medical benefits; unemployment insurance; and workers' compensation. Also, according to the Consolidated Omnibus Budget Reconciliation Act of 1986 (COBRA), employers with 20 or more employees must continue offering health insurance for up to 18 months for employees when they leave—either voluntarily or otherwise—and up to 36 months for widows, divorced or separated spouses, and employee dependents. While the former employee pays the cost of the insurance, employers must establish procedures for collecting premiums and keep track of former employees. Employers with 50 or more employees within a radius of 75 miles of their home office must provide for family and medical leave.

Social Security   Under the **Social Security** system, you act as both taxpayer and tax collector, as you must pay a tax on employees' earnings and deduct an equal amount from their paychecks. In 1999, the tax rate was 7.65 percent per employee (6.2 percent for Social Security and 1.45 percent for Medicare), and the taxable wage base was $72,600 for Social Security and unlimited for Medicare. Self-employed people must pay the entire cost themselves, which is twice the amount listed for employees.

> **Social Security** is a federal program that provides support for the retired, widowed, disabled, and their dependents.

There is currently considerable pessimism about the health of the Social Security system and its ability to maintain present benefit levels into the future. According to the 1996 Retirement Confidence Survey—as reported by the Employee Benefit Research Institute—79 percent of workers and 48 percent of retirees "are not confident that the system will continue to provide today's level of benefits when they retire."[51] A later survey by *USA Today* found that 58 percent of respondents looked to Social Security as only "a minor source of income," while 23 percent answered "not at all."[52]

Unemployment Insurance   State governments receive most of the **unemployment insurance** tax, which can be as high as 4.7 percent of a limited amount (which varies by state) of each employee's pay, while the rest goes to the U.S. government for administrative costs. If the business can lower its unemployment rate, the tax is reduced under a merit rating system. Using funds from the tax, the state pays unemployed workers a predetermined amount each week. This amount varies from state to state.

> **Unemployment insurance** provides some financial support to employees laid off for reasons beyond their control.

Workers' Compensation   Employee losses from accidents and occupational diseases are paid for under state **workers' compensation** laws. Each employer is required to pay insurance premiums to either a state fund or a private insurance company. The accumulated funds are used to compensate victims of industrial accidents or work-related illnesses. A firm's premiums depend on the hazards involved and the effectiveness of its safety programs. The amount paid to an employee or to his or her estate is fixed according to the type and extent of injury. According to the National Council on Compensation Insurance, the costs of these programs more than doubled during a recent six-year period, from just over $30 billion to over $60 billion, and the costs are still escalating. *This trend threatens small firms, which may not be able to bear the increasing costs.*

> **Workers' compensation** involves payments made to employees for losses from industrial accidents and occupational diseases.

Family and Medical Leave   Employers with 50 or more workers who live within 75 miles of the plant must guarantee workers up to 12 weeks of unpaid leave a year for births, adoptions, or the care of sick children, spouses, or parents. The **Family and Medical Leave Act** covers employees who have been on the job at least one year, but the employer can exclude the top-paid 10 percent of employees. Employees are required to give 30 days' notice when practical, such as for births and adoptions, and may be required to use vacation or other leave time first. Couples employed at the same place may be restricted to 12 weeks total leave each year. Employers must continue to provide health insurance during leave and guarantee workers the same or an equivalent job on return. In spite of the protection provided by the law, many workers find it too costly to use—both financially and professionally. Some don't use it because of the burden it places on fellow employees who must cover for them. Others cannot afford to miss their paychecks. A 1997 study by Coopers &

> The **Family and Medical Leave Act** requires employers with 50 or more employees to provide up to 12 weeks of unpaid leave for births or adoptions, and to care for sick children, spouses, or parents.

Lybrand (www.colybrand.com) found that the average number of employees per company using this leave was 5 percent.[53]

Some Other Popular Benefits

As shown in Figure 9–7, there are many voluntary benefits in addition to the legally required ones. Health, accident, life, and disability insurance are especially popular with small businesses and their employees. Yet in 1998 the Employee Benefit Research Institute found that 30.5 percent of employees in companies with fewer than 25 workers had no health coverage; 20.3 percent in companies with 25–99 workers had none; 15.3 percent in companies with 100–499 workers had none; and 11.8 percent in companies with over 500 had none.[54] Only 45 percent had some type of retirement plan.[55] Even when small firms do have health insurance, the cost is skyrocketing. A 1996 study by KPMG Peat Marwick (www.kpmg.com) found that employees who have family coverage at small firms saw their costs for coverage jump 23 percent a year from 1988 to 1996. And their share of the premium escalated from $408 a year in 1988 to $2,100 in 1996.[56] One of the best ways for small companies to provide these benefits is through membership in a professional association. For example, for a $149 annual membership fee, a small business owner who joins the Independent Business Alliance has access to affordable insurance and other financial services not available elsewhere.[57]

Other voluntary benefits are as varied as small businesses themselves. In trade and service businesses, discounts on the firm's goods or services are well received by employees. Some conscientious employers go much further.

> For instance, Truett Cathy, founder of Atlanta-based Chick-fil-A restaurant franchises (www.chick-fil-a.com), started a tuition program to help his employees get an education. The chain offers $1,000 in tuition assistance to all employees who have been with the company at least two years. To qualify, the employee must work 20 hours a week and maintain a C average in school. The company has handed out more than $10 million since the program started.[58]

A **defined-contribution plan** is a pension plan that establishes the basis on which an employer will contribute to the pension fund.

Pension programs were common in small firms until the passage of the Employee Retirement Income Security Act (ERISA) in 1974. Because the law proved too complex and difficult for small businesses to conform to, many of them gave up their voluntary pension programs, especially after the law was amended in 1989.

> Ronald Turner, of Clarksburg, West Virginia, dropped his employee pension plan and gave his employees the cash due them from the fund, saying that he had tried to obey the law, but quit after the required paperwork grew from 35 to 77 pages and the IRS (www.irs.gov) disqualified the plan "on a technicality."[59]

"Our pension plan is simple and portable. However, it does not involve much in the way of actual money."

(*Source:* From *AARP Bulletin,* November 1995, p. 2.)

Many small firms have decided to let their employees establish private pension programs. Most of them are now encouraging their workers to use a **defined-contribution plan,** which establishes the basis on which the employer will contribute to the pension fund. The contributions may be made through profit sharing, thrift plans, employer-sponsored Individual Retirement Accounts (IRAs), and various other means. The amount an employee receives at retirement is determined by the funds accumulated in his or her account at the time of retirement and what retirement benefits these funds will buy. The use of **defined-benefit plans,** with a fixed amount of payout at retirement, has drastically declined.

Finally, some employers have **401(k) retirement plans,** which permit workers to place a certain amount of their wages annually in tax-deferred retirement savings plans. Employers can match the employees' contributions (and often do) on a one-for-one basis, up to $6,000 of salary (indexed for inflation) for each employee. An employer's contribution may, however, vary from zero up to double the employee's contribution.

> A **defined-benefit plan** is a pension plan whereby the amount an employee is to receive at retirement is specifically set forth.
>
> **401(k) retirement plans** permit workers to place up to a certain amount of their wages each year in tax-deferred retirement savings plans.

Flexible Approach to Benefits

A **cafeteria-style benefit plan,** also known as **flexcomp,** can help you reduce your annual increase in benefit costs. Under this system, you tell your employees the dollar value of benefits they are entitled to receive. Each employee then tells you how to allocate the money among a variety of available programs. This system increases employee awareness of the value of the benefits and offers freedom of choice and a personalized approach. These plans are now a viable option for small firms because third-party administrators can take care of the paperwork.

(*Source:* © 1996 by Margaret P. Megginson. Used with permission.)

■ PROTECTING EMPLOYEES' HEALTH AND SAFETY

Totally safe working conditions are impossible to provide, so employee safety is a condition involving *relative* freedom from danger or injury. In this section we look at how small business owners can maintain working conditions in which employees not only *are* safe but also *feel* safe. *In other words, employees need to know that you care about their safety.*

Unlike large firms, which employ specialists to be responsible for health and safety activities, small businesses must rely on employees with various job responsibilities to cover this area as well as most of the other areas of human resource management we have discussed. There are, however, consulting firms that specialize in helping small businesses provide healthy and safe work environments, as the following example shows.

> A **cafeteria-style benefit plan,** or **flexcomp,** allows the employer to provide all employees with the legally required benefits, plus an extra dollar amount that each employee can choose how to use.

> Stephenson & Brook, based in Marblehead, Massachusetts, offers its services for a small monthly fee to small companies—those with fewer than 50 employees. Although this firm specializes in workers' compensation issues, hot-line staffers will address other human resource topics as well.[60]

Factors Influencing Workers' Health and Safety

There are many and varied factors bearing on the maintenance of healthy, safe working conditions. We cover only the most significant ones: (1) organization size, (2) type of industry, (3) type of occupation, and (4) human variables.

Organization Size   According to the New York State Department of Labor (www.labor.state.ny.us), the smallest and largest organizations have tended to be the safest places to work. Companies with *under 20 or over 1,000* employees have been found to be safer than those in between.[61] Statistically, the most dangerous organizations are those with *50 to 1,000 employees.*

Type of Industry   Although the safety records of industries vary periodically, the type of industry does have a correlation with safety. For example, the least safe industries usually include meat-packing plants, shipbuilding and repair, and metal sanitary ware.[62]

Type of Occupation   The type of occupation also affects safety. Workplace dangers and injuries that once were considered likely—or were reported—only in construction and factories have now spread to a variety of operations. For example, back injuries are quite prevalent among health care workers, who must frequently lift patients or heavy bedding, and among shipbuilders. According to the Bureau of Labor Statistics, health services and shipbuilding have higher rates of illness and injury than the average for the private sector.[63]

Repetitive stress injuries (RSIs), or **cumulative trauma disorders (CTDs),** are muscular or skeletal injuries to the hand, wrist, or other areas that bear the brunt of repeated motions. Among the most common is **carpal tunnel syndrome.**

A growing health problem for small firms, especially in offices, is **repetitive-stress injuries (RSIs),** also known as **cumulative trauma disorders (CTDs)** (one of the best known is **carpal tunnel syndrome**). According to the Bureau of Labor Statistics, these muscular or skeletal injuries to the hand, wrist, and other areas that bear the brunt of repeated motions caused over 31,000 absences from work in 1995.[64] Aetna Life & Casualty (www.aetna.com) estimates that workers' compensation claims from employees such as reporters, telephone operators, data processors, and checkout clerks using scanners may soon cost as much as $20 billion a year. And the Americans with Disabilities Act may make it easier for victims of RSIs to sue their employers.

According to one recent study, the increasing use of independent contractors and temporary employees has led to an increase in the accident rate in U.S. industries. The study suggests that employers should develop better ongoing relations with these workers and orient them better to job risks and dangers.[65]

The most common work-related problem for both men and women is back injuries—38 percent for women and 34 percent for men. The second most common for women is wrist injuries, 20 percent (as opposed to 12 percent for men, making it the third most common for them). Burns, cuts, and bruises are second for men (16 percent) and third for women (6 percent).[66]

Human Variables   The most important human variables influencing safety are job satisfaction, personal characteristics, and management attitudes. Studies indicate a close relationship between safety and employees' satisfaction with their work. Other studies indicate that where top management actively supports safety programs, the accident frequency and severity rates are lower. Finally, research shows that most industrial injuries occur in persons 20 to 24 years old, especially males; fewer occur among the married and females.[67]

The Role of the Occupational Safety and Health Act

The **Occupational Safety and Health Administration (OSHA)** establishes specific safety standards to assure, to the extent feasible, the safety and health of workers.

The Occupational Safety and Health Act created the **Occupational Safety and Health Administration (OSHA)** (www.osha.gov) to assure—to the extent feasible—safe and healthful working conditions for U.S. employees. The law covers businesses that are engaged in interstate commerce and have one or more employees, except those covered by the Atomic Energy Act (www.em.doe.gov) or the Federal Mine Safety Act.

Employee Rights   OSHA encourages increased examination and questioning of management's staffing decisions and equipment selection. If workers believe their employer's violation of job safety or health standards threatens them with physical harm, they may request an OSHA inspection without being discharged or discriminated against for doing so. They can participate in any resulting hearings and can protest if they think the penalty is too light. And they can request that the Department of Health and Human Services (www.dhhs.gov) check to see if there is any potentially toxic substance in the workplace and have safe exposure levels set for that substance.

Employer Obligations and Rights   Even though many accidents result from employees' own lack of safety consciousness, employees usually don't receive citations. Instead, OSHA holds employers responsible for making employees wear safety equipment (for an example, see Case 9–2, "The Case of Sam Sawyer," at the end of the chapter).

Employers are subject to fines for unsafe practices regardless of whether any accidents occur. Therefore, you should provide safety training for your employees, encourage and follow up on employee compliance with safety regulations and precautions, and discipline employees for noncompliance. Assistance may be obtained from OSHA and National Safety Council (www.nsc.org) chapters. Also, your workers' compensation carrier may suggest ways to improve safety and employees' health. You may obtain useful information from equipment manufacturers, other employers who have had an inspection, trade associations, and the local fire department.

Thousands of small business owners call OSHA each year requesting a visit from one of the OSHA consultants. These inspections are free for organizations that have fewer than 250 employees and are classified as "high hazard" under the government's Standard Industrial Classification (SIC) code, but may not always be possible to schedule.

Some Generalizations about OSHA Enforcement   Firms with fewer than eight employees do not have to maintain injury and illness records, except when a fatality occurs or an accident hospitalizes five or more persons. Also, OSHA doesn't inspect firms with 10 or fewer employees in "relatively safe" industries, which exempts nearly 80 percent of firms from inspections. Finally, inspectors concentrate on workplaces with unsatisfactory records. In late 1997, OSHA launched a cooperative compliance program. Under this program, about 500 companies with the highest rates of illness and injury—or the most OSHA citations—get full inspections. But another 12,250 companies with more modest rates were asked to create safety-and-health programs to avoid tough inspections.[68] In 1998, the U.S. Chamber of Commerce filed a federal suit to strike down the program. It claimed that OSHA was trying to coerce the companies to join the program by threatening to inspect them if they didn't join.

Since 1988, small businesses have found that the paperwork burden makes it especially difficult for them to comply with OSHA's Hazard Communications Standard, which requires every employer in the country to identify hazardous substances in the workplace, list them, and train employees to use them safely. At first, the law applied only to manufacturers, but now the rule applies to nearly all employers. Dry-cleaning establishments, especially, find the rules onerous.

Because the inspection program and its technical nature constantly change, you're advised to use the resources suggested previously, as well as local chambers of commerce, area planning and development commissions, and local offices of the SBA and OSHA.

Environmental Protection

The Environmental Protection Agency (EPA) (www.epa.gov) was created to help protect and improve the quality of the nation's environment. Its mandate includes solid-waste disposal, clean air, water resources, noise, pesticides, and atomic radiation. Environmental protection, though beneficial to society, can be hard on small firms. Many marginal plants have closed because of EPA requirements that pollution control equipment be installed. You owe it to your employees, for humanitarian reasons as well as financial ones, to protect their environment. Environmental protection efforts may also give your company a competitive edge.

WHAT YOU SHOULD HAVE LEARNED

■

1. The most important resource for any business is its people. Therefore, you must determine the needed number and skills of employees and the sources from which to recruit them. This process begins with a job description and job specifications.

   Employees can be recruited from either internal or external sources. When feasible, it is best to upgrade, transfer, or promote from inside the business, all of which increase employee morale and save time and money; also, employees' past performance is known. External sources include former employees, applications, friends and relatives of present employees, competing firms, social and professional organizations, schools and colleges, retirees and older workers, those with disabilities, and part-time and temporary workers.

2. Employees can be recruited through advertising, employment agencies, temporary help services, networking, employee referrals, scouting, and temporary help services. Newspaper want ads are the most common method of recruiting.

   You can evaluate prospective employees by (*a*) a preliminary screening interview or review of the candidate's application or résumé; (*b*) biographical information from the application or résumé and from school, military, and other records; (*c*) some form of testing; (*d*) verifying references; and (*e*) giving a physical examination after a preliminary job offer is made.

   Ultimately, the decision regarding whom to employ involves your personal judgment. Once the decision has been made, a clear—preferably written—job offer should be extended. Orientation can range from a simple introduction to co-workers to a lengthy training process.

3. After employees are hired, they should be retrained and developed periodically. Training methods include (*a*) on-the-job training (OJT), (*b*) apprenticeship training, (*c*) internship training, and (*d*) cross-training.

4. In selecting managers, you should look for *managerial qualities,* which are not the same as an individual's *nonmanagerial competence.* Techniques used for developing managers include (*a*) coaching, (*b*) planned progression, (*c*) job rotation, and (*d*) executive development programs—especially these developed by universities.

5. You must conform to federal and state laws in your dealings with current and prospective employees. The equal employment opportunity (EEO) provisions of the Civil Rights Act and the requirements of the Americans with Disabilities Act are especially important. Legislation has been passed to prevent discrimination on the basis of race, creed, color, sex, age, religion, disabilities, or national origin. The Equal Employment Opportunity Commission (EEOC) and the Office of Federal Contract Compliance Programs (OFCCP) enforce these laws. Age, sex, and language discrimination charges are particularly troubling to small firms.

6. Money is an important motivator, so you must pay your employees not just the minimum wage, but also enough to attract and keep them. You can use merit increases, incentive payments, and profit sharing to motivate your employees.

   Employee benefits, which are increasingly significant to both employees and employers, are quite costly. While Social Security, Medicare, unemployment insurance, workers' compensation, and family and medical leave are legally required, pension plans—especially 401(k) savings plans—and various kinds of insurance are popular voluntary benefits. Cafeteria-style benefit plans (sometimes called flexcomp) are now feasible for small companies.

7. Employee health and safety varies with the size of the organization, the type of industry, the type of occupation involved, and personal and human variables. Repetitive stress injuries are becoming a serious health problem for small firms, especially in their offices. OSHA, the government agency responsible for promoting safe and healthful working conditions, concentrates on the businesses most likely to be unsafe or unhealthy.

   While environmental protection is undoubtedly beneficial for everyone, the costs of required equipment and/or procedures can be a hardship for small businesses.

QUESTIONS FOR DISCUSSION

1. Which external sources are usually used by small businesses for finding new employees?
2. What are some advantages and disadvantages of filling job openings from within the company?
3. Distinguish among upgrading, promoting, and transferring employees.
4. What does the personnel selection procedure involve?
5. Describe the methods used to gather information about prospective employees.
6. What are the primary methods used to train employees? Explain each.
7. What should you look for in a potential manager?
8. How do EEO laws affect recruiting and selecting employees?
9. Which agencies enforce EEO laws? How do they enforce them?
10. What are some factors that affect the amount and form of compensation paid to employees?
11. Explain the five legally required employee benefits. What are some other benefits frequently used by small businesses?
12. Explain what cafeteria-style benefit plans are and why they are used.

C A S E   9 – 1

SUPREME PLUMBING AND HEATING COMPANY: WHERE ARE THE WORKERS?

In the late 1950s, two friendly competitors formed the Supreme Plumbing and Heating Company as a partnership in a rapidly developing industrial area southwest of Houston, Texas. At first, the partners did most of the work themselves, including plumbing, heating, and wiring for both commercial and residential buildings. The business grew rapidly, and several craftsmen and other employees were added. This left the partners devoting almost all their time to managing the business rather than doing the work themselves.

Supreme competed with six other companies within a 50-mile radius both for business and for the best craftsmen. This became difficult in the 1960s when the Lyndon B. Johnson Space Center was built nearby. Most of the area's skilled workers left their jobs with the companies to work at the center for better pay and benefits, causing a great shortage of craftsmen in the area. At the same time, demand for plumbing, heating, and wiring was increasing. It would have been a good opportunity for Supreme to expand its operations—if the needed workers could have been found.

The partners decided the only way to have an adequate supply of trained craftsmen was to do their own training, so they started an apprenticeship program.

The plan was to hire high school graduates or dropouts to work with some of the older craftsmen as apprentice plumbers and electricians, at the prevailing wage rate, until they learned the trade. When they finished their training, they would train others so there would be a continuous training program.

Although the program gave the young people an opportunity to learn a trade that would be valuable to them in future years, the plan didn't work. The trainees would work for Supreme just long enough to be trained; then they would quit to take another job, go into the armed services, or go back to school. The partners had to reduce the amount of construction work they bid on because of their limited work force. To compensate for this loss of revenue, they started a wholesale plumbing, heating, and electrical supply business.

The worker shortage at Supreme continued until there were only three plumbers, three plumber's helpers, two electricians, and two electrician's helpers left. Because the craftsmen were nearing retirement age and the helpers weren't interested in learning the trade, the owners had to go on with the wholesale business, although they would have preferred to continue in construction.

Questions

1. Supreme Plumbing and Heating Company limited itself to hiring only high school graduates and even dropouts. What type of preliminary screening should there have been for this type of job, if any? Explain.

2. What types of recruiting methods could have been implemented by the two partners?

3. When the new Space Center was built nearby, what kind of actions should the partners have taken?

4. Although the apprenticeship program seemed to be the route to take, what other options were there?

CASE 9-2

THE CASE OF SAM SAWYER

Sam Sawyer was a top-rated operator in a building where a material with caustic soda was processed. The five stages of the process were located on five separate floors. Operators moved the material in open buggies from the first stage to a chute in the floor and dumped it onto equipment on the floor below, where the next stage began.

Because of the corrosive nature of the material, close-fitting goggles were provided. Until a year earlier, safety rules had required that goggles be worn only when removing material from equipment, because that was when the greatest possibility of injury existed. Their use at other times was up to the discretion of each operator.

At two stages in the process, though, the material was light and fluffy, and occasional backdrafts through the chutes caused it to fly. After this had resulted in three cases of eye irritations, the rules were changed, and operators were required to wear goggles whenever they were near exposed material.

Dave Watts, supervisor of operations for two years, had worked on all stages of the operation his first year out of engineering school. He had gotten along well with the men, was grateful to them for teaching him the "tricks of the trade," and might have been tempted to be lenient with them. Watts's boss, however, was very safety minded and insisted that safety rules be followed to the letter.

Sam Sawyer, who had worked on the operation for 20 years, was an outstanding operator and was looked up to by his fellow workers. His safety record was one of the best in the plant, as he had had only one minor injury in all his years of service.

When the new safety rule went into effect, Dave was bothered because everyone went along with it except Sam, who contended that it was unnecessary to wear goggles except when unloading equipment. This caused problems for Dave, because the others followed Sam's example. After much discussion, however, Sam agreed to go along with the rule.

Dave had a strong feeling that Sam was complying with the rule only while he was around. On half a dozen occasions he thought Sam had put on the goggles just as he came on the floor. Before the rule change, Sam had worn the goggles around his neck when they weren't needed, but he had recently started wearing them pushed up on his forehead.

Dave's doubts were confirmed today when he came on Sam unexpectedly and saw him bob his head to shift the goggles from his forehead to his eyes.

Questions

1. What does the case show about the need for management emphasis on safety?

2. How can you explain the workers' lack of interest in their own safety?

3. What would you do if you were the supervisor?

4. How would you explain it to an OSHA inspector?

5. What does this case illustrate about the role of informal leaders?

Source: Prepared by Bruce Gunn, Florida State University. Used with permission.

10

MAINTAINING RELATIONSHIPS WITH YOUR EMPLOYEES AND THEIR REPRESENTATIVES

The only difference between chaos and a smoothly functioning operation is leadership.

David P. Campbell

You can't manage people—you can only work with them. For your business to succeed, you must work closely with them and take exceedingly good care of them.

Paul Hawken, *Growing a Business*

The good boss selects people with demonstrated capabilities, tells them what results are expected, largely leaves them alone to decide the means by which they can be obtained, and then monitors the results.

Sanford Jacobs, entrepreneur

LEARNING OBJECTIVES

After studying the material in this chapter, you will be able to:

1. Discuss basic organizational concepts and show how small firms can use them.

2. Explain how managerial assumptions affect human relationships with workers.

3. Explain why exercising effective leadership is so important in small business.

4. List some barriers to effective communication and show some ways to improve communication.

5. Explain how to improve employee motivation.

6. Tell why employee appraisals are used, and how they are done.

7. Define counseling and discuss areas in which it may be needed in small firms.

8. Outline procedures for handling employee complaints and imposing discipline.

9. Discuss some complexities of dealing with unions.

10. Understand the difficulty in terminating employees.

Cathy Anderson-Giles: Master Motivator

Good leadership, whether in the military, in sports, or in business, is not a one-way street in terms of communication and motivation. Effective leaders know not only how and when to speak, but how and when to listen.

Judging from the success of her small business, Equity Technologies Inc., and the feedback from her employees, Cathy Anderson-Giles, the company's CEO, is a tremendous leader and motivator who employs a progressive management style. Equity Technologies specializes in removing, repairing, and cleaning telecommunications equipment.

An important aspect of Anderson-Giles's leadership is having a very informal, friendly working atmosphere. Employees wear jeans and enjoy an open-door policy. One employee noted that it was Anderson-Giles's extra touches—such as using fine china at the company Christmas party, putting fresh flowers in the office, and letting employees choose the colors in their offices—that made work and the working atmosphere pleasant. "I call it employee-friendly. We're sort of a family here," remarked Reginald Croshon, repair technician coordinator. "We try not to look at it as 'I'm the boss, you're the employee.'"

Anderson-Giles's background in Vicksburg and Jackson, Mississippi, is just as nontraditional as her management style. Because her son had a disability, she originally decided to pursue a career in physical education for the handicapped. So she went back to school at Jackson State University (www.jsums.edu).

After a brief teaching stint, however, she realized this was not the profession for her. So she worked in the insurance industry while she attended law school at night. After receiving her law degree, she set up in private practice in her hometown of Jackson.

In 1984, her husband, who worked for AT&T (www.att.com), was transferred to Mobile, Alabama. It was then that she and her husband started their own company, Business Communication Distributors, which he continues to run. Six years later, they and two other investors started Equity Technologies Inc. with Anderson-Giles at the helm. "It was the logical step for me," she said. "I enjoy the process of creating businesses."

Anderson-Giles's employees seem to enjoy working for her. Perhaps her most important key to success is that she listens to and actively seeks the advice of her employees. Chip McNeill, manager of information services, states: "We have a lot of input in the day-to-day operation of the company." This style of leadership not only motivates employees but also makes them feel valued.

Anderson-Giles seeks advice from her employees because she believes in them, and they believe in—and perform for—her. Another motivating factor is that the employees know performance means advancement in the company. "We know the growth's here and there are opportunities for advancement," says Darrell Coxwell, assistant manager in the auditing department.

LaKeshia Joiner was one of the original employees hired by Anderson-Giles. Although LaKeshia had no work experience and only a high school diploma, Anderson-Giles saw considerable potential in her and continues to encourage her. Now LaKeshia has completed a degree at Southeast College of Technology (www.sect.com), is the supervisor of the company's auditing division, and is working on a business degree. Enthusiastically, LaKeshia declares, "I haven't reached my peak yet."

Neither has Equity Technologies Inc., which had to move four times in five years in order to expand. The company grew from 10 to 48 employees in the 1990s. Because of the company's excellent growth at that time, Equity Technologies won the Small Business Technology Award given by the Business Council of Alabama (www.bcatoday.org).

Anderson-Giles says that the key to her leadership and motivational skills is that she realizes "there's so much undiscovered talent in everybody." Apparently, she is adept at finding it, as evidenced by the fact that in 1999 she was appointed to a three-year term on the board of directors of the Business Council of Alabama.

Source: Prepared by William Jay Megginson from various sources, especially Sara Lamb, "Workplace Is People-Friendly," *Mobile* (Alabama) *Register,* November 12, 1995, pp. 1-F, 2-F;-"Transitions," *Mobile* (Alabama) *Register,* January 17, 1999, p. 2 F.

In previous chapters you have seen how to recruit, select, train, and compensate employees, as well as maintain their health and safety. You will now find out how to organize them, communicate with and motivate them, counsel them, discipline them, and deal with the labor unions that serve as their representatives.

■ SETTING UP THE ORGANIZATIONAL STRUCTURE

Organizing is determining those activities that are necessary to achieve a firm's objectives, and assigning them to responsible persons.

The organizational structure of a business governs relationships between the owner, managers, and employees. **Organizing** involves determining the activities needed to achieve the firm's objectives, dividing these activities into small groups, and assigning each group to a manager with the necessary authority and expertise to see that they are done. A major problem for many small business owners is that they don't organize their activities properly. The following discussion should help you understand how best to organize a business.

Some Basic Organizational Concepts

There are at least three basic organizational concepts that apply to growing small businesses: (1) delegation, (2) span of management, and (3) specialization. It must be added that *while these concepts should be applied to businesses as they grow larger, they must often be adjusted when applied to mom-and-pop businesses.*

Delegation is assigning responsibility to subordinates for certain activities, and giving them the authority to perform those activities.

Delegation   **Delegation** means assigning responsibility to subordinates for doing certain activities, giving them the authority to carry out the duties, and letting them take care of the details of how the job is done. Many owners and managers of small firms find it difficult to delegate authority. Yet you need to learn to delegate if you answer yes to most of the questions in Figure 10–1. When you delegate work to subordinates, try to delegate sufficient authority to them to carry out their responsibilities. Otherwise, they lack the means of performing their duties.

Except in very small mom-and-pop shops, you should give employees a *job description,* which is a written statement of duties, responsibilities, authority, and relationships (see

---

Figure 10–1
How Well Do You Delegate?

- Do you do work an employee could do just as well?
- Do you think you are the only one who actually knows how the job should be done?
- Do you leave work each day loaded down with details to take care of at home?
- Do you frequently stay after hours catching up?
- Are you a perfectionist?
- Do you tell your employees how to solve problems?
- Do you seem never to be able to complete the work assigned to you?

Source: Adapted from Claude S. George, *Supervision in Action: The Art of Managing Others,* 4th ed., © 1985, p. 283, reprinted by permission of Prentice Hall, Inc., Englewood Cliffs, New Jersey; and "Why Managers Fail to Delegate," in Donald C. Mosley, Paul H. Pietri, and Leon C. Megginson, *Management: Leadership in Action,* 5th ed. (New York: HarperCollins College Publishers, 1996), pp. 262–63.

Chapter 9 for details). When you delegate authority to employees to do certain duties, you must be willing to let them do it; yet you can't relinquish your responsibility for seeing that those duties are performed.

Span of Management   A manager's **span of control,** often called the **span of management,** which is the number of employees reporting directly to him or her, should be limited. In general, managers with fewer activities to control can successfully manage more people, and vice versa. For example, supervisors may have 10 or more employees reporting to them because of the similarity and repetitive nature of their work. On the other hand, middle managers may have fewer subordinates, doing very dissimilar jobs. Don't try to supervise too many people personally, or the operation of the business could be severely hampered.

> **Span of control (management)** is the number of employees that report directly to a manager.

Specialization   You should try to use **specialization,** whereby employees do the work they are best suited for. This concept is hard to apply in very small businesses, where rigid specialization can result in some employees being idle while others are overworked. You must exercise judgment in assigning job responsibilities according to employees' talents and desires, without neglecting an equitable distribution of work.

> **Specialization** is using employees to do the work that they are best suited for.

Some Organizational Problems in Small Firms

A common problem in small firms is the owner's reluctance to delegate authority. This practice prevents the owner from devoting time to more pressing needs while also preventing others from developing into well-rounded workers.

> For example, the owner of a small wholesale company was chairman of the board, president, and treasurer. He handled all financial affairs; supervised accounting operations, wages, salaries, and sales commissions; and made recommendations to the board on the payment of dividends. Yet the company also had a vice president, sales manager, and operations manager.

This example describes an owner who does not delegate authority. Another kind of problem is an owner who is afraid to make decisions, so the business becomes paralyzed. Then there's the owner who reverses decisions made by others. Perhaps he has not developed policies to cover the major repetitive situations and business functions.

The following are other indications of organizational trouble:

- The owner holds too many meetings attended by too many people, resulting in wasted hours and excessive costs.
- Administrative expenses grow more rapidly than sales.
- The owner spends too much time following proper procedures or resolving conflicts rather than "getting production out."
- The attention of key people is not directed toward key activities of the firm and their performance.

Failure to delegate places an immense burden on you, making it difficult for you ever to be absent from the business. Also, it virtually guarantees the failure of the business if you become incapacitated for a long time, because no one else has been trained to perform management tasks.

Some Ways of Organizing a Small Business

You can organize your business in many ways, but the most frequent ways are (1) by types of authority granted and (2) by activities to be performed. As we discussed earlier in the book, there is now a movement in small businesses toward using teamwork to bolster effectiveness, as larger companies have been doing for some time.

Organizing by Types of Authority   The organizational forms based on types of authority are (1) the line organization and (2) the line-and-staff organization. Within these types of organization is found another type—the informal organization.

As was shown in Figure 2–9, a business may start with the owner doing all the work and then hiring a few people who do a variety of duties in producing, financing, and selling the firm's product. The owner is directly responsible for seeing that the employees do these things. This is called a **line organization,** as shown in Figure 10–2.

As the firm grows and becomes more complex, specialized workers—called staff—are hired to advise and perform services for those doing the operations, financing, and selling. Some examples are accountants (or controllers), personnel officers, and legal staff. This type of organization is called a **line-and-staff organization** (see Figure 10–3).

In a **line organization,** the owner has a direct line of command over employees.

A **line-and-staff organization** is one that has specialists to advise and perform services for other employees.

Figure 10–2
A Simplified Line Organization

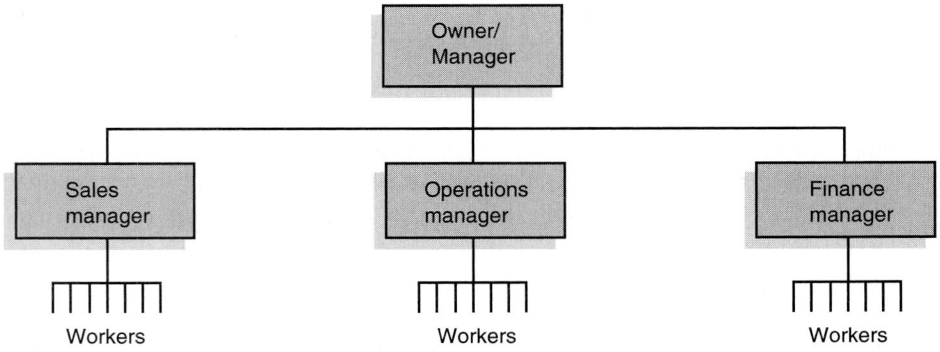

If the business is small and unincorporated, a tight, formal organization structure could stifle creativity and reduce initiative. Instead, you might have a structure similar to that shown in Figure 10–4.

An **informal organization** always exists within the formal structure of a business. It involves the many interpersonal relationships that arise on and off the job. Two examples are the *informal-leader* and *grapevine-communication* systems. *You can't fight it, so if you're wise, you'll determine who the informal leaders are and get their support for your activities.*

The **informal organization** is the set of interpersonal relationships that come about as a result of friendships that develop on and off the job.

What informal organizations do you belong to? A morning coffee group? A study group? A social get-together once a week?

Organizing by Activities to Be Performed   When you set up your formal organization structure, you can group the activities into small, workable groups according to:

1. *Function performed,* such as production, sales, or finance, as shown in Figure 10–2.
2. *Product sold,* such as menswear, ladies' wear, and so forth.
3. *Process used,* such as X-rays, operating room, and food service in a hospital.
4. *Area served,* such as urban, suburban, or rural.
5. *Types of customers served,* such as industrial, commercial, institutional, or governmental.
6. *Project being managed,* such as constructing a store or an apartment complex.

Preparing an Organization Chart

There is no one structure that is best for all businesses, either large or small. However, the following discussion may help you organize your business to achieve its objectives.

Figure 10–3
A Simplified Line-and-Staff Organization

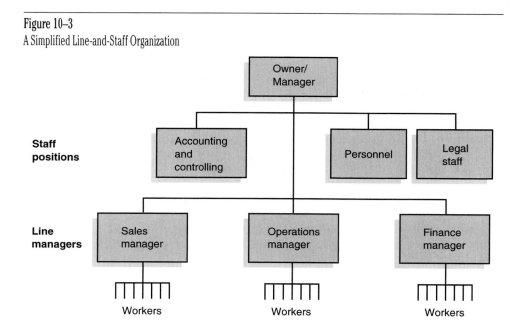

Figure 10–4
Organization of a Small, Unincorporated Mom-and-Pop Business

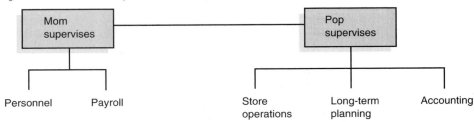

Begin by setting up a series of authority and responsibility relationships expressed in a formal **organization chart,** as shown in Figures 10–2 and 10–3. Even in a small business, a chart can be useful in establishing present relationships, planning future developments, and projecting personnel requirements (Figure 10–4).

An **organization chart** shows the authority and responsibility relationships that exist in a business.

Using Team Management to Improve Performance

The use of team management has become an important stepping-stone in the growth of many small businesses. Of all the methods used, quality improvement and teamwork may be the ones best suited to small firms. The goal of teamwork is to improve performance by involving employees in meeting customers' needs. When each member of each team fully understands the business's products, services, and culture,[1] team members then have a better grasp of the contribution their work makes to fulfilling the company's mission. And by doing more of the work formerly done by managers, they broaden their scope in the business by acquiring new skills.

> A unique type of team is St. Luke's, a new, upbeat advertising agency located in a renovated toffee factory in London's Bloomsbury district. None of the agency's "100 or so" workers have their own offices—or even their own desks. Instead, in the morning they pick up portable phones when they come to work, seat themselves wherever they please, and start calling clients.
>
> Everything about the agency is designed to foster creativity. There is "almost no corporate hierarchy and an entity [where] every employee receives an equal share of the profits," but not equal salaries. Among the unique features of the organization is the "Chillout Room," where the staff can go to escape the intense office atmosphere—perhaps by getting a massage.[2]

Problem-solving teams meet on a regular basis to discuss ways to improve quality, efficiency, and the work environment.

While teamwork may not be feasible for small mom-and-pop operations, several types of teams are found in larger, entrepreneurial-type small businesses.[3] The more important types of teams are:

Self-managing work teams take over managerial duties and produce an entire product.

- **Problem-solving teams,** which meet for an hour or two a week to discuss ways to improve quality, efficiency, and the work environment.
- **Self-managing work teams,** which take over some managerial duties, such as work and vacation scheduling, hiring new members, and ordering materials.

Cross-functional teams cut across different parts of the organization to monitor, standardize, and improve work processes.

- **Cross-functional teams,** which are formed to monitor, standardize, and improve work processes that cut across different parts of the organization, to develop products, or to otherwise address issues calling for broad representation and expertise.

■ GOOD HUMAN RELATIONS IS NEEDED IN SMALL FIRMS

The opening quotations and Profile illustrate the importance of good human relations in small firms.

Defining the term *human relations* is difficult, for it means different things to different people. Dr. Alfred Haake, lecturer for General Motors, would begin his lectures on human relations by saying, "Some people say that good human relations is treating people as if it were your last day on earth. Ah, no!" he would continue. "Good human relations is treating people as if it were *their* last day on earth." This thought is also expressed in the Golden Rule, which states: "So in everything, do to others what you would have them do to you."[4]

Human relations involves the cooperative and friendly interaction of people in an organization, especially in the areas of leadership, communication, and motivation. Regardless of the definition used, your success as a small business owner is based on practicing good human relations, according to the late Douglas McGregor,[5] and as the following example illustrates.

> Keith Dunn started his own restaurant because of the poor treatment he'd received from his employers. After he tried and failed at using motivational techniques, such as contests and benefits, he started including his employees in decisions affecting the business. After they became a vital part of the business, the annual turnover rate dropped from 250 percent—normal for the industry—to 60 percent.[6]

Finally, good human relations occurs when both the employees and the small business owner develop a form of social contract, which outlines their rights and duties to each other. Employees are happier and more productive when they know why their company exists, and what their roles are.[7] There are five topics to address with employees, namely:

- Reasons for being in business
- Growth goals
- Product goals
- People involvement
- Ethics statement

■ EXERCISING EFFECTIVE LEADERSHIP

Leading, one of the basic management functions, is getting employees to do the things you want them to do, by means of communicating with, motivating, and disciplining them.

While management and leadership are similar, there are some significant differences. Leading is an important part of managing—but not the whole of it. **Leadership** is the ability of one person to influence others to strive to attain goals or objectives. Management, while requiring the use of leadership, also includes the other functions of planning, organizing, staffing, and controlling. Leadership is especially important for small business owners. Without it, they can't get workers to strive to achieve their goals or the business's objectives.

The three most popular theories of leadership are traitist, behavioral, and contingency-situational theories. Most researchers now conclude that there is no specific style of leadership that can be used in all circumstances. Instead, our ever-changing and dynamic environment causes all situations to be different.[8] The best advice for small business owners would be to continue the educational process and learn by example how to adapt leadership styles to the situation at hand.[9]

According to Roderick Wilkinson, a fellow of the prestigious (U.K.) Institute of Personnel Management, a country's ability to survive depends on its ability to make things

Human relations involves the interaction among people in an organization.

Leading is the management function of getting employees to do what you want them to do, by communicating with, motivating, and disciplining them.

Leadership is the ability of one person to influence others to attain objectives.

and to trade them. Wilkinson, the longtime human resource director of Caterpillar Tractor Company, Ltd., says that, while scientists may invent (or discover) new products, it is businesspeople who have "an understanding of how to motivate people, an ability to work together [in order] to earn more, to live better, and to become whole people" that make a nation great.[10]

> This lesson was learned the hard way by Bill and Don Budinger, owners of Rodel, Inc., a supplier to the electronics industry. After experiencing internal battles, mistrust, and deteriorating customer relations, they "stumbled into a solution—the value of leadership training." They instituted a program with three basic beliefs: speak straight, listen generously, and be there for each other. This doctrine was taught to employees in off-site classes, daily departmental meetings, and monthly meetings with extensive dialog. Over time, a new sense of "ownership" developed within the company and is "starting to show in the bottom line."[11]

It is tempting to say that one leadership style is better than another for small business owners. Yet experience has shown that no one style is ideal at all times. Instead, the best approach depends on the situation and the characteristics of the people involved. A Chinese proverb expresses this thought by saying, "Of the best leader, when he is gone, the people will say: We did it ourselves."

Today, effective small business owners are recognizing the role played by diversity in exercising effective leadership. In our competitive global environment, managers must realize that at work, how humans behave and interact with others is governed by their beliefs, thought patterns, and values. While these may be largely subconscious, they are often so ingrained into our brains that they generate almost reflexive behavior. And there is a growing sense among progressive owners and managers that this diversity can be successfully managed.

■ COMMUNICATING WITH EMPLOYEES AND OTHERS

Communication is the transfer of meaning from one person to another.

Communication, the process of transferring *meaning*—that is, ideas and information—from one person to another, is your number one job. Classic studies have shown that verbal communication takes up about 80 percent of a manager's time.[12]

Communication is so important because people need and want to know what is going on so they can do their jobs properly. Owners, employees, customers, vendors, and others need to coordinate their work, so communication must be clear and complete. In addition, speaking pleasantly and persuasively makes people want to do good work, for, as a Japanese proverb says, "One kind word can warm three winter months."

What Happens When You Communicate?

While explaining a process as complex as communication is difficult, Figure 10–5 shows that the process involves: (1) someone (the source) having an idea, thought, or impression that (2) is encoded or translated into words or symbols that (3) are transmitted, or sent as a message, to another person (the receiver), who (4) picks up the symbols and (5) decodes, or retranslates, them back into an idea and (6) sends some form of feedback to the sender. Feedback completes the process, because communication cannot be assumed to have occurred until the receiver demonstrates understanding of the message. *Since communication is an exchange of meaning (rather than words or symbols), many forms of nonverbal communication convey meaning through signals, signs, sounds (other than words), and facial expressions.*

Figure 10–5
The Communication Process

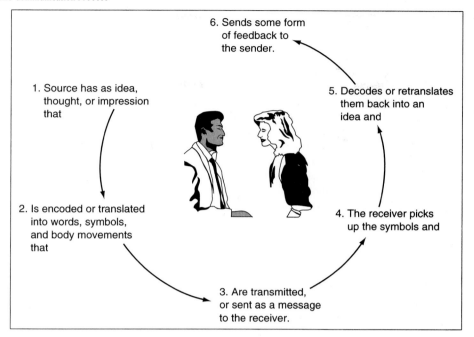

Barriers to Effective Communication

Despite the importance of communication and the amount of time we spend communicating, the transfer of meaning is not always effective. One prototype study showed that up to 70 percent of all business communication fails to achieve the desired results.[13] There are many causes of this ineffectiveness, especially some barriers erected by the business itself or by the people involved.

First, because of the owner's position of authority, employees tend to believe what the owner says, regardless of whether it is true or not, when they might be better off thinking through a problem on their own. The status of the communicator either lends credibility to what is being said or detracts from it; messages of higher-status people automatically tend to carry greater credibility than those of lower-status people. The individuals in authority themselves may get carried away by this tendency and not listen to their people, who may be closer to a problem.

The imprecise use of language also serves as a barrier. Have you noticed how frequently people use the expression "you know" in daily communications, lazily hoping their listener really does know, or adopt buzzwords (especially those from high-tech fields) without caring what they mean? For example, an employee being dismissed is sometimes said to be "outplaced" or "re-placed," often as a result of a "downsizing" (or "rightsizing") effort in the company, whether or not such jargon is applicable in the particular case.

Again, there is the differing meaning of words. *Random House Webster's College Dictionary* has the number of meanings shown for each of four frequently used words: *run,* 101 different meanings; *take,* 91; *break,* 84; and *turn,* 84.[14]

Perhaps the greatest barriers to effective communication are simply inattention and poor listening. Small business owners, as well as managers of bigger companies, are often so preoccupied with running their businesses that they may not pay attention to employee feedback.

How to Improve Communication

You can become a more effective communicator by clarifying your ideas, considering the environment in which the communication occurs, considering emotional overtones as well as the message, following up on communication, and being a good listener. As we have emphasized, communication is a two-way street. Even more important than getting your meaning across are listening to and understanding what the other person says. If you will pay attention to the communication process, then you will be in position to take advantage of the new technologies.

The computer is revolutionizing communication. First there was interpersonal, face-to-face communication. Then came the telephone, followed by cable, cellular, and satellite communications. Now the Internet is threatening to "blow the global telecoms market apart by slashing the cost of international phone calls, videoconferencing, and online document sharing."[15] This new technology provides small business owners with cost savings, access to new markets, and the ability to respond more rapidly to changing customer and supplier demand.

(*Source:* © 1996 by Margaret P. Megginson. Used with permission.)

Radiant House (www.li.net/~dminiero/rad.html), which imports cosmetics and toiletries, used to rack up monthly phone bills of $1,000–$1,200 for calls to Hong Kong and the United Kingdom. It also spent several months exchanging drawings and samples with its Hong Kong agents. Now, using Internet telephony, its personnel can talk to the agents via the computer screen, hold up samples, and describe needed alterations. Radiant House pays only the $20 monthly subscription fee to its Internet service provider for unlimited international calls and videoconferencing.[16]

Teleconferencing, also known as **videoconferencing,** is holding a virtual meeting using telephone, radio, closed-circuit TV, or computer communication connections.

For many small businesses—as well as larger ones—**teleconferencing** (also called **videoconferencing**) has become an effective cost- and time-saving way to communicate. Teleconferencing consists of a group of people in one area using a phone, radio, closed-circuit TV, or even computers to communicate with people in another area—near or far. This technique not only saves on travel costs and time but can also increase productivity. It permits more concerned people in the business to participate in high-tech meetings, thus reducing the time supervisors spend reporting back to their people. According to New York management consultant Karen Berg, company meetings tend to be more structured when using teleconferencing, resulting in 20 to 30 percent shorter meetings.[17] That is, the technology may have the effect of focusing people and making them better communicators, speakers and listeners. However, good communication skills must still be practiced.

■ MOTIVATING EMPLOYEES

Before reading the following material, complete the exercise in Figure 10–6. This exercise helps explain why motivation is so complex and why it is so difficult to motivate some

Figure 10–6
What Do You Want from a Job?

Rank the employment factors shown below in their order of importance to you at three points in your career. In the first column, assume that you are about to graduate and are looking for your first full-time job. In the second column, assume that you have been gainfully employed for 5 to 10 years and that you are presently employed by a reputable firm at the prevailing salary for the type of job and industry you are in. In the third column, try to assume that 25 to 30 years from now you have "found your niche in life" and have been working for a reputable employer for several years. (Rank your first choice as 1, second as 2, and so forth through 9.)

Ranking of selected employment factors

Employment factor	As you seek your first full-time job	Your ranking 5–10 years later	Your ranking 25–30 years later
Fair adjustment of grievances			
Good job instruction and training			
Effective job supervision by your supervisor			
Promotion possibilities			
Recognition (praise, rewards, and so on)			
Job safety			
Job security (no threat of being dismissed or laid off)			
Good salary			
Good working conditions (nice office surroundings, good hours, and so on)			

employees. You must use different incentives to motivate different people at different times in their working lives. Yet it is difficult for us to always know what a given employee wants at a given time. Understanding those needs and understanding how to use the appropriate motivation are the secrets of successful small business ownership and management.

What Is Motivation?

You can use **motivation** to bring out the best in your employees by giving them reasons to perform better, but it's not easy. *You are always motivating employees—either positively (to perform) or negatively (to withhold performance)—even when you're not conscious of doing so.* When you give employees a reason to perform better, you create positive motivation; on the other hand, if you say or do something that annoys, frustrates, or antagonizes employees, they'll react negatively and either withhold production or actually sabotage operations.

Motivation is the inner state that activates a person, including drives, desires, and/or motives.

> For example, a customer went into an ice cream shop in a college town and ordered a banana split. When it came, something was obviously wrong. There were five scoops of ice cream, double portions of fruit and nuts, and a huge serving of whipped cream, with several cherries on top. The customer, who was a management professor at a local university, asked the young employee, "What's wrong?" The young man didn't even pretend not to understand. "I'm mad at the boss," he promptly replied. A few months later, the shop went out of business.

The best way for you to succeed in business is to increase employee productivity and efficiency. While there is a limit to improvements in employee productivity, effective motivation can have a positive effect. However, *because many factors affect productivity, motivation alone is not enough.*

In general, employee performance is a product of the employee's ability to do the job and the application of positive motivation; that is,

$$\text{Performance} = \text{Ability} \times \text{Motivation}$$

or

$$P = A \times M$$

Most employees go to work for a company expecting to do a good job, receive a satisfactory income, and gain satisfaction from doing a good job. However, performance and satisfaction are dependent on the *ability* to do the job. If your employees are not performing as you would like them to, they may be unsuited for the job, inadequately trained, or unmotivated. If they are unsuited, move them to a more suitable job, and if untrained, train them. If they are both suited and trained, try harder to motivate them.

Why Motivate Employees?

One reason managerial motivation is so difficult to use is that there are different purposes for motivating people, each of which requires different incentives. Usually managers use motivation to (1) attract potential employees, (2) improve performance, and (3) retain good employees.

Attracting Potential Employees   If you want to encourage potential employees to work for you, you must find and use incentives that appeal to a person needing a job. These incentives usually include a good income, pleasant working conditions, promotional possibilities, and sometimes a signing bonus.

The exercise in Figure 10–6 has been used with junior- and senior-level business students since 1957. With very few exceptions, "good salary" has been the primary consideration in looking for a first job in over 200 surveys reviewed, while "promotion possibilities" and "good working conditions" are a close second and third. How did you rate these factors?

Improving Performance   You can also use motivation to improve performance and efficiency on the part of present employees. You can do this by praising good work, giving employees more responsibility, publicly recognizing a job well done, and awarding merit salary increases.

> Notice in the Profile at the beginning of the chapter that Cathy Anderson-Giles treats her people well to bring out the best in them. She gives them personal attention, helps them with their problems, and gives them challenging work to do.

Retaining Good Employees   Motivation can also be used to retain your present employees. This is accomplished primarily through the use of employee benefits, most of which are designed to reward employees who stay with the company. However, many other incentives can help explain today's work force retention, many of them individual and personal.

> For example, Cal Ripken, the shortstop for the Baltimore Orioles baseball team (www.theorioles.com), had not missed playing in a scheduled game from 1982 until September 6, 1995—when he broke Lou Gehrig's record of 2,030 consecutive games played.
>
> There is also Elena Griffing, at Bates Medical Center (www.altabates.com), who took her last sick day in 1952. She explained her feat by saying: "Watching the healing process makes it worth going to work."
>
> Then there is Francis Longobardi, a technical analyst at Genix Group, who is motivated by the "hustle and bustle" at work. She hasn't missed a day since she was employed in 1953.[18]

How to Motivate Employees

The theory of motivation is relatively simple (as shown in Figure 10–7).* An employee has a need or needs, and you apply some kind of incentive (or stimulus) that promises to satisfy that need. Your main problem in motivating employees is to know them well enough to know what they need and what incentives will stimulate them to perform.

Some Practical Ways to Improve Motivation

While we cannot give you a "cookbook" answer as to how to motivate your people, we do know that the old ways of motivating people through "command and control" are no longer viable options.[19] Instead, we must turn to the "real world" to see how the more progressive managers motivate their employees.

Some of the progressive methods that have shown good results in motivating employees, especially in small businesses, are: (1) quality circles, (2) zero-defects programs, (3) job enrichment, (4) variable work schedules, and (5) job splitting and sharing.

Figure 10–7
The Motivational Process

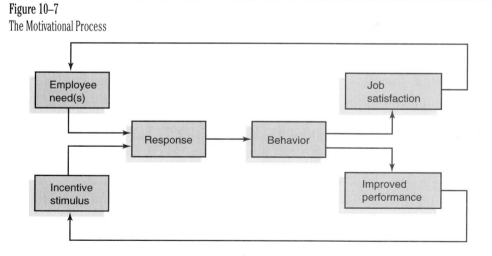

---

*For a review of the more popular theories of motivation, see any basic management text, such as Richard M. Steers, Lyman W. Porter, and Gregory A. Bigley, *Motivation and Leadership at Work,* 6th ed. (New York: The McGraw-Hill Companies, 1996).

Quality circles (QCs) are small employee groups that meet periodically to improve quality and output.

A **zero-defects** approach uses pride in workmanship to get workers to do their work "right the first time."

Job enrichment is granting workers greater responsibility and authority in their jobs.

A **variable work schedule** (also called a **flexible work arrangement**) permits employees to work at times other than the standard five 8-hour days.

Flextime is an arrangement under which employees may schedule their own hours, around a core time.

Job splitting occurs when employees divide a single job into two or more different parts, each one doing one of the parts.

Job sharing occurs when a single full-time job is retained, but its performance is shared by two or more employees working at different times.

Quality circles (QCs) are small, organized work groups that meet periodically to find ways to improve quality and output. They motivate by getting employees involved and taking advantage of their creativity and innovativeness.

The **zero-defects** approach is based on getting workers to do their work "right the first time," thus generating pride in workmanship. It assumes that employees want to do a good job—and will do so if permitted to.

Job enrichment emphasizes giving employees greater responsibility and authority over their jobs as the best way to motivate them. Employees are encouraged to learn new and related skills or even to trade jobs with each other as ways of making jobs more interesting and therefore more productive.

Variable work schedules (also called **flexible work arrangements**) permit employees to work at times other than the standard workweek of five eight-hour days.[20] Such schedules are being extensively used by small firms to motivate employees. **Flextime** allows employees to schedule their own hours as long as they are present during certain required hours, called *core time*. This gives employees greater control over their time and activities.

Job splitting is dividing a single full-time job into distinct parts and letting two (or more) employees do the different parts. In **job sharing,** a single full-time job is shared by two (or more) employees, with one worker performing all aspects of the job at one time and the other worker doing it at another time, as the following example shows.

Cheryl Houser, burned out after selling ads for the *Seattle Weekly* (www.seattleweekly .com) for four years, wanted time to travel, do volunteer work, and eventually have a baby. Carol Cummins, a co-worker expecting a baby, also wanted to work part time. Being good salespeople, they talked their boss, Jane Levine, vice president of advertising and marketing, into letting them share one full-time job. Houser worked on Mondays and Thursdays, Cummins worked on Wednesdays and Fridays, and both came in on Tuesdays. In exchange for lighter work duties, since the two women each worked only three days a week, the paper gets two seasoned workers for the price of one.[21]

Small business owners are faced with a dilemma when considering such motivational programs. They may believe that using one or more of the new methods will improve employee performance and hence increase profits. But they may not have the knowledge, time, money, or personnel to implement the method or methods.

Does Money Motivate?

Some studies have concluded that money doesn't motivate and that psychological rewards may be more significant than monetary rewards.[22] But, as shown, our research indicates that most students say "good salary" is the first thing they'll be looking for in their first job. Also, several studies indicate that money does motivate. For example, one study revealed that 60 percent of women say money motivates them to achieve a better life.[23] In summary, we believe that money motivates, but so do many other factors, as indicated in the Profile.

Motivation Is More than Mere Technique

Successful motivation of employees is based more on a managerial philosophy than on using a given technique. Thus, you should try to create an environment in your firm in which employees can apply themselves willingly and wholeheartedly to the task of increasing productivity and quality.

This thought was expressed soon after World War II by Clarence Francis, chairman of General Foods, when he said, "You can buy a man's time; you can buy a man's physical presence at a given place; you can even buy a measured number of skilled muscular motions per hour or day; but you cannot buy enthusiasm; you cannot buy initiative; you cannot buy loyalty; you cannot buy devotion of hearts, minds, and souls. You have to earn these things."[24]

■ APPRAISING EMPLOYEES' PERFORMANCE

If your employees' actual output cannot be measured, you need an effective system of **performance appraisal** (also called *employee evaluation* or *merit rating*) to help you answer the question "How well are my people performing?" Under such a system, each employee's performance and progress are evaluated, and rewards are given for above-average performance.

> **Performance appraisal** is the process of evaluating workers to see how well they're performing.

Often, this technique is used in determining merit salary increases, special merit raises, training decisions, layoffs, or promotions or transfers. Appraisals can also be used for disciplinary actions such as reprimands, suspensions, demotions, or discharges. Finally, the results of formal appraisals can be used to support or refute disciplinary documentation in proceedings before such bodies as the EEOC (www.eeoc.gov) and in Unemployment Compensation Appeals hearings.

Employee appraisals are usually based on such factors as quantity and quality of work performed, cooperativeness, initiative, dependability (including attendance), job knowledge, safety, and personal habits. While appraisals are usually done by the employee's direct supervisor, they may also be done by the affected employee, his or her peers, or subordinates, or by the use of electronic devices.

Employee evaluations should be related to promotions and salary increases in addition to identifying marginal workers and designing training activities for them. They can also be used to motivate employees, if the evaluations are adequately translated into rewards.

"In the interests of a fair and equitable gratuity, your service is being evaluated."

(*Source:* Cartoon by Fred Maes. Copyright 1996 by Fred Maes.)

Performance appraisals are based on the assumption that employees have (1) personal abilities and qualities that lead to (2) job behaviors that (3) result in work performance that (4) can be identified and measured. Therefore, as shown in Figure 10–8, you need to (1) determine which personal qualities an employee has that result in (2) his or her behaving in a certain way on the job that (3) results in a certain level or quality of work being performed. You must evaluate, measure, or rate work performance in order to take some type of human resource management action involving that worker.

Although employee appraisals themselves are important, it is the feedback from them that really leads to improved performance. An early research study found that those who took some form of constructive action as a result of performance appraisals "did so because of the way their superiors had conducted the appraisal feedback interview and discussion."[25] Yet a recent study of 9,144 workers by benefits consultant Watson Wyatt Worldwide (www.watsonwyatt.com) found that only 38 percent of them get "regular performance feedback."[26]

Figure 10–8
How Performance Appraisals Operate

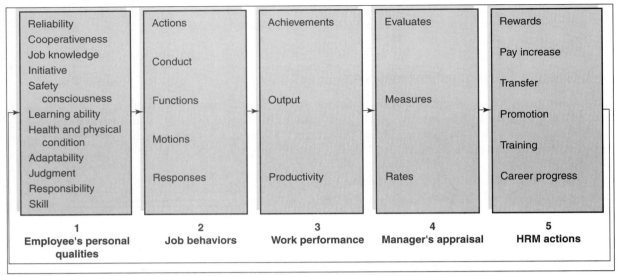

Reliability
Cooperativeness
Job knowledge
Initiative
Safety
    consciousness
Learning ability
Health and physical
    condition
Adaptability
Judgment
Responsibility
Skill
	Actions
	
	Conduct
	
	Functions
	
	Motions
	
	Responses
		Achievements
		
		Output
		
		Productivity
			Evaluates
			
			Measures
			
			Rates
				Rewards
				
				Pay increase
				
				Transfer
				
				Promotion
				
				Training
				
				Career progress

1 **Employee's personal** **qualities**	**2** **Job behaviors**	**3** **Work performance**	**4** **Manager's appraisal**	**5** **HRM actions**

■ COUNSELING TROUBLED EMPLOYEES

Counseling helps to
provide people with an
understanding of their
relationships with their
supervisors, fellow
workers, and customers.

Counseling is designed to help employees do a better job by helping them understand their relationships with supervisors, fellow workers, and customers. While most small firms don't have formal counseling programs, they counsel employees on a day-to-day basis. The points for discussion with a troubled employee in Figure 10–9 may help you do informal counseling. If you don't feel qualified to perform this counseling activity, specialized employees may be used. Or free one-on-one counseling may be obtained from SCORE executives, who have had hands-on experience.[27]

While counseling may benefit all areas of employee relations, most counseling needs fall into the categories of (1) job-related activities, (2) personal problems, and (3) employee complaints.

Job-Related Areas Needing Counseling

The areas that may most need counseling are (1) health and safety, (2) retirement or termination, (3) stress, and finally, (4) discipline, which will be treated separately in the next section.

Health and Safety   As shown in Chapter 9, the whole complex area of health and safety requires considerable counseling and guidance. Because safety is largely a matter of attitude, your role is to counsel employees on the need for safe operations and to actively support all safety efforts.

Retirement or Termination   Employees need considerable preparation for retirement, especially with regard to the benefits coming to them. But counseling is even more urgently needed when an employee must be terminated—with or without cause. Now that U.S. businesses are more concerned with cost saving, primarily because of foreign competition, terminations are more frequent.

When employees just can't produce or when the business can't afford to keep them, termination, often called *outplacement,* is sometimes the only option. But, as will be shown

Figure 10–9
How to Approach a Troubled Employee

1. Establish the standards of job performance you expect.
2. Be specific about behavioral criteria, such as absenteeism and poor job performance.
3. Restrict criticism to job performance.
4. Be firm and consistent.
5. Be prepared to deal with resistance, defensiveness, or even hostility.
6. Point out the availability of internal or external counseling services.
7. Explain that only the employee can decide whether or not to seek assistance.
8. Discuss drinking only if it occurs on the job or the employee is obviously intoxicated.
9. Emphasize the confidentiality of the program.
10. Get a commitment from the employee to meet specific work criteria and monitor this with a plan for improvement based on work performance.

later, you might want to help the worker find other employment. Even with such help, though, termination is still traumatic for the worker, and counseling is needed.

Stress   Stress is becoming a nasty buzzword in late 20th century workplaces. Nearly everyone feels the presence of stress, and few can fully escape it. One study found that 20 percent of all visits to doctors are related to stress.[28] Stress can arise suddenly or gradually and can last for a short time or can persist for years. Whatever its nature, job-related stress often begins when individuals are placed in a work environment that is incompatible with their professional work style and/or temperament. And stress becomes aggravated when individuals find that they can exercise little control over their work environment. Stress is now getting new attention as "a costly workplace hazard."[29]

Contrary to popular belief, a fast-paced, chronically pressured work environment alone is not the primary cause of stress; instead, stress begins when individuals and environments are mismatched. Some people thrive on a fast-paced, even frenzied work atmosphere, while others prefer a slow-paced environment.

Stress can be a killer for a small business. One study found that 75 percent of U.S. workers polled called their jobs "stressful."[30] When stress becomes great enough, it can result in **job burnout,** which is physical or mental depletion significantly below one's capable level of performance. Stress of such intensity is a major cause of absenteeism and work site antagonisms.*

"Well, back to the old stress-buster seminars."

(*Source:* Cartoon by Fred Maes. Copyright 1996 by Fred Maes.)

Personal Problems Needing Counseling

It has been estimated that about a fifth of employees suffer personal problems, which reduce productivity by as much as 25 percent and result in huge dollar losses.[31] Two-thirds of those

Job burnout is a physical or mental depletion significantly below a person's capable level of performance.

*See Victor M. Parachin, "Tension Tamers," *The Rotarian,* July 1997, pp. 18–19, for some tips on how to control stress.

problems are drug and alcohol related, while the others tend to be emotional problems. Some problems that can result from drug abuse are absenteeism, accidents, increases in medical expenses, insubordination, thefts, and product or service quality problems. Employers are coping with these problems through counseling, referral to trained professionals, and employee-assistance programs (EAPs).

Since 1989, small businesses with federal contracts and grants have been required to have a substance abuse policy that conforms to the Department of Defense's (www.defenselink.mil) "Drug-Free Workforce Rules." These rules impose sweeping new obligations on contractors and grantees.* While the cost of such a drug-free environment is unknown, many small firms may be unable to bear the cost.

Handling Employee Complaints

Because complaints will inevitably occur, you should encourage employees to inform you when they think something is wrong and needs to be corrected. An effective procedure to do this should provide (1) assurance to employees that expressing their complaints will not jeopardize their employment, (2) a simple procedure for presenting their complaints, and (3) a minimum of red tape and time in processing complaints and determining solutions.

Unresolved complaints can lead to more problems, so you should listen patiently and deal with them promptly even if they seem to be without foundation. You should analyze the complaint carefully, gather pertinent facts, make a decision, inform the employee of it, and follow up to determine whether the cause of the problem has been corrected. Detailed, written records of all complaints (and disciplinary actions), as well as how they were resolved, should be maintained in employees' files as a defense against legal charges that may be brought against you.

> One reason to try to maintain good relations with employees is the emergence of Web sites offering employees "a chance to vent about their unsatisfactory work life." For example, one site, www.disgruntled.com, posts anecdotes sent in by employees about their bosses' antics and features a satirical advice column.[32]

If good human relations practices and complaint procedures don't work, then the manager must resort to counseling. If counseling is unsuccessful, then discipline must be used in order to get the job done, as the following example illustrates.

> When Alan Robbins built Plastic Lumber Co. (www.plasticlumber.com) to convert old milk and soda bottles into fake lumber, he tried to be both "boss" and "pal" to his workers. But the Akron, Ohio, entrepreneur almost immediately ran into problems with his people. He tried counseling, but that didn't succeed either. Then he developed a "thick employment manual built around a point system." Even that didn't work. Finally he had to resort to strict discipline. In one recent month, he had to fire four employees, including two who tested positive for cocaine.[33]

■ IMPOSING DISCIPLINE

Discipline involves fairly enforcing a system of rules and regulations to obtain order.

Employees like to work in an environment where there is **discipline**—in the sense of having a system of rules and procedures and having them enforced fairly. You can achieve such an orderly, disciplined environment by either (1) motivating employees to exercise self-discipline or (2) imposing discipline on them.

---

*Contact your nearest SBA office for more information on these laws.

Encouraging Self-Discipline

To be effective, your employees should have confidence in their ability to perform their jobs, see good performance as compatible with their own interests, and know you will provide support if they run into difficulties. Therefore, you should encourage self-discipline among employees rather than rely on direct control. In this respect, the personal example of the owner is important in influencing employee discipline, as the following example illustrates.

> The owner of a small firm selling and installing metal buildings had a problem with employees taking long lunch breaks. When he asked his supervisors to correct this practice, one of them had the courage to say, "That would be easier to do if you didn't take two-hour lunches yourself."

Using Positive Discipline

We've heard managers of small firms say that traditional discipline doesn't work for them. Instead, some are using **positive discipline** to improve morale and lower turnover. Under this approach, employees who commit some breach of conduct receive an oral "reminder," not a reprimand. Then there is a written reminder, followed by a paid day off to decide whether they really want to keep their job. If the answer is yes, the employee agrees in writing to be on his or her best behavior for a given period. The employee who doesn't perform satisfactorily after that is fired. Since the cases are fully documented, employees usually have little recourse.

Positive discipline deals with an employee's breach of conduct by their receiving an oral "reminder" (not a reprimand), then a written reminder, followed by a paid day off to decide if they really want to keep their job. If the answer is "yes," the employee agrees in writing to be on his/her best behavior for a given period of time.

How to Discipline Employees Legally

Most employees rarely cause problems. Yet if you don't deal effectively with the few who violate rules and regulations, employees' respect for you will decline. Therefore, *an effective disciplinary system that meets union and legal guidelines involves:*

*   Setting definite rules and seeing that employees know them.
*   Acting promptly on violations.
*   Gathering pertinent facts about violations.
*   Allowing employees an opportunity to explain their behavior.
*   Setting up tentative courses of action and evaluating them.
*   Deciding what action to take.
*   Taking disciplinary action, while observing labor contract and EEO procedures.
*   Setting up and maintaining a record of actions taken and following up on the outcome.

This type of discipline system follows the pattern established for **judicial due process.** The procedure should distinguish between major and minor offenses and consider extenuating circumstances, such as the employee's length of service, prior performance record, and the amount of time since the last offense.

The **judicial due process** of discipline involves (1) establishing rules of behavior, (2) setting prescribed penalties for violating each rule, and (3) imposing the penalty(ies) only after determining the extent of guilt.

■ DEALING WITH UNIONS

The percentage of the U.S. work force that is represented by unions has been declining for the last four decades. It dropped from 39 percent in 1954 to 24 percent in 1979 and is now only 14 percent.[34] The percentage of the private-sector work force belonging to unions has dropped even more dramatically—from over 33 percent in 1955 to around 10 percent now. Yet unions are quite powerful economically and politically, as they represent 37 percent of public-sector workers,[35] so they affect small businesses in one way or another.

While union organizers have tended to concentrate their organizing efforts on larger firms, because they are easier to unionize, they're now also trying to organize smaller firms, because that's where potential new members are. Also, small business owners are more active in lobbying Congress and state legislatures, through groups such as the National Federation of Independent Business (NFIB) (www.nfibonline.com), for laws and regulations unions oppose.[36] Therefore, you need to know something about unions and how to deal with them.

Laws Governing Union–Management Relations

The *National Labor Relations Act (NLRA)* (also called the *Wagner Act*), as amended, requires management to bargain with the union if a majority of its employees desire unionization. (See Table 10–1 for the provisions of this and related laws.) Managers are forbidden to discriminate against employees in any way because of union activity. The *National Labor Relations Board (NLRB)* (www.nlrb.gov) serves as the labor court. Its general counsel investigates charges of unfair labor practices, issues complaints, and prosecutes cases. The union or management can appeal a ruling of the board through a U.S. circuit court all the way up to the U.S. Supreme Court.

Right-to-work laws permit states to prohibit unions from requiring workers to join a union.

In some states a *union shop clause* provides that employees must join the recognized union within 30 days after being hired. But under **right-to-work laws** in effect in 21 states, the union shop is not legally permitted. Figure 10–10 shows the states with those laws in effect in 1999.

What Happens When the Union Enters

Unions exist to bargain with the employer on behalf of their members for higher wages, fringe benefits, better working conditions, security, and other terms and conditions of employment. To do this, the union must first organize the company's employees.

The first thing you should do if your employees want to form a union is to recognize that it's because they believe they need the protection the union offers. You should therefore ask yourself such questions as: Why do my employees feel that it is necessary to have a union to represent them? Is it a lack of communication, or have I failed to respond to their needs? Am I treating them arbitrarily or unfairly? Studies of successful nonunionized companies find that management and employees participate in the business process as a team rather than as adversaries.

The second thing you should do is call in a competent consultant or labor lawyer. Small firms are increasingly turning to advisers to deal with unions, as the following example indicates.

> When employees tried to organize Persona Inc., a Watertown, South Dakota, manufacturing firm, its president called in Henry N. Teipel of St. Paul, Minnesota, as a consultant. He helped the personnel manager prepare for meetings with union representatives. The advice, which cost $4,000, "saved a tremendous amount of money . . . by keeping the battle short and the union out," according to the president.[37]

If your company is unionized, you should be prepared for certain changes. Your actions and statements may be reported to union officials, and the union may file unfair labor practice charges with the NLRB. Your best defense is to know your rights under the prevailing laws—and to maintain favorable relationships with employees.

Table 10–1

Some Laws Governing Union–Management Relations

Laws	Coverage	Basic Requirements	Enforcement Agencies
Railway Labor Act of 1926	Nonmanagerial employees of private railroads and airlines	Provides that employees are free to choose their own representatives for collective bargaining, and to settle disputes by mediation, arbitration, and emergency boards.	National Mediation Board; National Railroad Adjustment Board
National Labor Relations Act of 1935, as amended (also called the Wagner Act)	Nonmanagerial employees in nonagricultural private firms not covered by the Railway Labor Act, and postal employees	Employees have the right to form or join labor organizations (or to refuse to), to bargain collectively through their representatives, and to engage in other concerted activities such as strikes, picketing, and boycotts. There are unfair labor practices in which the employer and the union cannot engage.	National Labor Relations Board (NLRB)
Labor–Management Relations Act of 1947, as amended (also called the Taft-Hartley Act)	Same as above	Amended NLRA; permits states to pass laws prohibiting compulsory union membership; sets up methods to deal with strikes affecting national health and safety.	NLRB; Federal Mediation and Conciliation Service
Labor–Management Reporting and Discourse Act of 1959, as amended (also called the Landrum-Griffin Act)	Same as above	Amended NLRA and LMRA; guarantees individual rights of union members in dealing with their union; requires financial disclosures by unions.	U.S. Department of Labor

Source: Various government and private publications.

Negotiating the Agreement

Negotiating an agreement with the union requires much preparation, as well as the actual bargaining, and these require patience and understanding, so again it's advisable to consult your labor lawyer.

Preparing for the Bargaining   Preparation may well be the most important step in negotiating the agreement. Obtaining facts about the issues before sitting down at the bargaining table should improve your position. You should collect information on other contracts in the industry and in the local area. Disciplinary actions, complaints, and other key matters that arose before the union's entry should be studied. Current business literature concerning business in general and the status of union–management relations in the industry can be useful. A carefully researched proposal should be developed well in advance of the first bargaining session.

Figure 10–10
States With and Without Right-to-Work Laws

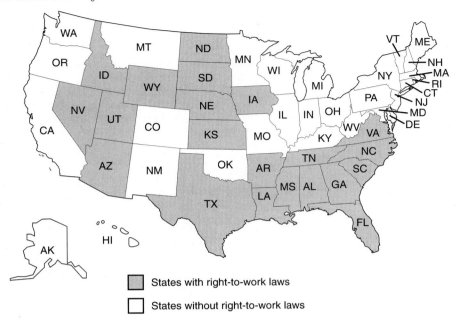

States with right-to-work laws

States without right-to-work laws

Bargaining with the Union   If you've prepared properly, you should be in a positive negotiating position instead of a defensive stance against the union's proposals. The "I don't want to give away any more than I have to" attitude generally leads to poor bargaining. All too frequently, however, fear seems to overcome the owner's willingness to develop in advance a proposal with attractive features that will appeal to employees, while protecting the company's position.

You should recognize the negotiation step as critical: It must be handled properly, preferably with outside assistance. Also remember that anything given away will be difficult to take back.

Be prepared to bargain over at least the following:

- Union recognition.
- Wages.
- Vacations and holidays.
- Working conditions.
- Layoffs and rehiring.
- Hours of work.
- Management prerogatives.
- Seniority.
- Arbitration.
- Renewal of the agreement.

The **management prerogatives clause** defines the areas in which you have the right to act freely as an employer, without interference from the union.

Specific agreements must be reached in each of these areas, and rules established that should be obeyed by the company and the union. The **management prerogatives clause** is very important because it defines the areas in which you have the right to act freely as an employer, without interference from the union.

Living with the Agreement

Because the agreement becomes a legal document when it's signed, you must learn to live with its provisions until time for renegotiation. Your managers should be thoroughly briefed on its contents and implications. The meaning and interpretation of each clause should be reviewed and the wording clearly understood. Supervisors' questions should be answered to better prepare them to deal with labor matters.

Information and advice can be obtained from government sources, such as federal and state mediators, NLRB regional offices, state industrial relations departments, and members of SCORE. Private sources include employer groups, trade associations, labor relations attorneys, and labor relations consultants.

■ TERMINATING EMPLOYEES

Although you still have the right to terminate employees for cause, the concept of "employment at will" is losing acceptance in courts and legislatures. **Employment at will** essentially means employers may fire employees with or without cause at any time they choose. Courts and legislators are now applying the "good faith and fair dealing" concept, whereby termination must be "reasonable" and not "arbitrarily" or "indiscriminately" applied. Violating this concept may lead to punitive damages in addition to actual damages that have been sustained by one of the protected employees. The trend away from employment at will is forcing even more paperwork on employers—causing time and money losses, especially if they're found to have terminated an employee "unreasonably."[38]

Employment at will means that employers may hire or fire workers with or without cause.

WHAT YOU SHOULD HAVE LEARNED

1. Some important organizational concepts that apply to small firms as they grow are delegation, span of management, and specialization. Following these principles helps you delegate authority so as to get the best from employees, tends to eliminate tensions, and eases employee frustrations.

    You can organize your business by (*a*) type of authority used or (*b*) activities performed. The simplest structure is the line organization, where orders are handed down from the top to the bottom. With growth, specialized people are needed to perform tasks not strictly related to operations, selling, or finance, resulting in a line-and-staff structure. Informal organizations, found in all businesses, shouldn't be ignored, because their informal leaders and grapevine communications can affect your bottom line. Team management can also be used to improve performance.

2. Good human relations implies the cooperative and friendly interaction of people in an organization,

resulting from good leadership, communication, and motivation.

3. Leadership is the ability of one person to influence others to attain organizational objectives. There is no one ideal leadership style; the most effective one depends on the situation and the characteristics of the people involved.

4. Managers spend 80 percent of their time communicating, that is, attempting exchanges of significant meaning, but not always succeeding. Barriers to effective communication include, among others, imprecise use of language and poor listening. You can become a better communicator by identifying your audience and the environment of the communication so as to frame your message clearly and by practicing being a good listener.

5. You can increase employee productivity and improve employee satisfaction through effective motivation. Your challenge is to know your employees well enough to know what incentives

will stimulate them to perform. Different incentives must be used according to the purpose of the motivation.

Some currently popular motivational techniques include quality circles, zero-defects programs, job enrichment, variable work schedules, and job splitting and sharing. Motivation is more than mere technique, however, and the best motivators recognize the worth of employees and expect the best from them.

6. Performance appraisals—also called *employee evaluations* or *merit ratings*—are used to answer the question "How well are my people performing?" Essentially, appraisals look at employees' personal qualities that lead to their job behaviors which affect work performance. Evaluating all these, the manager can not only estimate how well the employee is doing but give feedback and prescribe improvement.

7. Counseling may involve listening to an employee gripe about some petty grievance, or it may be needed to correct a serious work problem. Counseling is needed in the job-related areas of health and safety, retirement or termination, and job stress, as well as the personal areas of illness, mental and emotional problems, and substance abuse. Counseling assistance can be obtained from SCORE.

8. While some complaints from employees are inevitable, they can often be handled informally.

To discipline unsatisfactory employees, however, an established procedure is needed. In the ideal work situation, employees discipline themselves, but for those who don't, a procedure should be set up to take into account the severity of the offense and the number of times it has been committed, as well as other factors and extenuating circumstances. Positive discipline, which challenges employees to discipline themselves, is being used in many small firms.

9. Dealing with a union is a challenge most owners and managers of small businesses don't want to face, and most will try to keep the union out. However, when a union does enter, many things change. Many laws govern labor–management relations, so hire a good consultant to help you. Negotiating an agreement with the union requires much preparation. After agreement is reached, supervisors should be briefed on the terms of the contract and instructed on how to deal with labor matters. Managers can get help in dealing with a union from many government and private sources.

10. Because of civil rights legislation and court decisions, it is becoming increasingly difficult to terminate even the most ineffective employees. This trend is costing small businesses much in lost time and money.

QUESTIONS FOR DISCUSSION

1. Explain some of the basic organizational concepts used in organizing a small business.

2. How would you define (or explain) *good human relations?*

3. What is leadership? Why is it so important in small business?

4. Why is communication so important in a small business? What are some barriers to effective communication? How can these barriers be overcome?

5. What is motivation? Why is it so important to a small business manager?

6. What are some practical ways to improve employee motivation?

7. What is the purpose of performance appraisals? Why are they so important?

8. Discuss the areas requiring counseling. What, if anything, can a small business manager do to improve counseling in those areas?

9. Explain the differences between self-discipline and externally imposed discipline.

10. Explain how national labor laws affect small businesses. Should you, as a small business owner, favor or oppose your employees' unionizing? Defend your answer.

11. Explain why it is becoming so difficult to terminate employees.

CASE 10-1

PERSONNEL POLICIES HELP INTERMATIC GROW

Intermatic, Inc., is a Spring Grove, Illinois, producer of timing devices and low-voltage lighting. Jim Miller, CEO, claims his company's personnel policies and programs have been the key to its growth, profitability, and survival and thinks they saved it from disaster.

Several years ago, when Intermatic was on the verge of bankruptcy, Miller, a former employee, was asked to return as president. To save the company, he reduced the work force by 50 percent, closed one division, restructured the staff, consolidated positions, and instituted the employee relations policies and programs that have since assured the firm's success.

An incentive system for production workers earns them about 135 percent of their base pay, and some of the unusual employee benefits are (1) programs that pay workers to shed pounds, (2) free eye examinations and glasses, (3) aerobics classes, (4) golf lessons, (5) an outside exercise course, (6) an indoor track, (7) tennis courts, (8) membership in arts-and-culture clubs, (9) shopping at company-subsidized stores for items such as jeans, T-shirts, and baseball caps, and (10) reimbursement of tuition for college courses.

In addition, Miller is quite open in his communications with employees, telling them what has to be done and why it must be done. He also is available to help people with personal problems, knows them by name, and knows their family situations. The payoff? Turnover is only 3 percent, compared to over 5 percent for similar firms, and it has become such a popular place to work that there's a waiting list of people seeking employment with Intermatic.

Questions

1. How do you explain the improved performance at Intermatic?

2. Would Jim Miller's methods work at all companies? Explain.

3. Would you like to work at Intermatic? Why or why not?

Source: Author's correspondence with Intermatic, Inc.

CASE 10-2

CARLOS EXPANDS HIS BUSINESS

Carlos, a business school graduate, manages Don & Company, a small business that makes dolls and markets them in local stores. The company, which has nine full-time employees, not only deals with production and sales but also purchases the raw materials from which to make the dolls.

Carlos has managed to get a contract from overseas to provide a customer with a large number of dolls. Since he now has to increase his production capacity to meet the new orders, he has added a lawyer to his staff, along with an accountant who advises him on various aspects of the business. He has also approached legal firms, accounting firms, and firms that lease manpower for counseling.

Questions

1. What kind of organizational structure does Carlos have after expansion?

2. Do you think he made the right move? Why or why not?

V

OPERATING THE BUSINESS

Up to this point, we have examined various challenges of owning a small business: planning for, organizing, and managing the business; marketing the product; and organizing and managing the work force. Now it is time to look at the process of actually operating the business.

Many different activities are required to carry on operations. Your business must determine what products to sell; decide whether to purchase them from someone else or produce them; plan, acquire, lay out, and maintain the physical facilities needed for operations; procure and produce the right quality of the right products, at the right time and at the right cost; control the quality and quantity of inventory; control the quality of your output; maintain a work force; and do *all of this as efficiently and economically as possible!*

All these activities make operating a business interesting and rewarding—but also quite challenging. To help meet this challenge, this Part will cover designing operating systems for production and service, and the control of those systems. Chapter 11 discusses developing operating systems, choosing the right location—especially for retail stores and manufacturing plants—planning physical facilities, and improving operations. Chapter 12 examines purchasing and inventory control, as well as planning and controlling operations and quality.

CHAPTER

11

LOCATING AND LAYING OUT OPERATING FACILITIES

Production is not the application of tools to materials, but logic to work.

Peter F. Drucker

You know your company is ready for robots when you recognize that automating is cheaper than relocating in South Korea or Taiwan.

Bruce H. Kleiner, management professor

LEARNING OBJECTIVES

After studying the material in this chapter, you will be able to:

1. Explain what an operating system is and how it functions.

2. Discuss how to determine the right location for a small business.

3. Describe the important factors involved in choosing a retail location.

4. Describe the most important factors involved in choosing a manufacturing site.

5. Identify the steps in planning the layout of physical facilities and show how to implement them.

6. Explain the emerging role of telecommuting in small firms.

7. Discuss some ways of improving operations.

8. Explain how to set and use performance standards.

Oakwood Inn: It's Location, Location, Location!

Bill and Darlene Smith, owners of The Oakwood Inn in Raleigh, North Carolina, agree with many commercial real estate brokers that the three most important factors to consider in establishing a business are "location, location, and location." If that is true, then their activities in operating their bed-and-breakfast (B&B) establishment are destined to be successful.

The Inn is located near the Raleigh/Durham Airport, Chapel Hill and the University of North Carolina, Durham, Duke University, and North Carolina's famed high-tech Research Triangle Park. This strategic location is enhanced by the fact that the Inn is situated in the heart of the Historic Oakwood District only a few minutes from downtown Raleigh and the State Capitol.

The 1871-vintage Victorian home was converted into a bed-and-breakfast in 1984. Bill and Darlene, the current owners and resident innkeepers, purchased the property in the spring of 1997. The transition has been a smooth one, as they have continued the previous owner's high standards of excellence for their B&B operation.

Each of Oakwood's six guest rooms, all with bath en suite, bears the name of a street in Oakwood's historic district. Two are on the ground floor, and the remaining four are upstairs. In the East Room, names and a date can be seen to have been scratched on a windowpane in 1875 by a Victorian-era youngster who wanted to see if the diamond in his grandfather's ring was real. It was!

The Polk Room, a large, secluded ground-floor guest room, is typical of the accommodations. A massive, elegantly carved Victorian walnut bed stands out as the focal point of the room. The bed is believed to have been designed as a "traveling bed," with hinges for easy disassembly. Upholstered in emerald velvet and accented with matching tapestry pillows, an unusual mahogany Adam and Eve sofa serves as the center of the room's sitting area. Elaborately carved Victorian side chairs complete the ensemble. Luxurious velvet draperies with scalloped cornices, a period light fixture, and a coordinated green and cranberry area rug add the final touches. The color-coordinated bathroom is also spacious and equipped with a pedestal lavatory, a claw-foot tub with shower, and a pull-chain toilet—with an oak tank and toilet seat. There is also a private porch.

Although The Oakwood Inn is designed as a nostalgic recreation of Victorian splendor and leisure, the more mundane needs of today's travelers are not neglected: in addition to private telephone lines, harried business guests are also offered the use of fax and copy machines. The menu varies daily, but a typical breakfast at Oakwood includes a choice of fresh fruit compote, fruit juice, baked apple, French toast, sausages, and coffee, served in the spacious dining room. Guests are given the option of either privacy or company, sitting either at a large table or one of two small ones. A newspaper is delivered to each guest room before breakfast. Each afternoon, tea—with delicious cookies, cheese, and crackers—is set up and served in the dining room. In the summer, guests enjoy their afternoon tea sitting in wicker rockers on the tree-shaded front porch.

The Smiths are well equipped to operate Oakwood. First of all, their talents and tastes complement each other well. Bill likes to cook—especially breakfast—and enjoys experimenting with new dishes. He is also an excellent handyman who does the many repair jobs required by a 126-year-old wood-frame house. "There is always something that needs to be repaired or replaced," he says. He also does the work in the landscaped yard.

Darlene does the serving of breakfast and teas, as well as most of the other housework. She takes reservations; greets, registers, and caters to the guests; and does the house cleaning. A part-time employee helps for two hours a day, five days a week, permitting Darlene to clean house and make beds. (Making up the high old-fashioned beds is easier for two people working together, so Bill usually helps her.)

The Smiths came into the business with plenty of experience, although they admit they could have profited from taking a seminar or short course in the management of B&Bs before investing in the Inn. Also,

they say, "we should have done more research before taking over operation of Oakwood with only four days' training from the former owners."

The Smiths tend to operate on a 10-year cycle. Some years ago, they operated a mowing and landscaping business in De Land, Florida. They also opened and ran a doughnut shop at the same time. They then sold those businesses and moved to Flagstaff, Arizona, where they bought a small deli for $25,000, worked five days a week, doubled the space and business in five years, and sold it for $65,000.

With a son who has a degree in accounting and a daughter with a degree in hotel and restaurant management, the Smiths became interested in the B&B business. So they sold their house and deli in Arizona and purchased The Oakwood Inn in early 1997. Their daughter assisted them during the transition period.

The Smiths enjoy their new venture but find it more "confining" than previous endeavors, where they worked five days a week. They find the continuous operation of the B&B much more demanding in terms of time, so they plan to build up the business at Oakwood over the next 10 years, sell it, and retire. Whatever they do, with their ambition, initiative, drive, and work ethic, they will very likely succeed.

Source: Based upon a visit and subsequent communication with Bill and Darlene Smith

---

As the Profile illustrates, all businesses produce some product, either selling a good or providing a service. A retailer forecasts demand and then purchases merchandise and displays, sells, and delivers it to customers. A producer forecasts demand and then purchases material, processes it into products, and sells and delivers the products to customers. A service business tries to satisfy the needs of customers by providing a service. This is what the Smiths are trying to do with The Oakwood Inn.

This chapter examines what you must do to produce your product, how to choose the right location to produce it, how to plan and lay out physical facilities, and how to constantly improve operations. It also explores the new trend toward telecommuting.

■ DEVELOPING OPERATING SYSTEMS

The steps required to start a business, as discussed in Chapter 4, are: (1) searching for a product, (2) studying the market for the product, (3) deciding how to get into business, (4) making strategic plans, and (5) making operational plans, including planning the many aspects of operating the business once it's started. This last step involves setting up your operating systems and providing building(s), materials, equipment, and people to produce the product.

Operating systems in different businesses are really quite similar, although the sequence of events and activities may vary as each business adjusts the system to fit its own needs. Also, support systems, such as accounting, personnel, and cash flow systems, must be integrated into the overall producing system.

Operating systems have the following productive elements: (1) a system for changing form, place, or time; (2) a sequence of steps to change the inputs into outputs; (3) special skills, tools, and/or machines to make the change; (4) instructions and goods identification; and (5) a time frame within which the work is to be done.

What Are Operating Systems?

An **operating system** consists of inputs, processes, and outputs. The **inputs** include materials, people, money, information, machines, and other factors. The **processes** involve converting these inputs into the goods or services the customers want, using the employees, machines, materials, and other factors. The **outputs** consist of the goods and services required by the customers; desired outputs also include satisfying the needs of employees and the public.

Figure 11–1 shows some examples of how inputs are processed into outputs. The processes shown are for the major operations of the company: Cloth, thread, and buttons are sewn into shirts; or a computer program is derived from customer information through design, installation, and testing. In addition, each company has processes such as accounting, maintenance, and quality control that support its main activities. All processes are designed to result in proper operating systems.

How Operating Systems Work

Operations, or **production,** includes all the activities from obtaining raw materials through delivering the product to the customers. Thus, the word *operations* refers to those activities necessary to produce and deliver a service or good.

Operating systems consist of the inputs, processes, and outputs of a business.

Inputs are materials, people, money, information, machines, and other productive factors.

Processes convert these inputs into products customers want.

Outputs are the products produced and the satisfactions to employees and the public.

Operations, or **production,** is converting inputs into outputs for customers.

Figure 11–1
Examples of Operating Systems

Three activities must be performed by all businesses, regardless of their nature. They are (1) marketing, (2) finance, and (3) operations. In manufacturing and similar plants, operations is called production, but in retail and service-type firms the activity is called operations.

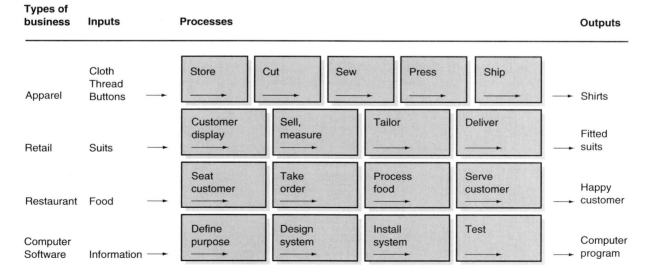

Types of business	Inputs	Processes					Outputs
Apparel	Cloth Thread Buttons	Store	Cut	Sew	Press	Ship	Shirts
Retail	Suits	Customer display	Sell, measure		Tailor	Deliver	Fitted suits
Restaurant	Food	Seat customer	Take order		Process food	Serve customer	Happy customer
Computer Software	Information	Define purpose	Design system		Install system	Test	Computer program

All businesses usually have systems other than the production system, and as the following example shows, these systems must be coordinated for the best production.

The objective of fast-food operations is to supply food quickly and with little customer effort. At Burger King, for example, there are three systems:

1. *A marketing system.* The order for a Whopper is taken from the customer and money received to pay for it.
2. *A production system.* The order is given to someone to prepare the hamburger and package it, while someone else prepares drinks.
3. *A delivery system.* The completed order is handed to the customer.

These three systems are coordinated to provide quick service and to keep the line moving. Figure 11–2 shows how the production system operates. Notice how the inputs—such as rolls, meat patties, mayonnaise, lettuce, onions, and pickles—are processed by cooking, assembling, and wrapping into the output—a Whopper—which is then delivered to the customer.

How to Begin Operations

After identifying the product (output), inputs, and processes, you are ready to begin operations, which involves: (1) choosing the right location, (2) planning physical facilities, (3) deciding on a layout, and (4) implementing your plans.

■ CHOOSING THE RIGHT LOCATION

As shown in Chapters 4 and 5, you must define the character of your business and decide on your objectives and strategies before you begin to investigate available locations for

---

Figure 11–2
Operations Involved in Producing a Whopper

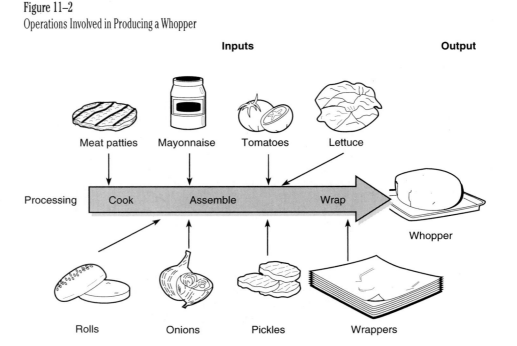

your business. Since company location is a major factor in success or failure, you must ask yourself such questions as: Do I plan to have just one location or to grow regionally or nationwide? Do I intend to concentrate on one product area or expand into several? The answers to these questions will focus your search.

Why Choosing the Right Location Is So Important

Location is one factor that can make the difference between success and failure for a small business. Sales come from customers who find it advantageous to buy from you rather than someone else. Have you, as a customer, patronized a business because it is near you? Or driven miles to obtain a special product? What factors caused you to live where you do now? Companies must consider similar factors to find suitable locations for their operations. Factors influencing the customer's choice of a business include variables such as convenience, time, cost, reliability, quality, and good service. These factors must be evaluated for each potential location before selecting the most suitable one.

When you choose a location, you usually expect to stay there for some time. Not only is it very expensive to move to another location, but also customers, who follow established patterns of activity and do not like changes, may not follow you to a new location. Employees are affected in much the same way.

Some Important Factors Affecting Location Choice

Information on which to base a location decision can come from a variety of sources, as discussed in Chapters 4 and 8. However, you should consider at least two sets of factors when choosing a location for your business: (1) general factors that affect all types of businesses and (2) specific factors that pertain to specific types of businesses.

General Factors Affecting All Businesses   The more important general factors are:[1]

1.   Access to a capable, well-trained, stable work force.
2.   Availability of adequate and affordable supplies and services.
3.   Availability, type, use, and cost of transportation.
4.   Taxes and government regulations.
5.   Availability and cost of electricity, gas, water, sewerage, and other utilities.

Specific Factors to Consider for Various Businesses   The type of business—retailing, producing, or service—influences most location decisions because it determines the relative importance of the general factors mentioned above. For example, location of customers may be more important to a large department store, while location of employees will be more important to a manufacturing plant. Table 11–1 shows some specific factors to be considered in making location decisions. Although the factors have been separated into retailer and producer, many of them apply equally to retailing, producing, and service organizations.

Retailers are concerned with people who come to, or are drawn into, the store to make a purchase. Therefore, location is concerned with people's movement, attention, attitudes, convenience, needs, and ability to buy. In other words, which location will provide sales at a reasonable profit?

Producers are concerned with converting, usually in considerable volume, materials, parts, and other items into products. They emphasize selling those products through intermediaries to the ultimate consumer, as discussed in Chapter 8. Compared to the merchandise of retailers, producing units are often larger and fewer and sold to a smaller number of customers. The plant and customer can be located some distance apart, so other factors

Retailers sell goods to the ultimate consumer.

Producers convert materials into products in considerable volume for others to sell to ultimate consumers.

Table 11–1
Some Important Location Factors

| | Factors affecting selection of | | |
City	Area in City	Specific Site
Retailer		
Size of trade area	Attraction power	Traffic passing site
Population trends	Competitive nature	Ability to intercept traffic
Purchasing power	Access routes	Compatibility of adjacent stores
Trade potential	Zoning regulations	Adequacy of parking
Competition	Area expansion	Unfriendly competition
Shopping centers	General appearance	Cost of site
Producer		
Market location	Zoning	Zoning
Vendor location	Industrial park	Sewer, effluent control
Labor availability	Transportation	Transportation
Transportation		Terrain
Utilities		Utilities
Government, taxes		Labor availability
Schools, recreation		

Source: U.S. Small Business Administration, *Choosing a Retailing Location,* Management Aid No. 2.021 (Washington, DC: Government Printing Office), p. 2.

become more important. Still, nearness to customers and suppliers helps to keep costs down and permits more satisfactory service. Primary emphasis on locating, though, is placed on cost and service.

Service companies, which provide a service for customers, have some characteristics of both retailers and producers.

Service companies have some characteristics of both retailers and producers. The performance of some services—such as those provided by hair stylists, dentists and doctors, and auto service stations—usually requires customers to come to the business's location, where the service is performed. The locations of service companies, therefore, depend on convenient and economical travel.

Some other services—such as home nursing care, landscaping and gardening, and plumbing and electrical repairs—require going to the client's home. But even those who perform these services should try to locate near where customers are clustered. However, some businesses that cannot attract enough customers to a central location may take all, or a part, of their activities "on the road" to obtain more income.

> For example, Sue Ley, the owner of CleanDrum, Inc., a company that straightens and cleans metal oil drums, tried using a mobile unit to clean drums at customers' locations. Although she found that this was too heavy a load for her limited work force at the time, she hopes to resume the service later.*

Many small service businesses start and continue to operate out of the owner's home. This is a logical arrangement since the owner may be tentative about going into business

---

*For more details, see Case 1–2 at the end of Chapter 1, and section IV, Sample Case: CleanDrum, Inc., in the Workbook for Developing a Successful Business Plan, at the end of this text on page 470.

Figure 11-3
Rating Sheet for Sites

Grade each factor: 1 (lowest) to 10 (highest)
Weight each factor: 1 (least important) to 5 (most important)

Factors	Grade	Weight
1. Centrally located to reach my market.	_____	_____
2. Raw materials readily available.	_____	_____
3. Quantity of available labor.	_____	_____
4. Transportation availability and rates.	_____	_____
5. Labor rates of pay/estimated productivity.	_____	_____
6. Adequacy of utilities (sewer, water, power, gas).	_____	_____
7. Local business climate.	_____	_____
8. Provision for future expansion.	_____	_____
9. Tax burden.	_____	_____
10. Topography of the site (slope and foundation).	_____	_____
11. Quality of police and fire protection.	_____	_____
12. Housing availability for workers and managers.	_____	_____
13. Environmental factors (schools, cultural, community atmosphere).	_____	_____
14. Estimate of quality of this site in five years.	_____	_____
15. Location of this site in relation to my major competitor.	_____	_____

Source: U.S. Small Business Administration, *Locating or Relocating Your Business,* Management Aid No. 2.002, p. 6. Copies of this and other publications are available from the SBA for a small processing fee.

and may not want to have the fixed expense of an office. Also, these owners tend to go to the clients to perform their service. Finally, as will be shown in Chapter 14, there are tax benefits.

At some point, the data collected must be analyzed to provide the information necessary for a decision. A score sheet like that in Figure 11-3 can be valuable in comparing possible locations. Evaluations can sometimes be quantitative, such as number of households times median income times percentage of income spent on store items times some special factor for this store. Others are ratings, grading factors from 1 for the lowest to 10 for the highest.

Some factors are very important and should be given more weight than others. One factor in a given site might be so intolerable that the site must be eliminated from consideration.

■ LOCATING RETAIL STORES

In choosing a site for a retail store, two interrelated factors are important: the type of store (i.e., the type of goods sold) and the type of location. There is a perception that market forces and the economies of scale enjoyed by big chains are relentlessly consuming small stores. A study by consultant Gary A. Wright, however, found this conclusion only partially valid. Instead, Wright found that "many small retailers who find a [specialized] niche and provide strong personal service to customers will survive and thrive into the next century."[2] In other words, *service, expertise, and location* are the dominion of small specialty retailers, as the following example illustrates.

The 17th Street Surf Shop targets males ages 8 to 28 with specialized surf gear. The store has expanded to a nine-store operation by selling surfing gear at a ratio of 90 percent soft goods to 10 percent hard goods.

Types of Stores

Customers view products in different ways when selecting the store from which to buy. Therefore, stores can be grouped into (1) convenience, (2) shopping, and (3) specialty stores, according to the type of goods they sell.

Convenience goods are products that customers buy often, routinely, quickly, and in any store that carries them.

Convenience Goods Stores **Convenience goods** are usually low-priced items that are purchased often, are sold in many stores, are bought by habit, and lend themselves to self-service. Examples are candy bars, milk, bread, cigarettes, and detergents. Although the term *convenience goods* may make you think of *convenience stores* (small markets with gas pumps), convenience goods stores are better typified by the grocery and variety stores where we regularly shop for consumable items. Convenience goods stores are interested in having a high flow of customer traffic, so they try to get people to want to satisfy their needs and come in to purchase the items currently on display. The quantity of customer flow seems more important than its quality. These stores are built where the traffic flow is already heavy.

For instance, our research has shown that nearly 70 percent of women patronize stores within five blocks of their residence. Convenient store hours were also found to be very important for this type of store.

Shopping goods are goods that customers buy infrequently, after shopping at only a few stores.

Shopping Goods Stores **Shopping goods** are usually higher-priced items, which are bought infrequently, and for which the customer compares prices. People spend much time looking for these items and talking to sales personnel about them. Therefore, capable salespeople with selling ability are required (see Chapter 8 for more detail). Examples of these goods are suits, automobiles, and furniture.

Specialty goods are bought infrequently, often at exclusive outlets, after special effort by the customer to drive to the store.

Specialty Goods Stores **Specialty goods** are high-priced shopping goods with trade names that are recognized for the exclusive nature of their clientele. By their very nature, specialty goods stores often generate their own traffic, but customer flow can be helped by similar stores in the vicinity. Some examples of specialty goods are quality dresses, precious jewelry, and expensive video and sound equipment. In essence, people do not comparison shop for specialty goods, but just buy the name on the item.

Types of Locations

In general, the types of locations for retail businesses are (1) downtown business districts, (2) freestanding stores, and (3) community shopping centers or malls.

Downtown locations attract business-oriented activities, as government, financial businesses, and head offices of large firms are usually located in the downtown area.

Downtown Business District Changes in retail locations have occurred as discounters have located their stores outside the downtown area. Now, governments, financial businesses, and the head offices of large firms provide most of the business for retail stores in **downtown locations.**

A downtown location has many advantages, such as lower rents, better public transportation, and proximity to where people work. But the disadvantages often include limited shopping hours, higher crime rates, poor or inadequate traffic and parking, and deterioration of downtown areas. In some cases, one or a few downtown areas are preferred to the exclusion of others.

A classic example of this trend can be seen in franchise locations in many Latin American countries such as Brazil, Chile, Colombia, and Mexico. According to Enrique Gonzales Calvillo, president of the Mexican Institute of Franchisers, Mexico is suffering from the tendency of economic activity to concentrate in the center of one city. He cites limited space, arbitrary and confusing zoning laws, the persistence of out-of-date and misguided real estate practices, and overwhelming demand as among Mexico's problems. The concentration of businesses in Mexico City has made investment in small and medium-sized businesses almost prohibitive.[3]

Freestanding Stores   **Freestanding stores,** found in many locations, may be the best for customers who have brand or company loyalty, or for those who identify with a given shop, where a business has a competitive edge over its competitors, where the character of customers and growth objectives blend well. Low costs, good parking, independent hours and operations, and restricted competition in these locations tend to fit the more entrepreneurial types of businesspeople. However, to attract customers, especially new ones, you may have to do considerable advertising. Moreover, acquiring a suitable building and land may be difficult.

Innovative entrepreneurs may find a lucrative location in neighborhoods formerly avoided by other businesses. But the market niche—product and clientele—must conform to the needs of the customers in the area, as the following example illustrates.

> Onyx Grocery, owned and operated by Albert Cooke and Rodney Tonge, is an example of such a fit. The partners opened the tiny store—only a little larger than a two-car garage—in Fort Lauderdale, Florida, in a neighborhood where there are few cars.
>
> Its shelves are crowded with convenience store essentials such as toiletries and cereals but also such nonessentials as hair weaves made from human hair, and the "drinks are cheap and cold."
>
> The store serves a special need, for there are no other neighborhood-owned or -operated businesses in the area. And the young African-American partners say their fledgling business is "a blueprint for achievement, a result of saving when spending was tempting—a result of preparation paying off."[4]

Shopping Centers   **Shopping centers** are planned and built only after lengthy and involved studies. These centers vary in size from small neighborhood and strip centers, to community centers, to the large regional malls. The largest of these in the United States is the Mall of America in Bloomington, Minnesota (www.mallofamerica.com). It occupies 4.2 million square feet, has four anchor stores—and 400 other retailers—dozens of restaurants, and an indoor amusement park.[5]

Why Shopping Centers Are So Popular   Shopping centers are designed to draw traffic according to the planned nature of the stores to be included in them. The design of the centers ranges from small, neighborhood convenience goods stores to giant regional centers with a wide range of goods and services, which may or may not be specialized. Shopping centers offer many services, such as specialized activities to bring in traffic, merchant association activities, parking, utilities, and combined advertising. A current trend is for large "power centers" to compete with one another to be the largest.

Another reason for the popularity of shopping centers is the growing interest in shopping. According to Tourism Works for America, a tourist trade group, "Shopping has become the most popular pastime of vacationers, surpassing outdoor activities such as hiking, swimming, or fishing."[6] This trend is especially noticeable in New England. For example, an ad in the local *New England Brochure* features "The Best Hiking in Vermont," but the description is of the crowded outlet malls, not the region's spectacular trails.

Freestanding stores, found in various locations, are usually best for customers who have brand or company loyalty.

Shopping centers vary in size and are designed to draw traffic according to the planned nature of the stores to be included in them.

Enclosed malls have eliminated weather problems for customers. Indeed, older people are encouraged to use the mall for exercise in a controlled climate.

The typical shopping center has two **anchor stores.** These stores, often large department stores, are usually located at the ends of the arms of the mall, where they are not only easily accessible from the parking lot but also generate heavy traffic for the small stores between them.

Within the malls, kiosks and carts often serve as magnets, occupying potentially prime selling spots. These small "stores" are fast growing in importance as malls increase in popularity. Carts and kiosks are also found in freestanding locations such as in parks, outside office buildings, and on street corners. They can provide a quick, easy, and inexpensive way to start a small business, as the following examples illustrates.

> In 1995, Wally Rizza, age 21, spent $25,000 to launch Shades 2000 Inc., a sunglasses cart in the Irvine Spectrum Entertainment Center in Irvine, California. Within a year he had sales of $184,000. By August 1998, he had three sunglasses carts, a jewelry cart, and a watch cart and expected to gross $500,000 for the year.[7]

Some malls may have a theme that stores are expected to conform to. The purpose of the theme is to pull the stores together and have them handle products of similar quality. For example, the center may have regulations on shopping hours, how to use the space in front of the store (what to display and how), and so on.

Drawbacks of Shopping Centers   Although the above advantages are considerable, there are also disadvantages to locating in a center. Some of the most significant of these are cost, restrictions imposed by the center's theme, operating regulations, and possible changes in the center's owners and managers, which could bring policy changes.

There is now a "total rent" concept for costs that must be considered in evaluating the costs of renting space in a shopping center. These costs may include dues to the merchants' association, maintenance fees for the common areas, and the cost of special events or combined advertising. The most common rental is a basic rent, usually based on square footage, plus a percentage of gross sales (usually 5 to 7 percent). In total, these costs tend to be high and often discourage tenants, as you can see from the following.

For example, if your mall space is 30 feet wide and 75 feet deep, you would have 30 $\times$ 75 or 2,250 square feet. If the entire mall space was 500,000 square feet, your store would occupy 2,250/500,000 or 0.45 percent of the entire mall. You could then project rent and related expenses as follows:

Annual Expenses		
Common area maintenance	$100,000 × .0045 =	$ 450
Real estate taxes	$20,000 × .0045 =	90
Rent @ $10 per square foot	$2,250 × $10 =	22,500
Merchants association fees @ 10%	$1 × 2,250 × 0.10 =	225
Total		$23,265

The average monthly amount would be $23,265 $\div$ 12 months = approximately $1,939. However, many landlords require additional "percentage" rent after a certain level of gross retail sales has been met. For example, in the above analysis, gross or annual rent equals 5 percent of $450,000 annually or $37,500 per month ($450,000/12). So when gross sales exceed $37,500 per month, you must pay an additional 5 percent on the excess!

■ LOCATING MANUFACTURING PLANTS

Manufacturing (or **production**) usually involves making or processing raw materials into a finished product. The materials may be extracted from the ground or harvested from the earth, or they may be outputs of other companies (such as metal plates, silicon chips, or ground meat for hamburgers), that are changed in form or shape, or assembled into a different type of product. The location of a manufacturing plant is usually selected with the aim of serving customers properly at the lowest practical cost. Of the factors to consider in locating a manufacturing plant (see Table 11–1), the most important are nearness to customers and vendors and availability and cost of transportation.

Of considerable importance to manufacturers are the time and cost of transporting finished goods to the customers and acquiring raw materials from vendors. The success of a given location can hinge on the availability and cost of the proper mode of transportation, as discussed in Chapter 8.

Manufacturing, or **production,** usually involves making or processing materials into finished goods.

■ PLANNING PHYSICAL FACILITIES

Once you've selected your location, you must begin planning, acquiring, and installing facilities. These **facilities,** which include the building, machines and other equipment, and furniture and fixtures, must be designed or selected to produce the desired product at the lowest practical cost.

Facilities are the buildings, machines and other equipment, and furniture and fixtures needed to produce and distribute a product.

There are five steps involved in this process: (1) determine the product to be sold and the volume in which it is to be produced, (2) identify the operations and activities required to get the product to the customer, (3) determine space requirements, (4) determine the most effective layout of the facilities, and (5) implement your plans.

Determine Product to Be Produced

Facilities should be planned for products to be produced now, but also for changes anticipated in the foreseeable future. Projections for five years are normal, and industry standards for the space required for planned sales or production volume can be a good start in planning.

Identify Operations and Activities to Be Performed

You will remember that operations include all the activities from buying the materials through delivering the finished product to the customer. These activities include (1) purchasing materials and parts for production or goods to sell, (2) performing operations needed to produce the product, and (3) carrying out support activities.

Sequences of operations may be fixed (e.g., producing the hamburger in Figure 11–2) or may change from order to order, as happens in retail stores or service businesses.

Determine Space Requirements

Space is required for materials, equipment, and machines, as well as the movement of customers and employees. Space is also needed for carts and trucks, inventory, displays, waiting areas, personal facilities, maintenance and cleaning, and many other services. The number and size of all these areas depend on the volume of output planned.

How Telecommuting Affects Physical Facility Needs

Telecommuting is the use of modern communication media, such as telephones, fax machines, computers, modems and fax/modems, and scanners, to work from an office, home, or any location.

Teleworkers are employees who work full or part time from their homes.

Determining space requirements is becoming easier—or more complicated, according to your point of view. The changing nature of production, operations, and service activities is also changing *where* people work, and therefore the amount of space needed. **Telecommuting,** which is using modern communication media—such as telephones, fax machines, computers with modems or fax/modems, and scanners—to work anywhere, has changed the concept of work.

According to a 1997 study by Find/SVP (www.findsvp.com), a New York research firm, "52 million Americans—about 40 percent of the total U.S. work force—are self-employed with home offices, work for companies as telecommuters, or simply put in after-hours time at home."[8] A later study by the same firm found that 11. 1 million of those people actually telecommute.[9] A study for *American Demographics* (www.demographics.com) found that 31 percent of U.S. homes had "a room that was used specifically as an office."[10]

With these kinds of workers, *work* is no longer *a place to go* to but *something you do.* According to June Langhoff, editor of *TeleTrends,* the official newsletter of the Telecommuting Advisory Council (TAC) (www.telecommute.org), use of the new technologies permits work to be done anywhere.[11] And recent studies show that telecommuters feel that they are 5 to 20 percent more productive when they work at home, simply because there are fewer distractions.[12] A 1997 study by Bell-South (www.bellsouth.com) found that 75 percent of telecommuters reported increased productivity in their work, and 83 percent reported a "significant improvement in their home lives."[13]

Who are these **teleworkers,** as telecommuters are now being called? An earlier survey found that 54 percent were men, while 46 percent were women.[14] There were nearly four times as many white-collar telecommuters as blue-collar ones.[15] In contrast to these professional, sales, or technical workers, however, are the many immigrants who speak little English, have no transportation, and must care for small children.[16]

Small businesses are particularly adaptable to telecommuting. An earlier survey found that *59 percent of telecommuters work for a company with five or fewer employees.*[17] Finally, a recent Gallup survey found that a growing number of Americans are "buying computers to start home-based businesses."[18] A considerable number of organizations have been established to aid the home-based business owner.*

"Mommy will take you potty as soon as she wraps up this business deal."

(*Source:* Copyright 1996 by Fred Maes.)

Decide on the Best Layout

The objective in layout planning is to obtain the best placement of furniture and fixtures; tools, machines, and equipment; storage and materials handling; service activities such as cleaning and maintenance; and places for employees and customers to sit, stand, or move about.

Figure 11–4 shows the layout of the previously mentioned CleanDrum, Inc., which cleans 50-gallon oil drums. Notice the movement of drums from one end of the plant to the other, the use of roller conveyors (even through machines), movement in a vat, and space

---

*Some examples are the American Association of Home-Based Businesses (www.aahbb.org), the National Association for the Self-Employed (www.nase.org), the Small Business Administration (www.sba.gov), and the Independent Business Alliance. You can call the Alliance at 1-800-559-2580 for further details about the assistance it provides in purchasing affordable insurance and other financial services.

Figure 11–4

Layout of the CleanDrum, Inc., Plant*

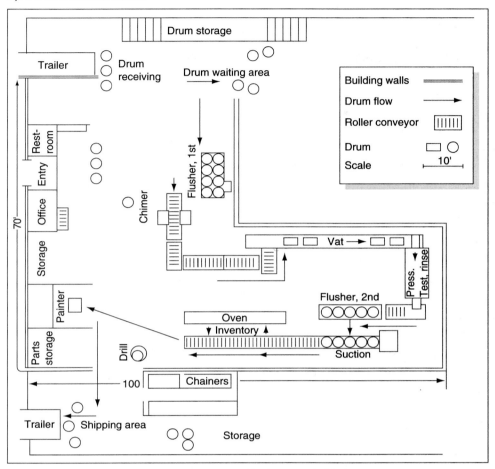

*See section IV, Sample Case: CleanDrum, Inc., in the Workbook at the end of the book.

for inventory, employees, and an office. Before installation, a model of the planned layout had been constructed and tested to iron out any kinks.

Types of Layout   The two general types of layout are *product* and *process*. In practice, however, layouts often combine the two types.

Product Layout   In a **product layout,** facilities are arranged so materials, workers, and/or customers move from one operation to another with little backtracking. This type is used in the school cafeteria shown in Figure 11–5A. The advantages of the product layout plan include specialization of workers and machines, less inventory, fewer instructions and controls, faster movement, and less space needed for aisles and storage. This arrangement tends to improve efficiency and maximize sales, especially in the automobile and fast-food industries.

A **product layout** has the facilities laid out according to the sequence of operations to be performed.

> Notice in the earlier Figure 11–2 that if you order a Whopper, its production moves forward from cooking the meat to assembling, wrapping, and delivering the Whopper to you.

Figure 11–5

Product and Process Layout Comparison of Cafeterias

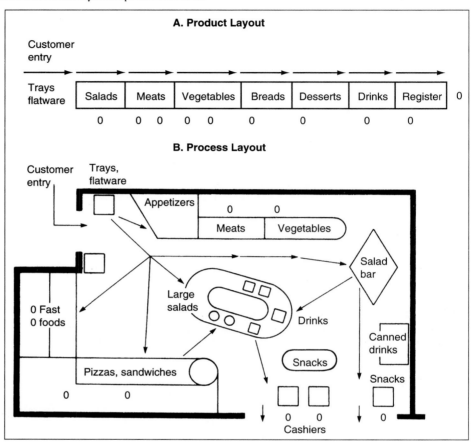

Process Layout   The **process layout** groups machines performing the same type of work and workers with similar skills such as the cafeteria shown in Figure 11–5B.

A **process layout** groups the facilities doing the same type of work.

The process layout requires more movement of material or people, as is shown by the figure, and requires a larger inventory. But it also provides flexibility to take care of change and variety, often can use the same general-purpose machines and equipment for several steps in the operation, and permits more efficient scheduling of equipment and workers.

Few layout plans are totally product or process layouts. Instead, most layout plans combine the two to obtain the advantages of both.

Determining the General Layout   The next step in the design process is determining the general layout by grouping machines, products, or departments. This helps to establish the general arrangement of the plant, store, or office before spending much time on details. Using similar layouts as an example, you can estimate the space needed. Space should also be provided, where appropriate, for maintenance, planning, and food and other needed services. Each service should be placed conveniently near the units that use it.

Entrance locations are important in the layout of retail and service establishments. Customers usually enter downtown stores from the street, parking lot, or corridors, and goods usually enter from the back. External factors to consider include entrances for employees, parking for customers, connections to utilities, governmental restrictions, and weather factors.

Figure 11–6
Questions to Ask about a Production Layout

---

1. *Space for movement.* Are aisles wide enough for cart and truck movement? Is there enough room for lines that form at machines and checkout stations? Can material be obtained easily and shelves restocked conveniently?

2. *Utilities.* Has adequate wiring and plumbing, and provision for changes, been planned? Has provision been made for proper temperature? Does the area meet Environmental Protection Agency (EPA) standards?

3. *Safety.* Is proper fire protection provided, and are Occupational Safety and Health Administration (OSHA) standards being met? Are there proper guards on machines, in aisles, and around dangerous areas?

4. *Working conditions.* Do workers have enough working space and light? Is there provision for low noise levels, proper temperature, and elimination of objectionable odors? Are workers safe? Can they socialize and take care of personal needs?

5. *Cleanliness and maintenance.* Is the layout designed for effective housekeeping and waste disposal at low cost? Can machinery, equipment, and the building be maintained easily?

6. *Product quality.* Has provision been made to assure proper quality and to protect the product as it moves through the plant or stays in storage?

7. *Aesthetics.* Is the layout attractive to customers and employees?

In manufacturing and large retail and wholesale warehouses, materials-handling devices such as conveyors, carts, hand trucks, and cranes are used to move materials. The objective is to move the items as quickly as possible, with a minimum of handling, and without increasing other costs (see Figure 11–4).

Determining the Final Layout   If your performance is to be efficient, the final layout must be planned in detail, so examine each operation to assure easy performance of the work. If workers spend too much time in walking, turning, twisting, or other wasted motion, the work will take longer and be more tiring. Tools and other items to be used should be located close at hand for quick service. Some specific factors to consider when doing your final layout are shown in Figure 11–6. Since the first of these, space for movement, is particularly important, you should ask questions such as: Is there enough room if a line forms? Can shelves be restocked conveniently? Are aisles wide enough for one- or two-way traffic?

> For example, grocery store aisles are designed to allow passage of two carts, but they often become blocked by special displays of new or sale items. Similarly, it may be difficult to squeeze between the display racks in department stores, and office planners often fail to allow enough space for storage of accumulated files.

The last consideration in the list in Figure 11–6, aesthetics, is also important, so ask yourself: Are the layout and surroundings attractive to workers and customers?

> The Gloucester, Virginia, ServiStar Hardware Store, which once was patronized primarily by men, was dank, dark, and ugly. With more women becoming do-it-yourselfers and buyers of more hardware store items, ServiStar decided to change its image. It installed bright lights, chrome gridwork, and even murals. "Some of the old guys come in and kid us about being a disco," says Robert Fitchett, whose family owns the store, "but our sales are up 33 percent from last year."

Layout is also important for those working at home. Susie Sherman, owner of Professional Office Solutions, Inc. (members.aol.com/ProfOffSol/), an interior design business, offers these suggestions: (1) design your workplace with you at the center, (2) use furniture with flexible spaces and cubbyholes, (3) keep a few supplies close at hand, and store the rest out of the way, (4) build shelves up to the ceiling, and (5) use the top of filing cabinets to hold peripherals, not as a place for paper collection.[19]

Implement Your Plans

Finally, you should test your layout plans to see if they are sound. One way to do this is to have employees, customers, or other knowledgeable people review the plans and make suggestions.

An important point to remember is that, although the layout of the interior of your facility is important, the walls and what is outside them can be equally vital to your success. Construction of a new building requires consideration of the type and method of construction, arrangements for vehicular movement and parking, provision for public transportation, if available, and landscaping.

■ HOW TO IMPROVE OPERATIONS

Products and methods of operation are constantly changing as competition pushes out obsolete or inefficient businesses. Some tools are available in the disciplines of work simplification and industrial engineering to help you keep up to date and constantly improve your operations.

The steps used in designing and improving work are: (1) state the problem, (2) collect and record information, (3) develop and analyze alternatives, and (4) select, install, and follow up on new work methods. Computers are now used to help improve operations, particularly through the use of software that simulates operations. Be sure to record your analysis on paper, tape, or disk for review.

State the Problem

As usual, it is best to begin by clearly stating *the problem—not a symptom of the problem.* Ask questions such as: Is the cost of the work too high? Is the quality of the service low? Is the service to customers delayed?

Collect and Record Information

This step consists of collecting information for the *what, how, where, who, why,* and *when* of the work being done. Observing the work being performed, talking with knowledgeable people, and studying available data are methods of obtaining information.[20]

Develop and Analyze Alternatives

Listing the available alternatives is basic to any type of analysis and a critical step in decision making. All work and services can be performed in many ways, and products can be made from many different materials.

Some questions that might be used in improving work performance include:

- Who performs the activity, what is it, and where is it being done?
- Why is the activity being performed?
- Can the activity be performed in a better way?
- Can it be combined with another activity (or activities)?

- Can the work sequence be changed to reduce the volume of work?
- Can it be simplified?

An example of improving work performance may now be seen in the food service industry. Many restaurants are turning to prepackaged frozen food instead of making menu items from scratch. Blaming price increases and the need for quality consistency, these restaurants are looking to others to prepare and freeze those items that are time-consuming to prepare.[21]

Select, Install, and Follow Up on New Methods

Using your objectives, such as lower costs or better service, as a guide, pick the method that best suits your goals. Installing this new method includes setting up the physical equipment, gaining acceptance, and training workers. Test the method to see that it works and follow up to see that workers are familiar with it and are following procedures.

■ SETTING AND USING PERFORMANCE STANDARDS

One of the most difficult problems you will face in your business is measuring the performance of employees, since there are few precise tools for establishing standards against which to measure performance. Instead, you must rely heavily on people's judgment. Physical work can be measured more precisely than mental work, but doing so still requires judgment.

Performance standards can be set by (1) estimates by people experienced in the work; (2) time studies, using a watch or other timing device; and (3) synthesis of the elemental times obtained from published tables. Most small business owners use the first method, using estimates of experienced people. These estimates should be recorded and given to workers for their guidance. The standards should allow for the time needed to do the work at normal speed, plus time for unavoidable delays and personal requirements. A good set of standards can be determined this way at a minimal cost.

WHAT YOU SHOULD HAVE LEARNED

■

1. All businesses have operating systems, which process (or transform) inputs of people, money, machines, methods, and materials into outputs of goods, services, and satisfactions.

2. Some general factors to be considered in locating any business are access to: (*a*) the work force, (*b*) utilities, (*c*) vendors, and (*d*) transportation, as well as (*e*) the effect of taxes and government regulations.

3. The most important factors to consider in choosing a retail location are the type of business and the type of location. The type of business largely determines the location. Convenience goods stores are usually located where the traffic flow is high, shopping goods stores where comparison

shopping can be done. Specialty goods stores often generate their own traffic but are helped by having similar stores in the vicinity.

The types of retail locations are downtown in the business district, in freestanding stores, and in shopping centers.

4. Among the most important factors in choosing a manufacturing site are nearness to customers and vendors and the availability and cost of transportation.

5. In planning physical facilities you: (*a*) determine the product to be sold and the volume to produce, (*b*) identify the operations and activities required to process it and get it to the customer, (*c*) estimate the space needed, and (*d*) determine the best

physical arrangement and layout of those facilities. The types of layout are product and process, or a combination of both.

Physical facilities must be laid out to provide for a smooth flow of work and activities, space for movement, adequate utilities, safe operations, favorable working conditions, cleanliness and ease of maintenance, product quality, and a favorable impression.

6. Telecommuting is becoming more important to small business because of the convenience and flexibility it provides employees—and even owners—of small businesses.

7. The methods used to improve operations include: (*a*) stating the problem; (*b*) collecting and recording information; (*c*) developing and analyzing alternatives; and (*d*) selecting, installing, and following up on the new methods.

8. Standards for measuring performance are needed. Standards can be set by (*a*) estimates by people experienced in the work, (*b*) time studies, using a watch or other timing device, and (*c*) using a synthesis of elemental times from published tables. Small businesses usually use estimates of experienced people.

QUESTIONS FOR DISCUSSION

1. What are some characteristics of an operating system? What are some inputs into an operating system? What are some outputs resulting from the operating processes?

2. Explain some of the more important general factors affecting location choice.

3. Explain the two most important factors in choosing a retail location.

4. Explain the two most important factors in locating a manufacturing plant.

5. Explain the steps involved in planning facilities.

6. Explain the three different types of layout.

7. What are some objectives of layout planning?

8. Explain the four steps involved in improving operations.

9. Which of the two cafeteria layouts in Figure 11–5 do you think would be more effective? Why?

10. Do you remember your movements during course registration at college the last time? What improvements could you make in the process?

11. What is telecommuting, and why is it growing in importance for small firms?

CASE 11–1

TELECOMMUTING IN THE ROCKIES

In today's world of notebook computers, tiny printers, cell phones, and fax machines, many of us work at home, on the road, and at the beach. There is even a town in Colorado that bills itself as a "telecommuting town."

Located in the southwest quadrant of Colorado, Telluride has only 1,500 residents, but one-third of them now have access to the Internet. One of the advantages of having the town wired for high tech is the relief of not having to leave home to go to work (the town's average annual snowfall is 300 inches). Another advantage is the savings to one's employer—$4,000 to $6,000 a year in reduced office space alone. These advantages are the result of $130,000 provided by the State of Colorado in 1993 to bring 21st century communications into the area.

Bernie Zurbriggen of Frisco, Colorado, is an example of how telecommuting works. After a brush with death, he resigned a highly stressful job and relocated in the Rocky Mountains. There he created U.S. Trans Comm (bernie@colo.com), the ultimate transportable company, through which he supplies customers, nationwide, with up-to-the-minute used car prices. In fiscal 1995, U.S. Trans Comm received 35,000 calls. As he adds new services, he predicts that call volume will rise significantly into the twenty-first century. His office (home) has 10 phones—and a breathtaking view of Buffalo Mountain and the Continental Divide.

Zurbriggen uses technology (both old and new) to provide the information services needed to keep in contact with customers—and he stays at home to do it.

Questions

1. Do you think this type of arrangement and location would be beneficial to a small business? Explain.

2. Do you think your productivity—in this situation and location—would be increased, be reduced, or stay the same? Explain.

Source: *Telluride Visitors Guide,* Telluride Publishing Co., Winter 1995–1996; Kerry Hannon, "A Long Way from the Rat Race," *U.S. News & World Report,* October 30, 1995, pp. 86–87; Andrew Feinberg, "Frisco System," *Forbes ASAP,* October 9, 1995, p. 21; and author's communication and conversations with Telluride Visitor Services, November 1995.

CASE 11-2

NELL HILL'S: AN ADVENTURE IN SHOPPING

In 1981, Mary Carol Garrity opened a gourmet food and gift shop in Atchison, Kansas. Because of her canny purchasing and creative displays, the shop soon evolved into a home furnishings store, Nell Hill's. While her goal was to serve the few residents of Atchison, her store soon began to attract customers from as far away as Kansas City, 60 miles distant.

For seven years the store made no profit, and Garrity took home a salary of only $12,000 a year. But then customers began to arrive from all over the state. For a store that does not advertise, is not listed in any Kansas City phone directory, and has received hardly any media attention, the influx of thousands of women driving long distances to shop is amazing. Nearly 95 percent of Nell Hill's sales are to shoppers who live more than 50 miles away, mostly in greater Kansas City. The number of shoppers is increasing, as evidenced by the fact that, in the last decade, sales have risen between 20 and 30 percent annually, reaching $1.7 million in 1996.

Garrity's success largely derives from her energy and dedication to not only finding unusual products but displaying them in creative ways. Because of her unique ability, Hallmark Cards, Inc., of Kansas City, Missouri, has added Atchison to its itinerary—along with New York and Paris—as a place for their artists to seek inspiration.

While Nell Hill's is not a discounter, it is able to keep prices low because its expenses are so low. The store itself and the warehouse where the merchandise is stored are in space that was abandoned when Garrity rented it.

Another attraction of Nell Hill's is the appeal of purchasing items directly from the store's owner and buyer. She greets most of her customers by name, will go to their homes to help them decorate, and has her customers send her photographs of their homes, which she then uses to help them remodel.

The success of Nell Hill's is part of a trend among upmarket shoppers. Convenience, value, and selection are no longer enough for many of these discriminating shoppers. Instead, they are looking for adventure. According to Nancy Ornce, creative director of gift wrapping and other specialty products at Hallmark Cards, "People are looking for shopping experiences that are off the beaten path." Apparently this trend is working in Garrity's favor. According to her, Nell Hill's has succeeded not in spite of its distance from customers, but because of it. "It's the romance of a small town," she says.

Like many other successful small business owners, Garrity plans to expand. Instead of opening Nell Hill's stores in other locations, however, her idea is to open as many as four additional stores in Atchison, each with a different name and theme. The first of these, a bed and bedding store, was scheduled to open in March 1998.

Questions

1. Evaluate the approach used by Mary Carol Garrity in developing and opening her store.

2. Do you agree with the statement that "The success of Nell Hill's is part of a trend among upmarket shoppers"? Explain.

3. What is your reaction to Garrity's plan to "open as many as four additional stores in Atchison, each with a different name and theme"?

Source: Kevin Helliker, "Word of Mouth Makes Kansas Store a Star," *The Wall Street Journal,* November 7, 1997, pp. B1, B9.

12

PURCHASING, INVENTORY, AND QUALITY CONTROL

Quality is never an accident; it is always the result of intelligent effort.

John Ruskin

Nothing can be produced out of nothing, any more than a thing can go back to nothing.

Marcus Aurelius

Resources must be employed productively and their productivity has to grow if the business is to survive.

Peter F. Drucker

LEARNING OBJECTIVES

After studying the material in this chapter, you will be able to:

1. Discuss the importance of purchasing.

2. Explain the need to choose suppliers carefully.

3. Describe how to establish an effective purchasing procedure.

4. Discuss how to establish and maintain effective inventory control.

5. Explain what is involved in operations planning and control.

6. Describe how to maintain quality control.

Anders Book Stores: Dealing with Hundreds of Suppliers

Bob and Kathy Summer find owning and managing Anders Book Stores (ABS) (www.mobis.com/~anders) "frustrating—but fun!" They purchased the store from Jim Anders in 1982 after spending several years working for him, during which time they learned some of the ins and outs of running a high-quality operation.

The Summers have divided the responsibilities so Bob specializes in college-level books and Kathy handles everything associated with textbooks and supplies for 14 private schools. After ordering and receiving the books, she groups them by grade, sells them, and returns unsold copies to publishers. In handling these activities, as well as being responsible for materials and supplies, she deals with over 1,000 suppliers each year.

Bob handles sales to students from the University of South Alabama (www.usouthal.edu), which has its own bookstore across the street, and from other colleges in the area. Bob receives the book orders from campus bookstores in the area; buys, receives, and sells the books; reorders if necessary; and returns unsold books to publishers.

A major problem Anders faces is estimating how many copies of each text to order. Each book order Bob receives has the estimated number of students in the class; so taking into consideration that some students will share a book and some won't buy a text, Bob estimates how many copies of each text to order.

Bob buys used books from students and used-book wholesalers; new textbooks come from the publishers. ABS has 1,200 publishers listed in its computer, although it regularly buys from "only" about 300 to 400 in any one year. When you consider that Kathy also buys from over 1,000 suppliers, you can understand why they say "buying and bookkeeping problems are horrendous."

About six weeks before classes start, orders are sent to publishers via computer modem. Publishers then ship the books, via UPS (www.ups.com), RPS (www.shiprps.com), or freight, sometimes as much as four weeks before they're needed.

Another problem is not having enough textbooks to meet student needs. When this happens, Bob reorders and books are shipped by UPS or RPS. The supplier usually ships the books one to seven days after the order is received. If needed immediately, a book can be shipped second-day express—at an additional charge. One year, enrollment increased so rapidly that Bob had to place over 50 reorders, for about 25 percent of the books sold.

Even worse is the problem of unsold books. Even when publishers allow returns for a refund, there is usually a restocking fee. And in the present economic climate of rapid mergers, sometimes the publisher that sold the books has been acquired by another house, so where should the books be returned? Given the already low gross profit margin of only 15 to 20 percent, returns put a severe financial strain on the business.

Poor-quality books pose another problem. In one order, some books had the first 78 pages glued together. In another, some sections came unglued and fell apart. Although the publisher replaces books, replacement is inconvenient and time-consuming.

Most of the large publishers send out an annual evaluation form for their dealers to complete. Since they've been doing this, Bob and Kathy have noticed an improvement in service from the publishers.

Like other small businesses, ABS has many personnel problems. For instance, increases in the minimum wage rate make a strong impact on operations. Such increases reduce the number of people who can be hired, with the result that there is more work to be done by fewer workers. The Summers used to employ many college students but now hire only a few. Also, they say, "the loss or death of a key employee can cripple a small business such as ours for an extended period of time. Therefore, we need to plan ahead and try to have a certain degree of depth to cover these employees. And usually these employees must be paid more in order to retain them."

Finally, taxes pose a problem for ABS. Not only are the taxes themselves a burden, but the amount of time and effort involved cut into core business activities.

Source: Author's discussions with Kathy and Bob Summer.

The Profile shows that the profitability of a small business depends largely on effective purchasing, inventory, operations, and quality control. Most small firms have many potential sources of supply for goods and services, each of which requires close study to secure the proper quality, quantity, timing, price, and service needed. This chapter emphasizes the strategies and procedures needed for effective purchasing, as well as inventory, operations, and quality control.

■ THE IMPORTANCE OF PURCHASING

Your business will need products provided by someone else, and the wide variety of items available requires careful study to ensure proper selection. Some items, such as electricity, come from only one supplier but even they require a careful analysis to obtain them at a favorable cost. Others, such as insurance, machines, and equipment, also require special attention because they are often expensive and are purchased infrequently. Still other items, such as paper clips and welding rods, are relatively cheap, and they're purchased routinely. Finally, materials that are part of the company's main product and have a high cost relative to revenue will take up a large amount of your time. This chapter is primarily concerned with this last group, those that are an important part of your main product. It also emphasizes that all aspects of purchasing must consider quality.[1]

What Purchasing Involves

Purchasing determines the company's needs and finds, orders, and assures delivery of those items.

Obtaining all items, including goods and services, in the proper form, quantity, and quality, and at the proper place, time, and cost, is the main objective of **purchasing**. Purchasing identifies the needs of the company and finds, negotiates for, orders, and assures delivery of those items. Thus, you should coordinate your needs with the operations of suppliers, establish standardized procedures, and set up and maintain controls to ensure proper performance. As you probably noticed, Bob and Kathy Summer do all these things in buying for Anders Book Stores.

In retail stores, buying requires coordinating the level of stock of many items with consumer demands, which change as styles, colors, technology, and personal identification change. (And many customers may expect to buy year-round certain "standard" items that don't reflect fashion changes.) Each type of item may be handled differently, so those doing the buying must work closely with those doing the selling to satisfy these differing needs.

Purchasing for a manufacturing plant involves getting the proper materials and processing them into finished goods, while maintaining proper control of inventory and quality. Thus, those doing the purchasing must work closely with those doing the production and selling.

Purchasing by the federal government has become so complex and costly that it discourages small businesses from trying to sell to it. At the urging of the SBA (www.sbaonline.sba.gov), though, the Federal Acquisition Streamlining Act was passed. It urges government agencies to buy off-the-shelf goods rather than items made to its own detailed specifications. The law also permits the government to communicate with vendors on-line rather than with paperwork. These changes should make it easier for small companies to bid on small federal contracts.[2]

Why Purchasing Is So Important

The cost of materials and other goods and services needed to produce a product is about half the revenue received for it. This means all other costs, plus profit, almost equal the cost of purchases. In many cases, the cost of purchases is as much as two-thirds of sales revenues.[3]

While the price of purchases is important, other aspects can be just as critical. For example, obtaining **just-in-time (JIT)** delivery—where the materials are delivered to the user just at the time they are needed for production—can save on inventory costs. Recent statistics, for example, suggest that JIT inventory management has helped keep warehouses from overflowing. For example, the U.S. Department of Commerce reports that the inventory-to-sales ratio for manufacturing has steadily declined since the early 1980s. Close coordination between you and your supplier can greatly improve efficiency by shifting inventory costs and management to the distributors. The distributor, in turn, usually discounts the price to the purchaser as a result of lower costs from increased production. These arrangements take on aspects of a partnership (as discussed in Chapter 3).

> For instance, Montreal-based Future Electronics (www.futureelectronics.com) is hooked up by an electronic data interchange system to Bailey Controls, an Ohio-based supplier of control systems. Every week, Bailey electronically sends Future its latest forecasts of what materials the Canadian company will need for the next six months. In this way, Future can stock up in time.[4]

Two current trends in purchasing that are causing considerable problems for small firms are supplier-base downsizing and fully integrated production networks. **Supplier-base downsizing,** which means reducing the number of suppliers to concentrate purchasing, is a result of corporate downsizing. This trend is especially harmful to businesses owned by women and minorities.[5]

The second problem, **fully integrated production networks,** is a primary problem for U.S. companies in global operations. For example, many primary competitors of U.S. firms have built up entire geographic regions where a fully integrated supply chain, from raw materials to finished products, involving hundreds of companies, is shutting out U.S. suppliers, especially smaller ones.[6] If small U.S. suppliers are to survive, they must assure that all suppliers in a supply chain achieve—and operate at—similar high standards and collectively market their skills to global competitors.

Just-in-time (JIT) delivery is having materials delivered to the user at the time needed for production.

Supplier-base downsizing means reducing the number of suppliers to concentrate purchasing.

Fully integrated production networks are entire geographic regions where a fully integrated supply chain, from raw materials to finished products, is built up.

Finally, not having the appropriate stock—the right style, at the right price, at the right time, and of the proper quality—properly displayed for customers can result in added costs, lower profits, and unhappy customers.

> For example, in the early 1990s, Chrysler (www.chryslercorp.com) had to recall the first 4,000 of its popular midsize LH cars to fix a 5-cent part. It was found that a defective washer in the steering system could disintegrate, making it harder to control the car.[7]

■ ASSIGN RESPONSIBILITY FOR PURCHASING TO ONE PERSON

While capable subordinates, such as specialty buyers, may be delegated the authority to order in their areas of expertise, in general *one person should be given the overall purchasing responsibility.* But that person should ask for—and get—the help of people knowledgeable in areas such as engineering and planning.

Stockouts are sales lost because an item is not in stock.

Those doing the purchasing should be aware of trends and special situations that can affect operations and should call situations such as the following to your attention:

"Sorry, girls! We just didn't order enough UltraToys. Can you come back next week?"

(© 1996 by Margaret P. Megginson. Reprinted with permission.)

1. *Expected changes in price.* Buying later for expected decreases in price or buying increased quantities for expected inflation in price can result in savings. However, **stockouts,** which are sales lost because an item is not in stock when customers want it, and inventory costs that are too heavy should be guarded against.
2. *Expected changes in demand.* Seasonal products and high-fashion items fall into this category.
3. *Orders for specialty goods.* The quantity ordered should match expected demand, so no material is left over. Because demand for these items is usually unknown, forecasts should include estimates of losses that may occur from stockouts or old and stale inventory.
4. *Short supply of materials,* as the following classic example illustrates.

> Sally Von Werlhof started Salaminder Inc. in 1974 to design, produce, and sell only top-of-the-line American-made western apparel. Growth was steady until the 1980 movie *Urban Cowboy* caused the demand for western wear to skyrocket. Salaminder was swamped with orders and expanded its work force to 60 employees. But sales plummeted in July 1981, when the fad died just as suddenly as it had begun.[8]

■ SELECTING THE RIGHT SUPPLIER

You will be more successful in purchasing if you can find several acceptable sources of goods and services. Because reliability in delivery and quality affects nearly all operations, suppliers can be valuable sources of information for various aspects of operations, and suppliers can provide valuable service.

You can find many good sources by consulting the Yellow Pages (www.yellowpages.com), the *Thomas Register of American Manufacturers* (www.thomasregister.com), the *McRae Bluebook,* newspapers, trade journals, and publications of research organizations. In addition, visits to trade shows and merchandise marts give you an opportunity to view exhibits and talk with salespeople. Internet and World Wide Web networks (to be discussed in Chapter 15) can be used to obtain information on possible sources. Many small firms are now hiring expert consultants when purchasing becomes complex.[9]

Types of Suppliers

As discussed in Chapter 8, you can purchase from brokers, jobbers, wholesalers, producers, or others. Each provides a particular type of service. Notice that Anders Book Stores buys new books from the producers (the publishers) but buys used ones from wholesalers (used-book companies) and students. Also, supplies and other items are ordered from a variety of sources.

Use Few or Many Suppliers?

Should you buy from one, a few, or many suppliers? A single source of supply can result in a closer and more personalized relationship, so if you use one source, when shortages occur you should receive better service than when many sources are used. Also, discounts may be obtained with larger-volume buying. If one seller can supply a wide assortment of the items needed, the cost of ordering is reduced. On the other hand, multiple sources provide a greater variety of goods and often better terms. Most small firms use several sources.

As indicated earlier, many companies are trying to reduce the number of suppliers used. However, a countertrend developed during the 1990s—namely, to bring minority suppliers into the vendor mainstream, as the following example illustrates.

> Ten years ago, 54-year-old Frank Brooks, CEO of Chicago's Economic Development Corporation, knew nothing about the food-processing business. Then a business associate told him McDonald's (www.mcdonalds.com) was looking for members of diverse groups to be vendors for its stores. So in 1985 Brooks established Brooks Sausage Company to produce and supply McDonald's midwestern outlets with pork sausages. First, however, Brooks learned the business as an apprentice—under the supervision of McDonald's—at OSI Industries.
>
> Brooks Sausage is now McDonald's "foremost minority-owned vendor," supplying several thousand restaurants. About 35 percent of Brooks's output goes to McDonald's outlets in Japan.[10]

Sometimes it's desirable—or even necessary—to use a single source for specialized items. The following example illustrates how this happened in one interesting development.

> Several years ago, Wynton M. and Carolyn Blount donated the land and money to build the Wynton M. Blount Cultural Park in Montgomery, Alabama, where the Alabama Shakespeare Festival is located (www.mainstreetusa.com/clients/al). Because they were great admirers of Queen Elizabeth II's beautiful black swans, they inquired as to where she had found them. The answer came back from England that they had been bought at a farm just a few miles from Montgomery—the only known source of supply of the beautiful birds.

Investigating Potential Suppliers

Potential supply sources can be checked for factors such as quality of output, price, desire to serve, reliability, transportation, terms of payment, and guarantees and warranties. Because all these factors affect your company's performance, a minimum standard must be set for each.

Suppliers should not be chosen on the basis of price alone, for quality and/or service may suffer if the supplier has to lower prices to obtain your order. Instead, suppliers should be chosen to meet carefully set quality and service standards. These standards can be used to ensure acceptable quality without paying for quality higher than needed.

Evaluating Supplier Performance

Just as you investigate potential suppliers, you should also evaluate their performance. Some services publish ratings of products. Also, while it requires some time and effort, you could develop a rating system of your own to use in selecting, evaluating, and retaining suppliers. Rating systems pick out important factors such as quality, service, and reliability, as well as price, and then use those to evaluate each supplier.

Sharp Corporation (www.sharp.usa.com) uses a rating system of this kind in its Memphis plant to evaluate its many suppliers, most of which are small firms. A copy of its creed, "Practice Sincerity and Creativity," is given to each potential supplier with a statement that Sharp "expects 100% quality parts," delivered precisely on schedule. Suppliers who agree to this stipulation become Sharp's suppliers and receive a periodic report card showing how they rate on satisfying quality, price, prompt delivery, and other standards.[11]

■ ESTABLISHING AN EFFECTIVE PURCHASING PROCEDURE

In addition to deciding on the suppliers to use, you must establish a purchasing procedure to ensure effective ordering and receiving of materials. While there is no one best way, Figure 12–1 presents a computer flowchart of a well-designed purchase order system. The procedure should accomplish several major objectives concerned with purchasing. The proper materials, parts, goods, and so forth needed to produce the goods or services must be obtained. The total price paid for the items purchased must be satisfactory for sale of the finished product. Moreover, the amount of resulting inventory should be in balance with customer demand to minimize total costs. Finally, a simple—yet effective—inventory control system should be established.

Requisitioning Goods or Services

Effective small companies establish standards for various aspects of the quality of their products and/or services. These standards are usually developed with the help of professional/technical people who are knowledgeable in technical, marketing, and production areas. The derived standards are then converted into specifications to be sent with orders to suppliers (see item 1 in Figure 12–1).

The request to purchase materials or services (called a purchase requisition) can originate from many sources. If a service is needed, the request usually comes from the user of that service, as when the accounting manager requests an outside audit, the personnel manager needs to install or change an insurance program, or the marketing manager needs to place an ad with an agency. But when materials are needed, the request can originate in any of several ways, such as when: (1) someone observes that inventory is low, (2) the system automatically identifies the need for an item, (3) an operating manager requests it, (4) a customer requests a given item, or (5) the purchasing manager observes some special conditions that indicate the need to purchase an item.

Purchasing by retailers poses different problems from purchasing by a producer. Figure 12–2 (on page 304) shows a suggested schedule for a retailer to buy and sell style goods. The procedure operates as follows.

Figure 12–1
Purchase Order Process Flowchart

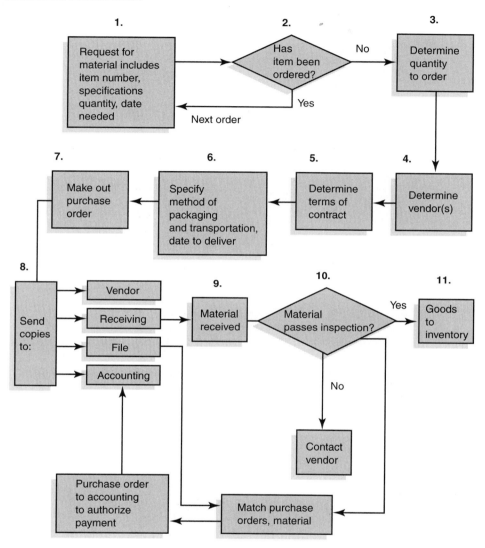

In the spring or summer of 1999, a retailer visits a trade show—or consults suppliers—and places orders based on evaluation of styles and plans. Between August—when the goods are received—and February, goods are sold, more goods are produced, and plans for the spring and summer are completed. Goods are received in time for the selling seasons; inventory and sales are checked to consider reordering. End-of-season sales late in the winter and summer can help reduce inventory. The cycle is repeated for each selling season.

Making and Placing the Purchase Order

There are many ways of placing orders for needed goods (item 7 in Figure 12–1), depending on your needs and the supplier's demands. Issuing **purchase orders** is very common, since they

A **purchase order** tells the supplier to ship you a given amount of an item at a given quality and price.

Figure 12–2
Schedule of Semiannual Production and Retail of Style Goods

Activity	Summer 1999	Fall 1999	Winter 1999–2000	Spring 2000	Summer 2000
Retailer plans and orders		Plans S&S 2000 sales		Plans F&W 2000–2001 sales	
		Selects styles and orders	Plans sales and promotion (*Reorders F&W 1999–2000*)	Select styles and orders	Plans sales and promotion (*Recorders S&S 2000*)
Retailer receives and sells goods	Receives F&W 1999–2000 goods	Sells F&W 1999–2000 goods			
		Regular sales	Markdown sales Receives S&S 2000 goods	Sells S&S 2000 goods	
				Regular sales	Markdown sales
Producer receives orders and produces goods		Produces S&S 2000 goods		Produces F&W 2000–2001 goods	

Note: F&W = fall and winter; S&S = spring and summer.

Standing orders set predetermined times to ship given quantities of needed items, at a set price.

become legal records for the buyer and seller. Establishing **standing orders** with the supplier simplifies the purchasing procedure and allows for long-range planning. It involves setting schedules for delivery of goods in predetermined quantities and times and at agreed-to terms.

Technology enters the picture at this point. As indicated earlier, many big purchasers are reducing the number of vendors they deal with. In the selection process, they are "eliminating companies that are behind the curve in technology."[12] In other words, if a vendor doesn't have the appropriate technology to adequately serve a purchaser, the purchaser will look elsewhere.

> For example, Aspen Publishers, Inc. (www.aspenpub.com), was only two years old when it hit $1 million a year in sales. One competitive edge was its ability to receive orders and payments electronically from customers such as J. C. Penney Company (www.jcpenney.com) and Dillard Department Stores Inc. (www.dillards.com). According to Aspen's CEO, Richard Feldstein, embracing computer and network technology "levels the playing field for small business."[13]

Paying a Satisfactory Price

The importance of the price of goods and services has been mentioned earlier in this chapter. *However, quality and price must be balanced against each other.* Customers naturally want high quality, but high quality tends to result in high production costs and a resulting high price. A low price is also attractive but generally reflects lower quality. Therefore, selection should not be made on the basis of price alone.

Prices set by suppliers are only one element of cost to be considered. There are added costs such as transportation, paperwork, reliability of the supplier, processing, and payment. Selection of a supplier should be based on total cost. Also, as discussed in Chapter 7, the possibility of discounts and allowances should be investigated.

Receiving the Items

Receiving the ordered goods and placing them in inventory (items 9, 10, and 11 in Figure 12–1), are the last steps in the purchasing procedure. A copy of the purchase order, including the desired specifications, is sent to those receiving the goods. On arrival, the condition of the goods is checked, and they are checked against the order to make sure they are the desired items, in the correct color, material, size, quantity, and so on. Computers and proper receiving procedures help detect deviations from these standards and speed up the process. As discussed in Chapter 8, transportation systems are constantly improving their service.

> For example, Rod and Kim Grimm recently drove their refrigerated Kenworth truck from Los Angeles to the small coastal town of Wells, Maine, stopping on the way only for "a few truck-stop meals" and fuel. The 3,195-mile, three-day trip was to transport 1. 5 million shrimp, which originated in Thailand, to Wells, where they had already been advertised by Shaw's Supermarkets Inc. (www.shaws.com), the New England chain buying them. The Grimms were four hours late leaving the warehouse in Los Angeles because the warehouse workers took four hours—including a dinner break—to load the 3,300 frozen boxes. Yet they completed their haul at 12:30 AM Tuesday, half an hour earlier than expected. The Grimms had averaged more than 1,000 miles a day.[14]

Using Computers to Aid Purchasing and Inventory Control

The recent great advances in electronic processing of all sorts of information and the drop in costs (as will be discussed in Chapter 15) have revolutionized the purchasing and inventory operations. Small companies are increasingly using computers to keep track of inventory items, spot replenishment needs, identify sources of supply, and provide information needed for ordering and checking the accuracy of receipts. Computers now largely provide the information needed by the buyer to use in the purchasing process. For example, use of the fax (in item 8 in Figure 12–1) speeds up the transfer of information. Steps 1 through 7 can also be performed automatically with a computer and selected programs.

■ CONTROLLING INVENTORY

An **inventory** is a formal list of property of a business, or—the way we will use the term— the property so listed. No business can operate without some kind of inventory, if only office supplies. Therefore, there is by definition no way to avoid carrying inventory—no matter how hard you may try—and *the best you can do is manage its movement and control its cost.*

An **inventory** is a formal list of all the property of a business, or the property so listed.

Many retailers tend to forget this truth, especially at Christmas. "Like a child who never finds the long-dreamed-about pony beneath the Christmas tree, [many] retailers hope every year for stupendous sales growth—and don't get it." Instead, they generally wind up with "an oversupply of goods," leading to inflated inventory and "hefty markdowns and pressures on profits."[15]

The Role Played by Inventory

Inventory is carried to disconnect one segment of the operating process from another so each part can operate at its optimum level. A crude example is in your home. If you did not have a supply of food, you would have to go out, find some, buy it, bring it home, and prepare it every time you were hungry. Having surplus food in your pantry or refrigerator,

Figure 12–3

Diagram of Material Flow and Inventory

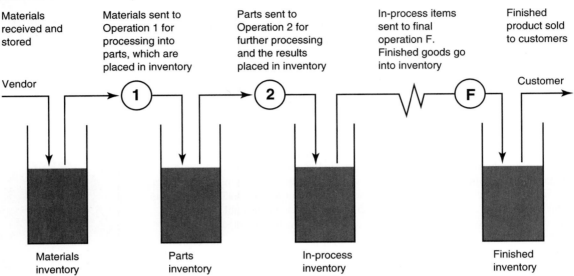

however, you can buy more food at your convenience, keep it as inventory, and then process it when you get hungry.

The same holds true in a producing plant. Figure 12–3 shows what happens from the receipt of raw materials, through each of three operations, to final sale to customers. Inventories are shown at different levels at different stages of the operation, and the inventory level at a given stage depends on what activities have occurred in the operations process.

A similar situation occurs in retail stores. Retailers receive goods, store them, put them on display for sale, sell them to customers, and then order more of the goods. The level of inventory at any given time depends on the amount of goods bought—and stored in inventory—relative to the quantity sold. Thus, a retailer must have enough goods in inventory after an order is received to last until the next order is placed and received. Figure 12–4 illustrates this process. When the goods on the left are received, they are stored with similar goods as inventory. Then, after being put on display and gradually sold, they are replaced by other goods.

Types of Inventory

Inventories exist in small firms at all times in one or more of the following forms: (1) finished items on display for sale to customers; (2) batches of goods, such as materials, parts, and subassemblies, awaiting processing or delivery; (3) repair parts awaiting use; (4) supplies for use in offices, stores, or shops, or for use in processing other goods; and (5) miscellaneous items, such as tools placed in a toolroom.

These inventories, especially the first two kinds, represent a major investment by all businesses—large ones as well as small. Many companies have failed because their inventory tied up too much money or the items in inventory became obsolete, damaged, or lost.

Figure 12–4

Goods Flow and Inventory in a Retail Firm

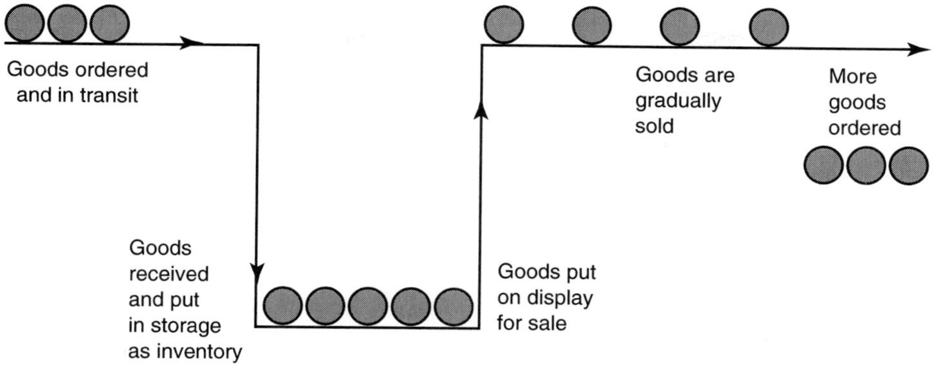

Goods ordered
and in transit

Goods are
gradually
sold

More
goods
ordered

Goods
received
and put
in storage
as inventory

Goods put
on display
for sale

Inventory Mix

According to the **80-20 rule,** approximately 80 percent of a company's income usually comes from 20 percent of its products. Companies having multiple products, parts, and services should therefore concentrate their attention on those items that have the greatest impact on costs and income. Similarly, 20 percent of the items in inventory represent 80 percent of the cost. Companies should be sure that these items are truly needed.

According to the **80-20 rule,** approximately 80 percent of a company's income usually comes from 20 percent of its products.

Costs of Carrying Inventory

Having inventory on hand costs a small business much more than most people realize. The costs of carrying inventory consist of: (1) the cost of providing and maintaining storage space, (2) insurance and taxes, (3) profits lost because money is tied up in inventory (called *opportunity cost*), (4) theft and destruction, and (5) obsolescence and deterioration of the items. Estimates of the sum of these costs range from 15 percent to over 100 percent of their value; 20 to 25 percent is the amount most frequently mentioned.

> One small Atlanta bookseller chain, called "Chapter 11, The Discount Bookstore Inc.," is able to compete with the giant chains by discounting best-sellers 30 percent—as the giants do—and *all books at least 11 percent.* Chapter 11, which stresses price in all its ads, has grown from one store to 11 over the past 7 years by putting *small stores* in low-cost strip malls that are "convenient to customers fatigued by Atlanta's . . . traffic." Chapter 11 stores are only 3,000 to 6,000 square feet, as compared to 20,000 or more for the superstores. Their inventory costs are low, as only a limited amount can be carried in the small space.[16]

Determining When to Place an Order

Figure 12–3 shows the changing inventory levels as materials are ordered, processed, stored, and sold. Figure 12–4 shows how levels change as a retailer orders goods, stores them, and then sells them. The real problem in both these instances is knowing when is the most appropriate time to order needed items.

The optimum inventory level can be maintained by having items arrive just in time for sale to customers. The actual system tries to approach zero inventory, but normally balances inventory carrying costs and stockout costs. This calculation is not easy, and you will make mistakes, but with rational analysis, practice, and a certain amount of intuition—and luck—you will make it.

Determining How Much to Order

The order quantity is determined by the level of inventory and the order interval. When orders are placed at *certain, regular intervals,* the order quantity should be set to bring the inventory level up to a predetermined amount. When *inventory level* determines the time to order, the order quantity is a fixed amount called the **economic order quantity (EOQ).**

The **economic order quantity (EOQ)** is the quantity to purchase that balances the cost of placing the order with the cost of carrying the inventory.

The EOQ model identifies the inventory order size that will minimize the annual costs of ordering and carrying inventories. In practice, there are many variations of the basic EOQ model. For example, the basic model assumes that the price of the inventory items will remain fixed. On the other hand, some EOQ formulas can take into consideration varying prices resulting from quantity discounts. Still other formulas can be used to determine the optimum lot size for items the company produces for itself. However, the basic EOQ model is useful in practice because it helps small business owners understand the role of the cost of ordering and carrying inventory.[17]

In summary, the EOQ is determined by balancing (1) the cost of placing an order for items to be placed in inventory with (2) the costs involved in carrying that inventory in stock. Refer again to Figure 12–2 which shows a situation in which the order size is determined by how much the company can sell during a season.

■ OPERATIONS PLANNING AND CONTROL

As shown in Chapter 5, operations planning and control begins when you determine what business you're going into, what product(s) you will sell, and what resources are needed to produce the quantity you expect. If you're to have products available when demanded by customers, you must carefully forecast and plan for sales. Predicting the sales of a small company with any degree of accuracy is difficult, but even crude estimates are better than none, since considerable cost is involved in trying to serve customers if the items they seek are not in stock.

Handling Variations in Demand

Demand for products varies from one period to another for such reasons as changing lifestyles, economic conditions, and seasons. Most sales of goods and services have seasonal variations. Therefore, you may be constantly hiring, training, and laying off employees; not using facilities efficiently; changing levels of inventory; and facing cash flow problems and product shortages.

Several operating plans may be used to cope at least partially with seasonal variations. The most popular such plans are these:

- Allow operations to rise and fall according to changing sales demands. This requires periodically hiring and laying off workers.
- Use self-service to reduce the number of employees and hire temporary or part-time workers during peak periods.
- Use inventory buildups (or drawdowns) to smooth out operations.
- Carry complementary products, such as winter and summer items.

- Subcontract production during maximum demand periods.
- Lose sales by not expanding operations to meet increased demand.
- Use special inducements to stimulate sales during periods of low demand.

Scheduling Operations

Scheduling involves setting the times and sequences needed to perform specialized activities, including when and how long it takes to do them. You are often faced with this problem of scheduling. For example, you try to schedule your classes to minimize inconvenience and for your greatest benefit. Then you have to schedule appointments with the doctor or dentist around them. Computers are now being used effectively by many firms to perform scheduling operations. Look again at Figure 12–2 which shows a schedule of the steps involved in selling style items.

A major entertainment event poses massive scheduling challenges, including scheduling the design and creation of clothing and costumes.

> For example, Miss USA Pageant (www.missusa.com) was such an event. The contestants' evening gowns were designed by Sherri Hill of Norman, Oklahoma. Some of the other costumes were designed and produced by Los Angeles costume designer Pete Menefee, who in addition took a dozen of Hill's dress designs and made them in different fabrics. Since each contestant required a different pattern, 120 different dresses were made for the women to choose from.
>
> The dresses, made in Los Angeles, were shipped to the contest site in Mobile, Alabama, where Menefee altered them with the help of local seamstresses. In addition, he saw that each young woman had the proper hosiery, shoes dyed to match, and costume jewelry to go with the gowns.[18]

Scheduling is setting the times and sequences required to do work.

Controlling Operations

Even if you make the best of plans, communicate them effectively, and use the best workers and materials to perform the work effectively, controls are still needed. Without adequate control over the operations, the process will fail.

In simple systems, the comparison of planned performance with actual performance can be made informally by personal observation. Usually, though, a system of formal checks is needed. Standards are set, data on actual performance are collected, standards and actual data are compared, and exceptions are reported.

■ QUALITY AND ITS CONTROL

In recent years, American consumers have shown increasing concern about the quality of U.S. goods and services, since so often foreign companies produce and sell products of superior quality. Now, though, many U.S. companies are taking steps to improve their products. This is particularly true of small companies, as shown in Chapter 8.

While small businesses must compete in the market with large companies, many are finding that emphasizing quality and reliability and designing output to match customer needs are better tactics than lowering prices.

> This is what is happening to the Morgan Motor Company in Malvern Link, Worcestershire, England, which has been selling its unique car since 1910. The company now produces 500 handmade cars each year to customers' individual orders. About 30 of these cars are sold to Americans. There is a long waiting list, and the wait time

from ordering to final delivery is four to five years in Europe and one to two years in the United States.

The company is trying to increase production to about 750 cars a year by expanding its factory operations and cutting waste. It also hopes to export more cars to the United States. But the company does not want to lose its quality advantage by increasing output beyond its staff's ability to maintain standards. An indication of the problem is the "thousands of colors, 40 different upholsteries, and four types of seats" the customer can choose from for each car.[19]

What Is Quality?

Quality refers to product characteristics and/or the probability of meeting established standards.

The term **quality** can have many meanings, two of which are significant to small business owners. First, it refers to characteristics of products being judged. Second, it means the probability that products will meet established standards. In the discussion that follows, we will use the meanings interchangeably.

Assessment of the quality of a product is relative; it depends on the expectations of the evaluator—the customer. Customers who are used to high-quality goods and services tend to be much more critical of purchases than those accustomed to lower standards. Because small companies usually cannot cater to all quality levels, they must set their sights on the level demanded by their customers and try to reach some level of total quality.

The idea of Total Quality (TQ) has not evolved as a theory but has developed from actual practice in manufacturing settings and has validated itself through the economic successes of adopting companies. In order for TQ to work, the principles and practices involved must be part of an organization's fabric and lifeblood.[20] The application of TQ is most commonly known as Total Quality Management (TQM) (www.tqmnet.com). TQM is used not only in manufacturing but also in services. One of the best-known organizations practicing quality service is Disney (www.disney.com).

The Disney Institute (www.disneyseminars.com) periodically offers three-and-a-half–day behind-the-scenes seminars at the Walt Disney World® Resort to give participants "new insights into customers, business, and operating systems." Disney's seminars, "The Disney Approach to Quality Service," are designed to show how Disney's best management practices can be applied to many service and retail organizations.[21]

Quality involves many characteristics of a product: strength, color, taste, smell, content, weight, tone, look, capacity, accomplishment, creativity, and reliability, among others. Part of the quality of a *service* are such factors as salespersons' smiles, attentiveness, friendly greetings, and willing assistance. Standards to meet the desires of customers must be established for each characteristic.

Customers tend to want high quality, but often they want to pay only a limited price for the product. Still, some qualities, such as a friendly greeting, cost little; others, such as precision jewelry settings, cost much. Quality-level analysis is thus based on the value of quality to the customer and the cost of producing that level of quality. To make the decision, you must ask the following questions: Who are my customers? What quality do they want? What quality of product can I provide, and at what cost?

How do you determine where to set the quality level? Market research, questionnaires, talking to customers, comparison with competitors' products, and trial and error are a few of the methods. Recent advances in technology have helped raise the level of quality attainable—while keeping costs low.

Figure 12–5
How Quality Circles Operate

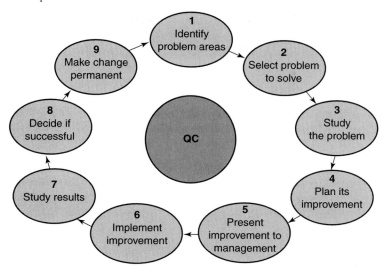

A quality circle consists of a few (usually 4 to 10) members who know the problem area. They proceed according to the above diagram.

Improving and Controlling Quality

There are many ways a small business can improve quality, but we will discuss only three: (1) setting up quality circles, (2) designing quality into the product and operations, and (3) installing a good quality control process.

Establishing Quality Circles   Many progressive companies report good results from using quality circle programs. As you can see from Figure 12–5, in **quality circles** small groups of workers meet regularly to identify and develop ways to solve company problems, especially quality. The members, who are usually not supervisors, receive training in areas such as problem identification, communications, and problem solving. Also, as they meet, they may have access to resource people who can provide further expertise. Quality circles seem to be more successful when top management gives them unrestricted support.

Designing Quality into the Process   Since quality is achieved during the production of a product, the processes must be designed to produce the desired quality. Machines must be capable of turning out the product within set tolerances, workers must be trained to produce that level of quality, and materials and goods must be purchased that meet the stated standards. In service companies, employees must be trained to understand a customer's needs and to perform the work to the customer's satisfaction. If the process or employees cannot produce the proper quality of output, no type of control can correct the situation.

Installing a Quality Control System   Quality control, or quality assurance, is a system used by a producer to ensure that the finished goods or services meet the expectations of customers, as advocated by the late W. Edwards Deming, the "Quality Guru."* Deming condensed his

Quality circles are small work groups meeting periodically to find ways to improve quality and performance.

---

*Deming died in 1993 at the age of 93, having achieved considerable fame as a quality expert in Japan, where the country's top quality award is the Deming Medal.

Figure 12–6
Deming's 14 Points

W. Edwards Deming distilled his self-developed methods of management into 14 points. Though they have been described and elaborated on in hundreds of books, videos, and seminars, in their original form they still provide the bedrock of most Deming processes.

1. Create constancy of purpose toward improvement of product and service.
2. Adopt the new philosophy.
3. Cease dependence on mass inspection.
4. End the practice of awarding business on the basis of a price tag.
5. Improve constantly and forever the system of production and service.
6. Institute training.
7. Institute leadership.
8. Drive out fear.
9. Break down barriers between departments.
10. Eliminate slogans, exhortations, and targets for the work force.
11. Eliminate quotas.
12. Remove barriers to pride of workmanship.
13. Institute a vigorous program of education and self-improvement.
14. Take action to accomplish the transformation. It's everybody's job.

Source: Reprinted from Loretta Owens and Mark Henricks, "Quality Time," *Entrepreneur,* October 1995, p. 161. Reprinted with permission of *Entrepreneur* magazine.

management philosophy and techniques into his famous "14 Points," as shown in Figure 12–6. These points stress the necessity for owners and top managers to become involved in continuous improvement processes, as the following example illustrates.

> Four brothers from Taiwan decided to open an instant-noodle factory in Lianjin, China, six years ago. At first they made very little profit because of the low profit margin—one-tenth of a cent per packet. The brothers then changed their tactics to answer one of the deepest anxieties of Chinese life: "When do I eat, and will it be clean?" They put their instant noodles in a shrink-wrapped Styrofoam bowl and sold it for 24 cents, which compared favorably to the 60-cent price of their only competitor, imported from Japan and Taiwan. The product was so successful that the factory had immediate shortages. To assure continued high quality, eldest brother Wei Ying-chan taste-tests his company's noodles every morning for breakfast.[22]

Regardless of what methods or techniques are used to achieve it, effective quality control involves at least the following steps:

- Setting standards for the desired quality range.
- Measuring actual performance.
- Comparing that performance with established standards.
- Making corrections when needed.

Some standards may be measured by instruments, such as rulers or gauges for length; but color, taste, and other standards must be evaluated by skilled individuals. Measurement may be made by selected people at selected spots in the process, usually on receipt of material and always before the product goes to the customer. Quality can also be controlled by feedback from customers, as shown in Figure 12–7.

Figure 12–7

Example of Feedback Quality Control in a Restaurant

Management Encourages Your Comments

Date 5/19/00

Waiter or waitress Phyllis

Please circle meal   Breakfast   (Lunch)   Dinner

	Yes	No
1. Were you greeted by host or hostess promptly and courteously?	✓	
2. Was your server prompt, courteous, and attractive in appearance?	✓	
3. Was the quality of food to your expectations?		✓
4. Was the table setting and condition of overall restaurant appearance pleasing and in good taste?	✓	
5. Will you return to our restaurant?		✓
6. Will you recommend our restaurant to your friends and associates?		✓

Comments:

Food was overcooked. Potatoes were left-overs. Meat was tough. This was my second visit and I brought a friend with me. We were both very disappointed.

Please drop this in our quality improvement box provided as you exit room.

Thank you and have a good day.

WHAT YOU SHOULD HAVE LEARNED

1. Purchases are a small company's largest single type of cost. Goods and services must be obtained at the proper price, quality, and time, and in the proper quantity. One person should be made responsible for the purchasing function.

2. Sources of supply must be found and investigated and one or more suppliers selected. Reliability in delivery and quality affect nearly all operations. You must also decide whether to use one or multiple suppliers.

3.   An effective purchasing procedure consists of (*a*) determining the items needed, in what quantity, from whom to purchase, and the terms of the contract; (*b*) sending the purchase order; (*c*) receiving the goods; (*d*) inspecting them; and (*e*) paying for them.

4.   Inventory is carried to disconnect one part of the operating process from another so each part can operate effectively. Inventory takes many forms, from raw materials to finished products. The cost of carrying inventory consists of providing and maintaining storage space, insurance and taxes, profits lost from money tied up in it, obsolescence and deterioration, and theft and destruction. The cost of inadequate inventory is dissatisfied customers from stockouts.

5.   Operations planning and control start with a forecast of sales from which operating plans are developed. Alternative plans for seasonal sales include: (*a*) producing to demand, (*b*) using self-service and part-time workers to help meet peak demand, (*c*) producing at a constant rate and inventorying for future demand, (*d*) carrying complementary products, (*e*) subcontracting high demand, (*f*) not meeting high demand, and (*g*) using off-season sales inducements.

Scheduling is setting the times and sequences required to do work. Control of operations is obtained by reacting to exceptions to plans.

6.   In small firms, the emphasis should be on quality of goods and services rather than on low price. The term *quality* refers both to acceptable characteristics and to reliability of the product. Quality circles have been used by small companies to improve performance.

Quality control involves (*a*) setting standards, (*b*) measuring performance, (*c*) comparing actual performance with standards, and (*d*) making corrections. Sampling inspections and customer feedback are used to check performance or quality.

QUESTIONS FOR DISCUSSION

1.   Discuss the advantages and disadvantages of buying locally versus buying from a distant seller.

2.   What are the advantages and disadvantages of shopping at a single store rather than at several?

3.   A company orders widgets in batches such as 1,000 units. The company uses a constant number each month (say 2,000) in production. Show how the inventory level changes over time between orders. What factors would cause you to change the order size up or down?

4.   How would you make an economic study to determine the quantity of a food item to buy for your family on each trip to the store? How often should purchases be made?

5.   In some parts of the country, building construction varies seasonally. Is this a problem for company management? What decisions must management make concerning these variations?

6.   Many times, sales personnel do not practice good selling relations. How would you control the quality of this type of service?

7.   What is quality? How can it be measured? How can it be controlled?

8.   Outline instructions for installing a new quality circle.

9.   In Figure 12–2, styles are changed twice a year. What changes would be required with seasonal changes of four or more styles?

10. What would you do if you received a large number of customer response forms with comments similar to those in Figure 12–7?

11. What effect on your company would the delivery of an increased percentage of defective parts have? What would you do about this?

UNIVERSAL FLEET SERVICES, INC. (UFS): SELLING A UNIQUE SERVICE

David V. deGruy, president of Universal Fleet Services, Inc. (UFS), graduated from college with a degree in finance and a concentration in math. Upon graduation, he accepted employment with International Paper Company (IP) as a computer programmer and systems analyst. Following his advancement to several positions of increasing responsibility, his last position with the company was procuring (by purchase or lease) and maintaining the company's fleet of forklifts. These are self-propelled machines for hoisting and transporting large rolls of paper or other heavy objects by means of steel fingers inserted under the load or a clamp around a roll of paper.

After becoming skilled in the field, deGruy developed a system for evaluating the purchase, use, and disposal of the company's equipment. He developed a process for managing the company's forklift fleet, which saved the company approximately $5 million a year. Additionally, he developed a system for evaluating the performance of forklifts offered by different manufacturers and employed this strategy in his evaluations for IP.

DeGruy developed a computer database to track information on all aspects of each truck forklift, including its purchase price, usage, maintenance, repair records,

useful life, and the most economical time to trade in the forklift. Figure 12–8 illustrates the inverse relationship between ownership cost and maintenance cost and the optimal replacement point. It's obvious that keeping a forklift in operation beyond its optimal replacement point would more than double its hourly cost.

In 1997, International Paper moved the operation in which deGruy was involved to a distant state, and deGruy decided to resign and start his own business rather than leave his hometown. The knowledge and experience he had gained at IP convinced him there was a need in industry for the kind of service he could provide. While at IP, he had been unsuccessful in locating an organization that could provide these services. If other organizations could also realize substantial savings in time and money and reduce interruptions in their productivity, surely they would be interested. He incorporated his company as Universal Fleet Services, Inc., with himself as president. He also has an associate who is a specialist in fleet operations. During the company's initial period, deGruy spent his time refining his earlier work and developing a comprehensive program of integrated services designed to provide the following services for a client:

Figure 12–8
Forklift Economic Life

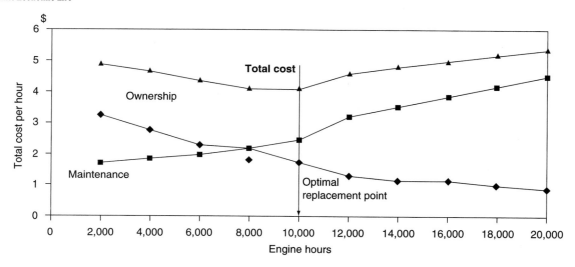

1. Survey and analyze the client's forklift fleet in order to properly establish and institute practices that will then become the standard for all its operations. In the process, procedures and safety requirements are determined in order to maximize the life cycle of each vehicle.

2. Evaluate the client's maintenance cost and the efficient utilization of its fleet. These findings are compared with UFS's data bank of comparable companies and operations to determine the proper parameters of acceptability and utilization of its capital. This includes an analysis of leasing versus buying the vehicles under specific, individual circumstances.

3. Effect other savings for the client by using the leveraged volume of forklifts and parts purchased for the multiple facilities and client base of UFS.

4. Provide monitoring and analysis to clients, which includes in-depth information and recommendations for equipment to buy, rotation of forklifts, and how to dispose of them when needed. It also deals with parts procurement, warranty issues, OSHA requirements, and training options for the client.

5. Reduce materials handling costs by implementing individualized programs for the client. Some of these entail forklift maintenance programs, including standby (extra) forklifts to be used in emergencies or during servicing of the regular equipment. From these programs, UFS issues interpretive reports to its clients. These reports include operating cost analyses showing average cost per hour for forklift operations and exception reports showing which forklifts are operating outside UFS's established norms. These can be sorted by individual departments or units to pinpoint responsibility.

6. Prepare a list of upcoming replacements. This list shows which forklifts should be replaced or, if they are under a lease agreement, those that are approaching the term to be turned back in. Then a "life cycle" report will identify graphically each forklift's current position in relation to its total useful life. Finally, if the client so desires, special reports can be made available with data identifying forklifts that have possibly been misused, abused, or neglected. Also included would be suggestions for what to do about these conditions.

Since UFS is an independent company, it can offer its clients an unbiased assessment of competitive pricing of multiple manufacturers' brands. While the client can choose the brand or brands that have proven valuable in the past, UFS offers standardized methods and practices for determining efficiency and reducing cost. Because this concept of service was new and applies primarily to large, well-established companies, deGruy had difficulty "selling" the idea to potential clients. It took nearly a year to generate enough interest in the new approach to attract a client. Recently, however, deGruy signed an agreement with a forklift manufacturer and a major steel company to service their large fleet of forklifts. Under the agreement the manufacturer will perform maintenance on all the steel company's forklifts. In addition, a standby forklift would be kept on the premises to use while scheduled maintenance or repairs were performed on the forklifts under contract. This standby forklift will also be available for the steel company to use for extra work. The company will have to pay only for the extra service time and not for when the standby forklift is replacing others being repaired or serviced.

UFS prepares reports on each of the company's forklifts, using a profile that includes the purchase date; the use, maintenance costs, and repair history of the unit; and when it is to be traded. When trade-in time comes, UFS acts on behalf of the company to purchase or lease new equipment at the most favorable price and terms. In effect, the company has turned over to UFS all responsibility for ensuring the proper management and efficiency of its fleet.

In late 1998, UFS attracted another major company as a client. With his experience and these two references, deGruy will now be able to attract other potential clients to his unique service. It seems the new company is on its way to success.

Questions

1. To what extent did deGruy's education and work experience prepare him for his new venture?

2. Evaluate the way deGruy went about developing and operating his company.

3. Explain how the service being provided can help a client's purchases, inventory, quality control, and profit.

4. What suggestions would you make to UFS as to how to "sell" its service to potential clients?

Source: Prepared by Leon C. Megginson from discussions with, and information provided by, David V. deGruy.

EDDIE & COMPANY: EXCEEDING THE RELEVANT RANGE

Eddie & Company is a small manufacturer located in the North Central part of the United States. The company manufactures auto and truck axles for automobile producers. Most of its output is sold to one of the larger auto companies. Because its sales have recently increased beyond all expectation, that company now wants Eddie & Company to increase its production level to satisfy the increased demand.

This request poses a serious dilemma for the owners of Eddie & Company. It would have to considerably increase production in order to ship more axles to the automaker. However, it has already been operating at full capacity just to meet the demands of its customers, including the automaker, when sales were low. The only ways to satisfy the increased demand would be (1) to buy the needed new products from its competitors and resell them to the automaker—at no profit—or (2) to increase its own production capacity in order to satisfy the demand.

The first alternative would satisfy the short-run increase in demand, but not the long-range one. But the second alternative of increasing production capacity would pose different problems. First, there is no assurance that the increased demand from the automaker will be permanent, and Eddie & Company could find itself with unused capacity. Second, this alternative would mean increased fixed expenses, which would raise the company's break-even point. And this increase would continue even if the automaker cut back its orders to the original level.

Questions

1. What options are available to the company?
2. What would you do if you faced the same situation?
3. Would you buy the product from your competitor to meet the contract? Explain.
4. Would you add the additional capacity? Explain.

VI

FINANCIAL PLANNING AND CONTROL

As we have shown throughout this text, the requirements for success in small business include an understanding of the importance of financial management; knowledge of how financial relationships affect profit or loss; and the devotion of time, energy, and initiative to planning and controlling financial activities. We discuss in this part how such planning and control ensure that the business will not only survive but also grow and develop.

Chapter 13 explains the need for, and methods of, planning for a profit and guides you through the steps of planning the profit for a hypothetical company. It also covers the basic financial structure of a business.

Chapter 14 explores the basic structure of control and shows how to collect information and compare actual performance with standard performance. The design and use of budgets and budgetary control are also covered, along with the use of ratio analysis. The chapter focuses on the taxes that a small business must pay and how to collect, handle, and report those taxes.

Chapter 15 deals with information technology. It emphasizes the importance of gathering and maintaining information, and explains how to record it. It also emphasizes the need for, and explains how to use, computers in small firms.

13

PLANNING FOR PROFIT

Earning a profit—staying in business—is still the No. 1 thing. Unless you can make money, you cannot do any of the other things.

Irving Shapiro, on his retirement as chairman of Du Pont

Accounting is a tool and, like most tools, cannot be of much direct help to those who are unable or unwilling to use it or who misuse it.

Financial Accounting Standards Board

LEARNING OBJECTIVES

After studying the material in this chapter, you will be able to:

1. Explain the need for profit planning for a small business.

2. Discuss what causes changes in the financial position of a company.

3. Understand the financial structure of a business.

4. Learn how to plan to make a profit in a small business.

5. Plan for a profit for an actual small business.

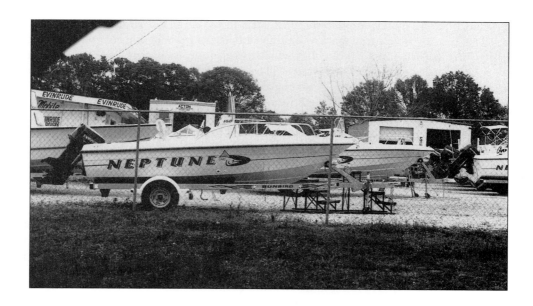

What Is Profit?

The Powell Company* had been started in a small metal building in Louisiana two years earlier to sell and service small boats. Now the company needed to hire some experienced personnel from an established competitor. Phil Powell, the owner, approached several of these people and offered them the same wages they were earning from their current employers. Because there were no immediate benefits from changing jobs, they were told of the advantages of getting in on the ground floor of the newer, though smaller, business. They were told that as the firm grew and sales and profits increased, it would be management's policy to pay a higher basic wage and also larger employee benefits. Several of these employees joined Powell.

During the subsequent year, sales didn't come up to expectations. Powell decided that to increase sales he should move to a more desirable location, where modern equipment and facilities could improve production. The search for a new location was begun, and the employees were excited at the prospect of being located in a newer building with expanded facilities and the latest tools and equipment.

While the new facilities were being readied, morale was high and employee performance was superior. When the facilities were occupied, morale improved even further. During the first few months, more orders were obtained by the sales force than the firm was able to fill, but production quotas were met and surpassed. It appeared to all concerned that the company was well on its way to becoming a leader in its field.

With the new and expanded facilities, though, came some problems. Overhead and the tax burden were greater. Costs incurred for insurance, utilities, and personnel had increased. So, while revenues were obviously getting larger, expenses were increasing faster, and the business wasn't even breaking even, much less making a profit.

Powell felt he couldn't keep his promise to increase wages and add more employee benefits. He told the employees they would have to wait until the financial position of the business improved before receiving what he had promised them. He told them their raises and new benefits wouldn't be given them until the company's sales were sufficiently higher than expenses to provide a profit.

Bob Benjamin, the production manager, agreed with Powell that wages couldn't be raised at that time, but he believed that unless the employees were shown a detailed report of expenses, they would continue to believe the firm was making a substantial profit and Powell had gone back on his word.

Powell realized this was true, but he felt the employees had no justification for looking into the company's books. The only course of action was the one he had outlined. He did not give the raise. Yet even so the business went bankrupt two years later.

*Name disguised at the request of the former owner.

Source: Prepared by Gayle M. Ross, Ross Publishing Company.

Profit cannot be left to chance in small firms. Yet all too frequently it is, because small business owners tend to know little about financial planning and control. Even when efforts *are* made to plan for profit, they are often inadequate, for owners tend to assume that history will repeat itself—that past profits will be repeated in the future. Instead, small business managers must learn to identify—and prepare for—all income and costs if they are to make a profit.

According to Marge Lovero, president of the Entrepreneurial Center, Inc., a business consulting and training company in Purchase, New York, "It's foolish to expect to generate revenue immediately."[1] Instead, it's best to play it safe by planning for all contingencies.

The type of business you are entering, for example, is critical in determining the amount of start-up funds you will require. While a retail business can generate income immediately, a service business may require a wait of 30 to 90 days. So you must factor this information into your estimate of the working capital you'll need.

Profit planning is particularly difficult for new entrepreneurs who have given up well-paying jobs in order to go out on their own. They realize they have given up their pension plan and insurance program(s), but they often fail to realize they've also given up such amenities as the former employer's copy and fax machines, subscriptions to professional literature, and seemingly insignificant incidentals such as stamps, memo pads, and pens, all of which may result in hundreds or even thousands of dollars in expenses.[2] These items must be included in your profit planning.

(*Source:* Reprinted with permission of Universal Press Syndicate.)

Eventually many corporate dropouts find it more attractive to start anew in the corporate world, and many of them succeed in the reverse transition. So if you are sure that you never want to work for "the man" again, you must be realistic about what you are giving up in exchange for your freedom and you must do some careful planning.

■ WHAT IS PROFIT PLANNING?

Profit planning is a series of prescribed steps to be taken to ensure that a profit will be made.

The definition of **profit planning** may seem obvious: planning for profit. To make a profit, however, your prices must cover all costs and include a markup for planned profit. This chapter will help you (1) determine how much profit you want and how to achieve it; (2) learn how to set up an accounting system for your firm and how to read, evaluate, and interpret its accounting and financial figures; and (3) evaluate, or estimate, your firm's financial position. Later in the chapter, we will outline a step-by-step process to follow to ensure that a profit results. The important thing to realize at this point is that, because it establishes targets, *profit planning must precede other activities.*

A lack of accurate cost information, a recurring problem among small business owners, usually results in profits of unknown quantity—or even a loss. Also, it can foster the illusion of making a greater profit than is really earned, if any is earned.

> The owner of Children's Party Caterer* illustrated this point. During the first interview with a SCORE counselor, she said she had "around $800 worth of party materials" in her pantry at home. But when asked the cost of materials used and the time involved in preparing for each party, she couldn't answer. The counselor gave her a homework assignment to determine the time she spent preparing for and giving each party, as well as the cost of materials.
>
> She was surprised to find she spent 18 to 20 hours per party, and the cost of materials ranged from $40 to $50. Also, she hadn't included the cost of transportation or the $10 to $12 baby-sitting cost for her two children. Yet she charged only about $40 to $50 for each party. To the suggestion that she raise her prices to cover these costs, plus a markup for profit, she responded, "People won't pay it." When the counselor replied, "You aren't in the charity business," her exuberant reply was, "Oh, but I enjoy doing it!"

■ How a Business's Financial Position Changes

The operations of a small business result from decisions made by its owner and managers and the many activities they perform. As decisions are made and operations occur, the firm's financial position constantly changes. For example, cash received from sales increases the bank balance; credit sales increase accounts receivable; and purchases of material, while increasing inventory, also increase accounts payable or decrease the bank balance. At the same time, machines decrease in value, materials are processed into inventory, and utilities are used. These constant changes in the financial position of the business must be recorded and analyzed.

Tracing Changes in a Company's Financial Position

Throughout all operations, the important question for small business owners is whether their business is improving its chances of reaching its primary objective—to make a profit. *However, some small firms make a profit and still fail, since profits are not necessarily in the form of cash.* Accounts receivable may reflect profits, but many of those accounts may not be collectible. Too much money may be tied up in other assets and not available to pay bills as they come due. In other words, focusing only on net income may be foolhardy unless other variables are also considered.[3] The "bottom line" is not an end in itself, but it is the beginning of the more difficult process of tracking cash flow. (See Chapter 14 for more on budgeting and controlling operations.)

First, we should trace the changes in our own small companies. Next, we should carefully monitor—or **benchmark**—those companies on which we depend. Benchmarking is setting up standards (for reference), and then measuring performance against them. Benchmarking has become so popular that several companies have been organized to help businesses get the most from their data.

> For example, Benchmark Research Inc. is a fully integrated market research firm that provides consumer, business, and social information to support improved business and organizational performance.[4]

Benchmarking is setting up standards (for reference) and then measuring performance against them.

---

*Name disguised.

The importance of cash flow may be illustrated with a home example—your personal finances. Your allowance, earnings, and/or other income may be adequate to pay for food, clothing, and other operating expenses, but you may have an unexpected expense, such as replacing a broken-down or worn-out car, for which you must make a cash down payment.

Say, for example, that your parents send you $500 per month for living expenses while at school, and you have the following expenses:

Cash allowance	$500
Food @ $10/day × 30 days	300
Gas for automobile	40
School supplies	50
Left to save or spend	$110

Now if your car breaks down and repairs will cost $175, do you walk or cut down on food?

If your funds are invested in a fixed asset, such as a loan on your car, they are not available for paying bills. The same is true of a small business. In fact, you can use the same computer programs to handle both your business and your personal finances.

Importance of Accounting

Accounting records are records of a firm's financial position that reflect any changes in that position.

Accounting is quite important in achieving success in any business, especially a small one. In fact, accounting is so tied to your financial well-being that, without it, you would not know what the bottom line is—or even whether it is a positive or negative amount.[5] Therefore, your **accounting records** must accurately reflect the changes occurring in your firm's assets, liabilities, income, expenses, and equity. The continued operation of your business also depends—as Irving Shapiro points out in one of the chapter's opening quotations—on maintaining the proper balance among its investments, revenues, expenses, and profit. Because profit margins are so critical to the success of a business, any decline in them should trigger an immediate search for the cause.

Many small business owners don't realize their business is in trouble until it's too late, and many fail without knowing what their problem is—or even that they have a problem. All they know is that they end up with no money and can't pay their bills. These owners fail to monitor all aspects of their businesses. They often consider financial statements "a necessary evil" and think everything is fine as long as sales are increasing and there is money in the bank. They don't realize that what they do in their day-to-day business activities is reflected in the financial statements. They tend to pay little attention to the information accountants give them. One young entrepreneur found this out the hard way.

"See no evil, speak no evil . . . I like that in an accountant, Mr. Farouche."

(Source: Management Accounting, January 1988, p. 13. Reprinted with permission.)

For Richard Huttner, the hardest problem in running New York's Parenting Unlimited Inc. was doing the accounting necessary to run its new acquisition, *Baby Talk* magazine. Although *Baby Talk* had revenues of several million dollars a year, it had no financial management, accounting system, general ledger, or bank account when it was acquired. Consequently, while trying to master an ongoing business, Huttner had to spend nearly a third of his time the first three months paying bills and doing accounting. He lamented, "Stanford didn't teach me how long it takes out-of-state checks to clear. At first, that caused us constant cash flow problems."[6]

In the discussion of financial management to come in this chapter, we have used an actual small business, which we have disguised as The Model Company, Inc., to illustrate the basic concepts. Assume throughout the following discussion that, while the company is owned by Mr. Model, you manage it for him. Therefore, you must make the management decisions.

■ WHAT IS THE FINANCIAL STRUCTURE OF A BUSINESS?

The assets, liabilities, and equity accounts of a business, which are interrelated and interact with each other, represent the **financial structure** of a firm, which changes constantly as business activities occur. Always keep in mind that *the total of liabilities plus owners' equity always equals the total assets of the firm.*

At regular intervals, a **balance sheet** is prepared to show the assets, liabilities, and owners' equity of the business. See Figure 13–1 for the arrangement and amounts of the accounts for our hypothetical business, The Model Company.

Remember, you can use the balance sheet as a gauge of the financial health of your company. It not only shows how assets are being used but also provides a snapshot of the company at a given moment. To keep you from getting bogged down in your daily activities, think of the following concepts:[7]

- Remember that "cash is king"—meaning that, if the balance sheet is correct, "current assets" should be easily convertible to cash.
- Keep your assets working for you—don't keep obsolete inventory or equipment.
- Make sure your business is properly financed.
- Have a financial plan—the goals in the financial plan should match the balance sheet.

To get a realistic look at your company, you should go over the balance sheet with your accountant instead of leaving everything up to her or him. Another good source of financial support would be a trusted banker.

Assets

Assets are the things a business owns. For accounting purposes, they are divided into current and fixed assets.

Current Assets **Current assets** are expected to turn over—that is, to change from one form to another—within a year. **Cash** includes the bills and coins in the cash register, deposits in a checking account, and other deposits that can be converted into cash immediately. A certain level of cash is necessary to operate a business; however, holding too much cash reduces your income because it produces no revenue. The question is, What is the correct level? The following example suggests a partial answer.

> Alan Goldstein, a partner in Touche Ross & Company's Enterprise Group in Boston, which helps small firms decide how much cash is needed, answers the question "When do everyday nuisances turn into disaster?" by saying, "When you're about to run out of cash."[8]

Accounts receivable result from giving credit to customers for less than a year, as shown in Chapter 8. While selling on credit helps maintain a higher level of sales, care must be taken to select customers who will pay within a reasonable time.

As discussed in Chapter 12, *inventory* provides a buffer between purchase, production, and sales. Therefore, you must maintain a certain amount of inventory to serve customers

Financial structure describes the relative proportions of a firm's assets, liabilities, and owners' equity.

A **balance sheet** is a statement of a firm's assets, liabilities, and owners' equity at a given time.

Assets are the things a business owns.

Current assets are those that are expected to change from one form to another within a year.

Cash includes bills, coins, deposits in a checking account, and other deposits that can be converted into cash immediately.

Accounts receivable are current assets resulting from selling a product on credit.

Figure 13–1

THE MODEL COMPANY, INC.
Balance Sheet
December 31, 20____

Assets

Current assets:		
Cash	$ 7,054	
Accounts receivable	60,484	
Inventory	80,042	
Prepaid expenses	1,046	
Total current assets		$148,626
Fixed assets:		
Equipment	$100,500	
Building	40,950	
Gross fixed assets	141,450	
Less: accumulated depreciation	16,900	
Net fixed assets		124,550
Total assets		$273,176

Liabilities and Owners' Equity

Current liabilities:		
Accounts payable	51,348	
Accrued payable	3,060	
Total current liabilities	$ 54,408	
Long-term liabilities:		
Mortgage payable	20,708	
Total liabilities		$ 75,116
Owners' equity:		
Capital stock	160,000	
Retained earnings	38,060	
Total equity		198,060
Total liabilities and owners' equity		$273,176

---

adequately. But carrying an excessive amount of inventory ties up capital, which then cannot be used for other income-producing assets. Thus, the amount of inventory to carry depends on a judicious balancing of income and costs.

Other current asset accounts often are called *short-term investments* and *prepaid expenses.* Usually, these make up only a small part of the current assets of a small business and need little attention (for an example, refer to Figure 13–1).

Fixed Assets   Items a business expects to own for more than a year—such as buildings, machinery, store fixtures, trucks, and land—are included among its **fixed assets.** Different types of fixed assets have different lengths of *useful life,* that is, the length of time that such assets, on average, may be expected to be used. Part of their cost is written

Fixed assets are relatively permanent items the business needs for its continued operations.

off each period as depreciation expense, with the result that the entire cost is spread over the asset's useful life.

As shown in Chapter 6, some small firms find it desirable to lease fixed assets instead of owning them. For example, a retailer may rent a store to reduce the need to make a large investment in it.

Liabilities

As discussed in Chapter 6, a business can obtain funds by owner investment and by borrowing, which is creating an obligation to pay. The first, which is necessary, increases *owners' equity,* or the *owners' interest* in the business. The second results in a **liability** of the business to pay back the funds—plus interest. Borrowing from creditors is divided into current and long-term liabilities.

> **Liabilities** are the financial obligations of a business.

Current Liabilities   Obligations to be paid within a year are **current liabilities.** They include accounts payable, notes payable, and accrued items (such as payroll), which are for services performed for you but not yet paid for.

> **Current liabilities** are obligations that must be paid within a year.

Accounts payable are obligations to pay for goods and services purchased and are usually due within 30 or 60 days, depending on the credit terms. Since any business should maintain current assets sufficient to pay these accounts, maintaining a high level of accounts payable requires a high level of current assets. Thus, you should determine whether or not early payment is beneficial; some sellers offer a discount for early payment, such as 1 or 2 percent if bills are paid within 10 days. This is a good return on your money!

> **Accounts payable** are obligations to pay, resulting from purchasing goods or services.

Notes payable, which are written obligations to pay, usually give the business a longer time than accounts payable before payment is due. An example is a 90-day note.

> **Notes payable** are written obligations to pay, usually after 90 days to a year.

Long-Term Liabilities   Bonds and mortgages are the usual types of **long-term liabilities,** which have terms of more than a year. A business usually incurs these liabilities when purchasing fixed assets. Long-term loans may be used to supply a reasonable amount of **working capital,** which is current assets less current liabilities. This type of borrowing requires regular payment of interest. The need to make these payments during slack times increases the risk of being unable to meet other obligations, so both short- and long-term strategies should be used. In general, small firms use long-term borrowing as a source of funds much less frequently than large ones do.

> **Long-term liabilities** are obligations to pay someone after one year or more.

> **Working capital** is a firm's current assets minus current liabilities.

Owners' Equity

Owners' equity is the owners' share of (or *net worth* in) the business, after liabilities are subtracted from assets. The owners receive income from profits in the form of dividends or an increase in their share of the company through an increase in retained earnings. Owners also absorb losses, which decrease their equity. (See Chapters 6 and 14 for further details.)

> **Owners' equity** is the owners' share of (or net worth in) the business, after liabilities are subtracted from assets.

As shown in Chapter 6, when owners invest in a corporation, they receive shares of stock, and the *owners' equity account*—common stock—is increased on the firm's balance sheet.

Retained earnings are the profits kept in the business rather than being distributed to the owners. Most firms retain some profits to use in times of need or to provide for growth. Many small firms have failed because the owners paid themselves too much of the profits, thereby reducing their assets. Definite policies should be set as to what part of your earnings should be retained and what part distributed to you as income.

> **Retained earnings** are profits kept in the business rather than distributed to owners.

■ PROFIT-MAKING ACTIVITIES OF A BUSINESS

The profit-making activities of a business influence its financial structure. These activities are reflected in the revenue and expense accounts, as shown by the following example:*

$$\text{Net income (profit)} = \text{Revenue (income)} - \text{Expenses (costs)}$$
$$\$46,700 = \$530,000 - \$483,000$$

During a given period, the business performs services for which it receives revenues. It also incurs expenses for goods and services provided to it by others. These revenues and expenses are shown in the **income statement,** also known as the **profit and loss statement** (see Figure 13–2).

Revenue and Expenses

Revenue (also called **sales income**) is the value received by a business in return for services performed or goods sold. The business receives revenue in the form of cash or accounts receivable.

An **income statement (profit and loss statement)** periodically shows revenues, expenses, and profits from a firm's operations.

Revenue (sales income) is the value received by a firm in return for a good or service.

Figure 13–2

THE MODEL COMPANY, INC.
Income Statement
January 1 through December 31, 20__

Net sales	$463,148	
Less: Cost of goods sold	291,262	
Gross income		$171,886
Operating expenses:		
Salaries	$ 83,138	
Utilities	6,950	
Depreciation	10,050	
Rent	2,000	
Building services	4,920	
Insurance	4,000	
Interest	2,646	
Office and supplies	6,550	
Sales promotion	11,000	
Taxes and licenses	6,480	
Maintenance	1,610	
Delivery	5,848	
Miscellaneous	1,750	
Total expenses		146,942
Net income before taxes		24,944
Less: Income taxes		5,484
Net income after taxes		$19,460

*Figures are from Figure 13–5.

Expenses, such as the costs of paying people to work for you (or for goods or services provided to you), include such items as materials, wages, insurance, utilities, transportation, depreciation, taxes, supplies, and advertising. As these costs are incurred, they are deducted from revenue.

There are two types of expenses (costs): (1) fixed and (2) variable. **Fixed expenses (costs)** are those that are incurred periodically, regardless of whether operations are carried on or not. These include such items as depreciation, rent, and insurance. **Variable expenses (costs)** vary according to the level of operations. Thus, if there are no operations, there are no variable expenses. These expenses include such items as labor and material to produce and sell the product, plus sales promotion and delivery costs.

Expenses are the costs of labor, goods, and services.

Fixed expenses (costs) do not vary with changes in output.

Variable expenses (costs) vary directly with changes in output.

Profit

Profit, also called **income,** is the difference between revenues earned and expenses incurred. Depending on the type of expenses deducted, profit may be called *gross income, operating profit, net income before taxes,* or *net income.*

Your profit margin indicates the relationship between revenues and expenses; therefore, a decline in profit margin should trigger a search for the cause. The problem could be a rise in expenses, a per unit sales revenue decline caused by discounting or pricing errors, or changing the basic operations of the business.

Profit (income) is the difference between revenue earned and expenses incurred.

■ HOW TO PLAN FOR PROFIT IN A SMALL BUSINESS

According to a Dun & Bradstreet report, a well-managed small business has at least the following characteristics:

*   It is more liquid than a badly managed company.
*   The balance sheet is as important to the owner as the income statement.
*   Stability is emphasized, instead of rapid growth.
*   Long-range planning is important.

Need for Profit Planning

As you study the income statement in Figure 13–2, you may interpret it as saying, "The Model Company received $463,148 in net sales, expended $291,262 for costs of goods sold, paid out $146,942 in total operating expenses, and had $24,944 left as net income (or profits) before income taxes." Under this interpretation, *profit is a "leftover," not a planned amount.* While neither you nor Mr. Model can do anything about the past, you can do something about future operations. Since one of your goals is to make a profit, you should plan the operations now to achieve your desired profit goal later. So let's see how you can do it!

Steps in Profit Planning

To achieve your goal during the coming year, you need to take the following profit-planning steps:

1. Establish a profit goal.
2. Determine the volume of sales revenue needed to make that profit.
3. Estimate the expenses you will incur in reaching that volume of sales.

4. Determine estimated profit, based on plans resulting from steps 2 and 3.
5. Compare the estimated profit with the profit goal.

If you are satisfied with the plans, you can stop at this point. However, you may want to check further to determine whether improvements can be made, particularly if you are not happy with the results of step 5. Doing steps 6 through 10 may help you to understand better how changing some of your operations can affect profit.

6. List possible alternatives that can be used to improve profits.
7. Determine how expenses vary with changes in sales volume.
8. Determine how profits vary with changes in sales volume.
9. Analyze your alternatives from a profit standpoint.
10. Select an alternative and implement the plan.

Need for Realism in Profit Planning

Be realistic when going through these steps, or you may be unable to reach the desired profit goal. You may feel the future is too uncertain to make such plans, but *the greater the uncertainty, the greater the need for planning.*

> For example, the president of a small firm said his forecasts were too inaccurate to be of any help in planning operations, so he had stopped forecasting. His business became so unsuccessful he had to sell out.
>
> The owner of another small business recently stated she can't forecast the next year's revenue within 20 percent of actual sales. However, she continues to forecast and plan, for she says she needs plans from which to deviate as conditions change.

■ PROFIT PLANNING APPLIED IN A TYPICAL SMALL BUSINESS

This section uses the above steps to plan profits for The Model Company. As manager, you must start planning for the coming year several months in advance so you can put your plans into effect at the proper time. To present a systematic analysis, assume you are planning for the company for the first time.*

Step 1: Establish the Profit Goal

A **profit goal** is the specific amount of profit one expects to achieve.

Your **profit goal** must be a specific target value. To begin with, as you manage the business, pay yourself a reasonable salary. Also, Mr. Model should receive a return on his investment—not only his initial investment but also any earnings left in the business—for taking the risks of ownership. To do this, compare what you would receive as salary for working for someone else and the income Mr. Model would receive if the same amount of money were placed in a relatively safe investment, such as U.S. government bonds or high-grade stocks. Each of these investments provides a return with a certain degree of risk—and pleasure. If Mr. Model could invest the same amount of money at an 8 percent return, with little risk, what do you think the return on his investment in The Model Company should be?

---

*Actually, you should be planning for each month at least six months or a year ahead. This can be done by dropping the past month, adjusting the rest of the months in your prior plans, and adding the plans for another month. Such planning gives you time to anticipate needed changes and do something about them.

Mr. Model originally invested $160,000 in the company and has since left about $40,000 of his profits in the business. He made about 10 percent on his investment this past year, which he thinks is too low for the risk he is taking; he believes about a 20 percent return is reasonable. So, as step 1 in Figure 13–3, you enter his investment, desired profit, and estimate of income taxes (from the past and after consultation with his accountant). You determine that he must make $52,000 before taxes, or a 26 percent return on his investment, if he is to reach his desired profit. After you and Mr. Model have set this goal, you should determine what the profit before taxes will be from your forecast of next year's plans.

Step 2: Determine the Planned Sales Volume

A **sales forecast** is an estimate of the amount a firm expects to sell during a given period. In preparing operating and sales budgets, these forecasts are used to estimate revenues for the next quarter, for the year, or perhaps even for three to five years. Learning how to forecast accurately can spell the difference between growth and stagnation for your business. But accurate forecasting is not always possible, especially for a product that is exploding in popularity, such as the cellular phone.

> A **sales forecast** is an estimate of the amount of revenue expected from sales for a given period in the future.

> Since the first successful test of cellular service in 1962 and the first introduction of such service in Chicago and Washington, D.C., in 1983, the cellular industry has exploded! The rate at which cellular phones were purchased increased from 14 percent in 1993 to 32 percent in 1997.[9] Now, with more than 1,500 cellular systems operating in the United States, analysts predicted that there would be close to 90 million subscribers by the year 2000.[10] This is the kind of information the entrepreneur must have as a basis for profit planning.

Different parts of the business use these forecasts for planning and controlling their parts of the operations. Thus, the forecasts influence decisions about purchasing materials, scheduling production, securing financial resources, purchasing plant or equipment, hiring and paying personnel, scheduling vacations, and planning inventory levels.

In our example, you would probably forecast sales for the coming year on estimates of several factors, such as market conditions, level of sales promotion, estimate of competitors' activities, and inflation. Or you could use forecasts appearing in specialized business and government publications. Also, your trade associations, banker, customers, vendors, and others can provide valuable information. Using all this information—and assuming 6 percent inflation for the coming year—you estimate that sales will increase about 8 percent, to $530,000 ($1,000 per unit × 530 units), which you enter as step 2 in Figure 13–3.

Step 3: Estimate Expenses for Planned Sales Volume

To estimate expenses for the coming year, first track your expenses closely for a month or two,[11] then record last year's figures as part of step 3. You should then adjust them for changes in economic conditions (including inflation), changes in expenses needed to attain the planned sales, improved methods of production, and a reasonable salary for the services of the owner.

You then compute that about 63 percent of your revenue is to pay for materials and labor used directly to produce the goods you will sell. Using this figure—adjusted 6 percent for inflation—you enter the result, $333,900, as "cost of goods." You then estimate the amount of each of the other expenses, recognizing that some expenses vary directly with volume changes, while others change little, if at all. Enter each expense figure in the appropriate place. The total of all expected expenses is $490,000.

Figure 13–3

THE MODEL COMPANY, INC.
Planning for Profit for the Year 20__

Step Description	Analysis	Comments
1. *Establish your profit goals.*		
Equity invested in company	$160,000	
Retained earnings	40,000	
Owners' equity	200,000	
Return desired, after income taxes	40,000	20% × $200,000
Estimated tax on profit	12,000	
Profit needed before income taxes	$ 52,000	
2. *Determine your planned volume of sales.*		
Estimate of sales income	$530,000	530 units × $1,000/unit
3. *Estimate your expenses for planned volume of sales.*	Estimated, 20__	Actual, last year
Cost of goods	$333,900	$291,262
Salaries	88,300	88,138
Utilities	7,100	6,950
Depreciation	10,000	10,050
Rent	2,500	2,000
Building services	5,100	4,920
Insurance	5,000	4,000
Interest	3,000	2,646
Office expenses	6,000	5,550
Sales promotion	11,800	11,000
Taxes and licenses	6,900	6,480
Maintenance	1,900	1,610
Delivery	6,500	5,848
Miscellaneous	2,000	1,740
Total	$490,000	$442,194
4. *Determine your estimated profit, based on steps 2 and 3.*		
Estimated sales income	$530,000	
Estimated expenses	490,000	
Estimated net profit before taxes	$ 40,000	
5. *Compare estimated profit with profit goal.*		
Estimated profit before taxes	$ 40,000	
Desired profit before taxes	52,000	
Difference	−$ 12,000	

6. *List possible alternatives to improve profits.*
   A. Change the planned sales income:
      (1) Increase planned volume of units sold.
      (2) Increase or decrease planned price of units.
      (3) Combine (1) and (2).
   B. Decrease planned expenses.
   C. Add other products or services.
   D. Subcontract work.

Figure 13–3 *concluded*

Expense Item	Sales volume of 364			Sales volume of 530		Sales volume of 700	
	Fixed Expenses	Variable Expenses	Total Expenses	Variable Expenses	Total Expenses	Variable Expenses	Total Expenses
7. Determine how expenses vary with changes in sales volume.							
Goods sold		$229,200	$229,200	$333,900	$333,900	$440,789	$440,789
Salaries	$50,000	26,304	76,304	38,300	88,300	50,585	100,585
Utilities	6,000	755	6,755	1,100	7,100	1,453	7,453
Depreciation	10,000		10,000		10,000		10,000
Rent	2,500		2,500		2,500		2,500
Building services	4,000	755	4,755	1,100	5,100	1,453	5,453
Insurance	5,000		5,000		5,000		5,000
Interest		2,060	2,060	3,000	3,000	3,962	3,962
Office expenses	2,800	2,198	4,998	3,200	6,000	4,226	7,026
Sales promotion		8,104	8,104	11,800	11,800	15,585	15,585
Taxes and licenses	5,000	1,305	6,305	1,900	6,900	2,509	7,509
Maintenance	800	755	1,555	1,100	1,900	1,453	2,253
Delivery		4,464	4,464	6,500	6,500	8,585	8,585
Miscellaneous	2,000		2,000		1,000		2,000
Total	$88,100	$275,900	$364,000	$401,900	$490,000	$530,600	$618,700

8. Determine how profits vary with changes in sales volume.

	Sales Volume of 364	Sales Volume of 530	Sales Volume of 700
Revenue @ $1,000 per unit	$364,000	$530,000	$700,000
Expenses			
Fixed	$ 88,100	$ 88,100	$ 88,100
Variable	275,900	401,900	530,600
Total	364,000	490,000	618,700
Estimated profit before income tax	$000,000 (Break-even)	$ 40,000	$ 81,300

9. *Analyze alternatives from a profit standpoint.*
   Increase income by increasing price? Decreasing price?
   Increase income by increasing advertising?
   Decrease variable costs?

10. *Select and implement the plan.*

Step 4: Determine the Estimated Profit

In this step, you first deduct the figure for estimated expenses from the estimated sales income; then add the total of any other income, such as interest. You calculate this amount and find that profit before taxes is estimated to be $40,000 ($530,000 − $490,000), which is higher than the $24,944 made last year.

Step 5: Compare Estimated Profit with Profit Goal

Next, you compare the estimated profit ($40,000) with your profit goal ($52,000). Because estimated profit is $12,000 less than you would wish, you decide to continue with steps 6 through 10.

Step 6: List Possible Alternatives to Improve Profits

As shown in step 6 of Figure 13–3, you have many alternatives for improving profits. Some of these are as follows:

A. Change the planned sales income by:
   1. Increasing planned volume of units sold by increasing sales promotion, improving the quality of the product, making it more available, or finding new uses for it.
   2. Increasing or decreasing the planned price of the units. The best price may not be the one you are currently using.
   3. Combining (1) and (2). On occasion, some small business owners become too concerned with selling on the basis of price alone. Instead, price for profit and sell quality, better service, reliability, and integrity.

> For example, several years ago Bert Olson stopped using pesticides on his 450-acre farm for two reasons. One was concern for the environment. The other consideration was cost: he was going broke as a conventional farmer. After the change, he started showing considerable profit as consumers' demand for organically grown foods increased.[12]

B. Decrease planned expenses by:
   1. Establishing a better control system. Spotting areas where losses occur and establishing controls may reduce expenses.
   2. Increasing productivity of people and machines through improving methods, developing proper motivators, and improving the types and use of machinery.
   3. Redesigning the product by developing new materials, machines, and/or methods for improving products and reducing costs.
C. Reduce costs per unit or add other products or services by:
   1. Adding a summer product to a winter line of products.
   2. Using idle capacity innovatively.
   3. Making some parts that are customarily purchased from the outside.
   4. Using the Japanese concept of **kaizen costing,** which sets in advance cost targets in all aspects of product design, development, and production. Kaizen costing requires each department—or cost center—to set specific cost reduction plans for each accounting period.[13]

Kaizen costing sets costs targets for all phases of design, development, and production of a product for each accounting period.

D. Subcontract work.

Having listed possible alternatives, you must evaluate each of them and concentrate on the best one or ones.

Step 7: Determine How Expenses Vary with Changes in Sales Volume

Although you have estimated your planned sales volume at 530 units (at $1,000 per unit), you will probably want to see what happens to expenses if you sell fewer or more units. This can be done by reviewing your expected expenses in step 3 and varying them up and down, remembering that some are fixed and some vary with level of sales. We've done this in step 7 at three levels: 364, 530, and 700 units. Notice that total expenses increase from $364,000 at 364 units, to $490,000 at 530 units, and to $618,700 at 700 units.

While an analysis of past costs is helpful in projecting future expenses, be aware that:

1. The relationships exist only within limited changes in sales volume. Very high sales volumes may be obtained by extraordinary and costly efforts; low volumes result in extra costs from idle capacity, lost volume discounts, and so forth.

2. Past relationships may not continue in the future. Inflation or deflation, changing location of customers, new products, and other factors can cause changes in the unit costs.

For example, cellular phones now account for about a quarter of the expense of maintaining company vehicles. Also remember that almost all such phone providers charge for usage time in addition to a flat monthly rate.[14]

Step 8: Determine How Profits Vary with Changes in Sales Volume

As you notice in step 8 of Figure 13–3, profit (or loss) can be estimated for different levels of sales. We've done that for the three levels—364, 530, and 700 units—using fixed expenses, variable expenses, and the resulting profit before income taxes.

These figures were then incorporated into a chart (Figure 13–4) to show what sales volume would result in The Model Company's neither making nor losing money on its

Figure 13–4
Break-Even Chart for The Model Company

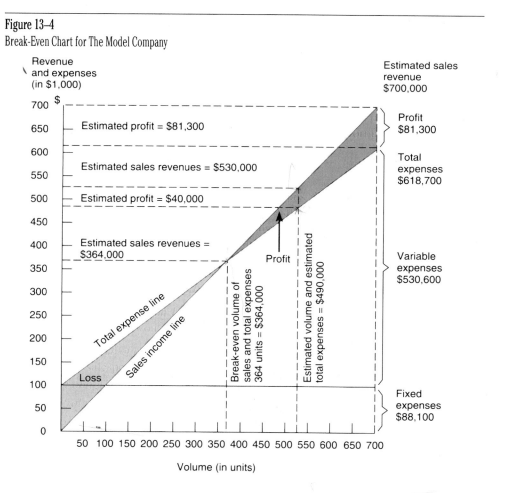

The **break-even point** is that volume of sales where total revenue and expenses are equal, so there is neither profit nor loss.

operations. This figure, called the **break-even point,** was 364 units, where sales revenues and total expenses were $364,000.

Step 9: Analyze Alternatives from a Profit Standpoint

Using the information you have generated so far, especially from steps 6, 7, and 8, can lead you to consider alternatives such as the following to increase profits:

- Change sales price.
- Change media—and/or amount budgeted—for advertising.
- Reduce variable costs.
- Change quality of products.
- Stop producing and selling low-margin products.

Other alternatives can be evaluated in much the same manner. Then, having made these economic analyses, you will be ready to make your final plan for action.

Step 10: Select and Implement the Plan

The selection of the plan for action depends on your judgment as to what will most benefit the business. The results of the analyses made in the prior steps provide the economic inputs. These must be evaluated along with other goals. Cost reduction may result in laying off employees or in reducing service to customers.

Mr. Model has just read this text and has been studying other management literature. After hearing you present the above analyses to him, he believes the company can reduce the cost of goods sold by about 2 percent. Figure 13–5 shows a simplified statement of the planned income and outgo for the next year, based on the work you and he have done. How does it look to you?

Figure 13–5

THE MODEL COMPANY, INC.
Income Statement for the Year 20__

Sales income		$530,000	
Less:			
Cost of goods sold	$327,200		
Other expenses	156,100		
Total expenses		483,300	
Net profit before taxes			$46,700
Pretax return on equity			23.4%
Pretax profit margin			8.8%

WHAT YOU SHOULD HAVE LEARNED

■

1. Not only do small business owners often fail to plan for a profit, but they also sometimes don't even know whether or not they are making a profit. Because healthy sales income doesn't guarantee a profit, it's important to determine the true cost of a product in order to set a fair price and budget and plan accordingly.

2. A business's financial position is not static. Assets and liabilities fluctuate every time a product is sold, money comes in, inventory is bought, or credit is given. Rapid growth and "paper profits" can be the downfall of small business owners who don't keep accurate records and don't listen to the conclusions accountants draw from the figures.

3. A company's financial structure consists of its assets, liabilities, and owners' equity. Assets are the things a company owns. Current assets, which turn over within a year, include cash, accounts receivable, and inventory, as well as short-term investments and prepaid expenses. Fixed assets—such as buildings, machinery, store fixtures, trucks, and land—are things the company expects to own for a longer time. Part of their cost is written off each year as depreciation expense.

   Liabilities are obligations created by borrowing or buying something on credit. Current liabilities, payable within one year, include accounts payable, notes payable, and accrued expenses. Long-term liabilities, with terms of a year or longer, should be used to pay for fixed assets and to acquire working capital.

   Owners' equity is the owners' share of a business after liabilities are subtracted from assets. Profits may be distributed to owners as cash or dividends, or accumulated in the business in the form of retained earnings.

4. A company's profit (net income) is what is retained after expenses—the costs of doing business—are subtracted from revenues—the proceeds from sales. When sales increase, not only does sales income rise, but variable costs change as well, and it may sometimes be necessary to increase fixed costs.

   To plan for a profit, you must have a profit target, which is your reason for being in business. Detailed profit planning includes at least the first 5 of the following 10 steps: (1) establish the profit goal, (2) determine the planned volume of sales, (3) estimate the expenses for the planned sales volume, (4) determine estimated profit for the planned sales volume, and (5) compare the estimated profit with the profit goal. If the results of (5) are unsatisfactory, (6) list possible alternatives that can be used to improve the profit position, (7) determine how expenses vary with changes in sales volume, (8) determine how profits vary with changes in sales volume, (9) analyze alternatives from a profit standpoint, and (10) select one of the alternative plans and implement it.

5. The chapter concluded by illustrating these steps for a hypothetical company.

QUESTIONS FOR DISCUSSION

■

1. Why is planning for profit so important to a small business?

2. In analyzing the changing financial position of a small business, what things should you look for?

3. "If a small firm is making a profit, there's no danger of its failing." Do you agree? Why or why not?

4. What is a firm's financial structure? What are the components of this structure?

5. Explain each of the following: (*a*) assets, (*b*) current assets, (*c*) fixed assets, (*d*) liabilities, (*e*) current liabilities, (*f*) long-term liabilities, (*g*) owners' equity, (*h*) retained earnings, (*i*) income (profit and loss) statement, (*j*) balance sheet, and (*k*) profit.

6. What steps are needed in profit planning?

7. How do you establish a profit goal?

8. How do you determine planned volume of sales? How does profit change with volume of product sold?

9. How do you determine planned expenses? Variable expenses? Fixed expenses?

10. What are some alternatives that could improve planned profits? Explain each.

CASE 13-1

EILLEN DORSEY AND WALTER HILL, JR., USE FINANCIAL PLANNING

Eillen Dorsey and Walter Hill, Jr., are successful entrepreneurs today because they learned early in life the importance of personal financial planning. Eillen, the youngest of eight children, was reared in Harford County, Maryland. Her parents taught her that if she dreamed long enough—and hard enough—and was committed to a dream, she would make it become real. But that meant saving her money for college and then for investment.

Dorsey attended Catonsville and Essex Community Colleges, where she began building a network of people who worked in corporate America and in local government agencies. She developed a particularly strong relationship with Walter Hill, Jr., who had attended Morgan State University and the University of Maryland—and also knew the value of savings.

Dorsey and Hill decided to use their savings to start a business in the Baltimore, Maryland, area when they noted that almost every corporation producing machinery had to buy some type of electrical components. They also knew that many of those companies were interested in doing business with a minority firm, so they saw an opportunity to become entrepreneurs.

Dorsey had been a salesperson for Technico, an electrical component company, and was familiar with firms that wanted electrical components. Hill, who was working at Westinghouse, also knew people in the industry. So they quit their respective companies to form ECS Technologies.

Each partner contributed $5,000 to get the business started, and they secured a $35,000 loan by using their homes as equity. Their homes thus became an important investment vehicle as well. The partners had already won a contract before they applied for the loan, making it easier for the lender to grant their request. Because the partners had invested their own money and assets, the banks were willing to give them a line of credit totaling $200,000.

Questions

1. Evaluate the way Dorsey and Hill did their financial planning.

2. Do you think their early personal financial planning influenced their professional financial planning? Explain.

3. To what extent do you think the two entrepreneurs will succeed in their venture? Explain.

Source: Reprinted from William G. Nickels, James M. McHugh, and Susan M. McHugh, *Understanding Business,* 4th ed. (Burr Ridge, IL: Richard D. Irwin, Inc., 1996), p. 667.

CASE 13-2

THE NEED FOR A CASH BUDGET

A small firm in Wichita, Kansas, specialized in the sale and installation of swimming pools. The company was profitable, but the owners devoted very little attention to the management of working capital. The company had never prepared a cash budget.

To be sure that money was available for payments as needed, the owner of the firm kept a minimum of $25,000 in a checking account. At times, this account grew larger, until at one time it totaled $43,000. The owner felt that this practice of cash management worked well for a small company because it eliminated all the paperwork associated with cash budgeting. Moreover, it had enabled the firm to always pay its bills in a timely manner.

Questions

1. What are the advantages and weaknesses of the minimum-cash-balance practice?

2. There is a saying, "If it ain't broke, don't fix it." In view of the firm's present success in paying bills promptly, should it be encouraged to use a cash budget? Defend your answer.

14

BUDGETING AND CONTROLLING OPERATIONS AND TAXES

If you think your business can fly without a budget, you may be in for a crash landing.

Bob Weinstein

Noah must have taken two taxes into the ark—and they have been multiplying ever since!

Will Rogers

LEARNING OBJECTIVES

After studying the material in this chapter, you will be able to:

1. Explain how managers exercise control in a small business.

2. Tell what a budget is, explain the different types, and tell how they are prepared and used.

3. Discuss how information on actual performance can be obtained and used.

4. Explain how ratios can be used to evaluate a firm's financial condition.

5. Explain how the U.S. tax system operates.

6. Name and describe the taxes imposed on the small business itself.

7. Explain how the ownership of the business results in direct taxation of the owner.

8. Understand the importance of record keeping and tax reporting.

Herman J. Russell: On Time and Within Budget

When Herman J. Russell, founder and chairman of the highly successful Atlanta-based H. J. Russell & Company (www.hjrussell.com), thinks of his entrepreneurial achievements, he thanks his father, who owned a small subcontracting business. Using lessons learned from his father as his keys to success, Russell turned a small brick and mortar business he formed in 1956 into a diversified construction and engineering company that is one of the largest black-owned businesses in the United States.

Russell, who grew up in Summerhill, one of Atlanta's oldest neighborhoods, learned from his father the trade of plastering and the value of saving. At the age of 16, while still in junior high, he bought a small plot of land from the City of Atlanta for $125. During his senior year in high school, he started building a duplex on his property and finished it during his first summer break from Alabama's Tuskegee Institute, where he paid his own tuition from his savings.

On graduation from Tuskegee, he converted his part-time building activities into H. J. Russell Plastering Company. After earning an excellent reputation Russell moved into building apartment complexes.

Russell has been involved in numerous joint-venture projects with many other contractors, including the Georgia-Pacific headquarters building in Atlanta, many other office buildings and apartment complexes throughout the Southeast, four underground stations for Atlanta's rapid-rail system, the Martin Luther King Community Center, the underground people mover at Atlanta's Hartsfield International Airport, and many projects for the 1996 Olympics. His mark is also on the Atlanta Botanical Gardens, the Carter Presidential Center, and the Georgia Dome Stadium, just to mention a few.

Russell says his extensive knowledge of the construction industry—which he learned the hard way, from the ground up—has been a vital factor in his success. Another important key to his success is his consistent dependability. He is well known for completing high-pressure projects on time and—probably more importantly—within budget.

Although committed to business, Russell is quite active in many local, state, and national charities. One of these is the Herman J. Russell Entrepreneurial Scholarship Foundation, Inc.

Russell's hard work and dedication have won him numerous honors. In 1962 he became the first black member of the Atlanta Chamber of Commerce; he became its president in 1981. He was named "1990 Entrepreneur of the Year" by the National Black MBA Association, Inc.; received the " Horatio Alger Award" in 1991; was inducted into the Junior Achievement 1992 Atlanta Business Hall of Fame; and won the Ronald McNair Challengers Award in 1995. He also holds the honorary Doctor of Laws degree from Morehouse College and an honorary doctorate in Humane Letters from Morris Brown College.

Russell has expressed his business philosophy in these words: "I've always believed in a philosophy of controlled growth. There is no quick fix to success; it requires lots of hard work and sacrifice."

He tells young people to "Be honest to yourself and others."

Source: Prepared by Leon C. Megginson from communications and correspondence with H. J. Russell & Company.

The Profile illustrates what this text has stressed throughout, namely, the importance of controlling your firm's operations. In this chapter, we emphasize the nature, objectives, and methods of control; the design and use of budgets; the importance of budgetary control; and the role of taxes.

■ WHAT IS INVOLVED IN CONTROL?

Profit planning alone—as discussed in the previous chapter—is not enough! After developing plans for making a profit, you must design an operating system to implement those plans. As you will see, that system, in turn, must be controlled to see that plans are carried out and objectives, such as profit and customer satisfaction, are reached.

The Role of Control

Control is the process of assuring that organizational goals are achieved.

We continually exercise **control** over our activities and are, in turn, subject to controls. We control the speed of the car we drive; signal lights control the traffic flow. We control our homes' thermostats, which keep the temperature within an acceptable range. Ropes in an airport terminal guide passengers to the next available clerk. Controls that have been established to help accomplish certain objectives are found everywhere.

> For example, as discussed in Chapter 12, Barbara B. Kaufman, president of Chapter 11*, The Discount Bookstore, Inc. (www.chapter11books.com), controls overhead by keeping her stores small. They each are 3,000 to 6,000 square feet, as compared to 20,000 square feet or more in book superstores.[1]

As shown in Chapter 4, planning provides the guides and standards used in performing the activities necessary to achieve company goals. Then, a system of controls is installed to ensure that performance conforms to the organization's plans. Any deviation from these plans should point to a need for change—usually in performance, but sometimes in the plans themselves.

Steps in Control

The control process consists of five steps:

1. Setting up standards of performance.
2. Measuring actual performance.
3. Comparing actual performance with planned performance standards.

4. Deciding whether any deviations are excessive.
5. Determining the appropriate corrective action needed to bring actual performance into conformity with planned performance.

These steps are performed in all control systems, even though the systems may be quite different. Later in this chapter, these five steps are covered in detail, but the first step should be strongly emphasized at this point.

Setting Performance Standards

Performance standards tell employees—in advance—what level of performance is expected of them. They also measure how well employees meet expectations. Performance standards are usually stated in terms of (1) units consumed or produced or (2) price paid or charged. Some examples are *standard hours per unit* to produce a good or service, *miles per gallon* of gasoline used, and *price per unit* for purchased goods. There are many ways of developing these standards, such as intuition, past performance, careful measurement of activities, and comparison with other standards or averages.

Once standards of performance are set, they should be communicated by means of written policies, rules, procedures, and/or statements of standards to the people responsible for performance. Standards are valuable for stimulating good performance, as well as in locating sources of inefficiencies.

Performance standards set—in advance—acceptable levels to which employee achievement should conform.

■ CHARACTERISTICS OF EFFECTIVE CONTROL SYSTEMS

Effective control systems should be: (1) timely, (2) cost-effective, (3) accurate, and (4) quantifiable and measurable, and they should (5) indicate cause-and-effect relationships, (6) be the responsibility of one individual, and (7) be generally acceptable to those involved with them.

■ USING BUDGETS TO COMMUNICATE STANDARDS

Performance standards serve as building blocks for the preparation of a **budget,** which is a detailed statement of financial results expected for a given future period. The time period may be a month, a quarter, or a year. The budget is expressed in monetary terms but may also include other measurements, such as number of units expected to be sold, units of inventory used, and labor hours worked. The budget should be based on realistic and attainable goals and should be applied to items needing control. In essence, *budgets are the communication devices used to tell people responsible for performing tasks what is expected of them.*

A **budget** is a detailed statement of financial results expected for a given future period.

Types of Budgets

The three most important types of budgets are (1) capital budgets, (2) operating budgets, and (3) cash flow budgets.

The **capital budget** reflects a business's plans for obtaining, expanding, and replacing physical facilities. It requires that management preplan the use of its limited financial resources for needed buildings, tools, equipment, and other facilities.

A **capital budget** plans expenditures for obtaining, expanding, and replacing physical facilities.

An **operating budget** forecasts sales and allocates expenses for achieving them.

A **cash flow budget** forecasts the amount of cash receipts and cash needed to pay expenses and make other purchases.

The **operating budget** is based on profit plans for the budget period (as shown in Chapter 13). It contains a forecast of the amounts and sources of sales income and the materials, labor, and other expenses that will be needed to achieve the sales forecast.

The **cash flow budget** is a forecast of expected cash receipts and expected cash payments. It shows whether sufficient cash will be available for timely payment of budgeted expenses, capital equipment purchases, and other cash requirements. It also tells whether arrangements need to be made for external sources of cash, such as borrowing or owner investments.

Preparing the Operating Budget

The objective of the operating budget is to plan and control revenue and expenses to obtain desired profits. Therefore, the *sales budget* is planned first, giving consideration to the production and personnel functions.

> For example, Ron Christy, associate director of the Center for Entrepreneurship at Wichita State University, advises start-up entrepreneurs that "a budget is an integral part of a company's planning process, the heart and soul [of it] being an accurate sales forecast."[2]

The *production budget* is then set so that the sales budget plans can be met. This budget includes production, purchasing, and personnel schedules as well as inventory levels. It includes units such as amount of materials and personnel time, as well as their costs.

Next, a *personnel budget* is developed for the number of people needed to produce the product, any costs of training them, their pay and benefits, and other factors needed. The amount of detail in each of these budgets depends on its value to the company.

The *sales budget* is the most basic plan to consider. As you saw in Figure 13–3, step 2, the sales budget must be prepared before you can plan your production and personnel budgets. Because it was discussed in detail there, we will not discuss it further in this chapter.

Preparing the Cash Flow Budget

It surprises some small business owners that their businesses may be making profits and yet fail because they do not have the cash to pay current expenses. But a cash flow crisis can be triggered by many and varied factors, such as a major equipment breakdown, seasonal business fluctuations, and customers who pay late—or not at all. Therefore, *provision must be made for adequate cash to pay bills when they are due and payable.* This cash planning takes two forms: (1) the daily and weekly cash requirements for the normal operation of the business and (2) the maintenance of the proper balance for longer-term requirements.

Planning Daily and Weekly Cash Needs   The first type of planning tends to be routine and is done on a daily or weekly basis. For example, you may have a fairly constant income and outgo, which you are able to predict with fair accuracy. Thus, you can establish policies for the amount of cash to maintain and set up procedures to control that level of cash. These routine demands represent a small part of the needed cash on hand, and they tend to remain fairly constant.

Planning Monthly Cash Needs   The second type of planning requires a budget for each month of the year. Payments for rent, payroll, purchases, and services require a regular outflow of cash. Insurance and taxes may require large payments a number of times each year. A special purchase, such as a truck, may place a heavy demand on cash. So, it takes planning to have the *right* amount of cash available when needed. Robert Hackley, executive vice president of Hotsy, a Central Florida dealership that sells industrial pressure cleaning equipment and detergents, offers the following advice on how to prepare for cash flow crises:[3]

- Establish and maintain a good credit rating.
- Set aside some funds in an interest-bearing account that you can draw on in an emergency.
- Schedule your payments to your maximum advantage; that is, don't pay anything before you have to, but also watch for early-payment discounts.
- Keep your fixed costs low and your variable expenses tied to revenue so that, if income drops, so do expenses.

Procedure for Planning Cash Needs

Figure 14–1 shows the form used by The Model Company to budget its cash for three months ahead. Each month is completed before the next month is shown. Items 1 through 4 give estimates of cash to be received. For example, The Model Company expects to receive 20 percent of its monthly sales in cash (item 1). A check of its accounts receivable budget can provide an estimate of the cash to be received in January (item 2). Other income (item 3) might come from sources such as interest on investments or the sale of surplus equipment. Item 4 shows the expected total cash to be received.

Expected cash payments, items 5 through 18, show the items The Model Company might list in its planned budget (see step 3 in Figure 13–3). Cash is often paid in the month during or after which the goods are received or the service is performed. Examples include payments for electricity and for material purchases. Some cash payments can be made at any one of several times. For example, payments on a new insurance policy can be set up to come due when other cash demands are low.

As shown in Figure 14–1, the cash budget shows when payments are to be made. For example, the cash balance on the first of January (item 20), plus the month's receipts (item 4), less the month's cash payments (item 19), provide an expected cash balance at the end of January as follows:

$$\text{Balance at beginning of month} + \text{Total cash receipts} - \text{Total cash payment} = \text{Balance at end of month}$$

A negative balance will require an increase in cash receipts, a decrease in payments, or the necessity of a short-term loan. A company should have a certain amount of cash to take care of contingencies. Item 23 in Figure 14–1 shows the desired amount of cash needed as a minimum balance. A three-month projection is probably the optimum time estimate for a cash budget. If sales are seasonal, or you expect heavy demands on the cash balance, longer periods may be necessary.

■ USING BUDGETARY CONTROL

By itself, a budget is only a collection of figures or estimates that indicate plans. But when a system of budgets is used for control purposes, it becomes **budgetary control.** This process involves careful planning and control of all the company's financial activities. It includes frequent and close controls in the areas where poor performance most affects a company. Other areas may be controlled less often. For example, the cost of goods sold by The Model Company is planned for 63 percent of the sales dollar, and utilities are 1.34

Budgetary control is the system of budgets used to control a company's financial activities.

Figure 14–1

	January		February		March	
THE MODEL COMPANY Cash Budget For Three Months Ending March 31, 20__						
Items that change cash level	Budget	Actual	Budget	Actual	Budget	Actual
Expected cash receipts 1. Cash sales						
2. Collections—accounts receivable						
3. Other income						
4. Total cash receipts						
Expected cash payments 5. Goods purchases						
6. Salaries						
7. Utilities						
8. Depreciation						
9. Rent						
10. Building services						
11. Insurance						
12. Interest						
13. Office expenses						
14. Sales promotion						
15. Taxes and licenses						
16. Maintenance						
17. Delivery						
18. Miscellaneous						
19. Total cash payments						
Cash balance 20. Cash balance—beginning of month						
21. Change—item 4 minus item 19						
22. Cash balance—end of month						
23. Desired cash balance						
24. Short-term loans needed						
25. Cash available—end of month						
Cash for capital investments 26. Cash available—line 25						
27. Desired capital cash						
28. Long-term loans needed						

percent of sales (see steps 2 and 3 in Figure 13–3). Cost of goods sold may be divided into material and labor and checked weekly, while utilities might be checked monthly.

Controlling Credit, Collections, and Accounts Receivable

As shown in Chapter 8, extending credit increases the potential for sales—and losses from bad debts. You may have found that the amount of accounts receivable for The Model Company was large relative to its credit sales (see Figures 13–1 and 13–2). Waiting until the end of the year to find this out is potentially dangerous, since the average retailer loses more from slow accounts than from bad debts. Checks should be made often enough to identify customers who are slow in paying and to determine the reason for it. In general, the longer an account goes unpaid, the less the chance of collection.

The best control of bad-debt losses starts with investigating the customer's ability and willingness to pay and by providing clear statements of terms. Then, monitor past-due accounts each month so that each slow account is followed up promptly.

You may decide to write off some accounts as a bad-debt expense, while providing some incentive for earlier payment by slow-paying customers. Uncollectable accounts receivable create a misstatement of income and therefore an unjustified increase in business income tax liability.

Other Types of Budgetary Control

Many other types of budgetary control can be used to restrain a company's activities and investments. Any expense item can increase gradually without the change being recognized. Have you noticed how fast the cash in your pockets disappears? A small business has similar problems. Contributing to this creeping increase in the firm's costs may be such diverse situations as a clerk added to process increased paperwork, a solicitor asking for donations, a big customer requesting special delivery, an employee or union demand for additional services, rising energy costs, and inflation-increased costs. These costs must be controlled if the firm is to survive.

> For example, many areas offer free trade zones. The Argentine government has developed a network of free trade zones in each of its 23 provinces. These areas provide generous tax breaks to zone users so that they may store goods to be reexported without having to pay the required 21 percent value added tax or any other charges. Utilities are much cheaper because they are tax free.[4]

Using Audits to Control the Budget

An **audit** of a company consists of a formalized, methodical study, examination, and/or review of its financial records, with the intent of verifying, analyzing, informing, and/or discovering opportunities for improvement. There are three main types of audits: (1) financial, (2) internal, and (3) operations audits.

An **audit** is a formalized examination and/or review of a company's financial records.

In *financial auditing,* an outside certified public accountant (CPA) verifies the records and financial statements of a company once a year. This audit furnishes the owner(s), creditors, potential and current investors, and regulatory agencies with information on the company's financial status and operations.

Internal auditing is an appraisal of accounting, financial, and/or operations activities with the intention of measuring and evaluating the effectiveness of controls. Such audits function primarily as a service to management for the improvement of its financial controls.

An *operations audit* studies the basic operations of a company in order to identify problem areas. It may include studies of functional areas (marketing, finance, production, organization structure, personnel, and planning). Closely related to internal auditing, operations auditing emphasizes operations more than financial activities.

In summary, a company should be audited annually to ensure continued proper financial reporting. Bankers often require financial statements audited by a CPA before they will grant a loan. If any questions arise as to proper controls, inefficient operations, or lost opportunities, some form of internal or operations audit should also be considered.

■ OBTAINING AND USING PERFORMANCE INFORMATION FOR CONTROL PURPOSES

Feedback is the response a receiver gives through further communication with the sender of the message or some other person.

Information on actual operational performance comes through some form of **feedback:** observation, oral reports, written memos or reports, and/or other methods.

Obtaining the Information

Observation will probably be most satisfying because you are at the scene of action and have direct control over the situation. However, this method is time-consuming, and you cannot be in all places at one time. But you can justify using this method if your knowledge is needed, your presence may improve the work, or you are present for other purposes.

Oral reports, the most prevalent type of control used in small firms, are also time-consuming, but they provide two-way communication. Rumors are an informal form of feedback and can be useful so long as one can "separate the wheat from the chaff."

Written memos or reports are prepared when a record is needed or when many facts must be assembled. This type of feedback is costly unless the reports are the original records. A good record system, as will be discussed later, is a valuable aid, and it should be designed to be a ready source of reports.

Comparing Actual Performance with Performance Standards

The ability to keep costs low is a primary advantage of small businesses. To do this, an effective record-keeping system and cost-sensitive controls are vital. Information about actual performance, obtained through feedback, can be compared with predetermined standards to see if any changes are needed.

Simple, informal controls can usually be used by small firms, comparisons are made as feedback is received, and decisions are made accordingly. Examples of the use of standards were discussed in Chapter 12 and follow the same pattern as control through the use of budgets.

Determining Causes of Poor Performance

Poor performance can result from many factors, both internal and external, including the following:

- Having the wrong objectives.
- Customers not buying the company's product.
- Poor scheduling of production or purchases.
- Theft and/or spoilage of products.
- Too many employees for the work being performed.
- Opportunities lost.
- Too many free services or donations.

Once management isolates the true causes of the firm's poor performance, remedies can probably be found.

■ EVALUATING THE FIRM'S FINANCIAL CONDITION

Having considered the financial structure and operations of a company, we now consider the methods of evaluating its financial condition. Look at Figures 13–1 and 13–2, which show the financial statements of The Model Company. Is the company in a good financial position? How can you tell? You can do so by establishing and analyzing **ratios,** which are relationships between two or more variables. For example, the amount of current assets needed depends on other conditions of a company, such as the size of its current liabilities. So the **current ratio**—current assets divided by current liabilities—shows how easily a company can pay its current obligations.

> **Ratios** are relationships between two or more variables.

> The **current ratio** is the amount of current assets divided by the amount of current liabilities.

Unfortunately, no standard figures have been determined for successes or failures, but reasonable evaluations are possible. Two sets of values can be used for evaluation purposes: (1) a comparison of the current value of your firm's operations with those of the past and (2) a comparison of your operations with those of similar businesses and the industry.

■ SOME IMPORTANT RATIOS AND THEIR MEANINGS

Some of the more important ratios, and the ways to compute them, are shown in Table 14–1. Spaces are provided for computing the ratios for The Model Company, using the data provided in Figures 13–1 and 13–2. Comparable figures for the industry are provided for comparative purposes.

These ratios will help you answer such questions as the following: (1) Are profits satisfactory? (2) Are assets productive? (3) Can the business pay its debts? (4) How good are the business's assets? and (5) Is your equity in the business satisfactory?

Are Profits Satisfactory?

Is the owner of The Model Company getting an adequate or reasonable return on investment? The ratio of *net profit (income) to owners' equity* (Ratio 1 in Table 14–1)—often called **return on equity (ROE)**—is used to evaluate this, but several other ratios should be considered in profit planning and decision making.

> **Return on equity (ROE)** is the percentage of net profit your equity earns, before taxes.

How much return does your company make on its sales dollar? The ratio of *net profit (income) to net sales* (Ratio 2) provides this information. Suppose The Model Company now makes 4.3 cents profit (after taxes) per dollar of sales. Is the trend up or down? How does it compare with the experience of similar companies? If it is dropping, why? Costs may be increasing without an increase in price; competitors may be keeping their prices lower than The Model Company; it may be trying to obtain a large sales volume at the expense of profit. An increase in sales volume with the same investment and net profit per dollar of sales will increase ROE; a decrease will reduce ROE.

Are Assets Productive?

Does your company obtain enough sales from its producing assets? The answer is reflected in the ratio of *net sales to fixed assets* (Ratio 3)—fixed assets representing the producing units of the company. So many variables exist (such as leasing instead of owning fixed assets) that this ratio can change with changes in policy.

Table 14–1
Financial Ratios

Ratio	Formula	The Model Company	Industry Average*
1. Net profit to owners' equity	$\dfrac{\text{Net profit before taxes}}{\text{Owners' equity}}$	= _____	18.4%
2. Net profit to net sales	$\dfrac{\text{Net profit before taxes}}{\text{Net sales}}$	= _____	3.1
3. Net sales to fixed assets	$\dfrac{\text{Net sales}}{\text{Fixed assets}}$	= _____	5.8
4. Net sales to owners' equity	$\dfrac{\text{Net sales}}{\text{Owners' equity}}$	= _____	7.5
5. Current ratio	$\dfrac{\text{Current assets}}{\text{Current liabilities}}$	= _____	1.3
6. Acid test (quick ratio)	$\dfrac{\text{Current assets} - \text{Inventory}}{\text{Current liabilities}}$	= _____	1.0
7. Receivables to working capital†	$\dfrac{\text{Accounts receivable}}{\text{Working capital}}$	= _____	1.2
8. Inventory to working capital	$\dfrac{\text{Inventory}}{\text{Working capital}}$	= _____	0.4
9. Collection period	$\dfrac{\text{Accounts receivable}}{\text{Average daily credit sales}^{‡}}$	= _____	43.0 days
10. Net sales to inventory	$\dfrac{\text{Net sales}}{\text{Inventory}}$	= _____	22.0
11. Net sales to working capital	$\dfrac{\text{Net sales}}{\text{Working capital}}$	= _____	10.0
12. Long-term liabilities to working capital	$\dfrac{\text{Long-term liabilities}}{\text{Working capital}}$	= _____	0.7
13. Debt to owners' equity	$\dfrac{\text{Total liabilities}}{\text{Owners' equity}}$	= _____	1.6
14. Current liabilities to owners' equity	$\dfrac{\text{Current liabilities}}{\text{Owners' equity}}$	= _____	1.1
15. Fixed assets to owners' equity	$\dfrac{\text{Fixed assets}}{\text{Owners' equity}}$	= _____	1.2

*Times unless otherwise specified.

†Working capital = Current assets − Current liabilities.

‡If 80 percent of sales are on credit, average daily credit sales are: Annual sales ÷ 365 × 0.80 = _____.

Does your company have enough sales for the amount of investment? The ratio of *net sales to owners' equity* (Ratio 4) provides an answer. This ratio can be combined with the *net profit to net sales* ratio (Ratio 2) to obtain the *return on equity (ROE)* ratio (Ratio 1).

Can the Business Pay Its Debts?

Can your business pay its current obligations? A number of ratios can help answer this question. As mentioned earlier, the best known is the *current ratio* (Ratio 5), which is the ratio of current assets to current liabilities. You may be making a good profit but not be able to pay your debts, for cash does not necessarily increase when you make a profit. The **acid test (quick) ratio** (Ratio 6), which is the ratio of current assets minus inventory to current liabilities, is an even more rigorous test of the ability to pay debts quickly.

The **acid test (quick) ratio** is the ratio of current assets, less inventory, to current liabilities.

Another check is obtained by using **working capital,** or current assets less current liabilities, as a basis. Working capital indicates the ability a company has to pay its current liabilities. The ratios of *accounts receivable to working capital* (Ratio 7) and *inventory to working capital* (8) provide an insight into the riskiness of the company's ability to make current payments.

Working capital is the amount of current assets less current liabilities.

How Good Are the Business's Assets?

How good are your assets? Cash in hand is the best asset, but it does not produce any revenue. *Accounts receivable* represent what you will receive in cash from customers sometime in the future. However, as indicated earlier, the older an account, the greater the chance of loss. So the *collection period* ratio (Ratio 9), accounts receivable to average daily credit sales, provides a guide to their quality.

Inventories can be evaluated in about the same way as accounts receivable. Because goods in inventory become obsolete if not sold within a reasonable time, they should generally be turned over as many times as necessary during the year to keep the product either fresh (as in milk and eggs) or desirable (such as changing technology). The turnover rate is expressed by the ratio of *net sales to inventory* (Ratio 10). If your company turns its inventory over too slowly, you may be keeping obsolete or deteriorating goods. Too high a ratio may result from an inventory so low that it hurts production or from not providing satisfactory service to customers.

> For example, as discussed in Chapter 12, Rod and Kim Grimm stay on the road in their black refrigerated Kenworth to get a load of frozen shrimp from Los Angeles to Massachusetts in just 73 hours. Due to the nature of the product, it must have a rapid inventory turnover in order to provide the freshest shrimp possible to the consumer.[5]

To get an idea of the support that you receive from your current assets, compute the ratio of *net sales to working capital* (Ratio 11). Accounts receivable and inventory should increase with an increase in sales, but not out of proportion. Increases in payroll and other expenses require a higher level of cash outflow. On the other hand, too low a ratio indicates available surplus working capital to service sales.

Is Your Equity in the Business Satisfactory?

How much equity should you have in your company? Assets are financed either by equity investments or by the creation of debt—a liability. Thus, any retained earnings, which are part of your equity, can be used to increase your assets or decrease your liabilities. You can maintain a high level of equity, with a relatively low level of risk, or a relatively high level of liabilities with a higher expected return on equity—but greater risk.

Most small companies do not like to maintain a large amount of long-term debt, since the risk is too great. The ratios commonly used to check the company's source-of-funds relationships are *long-term liabilities to working capital* (Ratio 12), *debt to owners' equity* (Ratio 13), *current liabilities to owners' equity* (Ratio 14), and *fixed assets to owners' equity* (Ratio 15). An extremely high value for any of these puts your company in a risky situation. While a bad year will probably decrease your income, the obligation to pay continues. On the other hand, a very good year results in large returns to you.

Ratios Are Interrelated

While each ratio indicates only part of the firm's position, the ratios overlap because a company is a complex system. Thus, a change in the size of one of the accounts, such as cash, affects other values.

The financial ratios for the items on the profit and loss statement can be expressed in percentages of sales. This information is usually hard to obtain from competing small firms. High cost of goods sold as a percentage of sales income may indicate a poor choice of vendors, inefficient use of material or labor, or too low a price. A high percentage of salaries may indicate overstaffing of the company.

■ THE U.S. TAX SYSTEM

The U.S. tax system includes all the federal, state, and local tax systems, each of which has at least two parts. The first part is the system for determining what the taxes will be and who will pay them. The second part is the system for collecting the taxes. Information about federal taxes can be found on the Internet at www.irs.ustreas.gov.

Who Pays the Taxes?

Indirect taxes are not paid by a person or firm, but by someone else.

Taxes can be either indirect or direct. **Indirect taxes** are paid not by the person or firm against which they are levied but by someone else. Since indirect taxes are part of the cost of doing business, they must either be added to the price of the firm's product or shifted backward to the persons who produced the product.

Direct taxes are those paid directly to a taxing authority by the person or business against which they are levied.

Direct taxes are paid directly to the taxing authority by the person or business against which they are levied.

> For example, the owner of a building containing a retail shop pays the property tax (direct) to the tax collector, but the amount of the tax is included in the rent paid by the retailer to the owner (indirect). In turn, the retailer includes this tax in the price a customer pays for the goods or services being sold (indirect).

Also, as will be shown later, you pay tax on your income (direct) even though your employer may withhold it and send it to the tax collector for you.

Table 14–2 gives an overview of some selected taxes on small businesses. It shows the kind of tax, the taxpayer, the point of collection, and the governmental unit collecting the tax.

How Taxes Affect Small Businesses

Taxes affect almost every aspect of operating a small business. First, there is the direct taxation of business income as an income tax on corporate profits.

Second, employers must withhold—and often match—a variety of employment-related taxes levied on their employees, such as federal and state taxes on personal wage and salary incomes, and federal taxes levied to fund the Social Security and Medicare systems.

Third, owners must pay personal taxes on their salaries and other ownership-related income they withdraw from the business. And if part of their wealth is invested outside the business, they face taxes on the investment income they receive.

Fourth, taxes are levied on the transfer of ownership of the business, so the owner must do careful estate planning to minimize the tax bite on an inheritance as will be discussed in Chapter 18.

Fifth, taxes also affect business decisions on other levels as well. For example, as shown in Chapter 3, the choice of the best form of business entity largely depends on the profitability of the business and the tax status of the owner(s).

Finally, the administrative cost of being a tax collector for the government is becoming burdensome. As shown in Table 14–2, it is the responsibility of the business owner to

Table 14–2
Selected Direct Taxes Paid by Small Firms

Kind of Tax	Taxpayer	Point of Collection	Collecting Agency
Corporate income tax	Corporations	Tax collectors	Internal Revenue Service State revenue departments City tax collectors
Corporate franchise tax (on capital stock)	Corporations	Tax collectors	States
Undistributed profits tax	Corporations	District IRS office	Internal Revenue Service
Customs duties	Corporations	Customs agents	U.S. Customs Service
Excise taxes	Businesses Customers	Utility companies Wholesale distributors Tax collectors	Internal Revenue Service State revenue departments
Motor fuel taxes	Businesses	Wholesale distributors	Internal Revenue Service State revenue departments
Highway use tax	Motor transport businesses	Interstate Commerce Commission	Interstate Commerce Commission
Unemployment compensation	Employers	Internal Revenue Service	Internal Revenue Service
Licenses, permits	Businesses	Tax collectors	City tax collectors State revenue departments CAB, ICC, FCC, etc.
Old Age, Survivors, Disability, and Hospital Insurance (OASDHI)	Employers Employees	Businesses	Internal Revenue Service
Sales and use taxes	Customers	Businesses	City and state revenue departments
Property tax	Businesses	Local tax collectors	City and county tax collectors
Inventory or floor tax	Businesses	Local and state tax collectors	City and county tax collectors
Public utility taxes	Utility companies	City, county, and state tax collectors	City, county, and state tax collectors

Note: This table applies to direct taxes only; the shifting of taxes from the point of collection backward or forward is not considered.

collect several taxes for the government by withholding sums from employees' paychecks or by adding the tax (such as sales or use taxes) to the price of products sold to customers. These administrative costs become very expensive in terms of personnel, time, and money.

Get Professional Help!

One of the purposes of this chapter is to make you aware of the current tax environment in which you will operate and to raise some basic tax issues important to every business owner. *It is very important for someone in every small firm to understand the tax system in order to take advantage of the opportunities available for deductions, credits, and tax savings.* Therefore, it is wise to hire a competent adviser on tax and other important financial matters. The IRS has many programs to educate and assist the owners of small businesses such as the Small Business Tax Education Program, which includes *Your Business Tax Kit* (www.irs.ustreas.gov).[6]

While the U.S. Internal Revenue Service, as well as state and local agencies, will willingly help you determine whether you owe additional taxes, *they accept no responsibility for the accuracy of their advice. The responsibility is yours, so get professional help!* Also, you should familiarize yourself with the *Tax Guide for Small Business,* which covers income, excise, and employment taxes for individuals, partnerships, and corporations. Remember, *the final responsibility for determining and paying your taxes rests with you.*

Types of Taxes

Since it is impossible to discuss all the taxes you will have to pay, we have grouped them into four categories: (1) taxes imposed on the business itself, (2) employment-related taxes, (3) personal taxes that owners pay, and (4) estate taxes (discussed in Chapter 18).

■ TAXES IMPOSED ON THE BUSINESS

Numerous taxes are imposed on the small firm as a condition of its doing business. We have grouped these together as (1) taxes and fees paid for the "right" to operate the business; (2) excise and intangible property taxes; (3) state and local taxes on business receipts; and (4) federal, state, and local income taxes.

Taxes and Fees Paid to Operate the Business

Some license fees, incorporation taxes, and the cost of permits must be paid before the business begins operating. Figure 14–2 lists some of the most important of these. These fees and permits are often intertwined with taxes, insurance, capital requirements, and the nature and scope of the business itself.

Excise and Intangible Property Taxes

An **excise tax** is an additional tax on certain items imposed by the federal government.

The federal government places an **excise tax** on many items such as tires for automobiles and other moving vehicles, cigars and cigarettes, and alcoholic beverages. Many states also apply such taxes. Taxes on intangibles such as copyrights, patents, and trademarks are another source of income for many states. Some states even have a tax on inventories in stock.

State and Local Sales and Use Taxes

A **use tax** is a tax on the use, consumption, or storage of goods within a taxing jurisdiction.

Many states and localities have sales and use taxes, which generate large sums. **Use taxes** are usually imposed on the use, consumption, or storage of goods within the taxing jurisdiction. This type of tax is often applied to automobiles and other moving vehicles that are purchased outside the jurisdiction and brought in for future use or for inventory items that are removed and used by the company itself instead of being sold.

A **sales tax** is a tax added to the gross amount of the sale for goods sold within the taxing jurisdiction.

Sales taxes are usually based on the gross amount of the sale for goods sold within the taxing jurisdiction. A new trend is to tax sales in other locations as well, so you will need to check for your liability for sales taxes in those locations. Exemptions from sales taxes are often provided for goods to be resold and for machinery or equipment used exclusively in processing or assembling other goods. Service businesses are often exempt, as are drugs, unprepared foods, and agricultural products in certain states. The application of sales taxes can be extremely complex.

Figure 14–2
Selected Licenses, Permits, and Registrations Required of Small Firms

- *Business license (city, county, state).* Generally, you must apply for one or more business licenses. Often a tax identification number will be printed on your business license, and you'll use the number when filing various tax returns. Your state department of revenue can assist you in defining your reporting requirements.

- *Employer's federal ID number (SS-4) (federal).* A federal ID number is needed to identify an employer on all federal tax filings. Some local jurisdictions also require the federal ID number on various filings. The SS-4 form is available from the IRS.

- *Incorporation or partnership registration (state).* You should plan on using an attorney to assist with registering your company as a corporation or partnership. If it is a corporation, you'll also need articles of incorporation, bylaws, stock certificates, a corporate seal, and other items.

- *Trade name registration (state).* You'll need to register any trade names used in your business (e.g., if your legal incorporated name is Superior Semiconductors of California, Ltd., but you generally go by the name "Superior," you'll need to register your alternative name).

- *Zoning permits (city or county).* If your business constitutes an "alternative use" or other special case, you'll need appropriate zoning permits.

- *Building permits (city or county).* If you are doing any remodeling, construction, or related work, be sure you have the appropriate permits.

- *Mailing permits (federal).* Check with your post office about any bulk, presorted first class, business reply mail, or other mailing permits.

- *Professional registrations (state).* Generally, these are employee specific, such as registered engineer, notary public, and so forth. You may, however, wish to reimburse employees for any job-related expenses.

Source: Building the High Technology Business: Positioning for Growth, Profitability, and Success (New York: Peat Marwick Main & Co., 1988), p. 59.

For example, in Maryland, services, prescription drugs, and food items in grocery stores are exempt from the state's 5 percent sales tax, but in 1992 the General Assembly imposed a sales tax on "snacks" (potato chips, pretzels, popcorn, and the like). Effective July 1, 1997, this tax was repealed for sales by grocery and convenience stores for off-premises consumption and for vending machine sales. Other food items, such as soft drinks, alcoholic beverages, and candy, as well as single servings of ice cream and frozen yogurt, continued to be taxed. The Maryland State Comptroller's Office reported getting 300 to 400 phone calls a day during the first week after the tax was repealed.[7]

One word of caution: Even if you do not collect these taxes from your customers or clients, you will probably be held liable for the full amount of the uncollected taxes.

Federal, State, and Local Income Taxes

Almost everyone, businesses and individuals alike, is concerned about income taxes—those presently in effect and those that may result from proposed changes. Because of the variation and complexities of the state and local laws, we will discuss only the federal law.

From the very beginning of your business, you should have a qualified accountant to provide you with information and help you make important decisions, compile facts for accurate tax returns, and protect you from costly errors. There are three major decisions involving these taxes that you must make at the start, namely: (1) the method of handling your income and expenses, (2) the time period for paying taxes, and (3) the form of business to use.

How the Form of a Business Affects Its Taxes

As discussed in Chapter 3, the amount and methods of handling income taxes affect the choice of business form. Thus, you may choose a partnership or proprietorship rather than pay higher taxes on corporate income and then pay additional individual taxes on dividends.

U.S. tax laws permit some corporations to seek S corporation status. S corporation shareholders (individuals, estates, and certain trusts) are taxed at individual rates, which are lower than corporate rates; yet they still enjoy the legal protection that comes with corporate status. But remember: S corporations do have disadvantages, such as restrictions on benefit plans and a limit of 75 shareholders.

Another relatively new type of organization that may be helpful to a small business owner is the limited-liability company (LLC). As discussed in Chapter 3, it combines the benefits of a partnership and a corporation.

Finally, as shown in Chapter 9, the use of employee stock ownership plans (ESOPs) can lead to tax advantages as well as cash flow advantages.

Treatment of Federal Corporate Income Taxes

There are three questions small corporations need to answer when handling their federal income taxes: What tax rate applies to the business? What is taxable income? What are deductible expenses?

A corporation's tax rate is based on its income, with progressively higher rates at greater income levels. Since these rates are subject to frequent revision, you should consult your tax accountant or IRS literature for the current rates.

Taxable income is total revenues minus deductible expenses.

For income tax purposes, **taxable income** is defined as total taxable revenues minus deductible expenses. While this definition sounds simple, problems arise in measuring both income and expenses. While the government has set the rules for calculating income for tax purposes, the firm may have discretion in reporting income to its stockholders.

Many not-for-profit businesses generally pay little or no tax. The growing trend toward nontaxpaying competitors has become a source of concern, frustration, and anger on the part of some small business owners.

Normally, deductions from income are classified as *cost of goods sold, selling expenses,* and *administrative expenses.* Administrative expenses are those needed to run a business office, such as rent, accounting and legal expenses, telephone and other utilities, dues and subscriptions to business publications, and professional services.

Inventory Valuation   Another accounting decision you must make is how to value inventory that is used during the year (and included in cost of goods sold). The problem is particularly acute when prices are changing rapidly and/or when a firm holds inventory for long periods. The three methods of computing inventory used in production are (1) the *first-in, first-out (FIFO) method,* (2) the *last-in, first-out (LIFO) method,* and (3) the *average-cost method.* In general, when prices are rising, small firms tend to use the LIFO method to save taxes.

Interest Payments   The U.S. Revenue Code favors the use of debt by small firms, since interest on debt is deductible while dividends paid to stockholders are not. The total amount of interest paid is deducted from revenue to find taxable income.

Business Lunches, Entertainment, and Travel   Allowances for meals and entertainment are subject to frequent changes by the Internal Revenue Service. According to IRS Code Sec. 274(K)(1)(B), "Any business meal is deductible only if the following conditions are met: (1) The meal is directly related to or associated with the active conduct of business. (2) The expense is not lavish or extravagant. (3) The taxpayer is present at the meal."

> For example, Robert Bennington says he writes off the cost of taking his mother out to lunch every week to talk about business; in addition she talks about his business to others and passes out his business cards.[8]

Automobile, Home, and Computer Expenses   Many small business owners operate out of their homes, and certain expenses—such as automobile, utilities, repairs and maintenance, computer operations and maintenance, and home insurance and taxes—can be deducted from income taxes if they are business related. The deductions are quite beneficial to the owner, but there are restrictions, which are enforced. For an automobile, you can either deduct the actual cost of running your car or truck, or take a standard mileage rate. You must use actual costs if you use more than one vehicle in your business. In 1999, the standard mileage rate was 31.5 cents, in addition to parking fees and tolls.[9]

When you work out of your home, you can claim *actual business-related expenses,* such as telephone charges, business equipment and supplies, postage, photocopying, computer paper and magnetic media, and clerical and professional costs. A deduction is also allowable for any portion of your home used "exclusively" and "regularly" as your principal place of business.

> For example, you can deduct expenses for taxes, insurance, and depreciation on that portion of your home that is used exclusively as your office. The IRS rule is this: The home must be the principal place of business for your trade or business, or a place of business used by clients, patients, or customers.[10]

The Deficit Reduction Act of 1984 limits the conditions under which computers used in the home can be deducted as business expenses. The simple test is this: If you use a home computer for business purposes over 50 percent of the time, it qualifies for the appropriate credits or deductions.

■ EMPLOYMENT-RELATED TAXES

As shown in Chapter 9, employers are legally required to provide their employees with Social Security and Medicare, unemployment compensation insurance, and industrial insurance (commonly called workers' compensation). In addition, the employer must withhold taxes from employees for city, county, state, and federal income taxes. Also, since 1986, the Employee Retirement Income Security Act (ERISA) has required employers with 20 or more employees to continue health insurance programs for limited periods for employees who are terminated and for widows, divorced spouses, and dependents of employees.

Income Tax Withholding

The IRS and certain states, counties, and localities require you to withhold the appropriate amount of income tax from each employee's earnings during each pay period. The amount of this pay-as-you-go tax depends on each employee's total wages, number of exemptions claimed on his or her withholding exemption certificate, marital status, and length of pay period. Each employee must complete and sign a W–4 form for your files.[11] See Figure 14–3 for the important employee-related forms needed by small firms.

The amount withheld from all employees must be submitted to the IRS, along with Form 941, on a quarterly basis. However, if $3,000 or more has been withheld from employees during the month, that deposit must be made within three banking days following the end of the month.

Figure 14-3
Selected Employee-Related Tax Forms Needed by Small Firms

Federal tax forms

For companies with paid employees:

- Form SS–4, Application for Employer Identification Number
- Form W–2, Wage and Tax Statement
- Form W–2P, Statement for Recipients of Periodic Annuities, Pensions, Retired Pay, or IRA Payments
- Form W–3, Transmittal of Income and Tax Statements
- Form W–4, Employee's Withholding Allowance Certificate, for each employee
- Form 940, Employer's Annual Federal Unemployment (FUTA) Tax Return
- Form 941, Employer's Quarterly Federal Tax Return
- Form 1099–MISC, Statement for Recipients of Nonemployee Compensation

Income tax forms and schedules, which vary depending on your organizational status, type of income/losses, selection of various elections, etc.

ERISA Form 5500 series, depending on your status under the Employee Retirement Income Security Act

State and local forms

Income and/or business and occupation taxes

Industrial insurance ("workers' compensation")

Unemployment compensation insurance

Form W–2, "Wage and Tax Statement," must be completed and mailed to each employee by January 31 immediately following the taxable year. Employers submitting an annual amount of $50,000 or more must transmit to the IRS by electronic media transfer.[12]

Social Security/Medicare Taxes

As shown in Chapter 9, the Social Security program requires employers to act as both tax collectors and taxpayers. Therefore, not only do you have to withhold a certain percentage of each employee's income, but you must also match it with a payment of your own. These taxes are technically for the Federal Insurance Contributions Act (FICA) but are usually referred to as the Social Security and Medicare taxes. For example, in 1999, the employer had to collect 6.2 percent of an employee's total earnings—*up to a maximum of $72,600*—and then match that amount out of business revenues. Another 1.45 percent of the employee's total earnings must be collected for Medicare. These taxes are sent to the IRS each quarter, along with Federal Form 941, Employer's Quarterly Federal Tax Return. Self-employed people must pay the combined employee's and employer's amount of taxes, which amounted to 15.3 percent in 1999.

Unemployment Compensation Insurance

The **federal unemployment tax** is a tax paid to the federal government to administer the unemployment insurance program.

Unemployment compensation insurance has two parts. First, a small basic amount is paid to the U.S. government as a **federal unemployment tax** to administer the program. In 1999 the rate was 6.2 percent on the base wage of $7,000. A second part, which is determined by the states, builds up a fund from which employees are paid in case they are laid off. Federal Form 940, Employer's Annual Federal Unemployment (FUTA) Tax Return, must be filed annually. However, you may be liable for periodic tax deposits during the year.

Workers' Compensation

Employers are required to provide industrial insurance for employees who are harmed or killed on the job. These payments are usually funded through an insurance program, with higher rates for higher-risk employees.

■ PERSONAL TAXES PAID BY OWNERS

There are several ways of withdrawing cash from the business for your own use. Some of these are taxable to you, and some are taxable to the firm.

Taxes on Amounts Withdrawn from the Business

First, salaries and bonuses received from the business corporation are expenses to the business. But individual income taxes are also paid on those sums. You can also withdraw cash from a proprietorship or partnership, and these sums are also taxable to you as an individual.

When owners receive a dividend from a corporation, it is taxed twice. The corporation pays taxes on it but gets no tax deduction, and owners must pay taxes at their individual rates.

Employees can also receive tax-free benefits from the business, which are deductible by the firm. These include such noncash items as medical and legal reimbursements, tuition assistance, and other employee benefits, as well as travel and entertainment expense reimbursements.

Finally, there are many pension and profit-sharing plans, the payment of which is deductible by the business. Payments from the plans are not taxable to the recipients until they are received.

(*Source:* Cartoon courtesy of J. Nebesky. Used with permission.)

Taxes on Amounts Received from Sale of the Business

Usually, when entrepreneurs sell their companies, the contracts contain the following important provisions: (1) a noncompeting clause from the seller, (2) warranties and representations by the seller about the debt and liabilities of the company being sold, and (3) the purchase price—whether it is paid in cash, with a promissory note, in stock in the acquiring company, or with some combination.

Under the Tax Reform Act of 1986, most sales of assets are subject to double taxation, both corporate and personal, as shown earlier, so many such transactions now involve the exchange of stock. Therefore, the form in which the proceeds are to be received can be as critical as the price and should be included in negotiations between buyer and seller, as the following example illustrates.

> Jan and Al Williams started Bio Clinic Co. in their garage in Southern California in the early 1960s. By 1985, the business was so successful that Sunrise Medical Inc. (www.sunrisemedical.com), a Torrance, California, company, offered $7.2 million for it. The Williamses, who were in the process of divorcing at the time, wanted different things when they negotiated the terms of sale. Jan wanted stock, since she expected the stock of Sunrise to grow in value. Al, on the other hand, wanted as much cash as possible. The parties worked out a compromise—$2 million in stock, and $5.2 million in cash.[13]

In summary, the tax consequences from the sale of a business are that either (1) you pay an immediate capital gains tax on cash payments from the sale, or (2) if you receive part of the payment in stock, you may be able to defer some taxes to a later period.

■ RECORD KEEPING AND TAX REPORTING

The importance of record keeping has been emphasized throughout this text. There are essentially two reasons for keeping business records. First, tax and other records are required by law; second, they help you manage your business better. While the IRS allows some flexibility in records systems, it does require that records be kept, be complete, and be separate for each individual business.

Maintaining Tax Records

When you start your business, as shown in Chapter 4, you should set up the kind of records system most suitable for your particular operations. Also, keep in mind that the records should be readily available to compute, record, and pay taxes as they become due and payable. A variety of accounting software packages are available to help small businesses maintain the necessary records.

The IRS requires that tax records be retained for up to three years after a tax return is filed. If there's reason to suspect fraud, the IRS may look at your tax records for longer periods. While the IRS has up to three years to look at your records, you also have up to three years from the date of filing to straighten out tax matters as the circumstances demand. If changes are needed, you may file a one-page amended return on Form 1040X.

Reporting Your Taxes

All federal, state, and local governments having jurisdiction over your business require that you submit a written monthly, quarterly, or annual report on income. Since the requirements vary so much for state and local agencies, you must contact each agency for a current list.

WHAT YOU SHOULD HAVE LEARNED

■

1. After planning is done, a control system should be established to aid in carrying out the plans. The control process is composed of: (*a*) setting standards, (*b*) measuring performance, (*c*) comparing actual performance with standards, (*d*) deciding whether corrections are needed, and (*e*) acting.

2. The budgetary control system is designed and used for control of financial affairs. Items in the financial statements should be checked frequently, with emphasis on where poor performance most affects the company.

3. Information on actual performance can be obtained by observation or from oral or written reports.

Actual performance can be compared to standards to determine the causes of poor performance.

4. Various ratios can be used to compare the company's current and past performance, as well as its performance relative to competitors. They can help determine whether profits are satisfactory, whether assets are productive, how able the company is to pay its debts, how good its assets are, and how much equity the owners have.

5. The U.S. tax system is very complex. Federal, state, and local governments impose taxes directly on individuals and businesses and require them to collect taxes from others. The four types of business taxes are (*a*) those imposed on the

business itself, (*b*) employment-related taxes, (*c*) personal taxes paid by the owners, and (*d*) estate taxes.

6. You are required to provide Social Security, Medicare, unemployment insurance, and workers' compensation for your employees, and to withhold taxes from them. Each employee must complete a W–4 form. The withheld amounts must be submitted to the IRS periodically. A W–2 Form must be mailed to each employee by January 31 of the following year. Unemployment insurance payments build up a fund from which a state can pay employees if they are laid off.

7. From the time you begin your business, you should maintain complete and accurate tax records. For tax purposes, records must be retained up to three years after the date of filing the return. If for any reason the IRS suspects fraud, there is no time limitation.

QUESTIONS FOR DISCUSSION

1. What is control? List the steps in an effective control process.

2. What are performance standards? Why are they used? List some examples.

3. What is budgetary control? How can it be used by a small business?

4. How can information about actual performance be obtained in a small firm?

5. Compute the ratios listed in Table 14–1 for The Model Company, using the data in Figures 13–1 and 13–2.

6. Evaluate the financial condition of The Model Company.

7. Evaluate your personal financial situation and operations, using material developed in this chapter.

8. Name the three main types of taxes a small firm must pay.

9. How does the form of a business affect its taxes?

10. Name and explain the three types of employment-related taxes.

11. Why are records so important for tax purposes?

CASE 14–1

THEME RESTAURANTS

Theme restaurants were the biggest restaurant craze of the 90s, and they popped up everywhere from Boston to Bangkok to Berlin. The craze is believed to have started with the introduction of the Hard Rock Cafe in London, England; Hard Rock Cafes are now found in many of the major cities of the world, and the name is a much imitated and hotly defended trademark. Other theme restaurants include Planet Hollywood, the Harley-Davidson Cafe, Dive!, Fashion Cafe, and the Rainforest Cafe. By the end of the century diners were getting pickier and theme restaurants' stock prices slumped, creating fierce competition.[14]

The success of these restaurants can be attributed to a perfect balance between novelty and food. Many of the theme restaurants such as the Hard Rock Cafe and Planet Hollywood look to celebrities to bring in the crowds. Both of these restaurants feature artifacts from past and present celebrities. And celebrities often visit the restaurant, making a diner's experience even more enjoyable. Planet Hollywood restaurants are designed to fit the culture and customs of the region. The Harley-Davidson Cafe attracts customers with vintage motor-cycles, while the Rainforest Cafe mimics a peaceful outdoor setting. The Fashion Cafe has models strolling a runway, and the Dive! is a faux submarine backed by director Steven Spielberg and others.[15]

But novelty alone is not enough. According to one restaurant owner, theme restaurants draw their initial crowd with the "wow," but if the food isn't good, customers won't come back. To attract repeat customers, theme restaurants try to create attractive menus that follow the image suggested by the theme. The Rainforest Cafe, for example, offers food seasoned with spices from South America. The Harley-Davidson Cafe, on the other hand, has a general line of American fare with specialty drinks such as the Shock Absorber and Wheelie, while Planet Hollywood looks to its signature Chicken Crunch to bring people back.

To successfully provide the customer with the appropriate food, excellent service, and requested products, the manager must have specific guidelines for control. One area needing control is the budgeting process. Many operations use a food cost percentage (FCP) as a guideline for quality control. FCP is the comparison of the sales price to the cost of the materials necessary for production. For instance, if the FCP is too low, it could indicate unacceptable ingredients; on the other hand, if the FCP is too high it might indicate inventory shrinkage (employee theft), purchasing fraud, and lack of appropriations skills, or indicate a need to raise prices. The individual operations can also compare these data to the industry average or to competitors' data to establish a yardstick by which to measure and compare. For example, according to the National Restaurant Association, in 1997 the average FCP was 35.5[16] which was 5.5 percent higher than in 1995.

FCP is only one aspect of the budgeting process. Budgets should be realistic, flexible, and prepared for various time frames. For example, the capital budget that outlines major expansions and acquisitions may project five to seven years into the future, while the operating budget outlines the operating or fiscal cycle for one year.

How long will the theme restaurant craze last? No one can say, but Standard and Poor's Industry Surveys indicate that midscale sit-down restaurants are expected to benefit from increased demand. U.S. customers spent about $215 million in bars and restaurants in 1995—or more than $400,000 every day on eateries. For a restaurant chain there are basically three ways to grow: build sales at existing sites, open new units, and make acquisitions.

Can these restaurants be successful over a long time? That is still to be seen, but getting people to come back is what separates successful theme restaurants from the nice ideas that won't turn heads or profits.

Questions

1. Do you think theme restaurants are a permanent part of the restaurant industry? Why or why not?

2. What suggestions would you make to improve the attractiveness of these restaurants?

3. Would you like to own and operate a theme restaurant? Why or why not?

CASE 14-2

HOW TO DEAL WITH CASH FLOW PROBLEMS

Financial experts can suggest many ways to deal with cash flow problems. You, the small business owner, must remember to always make finances your number one priority. Constant monitoring is the best way to identify problems at the earliest possible stage. Many small business operators, and those who have at one time or another been involved with small business, will tell you that you can never spend too much effort or time on the financing aspect of operations.

Key areas to watch include:

- Cash balances.
- Accounts receivable turnover.
- Accounts payable balance.
- Interest payments and percentages.
- Worker productivity.
- Unnecessary expenses or excesses.
- Obsolete assets and inventory.
- Making sure that the people handling your cash are capable and honest.

Questions

1. Which of the above can you quantify?

2. Which of the above do you think is the most important point? Why?

3. Which of the above can be compared to a budget? Which budget?

4. What other suggestions do you have? Explain.

15

USING COMPUTER TECHNOLOGY IN SMALL BUSINESSES*

Technology enables me to change, and technology forces me to change.

David H. Freeman

Farms, factories, even tiny one-person businesses are reaping the benefits—and surviving the frustrations—of computerization.

Jared Taylor, business consultant

LEARNING OBJECTIVES

After studying the material in this chapter, you will be able to:

1. Explain the importance of information to a small business, and state which information is needed.

2. Discuss the need for—and how to choose—management information systems (MISs) for a small business.

3. Describe the growing role of computers in business.

4. Explain how the microcomputer (PC) has affected small business.

5. Discuss the origin, growth, and uses of the Internet.

6. Explain some of the potential problems with computer technology in small business.

7. Discuss how accounting is part of a small business's management information system.

---

*The authors thank Dr. Walter H. Hollingsworth of the University of Mobile for his revision of this chapter.

Tom Williams Is Off to a Heady Start in Computers

Imagine that you have a house by a lake, own a thriving business in the hot new world of technology, and work with recording artists such as Eric Clapton. Yet you still have time to hang out with friends, become one of Blockbuster's favorite customers, read a lot, and play the cello. Does this sound to you like the ideal life? And imagine having all that by the time you're only 16!

Tom Williams, as the owner of White Sands Software and marketing/technical consultant for *Head Tripp,* had it all—and he *was* only 16. He produced an Enhanced CD—music plus multimedia—featuring 10 artists from Polydor/A&M Records, which premiered in Tower Records stores in New York, Los Angeles, Seattle, Chicago, Boston, and Austin, Texas. The Enhanced CD, which was demonstrated at in-store Macintosh computer kiosks, featured audio and video from Clapton, the Velvet Underground, and such new artists as Gene, Fig Dish, Sensor, Shed Seven, and 8 Story Window. The *Head Tripp* promotion was also featured at several Web sites, including a downloadable screen saver at the Polydor site.

This was pretty heady stuff for a promotion launched by a youth who at the time was too young to drive. Williams, who has the poise and presence of a corporate vice president, explained his success by saying, "My first introduction to the multimedia business was at age 11, when my family got a computer at home. I was looking for the games. All I could find was a word processor and a thing called Hypercard, a basic programming environment. As the summer progressed, I started to teach myself Hypercard and make simple games for myself."

When he entered the seventh grade that fall, Williams discovered that his new school had a color Macintosh with a music keyboard, a scanner, and other hardware that enabled him and his friends to create more elaborate games. "It was not like the nerdy thing to do," he hastens to add. "We were all on the sports teams as well."

While Williams admits that the games they created were "rip-offs of TV shows and whatever," the entrepreneurial bug had bitten him. His classmates bought floppy disks and labels from a local store and began selling their games "like we were selling drugs." Total gross sales for the first venture were $100, " . . . which in grade seven was so very much money." The games improved as the skill level of the programming increased. So Williams founded White Sands Software in 1993.

Then, in July 1994, Williams, who had himself legally declared an adult, moved from his British Columbia home to Cupertino, California. There he began working as an intern for a San Francisco multimedia company to learn the business ropes. In November, Apple asked if he'd be a consultant in its interactive music development, which led him to the *Head Tripp* assignment.

"From an early age, even to be associated with Apple was a dream come true," he says. His youth was a plus, for he fit into a large demographic group that Apple was wooing. "They could get a feel [from me] for what makes a 'cool' Enhanced CD, what tools were needed."

Although he consulted for Apple, Williams was still developing White Sands, where his mother was chairman of the board. He was in the process of creating screen savers, Web sites, and Enhanced CDs. The company had also been talking to Capitol Records about potential work, and it had a lot of corporate clients.

Williams was also developing an edutainment CD-ROM, entitled *When Mother Nature Is Missing.* It was based on a concept learned at the dinner table when he was two years old. His mother would mix food he didn't like with food he did like, so he couldn't tell the difference. "If you take that same concept to edutainment, [kids will have] so much fun they [won't] realize they're learning."

While an advanced placement test got him out of high school, he wasn't ruling out college. He said he would "have to get a new set of goals, because a lot of them I have already accomplished. I consider myself very fortunate that I wake up every morning and I like what I do."

By late 1998, Tom Williams was Director of Creative Development for MultiActive Technologies' MultiActive Education Inc. (www.MultiActive.com).

Source: Adapted from Bruce Haring, "Teen Off to a Heady Start in Computer Business," *USA Today,* October 31, 1995, p. 8D.

The Profile illustrates the explosive nature of computers and related technologies. It also shows the great diversity now being found in small businesses. The computer industry may have been started by more mature individuals, such as J. Presper Eckert, Jr., and John Mauchly (developers of the first commercially successful electronic computer—the Univac), but it is bright, brash, and adventurous young people who are developing today's advancing technology. Older entrepreneurs and workers are learning to cope.

This chapter is designed to show how computers and related technologies are revolutionizing small business operations, while other systems—such as accounting, financial, and management information systems—are still needed for successful operations.

"I suppose you're just going to sit there and let this computer craze sweep right by you?"

(*Source:* Cartoon courtesy of J. Nebesky. Used with permission.)

■ THE ROLE OF INFORMATION IN SMALL BUSINESS

Have you ever considered how many records you keep or generate? You probably have in your possession at least a driver's license, credit card(s), student ID, Social Security card, and checkbook. Without these items, you would find it difficult to transact much of your daily business. Also, whenever you use one of these items, records (or entries in the records) are generated.

For example, when you use a credit card, it generates a sales or credit slip, a monthly statement, and a record of payment. You use the statement to write a check and to deduct the amount from your bank balance. All the while, you keep some information (such as your Social Security number) in your head to save time in filling out forms.

As you can see, information is a most important resource for a small business, as well as for a person. It should help provide answers to such questions as: Is the product selling properly? Will the cash flow be adequate? Are the employees paid the correct amounts—and on time—and are the employment taxes handled properly?

Obviously, these questions cannot be answered without the appropriate data. Just as your personal records provide data for your personal decisions, your company must also collect data for its operations.

Efficient accounting and information systems are needed by small firms—as well as large ones—to convert data to information so management can use it to operate success-fully. And as you will see, many of these information systems are now computerized—even in many small businesses.

■ ELEMENTS OF A MANAGEMENT INFORMATION SYSTEM (MIS)

As shown in Chapter 11, all types of systems involve the same basic elements: inputs, processes, and outputs. A **management information system (MIS)** is designed to collect, record, process, report, and/or convert data into a form suitable for management's use. For example, as will be shown later, an accounting system records and processes data and produces reports. A system may be entirely manual or, at the other extreme, almost entirely machine or computer operated.

All these systems start with inputs, process them, and furnish outputs. Whether or not computers are used, an organized MIS is necessary for the efficient operation of any busi-ness. Figure 15–1 diagrams a system that can be manually or computer operated—or can use some combination of both. Defining the needs of each part of a business for informa-tion and its processing and use is the first step in designing an information system.

> A **management information system (MIS)** collects, records, processes, reports, and/or converts data into a usable form.

What Information Is Needed?

Everyone in the small firm should consider the questions "What do I need to know in order to do my job better?" and "What information do I have that will help others do their jobs better?" The accumulation of these pieces of information, with analysis of what data are reasonably available, is the initial step in forming an information system. Emphasis should be on developing a system adapted to present needs—yet flexible enough to accommodate future changes. An obvious but often overlooked bit of advice: *Even the best information system is of no value if it is not used—and used properly.*

Purposes for Which Information Is Used In determining what information is needed, you should ask yourself why you want it. The usual answers are:

- *To plan a course of action,* such as deciding the number of items to purchase, the number of salespeople to hire, and/or the amount of accounts receivable to expect.
- *To meet obligations,* such as repaying borrowed money.
- *To control activities,* such as assuring that ordered materials have arrived.
- *To satisfy government regulations,* such as conforming to safety, employment, and ethical standards.
- *To evaluate performance.*

Figure 15–1
Accounting for Sales

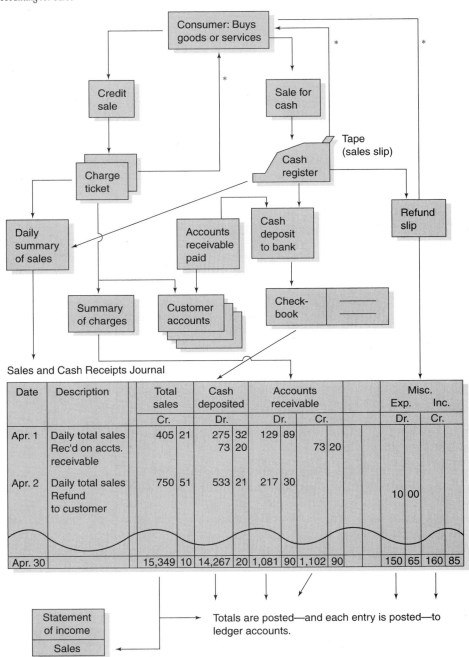

Date	Description	Total sales		Cash deposited		Accounts receivable					Misc. Exp.		Inc.	
		Cr.		Dr.		Dr.		Cr.			Dr.		Cr.	
Apr. 1	Daily total sales	405	21	275	32	129	89							
	Rec'd on accts. receivable			73	20			73	20					
Apr. 2	Daily total sales	750	51	533	21	217	30							
	Refund to customer										10	00		
Apr. 30		15,349	10	14,267	20	1,081	90	1,102	90		150	65	160	85

Totals are posted—and each entry is posted—to ledger accounts.

*Copy to customer

After determining the information needed, you must know how to use it. This involves classifying it into a usable form and establishing systems and procedures to assure the availability of critical information.

Examples of Needed Information   The kinds of information you might need are too numerous to discuss, but the most important are (1) records of service provided to customers and (2) records of services performed for the business.

Services to customers provide revenue in the form of cash, checks, or promises to pay. Figure 15–1 shows a diagram of a system for recording sales of goods or services. Both real-time and delayed transactions occur in this system. When products are sold, sales slips are made out to give to customers. Later, the slips are used as daily summaries of sales, sales taxes, and so forth, which are then recorded in journals. Unlike direct sales, rental of items requires additional transactions.

Services performed for the business must also be recorded. Goods sold to, or services performed for, a firm are its expenses of doing business, and payments must be made for them. In addition, payments are made to increase assets and reduce obligations.

Even very small businesses need formal systems for keeping records. In the past, very simple record-keeping systems such as manila folders, shoe boxes, and entries in a checkbook have been used for this purpose. These methods are simple and easy to understand but in many cases do not meet the demands of today's competitive marketplace.

Timing of Information Flow(s)

Data from activities may be needed (1) at the time of transaction (real-time processing) or (2) after transactions accumulate (batch processing). For example, as shown in Figure 15–1, a customer is given a sales slip on completion of the sale, which is *real-time processing.* An MIS can be designed to take care of such immediate feedback. For example, portable computers, modems, mobile phones, electronic wands or scanners, and radios can be used to collect and provide information quickly, as in the following example.

> Ernest Gore, an architect, visited Jean Soor, who was interested in building a house. During the discussion, Ernest opened his laptop computer and laid out the house plan as Jean described her ideas. Several times, they discussed "what ifs," and he made the changes to show their effects. He left with the plans well developed. Ernest attributes a great deal of his success in making the sale and satisfying the customer to this type of rapid feedback.

Batch processing is done after more than one transaction has occurred, such as at the end of an hour or at the end of the day, as shown in Figure 15–1, when the daily sales are summarized. Slower turnaround may meet the requirements of the system and be less expensive, so you should balance the speed and convenience of real-time processing with the economy of batch processing, as the following example illustrates.

> A chef in a restaurant is usually a highly skilled individual who schedules, cooks, and assembles meals. The server is a less-skilled person who uses an information system to transmit information from the customer to the chef. Many restaurants use turnstiles for placing orders. First, the orders are written. Then the slips are clipped to a turnstile that the chef can turn to read the order. The slips on the turnstile serve to schedule orders in sequence, and they may also become the customer's bill. The turnstile causes a brief delay in the MIS but is simple and effective. Also, being impersonal, it does not make the higher-status chef seem to be taking orders from the lower-status servers.

Now, many restaurants—especially fast-food chains—are using computers to convey orders from servers or front-counter order takers to the kitchen staff. In addition to eliminating bottlenecks in taking orders, computer systems can reduce waste and labor costs in food preparation and even serve as a marketing tool by tracking customers and their eating habits.

> For example, the assistant manager of a Boston Market Restaurant in San Francisco uses a computer program to track sales of every menu item hour by hour and to set cooking schedules. By consulting a computer printout, he can determine how much chicken to cook, when to put it in the rotisserie, and what time to serve it.[1]

Companies that apply computer technology effectively—as in the above example—stand a good chance of achieving a competitive edge. Unfortunately, there is no universal set of rules for bringing technology into a small business.[2]

Choosing an MIS

Figure 15–2 presents a checklist you can use to define your company and the types and volume of information it needs. Completion of this checklist should help you form a better idea of the system to install.

■ THE ROLE OF COMPUTERS IN BUSINESS

As their capabilities mushroom and costs decline, computers are rapidly taking over the roles of record keepers, clerks, and analysts. Through the use of computers, data can be quickly received, collected, processed, and reported. As a business grows, computers become more essential because of the increased volume of relevant information.

> **Hardware** consists of the CPU, monitor, keyboard, and other parts that you can see and touch.

A modern computer information system consists of hardware, software, and people. The **hardware** consists of a CPU, a monitor, a keyboard, and other parts that you can see, feel, and touch. (The *CPU* [*central processing unit*] is the part of the computer hardware that controls all other parts of the system.)

> **Software** is the programs, manuals, and procedures that cause the hardware to operate in a desired manner.

Software includes the programs, manuals, and procedures that cause the hardware to operate in a manner desired by the user. Of course, neither of these components is of any use without the people to use and operate them.

Early Business Use of Computers

The first computer used for a business application was the Univac, a giant *mainframe* installed by Sperry-Rand Univac at GE's Louisville, Kentucky, plant in 1954. Such computers were too big and expensive for small business use. They were in use until the 1960s.

Digital Equipment Corporation (DEC) produced the next development, the *minicomputer.* DEC marketed its first model in 1960 and, with a few other companies, dominated the market in the 1970s.

It was the *microcomputer,* however, that finally made computer technology feasible for small business use. Because of the abundance of inexpensive microcomputer hardware and software available to small firms, we will limit our discussion of computers to this type.

The Microcomputer—The Small Business Computer

> A **microprocessor** is a miniaturized computer processor designed and based on a silicon chip.

The terms *microcomputer, personal computer,* and *desktop computer* are used interchangeably to refer to computers based on the **microprocessor,** which is a miniaturized computer processor designed and based on a silicon chip. The significance of the microprocessor to

Figure 15–2
Defining What a Company Needs in an MIS

Type of business
Retail _____ Wholesale _____ Mfg. _____ Professional services _____
Real estate _____ Agriculture _____ Nonprofit _____ Other _____

Business size
Gross income _____ Net profit as percentage of gross income _____

Types of information needed
Numerical _____ Textual _____ Graphics _____ Communications _____

Location(s)
Single _____ Dispersed _____ Franchise _____ Subsidiary _____

Transaction volume
Invoices/month _____ Average accounts receivable _____ Average inventory _____
Inventory turnover _____ Number of inventory items _____
Number of customers _____ Number of employees _____

Current information system (Describe.)
_____
_____

Trouble areas (Rank each according to importance and number of people involved. Use more paper
if needed. Be as complete as possible.)
_____
_____
_____

Potential Future Needs (Include all possible needs, as they may be economically feasible in any
system designed.)
_____
_____

Applications

Business areas to be addressed (Number in order of priority.)
Accounting _____ Financial reporting _____ Inventory management _____
Cash flow planning _____ Market and sales analysis _____ Decision support _____
Billing _____ Scheduling _____ Quality control _____ Payroll _____
Employee benefits _____ Commissions _____ Customer tracking _____
Portfolio management _____ Legal defense _____ Long-term planning _____
Tax reporting _____ Word processing _____ Other (be specific)
_____

Computer skills available in company
_____

Proposed budget for MIS
$_____ Maximum _____

Time Frame
Desired start _____ Latest allowed start _____

small businesses is that it made them more competitive. The efficiency of their operations now approached that of larger competitors.

The first mass-produced microcomputer was the Radio Shack TRS-80, introduced in the early 1970s, which was soon followed by the Commodore Pet 2000. Then, in 1976, Steven Jobs and Stephen Wozniak opened a makeshift production line in Jobs's garage to produce the Apple—a small, easy-to-use computer to help families and small businesses. To raise the $1,500 needed for the start-up, Jobs sold his VW microbus, and Wozniak sold his Hewlett-Packard scientific calculator.

The development of the microprocessor made the development of the microcomputer possible. All of the so-called *personal computers (PCs)* have used these "computers on a chip" as the heart of their systems. Continuing improvement of the microprocessor chip has made possible more and more powerful computers in smaller and smaller boxes.

Apple (www.apple.com) and Commodore based their computers on a chip made by Motorola, rather than the one made by Zilog® Corporation that was used in the TRS-80. This chip required different software, since the computers were not compatible, and programs that would run on the Apple would not run on the TRS-80 and vice versa.

Because of the ease of entry into the computer market, the number of companies multiplied. Machines made by the emerging new companies were "hardware compatible" with the TRS-80 or Apple but not "software compatible" with either machine. Figure 15–3 shows how dramatically software for PCs has changed over the past two decades.

Figure 15–3
Key Dates in PC Software History

Here's a recap of how software for personal computers has changed since 1975.

1975	Bill Gates and Paul Allen adapt BASIC for microprocessors, the first language for programmers to develop PC applications software.
1979	*VisiCalc,* the first spreadsheet, unveiled for the Apple II.
1980	2.3 million PCs in use in the United States.
1981–82	IBM offers a PC using DOS, a Microsoft operating system. IBM licenses the system from Microsoft; Microsoft then licenses DOS to others.
1983	*Lotus 1-2-3,* the first heavy-duty business program, a detailed spreadsheet, introduced. As a result, IBM PCs are propelled into the office. Novell offers *NetWare* to link PCs on networks.
1984	The Apple Macintosh, the first popular computer with a user-friendly screen and mouse, makes its debut.
1985	First version of Microsoft's Windows, an operating system that uses on-screen icons and a mouse, introduced.
1990	Windows 3.0 introduced. More than 50 million PCs in use in the United States.
1992	Windows 3.1, an improved version of Windows 3.0, reaches the market.
1995	Windows 95 debuts.
1998	The debut of Windows 98 is cast into doubt by litigation over whether or not the Internet Explorer 4.0 browser can be included as an integral part of the operating system.

Source: William J. Cook, "Software Struggle," *U.S. News & World Report,* June 19, 1995, pp. 48–49. Adapted with permission.

In 1981, IBM (www.ibm.com) introduced its Personal Computer (IBM® PC), which soon became the industry standard. The IBM PC used the Intel 8088 chip, which was similar to the older chips already in use—except by Apple—so it was compatible with existing technology.

The introduction of the IBM PC gave instantaneous credibility to the personal computer market. While Apple and some others continued to use the Motorola chip, most of the other producers followed IBM's lead, using Intel® chips and operating systems created by Microsoft under the designation *MS-DOS*® or *PC-DOS*®. In rapid succession, 8088 computers were followed by those based on the 8086, 80286, 80386, and 80486 chips. The 80586—marketed under the trade name Pentium®—was introduced in early 1993, followed in 1996 by the Pentium Pro. The Intel Pentium III processor (code name "Katmai"), available at 450 and 500 MHz, will be Intel's highest-performance, most advanced, and most powerful processor for the desktops.

Most advances in computer technology have made the machines faster and more powerful, with more **random access memory (RAM),** larger disk storage, and a variety of efficient peripherals, including printers, modems, fax machines, and Internet access.

> **Random-access memory (RAM)** is the amount of usable memory (volatile storage) within the computer.

One of the computer industry's basic precepts is that *computer power tends to double every 18 months.*[3] In fact, today's top-of-the-line PC is over 400 times faster than the original IBM PC produced in 1981. And the typical high-end computer sold in 1998 had at least 64 MB of RAM, 1,000 times as much as the Commodore 64, introduced in 1982. Finally, today's hard drives, providing 8, 10, 14, or more gigabytes (i.e., approximately 8, 10, or 14 *billion* bytes) of storage, could not even have been comprehended by early computer users, who often had no hard disk at all and had to store everything on 360K floppies!

Indeed, changes in computer and related technologies are so swift and innovative that small business owners might consider leasing, rather than buying, computer hardware. While the new hardware is **backward compatible,** which allows existing programs to run on the new hardware, the latest software is written to take advantage of the most recent technological advances in hardware. These new programs, in many cases, *will not run* on computers based on the older microprocessors.

> **Backward compatible** hardware will run existing programs designed for older equipment.

If the user wishes to use the latest software, and thereby gain a possible competitive advantage, it is necessary to use the most recent and advanced hardware. As the stated goal of Intel® Corporation is to double computing power every 18 months, it will probably be necessary to upgrade hardware every 18 to 24 months to stay abreast of the newest and best information-processing technology. Intel's goal is not unrealistic in view of what has been happening in the past few years.

(*Source:* Cartoon by Fred Maes. Copyright 1996 by Fred Maes. Used with permission.)

A recent development being marketed with increasing success for business use is the "multimedia" computer, which includes, at a minimum, a sound card and a CD-ROM drive. **Read-only memory (ROM)** disks, which resemble audio CDs, can store whole encyclopedias of print information, plus pictures and sound—even moving pictures and animation. Even the most no-frills business computer, however, must include a CD-ROM drive, because CDs are now the usual distribution medium for new software. Likewise, the computer must have a modem, for today's business person could not function without Internet access and e-mail.

> **Read-only memory (ROM)** is unchangeable memory in the computer or on a disk that can be used for specialized applications.

The Laptop, or Notebook, Computer

A **laptop, notebook,** or **subnotebook computer** is a small, battery-powered package that can be used anywhere.

Perhaps the most revolutionary development is the **laptop** (or **notebook** or **subnotebook**) **computer.** Although they remain expensive compared to comparably equipped desktop models, these notebook-sized—and smaller—devices, in a battery-operated package, can be taken anywhere. For sales representatives on the road, engineers in the field, or employees taking inventory, laptops are ideal. While records or computations can be made on the spot, they can also be stored for later transfer to other computers either directly or by modem. Laptops have become standard carry-on luggage for "road warriors," who can use the hours spent on planes and in airports to stay on top of their paperwork.

> Some airlines, such as Delta (www.delta-air.com), American (www.aa.com), and United (www.ual.com), provide power ports for the work-obsessed traveler. Like any electronic device, however, laptops must not be used below 10,000 feet, as they interfere with avionics. A Walkman, Game Boy, or laptop radiates energy in a frequency band that can overlap radio frequencies used by a plane's communication and navigation equipment.[4]

Laptops are also popular with students because they can be taken to the classroom or library to facilitate note taking. Further miniaturization has resulted in "palmtop" computers, some of which fit in a shirt pocket, yet can run "light" versions of popular word processing, spreadsheet, and communications software.

Strengths and Weaknesses of Computers for Small Firms

The key to whether a computer is an asset or a liability in a small firm is the use made of it. The computer itself is not likely to be a limiting factor. The primary limitation is the availability of software that can economically accomplish the desired tasks. Figure 15–4 gives a list of the applications for which a computer is especially well suited and for which software is currently available (as well as a list of tasks not usefully delegated to computers).

Notice that the areas in which computer technology can be most useful are *repetitive, high-volume, quantitative tasks.* By contrast, the areas in which this technology is less

Figure 15–4
What Computers Do Best—and Worst

The computer is most helpful in the following applications, for which software is readily available:

- Repetitive, data-oriented operations, such as accounting, record keeping, or mailing lists.
- Organizing data into information, such as financial reporting.
- Codifying and monitoring procedures, such as technical manuals and production control.
- Calculations, such as financial ratios and tax analyses.
- Forecasting, such as trend projection and materials requirements planning.

The computer is less valuable, and may even be a liability, in operations of the following types:

- Solving unstructured problems or those that are not clearly defined, as in invention or innovation.
- Defining and/or establishing true authority in a company, such as leadership roles.
- Identifying new markets or products. The computer can be a major asset here, but only as a tool to assist human workers.
- Interpersonal relations, such as contract negotiations or establishing corporate culture.
- Defining the corporate mission.

useful are the *unstructured, open-ended activities in which human creativity or judgment is required.* While the latter are more innovative or people oriented, the former are the boring, detail-oriented jobs once performed by lower-paid employees. Smart business owners will delegate these activities to the computer, freeing competent staff to handle the more interesting, long-term problems.

> For example, four advertising veterans founded Rossin Greenberg Seronick & Hill, an advertising agency in Boston. Neal Hill, as CEO, was responsible for creating an organization to support the others so they could be creative. He soon found that most of the people's time involved moving information around, leaving little time to create ads.
>
> Hill computerized the noncreative work, but the employees resisted the change. Then Hill got top managers to use word processors. According to one partner, who used one only reluctantly, "My capacity to do the paperwork quadrupled." After that, the partners were able to motivate all the employees to use computers.
>
> In a year and a half, billings doubled, while personnel increased only 25 percent![5]

■ AND NOW—THE INTERNET!

The PC dominated business during the 1980s. But in the 1990s the Internet became the major attraction.

What is the Internet? Who owns the Internet? Who controls the Internet? These and other questions regarding the Internet are difficult—if not impossible—to answer. One fact is true, though: the Internet is here and will have a tremendous effect on our lives for many years in the future. A whole new business arena has grown up in and around the Internet.

What Is the Internet?

The **Internet** is a collection of computers and computer networks linked together to receive and distribute information around the world. Most colleges and universities, along with public schools, government agencies, businesses, and individuals, are connected to "the Net."

The Internet began as a means of communication between researchers, the military, and some parts of industry. In the early 1960s, scientists needed an efficient way to communicate the various aspects of their research efforts. Computers could process and print text very effectively. By networking computers (wiring them together so that each computer could communicate directly with the others), information could be shared very quickly and efficiently. Because the military needed a robust and secure computer network, the Department of Defense appointed the Advanced Research Projects Agency to design such a network. The result was the ARPANET, which was put in use in the late 1960s. This network was developed during the height of the cold war and was designed to survive and operate in the event of nuclear attack. The Internet is therefore a very robust system.

Academicians who wished to use the same type of networking technology did not have the same need for security as the military. Therefore, the academic community developed a network using the same basic development theory as the military but backed and primarily financed by the National Science Foundation (NSF). Eventually the military and academic networks—along with some others—were interconnected and became the Internet.

Ironically, the Net now has so much traffic that the scientists and researchers for whom it was designed can no longer rely on it. They have offered grants to university networks to find (or design) ways to assign priorities to data.[6]

The **Internet** is a collection of computers and computer networks linked together to receive and distribute information around the world.

How to Use the Internet

We will now attempt to answer the questions about what the Internet is and who controls it put forth above as best defined by current technology. The Internet collection of computer networks is ever changing. Each day hundreds—or even thousands—of new computers and networks come on line. There is no central control (although bills are currently pending in Congress to establish it) or ownership of the Internet. Corporations, educational institutions, government agencies, and individuals around the world join, use, and leave the Net in any way they wish every day. According to a wide-ranging report for the U.S. Department of Commerce, more than 100 million people were on line in April 1998, and the number "is doubling every 100 days."[7]

How many of these new users represent potential customers for the small business owner? Very early in the development of the Internet the likelihood of a large customer base did not seem to be very great. However, in the past few years the possibility of selling goods and services on the Net has demonstrated great opportunity. In 1997 customers spent $2.75 billion purchasing items on the Internet. This is estimated to exceed $1 trillion world wide by the year 2001.[8]

Every unit on the Net is free to use its own operating system and methods, but there is general agreement (protocols) as to how to ship information over the Internet. To be able to use it, however, you must have a service provider. There are many commercial providers, such as America Online® (www.aol.com), Prodigy® (www.prodigy.com), Genie® (www.genie.com), CompuServe® (www.compuserve.com), Sprint® (www.sprint.com), MCI® (www.mciworldcom.com), local phone companies, bulletin boards, and others. In fact, there were over 4,000 in 1997, up from 2,300 just a year earlier.[9] There are also freenets (free or nearly free service provided by a local government agency) and colleges and universities that provide Internet access service. The Internet itself is free, but you may have to pay a fee to your service provider.

The ability not only to network computers within the business but to connect to the Internet has provided business with an inexpensive means of access to a worldwide market. While still in their infancy, the Internet and its substructure the World Wide Web (WWW) have opened a vast new resource to the small business owner. The future of the Internet and the benefits and pitfalls are hard to predict at this time. Its use may be somewhat analogous to the very early days of radio when for the first time entertainment was being given away. Prior to the introduction of radio, performers had a tight control of their product. If you wanted to hear a band you had to pay admission to a "music hall." With the advent of commercial radio, however, music was transmitted free to anyone who had the proper receiver. There was some misgiving about how the performers were to be paid for their work. This problem was of course easily solved, with the result that we are inundated with commercials on our favorite radio and TV shows. Ample evidence of the rewards to successful entertainers is given by the cost of $1.6 million for each 30-second commercial for Super Bowl XXXIII and $1.5 to 1.7 million for the same time on the final *Seinfeld* show.[10] In the same way, Web sites are now being supported by advertising.

The World Wide Web

The World Wide Web is rapidly becoming the preferred method of navigating the Internet. The "Web" is a very powerful, yet easy-to-use interface to the many sites on the Internet. If the user has the proper computer hardware and software, the Web is capable of communicating not only text but also sounds, graphics, videos, and more. Many individuals, educational institutions, government agencies, and businesses have "home pages" on the Web. The user employs the "mouse" to "point and click" to move about a site on the Net or even between Web sites. But there must be some organized way of finding information on the Net. So some entrepreneurs have developed ways to do this. One of the most popular—and profitable[11]—of these systems is Yahoo! (www.yahoo.com), shown in Figure 15–5.

Entrepreneurship on the Net

Yahoo! is a prime example of new and successful businesses that have grown directly from a relationship with the Internet. Yahoo! was started by two graduate students at Stanford

Figure 15–5
Yahoo! Home Page

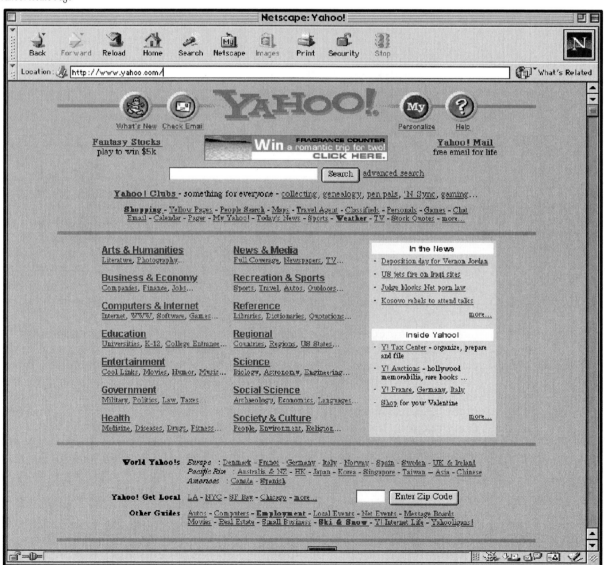

University—Jerry Yang and David Filo—who started indexing sites on the World Wide Web while working on their electrical engineering dissertations. At the time they started their endeavor, the Web was starting a rapid growth from what had been only a dozen or so sites in 1990 to the myriad of worldwide sites available today. Yang and Filo were soon working almost full time adding Web sites to their index. Soon Yahoo! was being accessed by thousands of people each day. What had started as a hobby (dare one say an obsession?) now had strong commercial possibilities.

The two young entrepreneurs were joined by Marc Andreesen, who, while a graduate student at the University of Illinois, had written the Web browser "Mosaic," which brought simple point-and-click commands and colorful graphics to the Net. With financing from Sequoia Capital, Yahoo! has grown to a search engine with over 15 million hits per day. With this number of users, Yahoo! is able to generate considerable income from advertising clients on its home page.

Marc Andreesen has also been quite successful with his other Internet ventures. He is the cofounder of Netscape Navigator, one of the most popular Web browsers. Any industry as dynamic as the computer industry experiences ever-changing fortunes. Netscape Communications, Inc., had revenues of $127.2 million for the quarter ending April 30, 1998, but because of intense competition and a two-for-one split in February 1996 the stock was trading in the $77 range during March 1999.

Other entrepreneurs are establishing businesses of all types on the Web. Figure 15–6 shows the CMPExpress Web site, which allows the customer to view the price and quantity on hand of any item in inventory. The customer may quickly view the technical specifications of the product by clicking on the product name text link or may order the product by clicking "Buy." About 90 percent of the orders for CMPExpress products come from the Internet. Of these orders, 40 percent are totally automated, and the products are shipped directly from the supplier to the purchaser so that the company does not have to keep an inventory.[12]

Another example is the Web site www.owners.com, which offers online real estate listings. A homeowner may choose one of three different listing plans with a range of costs from nothing for the most basic listing to $115 for the Premier plan. All listings are for four months, and the owner may update the listing at any time. The site also offers some very attractive additional services, such as access to books and articles, school district reports, and loan rates and analysis.

The Internet is like any other resource available to the entrepreneur. Those who use this tool in the most expedient and innovative way will reap the largest rewards from their efforts. Like all other tools, this one, used in the wrong way, will be of little or no value and may even be detrimental to the business. It is best to enlist the help of professionals to design Web pages and set up order-processing systems to be used on the Internet. A Web site that is difficult to navigate will be frustrating to the user and of little benefit to the firm. Likewise an automated system that is slow or inaccurate will be a liability to the firm rather than an asset.

Commerce on the Internet has exploded during the last few years. According to a Jupiter Communications study, total annual sales have increased from $710 million in 1996 to an estimated $9.9 billion in 1999.[13] In fact, at that time, *Internet traffic was doubling every 100 days,* as upwards of 7 million households go on line each year.[13]

By late 1998, about 25 percent of companies with fewer than 100 employees had a Web site. They used it to increase their visibility, find new customers, and give customers information about their businesses. Nearly half of them (46 percent) thought the site was worth their time and money, while only 6 percent thought it was not.[14]

From the small business owner's point of view, the Net can also lead to possible abuse by employees. For example, a survey by Yahoo! and Jupiter Communications of 73,000

Figure 15–6
Page from CMPExpress Web Site

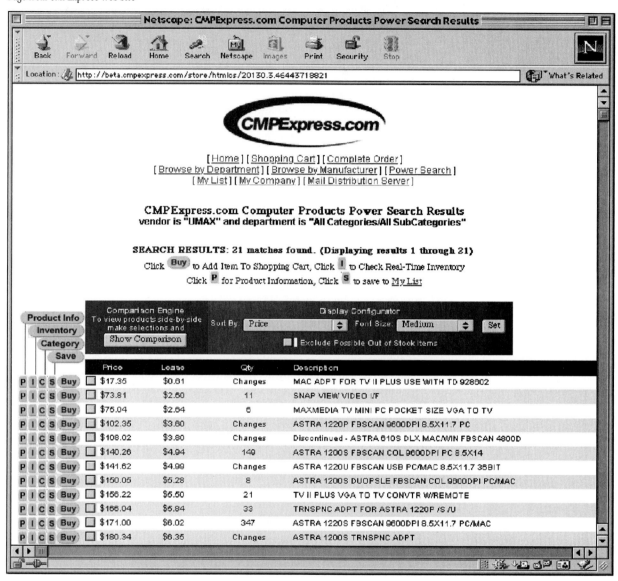

online users found that employees spent considerable time searching for—and viewing or engaging in or interacting with—entertainment, games, and "chat."[15]

■ SOME POTENTIAL PROBLEMS WITH COMPUTER TECHNOLOGY

There are many advantages and disadvantages to using computer technology. Therefore, careful planning is needed to assure accuracy, acceptability, and adaptability. Errors or inadequacies that develop in the system are much easier to detect and correct if the system is carefully designed and if employees are supportive and motivated to make it work. But even when errors and malfunctions are detected, they may not be easy to correct.

> Betty Shaffer, of Richardson, Texas, found that doing freelance bookkeeping in her home was "driving me insane." So she bought an IBM PC and an accounting program. Even after she learned to run the program—by reading the instruction manual—the system would not copy data from one diskette to another. Naturally, it had all worked fine at the outlet where she had bought it.
>
> After several painful months nursing the sick computer, Shaffer persuaded the store manager to make a house call. He found that the machine worked well when the display monitor was moved from the top of the drive unit and put on a table. He suspected the screen must have been mistakenly given a magnetic coating.
>
> With her computer "cured," Shaffer's business "took off." Because the computer does the calculations and prints the reports, she can do three times as much work—for three times the income.[16]

Another problem caused by the introduction of computerized operations is the need to upgrade your and your employees' skills. If this seems overwhelming to you, please take note. Help is available through other small companies specially set up to help you revamp or even get started in the computer world. Many computer retailers, including franchises such as Entré Computer Centers, provide software instruction, and some local Internet service providers offer free classes to get subscribers started "surfing."

Computers Require Added Security

Computers are used for generating and storing important—often confidential—records, which makes controlling access an important issue. In addition, as more people have access to information, it becomes more important to set up procedures to ensure that data are accurately entered and protected from being accidentally (or intentionally) destroyed or altered. This suggests that an important part of a computerized MIS are the procedures set up for entry, updating, and control (to be discussed more fully in Chapter 16). Some steps that can be taken to provide security, however, include:

- Physical control of facilities, such as guards and emergency power.
- Access control, such as identification of users and specifying who has the authority to use the equipment.
- Backups, such as appropriate saving of data.

Just as important as the security of the information you are storing is the integrity of that information. "Hackers" (computer programmers who experiment to see what mischief they can do) have created computer "viruses" that can destroy your data and programs without your being able to stop them. These are programs that "hide" in other programs and are transmitted from one computer to another through exchange of disks or by downloading files from a remote computer or network. *In order to protect your system, you need to get antiviral programs along with the system and minimize the use of programs and/or disks of unfamiliar origin.* Your antiviral program should be of the type that can be updated frequently.

The Y2K Problem or "Millennium Bug"

You've undoubtedly heard and read a great deal about the "millennium bug." By the time you read this, perhaps its effects will be history. But it is an example of how short-sightedness in software design can have disastrous repercussions down the line. During the 1960s, to save what was then extremely valuable memory, programmers lopped off the first two digits of the year. Therefore, many existing computers were unprepared for the turn of the century. Experts saw two scenarios for computer users who had not corrected the problem. First, the computer might reset to 01-01-00 but assume it was January 1, 1900. Second, the system might crash!

As late as mid-1998, a Wells Fargo Bank survey found that while 80 percent of companies with fewer than 100 employees were aware of the issue, half of them had no plans to address it. The study estimated that up to "330,000 small businesses would have to close" until the problem was corrected.[17] To prevent this scenario, the Small Business Administration (www.sba.gov) began a public service campaign of TV ads and mass mailings to small businesses on how to deal with the problem. Larger companies were also encouraging small firms to be prepared. For example, Boeing included a clause in its supplier contracts requiring that all the supplier's computers must be Y2K-compliant.[18]

But the seeming apathy of small business owners may not be unjustified. Those who use relatively new computers with modern operating systems (such as Windows 95 or NT) and rely entirely on commercial software from mainline publishers such as Microsoft, Lotus, and Corel will have little to worry about. Those who will be directly affected will be chiefly larger firms with proprietary software custom-written for their applications. Small businesses, however, stand to be inconvenienced, along with the general public, by the predicted failure of such vital entities as public utilities, government agencies, financial institutions, and major corporations. Worst-case scenarios foresee us helplessly stranded in the dark—without power, transportation, telephone communication, mail delivery, or insurance coverage, unable to use our ATM or credit cards or get a check validated, and so on. According to the Tate Bramald Consultancy of Great Britain, the industries most at risk are retail and transport.[19]

All of this should serve as a warning to present-day computer users to take the long view with regard to computer solutions that are being set up now. Although you may buy a new computer and software tomorrow, chances are that the database you set up yesterday will somehow be transferred to the new equipment—and this will happen many times. So be sure you structure the database to accommodate all the data you expect to need far into the future.

Reluctance of Some Owners to Use Computer Technology

In case we have led you to believe that most small businesses use computer technology, that isn't necessarily so! According to the Business Research Group Inc., of Newton, Massachusetts, only about a third of mom-and-pop operations use PCs. And only 57 percent of companies with up to 100 employees use them.[20]

Also, many middle-aged and older entrepreneurs have resisted computerizing their small businesses. In general, this reluctance derives from two sources. First, many small businesses use only the most basic forms of computerization because of the cost involved. Others, though, lack the self-confidence to venture far out into this new, and often bewildering, field.

Ben Satterfield, age 55, overcame his "fear of computers" only three years ago. That's when he realized he could no longer manage the bills and orders overwhelming his business, Mug-A-Bug Pest Control, Inc., of Lawrenceville, Georgia. While the move was tough, it was worthwhile. "The savings . . . I generated the first year paid for my computer and program."[21]

On the other hand, Earl B. Christy, the 72-year-old president of Christy Company in Fremont, Ohio, still resists the efforts of his children and 15 grandchildren to get him to computerize his 104-year-old pocketknife-manufacturing business. Ironically, in the late 1940s Christy "wrangled his father into buying an adding machine to help with the bookkeeping." Now, however, Christy fears losing his independence. "I can run any of the equipment in the factory," he says, "but I would need to hire someone computer literate to operate the computer."

While he "cheerfully tests computers at the local computer store with games of solitaire," his children and grandchildren "are eager to give him computer lessons."[22]

Choosing Software, Hardware, and Employee Training

The primary software applications likely to be needed by a small business include word processing, spreadsheet analysis, account processing, file management, and electronic mail/messaging. It is easy to assume that your business is unique and requires a specially designed system to match your needs. Be wary of this approach, however, because there are many "off-the-shelf" programs (already designed and available) that, while they may not satisfy all your needs, will likely provide a cost-effective solution to most of them.

Having defined your computer needs and the software desired, you must then choose the hardware. A wide range is available, from simple, inexpensive micros to complicated, expensive mainframes. Most small companies need a system somewhere in the middle—one that is not too costly but does the work satisfactorily. We suggest that you focus primarily on PCs because their speed and capacity make them capable of handling most of the needs of a small business, and it is increasingly easy to network several workstations at the same location. Figure 15–7 lists some selected sources of information to help you choose hardware, software, and employee training.

Figure 15–7
Sources of Information about Computer Hardware, Software, and Training

---

The following sources can be used to obtain information to help in choosing hardware, software, and training.

- *Computer stores and consultants.* These can provide need-specific advice, packaged systems, and ongoing support, but they may be more oriented toward their sale than to your needs. The quality of advice may vary. Future availability of recommended systems is critical.

- *Friends or peers, user groups, bulletin boards, and seminars or workshops.* These can give more specialized advice, though it may not match your needs. Since hands-on experience is often possible, you may gain a better understanding of your needs, if not a specific answer. These are good sources of answers to technical questions, but beware of sales pitches.

- *Magazines, books, and libraries.* Although these are good sources of background information and comparative evaluations of hardware and software, the volume and technical nature of the information may create information overload, and the information is usually not tailored to your needs.

- *Computer company promotional material and mail order.* This is more oriented to specific hardware and software than to your needs, but it permits comparison of detailed technical specifications. Some mail-order firms offer ongoing support, but be sure to check, because this is important.

- *Industry associations.* These may have systems already fully designed to handle your specific problems and data that could be useful to you, but they may include a membership cost or licensing fee.

- *Government publications and SCORE/SBA.* These are inexpensive sources of information, data services, consultant referrals, and possibly even funding, but the quality may vary and may not include the most recent technology.

It may be more satisfactory for a small business owner to have a machine custom-built by one of the estimated 100,000 small PC makers who operate out of their homes, warehouses, and small shopping centers. These small producers have carved out a market niche by offering personalized service and in some cases even designing and custom-building machines for anyone who walks in the door. Such small "systems builders" now ship around 30 percent of all PCs sold.[23] In fact, the "hand holding" that local PC builders and sellers can offer customers now gives them a special edge as home users and small businesses increasingly move into the PC world and the Internet.

> For example, when Jennifer Zihlman found a disturbing flicker in the monitor of her new PC, she didn't have to wait forever on a toll-free phone line, much less pay long-distance charges for support. Instead, she took the machine back to its manufacturer, Adam Computers Inc., located in Dallas. After 20 minutes watching a technician substitute some circuit boards, she was on the way back to her small embroidery business. The problem had been solved quickly and at no cost to her.
> Service such as this has kept Zihlman returning to Adam, a 16-employee company located in a strip shopping center. It is owned and operated by Aboo Talib, a former accountant.[24]

■ THE ACCOUNTING SYSTEM AS MIS

There are many parts to the MIS of a small business. Some of the more important of these are:

- Forecasting.
- Reporting to tax authorities, management, and workers.
- Inventory control.
- Human resources records.

These require collecting, storing, and analyzing data. One major MIS is the accounting system, which, because of its highly quantitative nature, has historically been the first system to be computerized even in very small companies.

The rest of this chapter traces the flow of data for selected transactions in the accounting system. The discussion is based on the flow shown in Figure 15–1. Note the level of detail needed to design systems and how the logical flow of data tends to lead to computerization. An expert may be needed to help on the more complex transactions.

Sales

Profits result from the sale of goods or the performance of a service, for which a record must be kept. Notice in Figure 15–1 how a record of sales and cash receipts can be made and accounted for.

The sale of a product generates a sales slip, on which the number and type of items, unit price, and total price are entered. When cash registers are used, cash sales can be recorded on a tape to be used as the sales slip. Cash registers and computers can record and total sales variables including types of product, salesperson, and department.

Information on the sales forms is used to accumulate the sales income, to reduce inventory, to make analyses for future plans, and—in the case of a credit sale—to enter in the accounts receivable a record for the customer. A computer is particularly useful in keeping records and warning of late-paying customers.

Daily summaries of sales, sales on account, cash received (including charges to bank credit cards), sales by department, and other vital data can be recorded on multicolumnar or computer paper. Then, periodically, the total is entered in the ledger account. An analysis of this sheet can provide valuable information on the sales trends, where the major volume is, or who is selling the most.

Cash Income and Outgo

Recorded sales totals must equal the total of recorded cash, credits, and other values if your accounts are to balance. Since cash is highly negotiable, the system for recording it should be designed and established with care in order to minimize mishandling and consequent losses. For cash sales, goods sold and cash received should be recorded independently of each other—if possible—for control purposes.

> For example, a waitress makes out the bill for a customer at a restaurant, and a cashier receives the money. The cash register, placed in view of customers paying their bill, allows them to check the cash recording.

Also, to maintain control, only certain people should be allowed to handle the cash and then only on an individual basis: each person starts with a standard amount for change, and the cash balance is reconciled each day—or more often, if feasible. The reconciliation assures that cash on hand equals the beginning cash on hand, plus cash sales, less cash returns.

At the end of each day, businesses usually deposit in the bank the cash received that day, less the change needed for the next day's operations. The deposited amount is added to the checkbook stub. The business then makes payments by check. Each check is entered in the cash journal to identify the account to which it is charged.

Accounts Receivable

When customers buy goods using open accounts or a store's credit card, each sale is entered on a customer account record, as shown in Figure 15–1. At the end of each period—usually a month—customers' accounts are totaled and bills sent requesting payment. As payments are received, the amount is posted to each customer's account and totaled for entry in the sales and cash receipts journal. Sales to customers using outside credit cards are treated as cash sales and processed as cash through the bank.

Accounts Payable

A business incurs many obligations for materials purchased, utilities, wages, and taxes. The bills and invoices for these are entered in the purchases or expense journal or computer and may be filed by date to be paid. The journals can be multicolumnar to show how the money is spent. Columns are for categories with many similar items, such as materials purchases, and the miscellaneous column is for categories, such as insurance, that require few entries. Individual files keep track of whom to pay, when to pay, and how much to pay. After payment, the bills are filed for future reference. The paid bill amount is entered on the check stub and in the purchases and cash disbursements journal.

Inventory

Among the most troublesome records to keep are those dealing with inventory. While the physical planning and control of inventory were discussed in Chapter 12, we will discuss here the accounting aspects of inventory handling and recording.

Figure 15–8
Examples of Recording and Adjusting Transactions

1. (a) Receive shipment of material X, $100, entered in books when received.
   (b) Used $80 of material X, entered at end of period.

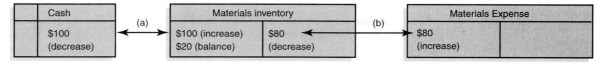

2. (a) Paid insurance policy premium of $600, entered when paid.
   (b) Monthly expense of insurance, $50 (1/12 of annual $600), entered at end of period.

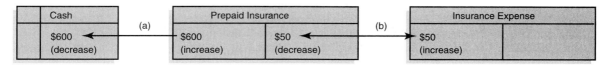

3. Have machine which cost $1,300. From machine records, machine expense, $20 = (Machine cost [$1,300] – Estimated scrap value [$100]) ÷ Estimated life (5 years [60 months]).

When materials are received, their costs are recorded as materials inventory and paid for with cash, as shown in 1(a) in Figure 15–8. Inventory increases by $100, and cash decreases by $100. As the materials are used, it's recorded as an expense of $80, leaving an inventory balance of $20 at the end of the month. In another method, often used by high-volume purchasers, purchases are charged to expense as they are received, and then, at the end of the month, the unused portion is moved to inventory.

A business selling a high volume of many items—a grocery store, for example—depends on periodic visual inspection of the items on the shelves. Holograph scanners or bar code readers, connected to a computer, are often used to read the product number, comparing the amount in inventory with expected needs and entering the amount that needs to be ordered. The introduction of computers and point-of-sale scanners has made the use of *perpetual inventory records,* for timely control, more feasible.

Expenses

A business purchases services and goods from other businesses, and these become expenses. Material is transformed and sold, electricity is used, machines decrease in value, and insurance protection lapses. The payment interval for these costs of doing business varies from one day to several years. To determine true profit—say for the month of March—income and expenses must be determined for that month. This can be done on a *cash* or an *accrual* basis.

Many small businesses compute their profit on the cash rather than accrual basis because the cash basis is simpler. The **cash basis** assumes that payments and use occur in

The **cash basis** assumes that payments and use occur in the same time period.

The accrual basis makes adjustments to income and expenses to reflect actual expenses incurred and income earned during the period.

the same time period. But payment is not always received (or made) in the same period in which services are performed—as in the case of credit sales, for example. The **accrual basis** makes adjustments to reflect the actual expense of a service and the income received for it in a given time period, not past expenses or anticipated income. In deciding which method to use, *balance the value of accuracy against the cost of each method.*

To calculate expenses by the accrual method, (1) obtain the values of all assets, payments, and obligations; (2) determine how much of each has been used during the period; and (3) transfer the used portion to expense and reduce the asset or increase the obligation. Items 2 and 3 in Figure 15–8 are examples of the accrual method.

Insurance may be paid monthly, quarterly, or annually. Usually, annual payments reduce the cost and are prorated as shown in example 2 of the figure. In the illustration, $600 is charged to prepaid insurance (an asset) when it is paid by the small firm, with one-twelfth, or $50, charged to expenses each month.

Depreciation is the gradual loss of value of a facility.

Machinery, equipment, and buildings are used over a number of years, so their value is only gradually used up. In order to assign a part of their expense to each period, an accounting method must reflect their **depreciation,** which is the amount of value a facility loses over a period of time. The most common method, *straight-line depreciation,* depreciates a machine at a constant rate over its useful life. The amount to be charged for each month may be determined by the following formula:

$$\frac{\text{Cost of machine} - \text{Disposal value (sell or scrap) at end of its expected life}}{\text{Expected life (in months)}}$$

The amount that has already been charged to *depreciation expenses* is called *accumulated depreciation.* Figure 15–8, example 3, shows the adjustment of the two depreciation accounts by the amount thus arrived at. Many other items of expense and income need the same types of adjustment just discussed.

Financial Statements

As shown in Chapter 13, financial statements, prepared from accounting records discussed in this chapter, aid you in making these analyses. They are usually the balance sheet and income statement. Income statements should be prepared monthly, while the balance sheets can be prepared less often. Tax reports are completed for the various government divisions many times during the year. These include reports for income, sales, Social Security, and excise tax.

WHAT YOU SHOULD HAVE LEARNED

∎

1. Information is an important resource for small businesses as well as for people. Companies collect and process data, make decisions, act on those decisions, and start the cycle anew.

2. A management information system (MIS) collects, processes, records, reports, and/or converts data into a usable form for management. Data can be processed in *real time,* with instantaneous feedback, or *batch processed* later at a lower cost.

3. Computers are increasingly important in business because they can process data so quickly. A computer—hardware—is physical equipment used for storing, processing, and presenting large quantities of data. Programs—software—direct the computer to process the data. Much of the value of a computer system comes from the software.

4. The microcomputer (PC) has made it feasible for a small business to process data related to such areas

as accounting, employees, forecasting, and operations. Most systems involve both manual and computer operations, and the choice of the appropriate system depends on output, cost, and the situation in the business. In choosing a computer system, analyze the present situation in terms of available software, hardware, and employee training.

5. The Internet is a collection of computers and computer networks linked together to receive and distribute information around the world. There is no central control or ownership, but companies, educational institutions, government agencies, and individuals around the world (some 30 million) can join, use, and leave the Net at will. It helps small firms do research, send and receive electronic mail, and order materials.

6. A potential problem with computer technology is that the possibility of errors and inaccurate information being turned out is magnified. Also, the owner and employees need to continually upgrade their skills. Greater security of the equipment and information is required. Some middle-aged and older owners are reluctant to install the technology for various reasons. Finally, some older computers

will have to be reprogrammed—at considerable expense—to enter the 21st century.

7. Accounting systems are part of a firm's MIS. The sale of goods starts a series of accounting entries using sales slips; cash register receipts; credit card receipts; multicolumnar paper (or computer files); and ledgers to record changes in cash, sales, and accounts receivable. Computers can facilitate this process and enhance its value. Secure systems must be designed to handle cash because stolen cash is not traceable.

When a sale is made on credit, the amount of the sale is entered into accounts receivable, and the customer is billed later.

Bills for purchases and other items used are recorded in suppliers' accounts for proper payment. Monthly, the amount used during the month is moved to an expense account. Keeping track of inventory can be one of the greatest challenges for any business. Expenses can be recorded on either the cash or the accrual basis. The simpler cash basis charges items as they are actually paid. The accrual basis assigns the amount of revenue and expenses to the period in which they occur.

QUESTIONS FOR DISCUSSION

1. What are some of the management decisions owners of small businesses must make?

2. What types of information do they need to make those decisions?

3. What are some of the sources of the needed information?

4. Explain how the use of computers by business has grown.

5. Explain how the microcomputer (PC) has affected small business.

6. What effect(s) do you think the Internet will have on small business?

7. What are some problems with computer technology for small firms?

8. Distinguish between the cash and accrual methods of handling expenses.

CASE 15–1

HERMAN VALENTINE: CUSTOMIZING COMPUTERS FOR MILITARY USE

Herman Valentine, chairman and president of Systems Management American (SMA) Corporation, remembers the time years ago when he shined shoes on the corner of Monticello and Market streets in downtown Norfolk, Virginia. His best customers were executives working in the four-story department store and the 16-story

Maritime Towers office building across the street. He now owns the entire block, including the store—which serves as headquarters for his company—and the office building.

SMA is a computer systems integrator serving the government and private industry. Its capabilities include manufacturing, installation, integrated logistics support, software/hardware development, configuration management, command and control, image processing, and data conversion services.

SMA has grown from a one-man operation in 1970 into a national corporation with a staff of 430. Not realizing how difficult it was going to be, Valentine "put in long hours, borrowed often from banks, and spent a lot of time on proposals for contracts he did not get." SMA is now one of the larger black-owned businesses in the United States.

An outstanding high school basketball player, Valentine wanted to play in college and the NBA, but he wanted a car more! So he took part-time jobs to buy one, finished high school, went into the army, married, and at age 23 returned to Norfolk. After earning a bachelor's degree from Norfolk State University in three years (paid for by more part-time jobs), he became an executive officer for the U.S. Department of Agriculture and later business manager for Norfolk State.

In 1970, he opened Systems Management Associates, a consulting firm for black businesses, with $5,000 he had saved. With an answering service, a post office box, and a part-time secretary, Valentine sold administrative and financial advice to black entrepreneurs and performed data processing and programming for them. Two years later, with 12 employees (mostly part-timers), he began bidding on—and winning—small government data processing jobs.

But his business really took off in 1981, when he snagged a contract to design, install, and maintain sophisticated record-keeping computers aboard Navy ships. The Navy thought the job was too big for him, but he persuaded them to send an evaluation team, which found no reason why he couldn't do the job. Revenues skyrocketed for a while, and they have been as high as $60 million. Valentine has pared down his operations somewhat, but SMA continues to bid on—and be awarded—government contracts.

Valentine is concentrating on more contract diversification, which includes the government as well as the private sector, as military budget cuts begin to affect the computer industry. After closing three small offices around the country and cutting $4 million out of overhead, he and his staff are "lean and competitive."

He trains his employees—many of whom are unskilled workers—to be computer technicians and high-tech specialists. He also encourages other minority individuals to become entrepreneurs.

Questions

1. How do you explain Valentine's success?
2. To what extent do you think his diversification plan will work? Explain.
3. What suggestions would you make to him for adjusting to the changing economic environment?

Source: Author's correspondence with Systems Management American Corporation.

CASE 15-2

LET YOUR FINGERS DO THE WALKING—TO LUNCH

Cassady's, a fast-food business, has been computerizing its drive-throughs and its ordering process. Customers can now order by using touch-screen computers, and the information is instantaneously relayed to the kitchen. Cassady's is doing this to be competitive in the market and is trying to prepare itself for the labor crisis in the near future, as predicted by some economists. These computer systems are expensive, but Cassady's has experienced a gain in sales in the stores where these computers are installed.

Questions

1. What are the factors that Cassady's should consider before implementing this program nationwide?
2. Do you think that Cassady's will get a competitive edge over other fast-food businesses by implementing this program?
3. Do you think that you would order more if you were entering your order through a computer?

PROVIDING PRESENT AND FUTURE SECURITY FOR THE BUSINESS

We have already covered most of the general information you need to manage a small business. Now we present some important special considerations.

Chapter 16 discusses your need to minimize the risks incurred in owning and operating a small business. Most losses can be minimized by establishing insurance and reserves. With properly planned operations and crime prevention, including security measures, the chances—or magnitude—of other losses can be reduced.

Chapter 17 looks at small business relations with governments and government agencies. It also discusses the need for social responsibility and the practice of business and managerial ethics.

Chapter 18 deals with the need to provide for management succession. It also discusses family and manager problems in small firms. Many business owners do not like to talk about the question of succession. However, to assure the continuance of your business or to provide a going concern for family members to operate, you must look at this question objectively and realistically.

16

RISK MANAGEMENT, INSURANCE, AND CRIME PREVENTION

Everything is sweetened by risk.

Alexander Smith

Carrying liability insurance these days is almost a liability in itself. . . . Premiums are rising at a fantastic rate . . . In fact, in some cases insurance coverage has become impossible to obtain—at any cost.

Charles W. Patchen, CPA and writer

LEARNING OBJECTIVES

After studying the material in this chapter, you will be able to:

1. Define risk and explain some ways of coping with it.

2. Explain what insurance is and show how it can be used to minimize loss due to risk.

3. Discuss some guides to be used in choosing an insurer.

4. Show how crime prevention can reduce risk and protect people and assets.

5. Discuss some techniques for safeguarding against theft.

6. Describe how to safeguard employees with preventive measures.

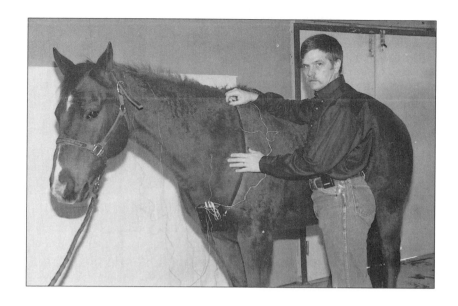

Dr. Jeffrey F. Van Petten: A Unique Entrepreneur

Jeff Van Petten's veterinary practice includes much more than traditional family pets and traditional pet care. When asked to describe his activities, he explains, "My practice is rapidly becoming an alternative medicine animal hospital that utilizes acupuncture, chiropractic, and homeopathy forms of treatment. As a professional, I like to look past the normal for better answers to problems."

Van Petten's interests and research have led to video productions, such as those dealing with "Barrel Horse Wellness." His films identify ways to diagnose musculoskeletal problems in horses and ways to prevent them.

Growing up in a rural environment gave Van Petten his love of animals and desire to keep them healthy. He is active in many associations that help him stay current on the latest discoveries and techniques in veterinary medicine. He is a member of the International Veterinary Acupuncture Society, was certified by the society in 1991, and serves on its Member Education Committee. Van Petten is also involved with the American Veterinary Chiropractic Association, the American Association of Equine Practitioners (www.aaep.org), the Kansas Veterinary Medical Association (in which he served on the Public Relations Committee), and the American Veterinary Medical Association (www.avma.org).

In addition to his many professional affiliations, Van Petten is very active in many local organizations.

He is a member of the local school board, the Jefferson County (Kansas) Health Board, the board of directors of the Kansas Horse Council, and president of Jefferson County Rural Water District Number One. Yet he still has time for hobbies such as hunting, fishing, roping, and riding horses.

When asked what motivates him to continue his practice, besides a love of animals, he will tell you that the pay is good. While there are approximately 66,000 veterinarians in the United States, most veterinary practices generate less than $500,000 in annual revenue.[1]

Van Petten's veterinary practice is an S corporation, employing an office staff as well as a second veterinarian, Dr. Rick Tanner. Van Petten purchased his practice in 1987 with 100 percent borrowed capital. The previous owner held a contract on the building, and a local bank financed equipment and start-up funds. The location on a highway, in a growing area, was very attractive, and near family and friends.

Being near family was important because, like many small businesses, Van Petten's practice is a family enterprise. Van Petten's wife, Jackie, daughter, Jolie, and son, Jarek, are supportive in many ways. Besides encouraging his involvement in professional activities and research—and tolerating the hours involved—they also pitch in as needed to help with client relations, clean cages, exercise animals, and perform any other needed support services.

The operation of veterinary medicine is affected by zoning laws and health department regulations on the size of and space available in the facilities, runoff animal waste, and handling of needles and prescription drugs. Regulations for prescription drugs for veterinary use are much the same as those for medical doctors and pharmacists.

Since there is an inherent danger in handling animals, the State of Kansas has passed the Kansas Livestock Liability Act, which was designed to create relief for both animal owners and handlers. Briefly described, it protects against liability for injury to people. This law has not been tested, so, to be on the safe side, veterinarians obtain a written release. Veterinarians also carry malpractice, professional liability, and errors and omissions insurance—in addition to the usual fire, theft, and similar coverage. Some of Van Petten's insurance is a form of self-insurance handled by the AVMA.

Source: Author's correspondence and conversations with Joyce Allen Baker and Jeffrey and Jackie Baker Van Petten.

In this chapter we will discuss some of the most prevalent risks facing you as a small business owner, such as the liability and omissions risks just mentioned in the Profile, and we will show how you can cope with them.

The first section of the chapter deals with risk and its management; the second section, with using insurance to minimize loss due to risk; the third, with crime prevention; and the last, with how to safeguard employees with preventive measures.

■ RISK AND ITS MANAGEMENT

Small business losses of money and property often occur as a result of fire, severe weather, theft, lawsuits, bankruptcy, politics, and other misfortunes, as well as the death, disability, or defection of key personnel. A hurricane, fire, or tornado may destroy your property outright. Remodeling, street repairs, or flooding may temporarily close your business and reduce income. Goods may be stolen, damaged, destroyed, or spoiled in transit, for which the common carrier isn't liable. Banks may either call in, or refuse to renew, loans. Customers may be unable to pay accounts receivable. The government may cut back on military spending. A competitor may hire one of your key employees. Given this rogues' gallery of lurking perils, what's a small business to do?

Risk management is the process of conserving earning power and assets by minimizing the shock from losses.

The answer is to use **risk management,** which is the process of conserving a firm's earning power and assets by minimizing the financial shocks of accidental losses. It lets a firm regain its financial balance and operating effectiveness after suffering an unexpected loss.

Types of Risk

Pure risk is the uncertainty that some unpredictable event will result in a loss.

There are two primary types of risk you will face as a small business owner. A **pure risk** is uncertainty as to whether some unpredictable event that can result in loss will occur. Pure risk always exists when the possibility of a loss is present but the possible extent of the loss is unknown. For example, the consequences of a fire, the death of a key employee, or a liability judgment against you cannot be predicted with any degree of certainty. Many of these risks, however, can be analyzed statistically and are therefore insurable.

Speculative risk is the uncertainty that a voluntarily undertaken risk will result in a loss.

On the other hand, a **speculative risk** is uncertainty as to whether a voluntarily undertaken activity will result in a gain or a loss. Production risks, such as building a plant that turns out to have the wrong capacity or keeping an inventory level that turns out to be too high or too low, are speculative risks. Speculative risk is the name of the game in business.

For example, Levi Strauss (www.levistrauss.com) tried to sell its jeans through mass merchandisers such as Sears (www.sears.com) and Penney's (www.jcpenney.com), only to have department stores turn to Lee jeans (www.leejeans.com).

Some business risks are insurable and others uninsurable. As you know, the greatest risk facing any small business—the possibility that it will be unprofitable—is uninsurable. Other uninsurable risks are associated with the development of new products, changes in customers' preferences, price fluctuations, and changes in laws. In this chapter we deal only with insurable risks.

Ways of Coping with Risk

There are many ways you can cope with risk.* The most common of these are:

- Risk avoidance.
- Risk prevention, or loss control.
- Risk transfer.
- Risk assumption, or self-insurance.

Risk avoidance is refusing to undertake, or abandoning, an activity in which the risk seems too costly. The following classic example illustrates a case where this was necessary.

> A New York bank experimented with having depositors of less than $5,000 either pay a fee to see a teller or use an automatic teller machine. When customers rebelled, the project was dropped as too risky.[2]

Risk avoidance is refusing to undertake an activity when the risk seems too costly.

Risk prevention, or **loss control,** consists of using various methods to reduce the probability that a given event will occur. The primary control technique is prevention, including safety and protective procedures. For example, if your business is large enough, you might try to control losses by providing first-aid offices, driver training, and work safety rules, not to mention security guards to prevent pilferage, shoplifting, and other forms of theft, as the following example illustrates.

Risk prevention (loss control) is using various methods to reduce the possibility of a loss occurring.

> Many malls are now using uniformed security guards to replace plainclothes officers. For example, New Orleans' Plaza Mall has moved its security station to a glass-enclosed room in the center of the mall. Passersby can see the officers monitoring closed-circuit TV sets. Some shopping centers are even having uniformed officers patrol their parking lots on horses or bicycles.[3]

Risk transfer means shifting the consequences of a risk to persons or organizations outside your business. The best-known form of risk transfer is **insurance,** which is the process by which an insurance company agrees, for a fee (a premium), to pay an individual or organization an agreed-upon sum of money for a given loss. But because of escalating health care costs, many companies are shifting part of the risk to their employees, who must pay higher deductibles and a larger percentage of nonreimbursed expenses.

Risk transfer is shifting a risk to someone outside your company.

Insurance is provided by another company that agrees, for a fee, to reimburse your company for part of a loss.

Risk assumption usually takes the form of **self-insurance,** whereby a business sets aside a certain amount of its own funds to meet losses that are uncertain in size and frequency. This method is usually impractical for very small firms because they do not have the large cash reserves needed to make it feasible.

Risk assumption (self-insurance) is setting aside funds to meet losses that are uncertain in size and frequency.

Generally, more than one method of handling risks is used at the same time. For example, a firm may use self-insurance for automobile damage, which costs relatively little, while using commercial insurance against liability claims, which may be prohibitively great.

---

*These methods have been summed up mnemonically by Professor Charles N. Armstrong, Kansas City Community College, who points out that you can TAME risk: that is, you can Transfer it, Assume it, Minimize it, or Eliminate it.

■ USING INSURANCE TO MINIMIZE LOSS DUE TO RISK

The principal value of insurance lies in its reduction of your risks from doing business. In buying insurance, you trade a potentially large but uncertain loss for a small but certain one (the cost of the premium). In other words, you trade uncertainty for certainty. But if the insurance premium is a substantial proportion of the value of the property, don't buy the insurance.

A well-designed insurance program not only compensates for losses but also provides other values, including reduction of worry, freeing funds for investment, suggestions for loss prevention techniques, and easing of credit.

In deciding what to do about business risks, you should ask yourself the questions about disasters shown in Figure 16–1. Often, when such disasters occur in small companies with inadequate or no insurance protection at all, either the owners are forced out of business or operations are severely restricted.

Types of Insurance Coverage

Because there are so many types of insurance, we will discuss only those you will need most as a small business owner.

The basic *fire insurance policy* insures only for losses from fire and lightning and losses due to temporary removal of goods from the premises because of fire. In most instances, this policy should be supplemented by an *extended-coverage endorsement* that insures against loss from windstorm, hail, explosion, riot, aircraft, vehicle, and smoke damage.

Coinsurance is having the business buy insurance equal to a specific percentage of property value.

To ensure reimbursement for the full amount of covered losses, most property insurance contracts have a **coinsurance** provision. It requires policyholders to buy insurance in an amount equal to a specified percentage of the property value—say, 80 percent.

Business interruption coverage should also be provided through endorsement, because such indirect losses are frequently more severe in their eventual cost than are direct losses. For example, while rebuilding after a fire, the business must continue to pay fixed expenses such as salaries of key employees and such expenses as utilities, interest, and taxes. You also need this type of insurance for other types of business interruption.

> For example, Ali Kamber, executive vice president for Ferromin International, a metals and minerals trading company with four employees, said his company lost $100,000 during the week following the bombing of the World Trade Center (www.wtca.org) in early 1993. The company "lacked insurance for business interruptions," he said.[4]

Figure 16–1
How to Determine Whether You Need Insurance

To determine how to handle business risks, ask yourself, What will happen if:

- I die or suddenly become incapacitated?
- A fire destroys my firm's building(s), machines, tools and equipment, and/or inventories?
- There is theft by an outsider, a customer, or an employee, or an employee embezzles company funds?
- My business is robbed?
- A customer is awarded a sizable settlement after bringing a product or accident liability suit against me?
- Someone, inside or outside the business, obtains unauthorized information from my computer?

Casualty insurance consists of automobile insurance (both collision and public liability) plus burglary, theft, robbery, plate glass, and health and accident insurance. Automobile liability and physical-damage insurance are necessary because firms may be legally liable for vehicles used on their behalf, even those they do not own. For example, when employees use their own cars on company business, the employer is liable in case of an accident.

A related type of insurance is known as *professional liability (malpractice) insurance.* This type of insurance protects the small business from suits resulting from mistakes made—or bad advice given—by someone in a professional context.[5]

Product/service liability insurance protects a business against losses resulting from the use of its product. It is particularly important for small firms because in conducting business, companies are subject to common and statutory laws governing negligence to customers, employees, and anyone else with whom they do business. One liability judgment, without adequate insurance, can easily result in the liquidation of a business. As a result, premiums for liability coverage are becoming almost prohibitive. In fact, the crisis has reached such proportions that some companies are dropping products rather than face the danger of bankruptcy.

Product/service liability insurance protects a business from losses resulting from the use of its product.

> After spending more than $100 million defending itself against charges that Bendectin, an antinausea drug used by millions of pregnant women for decades, caused birth defects, its only producer quit making it in 1983.[6]

The problem of product liability lawsuits has escalated since courts began interpreting "liability" so broadly.

> Jeanine Pelletier was awarded $40,000 by the Maine Supreme Court when she sued the Fort Kent Golf Club of Portland for nose and facial injuries. Her injuries resulted when her own golf ball ricocheted off railroad tracks that run through the course and hit her in the nose.[7]

Another growing problem for small firms is what to do about *liability when sponsoring athletic teams or some potentially dangerous activities.* Employers are facing the problem in two ways. Some are trying to get reasonably priced insurance coverage. When this isn't feasible, many small firms are abandoning the practice.

As discussed in Chapter 9, *workers' compensation* policies typically provide for medical care, lump sums for death and dismemberment, and income payments for disabled workers or their dependents. The workers' comp problem is rapidly getting out of control because of "unrestrained medical costs, excessive legal disputes in what is supposed to be a no-fault system, broadening definitions of what are job-related injuries, and rampant fraud and abuse."[8]

There are some things owners and managers of small companies can do to improve safety. These actions, which should also help reduce premiums, are:

- Involve employees in safety matters.
- Establish an open, two-way communication system.
- Make participation companywide.
- Make a big deal of the safety awards that are given, and be sure awards have a reasonable value.
- Keep the program exciting.
- Be especially watchful during high-risk periods.

Group health and life insurance for employees are also important in small firms. Life insurance provides protection for an employee's estate when he or she dies while still in the

Figure 16–2
Barriers to Being Your Own Boss

Two-thirds of adult workers have made plans for or seriously investigated working for themselves. What they say is the "greatest barrier" to doing it:

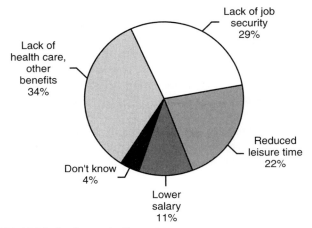

income-producing years, or lives beyond that time but has little or no income. Health insurance provides protection against the risk of medical expenses, including doctor and hospital bills and prescription expenses.

Health insurance is one of the most important benefits offered by small firms, but it's also one of the less frequently used. A major cause of low coverage by small firms is the cost. Health insurance costs have increased at more than twice the inflation rate for over a decade, and some small firms have experienced 25 to 50 percent annual increases. Widely recognized as an acute problem for the entire country, this is critical for small businesses, which usually do not provide such coverage for part-time (temporary) employees. In fact, as you can see from Figure 16–2, "lack of health care and other benefits" is one of the "greatest barriers" to people considering going into business for themselves.

In the mid-1990s, small firms' average health insurance costs rose 6.2 percent per year. Now, like all companies, they face a "crisis in health insurance."[9]

> In 1994, Judy and Joseph Weigner, of Louisville, Kentucky, were "downsized" from their jobs as nutrition aide and maintenance engineer. They moved to Jamestown, where they owned a vacation cabin, and started a business repairing small engines. The cheapest health insurance they could find cost $4,000 a year, with a $3,000 annual deductible. It also required the Weigners to pay 50 percent of all subsequent medical bills until expenses reached $9,000.
>
> They "reluctantly" bought the policy. The next year, when Joseph had surgery costing $5,000, the couple paid most of it out of their own pocket. Mrs. Weigner lamented that " . . . we sort of have the worst of both worlds. . . . We pay $4,000 a year for health insurance that does not cover much except a catastrophic illness. [And] we end up paying most of our medical bills."[10]

The Weigners' experience is not unique. In fact, it's not uncommon for proprietors of mom-and-pop businesses to be uninsured, as they can't afford the cost.[11]

Finally, insurance companies treat large and small businesses differently. If a big company has a bad year, with a high total health bill, the insurer regards it as a natural occurrence and assumes that costs will decline the following year. But it's common for rates at a very small business—one with 10 to 20 people covered—to skyrocket if just one employee racks up huge health claims during the year.

Business owner's insurance is another important protection you need. It consists of (1) protection of owner or dependents against loss from premature death, disability, or medical expenses and (2) provision for the continuation of a business following the death of an owner. Also, business continuation life insurance is used in closely held corporations to provide cash on the death of an owner. The cash can be used to retire the interest of a partner or, in case of death, to repurchase the stock of a closely held corporation.

A variation of this type of insurance, called *key person insurance,* insures the life (or lives) of important employees.[12] Key person insurance is used more often in small firms than in large ones, for a given individual can be more important to the well-being of a smaller company.

Insurers issue *fidelity and surety bonds* to guarantee that employees and others with whom the company transacts business are honest and will fulfill their contractual obligations. Fidelity bonds are purchased for employees occupying positions that involve the handling of company funds. Surety bonds provide protection against the failure of a contractor to fulfill contractual obligations. Problems with bonding restrict the growth of many small contractors.

> For example, in a poll of 150 contractors in New York and New Jersey, more than three-fourths of them said that difficulty in getting bonded limited their access to jobs, especially the bigger and more profitable ones.[13]

In summary, as important as it is for small businesses to carry many types of insurance, the cost is oppressive. Still, no prudent small business owner will be without the key types of insurance discussed, for one devastating claim could ruin the business.

Guides to Choosing an Insurer

In choosing an insurer, consider the financial characteristics of the insurer, the insurer's flexibility in meeting your requirements, and the services rendered by the agent. While insurance companies have agents representing them, independent agents represent more than one company. These independent agents use the following logo:

Some Red Flags to Look For   As in any industry, there are some black sheep or shady operators to look out for in choosing an insurer. To make sure you are being provided the coverage you have paid for, be on the lookout for the following red flags:[14]

- An agent who delays giving answers, fails to hand over a policy, or neglects to provide proof of endorsements.
- Routine answers such as: "Don't worry about it, it's a computer glitch."
- A delayed premium refund.
- A hand-delivered policy instead of one sent directly from the company.

- An adjuster who says it will cost you more to process the claim than the amount of your deductible.
- Delay tactics to encourage you into a lower settlement.
- Attempts to minimize your damages to save the company from having to pay on the claim.
- Request by the adjuster to keep the claim or proposed settlement a secret.
- An offer of a new policy to replace one that is flawed.

Financial Characteristics and Flexibility of Insurer   The major types of insurers are stock companies, mutual companies, reciprocals, and Lloyd's groups. While mutuals and reciprocals are cooperatively organized and sell insurance "at cost," in practice their premiums may be no lower than those of profit-making companies. In comparing different types of insurers, you should use the following criteria:

- Financial stability and safety.
- Specialization in your type of business.
- Ability to tailor its policy to meet your needs.
- Cost of protection.

Valid comparisons of insurance coverage and its costs are difficult to make, but your insurance brokers, independent insurance advisers, or agents can assist you. In addition, the following are a few things you can do to ease the pain when your insurance comes up for renewal:

- Consult your agent for methods of minimizing your premium.
- Consider boosting your policy deductibles to keep premium costs within manageable limits.
- Before renewal time arrives, shop around among several agents for coverage.
- Find out if your professional organization offers lower-cost coverage for its members.
- Check out the special-risk pools.
- Consider alternatives to insurance coverage, such as self-insurance or coinsurance.

Services Rendered by the Agent   Decide which qualifications of agents are most important, and then inquire about agents among business friends and others who have had experience with them. In comparing agents, look for contacts among insurers, professionalism, degree of individual attention, quality of service, and help in time of loss. Choose an agent who is willing and able to: (1) devote enough time to your individual problems to justify the commission, (2) survey exposure to loss, (3) recommend adequate insurance and loss prevention programs, and (4) offer alternative methods of insurance.

■ CRIME PREVENTION TO PROTECT PEOPLE AND ASSETS

Small business owners need to practice crime prevention to reduce risks and protect their assets. Not only do you need to prevent major crimes, such as armed robbery, theft, and white-collar crimes, but you also need protection from trespassing, vandalism, and harassment.

An awareness of the potential dangers helps to minimize the risks involved and reduces losses from crime. It's impossible to have a security program that will prevent all criminal acts, so you can only hope to minimize their occurrence and severity.

A study conducted by America's Research Group, Inc., revealed that more than a third of American customers have changed their shopping habits because of safety concerns. The study found that 42 percent of shoppers no longer shop after dark, 25 percent keep car doors locked, 15 percent refuse to shop alone, and 60 percent are very uneasy about carrying large amounts of money. Businesses are suffering as a consequence.

> Almost 40 percent of the respondents to another survey believed it was the responsibility of individual store owners to make shopping safer. Similarly, 31 percent felt shopping centers should be responsible, while 30 percent looked to local government for safety.[15]

Law enforcement agencies and the business community are learning to identify areas particularly susceptible to crime. Crimes appear to fall into patterns. Armed robbery may occur frequently in one type of neighborhood, theft in another, and both in a third. A prospective business owner needs to evaluate a potential site with this problem in mind. Examples of sites that appear to be particularly vulnerable to criminal acts are public housing projects, low-rent neighborhoods, areas of high unemployment, and areas with a high incidence of illiteracy.

Criminal acts have forced not only small but even large businesses into insolvency. Armed robbery, theft, and white-collar crimes are the major crimes affecting small firms.

Armed Robbery

In recent years, the number of armed robberies has increased significantly. The Bureau of Labor Statistics reports that "about 18,000 clerks are victims of nonlethal assaults annually."[16] An OSHA study found that "about half the more than 900 people killed on the job in 1996 were [convenience] store clerks."[17] In April 1998, OSHA issued suggested safety guidelines specifically for convenience stores. Included were (1) adequate lighting, (2) video cameras, (3) increased night staff levels, (4) alarms, and (5) bulletproof glass. OSHA also suggested better training for managers and clerks and emergency procedures for dangerous situations.[18]

An armed robber enters the premises with the intent of obtaining cash or valuable merchandise and leaves as quickly as possible to minimize the risk of identification or apprehension. Since time is critical in such circumstances, locations that afford easy access and relatively secure escape routes seem most vulnerable. This type of criminal usually wants to be in and out of the location in three minutes or less, and the pressure of the situation tends to make the robber more dangerous.

Several measures can be taken to reduce the chances of being robbed. They include modifying the store's layout, securing entrances, using security dogs, controlling the handling of cash, and redesigning the surrounding area.

Modifying Store Layout   Location of the cash register and high visibility inside and from outside the store are important in preventing armed robbery. If robbers cannot dash in, scoop up the cash, and dash out again within a short time, they aren't as likely to attempt the robbery, as the following example shows.

> One convenience food chain removed from the windows all material that would obstruct the view into the store. In addition, it encouraged crowds at all hours with various gimmicks and attracted police officers by giving them free coffee. The average annual robbery rate dropped markedly.

Securing Entrances   The security of entrances and exits is extremely important in preventing robbery. Windows and rear doors should be kept locked and barred. In high-crime neighborhoods, many businesses use tough, shock-resistant transparent materials in their windows instead of glass.

Using Security Dogs   Security dogs are trained to be vicious on command. Businesspeople have found these animals to be effective deterrents against armed robbers. When 589 convicted criminals were asked how best to foil burglars, the largest number—15.8 percent—said, "Have a dog."[19] However, health and sanitation regulations in some jurisdictions may prevent the use of dogs.

Controlling the Handling of Cash   Making daily cash deposits and varying the deposit time from day to day are highly recommended. Some cash registers signal "too much cash" and will not operate until an employee has removed the excess to a safe and reset the register with a key. Banks and other businesses rigidly enforce minimum-cash-on-hand rules for cash drawers to reduce losses in the event of an armed robbery.

Many businesses hide safes in unobtrusive places and limit knowledge of their combinations to only one or two people. It is not uncommon for a sign to be posted on the safe, or near it, advising that the person on duty does not have access to the combination or saying, "Notice: Cash in drawer does not exceed $50." Other stores, such as gas stations, use locked cash boxes and accept only correct change, credit cards, and/or payment through secured windows during certain hours.

"The salesman said it was the most effective home security system on the market."

(*Source:* Reprinted from *The Wall Street Journal,* permission Cartoon Features Syndicate.)

Redesigning the Surroundings   Well-lighted parking lots help deter robbers. If possible, try to keep vehicles from parking too near the entrance to your business. Armed robbery can be reduced by making access less convenient. For example, many convenience food store parking lots have precast concrete bumper blocks distributed so as to deter fast entry into and exit from the lot. Also, some businesses use silent alarms, video cameras to photograph crime in action, or video cameras tied to TV monitors in a security office.

The National Crime Prevention Council's Bureau of Justice Statistics (www. crimeprevention.org) has suggested a number of ways to make your workplace safer. In addition to those already mentioned, these include: (1) requiring identification from delivery or repair people or strangers seeking confidential information, (2) calling police or security people if you notice anyone—or anything—suspicious, (3) asking a co-worker or security guard to escort you to your car or a cab, and (4) when working late, trying to arrange for someone else to work—or stay—with you.[20]

Theft

Theft is always a serious problem for businesses. Because of the extent of the problem, many national merchandising businesses add 2 to 3 percent to their prices to cover the cost of theft, but even this may not be enough to compensate for the total loss. The two major types of theft are (1) theft by outsiders, usually known as shoplifting, and (2) theft by employees. (See Figure 16–3.) Retailers sometimes refer to losses from both kinds of theft as *shrinkage.*

Shoplifting   Shoplifting is a major hazard for retail establishments. Professional shoplifters, not amateurs and kleptomaniacs, cause the greatest prevention problems. The amateur may be a thrill seeker who takes an item or two to see whether or not he or she can get away with it. (This is often the case with children and teenagers.) The kleptomaniac has an uncontrollable urge to take things, whether needed or not. Kleptomaniacs and amateurs are more

Figure 16–3

Look Who's Stealing (Sources of Inventory Loss in the Retail Industry)

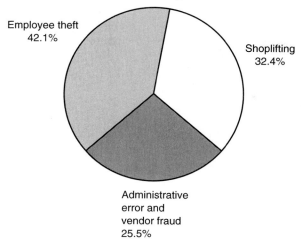

Employee theft
42.1%

Shoplifting
32.4%

Administrative
error and
vendor fraud
25.5%

Source: Adapted from Harrison Donnelly, "Store Security: The Retail Impact," *Stores,* November 1994, pp. 57–58.

easily detected than professional shoplifters, who may wear specially equipped clothing or baggy garments, carry large handbags, or use an empty box to conceal stolen merchandise to be picked up by an accomplice. Business owners and managers are often shocked by the techniques people use to remove merchandise from their premises, and by the people who do it.

> A well-known Houston matron was at the checkout counter. Upon inspection, her large purse was found to contain several prepackaged steaks and packages of luncheon meat. The store owner observed, "I thought she was one of our best customers. She has been coming here for years. I wonder how much she has taken."

Retailers are now striking back at shoplifters by means of a new tactic called *civil recovery,* or *civil restitution,* demanding payment of shoplifters or their parents for the items taken. Some states permit not only recovery of the amount stolen but also damage awards for additional costs of crime prevention, damage to displays, or injuries resulting from the crime. Civil Demand Associates, of Sherman Oaks, California, which specializes in this type of recovery, has clients nationwide.[21]

Employee Theft   As shown in Figure 16–3, employee theft is the major source of inventory loss in the retail industry. It may range from the simple act of an individual who takes only small items (such as pens or paper clips) to raids by groups that remove truckloads of merchandise. Surveys have found as many as 50 percent of employees admit stealing from their employer.[22]

Sometimes employees conspire with outsiders to steal from their employers—for example, by charging the outsiders a lower price or by placing additional merchandise in accomplices' packages.

Who Steals?   Research has shown that employees who think their income is too low, or stagnating, steal more often and in greater amounts than other employees. A study showed that those who steal tend to be young, full-time employees operating alone, and that they steal merchandise more often than cash.[23] A recent study found that the high turnover rate among temporary employees can cause serious security problems.[24]

Techniques for Preventing Theft   Retail establishments have found the use of the following measures effective in reducing theft:

- Wide-angle and one-way mirrors to observe employee or customer behavior.
- TV cameras, tied to monitors, to observe a large area of the store.
- Electronic noise activators—some visible to customers, some not—to warn of unprocessed merchandise leaving the store.
- Paper-and-pencil tests of a potential employee's honesty.
- Security guards, if economically feasible.
- Security audits, such as the following:

  Unannounced spot checks of critical activity areas, such as cash registers, employees' packages, car trunks, lunch pails, and waste disposal holding areas.

  Visible security surveillance of work activities.

  Weekly, monthly, or quarterly physical inventory checks.

In addition to using dogs and security guards, construction contractors have found the following measures effective:

- Scheduling operations and purchasing materials for just-in-time delivery.
- Scheduling lower inventory levels on weekends.
- Fencing and lighting storage yards and clearing the area adjacent to the fence.
- Using locking systems that are difficult to jimmy.
- Unannounced rotation of the person responsible for receiving materials.
- Assigning a trusted employee the responsibility for checking materials or equipment into the job site, to prevent problems such as that in the following example.

> A contractor purchased a mobile concrete mixer and sent it to the site of one of his jobs. Those responsible for the mixer left it outside the fenced-in area that night, and it was stolen. Later, the contractor found that a subordinate had failed to record it for insurance coverage.

White-Collar Crime

Another category of serious and rapidly rising abuse against business is white-collar crime. Reduced company loyalty, global economic turmoil, and more sophisticated technology are causing such crimes to boom worldwide.[25]

White-collar crimes
are those committed by managerial, professional, and technical employees.

Types of White-Collar Crimes   **White-collar crimes** are primarily committed by managerial, professional, and technical employees. They include the falsification of accounts; fraudulent accessing and manipulating of the computer; bribery of purchasing agents and other officials; collusion that results in unrecorded transactions; sale of proprietary information; and sabotage of new technology, new or old products, or customer relations. According to one survey, white-collar crime adds 15 to 20 percent to the price of everything we buy.[26]

The pirating of information and technology is particularly troubling, as it is mushrooming in scope and complexity. According to Kevin Reirson, president of the Minnesota branch of Ross Engineering (www.rosseng.com), a company that evaluates businesses for vulnerability to information theft, "All types of businesses are targets of espionage: large and small—even the local pizza parlor."[27]

According to a recent report by the American Society for Industrial Security, cases of intellectual property loss increased 320 percent worldwide from 1992 to 1995. For U.S.-based companies, the theft of research and development, customer lists, pricing information, and sales data adds up to about $24 billion a year.[28]

Computer security is becoming a real problem for small firms. Not only has the number of computer crimes increased, but so has their magnitude.[29] The two main problems are intentional destruction of data and fraudulent use.

> Someone broke into the payroll database at Pixar Animation Studios (www.pixar.com) in early 1998 and spun off a companywide e-mail listing the compensation of every employee. The culprit—who has not been found—tried to make the message appear to have come from Pixar's CEO Steve Jobs.[30]

This type of breach of security is not limited to small firms. Between 1991 and 1996, 254 employees of the Social Security Administration (www.ssa.gov) were caught selling confidential Social Security information to unauthorized people.[31] This weakness in the system increased the risks of "unauthorized access to and modification or disclosure of earnings, disabilities, and benefits records." Privacy concerns forced the suspension of a program to let people access their records online.

A survey of 73,000 online users by Yahoo! (www.yahoo.com) and Jupiter Communications (www.jup.com) found them averaging 9.7 hours a week "surfing the Net." In addition to using the Internet for business purposes, 50 percent of employees used it for "entertainment," 21 percent for "chatting," and 20 percent for "games."[32] Other surveys indicate that time lost due to leisure computer usage on the job amounts to about 1 hour per employee per day.[33] Thus, 25 employees could cost a small organization about $37,500 per year in unnecessary online charges. Even when connect fees are not an issue, obviously employers are not happy about this kind of use of "company time."

Another problem area is pirating software and computer disks. One indication of the magnitude of this problem is the fact that, according to the Software Publishers Association (www.spa.org), during one recent year software companies lost more money to piracy than McDonald's earned.[34]

Although it may be of limited value to small firms, top law enforcement officials from the world's major industrial nations have developed a cooperative strategy for combating "the growing problem of computer crime."[35]

Another form of white-collar crime is often committed against potential entrepreneurs. Scam artists, working with telephones and a "suckers list," tend to target individuals out of work as a result of corporate downsizing. These swindlers, pushing bogus get-rich-quick schemes, have cheated inexperienced entrepreneurs out of several hundred million dollars. "The victims are not greedy rich people but distressed middle Americans," says Deborah Bortner of the Washington State Securities Division.[36]

> For example, investors lost an average of $20,000 buying popcorn vending machines sold by Worldwide Marketing and Distribution. The FTA said the machines randomly dispensed "popcorn cups and half-cooked kernels."

Not only are scam artists preying on potential entrepreneurs, but they are increasingly using new methods to successfully execute old scams. Law enforcement officials say the Internet has come in handy as a vehicle for delivering fraudulent come-ons. Also, the Internet itself is being hawked as an attractive investment opportunity.[37] According to the Council of Better Business Bureaus Inc., a nonprofit umbrella group for its 135 regional offices, the number of complaints to its offices more than doubled (to 11,700) from 1990 to 1996. Figure 16–4 provides a breakdown of the complaints.

Figure 16–4
Let the Entrepreneur Beware

Complaints to Better Business Bureaus nationwide about promotions that typically target small business have been on the rise (figures in thousands). This table shows a breakdown of the complaints received in 1996.

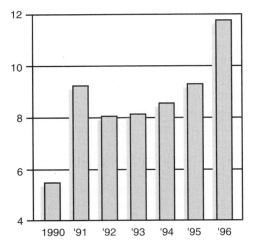

Type of Promotion	Complaints
Telephone service	5,682
"Paper pirates"/office supplies	1,662
Business opportunities	1,226
Loan brokers/advance-fee brokers	1,041
Phone solicitations	528
Advertising specialty companies	420
Directories (fake Yellow Pages, etc.)	339
Marketing-research companies	293
Advertising for charity publications	210
Promotions/prize offers	148
Franchise-selling companies	100
Police/fire/fraternal solicitations	79

Source: Council of Better Business Bureaus, as reported in *The Wall Street Journal,* May 21, 1998, p. R25. Copyright 1998 by *The Wall Street Journal.* Used with permission.

Ways to Minimize White-Collar Crime   Special measures must be taken to minimize crimes by white-collar personnel. Some deterrents you can use include audits, being aware of employee work habits, identification, and bonding. Also, as mentioned above, small firms that use computers may need the services of a firm with computer security expertise.

Audits of data such as past sales transactions, inventory levels, purchase prices, and accounts receivable may uncover undesirable activities.

You should be aware of your white-collar employees' work habits. They may all be open and aboveboard, but they should be checked. You should ask such questions as: Do they work nights regularly? Do they never take a day off? Do they forgo their usual vacation? Standards of living, dress, car, housing, entertainment, and travel that seem to cost more than an employee should be able to afford often signal economic misconduct.

Proper identification, along with a device that takes pictures of a check and the person cashing it, tends to discourage bad-check artists. Although this practice may be too expensive for your small firm, your bank may assist in developing effective identification procedures. Many states have passed bad-check laws, which permit a business that receives a bad check to collect not only its face value but also double or triple damages in small claims court. This financial penalty helps to reduce loss.

Since credit cards are frequently stolen, additional identification should be required. Be sure the signature corresponds to the one on the card. Also, you should be sure to ascertain the validity of trade documents, such as invoices and securities. Each year, millions of dollars are lost by businesspeople through carelessness that allows others to palm off bogus documents.

Fidelity bonding helps insure against employee fraud or theft. The employer pays a premium to an insurance company, which then assumes the risk and reimburses the company for any loss.

Document Security

Our personal experience working with small businesses, as well as press releases in recent years, has made us aware of the importance of document security. As shown in Chapter 15, *information is a vital factor in managing and controlling business activities,* and its management and maintenance help to assure the continuation of the business. The life of your business depends on the appropriate recording of information, its transmission to the appropriate persons, and its security. Records with confidential information should be stored in bank lockboxes, safes, or restricted areas, and only authorized persons should have access to them. And all records should be protected by backups.

The proprietary nature of confidential business records and various documents makes it essential that you protect them from unauthorized eyes and hands. The trade secrets and competitive advantage of your business may be lost if this information passes into the wrong hands. Therefore, a list of authorized personnel should be prepared and provided to those responsible for document security. Also, even the smallest companies should have security policies to protect sensitive business information.[38]

An unbending rule should be that under no circumstance is it permissible to remove confidential material from the restricted area or from the business premises. Some business owners think they can save on personnel costs by permitting material to be carried to an employee's residence where the employee works on the firm's records after hours. The chance of loss, the opportunity for access by unauthorized persons, and the risk of a claim for adequate compensation make this practice inadvisable.

■ SAFEGUARDING EMPLOYEES WITH PREVENTIVE MEASURES

Within a business, various types of accidents and health problems occur, causing potential losses. The use of insurance to eliminate or minimize disastrous financial losses to a company was discussed earlier in this chapter. In addition, safeguards can be instituted to reduce human suffering as well as costs to a company and employees.

> For example, after several pizza delivery men were shot in "high-crime areas," many pizzerias refused to deliver to these neighborhoods. This provided a market niche for Home Boyz Catering and Delivery, which set up a unique system in Birmingham, Alabama. It hires ex-gang members to deliver pizzas and other food items to high-crime areas, adding a $2.50 service charge (or "risk premium") for each delivery. The service has been so successful that the company has expanded into other cities.[39]

Employees are a valuable resource that you should protect through proper safety procedures as shown in Chapter 10. These procedures should be preventive in nature. Not only should you provide a safe workplace for workers, but, in addition, they must work safely, since most accidents occur because of human error such as driving an automobile carelessly or handling equipment improperly.

Guards over moving tools, devices to keep hands away or stop machines, employee protective gear, warnings of unsafe conditions, and medical treatment are some safeguards used to protect employees from accidents and health problems and to prevent lawsuits.

On April 28, 1998, the Occupational Safety and Health Administration (OSHA) (www.osha.gov) released a set of federal guidelines for curbing late-night retail crime. As homicide is the second-leading cause of work-related fatalities (912 deaths in 1996, or 15 percent of fatal work injuries), these guidelines are supposed to reduce that hazard. But Peter Eide, manager of labor law policy at the U.S. Chamber of Commerce (www.uschamber.com), said, "We see some problems with it [as] it could be cited as grounds for a lawsuit."[40] Lawyers say they are already getting calls from employers worried that they could be held liable if the "voluntary" guidelines aren't followed.

Two of the guidelines, recommending bullet-proof glass and surveillance cameras, may hit smaller employers hard. According to Mary Leon of the National Federation of Independent Business, "The costs are excessive for small convenience stores."[41]

WHAT YOU SHOULD HAVE LEARNED

■

1. One of the greatest challenges for small businesses is dealing with risk. Risk management minimizes financial shocks. Pure risk of losses is unpredictable and uncertain, but it is often measurable and insurable. Speculative risk is uncertainty about gain or loss from voluntary decisions and is not insurable. Risk may be avoided, prevented, assumed (self-insurance), or transferred through insurance.

2. Insurance can be used to minimize losses due to risks. Small businesses usually need the following types of insurance: (a) fire, (b) business interruption, (c) casualty, (d) professional liability, (e) product/service liability, (f) liability while sponsoring athletic teams and/or other dangerous activities, (g) workers' compensation, (h) health, (i) death or disability of owner, (j) key person insurance, and (k) fidelity and surety bonds.

3. In choosing an insurer, consider its financial characteristics, flexibility in meeting your requirements, and the services it renders. An insurance company can be judged on financial stability, specialization in types of coverage, ability to tailor policies to meet your needs, and cost of protection.

4. Although businesses should be insured against losses, they should also take steps to prevent crimes—armed robbery, theft, and white-collar crime, especially computer crimes. Measures that can reduce the chances of being robbed include modifying the store's layout, securing entrances, using security dogs, controlling the handling of cash, and redesigning the surrounding area.

5. Theft includes shoplifting by outsiders and employee theft. Security measures to reduce theft include wide-angle and one-way mirrors, bullet-resistant glass, TV cameras, electronic noise activators on merchandise, screening of prospective employees, security guards, and security audits.

   White-collar crime includes removal of cash; falsification of accounts; fraudulent computer access and manipulation; bribery; collusion resulting in unrecorded transactions; sale of proprietary information; and sabotage of new technology, products, or customer relations. Ways to minimize white-collar crime include auditing of records, observing employees' work habits, requiring proper identification with checks and credit cards, and fidelity bonding. Confidential documents should be stored in bank lockboxes, safes, or restricted areas.

6. A small firm has a special responsibility to protect employees, to provide a safe workplace, and to encourage employees to maintain safe work habits.

QUESTIONS FOR DISCUSSION

■

1. What is meant by risk management?

2. Distinguish between pure risk and speculative risk as they apply to small businesses.

3. Discuss four ways small firms can cope with risk.

4. What are some considerations in determining a small business's need for insurance?

5. What types of insurance are commonly carried by small businesses? Describe each type of coverage.

6. What criteria should you use in choosing an insurer?

7. Discuss some methods a small business can use to reduce the chances of being robbed.

8. What is meant by white-collar crime? What are some ways to minimize it?

9. What are some methods used to safeguard employees?

CASE 16-1

BEWARE OF "SOFTLIFTING"

These days, even the smallest of businesses are using computers. As mentioned in Chapter 15, the microcomputer has replaced the file cabinet, resulting in a great need for computer security. When we think about computer security we generally think in terms of protecting the equipment or the data on the hard disk. However, there is another type of computer security that business owners must be aware of, namely, guarding against "softlifting." A business owner who has more than one computer may be tempted to buy one copy of the needed software and install it on all the computers to save money. DON'T DO IT!

This is softlifting and it's a very common problem. According to the Software Publishers Association (SPA), one in five personal computer programs in use today is an illegal copy. Software bootlegging costs U.S. software publishers $1.2 billion each year, on sales of only $6 to $7 billion. This is why "Software Police" are cracking down hard and the penalties are harsh. Softlifting recently became a felony with penalties of up to $250,000 and five years in jail.

The University of Oregon Continuation Center in Eugene, Oregon, thought it would "save a few bucks" by softlifting. But it got caught and had to pay a $130,000 fine and hold a national conference on copyright laws and software use.

Parametrix Inc. of Seattle also learned the hard way. It was raided by the "Software Police," who had a search warrant and were accompanied by a U.S. marshal. The raid turned up dozens of bootlegged copies of software programs. Parametrix agreed to pay fines totaling $350,000. How does the SPA find out about these abuses? The tip-off usually comes from a call to the SPA's toll-free piracy hotline. Often the caller is an ex-employee or a disgruntled employee who is seeking revenge. More and more companies are getting caught. Obviously, thousands don't get caught, but since 1984 the SPA has conducted 75 raids and filed more than 300 lawsuits.

The best advice is: *Stay legal!* Don't risk losing the business you've worked so hard to build just to save a few bucks, because according to the SPA, if you're softlifting you are definitely living on borrowed time.

Questions

1. How severe do you perceive this problem to be? Why or why not?

2. Are you aware of any organizations that have participated in "softlifting"? If so, do they deserve to be caught and punished, in your opinion?

3. How can a small business owner prevent employees from making bootlegged copies of software programs for themselves?

4. You have a small business with five computers. Your old software is obsolete and must be replaced, but your business is struggling financially. Would you risk buying one copy of the software and installing it on all five machines? Explain why or why not.

Source: "Companies, Beware of 'Software Police,'" Associated Press release, in *Mobile* (Alabama) *Press Register,* November 16, 1992, p. 5B. Used with permission of Associated Press.

CASE 16-2

WHEN INVENTORY AND SALES DON'T BALANCE

Jeff Thomas, manager of a clothing store in Dallas, Texas, observed that over the past several months, inventory and sales were not equal. When he began to compare evening to daytime sales, he noticed that sales were staying the same, but the inventory count was lower in the evening than in the morning. Most of his 20 employees are on alternate schedules from daytime to evening. In an effort to curb possible stealing, Jeff began taking inventory more frequently and keeping a tighter control over the employees he put in charge of inventory counting and control.

Questions

1. What are some ways Jeff can improve security?

2. How can Jeff detect whether an employee is stealing?

17

BUSINESS-GOVERNMENT RELATIONS AND BUSINESS ETHICS

Small business owners spend an average of eight hours per week complying with federal and state regulations.

According to a study by MasterCard

Exercise caution in your business affairs, for the world is full of trickery. But let this not blind you to what virtue there is.

"Desiderata," plaque found in Old St. Paul's Church, Baltimore, Maryland

The dominant issues are the small business person's access to capital; and, second, the burden of regulation.

Philip Lader, SBA

LEARNING OBJECTIVES

After studying the material in this chapter, you will be able to:

1. Understand the legal system in which small businesses operate, and explain some basic business laws affecting them.

2. Discuss the role played by government assistance.

3. Describe some burdensome aspects of government regulations and paperwork.

4. Explain how to choose a lawyer.

5. Describe what is ethical and socially responsible behavior.

Zeiner Funeral Homes

Reuben Feuerborn is a third-generation funeral director and embalmer. If you ask him why he chose this particular career, he will tell you that he has "just always liked the service it provides to families." When we talked to him, Feuerborn was not affiliated with his family business but instead was employed by Zeiner Funeral Homes, a sole proprietorship located in the Midwest.

Zeiner Funeral Homes began in Marion, Kansas, in 1912 with the Thompson Funeral Home, which was sold to Gerald Harp in 1969. Harp in turn sold the company to Ty Zeiner in 1986. After purchasing the Thompson-Harp Funeral Home, Zeiner also acquired the Hillsboro Memorial Chapel (in Hillsboro, Kansas) in 1989 and the Florence Funeral Home (Florence, Kansas) in 1991. In January 1998 he purchased the Miller Funeral Homes, located in Hesston and Goessel, Kansas. The Marion location, where Feuerborn is employed, continues to be the center of operations, with the four other homes operating as branches, all under the name of Zeiner Funeral Homes.

When asked about ethical issues in the profession, Feuerborn said, "Nearly every issue is an ethical one that some unscrupulous undertaker has violated at one time or another. There are no questionable issues if you treat every family as if they were your own." The perception that morticians take advantage of the bereaved is an understandable result of the "sticker shock" experienced by families already traumatized by grief. The average cost of a funeral, according to the National Association of Funeral Directors, was $4,624 in 1997, in addition to a burial fee of approximately $3,500.[1] If cremation is chosen, the additional cost is a few hundred dollars. One way to prepare for funeral expenses is to purchase a pre-need burial policy, which is a prefunded funeral plan. All five Zeiner locations sell such policies, but 80 percent of Zeiner's business is "at-need services," which have no prearrangements.

Regulatory compliance is always an issue in any business—large or small—and funeral homes are no exception. In addition to all the zoning, business license, and other state and local requirements, the premises of funeral homes are regularly inspected by OSHA and—in Kansas—by the State Board of Mortuary Arts. The Board also inspects prefunded policies; Kansas state law requires that payments for each policy must be deposited in a separate account. The Board regulates the renewal of professional licensing for funeral directors, funeral establishments, and embalmers. In turn, the Federal Trade Commission requires all funeral homes to prepare a "General Price List" of all available services with their itemized prices. A copy of this list must be provided to anyone who asks for it, or before any funeral arrangements are made.

Source: Author's conversations and correspondence with Reuben Feuerborn and Ty Zeiner; and Sara Lamb, "Funerals Becoming Big Business," *Mobile* (Alabama) *Register,* January 26, 1997, pp. 1F, 2F.

Your small business will operate in a legal and political environment that sets rules and regulations for almost every activity from starting the business to terminating it. Throughout the book, we've talked about the operation of a small business within the framework of government assistance and regulation. Now we would like to go into greater detail about this environment. We will look at some of the most important government laws and regulations affecting small firms, as well as show how governments provide assistance and control. Then we will discuss how to choose a lawyer and how to maintain ethical and socially responsible behavior.

■ UNDERSTANDING THE LEGAL ENVIRONMENT

Because it is so important to know and obey government laws and regulations, we will give you an overview of the subject. For further coverage, you should obtain competent legal assistance from someone familiar with local business conditions.

You're already familiar with some of the most basic legal principles, such as *Everyone is equal under the law, Everyone is entitled to his or her day in court,* and *A person is presumed innocent until proven guilty.* Table 17–1 provides a closer look at some basic legal principles and terminology.

All laws affecting small businesses are based on the federal or a state constitution. However, the making, administering, and interpreting of laws are separated into three distinct branches of government: legislative, executive, and judicial. Moreover, laws are made at all levels of our government, including federal, state, county, and municipal levels. These levels are generally referred to as *multiple levels of government,* and each level

Table 17–1
Selected Basic Legal Terminology

Common law	Unwritten law derived from judicial decisions based on customs and usages accepted by the people.
Statutory law	Body of laws passed by federal, state, and local governments.
Interstate commerce clause	Gives Congress the right to "regulate commerce with foreign nations, and among the several states."
Police power	States' right to regulate business, including the right to use the force of the state to promote the general welfare of citizens. All laws must be based on the federal or a state constitution.
Due process	Implies that everyone is entitled to a day in court, and all processes must be equal and fair.
Legislative branch of government	The U.S. Congress, state legislature, country/city council, or any other body that passes laws.
Executive branch of government	President, governor, mayor, or any other who enforces the laws through regulatory agencies and decrees.
Judicial branch of government	The court system, or those who interpret the laws and supervise enforcement.
Public law	Deals with the rights and powers of the government.
Criminal law	Deals with punishing those who commit illegal acts.
Private law	Is administered between two or more citizens.
Civil law	Deals with violations against another person who has been harmed in some way.

administers its own laws. Occasionally some of these laws are contradictory, and they are often complex, so be prepared to retain competent legal representation, and practice the lesson shown in Figure 17–1.

■ SOME BASIC LAWS AFFECTING SMALL BUSINESS

It is beyond the scope of this book to name—much less explain—all of the many complex and often contradictory laws, old and new, affecting owners of small businesses, but we will hit the highlights. First we will discuss the Uniform Commercial Code, then torts and bankruptcy.

The Uniform Commercial Code

Since laws affecting business vary greatly from state to state, massive efforts have been made by the National Conference of Commissioners on Uniform State Laws to draft a set of uniform model statutes to govern business and commercial transactions in all 50 states. The result is the **Uniform Commercial Code (UCC),** consisting of nine parts. The Code has been adopted in 52 jurisdictions, including all 50 states, the District of Columbia, and the Virgin Islands. Louisiana, however, with laws still based on the Code Napoléon—the French civil code that has been in effect since the Louisiana Purchase in 1803—has adopted only Articles 1, 3, 4, 7, 8, and 9.[2]

The Code's nine articles are (1) General Provisions, (2) Sales, (3) Commercial Paper, (4) Bank Deposits and Collections, (5) Letters of Credit, (6) Bulk Transfers, (7) Documents of Title, (8) Investment Securities, and (9) Secured Transactions, including sales of accounts and chattel paper. Because of the complexity of these articles, we will not try to discuss them in detail. Instead, we refer you to any good basic business law text.

> The **Uniform Commercial Code (UCC)** is a set of uniform model statutes to govern business and commercial transactions in all states.

Torts

A **tort** is a wrongful act by one party that results in injury to a second party's person, property, or reputation, for which the first party is liable. In essence, tort law provides a means

> A **tort** is a wrongful act by one party, not covered by criminal law, that results in injury to a second party's person, property, or reputation, for which the first party is liable.

Figure 17–1
Good Advice

Source: Courtesy of Schieffelin & Somerset Co.

by which society compensates those who have suffered an injury as a result of wrongful action(s) by others.

Laws dealing with torts provide for the performance of duties and compensation for the physical, mental, or economic injuries resulting from faulty products or actions of others. This usually involves some form of economic restitution (monetary payment) for damages or losses incurred.

> For example, in March 1998, 26 independent bookstores in California, Florida, and other parts of the nation "threw the book" at several giant retail chains. The independents—and the American Booksellers Association—claimed that Barnes & Noble, Borders Group, and Borders' subsidiary Waldenbooks used their size to extract secret, illegal price discounts and advertising rebates from publishers.[3]
>
> The suit was built on grounds laid when Penguin Group WSA agreed to pay $25 million to the booksellers association because Penguin had given cash awards to large retailers "for paying their bills faster."
>
> The independents are asking for "triple their actual damage for the last four years, . . . and a judgment to stop the alleged special discounts."

Bankruptcy

Bankruptcy is a formal legal condition of inability to repay debts. People or businesses can petition the courts to be relieved of this financial obligation.

Chapter 11 provides for reorganizing a bankrupt business, whether the bankruptcy petition is filed voluntarily or involuntarily.

Under **bankruptcy** law, people or businesses can petition the courts to be relieved of the obligation to pay debts they can't repay. There are two types of bankruptcy: *ordinary,* or *straight, bankruptcy,* and *Chapter 11 bankruptcy,* or *reorganization.* Ordinary bankruptcy occurs when a debtor files an application with a court claiming that debts exceed assets and asks to be declared bankrupt. When one or more creditors file the bankruptcy petition against the debtor, it's called *involuntary bankruptcy.*

Chapter 11 of the Bankruptcy Reform Act of 1978 contains a provision for reorganizing the bankrupt business, whether the bankruptcy petition is filed voluntarily or involuntarily. Thus, the firm can continue to operate while its debts are being repaid. If the business is so far gone that it can't keep operating, it must be liquidated.

You should consult a lawyer as soon as possible if your business is ever faced with a bankruptcy situation. See "Choosing and Using a Lawyer" later in this chapter for more details.

■ GOVERNMENT HELP FOR SMALL BUSINESSES

Many examples of assistance to small businesses have been given throughout this text. Because most such help is provided by the SBA (www.sbaonline.sba.gov) and the U.S. Department of Commerce (www.doc.gov), their assistance will be summarized.

Small Business Administration (SBA)

As shown in Chapter 6, the SBA provides many types of direct and guaranteed loans for small firms. The SBA also provides help for small firms through publications such as its series of Management Aids, local workshops, small business development centers, and small business institutes. Information on overseas marketing is also provided. As shown in Figure 17–2, the SBA now has an "SBA Answer Desk" with a toll-free number.

In addition, the SBA sponsors the Service Corps of Retired Executives (SCORE). SCORE (www.score.org) is made up of volunteer members who specialize in helping people develop their business ideas. As was shown in Case 1–2, SCORE can match one or more of these counselors to a specific business. It can also call on its extensive roster of

Figure 17–2

SBA Answer Desk
1-800-U-ASK-SBA (800-827-5722)

The toll-free telephone number listed above is for the small business information and referral service being offered by the U.S. Small Business Administration. Call for information on starting a new business or for sources of technical and financial assistance for an already existing business.

Source: Journal of Small Business Management 32 (October 1994), p. 27.

public relations experts, bankers, lawyers, and the like to answer the important and detailed questions you might have about setting up a business. They'll even work with you as long as you need after you start your business. Some clients consult with SCORE counselors for several years.

Another way the SBA helps is by encouraging small business owners to try to perform more effectively. It does this by making state and national awards for the "Small Business Persons of the Year." The current President of the United States announces the winners and presents the awards at the White House.

U.S. Department of Commerce

As indicated in earlier chapters, the U.S. Department of Commerce also offers assistance through its International Trade Administration (ITA), its U.S. and Foreign Commercial Service Agency (USFCSA), and its Minority Business Development Agency (MBDA). Finally, the department's Census Bureau furnishes much demographic information. For small firms in a hurry, data may be obtained electronically.

Other Government Agencies

Among the other agencies helping small business is the U.S. Department of Agriculture, which provides assistance through the Cooperative Extension Service, the Federal Land Bank Association, the Production Credit Association, and the Farmers Home Administration.

> For example, when the North American Free Trade Agreement (NAFTA) went into effect in 1994, the SBA, in cooperation with USDA, started a program to guarantee hundreds of millions of dollars' worth of small business loans in 35 selected areas where NAFTA had led to job losses. The North American Development Bank (NADB), an international financial institution jointly capitalized and governed by Mexico and the United States, is coordinating the program. Small businesses in those areas can also apply to NADB for loans.[4]

■ HANDLING GOVERNMENT REGULATIONS AND PAPERWORK

As we mentioned in Chapter 1, if you want to see a small business person become incensed, mention government regulations and paperwork, which are a growing problem. At one time, smaller firms were exempt from many federal regulations and even some state and local ones. Today, though, these firms tend to be regulated the same as their larger competitors. While most small business owners are willing to comply with government regulations, compliance is often complex, costly, and time-consuming, and regulations are often confusing or contradictory, as the following example illustrates.

> According to Ron Smith, Colorado director of the National Federation of Independent Business (www.nfibonline.com), his state has taken steps to update its laws. However, there is still a regulation saying hospitals will be fined if they don't present their annual budgets to the Colorado Hospital. The only problem is, the Colorado Hospital was abolished several years ago.[5]

Dealing with Regulatory Agencies

In theory, a regulatory agency is more flexible and sensitive to the needs of society than Congress can be, since less time is needed for an agency to develop and issue new regulations than for Congress to enact new legislation. Experience, however, doesn't seem to support this theory. Many small business managers believe that on occasion an agency's findings may be arbitrary or may protect its own security or that of the industry it's supposed to regulate, as the following example illustrates.

> The Public Transit Authority of New York City (www.dot.state.ny.us/)refused to allow van or jitney services to operate in competition with established bus routes. Vincent Cummings started Brooklyn Van Lines to provide door-to-door service in his area. Although he won the approval of the Taxi and Limousine Commission (TLC) after five years of effort, his application was unanimously rejected by a New York City Council Committee.
>
> The City Council was set to hear Cummings's case in November 1996. When he arrived, he was told there would be no vote because the TLC had withdrawn its approval because of the "manner of operating of the vans and the effect on mass transit." In effect, *the city's transit monopoly must be preserved.*
>
> In fact, almost no new applications for jitney service have been approved since 1994, when the City Council passed a law dramatically restricting their operations. The law was recently challenged by the Institute for Justice, a free-market law firm that seeks "economic liberties for the poor."
>
> After Cummings took his case to court, the City Council reversed course and permitted him to operate 20 vans. His vans, which must meet all insurance requirements and pass safety inspections, will give 40 people employment in order to take passengers to and from production jobs.[6]

Some Benefits of Government Regulation

Do the benefits of government regulation outweigh the costs? Since there's no profit mechanism to measure this, as there is in private business, and since both costs and benefits are hard to determine, estimates must be made. Even with these measurement limitations, though, it's been shown that some regulations are truly cost-effective.

> For example, air pollution requirements have provided economic benefits that far outweigh the costs of complying with them, according to the White House Council on Environmental Quality.[7]

When regulations are imposed on one industry or business they often generate opportunities for other small entrepreneurs.

> When the EPA announced standards for replacements for automobile catalytic converters several years ago, it created a market for replacement models that could be made more cheaply because they didn't have to last as long. Perfection Automotive

"Sparky's found a way to get a bite back out of the government."

(*Source:* ©1996 by Margaret P. Megginson. Reprinted with permission.)

Products Corporation of Livonia, Michigan, broadened its product line to make them. It added nearly 100 employees, doubling its previous work force, to serve the market.[8]

Some Problems with Government Regulation

There are at least four areas of concern that small firms have with government regulations. The first problem is *the difficulty of understanding some of the regulations.* Many of them are often confusing and very restrictive.

Steve Forbes, editor-in-chief of *Forbes* (www.forbes.com) magazine, offers the following comment on our complex income tax system: "The Gettysburg Address runs to about 200 words. The Declaration of Independence has around 1,300 words. And the Holy Bible has about 773,000 words. But the U.S. federal income tax code has about seven million words and is growing longer every year."[9]

A second problem is *the enormous amount of paperwork involved in preparing and handling the reports needed to comply with government regulations and in maintaining the records needed to satisfy the regulators.* In 1996, Congress tried to help small businesses by passing the Small Business Regulatory Enforcement Fairness Act. The act requires each federal agency to set up compliance centers to help small businesses deal with pending legislation. The main thrust of the act is to get small business input as agencies are formulating new regulations, as it is easier to change a rule before it is written than after.

Karen V. Brown has been doing this for years at the Environmental Protection Agency. For instance, she has helped the wood-processing industry comply with regulations so they can get bank financing. And she recently wrote a memo— approved by the EPA's chief of regulators management—requiring EPA regulators to prepare simplified one-page explanations of 28 regulatory matters to be used in meetings with 25 small trade associations.[10]

A third problem is *the difficulty and cost of complying with the regulations.* According to Jack Faris, president and CEO of the National Federation of Independent Business, "The avalanche of federal regulations robs employers of 1 billion hours of productive time wasted filling out government paperwork."[11] The costs are greater than just the administrative expenses; bringing actual operations into compliance with the regulations is also expensive.

> Murray Wiedenbaum and Melinda Warren, economists at the Center for the Study of American Business (www.csab.wustl.edu), suggest that "industry-specific rules limiting entry or price . . . almost invariably cost the nation more than the benefits derived by the group these rules are designed to protect." They estimate that "regulations cost the economy $500 billion to $600 billion a year, or more than $2,000 per person." The two scholars stress that these regulations "save their greatest punishment for small businesses and low-income customers."[12]

Finally, a fourth problem is that *regulations tend to discourage small firms from hiring more workers as their employment approaches the cutoffs set by federal laws and regulations.* The following laws apply to small companies with the number of employees shown:

Occupational Safety and Health Act	10
Federal civil rights laws	15 or more
Americans with Disabilities Act	25
Family and Medical Leave Act	50
Worker Adjustment and Retraining Act	100

Discouraged employers are those who tend not to hire new people if it would make them subject to certain federal laws and regulations.

According to Wiedenbaum and Warren, these thresholds serve as a barrier to **discouraged employers** who tend not to hire new people if it brings them under one of these regulations. They report that "businesses with a work force of 49 report that they avoid hiring the [50th] person in order to avoid falling under the Family and Medical Leave Act regulations."[13]

Finally, a recent survey by U.S. Trust (www.ustrust.com) of the most successful U.S. business owners found that fully 85 percent of them believed that "government policies" had "made things worse" for them in recent years. Only 7 percent thought that "government intervention" had "made things better."[14] Table 17–2 shows what these business owners thought were "threats" to privately held businesses.

Table 17–2
Government Policies Perceived as the Most Serious Threats to Privately Held Businesses

Government Policy Perceived as a Threat	Percentage of Owners Who Perceived the Policy as a Threat
Government required paperwork	97%
Taxes on businesses, raw materials, final products or services	95
Environmental regulations	82
Health care reform	81
Product liability laws	78
Government pension laws, including ERISA	77

Source: A survey by U.S. Trust of affluent business owners, reported at www.ustrust.com/affbus.htm, accessed February 25, 1998, pp. 2–3.

How Owners of Small Firms Can Cope with Government Regulations

What can small business managers do about burdensome government regulations and paperwork? There are several approaches to consider.

1. Learn as much as you can about the law, particularly if it is possible that a law can help you.

> For example, over the years, the Alta Group, a titanium refiner in Fombell, Pennsylvania, has formed a partnership with OSHA to develop a comprehensive safety program. The OSHA Consultation Service, which is independent of OSHA's enforcement branch, provides free workplace safety reviews for small businesses—usually those with 250 or fewer employees at a worksite.[15]

2. Challenge detrimental or harmful laws, perhaps by joining organizations such as the National Federation of Independent Business, the National Small Business Association, or National Small Business United (www.nsbu.org). At the very least, you can get your message across to your elected representatives. For businesspeople too busy to write to officials, there are other entrepreneurs who will do it for them—for a price.

> For instance, Diane and Karl Woods, of Silver Spring, Maryland, launched a service for harried citizens who have something to say to their elected officials but are squeezed for time to say it. For a small fee, they will compose letters reflecting your feelings on a local or national issue, let you read and sign them, then send them off in your name to the appropriate official(s). The Woods want to "put the power back where it belongs—in the hands of the people—by acting as a private secretary to [their] clients."[16]

3. Become involved in the legal-political system to elect officials of your choosing who will help change the laws.

> A large number of entrepreneurs were elected to Congress in 1994 and 1996. They included the owner of a successful cellular phone business, the owner of a meat-packing business, an auto dealer, a trucking company owner, and a farmer.[17]

4. Find a better legal environment, if possible, even if it means moving to a different city, county, or state.

> Sam Chapman, an aquaculture specialist, had been breeding an exceptionally rare bright-blue lobster. When the research facility wanted to use his space for other activities, Chapman had the opportunity to start a small business based on 10 years of expensive research and to sell the crustaceans as rare pets. The state of Maine, however, had strict rules about possessing lobsters smaller than the state's legal eating size. Since Chapman's rare lobsters fell below this allowed size, he began to try to find a more conducive legal climate.[18]

5. Learn to live with the laws and regulations, even if it means forming an alliance with other companies or organizations.

Dealing with Private Regulators

Governments are not alone in posing a problem for small firms: Many professional organizations also establish standards of practice for their members. The guidelines are created to ensure professional conduct in various areas. Some of these areas include ethics, technical knowledge, competence, and compliance.

History indicates that government regulations are legislated when the business world neglects to regulate itself. However, sometimes the private regulators need to be regulated, as the following incident illustrates.

> A major professional society issued a "guideline" discouraging manufacturers from using a given product. As it turned out, a major supplier of a competing product was a member of the society.[19]

■ CHOOSING AND USING A LAWYER

You can see from the previous discussion that, from a legal point of view, it isn't easy to start and operate a small business. Therefore, one of the first things you should do when forming a business is to retain a competent lawyer. Actually, your attorney should be retained at the time you are developing your business plan, as well as when you are obtaining financing—not when you get into trouble.

Choosing the Lawyer

You should choose a lawyer as you would a consultant, an accountant, or anyone else who provides services. Comparison shop! Check the credentials of different attorneys! Discuss fees with them candidly! And, whatever you do, don't forget to talk with them about the wisdom of retaining legal counsel. For example, does it make sense to spend $500 in legal fees and court costs to recover a $300 bad debt?

Where to Look   How do you look for a lawyer? The first and most obvious step is to define the nature of your legal problem. Once you have defined the problem, there are a number of ways to find a lawyer to help you with it. The American Bar Association recommends four sources:[20]

1. *Personal referral* from someone whose opinion you value, such as your banker, your minister, a relative, or another lawyer.
2. The *Martindale-Hubbell Law Directory* (www.martindale.com), which includes professional biographies of most of the attorneys engaged in private practice throughout the United States.
3. *Lawyer Referral and Information Services (LRS),* which are provided by most bar associations in larger cities.
4. *Advertising,* since lawyers can now advertise certain information in newspapers and the Yellow Pages and on radio and television. (Very few do, however, except personal injury and workers' compensation attorneys.)

What to Look For   First, look for appropriate experience with your type of small business. While you may not necessarily rely on the lawyer for business advice, the one chosen should at least have sufficient background knowledge and information about the particulars of your business and its problems to represent you effectively.[21]

Second, since there should be compatibility between lawyer and client, observe the lawyer's demeanor, the style and atmosphere of his or her office, and any clients—if possible—before making your choice. Does the lawyer represent a competitor?.

Third, does the lawyer have time for you and your business? For example, if you have difficulty getting an appointment or are repeatedly kept waiting on the phone, you should probably look elsewhere.

Figure 17–3
A Sample Contract for a Lawyer's Services

I, John Doe, hereby agree to employ the law firm of Ruth Roe to represent me and act on my behalf and in my best interest in presenting a claim for any and all damages, including my personal injury, resulting from an accident which occurred on or about June 29, 1993, near Bethesda, Maryland.

I agree to pay to said firm an amount equal to 30 percent of any and all sums collected by way of settlement or from legal action. In the event of trial (as determined as of the time a jury is impaneled), I agree to pay said firm an amount equal to 50 percent of any amounts received.

Be it further understood that no settlement will be made without consent of client. It is understood that if nothing is obtained on client's behalf, then client owes nothing to said law firm, except for the expenses associated with handling this case.

Said law firm agrees to act on client's behalf with all due diligence and in client's best interest at all times in prosecuting said claims.

DATED this _____ day of _____ , 19____

John Doe _____

Ruth Roe, by: _____

Copyright 1998, *USA Today.* Reprinted with permission.

Finally, since cost is an important consideration, do not hesitate to discuss fees with the prospective attorney, for performance must be balanced against the cost of the service provided. Lawyers' time is expensive!

Maintaining Relationships with Lawyers

Lawyers usually have three basic ways of charging for their services. First, a flat fee may be charged for a specific assignment. Thus, the cost of the service is known, and funds can be allocated for it. Second, the lawyer may charge an hourly fee based on the type of activities to be performed and the amount of staff assistance required. Third, a contingency fee may be set. If the stakes are really high, and if time and risks are involved, the attorney may charge a percentage (say 30 percent) of the negotiated settlement, or even more if the amount is obtained through a trial (as high as 50 percent), as shown in the sample contract in Figure 17–3. Also, the lawyer will expect to be reimbursed for expenses. In long, involved cases, the lawyer should provide periodic reports, including a statement of expenses.

■ SOCIALLY AND ETHICALLY RESPONSIBLE BEHAVIOR

While most small business people have long accepted—and practiced—social responsibility and ethical behavior, considerable external emphasis is now being placed on these topics. Sometimes, however, small businesses are put at a disadvantage when they try to capitalize on being socially responsible.

For example, a group called Business for Social Responsibility (BSR) (www.bsr.org) was formed when many entrepreneurs took a media beating because a few journalists took a jaundiced view of the social responsibility movement. Immediately, responsible organizations were charged with the need to attain an unreachable set of standards, approaching perfection. BSR is a group of those targeted entrepreneurs who now fight for credibility in the eyes of the media.[22]

Social Responsibility

Social responsibility is a business's obligation to set policies, make decisions, and follow actions that are desirable in terms of the values and objectives of society. Whether that term is used or not, it means the business acts with the best interests of society in mind, as well as those of the business.

Socially responsible behavior can best be illustrated in terms of specific action programs that management undertakes. Thus, social responsibility as practiced by small firms usually takes the form of (1) consumerism, (2) employee relations, including providing equal employment opportunity to former unemployables, (3) environmental protection, and (4) community relations.

Consumerism   While the old saying that "the customer is always right" may not always be true, small business managers are now truly concerned about consumer needs and wishes. The movement to protect the valid interests of consumers (consumerism) is a major force in small business today.

Consumerism is the organized efforts of independent, government, and business groups to protect consumers from undesirable effects of poorly designed and poorly produced products. As shown in Chapter 7, the consumerism movement became popular during the 1960s and 1970s. The Child Protection and Toy Safety Act set up the Consumer Product Safety Commission (CPSC) to set safety standards, require warning labels on potentially unsafe products, and require recall of products found to be harmful. "Truth in advertising" is now also of paramount interest to small business owners.

Employee Relations   Enlightened **employee relations** involves a concern for employee rights, especially as to meaningful employment; training, development, and promotions; pay; and health and safety. As shown in Chapter 9, there is now a greater effort to hire qualified persons without regard to race, sex, religion, color, creed, age, or disabilities. While much is still to be done, small and large firms have made tremendous strides in this area.

> Marriott International Inc. (www.marriott.com) has a "welfare to work" program that trains former welfare recipients to become productive employees. It has put about 600 people through the program in the past few years, costing about $5,000 per employee (the government funds all but about $2,300 of it). Although there are sometimes problems with participants who have been evicted from their homes or welfare shelter, or commit crimes, the Marriott trainers nurture them through their difficulties. Those who complete the program receive full-time jobs, with Marriott or elsewhere.[23]

Other areas of employee relations include sexual harassment, family leave, care for children and elderly family members, and drug testing. While the courts and legislators are sorting out the legal aspects of these affairs, business owners must consider the ethical aspects.

Now that men and women are working alongside one another in almost equal circumstances, an emerging problem for managers is what to do about "office romances." A survey of firms of all sizes by the American Management Association found that more than 30 percent of employees reported having been involved with a co-worker at least once during their employment. While this situation poses a dilemma for managers, a rule of thumb is: If it appears in any way to involve sexual harassment, step in forcefully to prevent it.[24]

Environmental Protection   **Environmental protection** is trying to maintain a healthy balance between people and their environment. It takes two forms: (1) controlling pollution, and (2) conserving natural resources.

Social responsibility is a business's obligation to follow desirable courses of action in terms of society's values and objectives.

Consumerism is the organized efforts of independent, government, and business groups to protect consumers from undesirable effects of poorly designed and produced products.

Enlightened **employee relations** is showing interest in and concern for employees' rights.

Environmental protection tries to maintain a healthy balance between people and their environment.

Pollution control is trying to prevent the contamination or destruction of the natural environment. It is one of the most difficult problems facing not only small business but also all others in society. While efforts are being made to prevent—or control—air, soil, and water pollution, the problem is very complex. It involves balancing our current use of natural resources and conserving them for future use. The real problem—from a small business perspective—is balancing environmental needs with economic ones. This is becoming increasingly difficult; for example, court rulings have held that banks may be liable when their customers pollute, so banks have started demanding an environmental audit and proof that customers have never polluted.[25]

Conservation means practicing the most effective use of resources, while considering society's current and future needs. One form of conservation is **recycling,** which is reprocessing used items for future use. For example, the aluminum industry cuts its energy costs by 95 percent when it recycles instead of making aluminum from ore.[26] And in 1997, 98 percent of the iron and steel components in new cars came from recycled old cars.[27]

> One of the most popular—and successful—conservation programs is recycling paper. The savings from this practice are impressive: one ton of paper made completely from recycled scrap saves 3 cubic yards of landfill space, 17 trees, 7,000 gallons of water, and 4,100 kilowatt hours of energy.[28]
>
> Another example is New York Wa$teMatch (www.itac.org/industry/waste.html), which maintains a database of nonhazardous waste—electronic goods, food, metals, glass, wood, paper, plastic, rubber, and more—that firms can examine for needed raw materials to be used in manufacturing.[29] There is no charge for listing a material in the database, and services for small transactions are provided free of charge. For larger transactions, fees are based on a sliding scale.

Community Relations   There are several other areas of social responsibility in which small firms participate: (1) educational and medical assistance, (2) urban development and renewal, and (3) the arts, culture, and recreation.

Entrepreneurs and small business owners are very active in providing assistance to educational and medical institutions. The following example shows what one socially responsible owner is doing.

> Truett Cathy, founder and CEO of Atlanta-based Chick-fil-A, Inc. (www. chickfil-a. com), offers $1,000 college scholarships to all restaurant employees who have worked at least 20 hours per week for two consecutive years. Since 1973, Chick-fil-A has awarded more than $12 million in more than 10,000 scholarships at over 1,200 institutions.
>
> Another unique feature of Chick-fil-A is Cathy's refusal to open on Sundays. His "never on Sunday" policy gives him an edge in attracting and retaining a high-quality staff.[30]

Small business owners are particularly interested in urban development and renewal. First, it helps improve the environment in which they operate. Second, it helps provide them with a higher purpose.

> A 1997 Cone Roper survey of 2,000 consumers found that 76 percent of them would switch to stores or brands of products whose owners or producers seem concerned about the community.[31]

Most companies—from mom-and-pop stores to large corporations—contribute in some way to hometown arts, cultural, and recreational activities. These efforts include such activities as art workshops for children, civic orchestras or ballet or opera companies, and youth sports teams.

> When small merchants in Viroqua, Wisconsin, heard that Wal-Mart was building a 40,000-square-foot "Discount City" two miles north of town on the main highway, they decided to fight back. One owner offered discounts on sneakers to high school athletes and cheerleaders. The merchants banded together to renovate and modernize the town. The efforts resulted in so much pride that a welcoming sign was posted billing the town as "A Main Street City."[32]

Business Ethics

Business ethics are the standards used to judge the rightness or wrongness of a business's relations to others.

Business ethics are the standards used to judge the rightness or wrongness of a business's and its personnel's relations to others. Small business people are expected to deal ethically with employees, customers, competitors, and others. Ethical behavior is expected in decisions concerning cases of bribery, industrial theft and espionage, collusion, tax evasion, false and/or misleading advertising, and conflicts of interest, as well as in all personnel's conduct generally—loyalty, confidentiality, respect for others' privacy, and truthfulness are all expected.[33] Yet a recent study by the Society for Human Resource Management and the Ethics Resource Center found that 54 percent of human resource professionals "had observed employees running afoul of the law or of workplace standards."[34] Also, as shown in Table 17–3, 4 out of 10 workers in medium to large companies say they know of ethical or legal violations. Moreover, a recent study regarding pressure in the workplace indicated that 56 percent of workers surveyed felt some pressure to act unethically on the job, while 48 percent indicated actual participation in one or more unethical or illegal actions in the past year.[35]

Many large and small companies are embracing business ethics to be socially responsible, while others do it to enhance profits. Do practicing social responsibility and ethical behavior affect profits? While the final answer isn't in yet, the answer for now appears to be "maybe."

> One study found that many companies are discovering that doing good ethically and doing well financially go hand in hand.[36] Another study did not find a positive relationship between ethical behavior and profits, but such behavior did result in good public relations.[37]

Table 17–3
Ethics Lapses in Workplace

Four in 10 workers say they know of ethical or legal violations at their company in the past two years. Here's what they know of:

Reported Violation	Percentage Reporting
Sexual harassment	19%
Lying on reports/records	16
Conflict of interest	15
Stealing/theft	15
Lying to supervisor	15
Bias (race, age, etc.)	15
Drug/alcohol abuse	12

Source: Walker Information's Business Integrity Assessment, survey of companies with 100 or more employees from a variety of industries, as reported in *USA Today*, May 11, 1998, p. 1B. Adapted with permission.

In general, if you launch a business ethics program solely to enhance profits—*or* only to be socially responsible—the program will fail at the first sign of trouble.[38] Instead, socially responsible behavior and profits are *both* needed.

What course are you to follow, then? There are at least three levels of ethical behavior. At the lowest level is obeying the laws of the land. This is the very least that can be expected of the owners and managers of small businesses—as well as of large ones. The second level is governed by any codes of ethics issued by groups to which the business owner belongs. Finally, at the top level is the individual's **personal ethic.** This is the person's own belief system that tells him or her what to do if, as, or when the laws and/or any pertinent codes of ethics are silent.

As a minimum, the public expects small business owners and managers to obey both the letter and the spirit of laws affecting their operations. Finally, they should go beyond laws and social responsibility to behavior based solely on ethical considerations. Sometimes, it may seem difficult for the small business to act ethically and still satisfy the customer. Apparently, though, small businesses are succeeding better than big business executives, lawyers, and others. In the early 1990s, a Harris Poll of 1,256 adults found 64 percent of them thinking that small business owners have good moral and ethical standards. At the same time, only 39 percent thought the same of journalists; 31 percent believed the same about "business executives"; and 25 percent about lawyers.[39]

Perhaps your best test of ethical behavior is Rotary International's "Four-Way Test" of the things we think, say, or do:

1. Is it the TRUTH?
2. Is it FAIR to ALL concerned?
3. Will it build GOODWILL and Better Friendships?
4. Will it be BENEFICIAL to ALL concerned?

The great entrepreneur James Cash Penney, who became a Rotarian in 1942, tried a practical application of this test—even before Rotary was founded in 1905. In 1902, he opened his first Golden Rule Store—later known as J. C. Penney Company (www.jcpenney.com)—to provide top-quality customer service, treat his employees fairly, and apply ethical standards of the golden rule to business.

In 1913, he formalized his beliefs into the "The Penney Idea," which is spelled out as follows:[40]

*   To serve the public, as nearly as we can, to its complete satisfaction.
*   To expect for the service we render a fair remuneration and not all the profit the traffic will bear.
*   To do all in our power to pack the customer's dollar full of value, quality, and satisfaction.
*   To continue to train ourselves and our associates so that the service we give will be more and more intelligently performed.
*   To improve constantly the human factor in our business.
*   To reward men and women in our organization through participation in what the business produces.
*   To test our every policy, method, and act in this wise: "Does it square with what is right and just?"

One's **personal ethic** is one's own belief system that tells one what to do if or when the laws and/or any pertinent codes of ethics are silent.

WHAT YOU SHOULD HAVE LEARNED

■

1. The U.S. legal system is based on principles of fairness, including: (*a*) everyone is equal under the law, (*b*) everyone is entitled to a day in court, and (*c*) a person is presumed innocent until proven guilty. As there are multiple levels of government which create and administer the laws, small business owners may confront a body of complex and sometimes contradictory laws. The most important areas of business law for small firms are (*a*) sales, including leases, (*b*) commercial paper, (*c*) bank deposits and collections, (*d*) letters of credit, (*e*) bulk transfers, (*f*) warehouse receipts, (*g*) investment securities, and (*h*) secured transactions. Many of these laws, which differ in the various states, have been codified into the Uniform Commercial Code. Torts are wrongful injuries for which the law sets punishments and compensation. There are two types of bankruptcy: ordinary and Chapter 11.

2. Both the federal and local governments provide considerable assistance for small businesses. The SBA, U.S. Department of Commerce, U.S. Department of Agriculture, and other agencies provide assistance.

3. There is considerable regulation and paperwork from government agencies, which causes problems for small firms, including (*a*) the difficulty of understanding some of the regulations, which may be confusing and even contradictory; (*b*) the enormous amounts of paperwork needed to comply with them; (*c*) the difficulty and cost of complying with the regulations; and (*d*) that regulations tend to discourage small firms from hiring more workers as they near the cutoffs set by laws

and regulations. However, government also provides many benefits to small businesses.

Small firms can cope with regulation by (*a*) learning about the laws and using them for their benefit; (*b*) challenging detrimental or harmful laws and trying to get them modified or repealed; (*c*) becoming involved in the legal-political system; (*d*) finding a better legal environment, if possible; and (*e*) learning to live with the laws.

4. In choosing a lawyer, look for one who's familiar with small business activities, as well as with the problems you are facing. You can use a local or national lawyer referral service, talk to friends, or use word of mouth in searching for a competent lawyer. Some criteria for choosing a lawyer are to be sure that (*a*) the lawyer is knowledgeable about your type of business, (*b*) you and the lawyer are compatible, (*c*) the lawyer has time to deal with you and your business, and (*d*) the costs are not prohibitive.

5. Small businesses are expected to act in an ethical and socially responsible manner in dealing with employees, customers, and the public, and to consider not only the owners but also others in making decisions that affect them. Most small businesses have always acted ethically and responsibly, and continue to do so. At a minimum, small business owners are expected to obey both the letter and the spirit of laws affecting them. Further, they should adhere to any code(s) of ethics of groups to which they belong. Finally, their own personal ethic should guide their actions.

QUESTIONS FOR DISCUSSION

■

1. (*a*) What is the Uniform Commercial Code? (*b*) Explain what is included in it.

2. What is a tort?

3. Distinguish between (*a*) ordinary, or straight, bankruptcy and (*b*) Chapter 11 bankruptcy.

4. Describe some of the assistance available to small firms from government agencies.

5. Describe some of the problems involved in handling government regulations and paperwork.

6. Explain five ways in which small firms can cope with regulations.

7. (*a*) Describe the characteristics you should look for in a lawyer. (*b*) How would you find such a lawyer? (*c*) How are lawyers compensated for their services?

8. (*a*) What is social responsibility? (*b*) Why is it important to small firms?

9. (*a*) What are business ethics? (*b*) Why are they so important? (*c*) Quote Rotary International's "Four-Way Test."

CASE 17–1

"HANNADOWNS"

In 1983, Gun and Tom Denhart left the East Coast to found a new company in Portland, Oregon, to produce high-quality, high-priced children's clothing. They were neither inexperienced nor naive. Gun, who was from Sweden, had the equivalent of an MBA from her country's Lund University. Also, she had been a systems analyst, controller, and business law teacher for 15 years. Tom was an art director at a prestigious New York advertising agency.

The idea to produce a high-quality line of children's clothing came to Gun when people stopped her on the street to ask where she had gotten her son's colorful cotton clothes. In fact, they had been sent from Sweden by his grandparents. Gun decided to start producing a similar line of clothing.

The couple decided on the mail-order approach for Hanna Andersson, the Swedish name they chose for their new company. To counter the "sticker shock" caused by the high price, the company set out to demonstrate that the clothes would wear well enough to be passed from child to child. This was done by inviting customers to mail back outgrown clothing in good condition. Customers would receive a credit amounting to 20 percent of the garment's average retail price.

The program was so successful that "less than 1 percent" of the garments returned were rejected for recycling because of "poor quality." Hanna Andersson donates the usable returned clothing to needy children. In 1996 alone the program—called "Hannadowns"—shipped 133,000 garments and accessories to the company's warehouse in Louisville, Kentucky. They were promptly distributed to organizations for the needy, such as nonprofit schools, charities, and shelters.

In 1998, Hanna Andersson was doing quite well. It had 230 employees, five retail stores in four states, and a prosperous mail-order business in Japan, where it was considering opening retail stores as well.

The company is known for its enlightened employee program. In fact, *Working Mother* magazine has honored the company for six consecutive years for offering flextime to its employees. The company also pays 40 percent of employees' child care costs.

According to Gun Denhart, who is quite involved in philanthropic activities, the company is primarily a for-profit organization. The original idea for "Hannadowns," she says, was not "How can we save the world?" but a way to prove that her clothes were "really, really good."

Questions

1. Evaluate Gun Denhart's observation that her company's program of donating used clothes to needy children originated from the profit motive rather than considerations of social responsibility.

2. Do you think the company can continue the "Hannadown" program if it pursues its plan to expand its retail operation in Japan? Why or why not?

3. Would you say the company is following responsible business practices? Why or why not?

Source: Abstracted from Annette Spence, "Heroes in Our Time: Hannadowns," *Sky*, May 1998, pp. 107–11. Annette Spence is a writer and editor who lives in Knoxville, TN.

WHAT TO DO?

Matt Snipes has been with the Turner Foods grocery store chain for one year. During that time he has gone from assistant manager to manager of his own store in five months. The company is now promoting Matt to a store twice as big that does twice as many sales. Matt is 26 years old, married, and has one son. This company has been good to Matt and feels that he has a promising career with the company. Matt is hoping to move into the corporate office once he has his degree, which he is working on at night.

Bob Lindsey is the manager of another Turner Foods store in the district. Matt and Bob have become friends, and their families get together as often as their schedules permit. Bob may not be as good a manager as Matt, but he tries. Bob and his wife have two children,

with another on the way. They want to buy a bigger house and feel that, if they cut back and budget, they can afford an increase in house payments. Bob has worked with this company for seven years and doesn't have a lot of career options.

While visiting with the district manager, Matt was told that Bob was probably going to be demoted back to assistant manager. Matt feels that because Bob is his friend he should warn him. If Matt does this, however, he could lose his job.

Questions

1. What would be Matt's appropriate ethical action?
2. Should Matt have been privy to such information?
3. What responsibility does Matt have to Bob?

18

FAMILY-OWNED BUSINESSES: PLANNING FOR THE FUTURE

Time present and time past
Are perhaps both contained in time future,
And time future contained in time past.
> **T. S. Eliot**

Either you shape the future or the future will shape you.
> **John W. Teets, chairman and CEO, Dial Corporation**

LEARNING OBJECTIVES

After studying the material in this chapter, you will be able to:

1. Discuss some problems involved in organizing and operating small family-owned businesses.

2. Explain how family relationships can affect the business.

3. Discuss the importance and method of preparing for management succession.

4. Describe the activities needed to prepare the next generation to enter the firm.

5. Discuss the need for tax and estate planning in small companies.

Jan Weiler—Showing Tourists the Sites

Many people in the United States, if they think of Alabama at all, think of it as landlocked. Even many Alabamians are surprised to discover that their state offers many miles of beautiful sugar-sand beaches that rival those anywhere else on the Gulf Coast. But tourists have begun to discover Alabama's "Pleasure Island," and "snowbirds"—long-term winter visitors from states farther north, especially in the Midwest—return year after year to the beachfront communities of Gulf Shores and Orange Beach as well as elsewhere in Alabama's Baldwin County.

Needless to say, a flourishing tourist trade has developed. One of the major attractions is Riviera Centre, a giant outlet mall near the beach. But one person had the vision to see that the area had more to offer than "sand and Riviera Centre." Jan Weiler, owner/operator of Landmark Tours, Inc., provides small-group excursions to show visitors and residents alike some of the lesser-known features of Baldwin County, paying special attention to historic sites such as Blakeley, site of the last major battle of the Civil War. With a 15-passenger van that's custom designed with safety features and a sound system, she offers guided tours of Mobile Bay's Eastern Shore, Gulf Shores, and Orange Beach. The tours include historic homes and churches, artists at work, barnyard visits for children, walking tours of natural preservation areas, and down-

town shopping tours. Weiler also provides "step-on" service for tour groups traveling in larger chartered buses and develops custom tours for convention-goers and their spouses.

A native Iowan, Weiler discovered the area in 1987 when she and her husband retired and began to travel. In a "salty old trawler" named *Equal,* they cruised thousands of miles along the East Coast and through inland waterways until they discovered the Eastern Shore town of Fairhope, Alabama, about 30 miles from the Gulf. They "fell in love (doesn't everyone?)" with the area, sold the trawler, and settled there permanently in 1990. Weiler knew she wanted to start a business, but while she figured out what kind of business was needed she worked at Burris Farm Market in Loxley. From talking with the customers who came to buy produce, she realized that even long-time residents were unaware of some of the treasures their county had to offer. So she began to do research for a tour service.

In addition to the market research that must be done by anyone thinking of starting a business, Weiler had to gather material for her tour commentaries. She got this information by interviewing the locals, through exhaustive trips to local libraries, and from newspaper articles. She says there were no shortcuts in this process, and she purposely went slowly to guarantee a quality product.

She started business as a sole proprietorship in Fairhope on April 1, 1994, offering a variety of tours with the slogan "Let's go 'site' seeing!" Although many of the "sites" were in other parts of the county, it soon became evident that the customers—vacationers and especially convention-goers—were concentrated closer to the Gulf. After a year of success in Fairhope, she felt ready to expand her business to Gulf Shores. Her Fairhope operation had required only a city business license, but securing a franchise to operate in Gulf Shores took months and 17 pages of detailed information because she had to deal separately with state, county, and municipal government agencies. When she was finally cleared for takeoff in Gulf Shores, in July 1995, she reorganized as an S corporation.

Ironically, although she could operate in either Fairhope or Gulf Shores, she couldn't carry people between the two cities, as that would put her in competition with the common carriers. Persistence, tact, and careful establishment of a network of references helped her make her case before the Alabama Public Service Commission, and she is now free to operate throughout the county and to provide step-on guide service anywhere in the country (although she identifies "South Alabama" as her usual area of operation). She still has to be careful not to step on competitors' toes, but she has been able to carve a niche for her business by offering a unique mix of unusual destinations and personalized service. In contrast to the package tours offered by larger companies with many vehicles, Landmark Tours are all custom-planned for a particular group. In addition to her "historical" and "nature" tours, Weiler offers a variety of experiences she describes as "whimsy" tours. These can be shopping in downtown Fairhope or at a local pottery or candy kitchen, or tours of elegant homes and gardens. Most include a meal, often served at a historic site or quaint bed-and-breakfast. Still in the planning stages is a "pub crawl" Weiler dubs the Renegade Fun Run, which will take in two or more of the county's best-known night spots.

What does Weiler enjoy most about her career as a tour guide? "It has to be the people!" she says. "It's just a lot of fun."

This attitude has been largely responsible for her success. Other assets she cites are "long-term goals, patience, and—above all—quality." She's learned that the best way to guarantee quality is to hire the best and let them take charge. All her meals are catered, and all her equipment is leased. Although she believes in the "just-in-time delivery" concept, she recalls one bad experience that accounts for some of the "very little inventory" she maintains. She had taken a group to a B&B for a catered lunch. The menu had been carefully selected, and the table setting was elegant, with fine china and crystal. To her dismay, however, Weiler saw that, instead of silver or stainless cutlery, the caterer had supplied packets of plastic forks and paper napkins. Thoroughly mortified, Weiler wasted no time afterward in buying 88 forks, glasses, and trays and having 88 linen napkins custom-made.

In addition to this attention to detail, Weiler cites her flexibility and responsiveness to consumer demand. She is well aware that one hurricane could wipe out many of the sites she depends on for her tours, and she is constantly working to identify backup destinations and to diversify into other areas. One idea she's currently working on is a "slumber party": an all-expense-paid overnight trip to a destination outside the local area. This would be tailor-made for couples who want to take in the Selma Pilgrimage, for example, or attend a play at the Alabama Shakespeare Festival in Montgomery, without having to worry about securing or individually paying for tickets, accommodations, and meals.

Tour-goers are impressed with Weiler's curiosity about local history, geography, and people, coupled with her enthusiasm for sharing her knowledge with others. Satisfied customers have created a lot of good word-of-mouth advertising. Now, however, Weiler is casting a wider net through her new Web site (www.landmark-tours. com), which is especially geared toward convention planners. Extremely helpful to her in achieving the right marketing slant and understanding the needs of younger travelers is her son David Showers, who is currently being groomed as her successor. Although he has another full-time job, Showers has been able to take over some aspects of the business, as when he completely oversaw transportation for the University of Washington basketball team, in Mobile for an athletic contest. Since Landmark Tours is a corporation, Weiler will be able to bring Showers into the business by issuing shares of her stock to him. In addition, she foresees the possibility that her other son might also eventually join the firm. At this point she has not made specific plans for transfer of the company, but that is something she intends to do in the very near future.

Source: Prepared by Suzanne S. Barnhill from discussions with Jan Weiler.

The Profile of Jan Weiler is a good illustration of how a small business is started and grows. It also shows how a sole proprietorship can be expanded to take in family members, thus ensuring the future of the business.

■ ROLE OF THE FAMILY-OWNED BUSINESS

More than 46 million Americans work in home-based businesses, and, while family-owned businesses provide a living and personal satisfaction for many people, they must be managed just like any other small firms if they are to succeed.[1] Family businesses are the backbone of America, but they can also be a source of unresolved family tensions and conflicts, which can create obstacles to achieving even the most basic business goals. When close relatives work together, emotions often interfere with business decisions. Also, unique problems, such as the departure of the founder-owner, develop in family-owned firms. When more than one family member is involved, emotions and differing value systems can cause conflicts between members. In fact, most people-related challenges faced by family businesses—small or large—result from the interactions of business necessity with family values and relationships.[2]

The Family and the Business

We usually think of family businesses as being started, owned, and operated by the parents, with children helping out and later taking over. This has been the normal pattern, as many examples in the text have shown. Now, though, two contrary trends are developing. First, many young people are going into business for themselves—and tapping their parents for funds to finance their ventures. In return, the children often give one or both parents an executive position in the company, including a seat on the company's board. In fact, the average age of those involved in home-based businesses is 48.[3] Also, many retirees want to work part time for their children's businesses, without assuming a lot of responsibility.

> For example, the two brothers who run the Levy Organization in Chicago employ their mother as a hostess at one of their restaurants. They even named a deli after her and use her recipes. According to Mark Levy, the company's vice chairman, "My mom is a very integral part of our business."[4]

Another trend is the large number of spouses doing business together. This trend is expected to continue into the twenty-first century.

> Willie Foster, inspired by a desire to make biscuits that tasted as good as his aunt's, opened the very successful Biscuit King Café. When phenomenal sales growth necessitated adding another person, Willie's wife, Nancy, joined him in the operation. The Fosters say the key to their success was starting small and working hard.[5]

This is the kind of family business we traditionally think of: a married couple running a small neighborhood store, toiling long hours for a modest living. Now, though, a new breed of husband-and-wife entrepreneurs has emerged. They typically run a service enterprise out of their home and use computers, modems, and phone lines—even Web sites—as the tools of their trade. As shown in Chapter 2, the number of such firms nearly doubled in the 1980s, and this has been the fastest-growing category of new businesses during the 1990s. Figure 18–1 offers some tips on how to get along with your spouse while running a joint business.

A word of caution is needed at this point, however. While most modern marriages are built on a consensus model, with the assumption that neither spouse can make important

---

Figure 18–1
Making It in Business with Your Spouse

Following are some tips for spouses to follow in running a jointly owned business:

- Don't be blinded by romance; follow all the rules.
- Define each person's role and accentuate each other's talents.
- Don't ignore business conflicts in an attempt to spare a personal relationship.
- Agree to disagree—set the ground rules.
- Be clear and specific about your expectations of each other.
- Set aside family time, and stick to it.
- Set up a system for recognizing and rewarding hard work done by family members.

Source: Adapted from Paula Ancona, "Define Partners' Role in Family-Run Business," *Mobile* (Alabama) *Register,* June 6, 1993, p. 4-F. Column distributed by Scripps-Howard News Service.

decisions unilaterally, this is not practical in a business. Instead, one person should be clearly in charge, at least in a given management area, especially if other employees are involved. In business, a clearly defined chain of command is needed and expected.[6]

Although ownership of a small firm is usually controlled by one or a few family members, many others in the larger family are often involved. The spouse and children are vitally interested because the business is usually the source of their livelihood. In addition, some relatives may be employed by the firm, some may have investments in it, and some may perform various services for it. Involvement of family members should always be based on sound business practices, however, as the following example illustrates.

> The Hirzel Canning Company and Farm, Inc., produces all styles of canned tomato products—as well as its original product, sauerkraut. The company is led by 19 family members, including the fourth generation. But according to one member of the company, "Current and future individual growth in the business will depend on ability, contribution, and commitment to the success and continuation of the business, not one's family position."[7]

The founder-owner may set any one or more of a variety of goals, such as adequate income and perpetuation of the business, high sales, service to the community, support of family, and production of an unusual product, just to name a few. This variety of goals exists in all companies, but in family firms strong family ties can improve the chances of consensus and support, while dissension can lead to disagreement and/or disruption of activities.

Family Interactions

Usually the founder—or a close descendant—is the head of a small business. Relatives may be placed in high positions in the company, while other positions are filled by nonfamily members. In some cases, it is expected that the next head of the firm will be a family member and other members will move up through the ranks, according to their position in the family.

Asplundh Tree Expert Company (www.asplundh.com) is such a business. Asplundh defines itself as "a bunch of tree cutters." That may be true, but this "bunch" now operates in all 50 states and eight foreign

(*Source:* 1989 by Doug Blackwell. Reprinted with permission.)

countries. Outsourcing has enabled Asplundh to remain a family business since 1928. There are 65 members in the fourth generation, and a few will work in the company and help carry on the family work. When asked why they do not go public, Chris Asplundh replied, "Then we'd just have money—that isn't what this family is about."[8]

Family members' sense of "ownership" can be a strong, positive motivator in building the business and leading to greater cooperation. The opposite can also be true, however. Conflicts can occur because each relative looks at the business from a different perspective. Relatives who are silent partners, stockholders, or directors may see only dollar signs when judging capital expenditures, growth, and other important matters. On the other hand, relatives involved in daily operations may judge those matters from the viewpoint of marketing, operations, and personnel necessary to make the firm successful.

How to Deal with Incompetent Family Members   A related problem can be the inability of family members to make objective decisions about one another's skills and abilities. Unfortunately, their quarrels and ill feelings may spread to include nonfamily employees. One possible solution is to convince family members, as well as nonfamily employees, that their interests are best served by a profitable firm with strong leadership.

Some members want to become the head of the business but do not have the talents or training needed. Others may have the talents, but because of their youth or inexperience, these talents may not be recognized.

Family members with little ability to contribute to the firm can be placed in jobs in which they do not disturb other employees. Sometimes, though, relatives can demoralize the business by their dealings with other employees or customers or by loafing on the job, avoiding unpleasant tasks, or taking special privileges. They may be responsible for the high turnover rate of top-notch nonfamily managers and employees. Such relatives should be assigned to jobs allowing minimal contact with other employees. In some cases, attitudes may be changed by formal or informal education.

How to Compensate Family Members   Compensating family members and dividing profits among them can also be difficult because some of them may feel they contribute more to the success of the firm than others. Compensation should be based on job performance, not family position. When a family business decides to hire every relative who wants to work for the company—regardless of ability—it quickly becomes a welfare fund instead of a profit-making entity.

Fringe benefits can be useful as financial rewards, but they must conform to those given to nonfamily employees. Stock can be established as part of the compensation plan. Deferred profit-sharing plans, pension plans, insurance programs, and stock purchase programs can all be effective in placating disgruntled family members, as can a managerial title—if deserved!

When success leads a company into the second generation, titles start to matter to the children and younger relatives. A title is perceived as a confirmation of a job well done and also tends to serve as a motivator. This technique must be used carefully, however, to avoid counterproductive behavior in the future.

Family Limitations

Entrepreneurs tend to be specialists in an activity such as marketing, production, or finance, so they usually do not make good general managers. While managerial skills can be developed through training and/or experience, the skill of sometimes saying no to family members wanting to enter the business may still be missing.

Another problem is that family managers may feel it is necessary to clear routine matters with the top family member, regardless of his or her position or ability. Also, bottlenecks that work against efficient operations can be caused by personality clashes and emotional reactions. Therefore, lines of authority and responsibility in the company must be clear and separated from those within the family circle. This is an important distinction because a person's age often determines the lines of authority in a family, while *ability* must be the primary guide in a business.

The number of competent family members from whom to choose the managers of the company is usually limited. Some members do not want to join—or are not capable of joining—the company in any position; some are capable of filling only lower-level jobs; and some are not willing to take the time or expend the effort to prepare themselves for a management position. So it is amazing that so many family businesses in fact do have such good leadership—family and nonfamily. As the leader grows older, however, he or she must keep up with the times and guard against letting past successes lead to trying to maintain the status quo.

> For example, the five stockholders of Donald & Asby, engineers, established a policy of encouraging growth. One of the younger stockholders suggested using media advertising to obtain new business. But Donald, who had helped found the firm 30 years earlier, said this would produce an undesirable type of growth. He suggested that they continue to depend on the company's reputation to expand requests for job proposals. How do you think the stockholders decided? Why?

Some families organize their businesses into corporations and hire professional managers to run them when no family members are in a position to manage or no agreement can be reached on who should run the company. This solution has the advantages of using professional management, freeing family time for other purposes, reducing friction, and having employees treated more fairly.

> This new "portable CEO" is the antithesis of the 1950s-style "organization man." A Michigan State University study found that more than a third of the CEOs hired by major corporations in the 1990s came from outside the organization.[9]

The disadvantages of this arrangement, however, are reduced family employment, lower income, concentration of power in small cliques, difficulties in finding and keeping a good management team, and loss of the "personal touch."

Now that divorce is an unfortunate reality for 50 percent of U.S. couples, it poses special problems for the quarter-million husband-and-wife–run U.S. businesses. If you are

(*Source:* Reprinted with permission of King Features Syndicate.)

going through a divorce, your primary responsibility is to protect what is rightfully yours, based on your contribution to the business since its inception. You can best do this by (1) having the business appraised, (2) negotiating a buyout agreement, and (3) deciding what to do with any stock you might hold in the business. And you need competent professional help in order to do this without taking a tax "hit."[10]

Family Resources

The amount of capital available within the family may limit expansion. While family resources and contacts may be adequate for a small business, as the company grows, the borrowing power is limited by the amount of family assets. Then, family members may disagree about such issues as the following: Should money be obtained by borrowing, issuing stock, selling assets, or other financial techniques? Should planning be for the short or long run? Because of the diversity of opinion, even the choice of a consultant can be controversial.

Preparing the Next Generation

It might be assumed that children (or grandchildren) will automatically want to enter the family business. But this isn't always true. A growing problem facing many small family businesses today is apathy on the part of offspring. Often, children who are reared in a small business become bored or uninterested, or simply lack the drive and desire to succeed that motivated their parents. They may feel that since the business has supported them in the past, it will continue to do so in the future.

What leads children to follow in their parents' footsteps? In a significant early study, Nancy Bowman-Upton of Baylor University found that the two primary reasons were "to make money" and that they "like the business."[11] Helping children to "like the business" requires helping them discover what things they like to do and then matching those individual interests to the needs of the family business. The concept of doing what one likes is a motivator to meet the challenges of the business.[12]

Start at Part-Time or Full-Time Jobs?   One way to prepare children to take over the family business is to let them work on simple jobs, or on a part-time basis, which provides insights that may influence them into—or away from—the business. The experience often encourages them to finish their education to be better prepared when it's their turn to run the business.

Another form of preparation is working for another company to broaden their training and background. Such experience helps justify moving a family member into the family business at a higher level.

Start at Entry-Level or Higher-Level Positions?   Should a family member start in an entry-level job to learn the business from the ground up? There is some disagreement on this point, but none about the need for knowing the business, regardless of how it's done. The following are some techniques that should work for you:

- Never allow a child to work in senior management until he or she has worked for someone else for at least two years.
- Rotate the person in varying positions.
- Give promotions only as they are earned.
- Devote at least half an hour each day to face-to-face teaching and training.
- Don't take business matters home.

- If the newcomer is really to learn the business, true responsibility must be given. Otherwise, the person cannot learn to manage the business, as the following example shows.

> A son who took over his father's business said, "My father had difficulty trusting me. It's not what you might think. He just didn't want to see me fail. When he saw that something I was doing might not pan out, he would step in and take over. I never had a chance to fail."
>
> Thus, when he took over the business, making it work was very difficult, but he finally succeeded.[13]

■ PREPARING FOR MANAGEMENT SUCCESSION

Any business must be ready for changes in its top management. It's not enough to select a person to step into the top job when it becomes vacant. That key job requires much training and experience, because the decisions the person makes can vitally affect the company and its future. Thus, every transfer of ownership and power is an invitation to disaster. To prevent that from happening, the owner should do two things: *Plan early and carefully,* and *groom a successor!*

Why Succession Is a Problem

When preparing someone for management succession, many small business owners have concerns about passing the business on to their children. One survey found that the main concern was how to treat all children fairly; another was the reaction of nonfamily employees. And several respondents mentioned family communication, conflict, and estate taxes as concerns. A case study by Ivan Landsberg indicates that family business ownership in the future will experience a trend toward fewer owner-managed businesses and more run by sibling partners and syndicates of cousins.[14]

Another trend is having two or more children succeed the parent in running the business. A survey of owners of family-owned businesses with two or more children working for the company revealed that some groom one child from an early age to take over, while others plan to let children compete and to choose one or more successors with or without help from the board of directors. Still others plan to form an "executive committee" of two or more children or let the children choose their own leader(s). In essence, however, over half the respondents wanted to include two or more children in future ownership and management.[15]

If family members are going to be used to run the business, rather than bring in outsiders, ongoing training should begin early. One or more replacements should be started early on the path toward taking over the reins of the firm. This process sometimes does not work, as Case 18–1, at the end of the chapter, illustrates. But, as shown in the following example, sometimes it can work well.

> Charles O'Reilly began selling auto parts in 1914 (www.oreillyauto.com). Then, in 1957, he and his son "Chub" opened their own store. And, even though many family businesses don't survive to the third generation, this one still thrives.
>
> Chub's children started working and learning the business at an early age, working after school and on weekends. From the start, each of them was recognized for his or her own unique talents. At age 60, Chub began turning his business over to his well-trained children, and major decisions were made only after careful consultation with them.
>
> Now Chub's children are training the fourth generation of O'Reillys "to run this—or their own—business." The key to successful succession, they say, is to "get the inheritors to think like a team, rather than as sibling rivals."[16]

When the choice of replacements is limited, the owner may consider reorganizing the present assignments and using present managers more effectively. The job specifications for a new manager may be written more broadly to widen the range of choices. All present managers—family and nonfamily—should participate in this planning so they feel they have contributed to the decision.

An Overlooked Problem

In most firms, the development of managerial personnel and the provision for management succession are greatly neglected, often until it is too late to do anything about it. Research studies indicate that most entrepreneurs simply don't want to face the inevitable.

> For example, in interviews with 400 owners of small companies across the United States, Peter Collins, head of Buckingham Associates, a New York consulting firm, found that 85 percent *had no formal plan* to leave their business. Moreover, 31 percent had "no idea at all how they would exit their business."[17]

But this trend is changing. A growing number of entrepreneurs are turning to formal succession plans to save their heirs endless squabbles, according to Massachusetts Mutual Life Insurance Company (www.massmutual.com). Its annual survey of more than 1,000 family business owners found that 44 percent of them had written plans to guide the next generation's succession to control. That figure was up from 28 percent the previous year.[18]

■ PLAN AHEAD!

Management succession occurs when the family leader: (1) dies, (2) becomes incapacitated, (3) leaves the company—voluntarily or otherwise—or (4) retires. To avoid family succession problems, entrepreneurs should start planning early for their replacements. A comprehensive succession plan involves more than just laying out the role of the younger generation in the business and ownership of the business. Instead, operating authority must pass from one generation to the next. These plans should be flexible enough to include (1) a sudden departure or (2) a planned one.

Sudden Departure

A successful business must continue to operate even when the owner-manager leaves, for whatever reason. Plans can easily be made for vacations because they are of short duration, they require a limited number of decisions, and the vacationer is available if needed. When the owner takes a vacation, a form of on-the-job training is provided for those left in charge. Those persons can take over temporarily under those circumstances.

But the sudden death or incapacity of the owner can be very disruptive if not adequately provided for. If the owner has left no will or instructions on what to do, family members will probably have conflicting opinions about what should be done. For this reason, an owner should make a will and keep it current, including instructions about what should be done in—or with—the business.

As shown in Chapter 16, the firm can take out life insurance on the owners, the proceeds from which will go to the company in case of death. This money can be used to help the business operate until it recovers from the loss of its owner-manager.

Planned Departure

When owners plan to leave or retire, they have a number of options, as shown in Figure 18–2. If the company is a corporation, there will probably be less controversy, because the

Figure 18–2
Options for Replacing Family Management

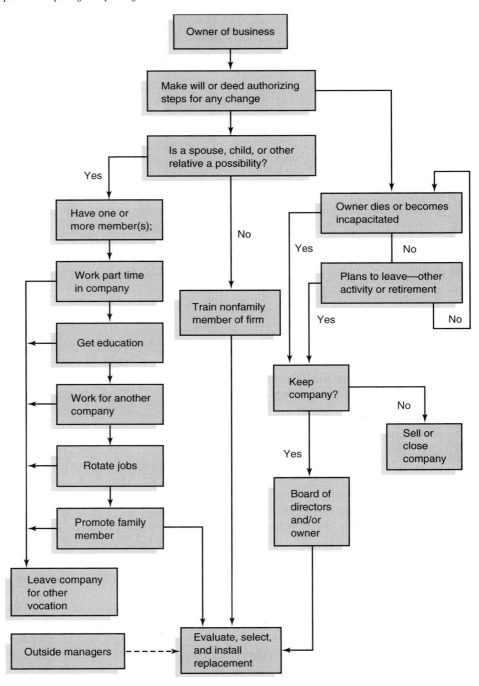

replacement top officer should be known by the time the owner departs, and the transition should go smoothly. The board of directors can select a family or nonfamily employee, or an outsider, for the top job. The handling of the stock can be delayed, but stock retention may give the new key executive the feeling that the departed one is still looking over his or her shoulder.

The entire family tends to become involved in the replacement decision in proprietorships and partnerships. Therefore, in planning for departure, the owner should look for someone in the family able and willing to take over. This person may already be recognized as the "heir apparent."

Bill Armstrong loves ambulances! Starting with one ambulance in 1946—bought with his mother's cashed-in life insurance policy—he now has 70. Many of these—costing $100,000 each—are crammed with the latest lifesaving devices, such as radios, cellular phones, a computer-driven defibrillator, and a triple-locked inventory of lifesaving drugs. He hires firefighters to man the ambulances because they've developed lifesaving skills.

Armstrong has been so intent on listening to alarm bells that he has failed to listen to the most important one—the need to provide a successor. However, he insists he is taking steps to ensure a smooth transition. His daughter, Gale Brady, runs the business side, while a technician, Brian Connor, functions as general manager.[19]

Selling to Family Members

If the transition is to be complete, the business should be sold to the offspring so that full responsibility is handed over to them. The advantages of this type of change for the original owner are as follows:

- The business stays in the family.
- It provides a source of employment for family members.
- The family's stature is maintained.
- The former owner is free to relax or travel.
- There is pleasure when the successor is successful.
- It can strengthen family bonds rather than produce additional family friction.

Sometimes, however, the business is sold to outsiders and later repurchased by one or more family members. This may occur when the owner wants to retire and the children are too young or lack interest, skills, or the funds needed to purchase the company.

For example, Charles Alfieri sold his hair replacement business to a Japanese company with a long-term employment contract. After disagreements with management, he retired from the firm.

Nine years later, the company was preparing to close, and Charles's cousin Andy (who had stayed on at the firm) bought the operation. Now Andy Alfieri is at the helm of the organization where he worked and learned from his cousin Charles while still in high school.[20]

Selling to Outsiders

If no relative will assume responsibility for the running of the business, the owner can sell out to a partner or an outsider, or can even close the business. Many small businesses are now being sold and moved offshore. Sometimes companies will see an opportunity for expansion in other countries, open businesses there, and later sell the established fledglings to locals. Mexico, where American interests continue to grow, is a good example.

There are many advantages to turning the reins over to an outsider. Among these are assured income, lack of worry about what subsequently happens, possible opportunity to consult, release of family tension, and relief from further responsibility. Selling to someone outside the family can mean loss of family identification and resulting sadness, since it marks the end of years of effort and the loss of something the founder built. Still, selling to outsiders can have a beneficial effect on family relationships, as the following example illustrates.

> When a troubled family business was sold, the reaction of one child was: "A number of financially enmeshed families were liberated to pursue individual courses. A company had shed its burdensome past and could look forward to a renewal under new leadership. Ray, Joyce, and I are no longer wrangling siblings polarized in an ugly triad. We are free to be friends."[21]

Making the Transition Easier

What preparations should you make when you plan to turn the business over to someone else? Too often, a small firm suffers under these circumstances, and sales may decrease or production lag.

To make transitions easier for themselves, owners need to broaden their focus. The narrower the owners' experience and skills, the more difficult it will be to make a smooth transition to other activities after leaving their business. Owners should begin to devote more time to hobbies and outside group activities, which should help them develop a sense of worth apart from the business. Finally, the transition can be made in phases, by gradually turning part of the business over to the successor(s).

■ TAX AND ESTATE PLANNING

As shown in Chapter 13, in projecting the future of your business, planning is needed to minimize estate taxes. A business and its assets may appreciate in value much more than the owners are aware, and inheritance taxes can be devastating. Therefore, estate plans should be reviewed frequently, along with possible estate tax liability and the provisions for paying such taxes.

Tax Planning

In planning your firm's future activities, consider the influence taxes will have on profits and the business's capital structure. Since tax laws and regulations change frequently, stay current in the knowledge of these matters. You should probably have annual planning conferences with a CPA well versed in business tax matters.

Estate Planning

Estate planning is preparing for the orderly transfer of the owner's equity in the business when death occurs.

Estate planning is preparing for the orderly transfer of the owner's equity when death occurs. The major concerns are usually the perpetuation of a family business and maintaining liquidity. Without sufficient cash to pay estate taxes, heirs may have little choice but to siphon cash from the business or even sell the business.

Tax rates on estates are now such that the assets bequeathed to beneficiaries may be needed to pay taxes, resulting in removal of equity from a business. By planning for the transition, this problem can be minimized.

From the small firm's standpoint, estate planning can (1) reduce the need for beneficiaries to withdraw funds, (2) help maintain beneficiaries' interest in keeping funds in the firm, and (3) provide for a smooth transition. Estate planning for the above objectives can be in the form of: (1) gifts to children, (2) stock sales to family members, (3) living trusts, and (4) **family limited partnerships.** This type of partnership allows business owners to pass assets to heirs with a minimum of income and estate tax costs—while retaining control of the assets during their lifetime.[22]

In carrying out those planning steps, appropriate steps should be taken to assure compliance with IRS regulations, especially the valuation of the business. Three methods for determining the true value of a business are (1) determining the value of a comparable business that is publicly traded, (2) ascertaining the business's value by capitalizing its earnings, and (3) estimating the business's value by determining its book value.

Certain actions are possible to assure that the IRS is bound by a predetermined agreement. One way of accomplishing this is to use a predetermined shareholder **buy/sell agreement,** whereby the corporation agrees to buy back the stock or sell it for the shareholder. Such an agreement becomes binding on the IRS; however, it must be in writing. Table 18–1 gives the regulations for a valid buy/sell agreement. In addition, a properly prepared buy/sell agreement assures a market for the stock. It also provides protection for the minority stockholder. If such a stockholder is terminated without such

> A **family limited partnership** allows business owners to pass assets to heirs with a minimum of income and estate tax costs while retaining control of assets during their lifetime.

> A **buy/sell agreement** provides for the corporation to buy back a shareholder's stock when he or she leaves the company.

Table 18–1
Buy/Sell Effectiveness

Internal Revenue Code Section 2803 regulations concerning buy/sell agreements:

- It must be a bona fide business arrangement.
- It must not be a device to transfer property to members of the decedent's family for less than full and adequate consideration.
- It is similar to comparable arm's-length transactions.

In addition, applicable case law has established several rules that must be followed:

- The estate must be obligated to sell at death.
- The agreement must have a fixed and determined sale price or a method for determining the price.
- The owner cannot sell the property during his or her lifetime without first offering it to the other owners.
- The price must be fair and adequate when the agreement is made.

A buy/sell agreement benefits both heirs and surviving owners.

Benefits to heirs

- Freedom from business worries.
- Guarantee of a fair purchase price.
- Possibility of avoiding probate delays.

Benefits to surviving owners

- Relief from concern about new and possibly unwanted partners.
- Advance knowledge of the purchase price.
- Retention of good relations with creditors and clients through a smooth transition of ownership.

Source: Author's conversations and correspondence with Alfred C. Corina, CLU, ChFC, July 1998.

an agreement, he or she may be placed at a serious disadvantage, as the following example illustrates.

> A young woman held 28 percent of the stock in her employer's corporation; a majority of her personal assets were tied up in the stock. Without warning, she lost her job, and her unsympathetic ex-employer was unwilling to redeem the stock.

A number of references may be used to aid in estate and tax planning, but we recommend using the services of a lawyer, accountant, and/or professional tax planner as well. If you wish to do your own planning, there are many software packages that can be of assistance.

■ ESTATE PLANNING TO MINIMIZE TAXES

No one wants to pay more taxes than necessary, especially when you are trying to pass the benefits of the estate you have built up over the years to your family. You want to reduce taxes to the minimum so they will get the maximum. Since family business owners frequently do not have the financial skills needed for estate planning, they should rely on a Certified Financial Planner (CFP).

Estate Planning Issues

For entrepreneurs, several issues are involved in estate planning. The most important of these are (1) trying to minimize taxes, (2) retaining control of the business, and (3) maintaining flexibility of operations.

Estate Planning Techniques

While it is impossible to avoid all estate taxes, the following can be used to minimize them: (1) family gifts, (2) family partnerships, (3) stock sales to family members, and (4) living trusts.

Make Gifts to Family   One way to reduce taxes on your estate is to start giving parts of it to your family as soon as feasible. The rules are:[23]

1. The gifts must be of "present interest," such as a direct cash gift, rather than a "future interest," such as gifts of cash that go into a trust fund for later distribution.
2. The first $10,000 given by each spouse to each person during the year is tax free. If both spouses contribute, the maximum is $20,000. Under provisions of the Taxpayer Relief Act of 1997, these tax-free limits for gifts were to be indexed from 1999 onward.[24]
3. Lifetime gifts of up to $312,500 by a single person, or $625,000 from a couple, are tax free. The maximum amount will increase to $1 million in 2006.[25]
4. The gifts, which are based on the fair market value of the property, can be cash, bonds, real estate, the family business, interest in a partnership, and so forth.

Establish a Family Limited Partnership   You can form a family limited partnership to take money out of your company at lower tax rates. It must be a passive partnership that owns some type of property but does not operate the business. For example, a business owner may elect to set up a family limited partnership, retaining at least 2 percent of the stock as a general partner and giving the balance to the children as limited partners and subject only to gift tax. *Because this type of tax shelter is very complex, do not try to establish it by yourself; get professional help.*

Sell Stock to Children   You can also sell all or part of your business to your children, but, like establishing a family partnership, this is complicated. First, your children will need a source of income to make nondeductible payments to you for the stock. And second, you must pay capital gains tax on the stock you sell. You may want to combine this method with gifts to the family. If the value of your business is greater than the amount you can give as gifts during your lifetime, you may want to give up to the maximum and sell stock for the rest of the business.

Establish a Living Trust   A **living trust** resembles a will but, in addition to providing for distributing personal assets on the maker's death, it also contains instructions for managing those assets should the person become disabled. You can put property into a living trust while you are still alive. Then, when you die, the property automatically goes to the designated heirs without having to go through probate court, saving considerable time and expense.

A **living trust** resembles a will but, in addition to providing for distributing personal assets on the maker's death, it also contains instructions for managing those assets should the person become disabled.

Living trusts are more difficult to contest than wills. Also, the firm's assets can be immediately and privately distributed to the beneficiaries. Finally, a living trust can save on estate taxes.[26]

> For example, if you have a will for an estate valued at more than $625,000, federal estate taxes must be paid at your death, at a rate beginning at 15 percent and quickly escalating to a maximum rate of 39.6 percent. A living trust, on the other hand, lets you and your spouse pass on up to $1.25 million to your beneficiaries tax free. When one of you dies, the trust is divided into two separate trusts, each with a $625,000 estate tax exemption.[27]

But there are some disadvantages of a living trust. First, when you establish such a trust, you must also change the title on all real estate, securities, and other assets to the name of your trust. From a legal point of view, you no longer own these properties, so there is nothing to probate when it becomes time to distribute your assets. You (and your spouse) may find it advantageous to become joint trustees in order to bypass the probate process. Finally, if you need to refinance your home or other assets, some lenders may refuse to refinance it if it is in a trust.

To avoid the many pitfalls of this device, hire an experienced trust attorney and select a capable and trustworthy trustee. Also, carefully weigh the benefits against the time and effort required.[28]

WHAT YOU SHOULD HAVE LEARNED

∎

1. This chapter shows that members of family-owned firms have different viewpoints depending on their relationships in the family and the business. Founders expect that some family members, especially their children, will follow them into the firm.

2. To the extent feasible, ownership and management should be separated from family affairs in order to be fair to nonfamily employees and to reduce friction. Accepted upward movement of family and other employees in the business can generate positive motivation, but evaluation of family members' skills is often difficult. Disruptive members should be isolated, delegation should be practiced, and compensation should be based on job performance—not personal or family relationships—if possible.

3. Family businesses are usually limited in the number and caliber of people from whom to choose managers, and in the money available for such purposes. Age may hamper the progress of younger family members and may lead to

disagreements on money matters. Forming a corporation tends to lessen family stress within the company. Ongoing training, including early employment in the business and personal contact with the owner, is recommended for developing younger members.

4. Start planning for succession early in the game to help smooth any sudden transition. If the new CEO is known early, planning has been good; if not, selection may have to be made under adverse conditions. Transfer of the firm to other family members has many advantages, including continuity and family support.

5. Planning for the future should also include estate planning to minimize the tax burden of the business owner's heirs. Strategies to reduce beneficiaries' need to withdraw funds, maintain their interest in leaving funds in the firm, and provide for a smooth transition include gifts to children, selling stock to family members, setting up a living trust, and setting up a family limited partnership. In all such planning, owners are advised to consult professionals such as lawyers, accountants, or professional tax planners, and to assure that IRS regulations are met.

QUESTIONS FOR DISCUSSION

1. Why is management succession so important an issue for any small firm? For a family firm?

2. Why is it often difficult to make reasonable decisions in a family business? What problems are caused by a family organization structure?

3. What problems face a company when a key officer leaves suddenly?

4. If you start a business when you are in your 20s or 30s, should you do anything about your replacement? Explain.

5. Suppose you have a successful business now but decide you want to leave it. What might be some reasons for leaving it? What alternatives do you have for the business?

6. How important is estate planning? How can you do it?

CASE 18–1

THE SON-IN-LAW

Fred Clayton, a college graduate with a degree in sociology, was inducted as a commissioned officer in the U.S. Navy. While in the service, he married the daughter (and only child) of Art Carroll, a prosperous manufacturers' agent in the electronics industry.

When Fred completed his military service, he accepted a sales position in his father-in-law's organization, the Carroll Sales Company. Carroll had high hopes that Fred would take an interest in the business and eventually relieve him of some managerial responsibilities. Fred was trained for a short while in the home office and was assigned a territory in which to make sales calls and promote the products offered by the company. A

new car and a liberal expense account were provided him. Fred presented a pleasing personal appearance to the customers. However, it was soon evident to Carroll that Fred did not possess the necessary characteristics to become a good salesman.

For quite a number of years, Fred continued to receive a share of the available business in his area with little sales effort, primarily as a result of the tremendous demand for electronic equipment, which far exceeded the supply at that time.

Carroll was concerned that Fred was not spending sufficient time in his territory. He would frequently leave town on Tuesday and return home on Thursday to cover an area that should normally take from Monday through Friday to properly service. Fred's expenses were extremely high for the time he spent in the field. On occasion, Carroll would discuss Fred's progress with him. Carroll requested that his son-in-law, as a future officer in the company, set an example for the other sales personnel by putting in more time in his territory and by cutting down on his weekly expenses. After these talks, Fred's behavior would improve, but within a short time would return to his old habits.

The company prospered and expanded as a result of a good sales effort from most of the sales force and because of the demand for their products. At this time—five years ago—when the company enjoyed a sales area comprising nine states, Fred was appointed district sales manager of a two-state territory and was responsible for the supervision of a warehouse and five salespeople. Although Fred did not work closely with any of his sales personnel, he took time to scrutinize all expense accounts and often returned them with items marked "not approved." The salespeople felt he was very petty about this and were frequently infuriated by him. He also controlled all their correspondence and information flowing to and from the territory. The other sales districts within the company had more liberal expense accounts, and salespeople could make decisions on their own. The district under Fred's supervision never led the company in sales, although it had the greatest potential of all the districts.

Art Carroll was more and more disappointed in the lack of sales progress in his son-in-law Fred's division. He was also very concerned over the results of a survey indicating that Fred's district had an unusually high turnover of sales personnel.

Finally, about a year ago, Carroll took his son-in-law out of sales. He still hoped that there might be some position in the firm in which the younger man would be a real asset. With this thought in mind, he placed Fred in charge of operations of the warehouses. Fred now controlled inventories. He continued to have problems with personnel, causing so much unrest among employees that a number of key employees talked of leaving.

Carroll realizes that the situation is critical. He asks himself, "Why, after all these years with the company, is Fred unhappy? Is he completely unmotivated to succeed because he thinks he doesn't have to? Doesn't he feel at least a moral obligation to try to get along with his associates? How have I failed to give his best abilities an opportunity? How far must I go in trying to fit him into the situation?"

Questions

1. Comment on Fred's capabilities for managing a small business.

2. What could Carroll do to help Fred become a better manager?

3. Who was responsible for developing Fred into a capable executive? Has Fred or Carroll succeeded or failed? Explain the success or failure of each.

4. How would you answer each of Carroll's present questions?

5. What does this case show about the problem of management succession in a small family-owned business?

Source: Prepared by Gayle M. Ross of Ross Printing Company.

CASE 18–2

CHOOSING A SUCCESSOR

John and Barbara Smith have operated a farming business for over 30 years. Now, after great success, it is time to turn the business over to one of their three children. The business is now operating as a brokerage firm for wholesale produce and has a strong customer base. The Smiths have built the company up over the years, but they feel that new management would increase profits.

All three of the Smith children have been working in the business. Tim, the oldest, with a degree in business administration, has handled the paperwork and administrative duties.

Sarah, who has a degree in sales, recently came to work for her parents. She was one of the top five salespeople with her previous company but decided to quit because the paperwork was becoming too much. Her previous employer expected her to supervise a new sales force.

The third son, Bert, has some college but primarily has worked with his parents. Bert has more knowledge about produce than the other two, as his primary job has been to buy the produce for the business from the other farmers. Bert is not a very good salesperson or administrator, but he has a great deal of knowledge about the product and the growers.

All three children have agreed to stay on with the company regardless of which one of them is chosen to head the business. They are perfectly willing to abide by their parents' decision; they want only what is best for the company and the family.

Questions

1. How should the Smiths choose their replacement in managing their business?

2. What qualifications do you think are the most important in choosing the successor? Why?

WORKBOOK FOR DEVELOPING A SUCCESSFUL BUSINESS PLAN

I. INTRODUCTION

A. What Is a Business Plan?

The business plan is probably the most useful and important document you, as a present or prospective small business owner, will ever put together. It is a written statement setting forth the business's mission and objectives, its operational and financial details, its ownership and management structure, and how it hopes to achieve its objectives.

B. What Is the Purpose of a Business Plan?

A well-developed and well-presented business plan can provide you with a "road map to riches"—or at least a pathway to a satisfactory profit. There are at least five reasons for preparing a business plan, which include the following:

1. It provides a blueprint, or plan, to follow in developing and operating the business. It helps keep your creativity on target and helps you concentrate on taking the actions that are needed to achieve your goals and objectives.
2. It can serve as a powerful money-raising tool.
3. It can be an effective communication tool for attracting and dealing with personnel, suppliers, customers, providers of capital, and others. It helps them understand your goals and operations.
4. It can help you develop as a manager, because it provides practice in studying competitive conditions, promotional opportunities, and situations that can be advantageous to your business. Thus, it can help you operate your business more effectively.
5. It provides an effective basis for controlling operations so you can see if your actions are following your plans.

In summary, the plan performs three important functions: (1) being an effective communication tool to convey ideas, research findings, and proposed plans to others, especially financiers; (2) serving as a blueprint for organizing and managing the new venture; and (3) providing a measuring device, or yardstick, by which to gauge progress and evaluate needed changes.

C. What Is Included in a Business Plan?

Regardless of the specific format used, an effective plan *should include at least* the following:

1. Cover sheet.
2. Executive summary.

3. Table of contents.
4. History of the (proposed) business.
5. Description of the business.
6. Description of the market.
7. Description of the product(s).
8. Ownership and management structure.
9. Objectives and goals.
10. Financial analysis.
11. Appendixes.

II. How to Prepare a Business Plan

You should start by considering your business's background, origins, philosophy, mission, and objectives. Then, you should determine the means for fulfilling the mission and obtaining the objectives. A sound approach is to (1) determine where the business is at present (if an ongoing business) or what is needed to get the business going, (2) decide where you would like the business to be at some point in the future, and (3) determine how to get there; in other words, determine the best strategies for accomplishing the objectives in order to achieve your mission.

The following is one feasible approach you can use in preparing a business plan:

1. Survey consumer demands for your product(s) and decide how to satisfy those demands.
2. Ask questions that cover everything from your firm's target market to its long-run competitive prospects.
3. Establish a long-range strategic plan for the entire business and its various parts.
4. Develop short-term detailed plans for every aspect of the business, involving the owner(s), managers, and key employees, if feasible.
5. Plan for every facet of the business's structure, including finances, operations, sales, distribution, personnel, and general and administrative activities.
6. Prepare a business plan that will use your time and that of your personnel most effectively.

III. How to Use This Business Plan Workbook

This workbook is a detailed, practical, how-to approach to researching and preparing an actual business plan. It is designed so that you can answer the questions that are asked or find the information that is called for, record it in the spaces provided, and prepare the final plan.

A. Sources of Information

There are several possible sources of information you can use in preparing this workbook. First, we have included a case study of an actual business (the name has been disguised at the request of the owner) that contains most of the information—except the location—that you will need to complete the workbook. A second source is a business with which you trade, the business of a friend or relative, or some other business that will be willing to provide the information.

Finally, you may want to come up with a possible business to start on your own. In that case, you would start from scratch, gathering the information you need to complete the workbook.

B. Completing the Workbook

The workbook should be completed essentially in two stages. The first stage is to gather the information beginning with Item 4, History of the (Proposed) Business, and going through Item 11, Appendixes.

After this information is gathered and recorded, come back and complete Item 1, Cover Sheet; Item 2, Executive Summary; and Item 3, Table of Contents.

Finally, type (or word process) the information from the worksheet into a final form (such as the example at the end of Chapter 8).

Item 1, Cover Sheet

On the cover sheet you should include identifying information so that readers will immediately know the business name, address, and phone number; the names and titles of the principals; and the date the plan was prepared.

   1. Cover Sheet
      Business name, address, and phone number:

_____

_____

_____

     Principals: _____

_____

_____

     Date: _____

Item 2, Executive Summary

The executive summary should be a succinct statement of the purpose of the plan. Thus, it should be designed to motivate the reader to go on to the other sections of the plan. It should convey a sense of excitement, challenge, plausibility, credibility, and integrity. Even though the summary is the second item in the plan, *it should be written last, after the rest of the plan has been developed.* Remember, *the executive summary is just that—a summary—so keep it short!*

   2. Executive Summary
      Brief summary of plan

_____

_____

_____

_____

_____

_____

_____

_____

Major objectives

_____

_____

_____

_____

_____

_____

Description of product(s)

_____

_____

_____

_____

_____

_____

Marketing strategy

_____

_____

_____

_____

_____

_____

_____

Financial projections

_____

_____

_____

_____

_____

_____

_____

_____

Item 3, Table of Contents

Because the table of contents provides the reader an overview of what is contained in the plan itself, it should be written and presented concisely, in outline form, using numerical and alphabetical designations for headings and subheadings.

3. Table of Contents (each section listed, with subheads)

_____

_____

_____

_____

_____

_____

_____

_____

_____

_____

_____

_____

_____

_____

_____

_____

_____

_____

_____

_____

_____

_____

_____

_____

_____

_____

_____

_____

_____

_____

_____

Item 4, History of the (Proposed) Business

The history of the (proposed) business should include a discussion of how the idea for the business, or product, originated and what has been done to develop the idea up to this point. If the owners or managers have been in business before, and their experience is pertinent to the success of the business, include that information. Other relevant background information on the persons, products, capitalization, source(s), funds, and anything else of potential interest to the readers should also be included.

4.   History of the Business
     Background of the principals, and/or company origins

_____

_____

_____

_____

_____

_____

_____

_____

     Background of the product(s)

_____

_____

_____

_____

_____

_____

_____

_____

Corporate structure

_____

_____

_____

_____

_____

_____

_____

Capitalization, or source of funds

_____

_____

_____

_____

_____

_____

_____

Brief outline of company successes or experiences, if any

_____

_____

_____

_____

_____

_____

_____

_____

Item 5, Description of the Business

Item 5 is the place to define your business, as you see it. Therefore, you should essentially answer such questions as: What business am I in? What services do I provide? This item should include more than just a statement of plans and a listing of activities. It should tell readers what customer needs the business intends to meet. In writing this component, try to put yourself in the position of the reader and include information that potential investors, customers, employees, and community members in general might need to assess your plan.

5. Description of the Business

_____

_____

_____

_____

_____

_____

_____

_____

Item 6, Description of the Market

The description of the market is one of the most important—but most difficult—items of the plan for you to develop. In it, you should try to answer such questions as: Who will buy my product? Where is my market? What is my sales strategy? What marketing strategy(ies) will I use? Who buys what, when, where, and why? What are my customers like? Who constitutes my target market (or what special niche am I aiming for)? You should also look at your competition and appraise it carefully, showing any weaknesses it has that you are able to, and plan to, exploit.

6.   Description of the Market
     Target market: Who? How many?

_____

_____

_____

_____

_____

_____

_____

     Market pentetration projections and strategies

_____

_____

_____

_____

_____

_____

_____

_____

Analysis of competition: How many? Strengths and weaknesses?

_____

_____

_____

_____

_____

_____

_____

Item 7, Description of the Product(s)

Item 7 should describe all of your existing or planned products, including services to be performed as well as goods to be produced. You should also look at any research-and-development activities and new plans to improve or redevelop the product, along with any patents, trademarks, and copyrights you hold—or that are pending.

7.   Description of the Product(s)
     What is to be developed or sold?

_____

_____

_____

_____

_____

_____

_____

_____

Status of research and development

_____

_____

_____

_____

_____

_____

_____

_____

_____

Patents, trademarks, copyrights

_____

_____

_____

_____

_____

_____

Item 8, Ownership and Management Structure

Item 8 is the place to describe the owner(s), including those you identified by name and title in Item 1. Here you would want to give more detail about their experience and expertise. Also, you should describe your management team, along with their abilities, training and development, and experience. Then, designate who will carry out the plan once it is enacted. Finally, something should be included about organizational structure, including employee policies and procedures.

8.   Ownership and Management Structure
      Owners and their expertise

_____

_____

_____

_____

_____

_____

_____

_____

Managers and their abilities, training and development, and experience

_____

_____

_____

_____

_____

_____

Organizational structure

_____

_____

_____

_____

_____

_____

_____

_____

Item 9, Objectives and Goals

In essence, your objectives and goals outline what you plan to accomplish in your business, as well as showing how it will be done. Include such items as sales and revenue forecasts; marketing plans, including how sales are to be made and what advertising, sales promotion, and publicity will be used; manufacturing plans, including provisions for quality assurance and control; and financial plans (but not the specific financial data, ratios, or analyses, which are in the next item).

9. Objectives and Goals
    Revenue forecasts

_____

_____

_____

_____

_____

_____

_____

_____

Marketing plans

_____

_____

_____

_____

_____

_____

_____

_____

How sales are to be made

_____

_____

_____

_____

_____

_____

_____

_____

Advertising and sales promotion

_____

_____

_____

_____

_____

_____

_____

_____

Manufacturing plans

_____

_____

_____

_____

_____

_____

Quality assurance plans

_____

_____

_____

_____

_____

_____

_____

_____

Financial plans

_____

_____

_____

_____

_____

_____

_____

_____

Item 10, Financial Analyses

Since one purpose of the plan is to attract prospective investors or lenders, Item 10 is the place in the plan where you can indicate the expected financial results of your operations. It should show prospective investors or lenders *why* they should provide funds, *when* they can realistically expect a return, and *what* the expected return on their money *should* be. While you must make assumptions—or educated guesses—at this point, you should at least try to include projected income statements and balance sheets for up to three years, as well as projected cash flow analyses for the first year by months. There should be an analysis of costs/volume/profits, where appropriate. Finally, you should provide projected statements of changes in financial position that you anticipate. If practical, you might want to provide some financial ratios.

10. Financial Data
    Projected income statements (three years)

_____

_____

_____

_____

_____

_____

_____

_____

Projected balance sheets (three years)

_____

_____

_____

_____

_____

_____

_____

_____

Projected cash flow analyses (first year, by months)

_____

_____

_____

_____

_____

_____

_____

Cost/volume/profit analyses, where appropriate

_____

_____

_____

_____

_____

_____

_____

_____

_____

Projected statements of changes in financial position

_____

_____

_____

_____

_____

_____

_____

_____

Financial ratios, if practical

_____

_____

_____

_____

_____

_____

_____

_____

_____

Item 11, Appendixes

In the appendixes you can include pertinent information about yourself and your business that is not included elsewhere in the plan. Some possible details to include are (1) narrative history of firm; (2) organizational structure (if not done in Item 8), including management structure, organization chart(s), and résumés of key people; (3) major assumptions you have made in preparing the plan; (4) brochures or other published information describing the product(s) and services you provide; (5) letters of recommendation or endorsement; (6) historical financial information, for the past three years (if not done in Item 10); (7) details of objectives and goals; and (8) catalog sheets, photographs, or technical information.

11. Appendixes
    Use separate sheet(s) of paper to write this information.

_____

_____

_____

_____

_____

_____

_____

IV. Sample Case: CleanDrum, Inc. (CDI)

For nine years, Sue Ley served as a forklift truck operator for a local oil company.* Then she drove a tractor-trailer for the company for four more years. Tiring of this type of work, and thinking she'd like to get into selling, she applied to participate in the company's education program, which paid tuition for employees taking college courses, and was accepted.

Sue enrolled in the marketing program at the local university. While continuing to drive the truck, she completed her marketing course work in three years and graduated with a bachelor's degree in business administration. But when she applied for a transfer to the marketing department, she was told that it would be "four or five years" before there'd be an opening for her.

Sue's uncle, who had taken over her grandfather's steel oil drum cleaning business, suggested that she start a similar business. Assuring her that she could make about $100,000 per year ($300,000 by the third year) if she founded a business of this sort, he offered to help her get the business started. She could not see any future with the oil company in marketing and did not want to drive trucks the rest of her life. Having saved $25,000 that she could put into the business, she decided to take a chance and start her own company.

History of the Business

Sue approached the local Small Business Development Center (SBDC) to find out if there was a large enough market for such a company in her area. The center arranged for two members of the local chapter of SCORE (the Service Corps of Retired Executives) to work with Sue. The Center's survey of 200 firms confirmed that a sufficient market existed for a "quality operation." While other firms were performing a similar service, their quality was not high enough to be considered true competition.

In 1993, using information provided by her uncle, Sue had an accounting firm prepare projected balance sheets, income statements, and changes in cash for five years. Sales projections were for 31,000 units in 1993 and up to 50,000 in 1998. Sales were estimated to be $367,000 in 1993, up to $558,000 in 1998, and net income was estimated to increase from $9,000 to $62,000.

Armed with these projections, and at the request of her banker, Sue approached potential customers and obtained letters indicating their willingness to do business with her "if high quality, good service, and competitive prices were offered."

Sue then prepared a business plan. On the basis of the plan, the SBDC report, financial projections, the letters, a personal history, and interviews with the loan officer, the bank approved a $60,000 loan. Adding her $25,000 as equity, Sue had a lawyer draw up incorporation papers for CleanDrum, Inc. (CDI). Sue was ready to enter the business of buying, straightening, cleaning, painting, and selling used 55-gallon steel drums; and buying, cleaning, and selling used plastic drums for transporting and storing oil, chemicals, and similar products.

She started by renting a building. Her uncle then arranged for purchase of the necessary machinery (at a "special" price of $59,000). (She later learned that he had bankrupted her grandfather's business and that the quality of the equipment he had purchased was "suspect.")

When the machinery arrived, her uncle failed to come to supervise its installation. It took Sue three months to hire mechanics, plumbers, and electricians to set up and connect the equipment, and to hire and train six laborers to operate the machinery. She studied her uncle's plant for two weeks to learn enough to enable her to run CDI. All these extra activities delayed her start-up and drained much of her cash.

Sue sold only 500 drums during the first month of operation, which did not provide sufficient income to cover her direct labor costs. In the first four months, she drove a truck during the daytime hours four days a week, and ran the drum-cleaning operations until 11 PM each night. The rest of the time, she was on the road selling CDI's drum-cleaning services.

She concentrated her sales activities on the people that had responded positively to the SBDC survey. But she had only limited success.

---

*See Case 1–2 for more details about the start of the business.

CDI's losses continued. She had expected her uncle to help her sell, but he didn't. Her banker insisted that she quit driving trucks and devote her full energies to her business or close it.

At the end of 1993, CDI had cleaned and sold about 18,000 drums, but it was still $30,000 in the hole. The bank loaned her another $12,000, and she mortgaged her home to obtain additional funds.

Management, Ownership, and Personnel

Early the next year, the financial situation was at its lowest point. At that time, a friend, Edie, invested $32,000 in CDI in return for 50 percent ownership.

Shortly thereafter, Edie expressed concern about the firm's losses and felt that labor costs should be reduced and a supervisor hired. Sue argued, however, that despite already low wages, the employees were efficiently producing a quality product. She said, "In the past, when I came to work, I often found a breakdown, a lack of materials, or that an employee hadn't shown up for work. Now, however, after their training, they have become productive."

By the eighth year, the number of workers had grown from six to eight, and the pay scale had grown from minimum wage to a range from minimum for recently hired employees to $8 per hour for the group leader. Social Security, workers' compensation, and unemployment insurance were the only employee benefits provided.

Sue had discussed with her SCORE advisers the possibility of giving the workers a bonus to recognize and encourage good work. "But," she added, "how do we pay for it?" She said that she was considering using temporary workers in order to avoid the problems of handling fringe benefits.

Product Line and Production Process

CDI performs two types of service. First, it buys steel and plastic drums with the intention of processing and selling them. This requires finding, pricing, purchasing, transporting, and selling drums. It then owns the drums until they are cleaned and sold.

Second, it has an ongoing drum exchange service, delivering processed drums and picking up old drums to be processed. CDI does not own those drums during processing. Sales are about evenly split between the two types of service, and steel drums make up about 85 percent of those handled.

The company rents a 5,000-square-foot building, where operations are conducted. (See Exhibit 1 for its layout.) Sue estimated that the machinery could process about 5,000 drums a month and that current production averaged about 4,000 drums per month. Machines are not fastened to the floor, but have electrical and pipe connections. The operations and their sequence for processing steel drums are shown in Exhibit 2.

The drums are brought to the plant in trailers, pulled by CDI's only tractor (267 drums make up a trailer load). The company has three trailers so that two can stay at the plant to be unloaded and loaded while the other is delivering clean drums to customers. CDI tries to move drums in full trailer loads which sometimes requires several stops. However, CDI has learned that orders for fewer than 50 drums are not profitable, so it does not accept them—unless the customer pays the transportation costs. The production process involves the following steps, in the order shown:

1. Drums are received and unloaded over a period of several days. The bungs (stoppers screwed in the tops of the drums) are removed and the drums checked for quality. The drums are stacked, moved to a waiting area, or moved to first flush. About 300 drums are in each of the receiving and shipping areas.
2. Each drum is upended on a pipe and flushed with steam and a chemical.
3. Each drum is righted, and a light is lowered into it so the drum can be inspected for rust. Rusty drums are rolled to a separate room where the rust is removed. They are then returned for further processing.
4. Drums needing straightening are run through the chimer.
5. Drums are placed on a conveyor, and rolled into a vat for cleaning. Six drums can be cleaned at the same time.
6. Drums are mechanically lifted, turned, and rolled into the outside rinser.

Exhibit 1

Layout of CleanDrum Plant

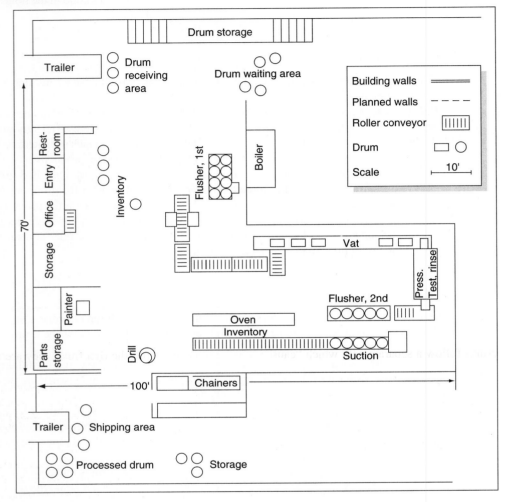

7. Drums are pressure tested. Those not meeting the pressure test are removed from the operation for further processing or discarding.

8. Drums roll down the conveyor where a worker lifts and upends each onto a steam pipe for final flushing.

9. Each drum is righted and placed on the floor where a suction pipe is inserted to dry the inside.

10. Final inspection for rust is made.

11. Drums are rolled to the paint booth for individual spray painting while being turned. A label is affixed to signify that the drum has gone through the entire cleaning process and conforms to established standards.

12. Drums are put into a waiting trailer for delivery or are moved to storage.

Freight can be a prime factor in the cost of some jobs. First, the distance that a tractor-trailer travels is a cost variable. And second, it is critical to keep empty or partial truckloads to a minimum. Therefore, *scheduling is very important.*

Exhibit 2
Sequence of Operations at CleanDrum

Steel Drums	Plastic Drums	Machines Used	Time in Drum
1. Receive	1. Receive	Trailer	
2. First flush	2. First flush	Flusher	3 minutes
3. Inspect for rust;		Visual	3 minutes
if so, clean with chain		Chainer*	15 minutes
4. Straighten		Chimer	1 minute
5. Clean		Vat	10 minutes
6. Outside rinse		Rinser	3 minutes
7. Pressure test;		Forced air	20 seconds
if not passed, cut out top		Hand cutter	10 minutes
	3. Pressure Test	Hand tester	2 minutes
8. Last flush	4. Flush	Flusher	4 minutes
	5. Wash outside	Hand washer	3 minutes
9. Dry		Suction/Oven	2 minutes
10. Inspect for rust;		Visual	2 minutes
if not passed, cut 9" hole		Drill press	10 minutes
11. Paint (90%)		Paint booth	4 minutes
12. Ship		Truck	

*About 5 percent.

Plastic drums follow a separate path which "causes some confusion." After the first flush, they are manually pressure tested, flushed again, and washed on a mobile cradle.

At times, space around the machines is crowded with drums (some stacked) awaiting the next operation. During the summer, the plant is extremely hot even with the draft through the open ends of the building. So, to help reduce the heat, a six-foot-diameter fan is placed in the wall by the vat. In rainy weather, workers in receiving and shipping wear raincoats or other protective wear.

Sue has considerably enlarged the production facilities since starting the company. She now feels that she needs to reduce the handling of the drums and, in the process, increase production capacity. She has found a larger first flusher, a larger chainer, a delivery trailer, and some roller conveyers at used-equipment prices that will give production the efficiency and capacity desired. Also, she needs a cutter-beader to get into the open top drum market. To rearrange the layout and reduce congestion, the plant needs to be enlarged.

Quality inspection of drums was recently combined with receiving drums to better tie the price to their condition. Sue feels that the changes are showing up in profits. They may also result in moving the chaining (rust removal) nearer the receiving area.

Recently, an outside firm made an environmental health and safety audit of the company. This audit included fire protection, human protection and movement, management policies, signs, and guards. Sue also explained that steps were being taken to make corrections that should avoid problems when OSHA inspectors come again. The $400 cost of the study should probably save from $1,500 to $2,000 in OSHA penalties.

Marketing and Sales Promotion

Since starting the company, Sue has spent part of her time on the road selling CDI's services. Currently, she spends two to three days each week on the road making contact with customers. Although she also makes many phone calls to her clients, Sue believes that these can't replace face-to-face contacts. She plans her itinerary to stay within a 200-mile radius in order to minimize travel time and mileage costs.

The 200-mile radius is considered the extent of CDI's market. This area is served by five companies, and total market demand is estimated to be 13,000 drums a month. Currently, CDI's sales volume places it in the lower middle of the group.

Sue estimates that she has over 100 customers, including about 50 percent of the companies that originally indicated a need for her services. About 75 percent of the sales have been drawn from competitors' customers.

Oil and chemical companies are CDI's major customers. Some call in to alert CDI to their need for its product. For example, one of the major customers recently called to tell her, "We have 100 drums ready to be cleaned, and will have 200 by the end of next week." Several companies order twice a month, while some order once every six months.

Sue has been selling about 3,500 to 4,000 drums a month, but her eye is set on sales of 5,000 per month. She explains that the goal is attainable for several reasons. First, the number of customers has steadily increased since CDI opened. Second, a competing company recently went bankrupt, and Sue picked up most of its customers. Finally, as will soon be discussed, several customers and sales reps from other noncompeting companies have "boosted" CDI to their customers.

Presently, Sue feels that quality and service should be her main selling emphasis. Even though CDI has chosen to compete on these points, however, it must also compete with price-cutting by some competitors. Pricing practices vary. Sue has heard reports that one competitor quotes a high price for the purchase of good drums and then finds enough wrong with them to drive the purchase price down so it can sell the processed drums for lower prices.

But Sue estimates the market for CDI drum cleaning is mainly among quality processors. She also believes that the market is restricted by freight costs, is expanding in the local market, and is stable, because several national companies need CDI's services.

Sue says she has seen delivered drums, processed by others, that have been carelessly processed, while others have not been pressure tested. Early on, CDI "almost lost a good customer because a part-time worker left some refuse in some drums."* Sue also cited a customer that was lost because somebody tampered with some of CDI's delivered drums. She hopes to convince potential customers who are currently buying substandard processing that it's in their best interest to obtain quality service.

CDI, which does only limited advertising and sales promotion, distributes magnetic calling cards and is the only company listed under "Barrels & Drums—Equipment & Supplies" in the Yellow Pages of the local telephone directory. Sue does not know of any other publication in which it would be worthwhile to advertise.

Some companies, having received poorly processed used drums, now use only new drums. Sue has approached some of these companies asking for a chance to demonstrate the quality of CDI's delivered drums. Although she hasn't had much success, she says she plans to continue trying this sales pitch. Also, her satisfied customers and others are referring other companies to CDI.

Financial Affairs

During the early years of the company, Sue used her checkbook to do the accounting. When cash was received, she entered it in the checkbook; when she paid a bill, she paid it by check. She used sales and shipping slips to keep track of sales and invoices received. At the end of the year, she took all the slips, invoices, and checks to the firm's accountant and received in return a financial package, plus completed tax forms.

Several years ago, however, a multicolumn income/expense form was introduced. Each column was designed for an item of income or expense and each sheet represented a month of activities. The form was summarized each month in order to obtain accounting information for management to use in decision making.

A computer has been installed and accounting programs are used for storage and processing data throughout the company. Costing and pricing have been simplified as well as the printing of statements, such as those shown in Exhibits 3 and 4.

During the early years, when annual sales were below $350,000, CDI incurred losses which accumulated and are now shown as a negative value in the equity section of the balance sheet. This negative value has been of grave

---

*Sue consistently emphasized to the authors how important the workers' performance was to the company.

Exhibit 3

CLEANDRUM, INC.
Balance Sheet
December 31, 1998
($000s)

	1996	1997	1998
Assets			
Current assets:			
Cash in bank	$ 6.7	$ —	$ 4.0
Accounts receivable	12.8	19.8	21.4
Inventory	7.7	27.2	31.0
Prepaid items	—	—	23.0
Total current assets	27.2	47.0	79.4
Property and equipment			
Equipment	156.6	178.8	203.7
Leasehold improvements	5.5	—	53.0
Less: accumulated depreciation	−102.2	−123.0	$−146.1
Net property and equipment	59.9	55.8	110.6
Total assets	$ 87.1	$ 102.8	$ 190.0
Liabilities and stockholders' equity			
Current liabilities:			
Accounts payable	$ 38.9	$ 50.5	$ 51.0
Current long-term debt	16.4	15.0	50.7
Notes payable	59.0	15.3	1.6
Accruals	11.8	6.9	14.4
Total current liabilities	126.1	87.7	117.7
Long-term debt	96.5	78.7	128.1
Total liabilities	222.6	166.4	245.8
Stockholders' equity			
Common stock	1.0	1.0	1.0
Added paid-in capital	16.7	108.3	108.3
Accumulated deficit	(153.2)	(172.9)	(165.1)
Total stockholders' equity	(135.5)	(63.6)	(55.8)
Total liabilities and stockholders' equity	$ 87.1	$ 102.8	$ 190.0

concern to Sue and she has discussed CDI's pricing policy many times with the SCORE counselors. Some counselors have suggested reducing the price to gain sales, while others have suggested raising prices to increase profit margins. Sue says, however, she cannot raise prices because of the competition.

CDI's pricing procedure is basically as follows: Used drums are purchased from various sources for about $4 each, depending on their condition. Those needing straightening and/or rust removal can be purchased at lower prices. After processing, a cleaned and painted drum is sold for about $12 to $13.

Customers' drums are processed and returned to them for about $7 a drum—again depending on the condition before processing. Drums sold for waste and parts storage are sold for about $5 each. Sue feels that CDI's pricing is in line with its competitors'. (One competitor sells drums at a lower price, but he doesn't pressure test them and appears to obtain dirty drums at lower prices than CDI.)

Exhibit 4

CLEANDRUM, INC.
Profit and Loss Statements
($000s)

Item	1996	1997	1998
Sales	$320.4	$436.2	$490.1
Cost of sales:			
Materials	99.1	175.4	183.9
Labor	74.6	87.3	104.9
Freight	42.0	11.3	23.3
Total cost of sales	215.7	274.0	312.1
Gross profit	$104.7	162.2	$178.0
Operating, administrative, and selling costs:			
Depreciation	16.7	24.3	23.1
Repair and maintenance	14.5	19.0	17.2
Rent	7.2	11.9	13.6
Utilities	18.0	19.0	24.9
Salary	20.9	25.0	25.0
Insurance	14.5	17.0	10.7
Office expense	3.6	2.6	3.8
General tax, legal, accounting	.5	14.2	13.6
Selling, travel, auto	10.4	10.3	14.6
Telephone	7.6	9.3	6.0
Miscellaneous	0.5	0.2	0.0
Total operating, administrative, and selling costs	$114.4	$152.8	$152.5
Operating profit	(9.7)	9.4	25.5
Income—legal	10.1	—	—
Interest expense	(19.9)	(11.7)	(17.9)
Net Income	$ (19.5)	$ (2.3)	$ 7.6

Recently, CDI obtained a contract to clean (only) a new type of drum that Sue feels will be profitable. Also, she sees a new market opening up for drums with removable tops, but this will require an investment in a cutter/beader. A year ago, CDI had a mobile cleaning unit made to service cleaning at drums' source. Sue feels there is a future in this business, but not now. The unit is used only as backup equipment.

While Sue has enlarged the production facilities in the past, she now feels they need to be expanded further—as noted earlier. Her plans would cost about $40,000, including machines and rearrangements. Rent would increase about $500 per month.

Sue has often spoken of CDI's difficulty with its cash flow. She is gathering information to use in a business plan to approach an investor or loan agent. As she has had difficulty in the past, Sue knows that she must present the most favorable impression of the company.

But Sue is optimistic, as she sees an expanding market, and 1998 showed that the company has a bright future. Also, she has found some sources of money where entrepreneurial women such as she are favored.

GLOSSARY

A

Accounting records Records of a firm's financial position that reflect any changes in that position.

Accounts payable Obligations to pay, resulting from purchasing goods or services.

Accounts receivable Current assets resulting from selling a product on credit.

Accrual basis This makes adjustments to income and expenses to reflect actual expenses incurred and income earned during the period.

Acid test (quick) ratio The ratio of current assets, less inventory, to current liabilities.

Advertising Advertising informs customers of the availability, desirability, and uses of a product.

Affirmative action programs (AAPs) These provide guidelines to help firms eliminate discrimination against women and minorities.

Agents Marketing intermediaries who market a product to others for a fee.

Allowances Allowances are given to customers for accepting quality or quantity reductions.

Americans with Disabilities Act (ADA) Law that requires the removal of many social and physical barriers to employing the disabled.

Anchor stores Those that generate heavy traffic in a shopping center.

Angel capitalists Wealthy local businesspeople and other investors who may be external sources of equity funding.

Apprenticeship training Training that blends OJT with learning of theory in the classroom.

Articles of copartnership These are drawn up during the preoperating period to show rights, duties, and responsibilities of each partner.

Articles of incorporation The instrument by which a corporation is formed under the corporation laws of a given state.

Assets The things a business owns.

Audit A formalized examination and/or review of a company's financial records.

B

Backward compatible Hardware that will run existing programs designed for older equipment.

Balance sheet A statement of a firm's assets, liabilities, and owners' equity at a given time.

Bankruptcy A formal legal condition of being unable to repay debts. People or businesses can petition courts to be relieved of financial obligation.

Barter Barter consists of two companies exchanging items of roughly equal value.

Benchmarking Setting up standards (for reference) and then measuring performance against them.

Bonds Bonds are a form of debt security with a standard denomination, method of interest payment, and method of principal repayment.

Bonus A reward—not specified in advance—given to employees for special efforts and accomplishments.

Break-even point That volume of sales where total revenue and expenses are equal, so there is neither profit nor loss.

Brokers Brokers bring buyers and sellers of goods together to negotiate purchases or sales.

Budgetary control System of budgets used to control a company's financial activities.

Budgets Detailed plans, expressed in monetary terms, of the results expected from officially recognized programs for a given future period.

Business angels See *Angel capitalists*.

Business ethics The standards used to judge the rightness or wrongness of a business's relation to others.

Business format franchising This grants the franchisee the right to market the product and trademark and to use a complete operating system.

Business incubators Old buildings that have been renovated, subdivided, and rented to new companies by groups desiring to assist young enterprises until they are healthy enough to go out on their own.

Business plan A business plan sets forth the firm's objectives, steps for achieving them, and its financial requirements.

Business services Services provided to another business or professional.

Buy-sell agreement Agreement that explains how stockholders can buy out each other's interest or how the corporation can buy back a shareholder's stock when he or she leaves the company.

C

Cafeteria-style benefit plan Allows the employer to provide all employees with the legally required benefits, plus an extra dollar amount that each employee can choose how to use.

Capital budget   Budget that plans expenditures for obtaining, expanding, and replacing physical facilities.

Carpal tunnel syndrome   See *Repetitive stress injuries.*

Cash   Bills, coins, deposits in a checking account, and other deposits that can be converted into cash immediately.

Cash basis   This assumes that payment and use occur in the same time period.

Cash budgets   Cash budgets project working capital needs by estimating what out-of-pocket expenses will be incurred and when revenues from these sales are to be collected.

Cash flow   The amount of cash available at a given time to pay expenses.

Cash flow budget   Budget that forecasts the amount of cash receipts and cash needed to pay expenses and make other purchases.

C corporation   A regular corporation that provides the protection of limited liability for shareholders, but whose earnings are taxed at both the corporate and shareholder levels.

Chapter 11   Provides for reorganizing a bankrupt business, whether the bankruptcy petition is filed voluntarily or involuntarily.

Chattel mortgage loan   Debt backed by some physical asset other than land, such as machinery, equipment, or inventory.

Coinsurance   Having the business buy insurance equal to a specific percentage of property value.

Combination franchising   In combination franchising, big-name operations offer both companies' products under the same roof.

Commission   Incentive compensation directly related to the sales or profits achieved by a salesperson.

Common stock   Common stock, representing the owners' interest, usually consists of many identical shares, each of which gives the holder one vote in all corporate elections.

Common stockholders   The owners of a corporation, with claims of a share of its profits and the right to vote on certain corporate decisions.

Communication   The transfer of meaning from one person to another.

Competitive edge   A particular characteristic that makes a firm more attractive to customers than are its competitors. Also called *competitive advantage.*

Complementary branding   See *Combination franchising.*

Conservation   Practicing the most effective use of resources, while considering society's current and future needs.

Consignment selling   With consignment selling, payments to suppliers are made only when the products are sold, rather than when they are received in stock.

Consumerism   Consumerism involves prodding businesses to improve the quality of their products and to expand consumer knowledge. It is the organized efforts of government, private, or , business groups to protect consumers from poorly designed or produced products.

Control   The process of assuring that organizational goals are achieved.

Convenience goods   Products that customers buy often, routinely, quickly, and in any store that carries them.

Cooperative   A business owned by and operated for the benefit of patrons using its services.

Corporate charter   States what the business can do and provides other organizational and financial information.

Corporation   A business formed and owned by a group of people, called stockholders, given special rights, privileges, and limited liabilities by law.

Cost-plus pricing   Basing the price on all costs plus a markup for profit.

Counseling   Helping to provide people with an understanding of their relationships with their supervisors, fellow workers, and customers.

Credit management   Setting and administering credit policies and practices.

Cross-functional teams   Teams that cut across different parts of the organization to monitor, standardize, and improve work processes.

Cross-training   Training in which workers learn many job skills so they are more versatile.

Cumulative trauma disorders   See *Repetitive stress injuries.*

Current assets   Those that are expected to change from one form to another within a year.

Current liabilities   Obligations that must be paid within a year.

Current ratio   The amount of current assets divided by the amount of current liabilities.

Customary price   What customers expect to pay because of custom, tradition, or social habits.

D

Debt financing   Debt financing comes from lenders, who will be repaid at a specified interest rate within a specified time span.

Defined-benefit plan   Pension plan whereby the amount an employee is to receive at retirement is specifically set forth.

Defined-contribution plan   Pension plan that establishes the basis on which an employer will contribute to the pension plan.

Delegation   Assigning responsibility to subordinates for certain activities and giving them the authority to perform those activities.

Depreciation   The gradual loss of value of a facility.

Diagnostic interviews   See *In-depth interviews.*

Direct taxes   Those paid directly to a taxing authority by the person or business against which they are levied.

Discipline   Fairly enforcing a system of rules and regulations to obtain order.

Disclosure statement   See *Prospectus.*

Discontinuance   A voluntary decision to terminate a business.

Discount   Reduction from the list price given to customers as an inducement to buy more of a product.

Discouraged employers   Those who tend not to hire new people if it would make them subject to certain federal laws and regulations.

Distribution   The physical movement of a product from the production line to the final consumer.

Distribution channel   A distribution channel consists of the marketing organizations responsible for the flow of goods and services from the producer to the consumer.

Diversification   Adding products that are unrelated to the present product line.

Diversity   Diversity in the work force is achieved by employing more members of minority groups, women, and older workers.

Downsizing (rightsizing)   Reducing the number of employees in order to increase efficiency.

Downtown locations   Downtown locations attract business-oriented activities, as government, financial businesses, and head offices of large firms are usually located in the downtown area.

Dual branding   See *Combination franchising.*

E

Economic order quantity (EOQ)   The quantity to purchase that balances the cost of placing the order with the cost of carrying the inventory.

80-20 rule   According to the 80-20 rule, approximately 80 percent of a company's income usually comes from 20 percent of its products.

Employee benefits   The rewards and services provided to workers in addition to their regular earnings.

Employee relations   Showing interest in and concern for employees' rights.

Employee stock ownership plans (ESOPs)   ESOPs allow small businesses to reap tax advantages and cash flow advantages by selling stock shares to workers; a form of profit sharing, they borrow money, purchase some of the company's stock, and allocate it to employees on the basis of salaries and/or longevity.

Employment at will   Employers may hire or fire workers with or without cause.

Empowerment   Giving employees experiences and responsibilities that equip them to function more effectively on their own.

Entrepreneur   The goals of an entrepreneur include growth, achieved through innovation and strategic management.

Entrepreneurial venture   In an entrepreneurial venture, the principal objectives of the owner are profitability and growth.

Environmental protection   Tries to maintain a healthy balance between people and their environment.

Equal Employment Opportunity Commission (EEOC)   Federal agency primarily responsible for enforcing EEO laws.

Equity   Equity is an owner's share of the assets of a company. In a corporation it is represented by shares of common or preferred stock.

Equity investors   Equity investors are those who actually become part owners of the business.

Estate planning   Preparing for the orderly transfer of the owner's equity in the business when death occurs.

Excise tax   An additional tax on certain items imposed by the federal government.

Executive summary   The executive summary is a brief overview of the most important information in a business plan.

Expenses   The costs of labor, goods, and services.

Exporting   Marketing our products to other nations.

F

Facilities   The buildings, machines and other equipment, and furniture and fixtures needed to produce and distribute a product.

Failure   A failure results from inability to succeed in running a business.

Family and Medical Leave Act   Law that requires employers with 50 or more employees to provide up to 12 weeks of unpaid leave for births or adoptions and to care for sick children, spouses, or parents.

Family limited partnership   Allows business owners to pass assets to heirs with a minimum of income and estate tax costs while retaining control of assets during their lifetime.

Federal unemployment tax   A tax paid to the federal government to administer the unemployment insurance program.

Feedback   The response a receiver gives through further communication with the sender of a message or some other person.

Financial leverage   Financial leverage is using fixed-charge financing, usually debt, to fund a business's operations.

Financial planning   Planning that involves determining what funds are needed, where they can be obtained, and how they can be controlled.

Financial resources   Cash flow, debt capacity, and equity available to finance operations.

Financial structure   This describes the relative proportions of a firm's assets, liabilities, and owners' equity.

Fixed assets   Assets that are of a relatively permanent nature and are necessary for the functioning of the business.

Fixed expenses   (costs) Expenses (costs) that do not vary with output, but remain the same.

Flexcomp   See *Cafeteria-style benefit plan.*

Flexible work arrangement   See *Variable work schedule.*

Flextime   An arrangement under which employees may schedule their own hours, around a core time.

Formal failures   Failures ending up in court with loss to creditors.

401(k) retirement plans   These permit workers to place up to a certain amount of their wages each year in tax-deferred retirement savings plans.

Franchise   An agreement whereby an independent businessperson is given exclusive rights to sell a specified good or service.

Franchisee   Independent businessperson who agrees to sell the product according to the franchiser's requirements.

Franchiser   The franchiser owns the franchise's name and distinctive elements and licenses others to sell its products.

Franchising   Marketing system whereby an individual owner conducts business according to the terms and conditions set by the franchiser.

Freestanding stores   Found in various locations, they are usually best for customers that have brand or company loyalty.

Fringe benefits   See *Employee benefits.*

Fully integrated production networks   Entire geographic regions where a fully integrated supply chain, from raw materials to finished products, is built up.

G

General partnership   In a general partnership, each partner actively participates as an equal in managing the business and being liable for the acts of other partners.

Global marketing   Marketing of products that are produced, bought, sold, or used almost anywhere in the world.

Green product   Environmentally friendly product offered for sale commercially.

H

Hardware   The CPU, monitor, keyboard, and other parts of the computer that you can see and touch.

High-knowledge industries   Those in which 40 percent or more of the human resources are professionals, technicians, or other "knowledge workers."

Human relations   The interaction among people in an organization.

Human resource planning   The process of converting the business's plans and programs into an effective work force.

Human resources   The personnel that make up the business's work force.

I

Immediate-response advertising   Advertising that tries to get customers to buy a product within a short time period so that response can be easily measured.

Importing   Purchasing and marketing other nations' products.

Incentive wage   Extra compensation paid for all production over a specified standard amount.

In-depth interviews   Detailed, probing, and penetrating interviews seeking to determine the applicant's character and other aspects of personality.

Indirect taxes   Taxes not paid by a firm or a person, but by someone else.

Infomercials   Long, usually half-hour, TV ads hosted by a hyper "sellevangelist" selling a relatively new product or service.

Informal organization   The set of interpersonal relationships that come about as a result of friendships that develop on and off the job.

Inputs   Materials, people, money, information, machines, and other productive factors.

Institutional advertising   Selling an idea about the company.

Insurance   Another company agrees, for a fee, to reimburse your company for part of a loss.

Intermediaries   Those units or institutions in the channel of distribution that either take title to or negotiate the sale of the product.

Intermediate-term securities   These mature in one to five years.

Intermodal shipping   Use of a combination of truck and rail to ship goods.

Internet   A collection of computers and computer networks linked together to receive and distribute information around the world.

Internship training   Training that combines OJT with learning at a cooperating school or college.

Inventory   A formal list of all the property of a business, or the property so listed.

J

Job burnout   Physical or mental depletion significantly below a person's capable level of performance.

Job description   Lists the duties and responsibilities of a given job.

Job enrichment   Granting workers greater responsibility and authority in their jobs.

Job sharing   When a single full-time job is retained, but its performance is shared by two or more employees working at different times.

Job specifications   Detailed written statements of work assignments and the qualifications needed to do the job acceptably.

Job splitting   When employees divide a single job into two or more different parts, each one doing one of the parts.

Joint venture   A form of temporary partnership whereby two or more firms join in a single endeavor to make a profit.

Judicial due process   The judicial due process of discipline involves (1) establishing rules of behavior, (2) setting prescribed penalties for violating each rule, and (3) imposing the penalty(ies) only after determining the extent of guilt.

Just-in-time (JIT)   Just-in-time delivery is having materials delivered to the user at the time needed for production.

K

Kaizen costing   This sets cost targets for all phases of design, development, and production of a product for each accounting period.

L

Laptop computer   A small, battery-powered device that can be used anywhere.

Leadership   The ability of one person to influence others to attain objectives.

Leading   The management function of getting employees to do what you want them to do, by communicating with, motivating, and disciplining them.

Lease   A contract that permits use of someone else's property for a specified time period.

Leased manpower   Employees obtained from an outside firm that specializes in performing a particular service.

Lenders   Lenders provide money for a limited time at a fixed rate of interest.

Liabilities   The financial obligations of a business.

Limited-liability company (LLC)   The LLC combines the advantages of a corporation, such as liability protection, with the benefits of a partnership, such as tax advantages.

Limited partnership   In a limited partnership, one or more general partners conduct the business, while one or more limited partners contribute capital but do not participate in management and are not held liable for debts of the general partners.

Line-and-staff organization   One that has specialists to advise and perform services for other employees.

Line of credit   This permits a business to borrow up to a set amount without red tape.

Line organization   In a line organization the owner has a direct line of command over employees.

Living trust   Resembles a will but, in addition to providing for distribution of personal assets on the maker's death, it also contains instructions for managing those assets should the person become disabled.

Long-term liabilities   Obligations to pay someone after one year or more.

Long-term securities   These mature after five years or longer.

Loss leader   An item priced at or below cost to attract customers into the store to buy more profitable items.

M

Management Information System (MIS)   Collects, records, processes, reports, and/or converts data into a usable form.

Management prerogatives clause   Defines the areas in which the employer has the right to act freely without interference from the union.

Manufacturing   Making or processing materials into finished goods.

Market research   The systematic gathering, recording, and analyzing of data related to the marketing of goods and services.

Market segmentation   Identifying and evaluating various layers of a market.

Marketing concept   The marketing concept involves giving special consideration to the needs, desires, and wishes of present and prospective customers.

Marketing mix   The proper blending of the basic elements of product, price, promotion, and place into an integrated marketing system.

Markup   The amount added to the product's cost to determine the selling price.

Merchandising   Promoting the sale of a product at the point of purchase.

Methods   Methods provide standing instructions to employees on how to perform their jobs.

Microprocessor   Miniaturized computer processor designed and based on a silicon chip.

Minority Vendor Profile System   A computerized database designed to match minority entrepreneurs with available marketing opportunities.

Mission   A business's long-term vision of what it is trying to become.

Mortgage loan   Long-term debt that is secured by real property.

Motivation   The inner state that activates a person, including drives, desires, and/or motives.

N

Net profit   The amount of revenue (sales) over and above the total amount of expenses (costs) of doing business.

Networking   The process of establishing and maintaining contacts with key persons in one's own or another organization as informal development or promotion systems.

Niche marketing   The process of finding a small—but profitable—demand for something and producing a custom-made product for that market.

Notebook computer   See *Laptop computer.*

Notes payable   Written obligations to pay, usually after 90 days to a year.

O

Objectives   The goals toward which the activities of the business are directed.

Occupational Safety and Health Administration (OSHA)   Establishes specific safety standards to assure, to the extent feasible, the safety and health of workers.

Off-price retailers   Those who buy designer labels and well-known brands of clothing at low prices and sell them at less than typical retail prices.

On-the-job learning (OJL)   See *On-the-job training.*

On-the-job training (OJT)   Training in which the worker actually performs the work, under the supervision of a competent trainer.

Operating budget   Budget that forecasts sales and allocates expenses for achieving them.

Operating systems   Operating systems consist of the inputs, processes, and outputs of a business.

Operational planning   Operational planning sets policies, procedures, and standards for achieving objectives.

Operations   Converting inputs into outputs for customers.

Organization chart   Chart that shows the authority and responsibility relationships that exist in a business.

Organizing   Determining those activities that are necessary to achieve a firm's objectives, and assigning them to responsible persons.

Outputs   The products produced and the satisfactions to employees and the public.

Owners' equity   The owners' share of (or net worth in) the business, after liabilities are subtracted from assets.

P

Partnership   A business owned by two or more persons who have unlimited liability for its debts and obligations.

Penetration price   Price set relatively low to secure market acceptance.

Performance appraisal   The process of evaluating workers to see how well they're performing.

Performance standards   Standards set in advance for acceptable levels to which employee achievement should conform.

Personal ethic   One's own belief system that tells one what to do if or when the laws and/or any pertinent codes are silent.

Personal (informal) failures   In personal (informal) failures, the owner who cannot succeed voluntarily terminates the business.

Personal services   Services performed by a business for consumers.

Physical resources   The buildings, tools and equipment, and service and distribution facilities that are needed to carry on the business.

Planning   The process of setting objectives and determining actions to reach them.

Policies   General statements that serve as guides to managerial decision making and supervisory activities.

Pollution control   The effort to prevent the destruction or contamination of the natural environment.

Polygraph   An instrument for simultaneously recording variations in several different physiological variables.

Positive discipline   Positive discipline deals with an employee's breach of conduct by their receiving an oral "reminder" (not a reprimand), then a written reminder, followed by a paid day off to decide if they really want to keep their job. If the answer is "yes," the employee agrees in writing to be on his/her best behavior for a given period of time.

Preemployment interviews   See *In-depth interviews.*

Preferred stock   Preferred stock has a fixed par value and a fixed dividend payout, expressed as a percentage of par value.

Preferred stockholders   Owners with a superior claim to a share of a firm's profits, but they often have no voting rights.

Problem-solving teams   Teams that meet on a regular basis to discuss ways to improve quality, efficiency, and the work environment.

Procedures   See *Methods.*

Process layout   Where facilities doing the same kind of work are grouped together.

Processes   Processes convert inputs into products customers want.

Producers   Producers convert materials into products in considerable volume for others to sell to ultimate consumers.

Product advertising   Product advertising calls attention to or explains a specific product.

Product and trademark franchising   This grants the franchisee the right to sell a widely recognized product or brand.

Production   See *Operations* and also *Manufacturing.*

Product layout   Where the facilities are laid out according to the sequence of operations to be performed.

Product life cycle   The product life cycle consists of four stages: introduction, growth, maturity, and decline.

Product/service liability insurance   Protects a business from losses resulting from the use of its product.

Profit   Revenue received by a business in excess of the expenses paid.

Profit goal   The specific amount of profit one expects to achieve.

Profit income   The difference between revenue earned and expenses incurred.

Profit motive   Expecting to make a profit as the reward for taking the risk of starting and running a business.

Profit planning   A series of prescribed steps to be taken to ensure that a profit will be made.

Profit sharing   An arrangement—announced in advance—whereby employees receive a prescribed share of the company's profits.

Promoting   Moving an employee to a higher position, usually with increased responsibilities, title, and pay.

Proprietorship   A business that is owned by one person.

Prospecting   Taking the initiative in seeking out customers with a new product.

Prospectus   Provides background and financial information about the franchiser and the franchise offering.

Publicity   Information about a business that is published or broadcast without charge.

Purchase order   A purchase order tells the supplier to ship you a given amount of an item at a given quality and price.

Purchasing   Purchasing determines the company's needs and finds, orders, and assures delivery of those items.

Pure risk   The uncertainty that some unpredictable event will result in a loss.

Push money (PM)   A commission paid to a salesperson to push a specific item or line of goods.

Q

Quality   Quality refers to product characteristics and/or the probability of meeting established standards.

Quality circles (QCs)   Small employee groups that meet periodically to improve quality and performance.

R

Random-access memory (RAM)   The amount of usable memory (volatile storage) within the computer.

Ratios   Relationships between two or more variables.

Read-only memory (ROM)   Unchangeable memory in the computer or on a disk that can be used for specialized applications.

Recruitment   Reaching out to attract applicants from which to choose one to fill a job vacancy.

Recycling   Reprocessing used items for future use.

Reengineering   The redesign of operations, starting from scratch.

Reinvention   The fundamental redesign of a business, often resulting in reduction of size and markets.

Repetitive stress injuries (RSIs)   Muscular or skeletal injuries to the hand, wrist, or other areas that bear the brunt of repeated motions. Among the most common is carpal tunnel syndrome.

Retailers   Retailers sell goods or services directly to the ultimate consumers.

Retained earnings   Profits kept in the business rather than distributed to owners.

Return on equity (ROE)   The percentage of net profit your equity earns, before taxes.

Revenue (sales income)   The value received by a firm in return for a good or service.

Right-to-work laws   Laws that permit states to prohibit unions from requiring workers to join a union.

Risk assumption   Setting aside funds to meet losses that are uncertain in size and frequency.

Risk avoidance   Refusing to undertake an activity when the risk seems too costly.

Risk management   The process of conserving earning power and assets by minimizing the shock from losses.

Risk prevention   (loss control) Using various methods to reduce the possibility of a loss occurring.

Risk transfer   Shifting a risk to someone outside your company.

S

Sales forecast   An estimate of the amount of revenue expected from sales for a given period in the future.

Sales promotion   Marketing activities (other than advertising or personal selling) that stimulate consumer purchasing and dealer effectiveness.

Sales tax   A tax added to the gross amount of the sale for goods sold within the taxing jurisdiction.

Scheduling   Setting the times and sequences required to do work.

SCORE (Service Corps of Retired Executives)   A group of retired—but active—managers from all walks of life who help people develop their business ideas.

S corporation   A corporation that is exempt from multiple taxation and excessive paperwork.

Selection   Choosing the applicant who has the qualifications to perform the job.

Self-insurance   See *Risk assumption.*

Self-managing work teams   Teams that take over managerial duties and produce an entire product.

Service companies   Companies that provide a service to customers and have some characteristics of both retailers and producers.

Shopping centers   Shopping centers vary in size and are designed to draw traffic according to the planned nature of the stores to be included in them.

Shopping goods   Goods that customers buy infrequently, after shopping at only a few stores.

Short-term securities   These mature in one year or less.

Skimming price   Price set relatively high initially in order to rapidly skim off the "cream" of the profits.

Small business   A business that is independently owned and operated and is not dominant in its field.

Small business investment companies (SBICs)   Private firms licensed and regulated by the SBA to make "venture" investments in small firms.

Small business owner   A small business owner establishes a business primarily to further personal goals, including making a profit.

Social objectives   Goals regarding assisting groups in the community and protecting the environment.

Social responsibility   A business's responsibility to follow desirable courses of action in terms of society's values and objectives.

Social Security   Federal program that provides support for the retired, widowed, disabled, and their dependants.

Software   The programs, manuals, and procedures that cause the hardware to operate in a desired manner.

Span of control   (management) The number of employees that report directly to an employer.

Specialization   Using employees to do the work that they are best suited for.

Specialized small business investment companies (SSBICs)   These assist socially and economically disadvantaged businesses with venture capital.

Specialty goods   Goods bought infrequently, often at exclusive outlets, after special effort by the customer to drive to the store.

Speculative risk   The uncertainty that a voluntarily undertaken risk will result in a loss.

Spiff   See *Push money.*

Staffing   Planning for recruiting, selecting, and training and developing employees, as well as compensating them and providing for their health and safety.

Standing orders   These set predetermined times to ship given quantities of needed items, at a set price.

Stock   Stock represents ownership in a corporation.

Stockouts   Sales lost because an item is not in stock.

Strategic planning   Strategic planning provides comprehensive long-term direction to help a business accomplish its mission.

Strategies   The means by which a business achieves its objectives and fulfills its mission.

Subnotebook computer   See *Laptop computer.*

Supplier-base downsizing   Reducing the number of suppliers to concentrate purchasing.

Synergy   The concept that two or more people, working together in a coordinated way, can accomplish more than the sum of their independent efforts.

System   In a system, all parts of the business work in unison.

T

Target market   The part of the total market toward which promotional efforts are concentrated.

Taxable income   Total revenues minus deductible expenses.

Telecommuting   The use of modern communications media, such as telephones, fax machines, computers, modems and fax/modems, and scanners to work from an office, home, or any location.

Teleconferencing   Holding a virtual meeting using telephone, radio, closed-circuit TV, or computer circuit connections.

Teleworkers   Employees who work full or part time from their homes.

Test marketing   Simulates the conditions under which a product is to be marketed.

Tort   A wrongful act by one party, not covered by criminal law, that results in injury to a second party's person, property, or reputation, for which the first party is liable.

Trade credit   Trade credit is extended by vendors on purchases of inventory, equipment, and/or supplies.

Transferring   Moving an employee from one job to another, without necessarily changing title or pay.

Transportation modes   Methods used to transfer products from place to place.

U

Unemployment insurance   Financial support to employees laid off for reasons beyond their control.

Uniform Commercial Code (UCC)   Set of uniform model statutes to govern business and commercial transactions in all states.

Unit pricing   Listing the product's price in terms of some unit, such as a pound, pint, or yard.

Upgrading   Retraining workers so they can do increasingly complex work.

Use tax   A tax on the use, consumption, or storage of goods within a taxing jurisdiction.

V

Variable costs   Costs that vary directly with changes in output.

Variable expenses   Variable expenses change in relation to volume of output; when output is low, the expenses are low, and when output is high, expenses rise.

Variable work schedule   Work schedule that permits employees to work at times other than the standard five 8-hour days.

Videoconferencing   See *Teleconferencing*.

W

White-collar crimes   Those committed by managerial, professional, and technical employees.

Wholesalers   Intermediaries who take title to the goods handled and then sell them to retailers or other intermediaries.

Workers' compensation   Payments made to employees for losses from accidents and occupational diseases.

Working capital   Current assets, less current liabilities, that a firm uses to produce goods and services, and to finance the extension of credit to customers.

Z

Zero-defects approach   Approach that uses pride in workmanship to get workers to do their work "right the first time."

ENDNOTES

Chapter 1

1. Suzie Amer et al., "Technology's 100 Richest," *Forbes,* October 6, 1997, pp. 58–76; and "World's Richest People," *USA Today,* June 22, 1998, p. 1B; and Janet Kornblum, "The $100 Billion Man to Be: Gates Draws Close to $100B," *USA Today,* January 21, 1999, p. 3B.

2. SBA, Office of Economic Research within the Office of Advocacy, *The Facts about Small Business, 1997,* www.sba.gov/ADVO/stats/fact1.html, p. 1, accessed March 18, 1998.

3. Amy Duncan, "Tapping the Small-Biz Mother Lode," *Business Week,* June 22, 1998, p. 206.

4. SBA Office of Advocacy, *The Facts about Small Business, 1997.*

5. *Imprimis* (published by Hillsdale College) 25, no. 6 (June 1996), p. 1.

6. SBA Office of Advocacy, *The Facts about Small Business, 1997,* p. 1.

7. Ibid.

8. Udayan Gupta, "New Business Incorporations Reached Record in 1994," *The Wall Street Journal,* June 6, 1995, p. B2.

9. "Business Beat: Brighter Days," *Entrepreneur,* July 1995, p. 16.

10. Ibid.

11. Jerry Langdon, "Small Businesses Shun Technology," *USA Today,* September 21, 1998, p. 9B.

12. "A Surprising Finding on New-Business Mortality Rates," *Business Week,* June 14, 1993, p. 22.

13. SBA Office of Advocacy, *The Facts about Small Business, 1997,* p. 1.

14. Ibid.

15. John Case, "The Age of the Gazelle," *Inc.* 18, no. 7, Special Issue: "The State of Small Business, 1996," pp. 44–45.

16. Robert J. Sherwood, "Profits," *Forbes,* April 21, 1997, p. 188.

17. Robert Boone, Jr., "Sales," *Forbes,* April 21, 1997, p. 180.

18. Eric S. Hardy, "Jobs and Productivity," *Forbes,* April 21, 1997, p. 220.

19. Robert L. Bartley, "On Clinton's Recipe for Growth," *The Wall Street Journal,* July 16, 1992, p. A10.

20. "Odds and Ends," *The Wall Street Journal,* July 17, 1992, p. B1.

21. SBA Office of Advocacy, *The Facts about Small Business, 1997,* pp. 1, 2.

22. Stephanie N. Mehta, "Entrepreneurial Spirit Enters High School," *The Wall Street Journal,* November 29, 1994, p. B2.

23. Linda C. Rhodes, "The Entrepreneurial Class," *The Wall Street Journal,* July 14, 1997, p. A14.

24. Amy Salzman, "Big Firm, Dead-End Career?" *U.S. News & World Report,* March 27, 1995, p. 62.

25. Stephanie N. Mehta, "It's Getting Easier for M.B.A.s to Find Jobs at Small Firms," *The Wall Street Journal,* July 8, 1997, p. B2.

26. Thomas Petzinger, Jr., "M.B.A.s at Anderson Often Seek Fortunes, Not Just Employment," *The Wall Street Journal,* June 13, 1997, p. B1.

27. American Booksellers Association BookWeb, "B&N Will Manage Harvard Coop Bookstores," *Book News,* September 11, 1995, found at www.bookweb.org/bookweb/btw/081195/art1.html; "[Harvard] History and Lore," found at www.news.harvard.edu/hno.subpages/intro_harvard/history/trivia.html; and various pages found at www.thecoop.com; all accessed March 20, 1998.

28. Information found at Harvard Student Agencies' Web site, http://hsa.net, including hsa.net/more_about_hsa/history/index.htm, accessed March 20, 1998.

29. Mehta, "Entrepreneurial Spirit Enters High School."

30. Ibid.

31. Lynn Brenner, "If You're Starting a Business . . . ," *Parade Magazine,* March 15, 1998, p. 22.

32. Stephanie N. Mehta, "Young Entrepreneurs Turn Age to Advantage," *The Wall Street Journal,* September 1, 1995, pp. B1, B2.

33. As told to Dr. M. Jane Byrd by Megan Crump.

34. Susan E. Kuhn, "Retire Today: Find a New Job Tomorrow," *Fortune,* July 24, 1995, p. 104.

35. Stephanie N. Mehta, "Retirees Starting Business Trip Over Stumbling Blocks," *The Wall Street Journal,* February 14, 1995, p. B1.

36. W. B. Barnes, *First Semi-Annual Report of the Small Business Administration* (Washington, DC: Small Business Administration, January 31, 1954), p. 7.

37. Information obtained during a visit to the Caudle House in October 1997.

38. Peter Nultz, "Serial Entrepreneur: Tips from a Man Who Started 28 Businesses," *Fortune,* July 10, 1995, p. 182.

39. U.S. Bureau of the Census, *Statistical Abstract of the United States, 1991,* 111th ed. (Washington, DC:

U.S. Government Printing Office, 1991), Table 861, p. 525.

40. SBA Office of Advocacy, *The Facts about Small Business, 1997,* p. 5.

41. David Kirkpatrick, "Now Everyone in PCs Wants to Be Like Mike," *Fortune,* September 8, 1997, pp. 91–92.

42. Jacqueline Love, "Smaller Businesses Offer Grads Broader Experience," *Mobile* (Alabama) *Register,* June 24, 1998, p. 7B.

43. Michael Hopkins and Jeffrey L. Seglin, "Americans @Work," *Inc.,* May 20, 1997, pp. 77–85.

44. Reported in Shelley Liles, "More Small Businesses Succeeding," *USA Today,* May 8, 1989, p. 1E.

45. Cited in *USA Today,* March 13, 1987, p. 13.

46. David S. Evans, "The Effects of Access to Capital on Entry into Self-Employment," *Small Business Research Summary,* no. 116 (November 1991).

47. Timothy Aeppel, "Missing the Boss: Not All Workers Find Idea of Empowerment as Neat as It Sounds," *The Wall Street Journal,* September 8, 1997, pp. A1, A10.

48. Laura Tiffany, "Basket Case," *Business Start-Ups,* April 1998, p. 78.

49. Aeppel, "Missing the Boss," p. A1.

50. Sue Shellenbarger, "In Re-Engineering, What Really Matters Are Workers' Lives," *The Wall Street Journal,* March 1, 1995, p. B1.

Chapter 2

1. Deborah Marchini, Stuart Varney, and Kelli Arena, "Strong Economy Is Placing Workers in the Driving Seat," CNN "Business News," September 1, 1997.

2. As reported in *USA Today,* June 13, 1995, p. 1B.

3. "Happiness Is Looking in the Mirror—and Seeing Yourself," *Business Week,* July 12, 1993, p. 22.

4. Kathy Jumper, "Couple Gets Balloon Company Off Ground," *Mobile* (Alabama) *Press,* July 14, 1993, pp. 1-E, 2-E; and "Champagne Hot Air Balloon Flights," at www.innisfree.com/ybs/attr.htm, February 28, 1998.

5. Amy Saltzman, "You, Inc.: Being Your Own Boss," *U.S. News & World Report,* October 28, 1996, pp. 66–73.

6. Tait Trussel, "The Untypical Typical Millionaire," *Nation's Business,* November 1988, p. 62.

7. "The Magic Touch," CNNfn, July 2, 1998; Janean Chun, "Magic Magic," *Entrepreneur,* July 1998, pp. 109–11; and Sylvester Monroe, "Post-Game Show," *Time,* March 17, 1997, pp. 38ff.

8. Kathy Chen, "Rags to Riches Story: How Rebiya Kader Made Her Fortune," *The Wall Street Journal,* September 21, 1994, pp. A-1, A-6.

9. Maggie Jackson, "Death's Sting: Families Opt for More Economical Funerals," *Mobile* (Alabama) *Register,* October 8, 1995, p. 54.

10. Nancy Madlin, "The Venture Survey: Probing the Entrepreneurial Psyche," *Venture,* May 1985, p. 24.

11. U.S. Trust, "Affluent Business Owners," www.ustrust.com/offbus.htm, February 25, 1998, p. 4.

12. Micheline Maynard, "Executives Claim Niche, Top Jobs," *USA Today,* September 20, 1994, p. 1B.

13. Scott Boeck and Marcy E. Mullins, "How Often Does Your Family Eat Dinner Together?" *USA Today,* October 23, 1995, p. 1D.

14. Stephanie Armour, "More Kids Putting Parents on Payroll," *USA Today,* April 29, 1998, pp. 1B, 2B.

15. John H. Johnson with Lerone Bennett, Jr., *Succeeding Against the Odds* (New York: Warner Books, 1989).

16. Lynn Langway, "Like Fathers, Like Daughters," *Newsweek,* January 16, 1984, pp. 78–80.

17. Donald C. Mosley, Paul H. Pietri, and Leon C. Megginson, *Management: Leadership in Action,* 5th ed. (New York: HarperCollins, 1996), p. 542.

18. Laurel Touby, "Dreams Come True: The $20 Million Success Story," *McCall's,* June 1998, p. 56.

19. Based on material provided by Levi Strauss & Co.

20. Janice Castro, "Big vs. Small," *Time,* September 5, 1988, pp. 48–50.

21. Kylo-Patrick Hart, "Tricks of the Trade," *Business Start-Ups,* September 1997, p. 124.

22. John H. Christy, "Market Value," *Forbes,* April 21, 1997, p. 212.

23. Michael Erbschloe, "Telecom Programs in the University: What's Available?" *Telecommunications* (American Edition), April 1997, pp. 59–60.

24. Paul Davidson, "High-Tech Help Wanted: No Experience Necessary," *USA Today,* December 23, 1997, p. 1B.

25. James Aley, "Where the Jobs Are," *Fortune,* September 18, 1995, pp. 53–54, 56.

26. Rusty Brown, "Women Entrepreneurs Dominate 80s," *Mobile* (Alabama) *Press Register,* January 18, 1986, p. 4-A.

27. Barbara K. Mistick and Deborah C. Good, "Value Systems of Women Business Owners: A Comparative Analysis," in *Proceedings of the Third AIDEA Giovani International Conference: Managing across Borders—Cross-Cultural Issues in Management Studies,* ed. Luca G. Brusati, Universitá della Svizzera Italiana (Lugano, Switzerland), June 4–6, 1998, p. 145.

28. Luisa Kroll, "Entrepreneur Moms," *Forbes,* May 18, 1998, p. 84.

29. Sharon Nelton, "Women Owners and Uncle Sam," *Nation's Business,* April 1998, p. 53.

30. "A Woman's Work," *Fortune,* August 24, 1992, p. 59.

31. SBA, "Women- and Minority-Owned Firms," *The Facts about Small Business, 1997,* at www.sba.gov/ADVO/stats/fact1.html, p. 2, accessed March 18, 1998.

32. Paula Mergenhagen, "Her Own Boss," *American Demographics,* December 1996, pp. 36–41.

33. As reported in *USA Today,* April 26, 1995, p. 1B.

34. Nelton, "Women Owners and Uncle Sam," p. 53.

35. Mark Robichaux, "Business First, Family Second," *The Wall Street Journal,* May 12, 1989, p. B1.

36. Kroll, "Entrepreneur Moms," p. 84.

37. Carol Hymowitz, "World's Poorest Women Advance by Entrepreneurship," *The Wall Street Journal,* September 5, 1995, p. B1.

38. "She's the Boss," *USA Today,* June 21, 1989, p. 1A.

39. Maria Puente, "Birth Rate in U.S. at a Record Low," *USA Today,* February 10, 1998, p. 4A.

40. Andrew S. Grove, "Immigration Pays," *The Wall Street Journal,* January 8, 1996, p. A18.

41. "Minority-Owned Businesses," *USA Today,* September 30, 1997, p. 1B.

42. Stephanie N. Mehta, "Big Companies Heighten Their Pitch to Minority Firms," *The Wall Street Journal,* October 23, 1994, p. B2.

43. Jeffrey A. Tannenbaum, "U.S. Firms Owned by Minority Women Grew by 153% in 9 Years, Report Says," *The Wall Street Journal,* June 25, 1997, p. B2.

44. "More Minority Women Owners," *USA Today,* June 23, 1997, p. 1B.

45. Randolph E. Schmid, "Black-Owned Firms Show Greatest Rise," *Mobile* (Alabama) *Press Register,* December 12, 1995, p. 7-B.

46. John Emshwiller, "Former TV Actor Stars as Entrepreneur," *The Wall Street Journal,* July 10, 1992, p. B1.

47. Stephanie N. Mehta, "Black Entrepreneurs Benefit," *The Wall Street Journal,* October 19, 1995, pp. B1, B2.

48. Tariq K. Muhammad, "From 'Buppie' to Biz Whiz," *Black Enterprise,* January 1997, pp. 47–48.

49. Elizabeth Lesley and Maria Mallory, "Inside the Black Business Network," *Business Week,* November 29, 1993, pp. 70ff.

50. Daniel Hager, "Minority Entrepreneurs Rediscover Booker T. Washington," *Human Events,* March 6, 1998, p. 18.

51. Ibid.

52. Kevin Johnson, "McDonald's Recruits Duo to Make Its McCroutons," *USA Today,* January 27, 1989, p. 7.

53. Marc Ballou, "Start-Up Mambos to Beat of Booming Market," *Inc.,* September 1997, pp. 56ff.

54. Nancy Archuleta, "Stand-In," *Inc.,* February 1995, p. 21.

55. Andrea Gerlin, "Radio Stations Gain by Going after Hispanics," *The Wall Street Journal,* July 14, 1993, p. B1.

56. "U.S. Asian and Pacific Islander Population," *The Christian Science Monitor,* July 27, 1993, p. 10.

57. As reported in Margaret L. Usdansky, "Asian Businesses Big Winners in 80s," *USA Today,* August 2, 1991, p. 1A.

58. Nathan Glazer, "Race, Not Class," *The Wall Street Journal,* April 5, 1995, p. A12.

59. Mortimer B. Zuckerman, "Beyond Proposition 187," *U.S. News & World Report,* December 12, 1994, p. 123.

60. Rochelle Sharpe, "Who Benefits: Asian Americans Gain Sharply in Big Program of Affirmative Action," *The Wall Street Journal,* September 9, 1997, pp. A1 and A8.

61. Timothy L. O'Brien, "Tribes Use Loans to Small Businesses to Create Jobs," *The Wall Street Journal,* August 27, 1993, p. B2.

62. Ibid.

63. Todd Logan, "Trapped," *Inc.,* January 1995, pp. 21–22.

64. SBA Office of Advocacy, *The Facts about Small Business, 1997,* at www.sba.gov/ADVO/stats/fact1.html, pp. 2, 17, accessed July 1997.

Chapter 3

1. Author's correspondence with Charlene Mitchell of Mel Farr Enterprises; and others, including Suzanne Telesmanich, "National Entrepreneur of the Year Awards," *USA Today,* November 21, 1997, p. 9A.

2. See Roger L. Miller and Gaylord A. Jentz, *Business Law Today: Alternate Essentials Edition,* 4th ed. (St. Paul, MN: West, 1997), pp. 408–9, for more detailed information.

3. Lee Berton and Joann S. Lublin, "Seeking Shelter: Partnership Structure Is Called in Question as Liability Rises," *The Wall Street Journal,* June 10, 1992, pp. A1, A9.

4. Frances A. McMorris and Michael Siconolfi, "Prudential's Limited-Partnership Woes Seem Near End as Legal Pact Advances," *The Wall Street Journal,* February 6, 1995, p. A12.

5. "Delaware Still Draws Corporations," *Mobile* (Alabama) *Register,* December 27, 1997, p. 7B.

6. "Legal Briefs: Is Delaware the Place to Go Broke?" *Business Week,* November 17, 1997, p. 6.

7. Harry Edelson, "Dispatch from the Boardroom Trenches," *The Wall Street Journal,* February 6, 1995, p. A12.

8. See "Small Businesses Set Up as S Corporations Get a Boost from Congress," *The Wall Street Journal,* August 14, 1996, p. A1, for further details.

9. "Corporate Structure: Protecting Subchapter S Status," *Inc.,* January 1992, pp. 107–8.

10. Internal Revenue Service, *SOI Bulletin,* Publication 1136 (rev. February 1997), Table 21, "Selected Returns and Forms Filed or to be Filed by Type During Specified Calendar Years, 1975–1997," found at www.irs.ustreas.gov.

11. William G. Nickels, James M. McHugh, and Susan McHugh, *Understanding Business,* 4th ed. (New York: McGraw-Hill, 1996), pp. 159–60.

12. Bellas & Wachowski, Attorneys at Law, "Comparison of Limited Liability Companies with Other Forms of Business in Illinois," at www.bellas-law.com/comparis.htm, p. 1, accessed March 4, 1998.

13. *West Federal Taxation: 1998* (Cincinnati: West, 1998), pp. 20–25.

14. Barbara L. Bryniarski, "Structuring for Limited Liability," *Nation's Business,* April 1992, pp. 46–48.

15. Adrian Ladbury, "KPMG May Give Up Partnership," *Business Insurance,* July 11, 1994, p. 17.

16. John R. Emshwiller, "SEC Sets Sights on Certain Limited Liability Companies," *The Wall Street Journal,* March 31, 1994, p. B2.

17. Author's correspondence with Carolyn Ann Sledge, assistant director of marketing for Delta Pride.

18. David R. Evanson, "Found Money," *Entrepreneur,* April 1995, pp. 112–13.

19. "Partners Produce," *The Wall Street Journal,* January 9, 1997, p. A1.

20. Leo Paul Dana, "Small Firms in International Joint Ventures in China: The New Zealand Experience," *Journal of Small Business Management* 32 (April 1994), pp. 88–102.

21. David Knott, "How a Small Producer Survives in Russia," *Oil and Gas Journal,* February 27, 1995, p. 24.

Chapter 4

1. This section is based on F. J. Roussel and Rose Epplin, *Thinking about Going into Business?* (U.S. Small Business Administration Management Aid No. 2.025). This and other publications are available from the SBA for a small processing fee.

2. An excellent guide to use is the SBA's *Checklist for Going into Business,* Management Aid No. 2.016. To obtain this aid, contact your nearest SBA office.

3. Keith H. Hammonds, "What B-School Doesn't Teach You about Start-Ups," *Business Week,* July 24, 1989, p. 208.

4. Thomas Petzinger, Jr., "Nurse Agency Thrives by Taking Hard Cases in the Inner City," *The Wall Street Journal,* September 26, 1997, p. B1, and the company's Web site.

5. Bruce Sims, "Phone Call Initiates Idea for Business," *Baldwin* (County, Alabama) *Press Register,* February 27, 1995, p. 3.

6. Anne Goodfriend, "10 Great Places to . . . Take Tea," *USA Today,* April 17, 1998, p. 3D.

7. Janean Chun, "Back in the Saddle," *Entrepreneur,* October 1995, p. 110.

8. Francis Huffman, "Living Large," *Entrepreneur,* October 1997, pp. 156–59.

9. Sharon Nelton, "Succeeding in a Walk," *Nation's Business,* January 1997, pp. 12, 14.

10. As reported in "Gallup Survey: 92 Percent Franchise Owners Successful," *USA Today,* March 11, 1998, p. 6B.

11. "Franchising: The Take-Out Recipe for Success," *Small Business Success* 11 (1989), p. 28.

12. Conducted by the International Franchise Association Education Foundation, and reported in "Buying a Franchise," *USA Today,* August 31, 1998, p. 1B.

13. As reported in *The Wall Street Journal,* July 17, 1997, p. B2.

14. Arthur G. Sharp, "Enfranchising Europe," *TWA Ambassador,* January 1991, p. 52.

15. "Franchising's High Rollers Hold Convention in Las Vegas," *USA Today,* February 11, 1998, p. 8A.

16. "Pop the Questions," *Business Start-Ups,* October 1997, pp. 62–68.

17. U.S. Department of Commerce, *Franchising in the Economy, 1988–1990* (Washington, DC: U.S. Government Printing Office), p. 4.

18. "Cowboy Not Interested in Joining the Herd: A Dying Breed," *USA Today,* December 26, 1997, p. 3B.

19. "Cruising the Internet to Buy a Vehicle: Web Sites Offer Buyers Trunkload of Options," *USA Today,* May 18, 1998, p. 3B.

20. Jeffrey A. Tannenbaum, "Dispute Grows over True Rate of Franchisee Failures," *The Wall Street Journal,* July 3, 1992, p. B2.

21. *Franchising Opportunities* (Babylon, NY: Pilot Industries, 1992), p. 76.

22. "Disclosure Documents Start to Become Available via the Internet," *The Wall Street Journal,* October 28, 1997, p. B2.

23. Nancy Kennedy, "Should You Franchise Your Business?" *Income Opportunities—The No. 1 Source of Affordable Money-Making Ideas,* February 1995, pp. 42–52.

24. Andrew A. Caffey, "Franchise 101: Up for Negotiation," *Entrepreneur,* September 1998, pp. 192F–G.

25. Jeffrey A. Tannenbaum, "Right to Retake Subway Shops Spurs Outcry," *The Wall Street Journal,* February 2, 1995, pp. B1, B2.

26. Jeffrey A. Tannenbaum, "Franchisees Balk at High Prices for Supplies from Franchisers," *The Wall Street Journal,* July 5, 1995, pp. B1, B2.

27. Jeffrey A. Tannenbaum, "To Pacify Irate Franchisees, Franchisers Extend Services," *The Wall Street Journal,* February 24, 1995, pp. B1, B2.

28. Jeffrey A. Tannenbaum, "Once Red-Hot PIP Faces Legal Assault by Franchisees," *The Wall Street Journal,* April 8, 1993, p. B2.

29. Jeffrey A. Tannenbaum, "Re-Emerging Risk? FTC Says Franchisers Fed Clients a Line and Failed to Deliver," *The Wall Street Journal,* May 16, 1994, p. A1.

30. Richard Gibson, "Court Decides Franchisees Get Elbow Room," *The Wall Street Journal,* August 14, 1996, p. B1.

31. Jeffrey A. Tannenbaum, "Focus on Franchising: A Federal Agency," *The Wall Street Journal,* January 23, 1995, p. B2.

32. As reported in *USA Today,* October 5, 1995, p. 1D.

33. Don L. Boroughs, "Serving Up Hot Profits," *U.S. News & World Report,* November 28, 1994, pp. 83–86.

34. "Lube Shops on Corner Stations," *Mobile* (Alabama) *Register,* October 4, 1992, p. 8E.

35. Audrey Genrich, "Small Businesses Drive Need for Support Services," *Franchising World,* November/December 1994, p. 24.

36. Jeffrey A. Tannenbaum, "Mergers between Strong Franchisees Begin to Catch On," *The Wall Street Journal,* May 4, 1995, p. B2.

37. Jeffrey A. Tannenbaum, "Mexican-Food Joint Venture Gives Arby's Indigestion," *The Wall Street Journal,* August 12, 1997, p. B1.

38. Jeffrey A. Tannenbaum, "Broiling Pace: Chicken and Burgers Create Hot New Class: Powerful Franchisees," *The Wall Street Journal,* May 21, 1996, p. A1.

39. Carol Steinberg, "Franchising: A Global Concept," *USA Today,* April 9, 1992, p. 5B.

40. "Bright Spot: Franchising Again Stands Out in the Trade-Balance Picture," *The Wall Street Journal,* November 9, 1995, p. B2.

41. "All the World's a McStage," *Business Week,* May 8, 1995, p. 8.

42. Kathy Chen, "KFC Rules Fast-Food Roost in Shanghai," *The Wall Street Journal,* December 2, 1997, pp. B1, B12.

43. Richard W. Stevenson, "Pepsi to Show Ad in Russian," *New York Times,* January 20, 1989, p. C5.

44. "Non-Kosher McDonald's Causes Jerusalem Stir," *Mobile* (Alabama) *Press Register,* June 10, 1995, p. 2E.

45. "All the World's a McStage."

46. Joyce Barnathan, "The Gloves Are Coming Off in China," *Business Week,* May 15, 1995, p. 61.

47. Jeffrey A. Tannenbaum, "Burger King Franchisees in Europe Are Growing Restive," *The Wall Street Journal,* October 3, 1995, p. B2.

48. Emory Thomas, Jr., "Chick-fil-A to Announce Expansion into Africa," *The Wall Street Journal,* September 27, 1995, p. S2.

49. "South Africa Draws More Franchisers, but Some Remain Skittish," *The Wall Street Journal,* December 8, 1993, p. B2.

50. "Moving South of the Border," *USA Today,* April 9, 1992, p. 7B; and Jeffrey Tannenbaum, "More Franchisers Try Alternatives to Stand-Alone Sites," *The Wall Street Journal,* November 10, 1994, p. B2.

51. U.S. Department of Commerce, *Franchising in the Economy, 1989–1992* (Washington, DC: U.S. Government Printing Office), p. 19.

52. As reported in Carol Steinberg, "Minority Recruitment Efforts Under Way," *USA Today,* June 25, 1992, p. 4B.

53. The actual term used by Walter Mondale in the early 1980s—and a few years later by Secretary of Labor Robert Reich in a lecture at Harvard—was "McDonald's jobs, burger flipper jobs." See Amith Shlaes, "About Those McDonald's Jobs . . . ," *The Wall Street Journal,* August 15, 1995, p. A17, for more details.

54. Ibid.

55. Ibid.

Chapter 5

1. Jacqueline L. Babicky, Larry Field, and C. Norman Pricher, "Focus On: Small," *Journal of Accountancy* 177 (May 1994), p. 41.

2. Hal Lancaster, "It's the Thoughts That Count in Putting Missions in Writing," *The Wall Street Journal,* October 28, 1997, p. B1.

3. "An Exterior View May Be What Some Companies Need in Their Strategic Plans," *The Wall Street Journal,* December 14, 1995, p. A1.

4. Hal Lancaster, "Fear of Flying Solo? Some Takeoff Tips from Two Consultants," *The Wall Street Journal,* February 28, 1995, p. B1.

5. Guy Kawasaki, "How to Drive Your Competitors Crazy," *The Wall Street Journal,* July 17, 1995, p. A10.

6. Theodore B. Kinni, "Process Improvement, Part II," *Industry Week,* February 20, 1995, pp. 45–50.

7. See "How to Start a Small Business: Focus on the Facts," AIG Library, WWW adaptation of SBA publication FF2 by Anjoch Investors Group, www.anjoch-investors.com, accessed September 1, 1998.

8. See *Keeping Records in Small Business,* Management Aid No. 1.017, which can be obtained free from the Small Business Administration, P.O. Box 15434, Fort Worth, TX 76119.

9. As reported in "Dig Deep to Open Business," *USA Today,* August 26, 1994, p. 1B.

10. Ibid.

11. Carrie Shook, "Making Haste Slowly," *Forbes,* September 22, 1997, pp. 220–22.

12. Melvin Gravely II, "Getting the Bank to Say 'Yes,'" www.tsbj.com/02-12/0212-07.htm, accessed November 21, 1997.

13. Timothy Aeppel, "From License Plates to Fashion Plates," *The Wall Street Journal,* September 21, 1994, pp. B1, B2.

14. The SBA has several free publications to help you in preparing a plan. For example, SBA Management Aid No. 2.007 is a Business Plan for Small Manufacturers.

15. William G. Nickels, James M. McHugh, and Susan M. McHugh, *Understanding Business,* 5th ed. (New York: McGraw-Hill, 1996), p. 189.

16. John G. Burch, *Entrepreneurship* (New York: John Wiley & Sons, 1986), pp. 377–82.

17. Carla Goodman, "The Big Time," *Business Start-Ups,* August 1998, pp. 26–29.

Chapter 6

1. Julie Candler, "Leasing's Link to Efficiency," *Nation's Business,* May 1995, pp. 30–34. See also Dean D. Baker, "Lease vs. Buy: Avoid Excess Costs," *Management Accounting,* July 1995, pp. 38–39, for some pitfalls to avoid when leasing.

2. Al Neuharth, "1999 Mood Will Shift; Carefree to Cautious," *USA Today,* January 8, 1999, p. 25a.

3. Donna Rosata, "Device Allows Stock Trading on the Run," *USA Today,* October 19, 1994, p. 2B.

4. David R. Evanson, "SCORing Points," *Entrepreneur,* June 1995, pp. 38–41. In 1995, only Connecticut, Georgia, Illinois, Maryland, New Jersey, New York, and Washington did not accept SCOR.

5. David Carnoy, "Smooth Sailing," *Success,* December 1996, pp. 47–48.

6. Tom Post, "Impossible Dream," *Forbes,* May 4, 1998, pp. 80, 82.

7. SBA Office of Advocacy, *The Facts about Small Business, 1997,* at www.sba.gov/ADVO/stats/fact1.html, p. 4, accessed March 18, 1998.

8. Udayan Gupta, "Seed Capital for Early-Stage Companies Grows Strongly," *The Wall Street Journal,* August 29, 1995.

9. Andy Reinhardt, "Nothing Jive about Juniper," *Business Week,* September 8, 1997, p. 38.

10. Gregg Wirth, "Industry Resources Edge Down," *Venture Capital Journal,* July 1995, p. 38.

11. Price Waterhouse National Venture Capital Survey, as reported in "Venture Capital Winners," *USA Today,* April 21, 1998, p. 1B.

12. Udayan Gupta, "Small Venture-Capital Firms Fill Void Left by Big Ones," *The Wall Street Journal,* July 13, 1995, pp. B1, B2.

13. "Venture Capital Winners."

14. Correspondence with the Vancouver Stock Exchange. Also see Cynthia E. Griffin, "Northern Exposure," *Entrepreneur,* May 1995, p. 15.

15. Michael Selz, "Finding Help: Anyone Need Cash?" *The Wall Street Journal,* May 21, 1998, p. R14; and Seth Fineberg, "Venture Capital Financings Reach Another High," *Venture Capital Journal,* February 1998, pp. 24–28.

16. Udayan Gupta, "Financing Small Business: A Foundation," *The Wall Street Journal,* March 10, 1995, p. B2.

17. Ellie Winninghoff, "The Trouble with Angels," *Working Woman,* March 1992, p. 37.

18. Julie Schmit, "Angels Spread Wings for Start-Ups," *USA Today,* August 27, 1996, p. 4B.

19. Communications from the National Business Incubation Association.

20. "New Study Shows Value of Business Incubators," *LSU Today,* November 7, 1997, p. 3.

21. Dale Buss, "Bringing New Firms Out of Their Shell," *Nation's Business,* March 1997, pp. 48–50.

22. Michael Selz, "Financing Small Business: A Venture Firm," *The Wall Street Journal,* July 1, 1997, p. B2.

23. Eleena De Lisser and Rodney Ho, "Barter Exchanges Say Future Looks Promising," *The Wall Street Journal,* November 12, 1997, p. B2.

24. *The Facts about Small Business, 1997,* p. 4, accessed March 18, 1998.

25. T. Carter Hagaman, "Why Can't Small Business Borrow?" *Managerial Accounting,* March 1995, p. 14.

26. Michael Selz and Udayan Gupta, "Lending Woes Stunt Growth of Small Firms," *The Wall Street Journal,* November 16, 1994, p. B1.

27. Michael Selz, "New Banks Are Loan-Friendly to Other Start-Up Firms," *The Wall Street Journal,* July 1, 1997, p. B2.

28. Anna Robaton, "Banking on Women," *Working Woman,* November 1997, pp. 66–70.

29. Arthur Andersen's Enterprise Group survey, as reported in "Putting Business on Plastic," *USA Today,* February 5, 1998, p. 1B.

30. Except where otherwise noted, this discussion is based on the SBA publications *Lending the SBA Way* and *Your Business & the SBA*. Since Congress periodically passes new legislation that determines the kind of assistance the SBA provides, contact the nearest SBA district office to ascertain what types of assistance are currently available to you, or visit the SBA Web site at www.sba.gov.

31. J. Tol Broome, Jr., "Borrowed Time," *OfficeSystems97,* December 1997, p. 14.

32. Michael Selz, "Venture Capitalists Fear the U.S. May Renege on SBICs," *The Wall Street Journal,* February 3, 1995, p. B2.

33. John Carey, "Teaching Old Crops New Tricks," *Business Week,* June 13, 1994, p. 48.

Chapter 7

1. "Secrets from the Market Pros," *Small Business Reports,* January 1994, p. 27.

2. Linda Lee Small, "Surviving the Superstore Steamroll," *Working Woman,* July 1994, pp. 62–64.

3. Jack Gordon, Marc Hequet, and David Stamps, "It's What You Know and Share That Counts," *Training,* February 1997, pp. 18–20.

4. Yumiko Ono, "Going Door to Door with Palazzo Pants," *The Wall Street Journal,* September 8, 1995, p. B1.

5. Tara Parker-Pope, "Avon Is Calling, with New Way to Make a Sale," *The Wall Street Journal,* October 27, 1997, p. B1.

6. Bob Levy, "The Prime Offender: Business Itself," *Washington Post,* May 12, 1988, p. D20.

7. Randy McClain, "Casual Gets Serious" (Baton Rouge, Louisiana) *Sunday Advocate,* February 15, 1998, pp. 1I, 5I.

8. Katrina Burger, "A Drink with an Attitude," *Forbes,* February 10, 1997, pp. 112–13.

9. Daniel Hill, "Love My Brand," *Brandweek,* January 19, 1998, pp. 26–29.

10. Alex Miller, *Strategic Management,* 3rd ed. (New York: McGraw-Hill, 1998), pp. 14–21.

11. "Edsel and Friends: Ten World-Class Flops," *Business Week,* August 16, 1993, p. 80.

12. Magrid Abraham, "Getting the Most out of Advertising and Promotion," *Harvard Business Review* 68 (May/June 1990), pp. 50–52.

13. Jim Buchta, "The Apartment of Tomorrow," (Minneapolis) *Star Tribune,* February 14, 1998, Star Tribune Online Top News (see www.startribune.com).

14. Stacy Krabetz, "Surprise! A Homebuilder (Finally) Surveys Buyers," *The Wall Street Journal,* June 24, 1997, p. B2.

15. Jacquelyn Lynn, "Survey Says . . . ," *Entrepreneur,* May 1995, pp. 60, 61.

16. AP bulletin, "Caller I.D. Aids Businesses," *Mobile* (Alabama) *Press Register,* January 30, 1995, p. 7-B.

17. Debra Phillips, "Touch of Class," *Entrepreneur,* October 1997, p. 23.

18. William C. Symonds, "Talbots Drops the Funkier Stuff," *Business Week,* October 6, 1997, pp. 164–66.

19. Reported in *USA Today,* November 28, 1989, p. 1A; and U.S. Department of Commerce, *Statistical Abstract of the United States, 1997,* 117th ed. (Washington, DC: U.S. Government Printing Office, 1997), p. 59, Table 66.

20. "The Aging of America," *USA Today,* July 21, 1998, p. 7A.

21. Sara Olkon, "For Deals, Don't Be Shy about Your Age," *The Wall Street Journal,* October 13, 1995, p. B7.

22. "Elderly on the Rise, but Not on the Move," *Employee Benefit Plan Review* 52 (November 1997), p. 45.

23. Faye Rice, "Making Generational Marketing Come of Age," *Fortune,* June 26, 1995, p. 110.

24. J. Allen Tarquinio, "King of Grits Alters Menu to Reflect Northern Tastes," *The Wall Street Journal,* September 22, 1997, p. B1.

25. Joseph Spiers, "Where Americans Are Moving," *Fortune,* August 21, 1995, p. 38.

26. Tom Shales, "It Came, It Thawed, It Conquered," *Washington Post,* April 16, 1987, pp. C1, C6.

27. Jim Salter, "Toymaker Plays Off Nostalgia," *Mobile* (Alabama) *Register,* February 8, 1998, p. 5F.

28. Meera Somasundaram, "Red Symbols Tend to Lure Shoppers like Capes Being Flourished at Bulls," *The Wall Street Journal,* September 18, 1995, p. B10a.

29. " 'Just Enough Packaging' and Right-Size Packages Carry Clout," *The Wall Street Journal,* September 7, 1995, p. A1.

30. Anne B. Lowery, "The Four Cs of Pricing: A Pricing Primer for Small Business," *TSU Business and Economic Review,* April 1994, p. 10.

31. William Rabb, "He Scrubs Up Sites No One Else Wants to Touch," *Mobile* (Alabama) *Register,* April 19, 1998, pp. 1B, 5B.

32. Allanna Sullivan, "Mobil Bets Drivers Pick Cappuccino over Low Prices," *The Wall Street Journal,* January 30, 1995, pp. B1, B8.

33. Author's discussion and correspondence with Ms. Brown.

Chapter 8

1. Tara Parker-Pope, "New Devices Add Up Bill, Measure Shoppers' Honesty," *The Wall Street Journal,* June 6, 1995, p. B1.

2. Ted Griggs, "Shopping for Shoppers" (Baton Rouge, Louisiana) *Advocate,* February 11, 1998, pp. 3C, 4C.

3. Letter from Virginia Scoggins to Suzanne Barnhill, May 1987.

4. Author's correspondence with Professor Russell Eustice, Husson College, Bangor, Maine.

5. Ted Tate, "Prospecting for Referrals and Leads," *OfficeSystems98,* June 1998, p. 26.

6. Carla Goodman, "You Make the Call," *Business Start-Ups,* April 1998, p. 22.

7. William M. Bulkeley, "Finding Targets on CD-ROM Phone Lists," *The Wall Street Journal,* March 22, 1995, p. B1.

8. Walter Kiechell, "How to Manage Sales People," *Fortune,* March 14, 1998, pp. 179–80.

9. Published by Career Press.

10. Distributed by Nightingale-Conant Corporation.

11. Author's correspondence with Sue Willis of Wendy's International, Inc.; and "Dave Thomas: What Makes for Success?" Hillsdale College's *Imprimis,* July 1996, p. 1.

12. Peter Pae, "Low-Power TV Expands, Fed by New Programming," *The Wall Street Journal,* May 30, 1989, p. B1.

13. Louis S. Richman, "Pioneers of a New Way to Sell," *Fortune,* October 31, 1994, p. 248.

14. Ibid.

15. "Spam That You Might Not Delete," *Business Week,* June 15, 1998, pp. 115ff.

16. As reported in *USA Today,* September 22, 1995, p. 1A.

17. Thom Grier, "But You Don't Get That Nice Musty Smell," *U.S. News & World Report,* November 3, 1997, p. 66.

18. Robert Maynard, "Managing Your Small Business—Getting Publicity Mileage from Company Trucks," *Nation's Business,* August 1997, p. 10.

19. "Spam That You Might Not Delete."

20. Thomas Petzinger, Jr., "Druggist's Simple Rx: Speak the Language of Your Customers," *The Wall Street Journal,* June 16, 1995, p. B1.

21. William M. Bulkeley, "Rebates' Secret Appeal to Manufacturers: Few Consumers Actually Redeem Them," *The Wall Street Journal,* February 8, 1998, pp. B1, B2.

22. "William Wrigley and Family," *Forbes 400,* October 16, 1995, p. 136.

23. Public Radio International's "Marketplace," June 29, 1998.

24. Joanne Lipman, "Nielsen to Track Hispanic TV Ratings," *The Wall Street Journal,* July 24, 1989, p. B4.

25. Andrew S. Grove, "A High-Tech CEO Updates His Views on Managing and Careers," *Fortune,* September 18, 1995, pp. 229–30.

26. Here are the answers to the questions in Figure 8–6:
    Made in China
    - Alarm clocks.
    - Sneakers—50 percent of all athletic shoes sold in the United States.
    - Cordless telephones—38.8 percent of imports from China.
    - Christmas ornaments.
    - Aladdin, the action figure.

    Made in the U.S.A.
    - Sheets and blankets—79 percent of cotton sheets sold here.
    - Vacuum cleaners—88.5 percent sold in the U.S.A.
    - Wonder Bra.
    - Office machinery.
    - Aladdin, the video.

    Source: Ellen Neuborne, "A 'Made in China' Day in the USA," *USA Today,* February 24, 1995, p. 1A.

27. "VCRs Cause Failure of Firm," *Mobile* (Alabama) *Register,* July 31, 1989, p. 2-A.

28. Robyn Meredith and Tammi Wark, "Does 'Made in USA' Label Fit?" *USA Today,* July 14, 1995, p. 4B.

29. Reported in William J. Holstein and Kevin Kelley, "Little Companies, Big Exports," *Business Week,* April 13, 1992, p. 70.

30. Bernard Wysocki, Jr., "The Global Mall: In the Emerging World, Many Youths Splurge, Mainly on U.S. Goods," *The Wall Street Journal,* June 26, 1997, p. A1.

31. Melanie Wells, "Foreign Markets Buy 'Made in America,' " *USA Today,* May 15, 1996, p. 1B.

32. See Richard Gesteland, "Do's and Taboos: Proper Etiquette in the Global Marketplace," *The Rotarian,* April 1998, pp. 26–29, 59, for an excellent discussion of what's proper and improper behavior in different countries.

33. AP bulletin, "McDonald's Bags Draw Complaints from Muslims," *Mobile* (Alabama) *Press Register,* June 8, 1995.

34. "The Forbes Four Hundred over $1,000,000," *Forbes 400,* October 16, 1995, p. 138.

35. De'Ann Weimer, Richard A. Mulcher, and David Case, "Turning Small into a Big Advantage," *Business Week,* July 13, 1998, p. 42.

36. Edwardo Lachica, "China Risks Losing Assistance for Electronics Industries," *The Wall Street Journal,* February 17, 1995, p. A5C.

37. Erika Kotite, "The Hot Zones," *Entrepreneur,* May 1995, p. 78.

38. Albert Warson, "Tapping Canadian Markets," *Inc.,* March 1993, pp. 90–91.

39. Holstein and Kelley, "Little Companies, Big Exports."

40. Marq Ozanne, "Managing Strategic Partnerships for the Virtual Universe," *Fortune,* September 29, 1997, p. 193.

41. Catherine Funkhouser, "SBA Upgrades Its Financial Assistance for Small Business Exporters," *Business America,* February 1995, pp. 10–15.

42. Its hotline can be reached at 800-872-8723.

43. Anyone interested in this program can reach the Eximbank's Business Development Group at 800-565-EXIM.

44. See "Railroad Facts," as reported in *USA Today,* June 25, 1992, p. 3A.

45. "UPS Delivers via Internet," *OfficeSystems98,* June 1998, p. 8.

46. Janet Guyon, "Smart Plastic," *Fortune,* October 13, 1997, p. 56.

Chapter 9

1. Thomas A. Stewart, "A New Way to Think about Employees," *Fortune,* April 13, 1998, pp. 169–70.

2. Barbara Marsh, "Small-Business Hiring Heads for the Roof," *The Wall Street Journal,* August 26, 1997, p. A1.

3. Population Division, U.S. Bureau of the Census, www.census.gov/population/estimates/nation/intfile 2-1.txt.

4. As reported in *The Aging of the Work Force* (Washington, DC: American Association of Retired Persons, n.d.), p. 7, Figure 1.

5. Michael Selz, "Small-Business Owners Find New Worries," *The Wall Street Journal,* December 6, 1994, p. B2.

6. Robert D. Hershey, Jr., "Blue-Collar Jobs Gain, but the Work Changes in Tone," *New York Times,* September 3, 1997, www.natcavoice.org/un/f97/ tone.htm, accessed April 15, 1998.

7. Mortimer B. Zuckerman, "Editorial: Who Does Feel Your Pain?" *U.S. News & World Report,* January 2, 1995, p. 126.

8. "Hard Times: High-Tech Help Wanted," *The Rotarian,* May 1998, p. 12.

9. Sue Shellenbarger, "Employers Are Finding It Doesn't Cost Much to Make a Staff Happy," *The Wall Street Journal,* November 19, 1997, p. B7.

10. "Job-Turnover Tab," *Business Week,* April 20, 1998, p. 8.

11. James E. Challenger, "Dispelling the Myths of Workers over 50," *The Rotarian,* July 1997, p. 8; and Christopher J. Farrell, "The Labor Pool Is Deeper than It Looks," *Business Week,* November 24, 1997, p. 39.

12. Rael Jean Isaac, "Invite the Guest Workers Back," *The Wall Street Journal,* November 9, 1995, p. A23.

13. Robert Lewis, "Escaping from the Jobless Maze," *AARP Bulletin,* October 1994, p. 2.

14. Carrie Beth Marston, "Temporary Insanity," *OfficeSystems95,* May 1995, p. 30.

15. Kevin Henbusch, "Temporary Liaisons," *American Demographics,* November 1997, pp. 36–37; and Stephanie Armour, "Bias Laws Also Apply to Temps," *USA Today,* December 26, 1997, p. 2B.

16. The National Association of Temporary and Staffing Services, "Who Are Temporary Workers? You May Be Surprised to Learn . . . ," www.natss.org/release4-3-98.htm.

17. Ken Gebfert, "Temps Changing Roles Mask Their Full Impact," *The Wall Street Journal,* August 2, 1995, p. S1.

18. Gail Edmondson, "A Tidal Wave of Temps in Europe," *Business Week,* December 1, 1997, p. 164J.

19. As reported in *USA Today,* December 13, 1995, p. 1B.

20. Selvin Gootar, "We Want You!" *OfficeSystems98,* February 1998, p. 47.

21. "Internet Expedites Employee Recruiting," *The Rotarian,* April 1998, p. 8.

22. "The Checkoff," *The Wall Street Journal,* September 16, 1997, p. A1.

23. Donna Fenn, "Hiring: Employees Take Charge," *Inc.,* October 1995, p. 111.

24. Marlene Brown, "Checking the Facts on a Résumé," *Personnel Journal Supplement,* January 1993, p. 6.

25. Peter Thompson, "Employee Screening Tests: Proceed with Caution," *The Rotarian,* May 1998, p. 6.

26. "References Not Always Honest," *USA Today,* June 6, 1994, p. 1B.

27. Haidee E. Allerton, "News You Can Use," *Training & Development,* December 1997, pp. 9–12.

28. Jerry McLain, "Practice Makes Perfect," *OfficeSystems 95,* April 1995, pp. 74, 75, 77.

29. Amith Shlaes, "About Those McDonald's Jobs . . . ," *The Wall Street Journal,* August 15, 1995, p. A17.

30. G. David Doran, "Revving Up Students," *Entrepreneur,* September 1997, p. 189.

31. Roberta Maynard, "Helping Employees Hone Their Skills," *Nation's Business,* July 1995, p. 12.

32. See, for example, Lynn Beresford, "McSchool Days," *Entrepreneur,* August 1995, pp. 200–202.

33. "New Managers Get Little Help Tackling Big, Complex Jobs," *The Wall Street Journal,* February 10, 1998, p. B1.

34. Stephanie Armour, "Disabilities Act Abused? Law's Use Sparks Debate," *USA Today,* September 25, 1998, pp. 1B, 2B.

35. Ibid.

36. Larry Reynolds, "Sex Harassment Claims Surge," *HR Focus,* March 1997, p. 8.

37. Equal Employment Opportunity Commission, *Guidelines on Discrimination Because of Sex,* 29 C.F.R., Section 1604.11 (July 1, 1992).

38. Susan B. Garland, "Finally, a Corporate Tip Sheet on Sexual Harassment," *Business Week,* July 13, 1998, p. 39.

39. Mary Ryder Brett, "Religious Discrimination," *OfficeSystems98,* April 1998, pp. 16, 25.

40. "English-Only Rules Become a Growing Problem in the Workplace," *The Wall Street Journal,* April 4, 1995, p. A1.

41. Peter Eisler, "Complaints Now Sit for at Least a Year," *USA Today,* August 15, 1995, p. 1A.

42. "Your Rights under the Fair Labor Standards Act," White House Publication 1088, rev. October 1996.

43. For more information, contact the nearest office of the Employment Standards Administration, Wage and Hour Division, of the U.S. Department of Labor.

44. Peter Nulty, "Incentive Pay Can Be Crippling," *Fortune,* November 13, 1995, p. 235.

45. E. Vogelly and L. Schaeffer, "Link Employee Pay to Competencies and Objectives," *HRMagazine,* October 1995, p. 75.

46. Donald L. McManis and William G. Dick, "Monetary Incentives in Today's Industrial Setting," *Personnel Journal* 52 (May 1973), pp. 387–89.

47. Frank Buckley and John Meehan, "Keeping Bad Taste in the Family," *Business Quarterly* 59 (Spring 1995), pp. 22–29.

48. Pam Robertson and Sue Matthews, "Like an Open Book," *CA Magazine,* May 1997, pp. 33–35.

49. To find out more about career opportunities with Lincoln Electric, contact its Human Resources Department by fax at (216) 383-4765.

50. Kathleen Madigan, "Here Come Hefty Hikes in Benefits," *Business Week,* May 18, 1998, p. 170.

51. "Worker and Retiree Views of Social Security Reform," *Working Age: An AARP Newsletter about the Changing Work Force,* November/December 1997, p. 4.

52. William M. Welch and Susan Page, "Special Report: Social Security Reform: System Is Face-to-Face with Change," *USA Today,* July 27, 1998, p. 7A.

53. Stephanie Armour, "Unpaid Leave Costly Proposition," *USA Today,* February 9, 1998, p. 4B.

54. "Survey: Most Small Businesses Providing Health Insurance, Even as Prices Rise" (Jackson, Mississippi) *Clarion Ledger,* June 20, 1998, p. 3C.

55. Robert McGarvey, "Something Extra," *Entrepreneur,* May 1995, pp. 70, 72–73.

56. Nancy Ann Jeffrey, "Health-Care Costs Rise for Workers at Small Firms," *The Wall Street Journal,* September 8, 1997, p. B2.

57. Lynn Brenner, "If You're Starting a Business . . . ," *Parade Magazine,* March 15, 1998, p. 22.

58. Charles Bartels, "Tuition Assistance Faces Uncertain Future," *Tuscaloosa* (Alabama) *News,* November 5, 1995, p. 1E.

59. Bryna Brennan, "Small Firms Dropping Pension Plans; Laws Too Complex," *Birmingham* (Alabama) *News,* December 17, 1989, p. 2D.

60. Rabina A. Gangemi, "FMLA? ADA? OSHA? HELP!" *Inc.,* April 1995, p. 112.

61. See Leon C. Megginson, Geralyn M. Franklin, and M. Jane Byrd, *Human Resource Management* (Houston: Dame Publications, 1995), p. 346, for more details.

62. U.S. Bureau of the Census, *Statistical Abstract of the United States, 1994,* 114th ed. (Washington, DC: U.S. Government Printing Office, 1994), p. 437.

63. Ibid., Tables 679 and 680.

64. "Carpal Tunnel Pain Drain," *USA Today,* October 9, 1997, p. 1B.

65. Dennis M. Rosseau and Carolyn Libuser, "Contingent Workers in High Risk Environments," *California Management Review,* Winter 1997, pp. 103–23.

66. "Sore Workers," *U.S. News & World Report,* April 24, 1995, p. 70.

67. Megginson, Franklin, and Byrd, *Human Resource Management,* p. 346.

68. "Carrot and Stick: OSHA's New 'Cooperation' Draws Mixed Reviews," *The Wall Street Journal,* December 16, 1997, p. A1.

Chapter 10

1. Thomas Petzinger, Jr., "A Couple Rescues Waremart from Throes of a Clash of Cultures," *The Wall Street Journal,* February 6, 1998, p. B1.

2. Andrew R. Sorkin, "Advertising: Gospel According to St. Luke's: Brash Agency Turns Old Rules Upside Down," *New York Times,* February 12, 1998, from *New York Times on the Web,* pp. 1–3.

3. For more information on teams and team management, see "Empowerment and Team Performance" in Chapter 1.

4. Matthew 7:12 (NIV).

5. Douglas McGregor, *The Human Side of Enterprise* (New York: McGraw-Hill, 1960).

6. Joshua Hyatt, "The Odyssey of an Excellent Man," *Inc.,* February 1989, pp. 63–69.

7. Stanley Bing, " 'All They Need Is Love,' " *Fortune,* April 14, 1997, p. 162.

8. Leon C. Megginson, Geralyn Franklin, and M. Jane Byrd, *Human Resource Management* (Houston: Dame Publications, 1995), pp. 266–70.

9. Richard L. Hughes, Robert C. Ginnett, and Gordon J. Curphy, *Leadership: Enhancing the Lessons of Experience,* 2nd ed. (New York: McGraw-Hill, 1996), p. 30.

10. Roderick Wilkinson, "We Need Leadership, Not Just 'Brains,' " *The Rotarian,* October 1994, p. 4.

11. Jay Finegan, "Rodel's Leadership Intensive Training Ended Internal Battling and Refocused the War

where It Belonged: On Competitors," *Inc.* (online), March 1997, pp. 1–9.

12. For more information on this topic, see Rosemary Stewart, *Managers and Their Jobs* (New York: Macmillan, 1967); and Henry Mintzberg, *The Nature of Managerial Work* (New York: Harper & Row, 1973), p. 38.

13. Ralph W. Weber and Gloria E. Perry, *Behavioral Insights for Supervisors* (Englewood Cliffs, NJ: Prentice-Hall, 1975), p. 138.

14. World Features Syndicate, in the *Mobile* (Alabama) *Press Register,* February 23, 1996, p. 2A.

15. Jane Bird, "The Great Telephony Shake-up and How It Affects Your Business," *Management Today,* January 1998, pp. 64–68.

16. "How the Cost of Calling Started Falling for Radiant House," *Management Today,* January 1998, p. 66.

17. "Lights, Camera, Meeting: Teleconferencing Becomes a Time-Saving Tool," *The Wall Street Journal,* February 21, 1995, p. A1.

18. "These Workers Would Make Cal Proud," *USA Today,* September 1, 1995, p. 2B.

19. Donald J. McNerney, "Creating a Motivated Workforce," *HR Focus,* August 1996, pp. 1 and 4ff.

20. Sue Shellenbarger, "More Corporations Are Using Flexibility to Lure Employees," *The Wall Street Journal,* September 17, 1997, p. B1.

21. Amy Saltzmann, "One Job, Two Contented Workers," *U.S. News & World Report,* November 14, 1988, pp. 74, 76.

22. Alfie Kahn, "Why Incentive Plans Cannot Work," *Harvard Business Review* 71 (September/October 1993), p. 55.

23. *U.S. News & World Report,* October 28, 1991, p. 16.

24. Clarence Francis, "Management Methods," speech given in 1952; reprinted in *Management Methods Magazine,* 1952.

25. H. H. Meyer and W. B. Walker, "A Study of Factors Relating to the Effectiveness of a Performance Appraisal Program," *Personnel Psychology,* August 1961, pp. 291–98.

26. "We Know What to Do, but We Need Skills and Authority to Do It," *The Wall Street Journal,* August 26, 1997, p. A1.

27. Melissa Campanelli, "Getting Good Advice," *Sales & Marketing Management,* March 1995, p. 42.

28. NBC "Evening News," November 11, 1997.

29. Stephanie Armour, "Workplace Hazard Gets Attention," *USA Today,* May 5, 1998, p. 1B.

30. Robert McGarvey, "On the Edge," *Entrepreneur,* August 1995, pp. 76–79.

31. Stuart Elliott, "Workers' Woes Give Firms Financial Fits," *USA Today,* June 13, 1989, p. 1B.

32. "Disgruntled Workers Find a New Place to Complain: The Internet," *The Wall Street Journal,* December 9, 1997, p. A1.

33. Timothy Aeppel, "Losing Faith: Personnel Disorders Sap a Factory Owner of His Early Idealism," *The Wall Street Journal,* January 14, 1998, pp. A1, A14.

34. Del Jones, "UAW Faces Cloudy Future," *USA Today,* June 17, 1998, p. 2B; and CBS "Evening News," September 7, 1998.

35. Jones, "UAW Faces Cloudy Future"; and CBS "Evening News," September 7, 1998.

36. Albert R. Karr, "Small Business Scores Big in Congressional Lobbying," *The Wall Street Journal,* October 3, 1988, pp. B1, B2.

37. Jeffrey A. Tannenbaum, "Consultants, Small Business Come to Need One Another," *The Wall Street Journal,* September 28, 1989, p. B1.

38. Del Jones, "Laws, Juries Shift Protection to Terminated Employees," *USA Today,* April 2, 1998, pp. 1B, 2B.

Chapter 11

1. Jan Norman, "How to: Find the Perfect Location," *Business Start-Ups,* February 1998, pp. 54, 56.

2. Paul W. Cockerham, "The Little Fish Survive," *Stores,* November 1994, pp. 64–65.

3. Justin Bicknell, "Where to Set Your Sites: On Location with Firms," *Business Mexico,* September 1994, pp. 6–7.

4. " 'Afrocentric Mind-Set' Part of Business," *Mobile* (Alabama) *Register,* July 31, 1994, p. 4-F.

5. William G. Nickels and Marian B. Wood, *Marketing: Relationships, Quality, Value* (New York: Worth, 1997), p. 453.

6. Danielle Reed, "A Tale of Two Leaves: Outlet Shopping," *The Wall Street Journal,* October 17, 1997, p. B12.

7. Julie B. Davis, "Deals on Wheels," *Business Start-Ups,* August 1998, pp. 37–40.

8. Harriet Webster, "Would You Like to Work at Home?" *Reader's Digest,* March 1998, p. 130.

9. Stephanie Armour, "Success of Telecommuting Dispels Myth," *USA Today,* April 17, 1998, p. 2B.

10. Howard Rothman, "Homeward Bound," Home Business article from Amazon.com, Inc., p. 1, accessed August 14, 1997.

11. June Langhoff, "Telecommute America: Get Ready for Business in the Fast Lane," *Fortune,* Special Advertising Section, October 30, 1995, p. 229.

12. Melanie Warner, "Working at Home—The Right Way to Be a Star in Your Bunny Slippers," *Fortune,* March 3, 1997, p. 166.

13. "The Way Things Work," *USA Today,* September 17, 1997, p. 1D.
14. "Who Works from Home," *USA Today,* September 21, 1994, p. 1B.
15. "Employees Who Prefer to Work at Home," *Personnel Journal* 71 (November 1992), p. 27.
16. "Unfinished Homework," *The Wall Street Journal,* January 6, 1993, p. A1.
17. "Employees Who Prefer to Work at Home," p. 27.
18. Udayan Gupta, "Home-Based Entrepreneurs Expand Computer Use Sharply, Study Shows," *The Wall Street Journal,* October 13, 1995, p. B2.
19. Lynn H. Colwell, "Elbow Room," *Business Start-Ups,* March 1998, p. 14.
20. Consult any basic industrial engineering or production/operations management text for a more detailed discussion of this process. There will probably be some sample forms you can use.
21. Yuniko Ono, "Would You Like That Rare, Medium, or Vacuum-Packed?" *The Wall Street Journal,* January 6, 1997, pp. A1, A14.

Chapter 12

1. Jeanne Lee, "Five Easy PCs," *Fortune,* November 10, 1997, pp. 311–12.
2. Laura M. Litvan, "Selling to Uncle Sam: New Easier Rules," *Nation's Business,* March 1995, pp. 46–48.
3. Leon C. Megginson, Donald C. Mosley, and Paul H. Pietri, Jr., *Management: Concepts and Applications,* 4th ed. (New York: HarperCollins, 1992), p. 662.
4. Myron Magnet, "The New Golden Rule of Business," *Fortune,* February 21, 1994, pp. 60–61.
5. "Minority Supplier Development, Part 3: Why Aren't Minority Supplier Programs More Successful?" *Purchasing,* February 16, 1995, pp. 97–100.
6. David Friedman, "The Enemy Within," *Inc.,* October 1995, pp. 47–52.
7. Micheline Maynard, "5-Cent Part Defect Forces LH Recall," *USA Today,* September 4, 1992, p. 1B.
8. Donna Fenn, "Growing by Design," *Inc.,* August 1985, p. 86.
9. "Consultants: For a Complex Purchase, an Outside Expert May Be Just What You Need," *Inc.,* October 1991, pp. OG 65–66.
10. Dale D. Buss, "Supply-Side Economics," *Income Opportunities,* January 1995, pp. 18–24.
11. Author's conversation with Alan Lowe, Department of Product Planning and Development, Sharp Corporation.
12. Gary McWilliams, "Mom and Pop Go High Tech," *Business Week,* November 21, 1994, p. 82.
13. Ibid.

14. Anna W. Mathews, "Mr. and Mrs. Grimm Get a Load of Shrimp Cross Country, Fast," *The Wall Street Journal,* February 3, 1998, pp. A1, A8.
15. Robert Berner, "Gift Rap: At Christmas, Retailers Are like Kids Who Ask Santa Claus for a Pony," *The Wall Street Journal,* October 27, 1997, pp. A1, A8.
16. Jeffrey A. Tannenbaum, "Small Bookseller Beats the Giants at Their Own Game," *The Wall Street Journal,* November 4, 1997, pp. B1, B2.
17. For a fuller discussion of EOQ, see Robert Albanese, Geralyn M. Franklin, and Peter Wright, *Management,* rev. ed. (Houston, TX: Dame Publications, 1997), p. 620.
18. Kathy Jumper, "Menefee Wants His Clients to Be Happy, Look Good," *Mobile* (Alabama) *Register,* February 20, 1989, p. 1-B.
19. Ken Cross, "A Chat with Charles Morgan," *Fortune,* October 2, 1995, p. 27.
20. Richard L. Hughes, Robert G. Ginnett, and Gordon J. Curphy, *Leadership: Enhancing the Lessons of Experience,* 2nd ed. (New York: McGraw-Hill, 1996), p. 518.
21. Author's correspondence with Craig Taylor, Director, Business Programs, Disney Institute.
22. Leslie Chang, "Eating Their Lunch: Coals to Newcastle, Ice to Eskimos; Now, Noodles to the Chinese," *The Wall Street Journal,* November 17, 1997, pp. A1, A10.

Chapter 13

1. Bob Weinstein, "Biz 101: On the Money," *Entrepreneur,* September 1998, p. 192A.
2. Paul DeCeglie, "Reality Check," *Business Start-Ups,* March 1998, p. 12.
3. Anne Fisher, "Starting Anew," *Fortune,* March 30, 1998, p. 165.
4. "Welcome to Benchmark Research Inc.," www.benchmark-research-inc.com/bmpres.html, accessed May 13, 1998.
5. Jeffrey Rothfeder, "Top Tips for the Bottom Line," *PC World,* December 1995, p. 198.
6. Roger Ricklefs and Udayan Gupta, "Traumas of a New Entrepreneur," *The Wall Street Journal,* May 10, 1989, p. B1.
7. Bob Weinstein, "Balancing Act," *Entrepreneur,* March 1995, pp. 56–61.
8. David M. Gumpert, "Don't Let Optimism Block Out Trouble Signposts," *USA Today,* May 8, 1989, p. 10E.
9. "Wireless Sets You Free," *Fortune,* March 16, 1998, www.pcia.com/fortune.htm, p. 2, accessed May 25, 1998.
10. Jeff Ducato, "The Cellular Explosion," *Greater Rochester Realtors Newspaper,* www.homesteadnet.com/homestead/newspaper/april97/grararti.html, p. 1, accessed May 25, 1998.

11. Paul DeCeglie, "Cut It Out," *Business Start-Ups,* February 1998, p. 14.

12. Phillip Piña, "Organic Can Mean Profits for Farmers," *USA Today,* September 19, 1995, p. B1.

13. Yasuhiro Monden and John Lee, "How a Japanese Auto Maker Reduces Cost," *Management Accounting,* August 1993, pp. 22–26.

14. PHH Vehicle Management Service Survey of 400,000 autos in business use, as reported in *USA Today,* August 2, 1995, p. 1A.

Chapter 14

1. Jeffrey A. Tannenbaum, "Small Bookseller Beats the Giants at Their Own Game," *The Wall Street Journal,* November 4, 1997, pp. B1, B2.

2. Bob Weinstein, "Let's Get Fiscal," *Entrepreneur,* June 1995, p. 68.

3. Jacquelyn Lynn, "Damage Control," *Entrepreneur,* March 1998, p. 37.

4. Larry Luxner, "Trade Zones Mark Strategy Shift," *The Wall Street Journal,* October 9, 1997, p. B20.

5. Anna Mathews, "Mr. and Mrs. Grimm Get a Load of Shrimp Cross Country, Fast," *The Wall Street Journal,* February 3, 1998, pp. A1, A8.

6. *Starting a Business and Keeping Records,* Publication 583, www.irs.ustreas.gov.

7. Controller of the Treasury, Compliance Division, "How Are Sales of Food Taxed in Maryland?" Business Tax Tip #5, www.comp.state.md.us/taxtips/bustip05.htm; and Susan Adeletti, "Snacks Pose Taxing Problem," *The Journal Online* (Journal Newspapers, Alexandria, Virginia), July 1997, www.jrnl.com/news/97/Jul/jrnl118090797.html, accessed June 29, 1998.

8. Bernie Kohn, "Toe-to-Toe with the IRS," *Tampa Tribune,* March 29, 1998, pp. 1–2, www.tampatrib.com.

9. Rev. Proc. 96-93, I.R.B. No. 53, 46.

10. David L. Epstein, "Prepare Your Heir," *Restaurant Business,* January 20, 1988, p. 34. See also Tom Herman and Rodney Ho, "Deducting the Costs of Home Office to Get Easier," *The Wall Street Journal,* July 31, 1997, p. B2.

11. "So You're Going to Take Over the Family Business," *Agency Sales Magazine,* July 1988, p. 34.

12. Publication 15, Circular E, *Employers Tax Guide.*

13. John R. Emshwiller, "Handing Down the Business," *The Wall Street Journal,* May 19, 1989, p. B1.

14. Mitchell Pacelle, "Skeletons, Subs, and Other Restaurant Themes Do Battle," *The Wall Street Journal,* May 21, 1997, pp. B1, B14.

15. Richard Gibson, "Planet Hollywood Reels as 'Entertainment' Fades," *The Wall Street Journal,* January 23, 1998, pp. B1, B7.

16. According to Kate McAloon, Information Services Library, May 19, 1998.

Chapter 15

1. G. Pascal Zachary, "Restaurant Computers Speed Up Soup to Nuts," *The Wall Street Journal,* October 25, 1995, p. B1.

2. David H. Friedman, "Plenty of Challenges, No Rules," *Inc. Technology,* Summer 1995, p. 9.

3. Erick Schonfeld, "The Squeeze Is On for PC Makers," *Fortune,* April 13, 1998, p. 182.

4. Katherine T. Beddingfield, "Laptops: Safe at Any Altitude?" *U.S. News & World Report,* November 3, 1997, p. 70.

5. Tom Richman, "Break It to Me Gently," *Inc.,* July 1989, pp. 108–10.

6. Mike Snider, "Searching for Ways to Direct Internet Traffic," *USA Today,* March 14, 1996, p. 1D.

7. Elizabeth Weise, "Net Use Doubling Every 100 Days," *USA Today,* April 16, 1998, p. 1A.

8. "Pro and Con: Should the Internet Be Tax-Free Commerce?" *Mobile* (Alabama) *Register,* May 28, 1998, p. 13A.

9. Heather Green, "All Roads Lead to the Web," *Business Week,* November 24, 1997, p. 150.

10. As reported by the Associated Press, May 14, 1998; and "Super Bowl Ad Rates," *USA Today,* January 20, 1999, p. 1B.

11. Edward W. Desmond, "Yahoo: Still Defying Gravity on the Web," *Fortune,* September 8, 1997, p. 154.

12. Correspondence with Bryn Kaufman, President of CMPExpress.com.

13. "Internet Sales," *USA Today,* July 20, 1998, p. 15A; and George Will, "The National Political Stage Becomes Irrelevant," *Mobile* (Alabama) *Register,* January 1, 1999, p. 11A.

14. "Small Business and the Web," *USA Today,* July 30, 1998, p. 1B.

15. As reported in *USA Today,* December 8, 1995, p. 1A; and George Will, "The National Political Stage Becomes Irrelevant," *Mobile* (Alabama) *Register,* January 1, 1999, p. 11A.

16. Jared Taylor, "Keeping Up with the Computers," *The Wall Street Journal,* Special Report, May 20, 1985, p. 84C.

17. Michael Diamond, "Small Firms Ignore 2000 Bug," *USA Today,* July 8, 1998, p. 2B.

18. Ibid.

19. Douglas Hayward, "Small Businesses Head for Year 2000 Disaster," *TechWeb News* (www.techweb.com), October 22, 1997, pp. 1–2.

20. "Mom and Pop, Unplugged," *The Wall Street Journal,* April 13, 1995, p. A1.

21. Stephanie Mehta, "Older Business Owners Ponder the New Technology," *The Wall Street Journal,* May 27, 1994, p. B2.
22. Ibid.
23. Doug Levy, "Personal Touch Drives Sales," *USA Today,* June 5, 1998, p. 1B. See also, "Firms Slipping the Grasp of Giants Intel, Microsoft," *USA Today,* June 11, 1998, p. 1B.
24. Evan Ramstad, "Defying the Odds: Despite Giant Rivals, Many Tiny PC Makers Are Still Doing Well," *The Wall Street Journal,* January 8, 1997, p. A1.

Chapter 16

1. U.S. Bureau of the Census, *Statistical Abstract of the United States, 1994,* 114th ed. (Washington, DC: U.S. Government Printing Office, 1994), pp. 254, 415; and Margaret Isa, "Pet Practice's Coming IPO May Not Have Much Bite," *The Wall Street Journal,* July 31, 1995, p. C1.
2. "Citibank's Test of Paying to See Tellers Doesn't Pay," *The Wall Street Journal,* May 26, 1993, p. 6.
3. Adapted from Shelly Reese and Ellen Neuborne, "Malls Sell Shoppers on Security," *USA Today,* December 20, 1994, p. 2B.
4. Rob Wells, "Trade Center Firms Struggle to Resume Business Activity," AP bulletin to *Mobile* (Alabama) *Register,* March 2, 1993, p. 6-A.
5. William G. Nickels, James M. McHugh, and Susan M. McHugh, *Understanding Business,* 4th ed. (New York: McGraw-Hill, 1996), p. 690.
6. Linda Chavez, "Suits Are Big Problem," *USA Today,* September 10, 1992, p. 14A.
7. "Hooking a Tort," *The Wall Street Journal,* July 20, 1995, p. A12; and "Only in America," *Fortune,* September 4, 1995, p. 127.
8. Roger Thompson, "Workers' Comp Costs: Out of Control," *Nation's Business,* July 1992, pp. 22–30.
9. Nickels, McHugh, and McHugh, *Understanding Business,* p. 689.
10. Elliot Carlson, "We Must Act—and Act Now," *AARP Bulletin,* May 1998, pp. 1, 14, 15.
11. Ibid.
12. Roger L. Miller and Gaylord A. Jentz, *Business Law Today,* 4th ed. (St. Paul, MN: West, 1997), p. 585.
13. Udayan Gupta, "Enterprise," *The Wall Street Journal,* April 21, 1992, p. B2.
14. Jane Easter Bahls, "Inside Jobs," *Entrepreneur,* June 1995, pp. 72–75.
15. Janean Huber, "Never Fear," *Entrepreneur,* May 1995, p. 14.
16. "Store Safety," *USA Today,* April 29, 1998, p. 1B.
17. Ibid.
18. Ibid.

19. "To Stop a Thief," *U.S. News & World Report,* May 1, 1989, p. 76.
20. Pat Carr, "How to Make Your Workplace Safe," *Mobile* (Alabama) *Register,* August 29, 1994, p. 1-D.
21. Author's conversation with Frank Luciano, December 12, 1995.
22. John R. Emshwiller, "Employers Lose Billions of Dollars to Employee Theft," *The Wall Street Journal,* October 5, 1992, p. B2.
23. *Security Management* magazine, as reported in *The Wall Street Journal,* November 11, 1986, p. 39.
24. John Goff, "Labor Pains," *CFO: The Magazine for Senior Financial Executives,* January 1998, pp. 36–44.
25. Thomas Omestad, "Bye-Bye to Bribes," *U.S. News & World Report,* December 22, 1997, pp. 39, 42–44; and Kim Clark, "The Detectives," *Fortune,* April 14, 1997, pp. 122–26.
26. Haidee Allerton, "Working Life Rock Bottom," *Training and Development,* September 1993, p. 87.
27. Allison Weiser, "Protecting Your Business Secrets," *The Rotarian,* August 1997, p. 14. See also Steve Casimiro, "The Spying Game Moves into the U.S. Workplace," *Fortune,* March 30, 1998, pp. 152, 154.
28. Weiser, "Protecting Your Business Secrets."
29. M. J. Zuckerman, "Computer Attacks Up 22% Since 1996," *USA Today,* March 4, 1998, p. 1A.
30. Del Jones, "Companies Grapple with Limiting Employee Abuse," *USA Today,* April 27, 1998, p. 1A.
31. Peter Eisler, "Audit: Social Security Files Not Secure," *USA Today,* December 5, 1997, p. 1A.
32. As reported in *USA Today,* December 8, 1995, p. 1A.
33. Del Jones, "On-line Surfing Costs Firms Time and Money," *USA Today,* December 8, 1995, pp. A1, A2.
34. As reported in *USA Today,* September 1, 1994, p. 1A.
35. Kevin Johnson, "Worldwide Strategy Set on Fighting Cybercrime," *USA Today,* December 10, 1997, p. 1A.
36. David Lynch, "Entrepreneurs Lose in Get-Rich Schemes," *USA Today,* July 19, 1995, p. 1B.
37. John R. Emshwiller, "Ripped Off," *The Wall Street Journal,* May 21, 1998, p. R25.
38. Baseline Software Inc. (www.baselinesoft.com) has a package for writing such policies. Its *Information Security Policies Made Easy,* priced at $495, consists of a book, accompanied by a CD-ROM or floppy disk, providing companies with 10 written policies concerning the Internet, intranets, e-mail, telecommuting, privacy, data classification, and PCs. See "Make Information Security Your Policy," *OfficeSystems98,* April 1998, p. 12, for more information.

39. Thomas J. DiLorenzo, "Pizza Driver Safety Transcends Civil Rights," *USA Today,* June 25, 1997, p. 13A.
40. Stephanie Armour, "Retail Anti-Crime Steps Spur Debate," *USA Today,* May 6, 1998, p. 5B.
41. Ibid.

Chapter 17

1. Sara Lamb, "Funerals Becoming Big Business," *Mobile* (Alabama) *Register,* January 26, 1997, pp. 1F, 2F.
2. Instead of trying to document each part of the Code, we suggest that you look up the topic in the index of any up-to-date business law text. Most of our information came from Roger L. Miller and Gaylord A. Jentz, *Business Law Today: Alternate Essentials Edition,* 4th ed. (St. Paul, MN: West, 1997), "Appendix B: The Uniform Commercial Code," pp. A-9–97.
3. Aissaton Sidime, "Independent Bookstores Sue Big Chains," *Tampa Tribune,* posted to www.tampatrib.com, March 18, 1998.
4. Rodney Ho, "Small Businesses in Areas Hurt by NAFTA Can Apply to New Loan Guarantee Plan," *The Wall Street Journal,* August 7, 1997, p. B2.
5. Brent Bowers, "The Doozies: Seven Scary Tales of Wild Bureaucracy," *The Wall Street Journal,* June 19, 1992, p. B2.
6. "Let the Vans Roll," *The Wall Street Journal,* July 14, 1997, p. A14; and "The Vans Roll," *The Wall Street Journal,* August 13, 1997, p. A14.
7. U.S. Department of Commerce, *Survey of Current Business* (Washington, DC: U.S. Government Printing Office, August 1983), p. 24.
8. Jeffrey A. Tannenbaum, "Government Red Tape Puts Entrepreneurs in the Black," *The Wall Street Journal,* June 12, 1992, p. B2.
9. Steve Forbes in a lecture at Hillsdale College, Hillsdale, Michigan, published as "The Moral Case for the Flat Tax," *Imprimis* 25, no. 2 (October 1996), p. 2.
10. John J. Fialka, "Finding Help: I'm from the Government . . . ," *The Wall Street Journal,* May 21, 1998, p. R18.
11. Jack Faris, "Give Small Biz a Break," *USA Today,* June 13, 1995, p. 11A.
12. Tony Snow, "Curtain Finally May Ring Down on Regulatory Follies," *USA Today,* December 19, 1994, p. 11A.
13. Ibid.
14. A survey by U.S. Trust of affluent business owners, reported at www.ustrust.com/affbus.htm, p. 2, accessed February 25, 1998.

15. Laura M. Litvan, "A Low-Stress OSHA Review," *Nation's Business,* January 1995, p. 37.
16. From *The Wall Street Journal,* as reported in "Couple Forms Letter-Writing Business," *Mobile* (Alabama) *Press Register,* February 19, 1995, p. 4-F.
17. Rodney Ho, "Mr. Entrepreneur Goes to Washington: Elections Give Smaller Firms New Power," *The Wall Street Journal,* November 17, 1996, p. B2.
18. William M. Bukeley, "If Someone Breeds a Purple Cow, They'll Have a Crazy Surf'n'Turf," *The Wall Street Journal,* March 15, 1993, p. B1.
19. Thomas Petzinger, Jr., "The Front Lines: He Ran Up Against Latest Business Foe: Private Regulations," *The Wall Street Journal,* September 22, 1995, p. B1.
20. *How to Choose and Use a Lawyer* (Chicago: American Bar Association, 1990). For information, contact the ABA at 750 N. Lake Shore Drive, Chicago, IL 60611.
21. Jeffrey A. Tannenbaum, "Small-Business Owners Must Pick a Lawyer Judiciously," *The Wall Street Journal,* February 15, 1989, p. B2.
22. "Good for Nothing," *Entrepreneur,* June 1995, p. 16.
23. Dana Milbank, "Real Work: Hiring Welfare People, Hotel Chain Finds, Is Tough but Rewarding," *The Wall Street Journal,* October 31, 1996, pp. A1, A10.
24. Carol Hymowitz, "Drawing the Line on Budding Romances in Your Workplace," *The Wall Street Journal,* November 18, 1997, p. B1.
25. Gary Hector, "A New Reason You Can't Get a Loan," *Fortune,* September 21, 1992, pp. 107–12.
26. The Aluminum Association, as reported in "Recycling: Earth Day Legacy," *USA Today,* April 21, 1995, p. 1B.
27. The Steel Recycling Institute, as reported in "Not Driving to the Landfill," *USA Today,* July 28, 1998, p. 1B.
28. Carolina Pad, as reported in *USA Today,* March 9, 1995, p. 1A.
29. Cynthia E. Griffin, "Don't Want Your Waste? Sell It!" *Entrepreneur,* September 1998, p. 194.
30. Diana West, "Profile: Pioneer Restaurateur Serves Big Helpings of Scholarships, Too," *The Rotarian,* July 1997, p. 50, and author's conversations with a Chick-fil-A manager.
31. Del Jones, "Good Works, Good Business," *USA Today,* April 25, 1997, pp. 1B, 2B.
32. Donald D. Jackson, "It's Wake-Up Time for Main Street when Wal-Mart Comes to Town," *Smithsonian,* October 1992, pp. 36–42, 46–47.
33. The Annenberg/CPB Project has an audio and video series entitled "Ethics in Business." A preview can be arranged by writing The Annenberg/CPB Project, c/o Intellimation, P.O. Box 4069, Santa Barbara, CA 93140, or by calling 1-800-LEARNER.

34. Geanne Rosenburg, "Truth and Consequences," *Working Woman,* July/August 1998, p. 79.

35. Jacquelyn Lynn, "Do the Right Thing," *Entrepreneur,* August 1998, p. 85.

36. Don L. Boroughs, "The Bottom Line on Ethics," *U.S. News & World Report,* March 20, 1995, pp. 61–66.

37. Kenneth Labich, "The New Crisis in Business Ethics," *Fortune,* April 20, 1992, p. 172.

38. W. Michael Hoffman and Edward S. Petry, Jr., "Abusing Business Ethics," *Phi Kappa Journal,* Winter 1992, pp. 10–13.

39. Harris Poll, as reported in Grant Yifusa, "Who Do We Trust?" *Reader's Digest,* January 1993, p. 109.

40. Thomas M. Goodsite, "The 'Golden-Rule' Rotarian," *The Rotarian,* October 1994, pp. 38–39.

Chapter 18

1. "Home Business Motivation," *USA Today,* March 13, 1997, p. 1A.

2. James Lea, "People-Related Challenges Crop Up in Family Companies," *Jacksonville Business Journal,* www.amcity.com;80/jacksonville/stories/031698/smallb2.html, p. 1.

3. "Home Business Motivation."

4. "The New Business: Smith and Parents," *The Wall Street Journal,* December 8, 1988, p. B1.

5. David Clothier, "Specialty Biscuits Hot Seller," *Mobile* (Alabama) *Register,* March 23, 1997, pp. 1F, 2F.

6. Kathy Marshack, Public Radio International's "Marketplace," October 14, 1998.

7. "Family Businesses of 1997," *Succeeding Generations* 1, no. 13 (Winter 1997). Published by The University of Toledo (Ohio) Center for Family Business.

8. Randall Lane, "Let Asplundh Do It," *Forbes 400,* October 16, 1995, pp. 56–64.

9. John Helyer and JoAnn S. Lubin, "The Portable CEO: Do You Need an Expert to Head a Widget Company?" *The Wall Street Journal,* January 21, 1998, pp. A1, A10.

10. Kimberly S. McDonald, "Getting Yours," *Fortune,* March 3, 1997, pp. 203–5.

11. Survey by Nancy Bowman-Upton, as reported in "Reasons Children Join Family Businesses," *The Wall Street Journal,* May 19, 1989, p. B1.

12. "Question of the Week: What Opportunities Are Out There?" *Home Business Resource Centre,* at www.describe.ca/yourbiz/yourbiz/htm, September 17, 1997.

13. "So You're Going to Take Over the Family Business," *Agency Sales Magazine,* July 1988, p. 34.

14. Scott McKimmy, "More Questions Are the Answers," *Succeeding Generations,* Fall 1996, p. 1.

15. John Ward, as reported in Buck Brown, "Succession Strategies for Family Firms," *The Wall Street Journal,* August 4, 1988, p. 23.

16. Ewing Terzah, "Highly Effective Management Team," *Forbes,* October 23, 1995, pp. 312–14.

17. "Entrepreneurs Neglect One Type of Planning," *The Wall Street Journal,* April 8, 1992, p. B1.

18. Michael Selz, "More Family-Owned Firms Make Plans for the Next Generation," *The Wall Street Journal,* September 8, 1995, p. B2.

19. Thomas Petzinger, Jr., "In Lifesaving Field, Tools of the Trade Earn Workers' Loyalty," *The Wall Street Journal,* October 25, 1996, p. B1.

20. Patricia Schiff Estess, "Good Buy?" *Entrepreneur,* May 1995, pp. 74, 76.

21. Jean K. Mason, "Selling Father's Painful Legacy," *Nation's Business,* September 1988, p. 30.

22. See Dianne S. Cauble, "Making Partners of Your Heirs," *Small Business Reports,* October 1994, pp. 54–57; and Mary Rowland, "Keeping It in the Family," *Nation's Business,* January 1995, pp. 63–64.

23. William H. Hoffman, Jr., William A. Raabe, James E. Smith, and David M. Maloney, *West's Federal Taxation: Corporations, Partnerships, Estates, and Trusts, 1998 Edition* (Cincinnati: West/Southwestern, 1998), p. 17; and "Estate Taxes Will Face Renewed Assaults in Congress Next Year," *The Wall Street Journal,* December 17, 1997, p. A1.

24. "Keep Your Money in the Family," *Baldwin* (County, Alabama) *Register,* July 27, 1998, p. 3.

25. "Taxpayer Relief Act of 1997 Benefits Almost Everyone," *Credentials Services International Bulletin* 2, no. 11, p. 1.

26. Louis Austin, Vicki Schumaker, and Jim Schumaker, "Living Trusts Replace Wills as Estate Planning Tools," *Small Business Reports,* March 1989, p. 93.

27. Hoffman et al., *West's Federal Taxation.*

28. Diane Weber, "A Living Trust Can Be Great if You Dodge These Pitfalls," *Medical Economics,* August 20, 1992, pp. 90–95.

Photo Credits

Chapter 1: Trillium House owners Ed and Betty Dinwiddie. Photo courtesy of Betty and Ed Dinwiddie, Trillium House.

Chapter 2: Bob and Mai Gu enjoy visiting with some of their favorite customers. Photo courtesy of Leon C. Megginson.

Chapter 3: Henry E. Kloss. Photo courtesy of Henry E. Kloss.

Chapter 4: Ray A. Kroc, founder of McDonald's Corporation. Photo courtesy of McDonald's Corporation.

Chapter 5: Sam and Teresa Davis. Photo by Shawn Scully, *The Tuscaloosa* (Alabama) *News,* May 7, 1995, p. E1.

Appendix B map: Courtesy of Tom Keith, Keith Map Service.

Appendix C map: Courtesy of Tom Keith, Keith Map Service.

Chapter 6: Roy Morgan. Photo courtesy of Air Methods Corporation.

Chapter 7: Gerald Byrd. Photo courtesy of Gerald Byrd.

Chapter 8: Juli Byrd, cruise counselor; Bob Bender, partner; Steve Cape, partner; and Kari Givens, corporate travel agent of Springfield Travel. Photo courtesy of Leon C. Megginson.

Chapter 9: Michael Levy and Mary H. Partridge. Photo courtesy of Michael Levy and Mary H. Partridge.

Chapter 10: Cathy Anderson-Giles talking to a customer. Photo courtesy of Cathy Anderson-Giles.

Chapter 11: Oakwood Inn. Photo courtesy of Leon C. Megginson.

Chapter 12: Bob and Kathy Summer. Photo courtesy of Leon C. Megginson.

Chapter 13: The "Powell Company." Photo courtesy of Leon C. Megginson.

Chapter 14: Herman J. Russell. Photo courtesy of H. J. Russell & Co.

Chapter 15: Tom Williams. AP photo by John Makely.

Chapter 16: Dr. Jeffrey Van Petten. Photo courtesy of Joyce Allen Baker and Jeffrey Van Petten.

Chapter 17: Reuben Feuerborn at Zeiner Funeral Home. Photo courtesy of Reuben Feuerborn.

Chapter 18: Jan Weiler and David Showers. Photo courtesy of Suzanne Barnhill.

Index